Home-School Collaboration:

Enhancing Children's

Academic and Social Competence

Edited by

Sandra L. Christenson
University of Minnesota

Jane Close Conoley
University of Nebraska-Lincoln

The National Association of School Psychologists
8455 Colesville Road, Suite 1000
Silver Spring, Maryland 20910

From the NASP Publications Policy Handbook

The content of this document reflects the ideas and positions of the authors. The responsibility lies solely with the authors and does not necessarily reflect the position or ideas of the National Association of School Psychologists.

First Printing: 1992

Published by:
  The National Association of School Psychologists
  8455 Colesville Road, Suite 1000
  Silver Spring, Maryland 20910

ISBN 0-932955-04-5

Printed in the United States of America

0 9 8 7 6 5 4 3 2 1

Dedication

Dedicated to professionals who have made heroic efforts to harmonize the important systems in children's lives.

SLC/JCC
Summer, 1992

Contents

Part I:
Conceptual/Empirical Bases for
Home-School Collaboration

Part II:
Programs and Models for the 90s

Part IV:
Implications for Facilitating Change Toward
Home-School Collaboration

Contributors

Deborah Anderson
Research Associate
Division of Child and Adolescent
    Psychiatry
University of Minnesota

Dianne Apter
Director of Early Childhood Direction
    Center
Syracuse University

Gerald J. August
Associate Professor of Child and
    Adolescent Psychiatry
University of Minnesota

Theresa Bahns
Doctoral Candidate
University of Nebraska-Lincoln

Kris O. Battaglini
Doctoral Candidate, Indiana University of
    Pennsylvania
School Psychologist
Cape Henlopen Schools
Susex Consortium
Lewes, Delaware

Michael L. Bloomquist
Research Psychologist
Minnesota Competence Enhancement
    Project
Division of Child and Adolescent
    Psychiatry
University of Minnesota

Andrew S. Bondy
State Director
Delaware Autistic Program
Newark, Delaware

Cindy I. Carlson
Associate Professor of Educational
    Psychology
University of Texas at Austin

Susan D. Chapman
Doctoral Student in School Psychology
University of South Carolina

Sandra L. Christenson
Associate Professor of Educational
    Psychology
University of Minnesota

Elaine Clark
Associate Professor of Educational
    Psychology
University of Utah

Jane Close Conoley
Professor of Educational Psychology
University of Nebraska-Lincoln

William J. Doherty
Professor of Family Social Science
University of Minnesota

Sanford M. Dornbusch
Director of Stanford Center for the Study
    of Families, Children, and Youth
Stanford University

Carl J. Dunst
Director of Family, Infant, and Preschool
    Program and Center for Family
    Studies
Western Carolina Center
Morganton, North Carolina

Martha E. Edwards
Social Psychologist
Ackerman Institute for Family Therapy

Joyce L. Epstein
Co-Director
Center on Families, Communities,
    Schools, and Children's Learning
Professor of Sociology
The Johns Hopkins University

Martha Farrell Erickson
Coordinator, All-University Community
    Consortium on Children, Youth, and
    Families
University of Minnesota

Mary Jo Franklin
School Psychologist
Stillwater School District
Stillwater, Minnesota

Craig L. Frisby
Assistant Professor of Educational
    Psychology
University of Florida

Jewelle Taylor Gibbs
Professor
School of Social Welfare
University of California at Berkeley

Debbie Hamby
Research Associate
Center for Family Studies
Western Carolina Center
Morganton, North Carolina

Julia Hickman
Psychologist
Private Practice
Bastrop, Texas

Connie Burrows Horton
Assistant Professor of School Psychology
Illinois State University

Larke Nahme Huang
Psychologist
College of Education and Human
    Services
George Mason University

E. Scott Huebner
Associate Professor of Psychology
University of South Carolina

William R. Jenson
Professor of Educational Psychology
University of Utah

Charlie Johanson
Director of Chugiak Children's Services
Chugiak, Alaska

Kenneth A. Kiewra
Associate Professor of Educational
    Psychology
Director of Academic Success Center
University of Nebraska-Lincoln

Daniel Olympia
School Psychologist
Jordan School District
Salt Lake City, Utah

Kathleen D. Paget
Professor of Psychology
University of South Carolina

Vida E. Peskay
School Psychologist
Robbinsdale School District
New Hope, Minnesota

Philip L. Ritter
Research Associate
Stanford Center for the Study of
    Families, Children, and Youth
Stanford University

Theresa Rounds
Doctoral Student in Educational
    Psychology
University of Minnesota

Nancy Russo
School Psychologist
Metuchen Public Schools
Metuchen, New Jersey

Susan Sheridan
Assistant Professor of Educational
    Psychology
University of Utah

Joan Silverstein
Associate Professor of Psychology
Montclair State College

Judith Springer
Crisis Counselor
Bernardsville Public Schools
Bernardsville, New Jersey

Susan McAllister Swap
Chair, Department of Professional
  Studies
Wheelock College

Deborah Tharinger
Associate Professor of Educational
  Psychology
University of Texas at Austin

Carol M. Trivette
Associate Director
Center for Family Studies
Western Carolina Center
Morganton, North Carolina

Michael R. Valentine
Educational Consultant
Long Beach, California

Margaret B. Walker
Director, Behavioral Skills Program
Lincoln Public Schools
Lincoln, Nebraska

Howard M. Weiss
Director of the Family-School
  Collaboration Project
Ackerman Institute for Family Therapy

Richard M. Wielkiewicz
Assistant Professor of Psychology
College of St. Benedict

Introductory Statement

The schooling of America's children and youth has become an increasingly complex process. Changes in the economic structure of our society combined with changes in the family structure in our communities have presented educators with significant challenges. These changes have resulted in a search for new approaches to the schooling process and additional resources to insure the success of that process. Perhaps the most under-utilized resource in the schooling of America's children and youth is the family. The critical role of families and communities for the success of schools in meeting national education goals has been recognized in America 2000. The success of the schooling process in the 21st century may well rely on our ability to link schools and families as effective partners in the education of children. This book is about the creation of such an effective partnership.

The National Association of School Psychologists is committed to facilitating the development of effective home-school partnerships and bringing the family into the school process as an equal partner. The historical relationship between educators and parents has not been one of "equal" partners. As the structure of the family and society changes and as schools undergo reform, there is an urgent need for schools and parents to modify their historical relationship and become partners in the education of all students. School psychologists and other mental health professionals can play a pivotal role in the establishment of this new relationship between home and school. The contents of this book make a significant contribution to the literature on how to nurture that relationship.

In this book you will find information that will facilitate the development of effective home-school partnerships. Your willingness to work to forge these partnerships will make a significant contribution to the schools, children, youth, and families with whom you work. The National Association of School Psychologists thanks you for your efforts.

George M. Batsche, Ed.D.
23rd President of the National
Association of School Psychologists
(1991–1992)

Preface

This book is about meeting children's needs. The focus is on creating partnerships between home and school so that children's educational and mental health concerns can be addressed effectively. Ecological theories of human development (Bronfenbrenner, 1979, Garbarino, 1982, Werner, 1990) are widely accepted in developmental psychology, but not always implemented when intervening for children. Home and school make up the two most powerful contexts in children's lives. Partnerships that move children and adults toward common goals of competence are critically needed (Seeley, 1985). The rhetoric is available, but the implementation of significant joint efforts for children is rather rare.

Seeley (1989) suggested that parents have overtly or covertly signaled their desire to be uninvolved in their children's schooling. This position does not receive historical support. Ties between parents and educators have not always been distant or tenuous (Berger, 1991). It may be the evolution of the teaching profession has had unintended consequences. The increased professionalization of teaching in the 1920s, 1930s, and 1940s (a good thing) may have had the unintended consequence of reducing parental responsibility for their children's education and their involvement in the educational process. From an ecological perspective, it is unlikely that educators could manage the education of children without the support of parents. The likelihood has been even further reduced, however, by the massive social changes that have affected the American family. The American family is often referred to as an imperiled institution. Economic and social changes have caused both educators and parents of the 1980s and 90s to say, "We can't do it all" (Lewis, 1991, p. 340). Rich (1987), of the Home and School Institute, contends that "Families and teachers might wish that the school could do the job alone. But today's school needs families and today's families need the school. In many ways, their mutual need may be the greatest hope for change" (p. 62).

What must be considered when planning partnerships? At least three very complex situations require attention. First, poverty cannot be overcome by the good intentions of educators. Poverty is a massive reality for children and families (Olson, 1990). As schools attempt to move from rhetoric to action, community agencies must be involved with both families and schools (Chrispeels, 1991). In line with such inclusiveness, school personnel must see a child's family as including grandparents, aunts, uncles, brothers, sisters, and neighbors (Davies, 1991). These may be the significant adults for children of poverty. Schools must seek partners in education—these partners may be parents, extended families, community agencies, business people—rather than relying on narrow conceptualizations of who make up a family (Merenda, 1989).

Second, Pett (1991) challenges schools to move from a deliverer of educational services to a broker of multiple resources that can foster and create successful, productive children. Educators may be unable to do it all, but they are faced with bringing it all together for children (Lewis, 1991). Every school must examine its picture of family to be sure guiding assumptions are accurate reflections of today's realities.

Third, a shift in expectations must occur. Rather than expecting parent involvement, schools must frame their missions as providing parent support. This reframing of home-school relationships reflects "a larger, growing interest in how government, employers, and mainline institutions can support families" (Powell, 1991, p. 307). Support may be a necessary precursor to true parent-teacher-community alliances.

These three points must be considered when planning or thinking about any home and school collaboration. Poverty is a real deterrent to parent involvement and school understanding. A failure to bring resources together will inevitably undermine intervention effectiveness, and support (not blame) is the key to bring systems into harmony with one another.

Addressing the topic of home-school partnerships is timely. Two forces were influential in the conceptualization of this book. The first force relates to school restructuring discussions and agendas. Conley (1991) defines restructuring as "activities that change fundamental assumptions, practices and relationships, both within the school and between the school and the community, in ways that lead to improved student learning outcomes" (p. 49). Making home-school collaboration a functional reality is a restructuring activity. The purpose of such collaboration is to increase the competence of children and youth.

The second force relates to prevention. One of the major principles for action adopted by the National Commission on Children (1991) is prevention. Children grow, learn, and develop in the context of home and school environments. Home-school collaboration aimed at increasing the competence of parents and decreasing the dysfunctional or dangerous aspects of children's environments is one avenue to prevent the development of problems. It is also of some pragmatic relevance that partnerships may be easier to develop before conflictual and crises patterns occur that damage the ties between families and schools.

This volume is divided into four sections: Conceptual/Empirical Bases for Home-School Collaboration, Programs and Models for the 90s, Approaches for Enhancing Home-School Collaboration, and Implications for Facilitating Change Toward Home-School Collaboration. Both restructuring and prevention concepts are evident in the chapters. It is our hope that school-based mental health practitioners, educators, and community-based mental health professionals will find this book a valuable resource for assisting families and schools to work collaboratively . . . or as partners . . . in educating and socializing children and youth. It is time for action. It is time for change.

REFERENCES

Berger, E. H. (1991). Parent involvement: Yesterday and today. *The Elementary School Journal, 91*(3), 209–220.

Bronfenbrenner, U. (1979). *The ecology of human development: Experiments by nature and design.* Cambridge, MA: Harvard University Press.

Chrispeels, J. H. (1991). District leadership in parent involvement: Policies and actions in San Diego. *Phi Delta Kappan, 72*(5), 367–371.

Conley, D. T. (1991). What is restructuring? Educators adapt to a changing world. *Equity and Choice, 7*(2, 3), 46–51.

Davies, D. (1991). Schools reaching out: Family, School, and community partnerships for student success. *Phi Delta Kappan, 72*(5), 376–382.

Garbarino, J. (1982). *Children and families in the social environment.* Hawthorne, NY: Aldine de-Gruyter.

Lewis, A. C. (1991). Coordinating services: Do we have the will? *Phi Delta Kappan, 72*(5), 340.

Merenda, D. W. (1989). Partners in education: An old tradition renamed. *Educational Leadership, 47*(2), 4–11.

National Commission on Children. (1991). *Beyond rhetoric: A new agenda for children and families.* Washington, DC: U.S. Government Printing Office.

Olson, L. (1990, April). Parents as partners: Redefining the social contract between parents and schools [Special issue]. *Education Week, 9*(28).

Pett, J. (1991). Pett peaves. *Phi Delta Kappan, 72*(5), 341.

Powell, D. R. (1991). How schools support families: Critical policy tensions. *The Elementary School Journal, 91*(3), 307–391.

Rich, D. (1987). *Schools and families: Issues and actions.* Washington, DC: National Education Association.

Seeley, D. S. (1985). *Education through partnership.* Washington, DC: American Enterprise Institute Studies in Education Policy.

Seeley, D. S. (1989). A new paradigm for parent involvement. *Educational Leadership, 47*(2), 21–23.

Werner, E. E. (1990). Protective factors and individual resilience. In S. J. Meisels & J. P. Shonkoff (Eds.), *Handbook of early childhood intervention* (pp. 97–116). Cambridge, MA: Cambridge University Press.

Acknowledgements

This book was made possible by the collaborative efforts of many people from several systems. We acknowledge gratefully their assistance and expertise. There would be no book without the generosity of the chapter authors whose cooperation and commitment to this project made editing a significant professional and personal event. They toiled for little reward and produced important pieces.

We relied on several people to provide us with reviews of the chapters and input into the conceptualization of the text. These people are thanked for their constructive, comprehensive, and timely feedback. Thank you: Sarah Allen, Andrea Bie, Lisa Bischoff, Ann Casey, Maureen Cleary, Collie Conoley, Brenda Cumming, Anne Goldberg, Terry Gutkin, Gladys Haynes, Jack Kramer, Deborah LaQua, Paula Laidig, Shui Fong Lam, Doug Marston, Anne O'Brien, Sheila Pederson, Jerry Tomlinson, Kathy Welch, and Carolyn Wright.

Without the efficient secretarial help of Bonnie Warhol, Arly Piri, and Chris Goldsby this book would not have been possible. Jane Carey and her staff at Boyd Printing are also acknowledged for their significant expertise in typesetting and printing.

The leadership of the National Association of School Psychologists deserve special mention. Bill Pfohl served as Publications Commitee Chair of NASP during 1990-91. Howard Knoff has been chair of the Publications Board during the production of the volume. All members of the Publications Board of NASP are thanked for their belief in the project and for their patience.

In the midst of publication we turned to Linda Murphy to assist us in the role of a technical editor. She has been invaluable to the production of the book and to the maintenance of our collective sanity. Linda's "day job" is as managing editor of the Buros *Mental Measurements Yearbook Series*. We were very fortunate to access her considerable expertise for this project.

Part I:

Conceptual/Empirical Bases for Home-School Collaboration

FAMILY SYSTEMS AND THE SCHOOL

William J. Doherty and
Vida E. Peskay

Like the rest of psychology, school psychology was founded with a focus on the individual. Unlike the rest of psychology, however, school psychology from its outset was concerned with the ecology of the individual child as represented by the school (French, 1990). Although early school psychologists certainly understood the importance of the child's family environment, it was not until the late 1970s and 1980s that more systematic attention began to be paid to how school psychologists can assess and work with families (Anderson, 1983; Conoley, 1987; Fine & Holt, 1983; Lombard, 1979; Wendt & Zake, 1984). This new interest in families may have been part of a larger cultural and professional movement, because other health professions, including social work, family medicine, and nursing, were simultaneously experiencing a similar quickening of interest in families in the early 1980s (Doherty, 1985).

As school psychologists were beginning to explore the family dimensions of their work, family therapists were moving the boundaries of their clinical work into community settings. Harry Aponte (1976) wrote the first article on how family therapists based in mental health settings can work directly with school systems and families. Evan Imber-Black (1988) and John Schwartzman (1985) developed models for family therapists to work with

families who were dealing with a variety of community institutions. Doherty and Baird (1983, 1986) and Christie-Seely (1984) contributed models for how family therapists could collaborate with family physicians in the delivery of family-centered health care. If in the 1980s, school psychologists "discovered" the family, family therapists at the same time "discovered" the school and other community systems (Green, 1989; Lusterman, 1985).

This chapter represents the combined efforts of a family therapist (the first author) and a school psychologist (the second author). The goals of the chapter are to provide an introduction to family systems theory, and to describe applications of a family systems model to school settings and the work of school psychologists. We use a minimum of systems theory jargon; readers interested in more technical descriptions of family systems theory are referred to Constantine (1986) and Montgomery and Feuer (1988). Throughout the chapter, we use illustrations related to the professional work of school psychologists.

The chapter begins with a justification for family systems thinking in schools, followed by an overview of family systems theory. The third section of the chapter describes the various interactional triangles that school psychologists face when dealing with families and schools, and the fourth section delineates a model for different levels of involvement that school psychologists can have with families.

WHY FAMILY SYSTEMS THEORY?

Families have always been recognized as a central influence on children's emotional well-being and school learning. However, the traditional training of school psychologists has not given them systematic ways of assessing and working with families (Fine & Holt, 1983; Kramer, 1990). Lacking an explicit conceptual framework for understanding family systems, school psychologists are apt to rely on kinds of evaluations that do not take family process into account or lead to effective action. Professionals who do not have formal means of assessing families often use cultural categories such as "overinvolved mother," "fathers who are too busy for their children," "neglectful parents," "broken home," and "bad home life." There are three problems with these kinds of concepts: (a) They are simplistic and unifactorial; (b) they are moralistic and parent-blaming; and (c) they fail to consider the possibility that the school has become part of the problem. To correct this situation, we are arguing that school psychologists need more explicit and sophisticated models for assessing families of children in schools.

Family systems theory, developed in the context of family therapy, is the major model currently used to assess families. However, as Anderson (1983) has pointed out, family systems theory has not been adequately translated into terms that school psychologists find useful within their role. Working with whole families around serious family problems is outside of the training and interest of most school psychologists—and outside of the traditionally defined constraints of their role in schools. This fact notwithstanding, we believe that, when properly translated to the school context, family systems theory offers a way to transcend the current atheoretical approach of many school psychologists to assessing families. The central advantages of family systems theory are (a) that it offers more complex, nonblaming ways of understanding troubled families; (b) it offers a way to understand the complex dynamics between families and schools; and (c) coupled with family systems interventions, it provides a useful way to promote positive changes in children and parents.

BASIC FAMILY SYSTEMS THEORY

This section describes nine principles of family systems theory in nontechnical language. As a preface we want to emphasize that contemporary family systems theory does not make claims to explain all of human behavior. Each individual is influenced by biological, temperamental, and larger environmental forces beyond the family. Family systems theory's conceptual niche falls in the domain of the individual's intimate environment, an area greatly neglected and deserving of emphasis, but not one that should be viewed as standing alone as a complete theory of human behavior.

1. *Family interaction patterns regulate the behavior of individuals, and tend to repeat across generations.* This idea of interaction patterns—repeated behavioral sequences that form a coherent whole—is the core of the theory. Families develop and perpetuate dozens of interaction patterns, from mealtime activities, holiday rituals, ways to manage angry or sad feelings, ways of handling secrets and privacy, and modes of dealing with outside systems such as schools. The image of a dance can convey the dynamic, flowing yet patterned quality of human behavior as viewed by family systems theory. Behaviors of an individual are moves in a complex family choreography, with other family members making complementary moves and the total family dance taking on an identity of its own.

Example: A 9-year-old girl presents a failing report card to her mother, who is upset and says "Let's tell Dad later." When Dad inquires of the child, the child equivocates. He discovers the cover-up, gets angry at the child, and the parents have a fight. Later Dad tells the child she will lose her summer camping trip if she does not pull up her grades. The child goes for comfort to Mom, who tells her she will handle it with Dad. Family systems theory views this scene as a set of spiraling moves involving at least three individuals. Either parent alone might be effective with this child, but the family dance is likely to lead to trouble for the child's school performance.

Gregory Bateson (1972), a founder of family systems theory, used the image of "vibrations" to characterize all living systems. In this metaphor, individuals vibrate to the oscillations of family patterns, which are in turn influenced by the oscillations of the individuals within the family. The historical aspect of family interaction patterns is the assumption that current family patterns tend to reflect the influence of past patterns, with families sometimes being stuck in dysfunctional interactional styles for generations.

2. *Family belief systems are powerful influences on individuals' behavior.* If interaction patterns represent behavioral sequences, family belief systems represent shared assumptions about the family and its relationship to the world. These beliefs involve implicit and explicit rules about how family members should behave. Family psychiatrist David Reiss (1981) has developed and validated a model for understanding how families view their social environment, along the lines of dangerous versus safe, predictable versus unpredictable, and controllable versus uncontrollable. Families also have organized beliefs about their internal dynamics—"what kind of family we are." For example, some families have beliefs about the high achievement potential of all family members, or the importance of a religious identity as a family. Family systems theory does not assume that every family member holds identical beliefs, but that there is generally a family "paradigm" around which family members cohere or dissent (Constantine, 1986). Fundamental disagreement about the family's paradigm or worldview, according to Reiss (1981), represents a major crisis for a family.

Examples: A family for generations has viewed schools as places of failure and punishment. Parents in the current generation refuse to meet either with teachers or with school psychologists. Another family has a history of successful interactions with school systems. Prior to going on a vacation during school time, these parents secure all assigned work their child will be missing, and then set aside time for the child to finish the work before returning to school.

3. *Key family interaction patterns occur in triangles.* Both psychoanalysis and traditional developmental psychology have focused on dyads—one-to-one dynamics. Family systems theory proposes that all dyadic relations occur in a field with other people, and that the triadic or triangular patterns are the minimum unit for understanding ongoing relationships. Family psychiatrist Murray Bowen (1978) was an early proponent of the centrality of triangles in human emotional systems. Applied to children's adjustment, a triangular perspective suggests that, in addition to relating to mother and father separately, the child relates to their relationship. That is, the child lives in a "force field" of pulls and pushes to and from each parent that is calibrated in part by the parents' own relationship. The notion of family triangles should not be taken as inherently pejorative; for example, a constructive triangle exists when two parents work collaboratively to raise a child. However, when parents are conflicted or very distant, the child is apt to be distressed even when one-to-one relationships with each parent are not conflicted or distant. Similarly, when a child is incorporated into a cross-generational coalition with one parent against the other—as when a parent tells secrets to the child about the other parent—the child has been "triangulated" into a highly dysfunctional pattern of relating to parents. On the other hand, a supportive alliance between the parents vis-à-vis the child represents a benign triangle in the family.

Examples: In one family, mother pushes her son to study and achieve academically, while father supports hockey over study. The boy cannot simultaneously please both parents. In another family, although the parents are divorced and share joint custody, both have instituted a study time in their respective households and allow television watching only after homework is completed.

4. *Family health requires clear family boundaries—knowing who is in or out of the family and its subsystems.* Family therapist Pauline Boss (1988) uses the term "boundary ambiguity" to describe the situation when family members are uncertain about who is in the family or how members belong or fit in. In a post-divorce family, the children may regard Dad as still a member of *their* family, while Mom regards the family as a "single parent" unit. In remarried families it is often not clear whether the mother's new husband should act like a father or like a friend; if like a father, what is the status of the biological father? Boss (1988) has demonstrated in her research that individuals and families experience stress when they are unclear about family boundaries.

Examples: In one family, the new stepmother becomes the adult who negotiates with the school when the child is in trouble. Neither the child nor the biological mother accepts her authority, and the biological father sometimes supports and sometimes undermines her position. In another family, both biological parents attend school conferences, arranging separate appointments. The new stepmother, although positively regarded by the child, does not assume leadership in relation to the school, and does not attend school conferences.

5. *Family health requires a balance between connection and individuation.* The idea here is that healthy family functioning involves a tightrope walk between group solidarity and individual autonomy. Families with too much connectedness—either in the whole family or in particular dyads or triads—will raise children who are oversocialized and have difficulty leaving home emotionally. Families with too much separateness will raise children who are undersocialized and have difficulty trusting others. Fam-

ily psychiatrist Salvador Minuchin (1974) developed the term "enmeshment" to characterize families with excessive emotional bonding, leaving individual autonomy sacrificed, and "disengagement" to characterize families with too little emotional bonding, with nurturing and monitoring sacrificed.

Examples: In some cases, parents react with great anxiety to their daughter being snubbed by other junior high students in a new school. Or parents tell the school that their adolescent son's destructive behavior is not their problem, and fail even to monitor his cooperation with the school. In a more positive example, after an eighth grade boy was suspended from school for the remainder of the day for fighting, his parents supported the school's decision and, rather than leave work to pick up the child, they instructed the school to allow the boy to walk 3 miles home, and to tell him to call a parent as soon as he arrived home. The parents were signalling that they were not going to "rescue" him at school when he broke the rules.

6. *Flexibility is a key safeguard against serious family dysfunction.* A cardinal systems theory principle is that healthy systems are flexible systems— able to change their rules, interaction patterns, beliefs, and roles in response to demands from inside the family or from the environment (Olson, Sprenkle, & Russell, 1979). Parenting involves continual adjustment as children change developmentally; a parent monitoring style that is appropriate for a toddler is inappropriate for an adolescent. In the face of a family crisis brought on by illness or unemployment, some families rally by adapting their roles and routines, whereas others become stuck in patterns that no longer work. Therefore, stressful events in themselves do not disable families; the family's flexibility often determines whether the event has a positive, neutral, or negative outcome for the family.

Examples: Some families are able to accept and accommodate to the news that their child is mentally handicapped, but other families do not assimilate the new information. They cling to previous beliefs that their child is learning disabled or resistant to learning, or is misunderstood by teachers. Because of this inflexibility, they have difficulty in sustaining collaborative relationships with school professionals.

7. *Individuals' symptoms frequently have meaning within the family's interaction patterns or worldview.* If family relationships are viewed as a complex choreography, then the "breakdown" of one member may be correlated with what is occurring with other family members or with the family as a whole. In family therapist Jay Haley's (1976) term, symptoms may be a "metaphor" for a hidden dimension of family interaction. In one family, an adolescent ran away from home at a time that one parent was agonizing over a decision whether to leave the marriage; the therapist concluded that the adolescent fled so that the parent did not have to. Family psychiatrist Don Jackson (1957) used the term "family homeostasis" to describe the ways in which symptomatic behavior can stabilize a family system, and how the removal of the symptom can destabilize families.

Example: A child's functioning at home and school deteriorates, prompting the divorced parents to cooperate for the first time since the divorce, after which the child's functioning improves immediately. The child's symptoms appeared to serve as a means of reconnecting the parents.

8. *Small perturbations can lead to major family change.* One of the hallmarks of systems theory is the notion that accidental "kicks" in a complex living system can lead to large scale unanticipated change. In science, the contemporary version of this is found in chaos theory (Glieck, 1987), which has shown how small perturbations—for example in air temperature—can be accelerated by other environmental conditions to lead to major changes that could not have been predicted in advance. In families who are coping adequately in a stressful environment, a perturbation such as the birth of a new, sickly child, the broken leg of a family wage earner, or the death of a beloved grandparent can trigger changes that render the family disabled and a child in trouble. Similarly, a family that has become dysfunctional may "turn around" after some event that initially is not so promising, such as a more satisfying or better paying job. Family systems theory emphasizes the power of small events for good or ill.

Examples: A new teacher relates well to a troubled child, who in turn is easier to manage at home, which gives the parents a respite to improve their marriage, which in turn takes pressure off the child, who then improves in other classes at school. In an example of a negative perturbation, think of a 14-year-old boy who had been attending school regularly, despite the fact that none of his older siblings had graduated from school, his father was a binge drinker and periodically abusive, and his mother was illiterate. The "kick" in the system occurred when his older brother moved back home, which was followed by his father's blood pressure going up, the father and the 14-year-old increasing their fights, and the boy's school attendance all but ceasing.

9. *Professionals become part of a new system with the family.* Family systems theory in the 1980s began to emphasize how professionals who work with families become incorporated into a "meta" system that can be examined with the same systems concepts as the family system (Keeney, 1983). Therefore, all of the family systems principles described above can be used to understand and assess the interactions between school professionals and families: repeated interaction patterns, beliefs, triangles, boundaries, flexibility, connectedness versus disengagement, the meaning of symptomatic behavior, and the role of small perturbations. The next section describes a number of examples of these home-school dynamics.

SYSTEMS DYNAMICS IN THE FAMILY/SCHOOL RELATIONSHIP

In this section we apply family systems principles to interactions that occur when school psychologists and other school professionals become involved with families. The fundamental assumption underlying our systemic view is that school psychologists are continually and inevitably involved in triangles involving various combinations of children, parents, teachers, guidance counselors, administrators, physicians, and other mental health professionals. Our most extensive treatment will be of the family/psychologist/child triangle. Then the discussion will turn to patterns of negative escalation in family/school dynamics.

The Family/Psychologist/Child Triangle

The fundamental implication of family systems theory for school psychologists is that every relationship with a child in a school involves a triangle that includes the child's family. There are no strictly one-to-one relationships of school professionals with children; families are always implicated, whether as active partners or silent partners. A balanced relational structure involves collaboration between parents and school professionals for the welfare of the child, with parents staying within their role as parents, not acting as professional educators, and school professionals within their role, not becoming parent substitutes. A balanced relational structure also involves school professionals establishing respectful and caring relationships with parents as persons, with sensitivity to their personal needs, as opposed to viewing parents merely as agents of accomplishing goals for their children. In a healthy home-school relationship, the boundaries of the family would be permeable enough to allow school psychologists "inside" in order to work effectively with parents and children, and the school's boundaries would be permeable enough to allow the parents to participate meaningfully in shaping the school environment for the child.

The family/psychologist/child triangle can be functional or dysfunctional, but it cannot be avoided. The triangle is functional when family and psychologist collaborate for the good of the child, or when the child turns to the psychologist for help and the parents respond supportively. The triangle becomes dysfunctional when a number of distortions occur in boundaries, responsibility, and communication. One kind of distortion occurs when parents abdicate responsibility for the children's welfare to the school. Parents may· fail to keep appointments with teachers and psychologists, they may fail to follow through on home-school agreements, or they may fail to require their children to attend school.

This pattern of parents' distancing creates difficult challenges for the school psychologist. From a family systems viewpoint, the twin dangers for the school psychologist are either to give up on the parents prematurely without understanding their context, and/or to try to serve as a substitute for the parents. The former approach—as when the school psychologist stops trying to talk with the parents—forecloses the possibility of a collaborative triangle, and the latter approach—as when the school psychologist meets daily with the child to work on family problems—involves the school psychologist in an impossible level of responsibility for the child. When parents create too much distance from the child's school, the challenge for the school psychologist is to search for an understanding of the family dynamics and the family/school dynamics, and to be alert for future openings toward collaboration. Villainizing and dismissing parents feels self-righteously rewarding, but it perpetuates the distance. A school psychologist who uses a systems perspective focuses on the parents' inaccessibility as occurring within a transactional field that involves actions by the school and probably other community systems.

Another kind of dysfunctional triangle occurs when parents are overinvolved in the child's school-related activities or problems. This pattern is most apt to occur in enmeshed family systems, in which a child's failure or distress reverberates through the family emotional system and shows itself in anxious preoccupation in one or both parents. Parents in such families are apt to be highly critical or demanding of teachers, administrators, and school psychologists. Whatever special education opportunities the school offers are not enough; whatever level of attention to the child is being offered is not enough. Far from being inaccessible, these parents seem intrusive and hovering. And the school psychologist, who is often the bearer of "bad news" about the child's learning limitations, is situated to be the target of the grief and anxiety of enmeshed family systems.

Example: A 15-year-old girl with cerebral palsy was placed in the 6th grade of an out-of-district school. The mother did not approve of the school program in the child's own district but wanted her daughter to be able to socialize with other children. She insisted on screening all special education materials, called the case manager and paraprofessional every day, and refused to allow any standardized testing.

A family systems view of parental overinvolvement can take several forms. First, the school psychologist can assess whether one or both parents are enmeshed with the child, and whether the other parent is disengaged or trying to maintain appropriate boundaries. Second, the overinvolved parent(s) can be viewed with compassion stemming from an appreciation for the anxiety they experience in dealing with their child— they feel too deeply responsible for their child's welfare—and thus should not be scapegoated for not "wanting" their children to be separate individuals. High levels of monitoring and involvement are necessary with handicapped children; it is inevitable that some parents will cross over the line to unhealthy forms of enmeshment.

Third, children can be assumed to be active participants in the parental overinvolvement, often through a pattern of underresponsibility for their own feelings or behavior. Any simplistic message to the parents to "back off" only stirs up more anxiety in them and the child. Often the child who complains about overinvolved parents becomes quite upset

when the parents become more distant, prompting a renewal of the child's troublesome behavior. Both the child's and the parents' feelings must be understood and worked with if the parents are to become more appropriately involved.

Fourth, it is important to examine how school professionals may have unintentionally contributed to a pattern of parental overinvolvement. For example, routinely holding parent conferences for special education students with only the mother present may accentuate her feeling of sole responsibility for her child, whereas flexible scheduling of meetings, combined with insistence that both parents be present, can partially neutralize the mother's anxiety by spreading the responsibility. Another example of indirect school contribution to this triangular problem occurs when school professionals engage in distancing maneuvers from the overinvolved parent(s), as in not returning phone calls promptly, postponing conferences, and dismissing parents' concerns as "over-reacting." When anxious parents sense school professionals' withdrawal, they are apt to increase their pressure for answers, changes in educational plans, or access to teachers and psychologists. A pursuer/distancer pattern thus becomes established, with both sides contributing to the dysfunctional dance.

The Family/Psychologist/ Teacher Triangle

Often the most painful triangles are those involving other professionals and the people being served. Teachers have responsibility for educating a large number of students, and often feel overwhelmed in dealing with children who have special needs or problems. The ideal relational structure involves appreciation and respect by the teacher and school psychologist for their mutual roles, with both oriented as a primary goal toward the welfare of the child and family. However, it is not uncommon for teachers to ask the school psychologist to "solve" the problem they are having with a child by "straightening out" the child and the parents. To use common parlance, teachers sometimes try to dump problem children and problem families on the school psychologist. When teachers are at their wits end, they can try to coerce the school psychologist to remove the child from the classroom, to hold the child back from promotion to the next grade, or to threaten the parents if they do not cooperate. The school psychologist then feels caught between loyalty to the teacher as a fellow school professional and professional obligation to the child and parent.

Example: A sixth grade boy frequently did not come to school. His mother vacillated between claiming helplessness and blaming the school for placing too much stress on her son. A psychiatrist found the boy to be extremely anxious and mildly depressed. Some school personnel felt the boy was "manipulative," the mother "negligent," and the school psychologist "rescuing." The school psychologist attempted to work with the boy and his mother to keep him in school, but other school professionals recommended filing charges against the mother with child protective services, having the boy repeat sixth grade, and having the boy placed in a full-time program for children with emotional disturbance.

Negative triangles lead to bashing of the various parties. In the case of the family/psychologist/teacher triangle, teachers can join forces to criticize and squeeze the school psychologist. The school psychologist who is not sensitive to the relational dynamics may respond by triangling with the parents against the teacher, by indicating that he or she is the only one really "for" the child, and by trying to convince the teachers to change their minds. School psychologists can also band with one another to bash teachers for being authoritarian and uncaring about troubled children. Not having to deal with disruptive children in classroom settings, school psychologists can be tempted to assume the moral high ground in dealing with teachers. Teachers naturally resent this patronizing attitude, and respond by assuming the pragmatic high ground, as

in "Somebody around here has to be concerned with teaching a classroom full of children." One way out of this tension between teachers and school psychologists is to join forces against the family by prematurely concluding that the parents and the child are hopeless and that school professionals have made no contribution to the problem.

The Teacher/Psychologist/Principal Triangle

The school principal has the most complex role in the organization, involving loyalties and responsibilities to children, parents, teachers, counselors, psychologists, other school support and community personnel, the superintendent, and the school board. The opportunities for troublesome triangles are nearly limitless. The most skillful principals continually balance among their constituencies and keep a focus on the mission of the school to promote the education and welfare of children. However, the need for compromises is ever-present, as when teachers are at the end of their rope with a child who disrupts classes, but the school psychologist wants more time to work with the child and the parents before suspending the child. The school psychologist is aware that suspensions and out-of-school placements typically do not promote long-term positive changes in children. In this case, the principal must balance the morale of the teachers with the needs of the child and the judgment of the school psychologist.

A special feature of triangles with principals is that the school psychologist who disagrees with the principal is differing with the boss. When the school psychologist and the teacher or counselor are at odds over a child, the principal is like the parent whose children are squabbling. All parties are tempted to tell secrets behind the backs of the others, and all are tempted to show a different face to each party. For example, the principal may imply to the teacher that the school psychologist should be humored because he or she does not "really understand" the needs of a classroom—and then imply to the school psychologist that the teacher is "over-reacting."

The school psychologist is fully capable of contributing to the negative relational dynamics as well. This can take the form of undermining the teacher to the principal, or of creating a new triangle with the principal and the parents. In this latter case, the school psychologist may undermine the role of the principal by subtly suggesting to the parents that the principal is acting for political reasons or out of ignorance—and that only the school psychologist really understands and cares.

Misattributions and Escalating Negative Interactions

One of the themes of this chapter is that a sophisticated systems approach involves appreciating the role of the school and its professionals in creating and perpetuating problems with children and families. Here we are not intending to villainize the school or to minimize family's responsibilities. Rather, our assumption is that frequently when problems become chronic and destructive in human relationships, all the involved parties are likely to be contributing—at least unwittingly—to maintaining the problematic interactions. More bluntly—we are all part of the loop when things go wrong and stay wrong. The advantage of this working assumption is that it gives the professional something to work on when all else seems hopeless—one's own attitudes and behavior.

In our view, one of the central mistakes that schools make in assessing the causes of problem behavior in children and uncooperativeness from parents is to view most problems as issues of *control*. That is, someone is deemed to be undermining legitimate authority of the school or the teacher, or is refusing for the wrong reasons to cooperate with the appropriate controls and expectations that the school has of children and parents. This point has been made in the family systems area by Doherty and Colangelo (1984), who propose that serious control/conflict problems in family relationships are generally secondary to problems in what they call "inclusion." Inclusion refers to issues of organization and bonding in social groups. It involves areas such as clarity of structure, adequate interpersonal connections, and a shared meaning about the purposes and values of the family or other social group. In their model, called the Family FIRO Model (after Schutz's [1958] FIRO theory), Doherty and Colangelo (1984) propose that it is often a mistake to focus initially only on the control dimension of interactional problems, because generally the control issues are being "fed" by problems of inclusion, such as unclear authority structures, children feeling neglected, and parental disagreement about values, priorities, or shared goals.

How does this theory relate to school interactions with families? We suggest that control issues such as conflict or noncooperation from parents most often stems from something awry in the inclusion aspect of the family/school relationship. Examples include parents feeling excluded by school professionals, parents getting different answers from different school professionals, parents' negative views of schools because of their family of origin experience, and parents being so overwhelmed with family problems that they cannot apply enough energy to engage the school constructively. Notice that none of those common examples involves the attribution that parents want to antagonize or undermine the school, or that they do not care enough about their children to cooperate with the school. Attributions that someone is deliberately trying to coerce or undermine lead to negative, punitive actions that may make the problem worse.

Negative attributions about parents' behavior, in the absence of sensitivity to underlying family dynamics and family-school dynamics, lead to escalating negative interactional sequences between school and home. Here is how we would script the dance, which can begin with a move from either side:

Disliked action > scapegoating > blaming > defensiveness > Non-cooperation >

More scapegoating, etc. > Punitive action or withdrawal > Counter-punitive action or counter-withdrawal—and onward.

Many of the examples we have used in this chapter fit this pattern nicely. When the school psychologist sees this pattern occurring, it is reasonable to conclude that something is awry in the family-school system, not just in some individuals in the system.

Summary

This section of the chapter has described some common dynamics of the family/school relational system. Many of these dynamics occur in triangles, and they involve attributions or explanations of other parties' actions, and the danger of runaway negative escalations. We hope we have conveyed the power of family systems theory to understand some of the interactional dances between families and school, and the advantage of seeing school psychologists and other professionals as part of the same system with the child and family. In our experience, seeing oneself and one's colleagues as potentially "part of the problem" in a complex home-school relationship gone awry can lead to more creative movement toward being "part of the solution."

In the next section we turn to the matter of how school psychologists can act upon systems understanding in the home-school relationship. Specific techniques for working with families in schools are addressed elsewhere in this book. Here we offer an outline of the various modes of involvement that school psychologists can have with families.

LEVELS OF SCHOOL PSYCHOLOGISTS' INVOLVEMENT WITH FAMILIES

Assuming the validity of the notion that school psychologists inevitably are involved with families when working with children, what kinds of involvement with families are appropriate within the context of the school psychologist's role? The idea of different levels of intensity and complexity in clinical work has a precedent in medicine. In obstetrical care, for example, medical professionals describe levels ranging from simple, uncomplicated deliveries through complicated vaginal deliveries through cesarean sections. Different degrees of training are necessary for each level of clinical complexity.

In the area of school psychologists' work with families, Anderson (1983) outlined several different kinds of involvement with families. In terms of intervention, a minimal level described by Anderson is awareness of the family context in which a child-oriented intervention occurs. A second level of family-oriented intervention involves performing liaison functions among home, school, and community. The most intensive level would be providing direct interventions for families through the school. Each of these three levels involves different degrees of sophistication in family assessment. Another levels model was presented by Conoley (1987), who focused on "progressively greater positive interdependence between family and school system" (p. 191).

In applying family systems ideas to family medical practice, Doherty and Baird (1986, 1987) outlined five levels of physicians' involvement with families, along with the knowledge base, personal development base, and skills needed for each level. Doherty and Baird's model has some similarities with Anderson's (1983) and Conoley's (1987) models, but makes distinctions between cognitive, affective, and systems-level orientations to work with families. Doherty and Baird's levels also deal explicitly with the competence needed by professionals in different kinds of family work. This model, which has been used widely in family practice education, may have heuristic value for school psychologists as well. We first briefly outline Doherty and Baird's levels of family involvement for physicians, and then adapt this model to school psychologists.

Doherty and Baird's Levels Model for Physicians

According to Doherty and Baird (1986, 1987), Level One of physician involvement with families is termed "Minimal Involvement with Families." Here families are not viewed as a conscious focus of professional clinical practice, but are dealt with for practical or legal reasons only, as in getting permission for surgery or obtaining information when the patient is not competent. Level Two is termed "Ongoing Medical Information and Advice." Here the physician meets with families and patients for the purpose of sharing diagnostic information, answering questions, and collaborating on treatment planning. However, the physician does not attempt to engage or work with affective issues of family members; Level Two has a cognitive orientation.

Level Three for physicians is termed "Feelings and Support." It involves the physician going beyond the cognitive level to elicit family members' emotional responses to the patient's illness and prognosis. The physician also educates the family about the normal stresses stemming from illness. Level Three, then, involves both cognitive and affective issues, but the physician is not attempting to intervene to bring about change in family interaction patterns. Level Four, "Systematic Assessment and Planned Intervention," goes beyond the previous levels by providing a brief, focused intervention into family patterns that are believed to be complicating the patient's medical situation or causing family strain. Level Four involves a "primary care" intervention based on a systems analysis of the family's difficulties. This might consist of one or a few family conferences focused on bringing about change in family patterns directly related to the patient's problems. Level Five is called "Family Therapy." This level is beyond the primary care training of most family physicians. It is a specialty service provided by therapists who are trained to engage seriously disabled families around a wide range of issues, both those related to a medical problem and those beyond the presenting problem.

As it has been used in family practice education, this model has demonstrated five advantages. First, it acknowledges several useful and appropriate ways to interact with families, as opposed to mandating one kind of involvement. Second, it stresses that the level of appropriate involvement depends on the physician's ability and time constraints, and on the family's openness and motivation. Third, it makes a relatively clear distinction between primary care counseling and specialized family therapy. Fourth, it lays out the knowledge and skill needed for each kind of involvement. Fifth, it offers a developmental sequence of competencies in working with families, with competency at Level Two informational dialogue seen as essential for Level Three affective conversation, which in turn is an essential competency before the physician should attempt systemic interventions.

Application of the Levels Model to School Psychologists

We now adapt these levels to the context of school psychologists, and include, in Table 1, a presentation of the knowledge base, personal development base, and skills required by school psychologists to practice at each level. The levels can be used both as a description of interactions between school professionals and families—demarcating the kinds of conversation that occurred at a family conference or private meeting with parents—and as a way to characterize the competency of school psychologists for different kinds of family work.

Level One "Minimal Emphasis on Family" consists of dealing with families only as necessary for practical and educational/legal reasons, but not viewing communicating with families as integral to the psychologist's role or as requiring special skills to develop. Rather, the family is relegated to a background factor. Examples of activities at this level include securing parental permission for assessment and meeting with the student individually or in a group on a regular basis without parental involvement beyond giving permission for the child's participation.

Level Two "Ongoing Psychoeduca-

TABLE 1
Levels of School Psychologists' Involvement with Families

Level 1: Minimal Emphasis on Family
This baseline level of involvement consists of dealing with families only as necessary for practical educational/legal reasons, but not viewing communicating with families as integral to the psychologist's role or as involving skills to develop. Rather, the family is relegated to a background factor.

Level 2: Ongoing Psychoeducational Information and Advice
Knowledge base: Primarily psychoeducational plus awareness of the triangular dimension of psychologist-child relationship. Awareness that families are valuable sources of information for the psychologist for diagnostic purposes and for tailoring interventions to the child's life situation.
Personal development: Openness to engage children and families in collaborative ways.
Skills:
1. Regularly and clearly communicating assessment results and intervention options to family members. This may include ongoing communication relating to the outcomes of interventions.
2. Asking family members questions that elicit relevant "diagnostic" and intervention information.
3. Attentively listening to family members' questions and concerns.
4. Advising families about their role in ongoing educational and remedial needs of the child.
5. For post-divorce or nontraditional families, knowing how to communicate with key family members who are involved with the child.
6. Identifying gross family dysfunction that interferes with school functioning and/or psychoeducational programming, and referring the family to a therapist.

Level 3: Feelings and Support
Knowledge base: Normal family development and reactions to stress.
Personal development: Awareness of one's own feelings in relation to the child and family.
Skills:
1. Asking questions that elicit family members' expressions of concern and feelings related to the child's school difficulties and their effect on the family.
2. Empathetically listening to family members' concerns and feelings, and normalizing them where appropriate.
3. Forming a preliminary assessment of the family's level of functioning as it relates to the child's difficulties in school.
4. Encouraging family members in their efforts to cope as a family with their situation.
5. Tailoring psychoeducational advice to the unique needs, concerns, and feelings of the family.
6. Identifying family dysfunction and fitting a referral recommendation to the unique situation of the family.

Level 4: Systematic Assessment and Planned Intervention
Personal development: Awareness of one's own participation in systems including clinical triangles, the educational system, one's own family system, and larger community systems.
Skills:
1. Engaging family members, including reluctant ones, in a planned family conference or a series of conferences.
2. Structuring a conference with even a poorly communicating family in such a way that all members have a chance to express themselves.
3. Systematically assessing the family's level of functioning.
4. Supporting individual members while avoiding coalitions.
5. Reframing the family's definition of their problem in a way that makes problem solving more achievable.
6. Helping the family members view their difficulty as requiring new forms of collaborative efforts.
7. Helping family members generate alternate, mutually acceptable ways to cope with their difficulty.
8. Helping the family balance their coping efforts by calibrating their various roles in a way that allows support without sacrificing anyone's autonomy.
9. Identifying family dysfunction that lies beyond the school difficulties and orchestrating a referral by educating the family and the therapist about what to expect from one another.

Level 5: Family Therapy
Knowledge base: Family systems and patterns whereby dysfunctional families interact with professionals and other community systems.
Personal development: Ability to handle intense emotions in families and self and to maintain one's balance in the face of strong pressure from family members or other professionals.
Skills: (Examples)
1. Determining treatment priorities when the family has multiple problems.
2. Addressing a wide array of family problems as they emerge during treatment, such as sexual problems and family of origin issues.
3. Managing severe family conflict that erupts during sessions.

tional Information and Advice" is the level at which the school psychologist has a conscious focus on families, believes they are important in working with children, collaborates with them in the psychoeducational area, and has good skills at conducting family conferences that focus on psychoeducational issues.

Example: A child who attends kindergarten in the afternoon regularly arrives looking angry. He stays by himself and refuses to participate. The kindergarten teacher is thinking of asking the parents to withdraw the child from kindergarten for the remainder of the school year in order to give him a chance to "grow up." During a conference with the parents and the teacher, the school psychologist asks the parents to describe their child's behavior at home. They indicate that, although he socializes well with neighborhood children, he has long periods of solitary play. The parents also volunteer the information that the boy begins his group day care early in the morning. Based on this information about the child's "style," the school psychologist suggests that the teacher establish a solitary play situation for the boy for a short time period after he enters the classroom.

Level Three "Feelings and Support" embraces the activities, knowledge, and skills of Level Two, but moves beyond them to deal with the affective responses of family members. Family conferences at Level Three generally involve switching back and forth between psychoeducational material and affective material. Parents are viewed as persons who may need emotional support and guidance, not just as agents of socialization or educational programming for their child. Family conferences become opportunities for addressing parents' fears, concerns, and personal stresses that bear on the child's school life. Even if teachers or other professionals at the conference are not oriented to a family approach, the school psychologist would have the skills to make the experience supportive to the parents. At this level of interaction, of course, school psychologists must deal with their own emotional reactions to

parents. Because Level Three interactions are so central to the work of school psychologists, we offer three examples.

Example 1: A second grade child was experiencing difficulty in both social and academic areas. The school psychologist met with the mother, who was a single parent living with her own mother. When the school psychologist inquired about the mother's own life, she tearfully told of her struggle with a decision about whether to place her aging mother in a nursing home because of her mother's deteriorating Alzheimer's disease. Because the mother had limited financial and emotional resources, ongoing support was provided to her through existing school services, and extensive programming was provided for the child.

Example 2: A Korean boy was experiencing emotional, social, and academic difficulties in sixth grade. Attempts to encourage the family to seek outside evaluation and counseling were unsuccessful. When the school psychologist turned her attention to the needs of the family, it became evident that the family was fearful that if their son was perceived as emotionally disturbed, they would be alienated from the Korean community. They preferred to view their son as "retarded," a diagnosis far more acceptable to their community. The school psychologist subsequently helped the boy obtain the services he needed, while being sensitive to the family's need for their own definition of the problem.

Example 3: A first grade girl, along with several of her friends, had "mooned" from the window of the school bus. Her middle class parents were appalled and asked to meet with the school psychologist. The mother cried as she questioned her ability to parent, the role that her full-time employment might have had in the child's behavior, and whether her child was ready for school. The school psychologist acknowledged her feelings, and proceeded to talk about peer pressure, how imitative 6-year-olds can be, and how interested in "potty talk" they are. After the mother calmed down, the father began to talk about his anxieties and unhappiness at work and how he had been withdrawn and irritable at home in recent months. The parents left feeling relieved about their child and with the resolve to talk more with each other about the anxieties that had surfaced in the conference.

Level Four "Systematic Assessment and Planned Intervention" subsumes Levels Two and Three but goes beyond by providing a focused family intervention aimed at changing family interaction patterns that interfere with the child's school performance or psychosocial well-being. Whereas Level Three interactions are generally limited to the expression and clarification of feelings, along with education about child development and family stress, Level Four is focused on bringing about family change. The school psychologist working at this level is able to conduct a few planned family counseling sessions, and would know when such counseling reaches its limit. Level Four competency requires a working understanding of family systems theory and supervised training in school-based family counseling. School psychologists who do this kind of counseling regularly should have a family therapist consultant to process cases with.

Example 1: The sixth grader's mother came to the school planning conference with her ex-mother-in-law, her ex-sister-in-law, and a volunteer advocate from a local nonprofit organization. It quickly became apparent that the mother and grandmother were in total disagreement about how to manage the child. The school psychologist listened to and clarified both of their feelings and positions, and then helped them through some difficult negotiations on areas of agreement for the good of the child.

Example 2: The mother of an eighth grade boy spoke rapidly about her history with the schools and how she had been forced to "fight" for everything for her son. After several hours of such discussions with the school psychologist, she agreed to invite her husband to a planning meeting. With her husband present, she was able to say that she wanted to share some of the responsibility she felt for her son with her husband and with

school personnel. The father was able to share some of his intense fears regarding his son, as well as his desire to become more involved in helping his son to improve in school. The school psychologist helped the parents to negotiate a new form of shared responsibility for their son's school activities.

Level Five "Family Therapy" involves an extended series of family sessions aimed at major systemic change. Whereas Level Four interventions focus on the family-school system and on parent-child problems, Level Five family therapy may extend more broadly into the parent's marriage, parents' problems such as depression and alcoholism, and the family's relationships with other community systems. This kind of involvement will probably not be pursued by a school psychologist in a school setting, unless that psychologist has a specially defined role and has sought intensive training in family therapy. The skills particular to Level Five are those involving dealing with families who are resistant to change and with families who have multiple problems requiring simultaneous attention. These skills will not be delineated in detail here, because they are generally outside of the training of school psychologists. Examples include: (a) determining treatment priorities when the family presents the problems in multiple subsystems and with multiple community systems, (b) managing severe family conflict that erupts in therapy sessions, and (c) stirring up family conflict in order to unbalance a "stuck" family system.

These five levels do not constitute a prescription for school psychologists, but rather a set of alternatives in working with families. The level of the school psychologist's involvement with a particular family will depend partly on the family's wants and needs. Some families do not want interventions into their family dynamics, rendering Level Four involvement inappropriate. Similarly, some families are reluctant to talk about their feelings in a school setting. Although at least Level Two involvement is almost always desirable and worth working toward, at times the school psychologist might have to settle for minimal parental participation such as signing consents.

The appropriate level of involvement will also depend on the school psychologist's sense of confidence and competence in dealing with families. Few school psychologists would be expected to pursue Level Five family therapy competence, but many might be interested in obtaining Level Four competence. Even for the school psychologist who has Level Four competence, however, contextual constraints may require a different level of involvement, as when there is not enough time for a longer family conference or when the family already has an outside therapist.

Finally, the levels model can help professional training programs develop curriculum goals in the family area by suggesting the knowledge and skill needed for different degrees of family work that are appropriate for the school psychologist, but that are less intensive than would be required of a specialist in family therapy. Professionals in some training programs might regard Level Three as minimum competency for school psychologists—the ability to work collaboratively with families around psychoeducational and emotional issues—whereas those in charge of other programs might decide to enhance the family curriculum and training opportunities to help students achieve Level Four competency—the ability to do brief, focused systems interventions with families. The latter requires, however, that the school psychologist have access to a Level Five family therapist for consultation and referral.

OBSTACLES TO A FAMILY SYSTEMS ORIENTATION IN THE SCHOOLS

Any systems analysis of change efforts requires an exploration of the contextual obstacles. Here we discuss five barriers to the implementation of a family systems model by school psychologists: time constraints, role perceptions, structural incongruency, training, and boundary issues with other professionals.

1. *Time constraints.* Most school psychologists we know already have a full "dance card." Adding regular and perhaps lengthier family conferences to the schedule means that some other activity must be decreased, such as consultation, testing and assessment, research, or direct services to individual children. Our belief is that working with families tends to decrease demand for some of these other activities, but in the short run priorities must be rearranged.

2. *Role perceptions.* Traditionally school psychologists have occupied the role of "gatekeeper" for special education services in the schools. Despite attempts by school psychologists and training programs, it has been difficult to transcend the limitations of this role. State legislators continue to mandate specific assessment information that is typically provided by school psychologists. Teacher training programs generally do not educate teachers about how to use psychologists beyond assessment and consultation about behavior modification in the classroom. And school psychologists themselves, trained to focus on the individual child, have difficulty assuming a new family-oriented image of their role in the schools. In this chapter we have called not just for expanded activities with families, but for a new definition of the school psychologist's role in the schools. Such a change collides with entrenched role perceptions that will not easily change.

3. *Structural incongruency.* Consider the situation of a school psychologist with Level Four competency and a systems orientation toward home and school. That psychologist will attempt to create structures that allow family involvement, structures that may collide with those of a school that is oriented to Level One family involvement. An obvious example is a school system that expects single parents and two-parent blue collar workers to regularly attend meetings during the workday. Another example occurs when the principal expects the school psychologist to assume such a heavy assessment load that family work is precluded. In this situation, the

school psychologist may have to negotiate a new job description. An additional incongruency may occur among the group of school psychologists in a school district, when some support, and others do not support, a family-oriented approach. The latter group may feel that their professional self-concept and their work day are being infringed upon. Ultimately, for a systems approach to work in any organization, there must be congruency at all levels of the organization.

4. *Training limitations.* Those providing training programs for school psychologists already complain about the amount of coursework that must be provided within given time constraints. Currently, universities must provide training in traditional assessment, research, consultation, counseling, psychopathology, and more. If the curriculum were to provide a thorough grounding in working with families, something else would have to be reduced in the curriculum or the length of the program increased. Similarly, internship experiences would have to be altered to create space for family training, with the consequent loss of training in other areas. Clearly, our view is that such adjustments are worth the effort, but the faculty would have to be quite committed to accept reductions in their own, more traditional areas of interest.

5. *Boundary issues with other professionals.* There is a degree of ambiguity about role expectations between school psychologists and other mental health professionals who work inside and outside the schools. For example, in some schools the school social worker regards family work as social worker professional turf, and might be threatened by the school psychologists' activities with families, at least those at Level Four. Without mutual education and collaboration, there can also be misunderstanding and conflict between family therapists in the community and school psychologists, with the former seeing the latter as amateur family therapists. Ideally, partnership models can be created among these professional groups, with each

functioning within its own expertise but relying on the others as well. In our view, family work is inherently team work.

SUMMARY AND CONCLUSION

We have made a case for a family orientation for the school psychologist and for family systems theory as an orienting framework for the school psychologist in working with families. We have described the various triangles that the school psychologist works with every day, and suggested that a systems analysis is essential to avoid damage to children and families and school professionals in these triangles. We have argued that the hallmark of a systems orientation is the willingness to examine how the school and its professionals often become part of the problem in trying to be part of the solution. We have described a model for qualitatively different levels of involvement by school psychologists with families, and we have delineated obstacles to implementing a family systems approach to the schools.

The proposals in this chapter create a fundamental identity dilemma for the school psychologist: Who is the client when the school psychologist has a family orientation? Briefly, our resolution of this issue from a systems perspective is that the child is *always* the client, but that the child is never the *only* client. Even with identity issues partly resolved, the obstacles described above leave important questions about how to implement a family systems approach to the schools. How can school psychologists redefine their role if school officials do not have a family orientation? How does the school psychologist with a family orientation and Level Four competency function within a system oriented to individual children and Level One family competency? How can training programs foster a family perspective and teach family skills if the structures of school psychologists' work in schools frustrate this perspective? In a more family-oriented school district that may expect Level Four family involvement by school psychologists, how can they obtain the training and ongoing consultation needed to practice competently at this level? And how can family therapists and school psychologists learn to collaborate in providing services to troubled families, given the lack of training of family therapists in understanding schools and the lack of training of school psychologists in understanding families? A family systems model in the schools will work only if family therapists become more involved as support and referral resources for school psychologists.

These larger contextual issues do not lend themselves to ready solutions. However, consistent with family systems theory, we suggest that family-oriented school psychologists take a non-scapegoating and collaborative stance toward structural change. There are no villains standing in the way of meaningful involvement of families in the work of school psychologists. Instead there are larger systemic and cultural issues in schools and American society that create obstacles to viewing individuals in their social context and to sharing social power and responsibility with the clients of professional services. *The family systems approach we have described for the schools is fundamentally social and collaborative. It involves a different paradigm for practice, not just an extra set of concepts and techniques to be grafted onto the old paradigm.* Hence, it is countercultural in the late 20th century. But the winds of change are blowing, and the current educational system seems no longer to have a broad social mandate. If, in conjunction with family therapists and other professionals in and out of the schools, school psychologists can provide leadership for involving families in an inviting, collaborative way in the care and education of children, the role of the school psychologist will be transformed. The new role will be more challenging and more complex than the old one, but it will also be more consistent with the ecological vision of the men and women who pioneered the field nearly a century ago.

REFERENCES

Anderson, C. (1983). An ecological developmental model for a family orientation in school psychology. *Journal of School Psychology, 21*, 179–189 .

Aponte, H. J. (1976). The family-school interview: An eco-structural approach. *Family Process, 15*, 303–311.

Bateson, G. (1972). *Steps to an ecology of mind*. San Francisco: Chandler.

Boss, P. G. (1988). *Family stress management*. Newbury Park, CA: Sage.

Bowen, M. (1978). *Family therapy in clinical practice*. New York: Aronson.

Christie-Seely, J. (Ed.). (1984). *Working with the family in primary care*. New York: Praeger.

Conoley, J. C. (1987). Schools and families: Theoretical and practical bridges. *Professional School Psychology, 2*, 191–203.

Constantine, L. C. (1986). *Family paradigms*. New York: Guilford.

Doherty, W. J. (1985). Family interventions in health care. *Family Relations, 34*, 129–137.

Doherty, W. J., & Baird, M. A. (1983). *Family therapy and family medicine: Toward the primary care of families*. New York: Guilford.

Doherty, W. J., & Baird, M. A. (1986). Developmental levels in family-centered medical care. *Family Medicine, 18*, 153–156.

Doherty, W. J., & Baird, M. A. (1987). *Family-centered medical care: A clinical casebook*. New York: Guilford.

Doherty, W. J., & Colangelo, N. (1984). The Family FIRO Model: A modest proposal for organizing family treatment. *Journal of Marital and Family Therapy, 10*, 19–29.

Fine, M. J., & Holt, P. (1983). Intervening with school problems: A family systems perspective. *Psychology in the Schools, 20*, 59–66.

French, J. L. (1990). History of school psychology. In T. B. Gutkin & C. R. Reynolds (Eds.), *The handbook of school psychology* (2nd ed., pp. 3–20). New York: Wiley.

Glieck, J. (1987). *Chaos*. New York: Viking.

Green, R. J. (1989). "Learning to learn" and the family system: New perspectives on underachievement and learning disorders. *Journal of Marital and Family Therapy, 2*, 187–203.

Haley, J. (1976). *Problem solving therapy*. San Francisco: Jossey-Bass.

Imber-Black, E. (1988). *Families and larger systems*. New York: Guilford.

Jackson, D. (1957). The question of family homeostasis. *Psychiatric Quarterly Supplement, 31* (part 1), 79–90.

Keeney, B. P. (1983). *The aesthetics of change.* New York: Guilford.

Kramer, J. J. (1990). Training parents as behavior change agents: Successes, failures, and suggestions for school psychologists. In T. B. Gutkin & C. R. Reynolds (Eds), *The handbook of school psychology* (2nd ed., pp. 683–702). New York: Wiley.

Lombard, T. J. (1979). Family-oriented emphasis for school psychologists: A needed orientation for training and professional practice. *Professional Psychology, 10,* 687–696.

Lusterman, D. D. (1985). An ecosystemic approach to family-school problems. *The American Journal of Family Therapy, 13,* 22–31.

Minuchin, S. (1974). *Families and family therapy.* Cambridge, MA: Harvard University Press.

Montgomery, C., & Feuer, L. (1988). *Family systems and beyond.* New York: Plenum.

Olson, D. H., Sprenkle, D. H., & Russell, C. S. (1979). Circumplex model of marital and family systems: I. Cohesion and adaptability dimensions, family types, and clinical applications. *Family Process, 18,* 3–28.

Reiss, D. (1981). *The family's construction of reality.* Cambridge, MA: Harvard University Press.

Schutz, W. (1958). *FIRO: A three dimensional theory of interpersonal behavior.* New York: Holt, Rinehart & Winston.

Schwartzman, J. (Ed.). (1985). *Families and other systems: The macrosystemic context of family therapy.* New York: Guilford.

Wendt, R. N., & Zake, J. (1984). Family systems theory and school psychology: Implications for training and practice. *Psychology in the Schools, 21,* 204–210 .

2

HOME-SCHOOL COLLABORATION: EFFECTS, ISSUES, AND OPPORTUNITIES

Sandra L. Christenson, Theresa Rounds, and Mary Jo Franklin

Trying to educate children without the involvement of their family is like trying to play a basketball game without all the players on the court. (Bradley cited by Olson, 1990, p. 17)

The crucial issue in successful learning is not home or school—teacher or student—but the relationship between them. Learning takes place where there is a productive learning relationship. (Seeley, 1985, p. 11)

Shifting the blame for children's school problems from the school to the home is not a satisfactory solution. Mutual support is the answer. (Scott-Jones, 1988, p. 66)

The first five years of life are a very important period . . . it's become counterproductive in that it's become a magic period: If we just do everything we can during the preschool years, then everything is going to be wonderful during school. That's just not true. . . . Changing the trajectory of development of a child really calls for a lot of effort, and it has to be done year after year after year. That is why the family is so important, because the family is there year after year after year. (Zigler cited by Olson, 1990, p. 22)

Quotes are worth a thousand words! The predominant theme of these quotes is: Partnership is integral to the educational success of children and youth. These quotes imply that academic outcomes will improve when parents and educators collaborate throughout students' educational careers. In this chapter, theoretical and empirical support for home-school partnerships is reviewed.

Why a partnership? Why a shared responsibility among home, school, and community for promoting positive academic and socialization outcomes for children and youth? Why should school psychologists and other mental health professionals be interested in or concerned about collaboration? The theoretical underpinnings of a partnership approach for improving student learning include at least three points:

1. In today's society, schools alone cannot meet all children's needs. The sheer number of at-risk children, problem situations, and changing demographics of American society dictate a collaborative stance.

2. Children learn, grow, and develop both at home and at school (Bronfenbrenner, 1979). There is not a clear-cut boundary between home and school experiences for children and youth, rather

there is a mutually influencing quality among home and school experiences. Epstein (1987) notes that time in school is not purely school time; time at home not purely family time.

3. A learning environment is educative when it enables the individual to learn and develop specialized skills; it is miseducative when it fails to encourage positive human development. The educative community, according to Fantini (1983), is produced when learning environments of the home, school, and community are linked together and carefully coordinated to serve the developmental needs of individuals.

Recent parent involvement in education mandates in 20 states (Nardine & Morris, 1991) and the salience of the topic in educational journals are two signs that educators are responding to the importance of the home-school relationship. Within the last 4 years, home-school collaboration has been a topic of special issues in five publications: "Parents and Schools" in *Educational Horizons* (Epstein, 1988b); "Strengthening Partnerships with Parents and Community" in *Educational Leadership* (Brandt, 1989); "Parents as Partners" in *Education Week* (Cohen, 1990; Olson, 1990); "Tapping Parent Power" in *Phi Delta Kappan* (Gough, 1991); and "Educational Partnerships: Home-School-Community" in *The Elementary School Journal* (Hoffman, 1991). Although there is strong interest in partnerships, the field is characterized more by rhetoric than reality. Fortunately, there are innumerable opportunities and challenges to change the rhetoric to reality.

The purpose of this chapter is to review literature on the effects of, issues related to, and opportunities for creating effective home-school partnerships. A "review of reviews" approach of the literature has been adopted. Our intent is to provide readers with substantiated generalizations. In this chapter we summarize literature in an attempt to answer five questions: (a) What is home-school collaboration? (b) Why should parents and educators collaborate? (c) What is the current state of practice? (d) What factors influence collaboration? and (e) How can school psychologists and other mental health professionals strengthen home-school-community partnerships?

WHAT IS HOME-SCHOOL COLLABORATION?

To collaborate means "to work jointly with others or together . . . to cooperate with an agency or instrumentality with which one is not immediately connected" (Merriam-Webster, 1985, p. 259). This definition seems simple and straightforward; however, most individuals believe collaboration is difficult to define. Collaboration refers to the process of or the product resulting from collaborating. What does that mean exactly? What does collaboration look like in practice?

Families as Allies Project engaged parents of children with emotional disturbance and educators in a number of training activities, out of which emerged several key elements of collaborative relationships. These include: mutual respect for skills and knowledge, honest and clear communication, two-way sharing of information, mutually agreed upon goals, and shared planning and decision making (Vosler-Hunter, 1989). Putting these elements or basic building blocks together requires patience, desire, and commitment. Knitzer and Yelton (1989) identified a realistic sense of time, a set of shared goals, and leadership as ingredients of successful collaboration. Similarly, Seeley (1985) in his book, *Education through Partnership*, offers an excellent, simple-to-the-point definition of partnership. He defined partnership as "a common effort toward a common goal" (p. 65). In a subsequent article, Seeley (1991) opines that "the concept of educational partnership calls for making education a shared responsibility of families, schools, and communities rather than a function delegated to bureaucratic agencies, and it calls for collaborative rather than bureaucratic structures for carrying out this responsibility" (p. 31). Dunst and his co-authors (this volume) provide a data-based definition of partnership, and a component analysis of partnerships between parents and professionals. It is noteworthy that the defining characteristics of collaboration and partnership are consistent with characteristics of Cochran's (1987) empowerment process including: mutual respect, critical reflection, caring, and group participation.

The goal of collaborative relationships is optimal school success for all students. Rich (1987) has shown that "parent participation is most widespread and sustained when parents view their participation as directly linked to the achievement and performance of their children" (p. 63). Collaborative relationships are complementary relationships. Parents and teachers do not need to perform the same task or behavior to assist a child's school productivity. What is important is that they complement each other's efforts by working toward similar goals. According to Vosler-Hunter (1990), "Clear and open communication, when conducted in an atmosphere of respect and sensitivity to the other person will provide a basis for mutual understanding and action" (p. 3) or complementary relationships between home and school, parents and professionals.

The term home-school collaboration is related to parent involvement but is broader and more inclusive. Parent involvement focuses on the parents' role in becoming involved in their children's education, whereas home-school collaboration focuses on the relationship between home and school and how parents and educators work together to promote the social and academic development of children. Although home-school collaboration implies parent involvement, the reverse is not always true. Home-school collaboration implies that there is a partnership between the two systems and both systems are working toward a common goal. The underlying philosophy of home-school collaboration is the recognition that two systems working together can accomplish more than either system can accomplish separately, and that both parents and educators have legitimate roles and responsibilities in the partnership. The activity in which parents and teachers are involved does not distinguish home-school collaboration from parent involvement. Rather, it is the philosophy of partners working toward a common goal and with shared power that characterizes home-school collaboration. Thus, activities can be similar in parent involvement and home-school collaboration programs, however, the attitude with which the activities are implemented is different.

The differentiation of the terms parent involvement, parent education, and home-school collaboration is essential for understanding the literature and current practice. Most research has focused on parent involvement, a term that has been defined in different ways and is currently being redefined. Most practice is focused on parent involvement or parent education. Parent involvement was the common term during the period of the 1960s to late 1980s. The 1990s began with the recognition that creating effective home-school partnerships should be the goal of educators' efforts.

Chavkin and Williams (1985) define parent involvement as "any of a variety of activities that allow parents to participate in the educational process at home or in school, such as information exchange, decision sharing, volunteer services for schools, home tutoring/teaching, and child advocacy" (p. 2). Epstein (1987) offers a well-researched classification of types of involvement that characterize schools' comprehensive programs to share responsibilities with families for the education of their children. The five types are: (a) basic obligations of families (e.g., provide for health, build positive home conditions that support learning), (b) basic obligations of schools (e.g., communication about school programs and children's progress), (c) involvement at school (e.g., attend school functions, volunteer), (d) involvement in learning activities at home (e.g., monitor, discuss, and help with homework), and (e) involvement in decision making (e.g., participatory roles in PTA or advisory councils). A sixth type of involvement has been identified as an important component in schools' programs: collaboration and exchanges with community organizations (e.g., business partnerships, access to community services) (Epstein & Dauber, 1991).

A common thread that runs through these definitions of parent involvement is the focus on parents' role in educating their children. Involvement can take many different forms, including actual presence at school, teaching at home, reading to children, or communicating with teachers. Regardless of the specific form, the essence is an active interest in and encouragement of children's education. This interest is then communicated to children through various parental behaviors that show children their parents are concerned and interested in their learning.

Davies (1991) notes that schools, particularly urban schools, are putting together new and broader definitions of parent involvement. These definitions more closely resemble definitions of home-school collaboration. The new definitions emphasize involvement of family (e.g., grandparents, brothers, aunts) and community agencies, encourage educators to actively reach out to all parents— uninvolved and those who readily respond to school requests, and underscore the importance of recognizing the inherent strengths of all families and addressing priorities of families and teachers. New definitions recognize the importance of providing success for all children, serving the whole child, and sharing responsibility so that all families can be more effective in all aspects of child rearing. These definitions were influenced by the family support movement that has been advocated by researchers at major universities, including Edward Zigler and Sharon Lynn Kagan of the Bush Center in Child Development and Social Policy at Yale, Heather Weiss of the Family Research Project at Harvard, and Moncriff Cochran and his colleagues at Cornell (Davies, 1991). Goals of the family support movement are to strengthen all aspects of the child's development, stress parent education at home, and help parents connect with natural support systems.

Unfortunately, the distinction between parent education and parent involvement in education is often blurred (Epstein, cited by Cohen, 1990). Parent education refers to educating or training parents about parenting or dynamics of family life, without exploring the relation to schooling. Epstein (cited by Cohen, 1990) opines that "parent education programs have to make stronger connections with schooling and with the child as a student. That's the kind of continuing education parents want and need and often do not have access to" (p. 19). Parent education programs connected to children's schooling would exemplify Zigler's quote about changing the trajectory of the development of the child (see beginning of this chapter).

In summary, parents can be involved in their child's schooling without collaborating with educators. Home-school collaboration is an attitude not an activity, and occurs when partners (parents and educators) share common goals and responsibilities, are seen as equals, and contribute to the collaborative process.

WHY SHOULD PARENTS AND EDUCATORS COLLABORATE?

The quotes by Bradley and Seeley at the beginning of this chapter suggest that students' learning is enhanced when collaboration between home and school exists. What is the evidence for these quotes? Four comprehensive literature reviews on the effects of parent involvement in education have been written in less than a decade (Becher, 1984; Henderson, 1989; Kagan, 1984; Sattes, 1985). Countless articles concluding that parent involvement has positive benefits for students' success in school have been published. Henderson (1989) reviewed 48 studies; the other authors either duplicated or added other studies. The earliest article we found for this chapter came from a presentation by Rankin (1967) at the annual meeting of the American Educational Research Association. For an inner-city elementary sample, Rankin found high achievement related to greater parent contact with schools. High-achieving children from the Detroit area were much more likely to have active, interested, and involved parents than low-achieving children. Parents of high achievers provided experiences for children (e.g., games, talking), showed interest in their children's activities (e.g., talked about schoolwork, helped with homework, set expectations for school), developed children's interest in reading, and took the initiative to contact school personnel. These findings have been replicated.

The following conclusions about the effects of parent involvement in education can be made as a result of the four literature reviews:

1. Parent involvement is correlated with student achievement. When parents are involved, students have higher grades and test scores and better long-term academic achievement.

2. Parent involvement affects non-cognitive behavior: Student attendance, attitudes about school, maturation, self-concept, and behavior improve when parents are involved.

3. There are benefits for parents, teachers, community, and schools when parents are involved. In general, there are more successful educational programs and effective schools.

4. All forms of parent involvement strategies seem to be useful; however, those that are meaningful, well planned, comprehensive, and long lasting offer more options for parents to be involved, and appear to be more effective. Student achievement is greater with meaningful and high levels of involvement.

5. Achievement gains are most significant and long lasting when parent involvement is begun at an early age.

Overall, data on parent involvement in education suggest that it is a viable, worthwhile intervention or avenue for improving educational outcomes. In this section, we describe the effects of parent involvement in education in three categories: home-school collaboration, parent involvement, and family process, high-lighting representative studies in each category.

Home-School Collaboration Effects

Little research to date has focused on the mutual effects of home and school influences on student performance in school. One exception is research conducted by Hansen (1986). Hansen examined the extent to which the interplay of family interactions and classroom interactions influence children's success in elementary schools. The focus of his investigation was on continuities and discontinuities between families and classrooms in their forms of interaction rules. Thus, he was not studying differences in what is done (attitudes or conversational content) in families compared to classrooms, but rather how things are said and done. Particular attention was paid to mismatches in the way family members and classroom participants related to one another. Rule structures of home and classroom environments were categorized into exchange and communal rules for 196 children in eight elementary school classrooms in suburban New Zealand. Three broad categories were used to describe home and classrooms as: cohesive, coercive, or laissez-faire, a classification similar to Baumrind's (1966) parenting styles. Hansen hypothesized that children perform best in school situations in which the rule structures parallel those of their homes. He found that the greater the discontinuity in interaction rules in home and school, the more children's academic grades declined. He also found that there was no preferred classroom or home type; rather, the *match* between home and school was the critical factor for children's academic success. Children from cohesive families showed improved grades in cohesive classrooms, and a decline in coercive and laissez-faire classrooms. This pattern was similar for the other two types, allowing Hansen to conclude "there is an interactive influence of families and classrooms; children are relatively advantaged in classrooms that are similar to their families in rules of interaction, and relatively disadvantaged in classrooms that are dissimilar" (Hansen, 1986, p. 656).

Additional evidence for the effect of home-school collaboration on children's school performance and social development is provided by a review of selected partnership programs in large cities conducted by Collins, Moles, and Cross (1982). The researchers recognized that several home-school partnership programs had been developed and implemented for preschool and early elementary school-age children and that an overarching conclusion from studies of these programs (e.g., Head Start, Follow Through, Family Matters) was the necessity for parents to be involved at home in educational activities to support and maintain educational and developmental progress (Bronfenbrenner, 1974; Goodson & Hess, 1975). Therefore, they identified programs and practices for grades 4 to 12, where parents and teachers worked collaboratively to promote students' educational success. As part of the work of the Families as Educators Team, supported by the National Institute of Education, 28 home-school collaboration programs, all of which helped parents act in educational capacities such as home tutors, homework and attendance monitors, or participants in home learning activities, were systematically studied in the 1980–81 school year. The programs were situated in 12 states and 24 cities with populations of 500,000 or more.

Programs had multiple goals and modes of contact with homes. Increased reading and math achievement was a major emphasis of 24 programs, improved social development including conduct, interpersonal relations, and self-concept was a major emphasis of 14 programs, and 17 programs were concerned in a major way with school attendance. To involve parents, 15 used individual conferences, 17 used workshops, and 15 made home visits or frequent use of telephoning. Seventy-five percent of the programs supported parents in home tutoring, monitoring of homework and attendance, and participating in home activities to promote student learning. Twenty-two of the programs were at the secondary level. This suggests that school districts have made a concerted effort and are interested in working with families of older students. Fifty percent of the programs targeted low-income families; another four programs targeted minorities. Nine programs reported no evaluation data. The remaining 19 programs surveyed reported the following results: reduced absenteeism, higher achievement scores, improved student behavior, and increased confidence and participation among parents. Specifically, 12 programs indicated student achievement gains, 8 indicated improved academic self-concept, 7 better attendance, and 5 better school conduct. Eighteen programs reported greater parent support of and communication with schools and 11 programs reported greater parent involvement in students' learning. The authors' caveat that the reported gains and changes in behavior cannot be attributed entirely to strengthened home-school relationships is characteristic of research in the field. Home-school collaborative efforts are usually embedded in more comprehensive efforts to improve school learning.

Two frequently cited home-school collaboration efforts with a rich variety of parent participation that have shown dramatic achievement gains are the New Haven Primary Prevention Project (Comer, 1980) and Operation Higher Achievement (Walberg, Bole, & Waxman, 1980). Comer's (1980) long-term program to alter the governance and organization of two inner-city New Haven schools resulted in significant and long-lasting gains in student achievement for minority socially disadvantaged children (see Swap, this volume). Both schools attained the best attendance records in the city, greatly reduced student behavior problems, minimized parent-staff conflict, and achieved near grade level academic performance. The program was begun in 1968 and has been replicated in other districts. More than two decades later, Comer and Haynes (1991) contend:

> meaningful parent participation is essential for effective schooling. We premise

our view on the notion that families *and* schools constitute important sources of influence on the psychoeducational development of children and that the best results are achieved when these two institutions work together. (p. 278)

At the Grant School in Chicago, a steering committee composed of parents and educators was created to meet seven goals (e.g., increase parents' awareness of the reading process, improve parent-school-community relations) of the program called Operation Higher Achievement (Walberg et al., 1980). Committee members developed contracts that were signed by the district superintendent, principal, teachers, parents, and students in grades 1–6. Contracts stated the specific details of individuals' roles and responsibilities. For example, educators signed contracts that specified the educational services to be provided the student. Parents agreed to provide a quiet place for home study, encourage their child by discussing school work daily, recognize their child's progress, and cooperate with educators on matters of school work, discipline, and attendance. Ninety-nine percent of the students in 41 classes (826 students in grades 1–6) signed contracts with their parents and teachers. Students of teachers who were rated by principals as intensely involved in the home-school intervention gained .5 to .6 grade equivalents in reading comprehension, as measured by the Iowa Test of Basic Skills, as compared to students whose teachers were less intensely involved in the home-school intervention. Students in the intensely involved group gained 1.1 grade equivalents; students in the less intensively involved gained a .5 grade equivalent. Walberg et al. (1980) concluded that inner-city children can make middle-class progress if educators work cooperatively with parents in pursuit of common goals.

Parent Involvement Effects

It is difficult to interpret the effects of parent involvement because studies use different definitions, different programs or types, and different outcome measures.

Parent involvement is often one component of a more comprehensive intervention plan. The fact that parent involvement is unique from school to school and study to study has made systematic evaluation difficult and problematic (Kagan, 1984). Programs are tailored to local needs and are continuously modified. Kagan indicates that "parent involvement research is done in bits and pieces by different scholars . . . and the emphasis of research has been on producing quantitative studies" (p. 15). In part, the plethora of program designs and goals that exist in school settings has forced researchers to examine isolated elements, such as the effects on different stakeholders. The cumulative effect of many studies has been considered the best way to interpret the effects of parent involvement in schooling.

Concurrent with the development of empirical studies, some researchers have studied parent-school relations by examining factors that create patterns of involvement. This research is referred to as models of parent involvement, because models or programs that practitioners can consult or replicate are developed. Examples include models developed by Gotts (1979), Gordon (1977), and Kroft (1989). Gotts (1979) created the most comprehensive model by classifying different types of parent involvement programs according to the roles played by parents and the degree to which the program was preventive, comprehensive, and viewed parents as resourceful. According to Kagan (1984), the many models verify the complexity of the practice of parent involvement. Because no one model is fully predictive under a full range of circumstances, models are "guides, not rule books, for practice" (p. 8). In this section, we describe the effects of different models of involvement and the effects on different stakeholders.

Effects of models of involvement. Factors that create patterns of involvement between parents and educators are studied in models research. Gordon (1977) identified three models of parent involvement that are differentiated on the basis of their direction of influence: Parent Impact Model, School Impact Model, and Community Impact Model (see Frisby, this volume). In the Parent Impact Model, most of the influence goes from the school to the home. The impetus for this model came from research conclusions that the home environment accounts for almost 50% of the variance in children's school achievement (Coleman et al., 1966; Mayeske, Okada, Cohen, Beaton, & Wisler, 1973). Many parent education efforts are based on this model, which has been described by Leler (1983) as a one-way model. In this model, the rich knowledge and experience of parents tend to be ignored by teachers. Although many programs designed to create a positive learning environment at home (home visitor programs, group classes, Head Start parent involvement, Home Start, and Title III) are primarily characteristic of this model, recognize that some of these programs have acknowledged the input of parents.

In general, researchers found that the parent impact model had a powerful impact on student achievement. Of the 18 studies reviewed by Leler (1983), 13 showed positive gains in achievement as a result of parent involvement, 5 showed no difference between experimental and controls on any measure, and none showed negative results. These findings have been evident for over two decades (Gordon, 1978; Palmer, 1977). For example, in a widely quoted study by Smith (1968), the efficacy of a parent support program to improve the reading achievement of elementary school children from low-income, inner-city families was examined. Parents of second and fifth graders in the experimental group attended group meetings at school and were instructed to establish homework routines at home, read to their children, read in the presence of their children, ask questions about their children's work and praise their efforts, and arrange a quiet place for daily study. Children in the experimental group made greater gains in reading vocabulary over the 5-month period than the matched comparison group. Although there were no significant

differences in reading comprehension for the groups, parents from the experimental group were overwhelmingly favorable toward the program, suggesting the potential for gains to be measured later.

Also, Graue, Weinstein, and Walberg (1983) evaluated the efficacy of 29 controlled studies of elementary school-based programs for increasing the educationally stimulating qualities of the home environment. They concluded from their meta-analysis that school-based home instruction programs have large positive effects on children's academic learning. The researchers suggested that reasons for increased positive learning outcomes may include: (a) the quality and quantity of academic instruction is extended, (b) children's efficiency and motivation for classroom learning is increased because of parent support, (c) children watch less television, and (d) closer and more constructive family relations are encouraged. The effects of this model continue well beyond the short term. Lazar (1978), in his longitudinal study of 11 early childhood projects, documented measurable differences in achievement and significantly fewer assignments to special education classes and grade retentions for economically disadvantaged high school seniors who had graduated years before from preschool programs with high parent involvement.

Most of the influence goes from home to the school in the School Impact Model, in which a major goal is to make schools and other agencies more responsive to parents. Activities are aimed at modifying teachers and school systems; typical activities include parents serving on advisory councils or boards. Leler (1983) indicated that no studies looked at the effect of this model on achievement; however, information on attitudes has been investigated.

From 10 investigations of parent involvement in decision making conducted in the late 1970s, Leler (1983) concluded that there is substantial evidence that parents, teachers, principals, administrators, and school board members desire greater involvement of parents in schools, including some participation in decision making. Other findings across the studies reviewed include: (a) advisory councils are most influential when members have support from outside, and within the school (principal), and when council members focus on specific and limited tasks; (b) parents, educators, and students become more understanding of each other, the school, and the home when parents are frequently and meaningfully involved; (c) public confidence in schools is increased through meaningful home-school relationships; and (d) ideal parent involvement from both parents' and teachers' perspectives did not exceed the level of "making suggestions."

A study by Whittaker (1977) revealed agreement on the importance of citizen involvement in educational decision making, but disagreement among parents and educators on specific involvement. Responses to a citizens participation inventory from 697 Black mothers with a high school education and 248 Black male administrators in Atlanta indicated that parents perceived no active roles for parents in educational decision making. In contrast, administrators perceived a more active role in both administrator-perceived duties (e.g., evaluating principals, deciding on textbooks) and citizen-perceived duties (e.g., planning school events or parent involvement programs). Administrators identified community apathy as the major barrier and parents identified difficulty in getting information about school policies as the major barrier to effective participation. Chavkin and Williams' (1985) results from a survey of over 2,000 parents support the parents' perspective in Whittaker's (1977) study. Between 11% and 27% of the parents participated in the following activities: helping to hire or fire teachers and principals, working as part-time paid staff, helping to evaluate teachers' and principals' performance, planning the school budget, and making curricular decisions.

Henderson (1989) suggests that the effects of introducing a parent involvement component into a school-based program is an example of Gordon's School Impact Model. When there are many options and roles for parents (paraprofessionals, decision makers, home tutors, volunteers, or co-learners), student achievement seems to vary directly with the level of involvement. The more comprehensive and long lasting the involvement, the greater the effect on student achievement (Gross, Ridgley, & Gross, 1974; Herman & Yeh, 1980; Irvine, 1979). In a study of three Michigan school districts that involved parents in performance contracts, Gillum (1977) found that the district with the most comprehensive parent program had the greatest improvement in reading for disadvantaged students in grades 2–6. Gillum stated, "For most districts where parent involvement was 'pro forma' and consisted either of filling out a questionnaire or attending large group meetings, the achievement of the pupils was similar, but less than the achievement in the district where parents participated in deciding what was taught and had responsibility for working with the teachers and children" (cited by Henderson, 1989, p. 35).

The Community Impact Model is characterized by a strong relationship between community and school for the purpose of improving school effectiveness and student achievement. The most intensive parent involvement effort in public schools that follows this model is the Follow Through Program, a community services program established in 1967 under an amendment to the Economic Opportunity Act of 1964 for children in kindergarten and primary grades who come from low-income families (Olmsted, 1991). Quantitative and qualitative data from the first 20 years of Follow Through indicate benefits for students, parents, and teachers when parents use their skills in advocacy, decision making, and instruction. Other examples of the Community Impact Model are efforts to improve the school performance of socially disadvantaged minority students in grades K–6 in New Haven (Comer, 1980), to provide bilingual multicultural education to children, preschool through third grade, of migrant and seasonal farm workers in Washington and Texas (McConnell, 1979), and to improve the school performance of disadvantaged students in elementary school in Washington, DC (Gross et al., 1974). Evaluation of these efforts showed the following results: Achievement of students in reading and mathematics improved. Increased positive attitudes among parents, teachers, and students about school goals were evident. The number of parents involved in the total school program increased. Student attendance improved. Behavior problems decreased. In addition, the Washington, DC program obtained data on adult outcomes; the number of parents receiving credit toward a high school diploma or General Education Development (GED) certificate increased.

Henderson (1989) reported that some researchers assess the impact of the community and community-school partnerships on student achievement by examining whether schools with high achievement have more community involvement and support than schools with low achievement. She summarized the results of three studies conducted between 1969 and 1985 that illustrate the importance of parent and community interest in education. McDill, Rigsby, and Meyers (1969) surveyed students, teachers, and principals in 20 randomly selected high schools in eight states. Parent involvement, defined by the degree to which parents were apathetic to school policies, interested in their children's progress, and asked for appointments with teachers to discuss their child's schoolwork, was identified as a "Climate Source Variable" and correlated with math achievement measures and college plans when the effects of ability and family educational background were controlled. They concluded that the degree of parental and community interest in education was the critical factor in explaining the impact of the high school environment. Wagenaar (1977) found that public schools in a large midwestern city with high achievement levels more actively encouraged parent and community involvement than schools with lower achievement. He gathered data from 135

schools to determine levels of community involvement and support. There was a positive, moderate relationship between community involvement and support and schools' average reading and math scores when the effects of socioeconomic status (SES) were controlled. Measures of community group support, number of and attendance at school functions, and number of community groups using school facilities were strong, positive correlates of achievement. Citizen participation in policy factors and decision making were unrelated to achievement. Wagenaar concluded that behavioral involvement at school, use of school facilities, and an open communications atmosphere are important for high success in schools. Identical conclusions were reached by Phillips, Smith, and Witte (cited by Henderson, 1989), who studied 22 school districts in the Milwaukee metropolitan area in 1985 and found parent involvement was associated with high school performance regardless of family income level, grade level of the school, or school location. The authors concluded:

> What these findings suggest is that it is not simply the amount of time parents spend interacting in schools or the effectiveness of that interaction . . . the findings mean that parent actions in the home and the psychological process of creating positive expectations also are likely to matter in school performance. Those schools that do well are likely to have active parent organizations, numerous volunteers, and a high frequency of positive interactions between parents and teachers, but those actions will be backed up by and begin with early educational nurturing and positive educational expectations for the child. Poor, uneducated single parents are less likely to be able to afford, or perhaps understand the importance of, either school or home involvement. Thus without fundamental changes, the reinforcing cycle will continue. (cited by Henderson, 1989, pp. 51–52)

Effects on stakeholders. Literature on the effects of parent involvement is concerned with how parent involvement affects key stakeholders: students, parents, teachers, and the school as a whole.

This question is probably the most researched area in the parent involvement field, and the conclusions of most of the studies are similarly positive. A variety of outcomes have been assessed including achievement, attitudes, and school climate; however, the most common outcome variable investigated is achievement. The vast majority of researchers found positive effects for all key stakeholders.

Most of the research that examines the effects of parent involvement on students is interested in how it impacts student academic achievement. Epstein (1988a) and her colleagues at Johns Hopkins University, research leaders in this area, conducted a series of studies with 3,700 first, third, and fifth grade teachers and their principals in 600 schools in Maryland. They surveyed parents, teachers, principals, and children concerning parent involvement, and collected longitudinal achievement data on a subset of students. In a study of 293 third and fourth graders, Epstein (1988a) found that students who had teachers who frequently used parent involvement activities had larger reading achievement gains from fall to spring on the California Achievement Test than did students who had teachers who did not use parent involvement. This effect was independent of teacher quality, students' initial achievement, parents' education, parents' improved understanding of the school program, and the quality of students' homework. Interestingly, these children did not have similar gains in math achievement. Epstein found that the type of parent involvement most often used by these teachers was home learning activities that involved reading. She hypothesized that the kind of learning activity directly affected the type of academic gains. In a related study of 613 fifth graders, Epstein (1982) found that students who had teachers who frequently used parent involvement activities were more likely to be nominated by their teachers as "homework stars."

Several literature reviews corroborate Epstein's conclusion that parent involvement has positive effects on student achievement. In a review of 18 parent involvement studies, Henderson (1989) concluded that parent involvement correlated highly with student achievement. However, she reported that simply involving parents at home was not enough to improve a school's average level of achievement. In order for the school as a whole to benefit, parents must also be involved at school. In another review of the literature, Kagan (1984) found that the type of parent involvement determines how well it correlates with achievement, and that a combination of home and school involvement seems to be the most effective. Becher (1984) concluded in her review that there is "substantial evidence indicating that children have significantly increased their academic achievement and cognitive development" (p. 19) as a result of parent involvement.

In addition to increased academic achievement, other positive effects of parent involvement on students are documented. Epstein (1982) found that fifth grade students who had teachers who emphasized parent involvement had: better attitudes toward school, more regular homework habits, and more positive attitudes toward homework. These students also reported more similarities between home and school and more teacher familiarity with their parents. Kagan (1984) reported that parent involvement correlated with improved attendance, a reduction in suspension rates, and improved attitude toward homework.

Parent involvement has positive effects on parents as well as children. Kagan and Schraft (1982) investigated how different types of parent involvement may differentially affect parents. They found that parents at a low-income school showed strong correlations between level of involvement and personal aspiration. Similar correlations were not found at a middle-income school. They found that low-income parents who were paid a small amount for their involvement demonstrated higher aspirations and perceptions of power than their unpaid counterparts. Parent involvement with learning activities at home had positive effects on parents' attitudes and knowledge. Epstein (1986) found that when teachers frequently used parent involvement techniques parents felt teachers worked harder to involve them. Parents also had increased understanding of the school's program and rated their child's teacher higher on teaching quality and interpersonal skills.

Two literature reviews in parent involvement describe some of the benefits to parents. Becher (1984) reported that parents developed more positive attitudes about the school and the school personnel, helped muster community support for the program, and became more active in the community after becoming involved at school. Parents also developed more positive attitudes about themselves and improved their relationship with their child. Kagan (1984) discovered that some of the effects of participation on parents included attitudinal change, improved economic status, and increased political participation.

There is less research that examines the effects of parent involvement on teachers. There is some evidence that when teachers use parent involvement techniques they allocate more time to instructional activities and rely more on student-oriented activities than text-oriented activities (Becher, 1983). Epstein (1986) found that teachers who frequently used parent involvement rated parents as more helpful and willing to follow through than did teachers who infrequently used parent involvement activities. She also found that teachers who used parent involvement made equal demands of less educated and better educated parents; however, teachers who did not use parent involvement made more frequent requests of less educated than better educated parents.

Research has shown that parent involvement also has positive effects on the school as a whole. Comer (1984) and his colleagues at the Yale Child Study Center implemented a school improvement program in several elementary schools in the New Haven school system. His model has four components: a representative governance body, a parent program, a mental health team, and a staff and curriculum development program. As an integral part of the plan, parents were involved in the governance body, and participated as paid aides in the classroom and in a parent group with regular group activities. After 4 to 5 years, the schools in the program increased overall reading and math achievement, boosted attendance, and significantly reduced behavior problems. Comer (1984) wrote, "Parent presence in responsible and respected roles in the schools sent a message to the children: The school people and the program are important. In direct and indirect ways the parent aides and the parent group members conveyed the expectations to the children that they should behave well socially and achieve well academically" (p. 333). His model has been implemented in many schools nationwide. Comer and his colleagues have shown that students' and parents' perceptions of classroom and school climate in experimental schools are significantly improved when compared with students' and parents' perceptions in control schools (Haynes, Comer, & Hamilton-Lee, 1989). School climate is considerably enhanced when parents are included in the planning and organizing of school activities.

FAMILY PROCESS EFFECTS

Support for home-school collaboration also comes from studies examining the influence of the home environment on students' school success. These studies are characteristic of the Parent Impact Model described by Gordon (1977), and are referred to as family process studies in the child development and sociology literatures. Studies in this area support Epstein's (1987) parent involvement levels one and four.

In their seminal chapter, "Family and School as Educational Institutions," Hess and Holloway (1984) reviewed: (a) the family's effect on academic achievement and cognitive objectives that support classroom performance, (b) ways families influence achievement indirectly by nurturing cognitive behavior necessary for achievement in the classroom, and (c) family influences on social and motivational aspects of student behavior and their relationship to classroom performance. With the caveat that it is not easy to summarize these results because family process variables studied are defined differently and researchers use different instruments, data collection, and analysis procedures, they identified generally similar variables and argued that there is some convergence in the family process variables critical for students' success. According to this review, family process variables associated with achievement are: verbal environment of the home, parental expectations for child success or press for achievement, parental warmth and nurturance toward child, parental control, and parental beliefs and attributions. Studies show that families indirectly influence achievement, student motivation, and classroom performance (reading or math) for their children in many ways: fostering children's interest and skill in reading and math, providing quality reading material and math experiences, modeling learning by reading and using math in the home, reading with children, engaging in discussions about reading with their children, expecting children to learn math and to read, requesting verbal responses from their child, and believing their child's effort, not luck, will result in learning. The role of parent-child interaction in school-relevant tasks, such as language development or communicative competence, children's style in solving problems, and opportunities for memory and attention, is a relatively new research area. In general, parents' attempts to teach and guide their children's acquisition of language, develop a reflective problem-solving style, orient their attention, and emphasize memory of experiences and skills correlate with school-relevant outcomes. Hess and Holloway (1984) caution:

> The outcomes of these processes depend to a great degree on three features of the social world in which the child lives: the consistency (consensus) among socializ-

ing agents about the goals of education, the degree to which these goals are taken seriously, and the ability of the socializing agents to counter knowledge, values, and goals that come from competing sources—for example, television and peers. If multiple sources of information and reward are diffuse and contradictory, they erode the effectiveness of family and school; discontinuities between family and school can compromise the effectiveness of both. (p. 212)

Walberg's (1984) concept of "the curriculum of the home" is consistent with Hess and Holloway's conclusions. In a synthesis of 2,575 empirical studies of academic learning he found that parents directly or indirectly influence eight determinants of cognitive, affective, and behavioral learning: student ability, student motivation, quality of instruction, amount of instruction, psychological climate of the classroom, academic stimulation in the home environment, peer group, and television. Social and economic factors (class size, SES level, financial expenditures per student) influence school learning, but to a less prominent and tangible degree. Walberg argues that improvements by parents and educators in these eight determining factors hold the greatest hope for improving learning. Altering home conditions for academic learning and the relations between home and school should produce large effects on learning. According to Walberg (1984), "the curriculum of the home predicts academic learning, twice as well as the socioeconomic status of families" (p. 400). The curriculum of the home includes: informed parent-child conversations about everyday events, encouragement and discussion of leisure reading, monitoring and joint analysis of television watching, expression of affection, interest in children's academic and personal growth, and delay of immediate gratifications to accomplish long-term goals.

Clark's (1983) results from his frequently cited observational study of family life for poor Black secondary students supports the importance of the curriculum of the home. Certain patterns were evident in homes of high-achieving students. Family life of high-achieving poor students was characterized by frequent dialogues between parents and children, strong parent encouragement of academic pursuits, warm and nurturing interactions, clear and consistent limits, and consistent monitoring of how time is spent. Parents of high achievers feel personally responsible to help their children gain knowledge and basic literacy skills, communicate regularly with school personnel, and be involved in school functions and actions. Clark labeled this parenting style "sponsored independence"; the behaviors and attitudes of parents are similar to Walberg's concept of the "curriculum of the home" and Dornbusch's data on authoritative parenting style (see Dornbusch and Ritter, this volume).

In summary, there is a substantial body of literature that documents the positive effects of parent involvement in schooling. Home-school collaboration and meaningful parent involvement appear to be advantageous for students, parents, teachers, and schools. Some benefits include improved achievement, attitudes, and better relationships between teachers and parents. Despite the general consensus in this area of research, there are several methodological concerns that need to be addressed. A significant problem in this area is that most of the studies are correlational and causality is difficult to determine. As noted by Kagan (1984), "Correlation studies of school-based parent involvement and achievement are not sufficiently precise to determine the mechanism by which achievement is influenced" (p. 14). Parent involvement often is not clearly defined or it is defined differently in studies. There is not a clear understanding of which types of parent involvement lead to which outcomes.

What is most promising is that the parent involvement in education literature does not propose shifting educational responsibilities from the school to home. Henderson (1988) stated "schools can become more effective if they do involve parents, as long as they also do

the rest of their job" (p. 152). Parent involvement is seen as an additive if not synergistic effect, and home-school collaboration, as illustrated by Scott-Jones's quote (see beginning of this chapter) is the goal. In Bronfenbrenner's (1979) terminology, however, most studies have focused on the microsystem (e.g., family influences on student achievement), rather than on the mesosystem, the concrete linkage between a child's experience in home and school environments.

WHAT IS THE CURRENT STATE OF PRACTICE?

How involved are parents with their children's schooling? The amount and type of parent involvement in special and regular education are described in this section.

Parent Involvement in Special Education

There is a diverse body of literature that examines the amount of parent involvement at various schools or for a certain population. Many studies that examine amount and types of parent involvement are in the special education literature, specifically in the area of parent involvement in the Individual Education Plan (IEP) conference. Since the passage of Public Law 94–142 (Education of All Handicapped Children Act of 1975), schools have been required to involve parents of children with special needs. Although PL 94–142 mandates parent involvement at the IEP conference, researchers have found both superficial and low levels of involvement.

In a frequently cited study, Goldstein, Strickland, Turnbull, and Curry (1980) conducted an observational analysis to determine the dynamics of 14 IEP conferences. Goldstein and her colleagues found that parent involvement at these conferences was generally restricted to reviewing an already developed IEP. The parent was primarily a recipient of information; they generally talked about half as much as the resource teacher. Vaughn, Bos, Harrell, and Lasky (1988) conducted a follow-up investigation to the Goldstein study to determine if there was a similar level of involvement 10 years after PL 94–142 mandated parent involvement. Their data, strikingly similar to Goldstein et al., reflected a similar low level of involvement. In addition, Lynch and Stein (1982) found that although 75% of 400 parents felt they were active participants in the development of the IEP, 48% did not offer suggestions at the IEP meeting.

In addition to low levels of parent involvement at IEP conferences, other studies show a similarly low level of involvement in special education programs as a whole. In a survey of 325 parents of students with handicaps in a midwestern town, Leyser (1985) found that 10% to 20% of parents did not attend any parent-teacher conference or have any contact with the special education teacher. In addition, 30% to 40% of the parents did not know what an IEP was. Lusthaus, Lusthaus, and Gibbs (1981) asked parents to indicate their level of involvement in nine decisions made at school; their involvement was then classified as (a) no involvement, (b) giving and receiving information, and (c) having control over information. Parents most often found themselves giving or receiving information, or not involved; they seldom were in control of decisions. McKinney and Horcutt (1982) found in their sample of 36 parents of children with learning disabilities that one-fourth of the parents could not recall the IEP, and of those who could, few had any direct knowledge of the content.

Parent Involvement in Regular Education

The phenomenon of low levels of parent involvement is not restricted to special education programs. When researchers examined parent involvement in regular education they also found generally low levels of involvement (Cutright, 1984; Davies, 1987; Epstein, 1984), or involvement restricted to superficial types.

In a survey of 3,103 parents from the southern United States, Chavkin and Williams (1985) asked parents to indicate their actual participation and their degree of interest in seven parent involvement roles: paid school staff, school program supporter, home tutor, audience, advocate, co-learner, and decision maker. Parents were interested in many more roles than they were actually involved in. There was an especially large discrepancy between actual parent involvement in decision-making roles and the parents' interest in these roles. Seventy-four percent of the parents were interested in the role of decision maker, but only 21% actually participated in a decision-making activity. There was considerable discrepancy between interest in the role of advocate (meeting with school officials to ask for changes in the practices of the school or in the system) and participation in advocate activities. There was less discrepancy between role and participation in the roles of home tutor (91% interest and 86% participation) and audience (95% interest and 92% participation). In general, it seems that there was less opportunity for the parents in this survey to be involved in decision making and advocacy, even though their interest in these roles was high. Not surprisingly, the majority of teachers surveyed did not see decision making as an important role for parents. Similarly, Snider (1990) reported data from the Metropolitan Life Survey of the American Teacher that showed 47% of parents but only 18% of teachers believed having parents serve on curriculum decision committees was very valuable. More parents (51%) than teachers (26%) believe involving parents on management teams to determine school policies is valuable.

Parents tend to be more involved in their children's education at home than at school. Epstein (1985) reported that only 4% of parents in her sample—one to two parents per classroom—were active at school. In her survey of 1,269 inner-city parents, Epstein (1986) examined levels of involvement and found similar results. She divided involvement into four levels: basic obligations, school-to-home communications, involvement at school, and involvement in learning activities at home. She found that most parents were very involved at the first level: 97% of the parents supplied their children with necessary school supplies, and 90% said their children had a regular place to study at home. At the next level there were fewer parents involved: 16% had received no memos from the teacher; 35% had attended no parent-teacher conference, and 60% never spoke to the teacher on the phone. For the third level, parent involvement at school, there was even less participation: 70% of the parents were never involved in activities assisting the school staff. For the last level, involvement in learning activities at home, Epstein reported techniques used most frequently by teachers. All techniques involved reading: reading to the child or listening to the child read; encouraging the parent to go to the library; and loaning books or loaning materials to the parent to use at home. Techniques used the least included: discussions, informal learning activities, contracts, and parent observations.

Dauber and Epstein (1989) asked 2,317 inner-city parents about their involvement at school, with homework, and in reading activities at home. Parents rated their frequency of involvement on a 4-point scale indicating: never (1), not yet (2), once or twice (3), and many times (4). Parent involvement at school was the lowest with a mean of 2.36, involvement with homework had a mean of 3.54, and involvement in reading activities at home a mean of 3.0. The overall mean of all 18 items was 3.07. Survey results showed that parents in this population were more likely to be involved at home than school.

Parents tend to be involved at school in traditional ways. Jennings (1990) reported the results of the PTA/Dodge National Survey, which indicated that parents most often help with fundraising or extracurricular activities. About 50% of the parents who had at least one child in grades K–12 helped with discipline matters or served as classroom helpers. Parents were least involved with decision-making activities such as determining school building policies, making curricular decisions, and selecting textbooks.

Parent involvement tends to be highest at the elementary grade level, particularly in primary grades. There is a dramatic decline in parents' involvement in education around grade 4 (Epstein, 1986). Involvement is lowest at the secondary school level. Chavkin and Williams (1985) identified infrequent parent-teacher conferences, teachers' lack of request for parents to be involved, and parents' lack of understanding of high school course content as reasons for less parent involvement in high school.

Although most of the research in this area is concerned with involvement in public schools, there are some studies that examine parent involvement in non-public schools. Bauch (1988) investigated parent involvement levels in five inner-city secondary Catholic schools and found that about 30% of the parents helped with class trips or other activities, 12% served as school advisory board members, 14% helped in the classroom, 77% of the parents attended school meetings, and 79% made sure that homework was done. Eighteen percent of parents said they did not talk to their child's teacher during the year, and only 29% talked with their child's teacher more than twice in a year. Parent involvement in school decision making was low: About 51% say their advice was never sought concerning school decisions on topics such as curriculum, finances, personnel, school policy, or home-school relations. In another study of Catholic high schools, Coleman and Hoffer (1987) found that parents at Catholic schools were more involved in activities such as parent-teacher conferences, PTA meetings, visiting classrooms, and volunteer work than were parents in public high schools.

In summary, most schools have not yet worked with the home in a concerted, systematic manner (Rich, 1987). Parent involvement strategies have been implemented most frequently by teachers in lower grades and with larger class sizes (Becker & Epstein, 1982). Efforts to involve parents in the education of their children drops dramatically at grade 4

(Epstein, 1986). Despite decreases in parent involvement efforts, parents at all levels want to stay involved and informed. When parent involvement programs are present, upper grade level parents respond (Brandt, 1989).

It appears that the levels of involvement are lower than what many individuals would characterize as ideal. This seems true for special education programs in general, and especially for parent involvement in IEP conferences. In regular education programs, it appears that most parents who are involved participate at home; involvement at school is minimal. A number of studies found that although parents are involved most frequently in traditional ways, they are interested in other types of involvement, including decision making, but it appears that schools do not encourage this type of involvement.

WHAT FACTORS INFLUENCE HOME-SCHOOL COLLABORATION?

Research on the effects of parent involvement shows strong positive effects when parents are involved in their child's education both at home and in school. Research on levels of involvement, however, generally shows low levels of involvement or involvement that is limited to specific roles. If there are so many benefits to parent involvement, why aren't parents more involved? This question is addressed in literature examining moderating variables that influence the effects of parent involvement. In this section we discuss five categories of moderating variables: theories of home-school relationships, parent and child characteristics, school and teacher characteristics, parent and teacher attitudes toward involvement, and parent-professional interaction issues. The reader will note that many variables influence the effects of parent involvement in education and that there are interrelationships among variables. The many moderating variables illustrate our contention that home-school collaboration is an attitude. The moderating variables are the issues with which practitioners deal as they implement the process of creating effective partnerships between home and school.

Theories of Home-School Relationships

Of available theories on home-school relationships, the work of Coleman (1987), Epstein (1987), and Swap (1990) are most notable. Although these individuals are in the process of researching their proposed theories, they are careful to caution that no one empirically based theory or model exists, and that much data are needed. The degree to which educators and parents are influenced by a specific theoretical stance influences the extent to which collaboration exists. Coleman and Epstein's theories of home-school relationships are reviewed; Swap's three philosophies are covered in detail in this volume.

Coleman (1987) proposed that home and school provide different inputs for the socialization process of children. One class of inputs, opportunities, demands, and rewards, comes from schools. The second class of inputs, attitudes, efforts, and conception of self, comes from the social environment of the household. Educational outcomes result from the interaction of qualities that the child brings from home with qualities of the school. Schools do make a difference for children; however, they do not have an equal effect on children. According to Coleman (1987):

> Schools, of whatever quality, are more effective for children from strong family backgrounds than for children from weak ones. The resources devoted by the family to the child's education interact with resources provided by the school—and there is greater variation in the former resources than in the latter. (p. 35)

Schools can reward and demand and provide opportunities for children to learn; however, Coleman views families as providing the building blocks that make learning possible. Families provide the "social capital" needed by schools to optimize learners' outcomes.

Coleman argues that the social capital in homes is shrinking. As this occurs, school achievement will not be maintained or increased if we simply replace these resources with more school-like resources—those that produce opportunities, demands, and rewards. Rather, academic and developmental outcomes for children need to be maintained or increased by replacing them with resources that produce attitudes, efforts, and conception of self—those qualities from the home that interact with ones provided by the school.

Epstein (1987) proposed an integrated theory of family-school relations characterized by a set of overlapping spheres of influence that alter interactions of parents, teachers, and students as a function of three forces: changes in ages and grade levels of students; philosophies, policies, and practices of the family; and philosophies, policies, and practices of the school. These forces determine how much and what kind of overlap occurs between family and school. Epstein's model is based on a developmental framework that accounts for the continuity of family-school interactions across school years, and the changes in form and purposes of parent participation at different student ages and stages of development. According to Epstein, three perspectives influence assumptions of school personnel and parents concerning family-school relations. One perspective assumes that families and schools hold very different and separate responsibilities in the education of children. In this perspective, it is believed that families and schools have separate goals for educating and socializing children. These goals are best achieved when teachers keep a professional distance from and equal standards for children in their classrooms. Parents, on the other hand, develop personal relationships with and individual expectations for their children at home. A second perspective assumes that socialization and educational responsibilities for children are shared between home and school. Teachers and parents share common goals for children. These goals

are best achieved when everyone works together. In this perspective, an overlap of responsibilities between parents and teachers is expected. Finally, in the third perspective, the sequential perspective, parents and teachers contribute to children's development at different stages. Parents teach needed skills to children until the time of their formal education around the ages of 5 and 6. At that time, teachers assume the primary responsibility for children's education. These major theoretical perspectives on home-school relations have a profound effect and either encourage or discourage parent involvement in the schools.

According to Epstein (1987), when teachers and parents emphasize their shared responsibilities, their combination of labor pushes the spheres of family and school influence together, increases interactions between parents and school personnel about the developing child, and creates "school-like families" and "family-like schools" (see Epstein, this volume). Epstein illustrates that at any time, in any school, and in any family, parent involvement is a variable that can be increased or decreased by the practices of teachers, parents, administrators, and students. Parents and educators can interact with others in ways that include or exclude parents from their child's education or include teachers as influence on the family in relation to schooling.

Parent and Child Characteristics

Parent characteristics that may influence involvement, such as educational status, socioeconomic status (SES), marital status, and employment have been studied more than child characteristics that may influence involvement. Miller (1986) examined the relative influence of various independent variables on the amount of parent involvement. Three types of parent involvement were identified: visiting the school, active participation in the parent-teacher association, and interest and concern about local school issues. Based on telephone interviews with a national sample of 746 parents, he found that one-third of the parents had visited their child's school three or more times during the preceding year, one-third were active members of the PTA, and 43% said they were attentive to local school issues. Gender was the strongest predictor variable, with women being more involved. Miller also found that the child's grade level was a strong predictor with parents with children in the lower grades being more involved. Level of formal education of the parents was not predictive of school visits or active involvement in the PTA; however, it was slightly predictive of attentiveness to school issues. The amount of time parents worked had little influence on the amount the parent was involved.

Stevenson and Baker (1987) found similar results in their interview-based investigation of the relationship of maternal educational status, age and gender of the child, and maternal employment to parent involvement in a national sample of parents and teachers of 179 children. Their measure of parent involvement was simply having the teacher rate the parent on a scale of 1 to 5 according to how much they participated in activities at school (e.g., PTO and parent-teacher conferences). Maternal education and age of the child were significantly correlated with parent involvement, whereas sex of the child and maternal employment did not correlate significantly with parent involvement. The authors found some interesting relationships between the sex of the child and determinants of parent involvement. The association between maternal education and parent involvement was strong for boys but practically nonexistent for girls. Similarly, age was highly associated with parent involvement for boys, whereas there was little association with this variable for girls. The authors concluded that the findings that link maternal education and age of the child with parent involvement for boys and not girls are due to the "usual slow start of young boys in school and the general concern of middle-class parents with early school success" (p. 1354).

Revicki (1981) found SES and number of siblings correlated with parent involvement. He studied parent involve-ment among parents of second grade students from two Follow Through Projects. Parent involvement in this study consisted of parent classroom volunteering, and attendance at meetings and activities. Approximately 35.5% of the variance in parent involvement was explained by the contribution of SES, sibsize, and participation in the program. The higher the SES and the smaller the family the more active the involvement.

In their study of 2,317 parents of elementary and middle school students, Dauber and Epstein (1989) found similar results. Parents who are better educated and do not work outside the home are more likely to be involved at school. When the researchers focused on parent involvement at home, they found that parents with fewer children helped their child more at home than did parents with many children. Parent employment outside the home, however, was not a predictor of parent involvement at home.

School and Teacher Characteristics

Some researchers in the field of parent involvement investigate the influence of school and teacher characteristics on parent involvement. Dauber and Epstein (1989) comment on the relative importance of teacher and school practices:

> The strongest and most consistent predictors of parent involvement at school and at home are the specific school programs and teachers' practices that encourage and guide parents' involvement. Regardless of parent education, family size, student ability or school level, parents are more likely to become partners in their children's education if they perceive that the schools have strong practices to involve parents at school, at home on homework, and at home on reading activities. The sum of all 9 school practices has the strongest effect on parents' total involvement after all other factors have been statistically controlled. (p. 8)

It appears that parents often rely on the lead of schools to guide them in their involvement both at home and at school.

Hoover-Dempsey, Bassler, and Brissie

(1987) investigated the contributions of school characteristics to parent involvement. They examined several school characteristics: school SES level, teacher degree level, grade level, class size, teachers' sense of efficacy, principals' perception of teacher efficacy, organizational rigidity, and instructional coordination. In this study, teacher efficacy and school SES were most consistently associated with parent involvement. A high sense of self-efficacy among teachers was associated with greater parent involvement. The authors also found that school SES correlated positively with three parent involvement activities: parent-teacher conferences, parent volunteers, and support from parents. SES did not correlate with two home-based parent involvement activities: home tutoring and home instruction.

Teacher education has been associated with differential levels of parent involvement (Becker & Epstein, 1982; Chavkin & Williams, 1988). It appears that teachers with additional graduate training are more likely to involve parents to a higher degree than teachers with less education.

Hulsebosch (1989) conducted intensive interviews with teachers who involve parents in education (high involvers) and do not involve parents in education (low involvers) and described differentiating characteristics. Teachers who did not involve parents were found to emphasize rules and to be more structured and less flexible. Low involvers were more aware of and confined to the parameters of their jobs. Many felt they held total responsibility for any instruction or activities that occurred in the classroom. Low involvers believed that home and school should be separate, and viewed parents as having different and often conflicting values. Often, these teachers felt constrained by their careers as well as not appreciated. The teaching profession was seen by low involvers as autonomous, and they attempted to create "professional" boundaries between teaching and parenting. In contrast, high involvers believed education was closely tied to the home, and consequently they made efforts to have classroom activities fit with children's homes. High involvers described parents in positive terms, whereas low involvers described the negative influence of home events on school life. Both high and low involvement teachers perceived time and effort as a "cost" of parent involvement, however, they differed in their perception of the cost. High involvers indicated that the effort was a necessary and important part of their work, whereas low involvers implied the effort was an unnecessary add-on to the real world of teaching. According to Hulsebosch (1989), low involvers see parental involvement activities as ancillary to the real world of the classroom, whereas high involvers see parents as an asset that is a basic element of a child's education.

Parent and Teacher Attitudes

Parents' and teachers' attitudes toward parent involvement have been investigated in surveys. Parents and teachers share much common ground in their opinions about the role of parents in education (Williams & Stallworth, 1984). Both agree that teachers should: communicate frequently with parents about what is happening at school and how parents could assist their children's learning at home, work closely with parents, and be trained in parent involvement strategies and models. Both agree that parents should enforce rules about homework, cooperate with and help teachers, and attend school functions. There also appears to be agreement across home and school about what is important for encouraging and supporting students' success in school. In a survey of 300 parents and 84 teachers about parents' and teachers' roles and responsibilities in educating children, Christenson, Rounds, Roschelle, and Anderson (1991) found no significant differences in parents' and teachers' perceptions of their own and each other's responsibilities.

Although both parents and teachers believe that parent involvement is vital to a child's success in school, Williams and Stallworth (1984) also found no consensus about what kind of involvement is most useful. Principals and teachers favored parent involvement in traditional ways (e.g., chaperone field trips, supervise homework, fundraising) and rated nontraditional ways (e.g., setting discipline policy, curricular decisions) as inappropriate or less useful. Principals and teachers rated all but the most traditional nonthreatening roles (e.g., school program supporter, audience at school functions) to be unimportant. Parents, on the other hand, favored all forms of parent involvement, including tutoring at school and serving on school governance committees. Although teachers and principals rated decision making as the least important role parents play, superintendents and school board members rated parent decision making at school as important. Chavkin and Williams (1985) replicated these findings in their survey of parents and various educators (teachers, principals, superintendents, school board presidents, state education agency officials, and teacher educators). They also found that educators believed districts should make rules for involving parents and that parents do not have enough training to help make school decisions; parents did not agree with these statements.

Data reported from the Metropolitan Life Survey of the American Teacher by Olson (1990) suggest that both parents and teachers believe parents contribute to less than desirable educational outcomes for students. A majority of both parents and teachers agreed that many or most parents fail to discipline their children, fail to motivate them to learn, leave their children unsupervised after school, demonstrate too little interest in their children's education, and neglect to see that their children's homework is completed. Again, parents and teachers agree; it appears that opinions held by the two major forces entrusted with educating and socializing children in society, parents and teachers, are quite similar. Both see parents as important for their child's educational success; both see less than desirable follow-through by parents.

Parent-Professional Interaction

It is encouraging that parent-school connections as rated by parents and teachers appear to be more positive than negative. Data from more than 2,000 parents and 1,000 teachers from the Metropolitan Life Survey of the American Teacher conducted in 1987 (cited by Olson, 1990) showed that 70% of parents and teachers rated relations between parents and teachers in their school as good or excellent. Only 7% of parents and 5% of teachers rated parent-teacher relations as poor. More parents (76%) rated teachers' availability and responsiveness to personal requests as good or excellent than teachers' (54%) similar rating for parents' availability and responsiveness of teacher requests. Despite this discrepancy, only 12% of teachers and 8% of parents rated the other's availability and responsiveness as poor. At least 60% of parents and teachers felt supported by each other; only 10% of parents and teachers reported poor support for each other. Across all grade levels (K–12) 73% of parents and 80% of teachers agreed that their school does a good job of encouraging parent involvement in educational areas. A slight decline in percentages was directly related to higher grade levels in school.

Although the results from this survey suggest that parent-school connections tend to be more positive than negative, the results also reveal that connections are poor for a proportion of parents and teachers. Issues related to parent-professional interaction that may influence parents in general, and this group in particular, are communication, perceptions of other in the relationship, structural differences between home and school, and the concept of professional dominance. Each is discussed separately.

Communication. Effective communication between parents and teachers is a critical component in establishing effective home-school collaboration. Communication between home and school usually takes place formally through parent-teacher conferences, open houses, and PTO meetings or informally through notes and phone calls. The customary parent-teacher conferences, however, can often cause tension between parents and teachers. Conferences usually consist of a teacher's rushed reports of a student's progress. They are typically scheduled in blocks of time, one right after another. Most often conferences are one-way verbal report cards that do not encourage parents or teachers to develop relationships or contribute equally to effective communication or problem solving. Unfortunately, parent-school communications that are not productive can actually add to difficulties and problems later when parents and school people communicate in crisis or problem situations (Swap, 1987). It should be noted that some schools have implemented recommended changes in parent-teacher conferences (Chrispeels, 1988). The new format focuses on collaboration and the development of individual learning goals, and is most often used by primary grade level teachers (Minnesota State Department of Education, personal communication, September 8, 1991).

Parents frequently report having little or no communication with school personnel. When they do hear from educators, parents report that the communication is primarily negative and concerns problems at school (Davies, 1989). The major function of many of the school-to-parent contacts was to share negative information about behavior, attendance, academic performance, and monitoring children's progress. Often no intervention plan for the behavior of concern was developed (Leitch & Tangri, 1988). In their study of home-school communication, Tangri and Leitch (1982) report that both parents and teachers recognize that the majority of communication between them is negative—teacher messages about poor student performance and parent complaints regarding events in the school.

It appears that when there is little or no communication between parents and teachers, both parties interpret the others' lack of availability as a signal of their lack of concern for the child. As a result, the other is seen as the enemy. In reality,

teachers and parents of today's society alike are feeling stressed by multiple demands of their professional, family, and individual responsibilities, and the limited time that results (Swap, 1987).

Another factor influencing communication between parents and school people is the diversity of parent characteristics and needs of parents. Epstein (1987) suggests that parents differ dramatically in their knowledge of how to help children at home, their beliefs that teachers want them to help their children at home, and the degree of information and guidance they receive from their children's teachers in how to help their children at home. Teachers may use educational language that is foreign to parents, place unrealistic expectations on parents, or may not be sensitive to how parents are understanding the information communicated. Differences in parent characteristics and educators' sensitivity to parents' differential needs directly influence the amount and manner in which parents become involved in their children's education. Seeley (1989) suggested that many parents have signaled, either subconsciously or directly, that they do not have to be involved in their child's education because that responsibility has been assigned to the school.

Perceptions of other in the relationship. Studies that examine parents' and teachers' attribution for children's school problems suggest blaming exists between parents and teachers. Vernberg and Medway (1981) conducted interviews with 30 parents and teachers to ascertain their attributions for children's problems in school. They found that parents tended to hold teachers responsible for problems that their child had in school. Likewise, teachers tended to find parent-home variables as responsible for problems. Moses and Croll (1987) found that when teachers were asked to attribute a cause for a child needing special education services they tended to associate problems with parents or the home. The percentage of teachers who attributed causes to the home varied as a function of children's special education diagnosis. For children with an LD diagnosis 29.5%

of the time the cause was attributed to home, for children with behavioral or emotional problems 68% of the time the cause was attributed to the parent or home.

Epstein (1982) found that there was little correlation between teachers' attitudes toward parent involvement and their actual practices. Most of the teachers supported the idea of parent involvement; however, not all teachers actually were able to put their ideas into practice. Teachers may be hesitant to involve parents in their children's education for a variety of reasons. These reasons may include: the time investment required from the teacher to ensure productive parent participation, the absence of external rewards for efforts to involve parents, problems with low commitment, and the perception that parents lack the necessary skills to become effectively involved (Blase, 1987; Epstein & Becker, 1982; Moles, 1982). Teachers were concerned about the effect of parental tutoring on the parent-child relationship, and about creating inequality by using parent involvement activities because some parents were uninvolved. Finally, they were concerned about parents' teaching techniques, including parents doing too much of the assigned work. All these issues would discourage a teacher from using parent involvement techniques.

Some teachers feel insecure with parents because they perceive that parents, when involved, will challenge their professional competence, attack and criticize them, or blame them for their children's problems (Blase, 1987; Epstein & Becker, 1982; Power, 1985; Vernberg & Medway, 1981). Gibson and Dembo (1984) reported that lower levels of parent-teacher contacts may be due to teachers' feelings of high frustration and lower efficacy resulting from their reaction to characteristics of low-achieving students' parents. Teachers may also feel they cannot meet the demands placed upon them from parents and the school, are not adequately trained to deal with parents, and have difficulty relating to culturally different families (Moles, 1982). In addition, some teachers do not believe that encour-

aging parent involvement practices is a part of their professional role and often see it as interfering with the teaching tasks that have been entrusted to them (Seeley, 1989). According to Henderson (cited by Olson, 1990), "It's still not considered part of the professional portfolio of the educator to work with parents. Efforts to involve parents are seen as something supplementary to the school . . . a sort of luxury that is nice if you have the time and staff to do it" (p. 22).

In their interview study of 60 parents and their child's teachers in two urban junior high schools, Leitch and Tangri (1988) found that teachers primarily attribute low parent involvement to beliefs that parents do not hold or communicate the necessary educational values. Teachers identified feeling hopeless and overwhelmed by problems students and families bring to school and held low expectations regarding parents' follow-up efforts. These researchers concluded that the lack of knowledge about how teachers and parents can each use the other more effectively is a major barrier in developing home-school collaboration. Teachers, who must be acknowledged as the greatest potential link for effective home-school collaboration (Moles, 1982), need more knowledge and specific skills for involving parents in the education of their children.

A criticism of parent involvement efforts that consistently surfaces from school personnel is that even when parents are given opportunities to become involved in children's education, some parents still choose not to be involved. These parents are often labeled by school people as "hard-to-reach" and receive little encouragement to become involved in their children's education (Heleen, 1989). Teachers and administrators often assume that these parents are either too lazy, incompetent, or preoccupied to participate in school programs. They believe that low-income parents do not value or have little to offer to the education of their children (Davies, 1989). Although teachers commonly hold these beliefs, very few of these beliefs are actually valid and substantiated. The most common explanation teachers had for parent noninvolvement was the parents' high work demands. Research results, however, have demonstrated that working parents were just as involved as nonworking parents (Leitch & Tangri, 1988). Teachers attributed low parent involvement to parents who represent all levels of education (less well to highly educated) and income levels (financially stressed to financially secure). Leitch and Tangri (1988) conclude from their study that noninvolved parents exemplify not a few but a range of parental characteristics. They also conclude that teachers' unsubstantiated assumptions of parents who are noninvolved negatively influence home-school relations. These assumptions lead to bitter confrontations about children's academic and behavioral problems, cause distrust and alienation, and only contribute to the alienation felt between parents and school people (Comer, 1984; Lareau, 1987; Smrekar, 1989; Swap, 1987).

From parents' perspectives, there are many factors that prevent or limit productive involvement in children's education. These factors may include: lack of time, minimal opportunities for involvement, job or family demands, different cultural backgrounds, family health problems, work schedules, demands of families with small children, receiving only "bad" news from school, fears for their safety, late notices of meetings, not understanding the work their children bring home, and feeling unwelcomed by the schools (Becker & Epstein, 1982; Tangri & Leitch, 1982; Moles, 1982). Parents identified by school personnel as being "hard-to-reach" do not feel they are "hard-to-reach" and state they will come to school if there are good reasons to do so. Heleen (1989) suggested that from the perspective of low-income parents, the problem can be seen more as the school being "hard-to-reach" rather than the parent. It seems that the term "hard-to-reach" is much like placing blame on another for problems and difficulties; placing blame as illustrated by Scott-Jones's quote at the beginning of the chapter is not a solution.

There is a strong belief that educators need to do more to involve parents in education. Epstein (1986) found that parents had overwhelmingly positive attitudes toward public schools; 90% of parents believed that their child's school was well run and most parents felt comfortable at their child's school. At the same time, many parents believed teachers could do more to get parents involved in learning activities at home. They thought teachers should try to involve parents, and 80% of the parents believed they could spend more time helping their child if they were shown how. Similar results were revealed in a later survey conducted by Dauber and Epstein (1989) who showed that parents in an inner-city school wanted teachers to help them help their child at home and give them more information about their child's curriculum. Most doubt their own ability to help their children but still express a desire to help them. Parents also identified that at times, children's homework was beyond their understanding even when they wanted to understand (Leitch & Tangri, 1988). Many parents communicate they do not enjoy coming to school—often stating that they have bad memories of school and feel intimidated when discussing school issues with school personnel. Parents report that they have low expectations for themselves and for their children. A large majority of these parents report that they are satisfied with their children's school experiences even though their children are not experiencing success (Davies, 1989).

Parents' and teachers' perceptions of each other has contributed to individuals encouraging schools to move beyond rhetoric. Major reports on schooling, *A Nation at Risk* (National Commission on Excellence in Education, 1983) and *Turning Points* (Carnegie Council on Adolescent Development, 1989), emphasize the role of parents in making education work, but Davies (1991) delineates the need for schools to reach out to families who live under stress because of economic hardship or barriers of language and social custom. Parents of all SES and educational backgrounds can be involved productively (Dauber & Epstein, 1989; Epstein, 1986). Epstein (cited in Olson, 1990) contends that "a relatively small percentage of parents have personal problems so severe that they cannot work cooperatively with teachers, given the proper assistance" (p. 22). To date, however, parent involvement programs are too fragmented, narrow in scope, and only sporadically funded (Nardine & Morris, 1991).

Structural differences between home and school. With respect to parent-professional interaction, some authors have suggested that the structures of home and school differ, and that these differences make parent involvement in the school difficult (Seligman & Darling, 1989; Lightfoot, 1975; Litwak & Meyer, 1974). Lightfoot (1975), for instance, theorized that parents and teachers are naturally poles apart because of the differences in their societal roles and the way they view children. Parents have individual relationships with their children whereas teachers are concerned with how the child fits in the group. Parents hold particularistic expectations of the child and teachers hold universalistic expectations. However, Lightfoot also pointed out that parents and teachers share the job of socializing children, and that their roles sometimes overlap and are not always clearly defined, a finding replicated by Leitch and Tangri (1988). Lightfoot (1975) wrote:

> I believe that part of the distrust between parents and teachers emanates from the real differences in perspectives that evolve out of the definitions of their cultural and societal role. The parent is protective and highly invested in his/her child, sees the educational system as competitive and individualistic, and seeks to get the teacher to recognize the child's unique place and give favorably to him. . . . Teachers, on the other hand, view their cultural role as rational and universalistic. In their view, a teacher should create . . . the classroom that is ultimately a system of equalized attention and favors. (p. 41)

According to Lightfoot, if interaction and communication are encouraged, these differences will not necessarily lead to poor relationships.

Litwak and Meyer (1974) hypothesized that differences between families and schools are due to structural differences. They describe the structure of the family as: diffuse, noninstrumental, face-to-face contact, and relatively permanent relations. In contrast, they describe the school as a bureaucracy characterized by a hierarchy of authority, impersonal relations, a priori definition of duties and privileges, separation of policy and administrative decisions, and using rules to guide behavior. As a result of these different structures, families and schools vary in their efficiency at dealing with tasks. According to Litwak and Meyer, family and schools must work together but also remain separate because their basic organizational principles are antithetical. The solution to this paradox is a balance of cooperation between home and school. Families and educators cooperate but maintain a separateness, which is a characteristic of complementary, collaborative relationships.

Professional dominance. In her investigation of the relationship between schools and families in four school systems, Lindle (1989) showed that parents want a person-to-person relationship not a "professional-client" relationship with schools. Parents desire opportunities to dialogue with educators about their children's education, opportunities to share perceptions about their child with educators, and provision of timely information about their child's school performance on an informal basis. Parents indicated a dissatisfaction with school personnel who are "too business-like," "patronizing," or "who talk down" to them. Lindle found that parents believed a personal touch from a teacher was the most important factor in encouraging their involvement with and support of schools. Her finding that parents want to be equal partners in the education of their children is supported by parents who have children with special needs. Peterson and Cooper (1989) described the values and concepts that lie at the heart of true parent-professional teamwork for children with handicaps:

> (a) Active, sensitive listening to what parents say about their own needs and desires; (b) respectful acceptance of what parents say about their own values, needs, and desires concerning education and treatment of their handicapped child; (c) an attitude of partnership manifest through joint sharing, planning, and decision making; (d) alternative options for parents; (d) equal importance given to roles played by each party; (e) individualization and flexibility of parent and family services and parent involvement; (f) respect for the parameters of parenting responsibilities and the prerogatives of parents to control their own lives; (g) respectful acceptance of what parents say about their own values, needs, and desires concerning education and treatment of their handicapped child; (h) open, reciprocal, and honest communication; and (i) fair, appropriate distribution of decision-making powers among parents and professionals. (p. 232)

Garfunkel (1983), however, questions whether parents can achieve equality because there is no provision for parents to be enfranchised as equal partners in the educational process. Professional educators are responsible for fiscal, personal, curricular, and disciplinary activities of schools.

Professional dominance is a common image associated with many professionals, including educators (Friedson, 1970). Professionals are characterized by the traits of achievement, universalism, functional specificity, and affective neutrality. Mendoza and Cegelka of Project P-PACT in San Diego identified nine differences in perception between parents and professionals that interfere with communication and collaboration and were based on traits of professionalism (cited by Chrispeels, 1987). For instance, the professional role is achieved rather than ascribed; the professional chose to teach children, whereas parents were given and accept the child as he is. The professional role is universalistic. The professional is expected to be fair to all children, whereas parents adopt an individualized

perspective, wanting what is best for their child. Professionals become "specialized experts," noting one aspect of a child's development. Parents adopt a more diffuse orientation, focusing on the child's ongoing development. Professionals are expected to be affectively neutral, to be able to distance themselves from the child. The parent role is the antithesis of the professional role; emotional involvement is expected. Differences in the roles played by parents and professionals can lead to strained communication.

Attitudes contribute to difficulties in parent-professional interactions. According to Swap (1987), factors that restrict parents' and teachers' ability to use effective problem-solving strategies are blaming each other, denying problems, feeling a sense of failure in parenting or teaching, anticipating negative or punishing interactions, and feeling a sense of responsibility for children's difficulties. Guttmann (1982) found that teachers attributed causes for problem behavior to the child first and the parents second, and minimized or dismissed any reasons associated with themselves. In contrast, parents attributed responsibility almost equally to the child, teacher, and themselves. Guttmann cautioned that differences in attributional patterns may account for some of the difficulty parents and teachers have in dealing with school problems, delineating parent-teacher responsibilities, and arriving at constructive, mutually agreeable solutions. Rich (1987) interpreted the emphasis teachers placed on home life as a recognition of the significance of the home as an educational environment rather than as a deficit view of the child or blaming of the family. This interpretation is consistent with the current philosophical orientation toward home-school relationships.

The current status of affairs is that the rhetoric about partnership belies the reality (Seeley, 1985). According to Seeley, successful educational partnerships exist in some classrooms and schools; however, partnership for education is limited. It only occurs when parents, educators, and students think of their relationship differently (Seeley, 1989), or individuals engage in a paradigm shift—one which moves from the concept of relationships in terms of service delivery—of "provider" and "client"; of "professionals" and "target populations"—to one of complementary efforts toward common goals. Seeley (1985) argues:

> Partners may help one another in general or specific ways, but none is ever a client, because the relationship is mutual. Providers and clients can deal with one another at arm's length; partners share an enterprise, though their mutuality does not imply or require equality or similarity. Participants in effective partnerships may be strikingly different, each contributing to the common enterprise, particular talents, experiences, and perspectives and sometimes having different status within the relationship and control over aspects of the work to be done." (p. 65)

Seeley's perspective is supported by parents, parents who want a personal touch and want to be equal partners (Lindle, 1989; Peterson & Cooper, 1989). Rich (1987) has referred to this as the adult-adult approach in educating and socializing children. This paradigm shift in parent-professional interaction is evident in recent theories about home-school relationships.

In summary, parent-child characteristics, school-teacher characteristics, and attitudes toward parent involvement all affect parent participation. The most consistent parent-child characteristics that are associated with parent involvement are gender of the parent, SES, and age of the child. Women, higher SES groups, and parents of younger children all are more involved. On the other hand, some variables that individuals have hypothesized to be associated with parent involvement, such as maternal employment and formal education, are not clearly related. Although there is not a lot of research on school-teacher variables associated with involvement, it appears that more efficacious teachers are more likely to involve parents. Dauber and Epstein (1989) concluded that teachers' and schools' efforts to involve parents are among the most important influences on parent involvement. Teachers' beliefs about the importance of parent involvement, comfort level with parents, and ability to communicate with parents on an equal basis influence individual teacher practices. Finally, parents' and teachers' attitudes toward involvement are generally positive, although this does not seem necessarily to translate into behavior.

There is also some evidence that parents and teachers may blame each other for children's problems. Despite the evidence of barriers between parents and teachers, and poor relationships between many schools and families, the necessity of overcoming the tenuous quality of home-school relationships has been made clear by many researchers and practitioners (Bronfenbrenner, 1974; Hobbs, 1979; Lightfoot, 1978). Research indicates that barriers are present regardless of parental SES level or educational background. It appears, however, that attempts to break down barriers between schools and parents with lower SES and educational backgrounds requires additional commitment and work from school people. It also appears that for this parent group, the benefits of increased parent involvement—although present—may not be as consistent or strong (Henderson, 1988). Family involvement in the schools may, however, be most needed by these parents (Scott-Jones, 1988). Parents with lower SES and educational backgrounds can become effective and active participants in their children's education if school people are willing to provide them with clear, specific, and useful suggestions that they can easily and successfully implement. Seeley (1984) suggested that unproductive relationships result because schools do not take into account the variety of relationships and needs of students and their families. He states that educators must be committed to supporting, communicating, valuing, and listening to all parents.

In order to foster mutually supportive families and schools, everyone must share in the responsibility and avoid shifting the blame for children's problems on others (see quote by Scott-Jones at the beginning of the chapter). School personnel, parents, and students must be willing to work together toward a common goal to effectively change old attitudes and habits (Seeley, 1989). If schools, families, and communities are to be effective partners in contributing to children's development and education, it is imperative that ways of developing and encouraging productive home-school interactions be found and implemented.

HOW CAN COLLABORATION BE INCREASED?

The effects of parent involvement in education appear to be consistent and of a sufficient magnitude to be substantial. We know the product of parent involvement in education efforts: students' academic and socialization outcomes are higher when parents are meaningfully involved and programs are comprehensive. Student learning is enhanced when there is a match between the efforts of home and school. There is also evidence that discontinuities between family and school have a negative effect on student learning.

The issues related to home-school relationships for promoting school performance are documented. We know that both home and school characteristics and home and school practices affect the degree to which meaningful parent involvement in education occurs. Findings from research in this area serve as guidelines, not rulebooks, for implementing home-school collaboration programs. In sum, we do not know the process or "how to" for creating effective partnerships between parents and educators in all communities and around all educational concerns. However, we know parents rely on schools to guide their involvement at home and at school, the importance of the elements of collaboration, and that creating home-school partnerships based on known guidelines holds promise for students' school performance.

The decade of the 90s has the potential to make a difference for children, youth, and their families (National Commission on Children, 1991). Opportunities to increase educational achievement by strengthening and supporting families are evident from the home-school collaboration literature. Based on our review, we propose that there are at least four areas of opportunity to change the rhetoric about home-school collaboration to reality: training, development of comprehensive parent involvement programs at a school level, interventions for groups of or individual children and their families, and research.

There is an opportunity to provide training for teachers, administrators, and parents. Training in preservice and inservice programs about school and family connections is a topic that requires special attention. Knowledge about the benefits of involving parents as well as specific parent involvement practices have been identified as essential components in teacher/administrator training and inservice (Chavkin & Williams, 1988). According to Epstein (1989), "Of all the problems that prevent educators from moving from rhetoric about parent involvement to more successful practice, none is more serious than the lack of teacher and administrator education and training in this topic" (p. 7). And yet, few school districts or states are systematically supporting training efforts (Nardine & Morris, 1991). In particular, training to enhance clear, nonblaming parent-professional interaction and improve school-to-home and home-to-school communication is essential.

There is an opportunity to develop comprehensive parent involvement programs for schools. Programs need to provide options at different levels of involvement (e.g., Epstein, 1987), and work toward involving community and business partnerships. The benefits of each school planning and implementing home-school collaboration efforts to meet the specific needs of their students, parents, and teachers may be far reaching.

There is an opportunity to develop and implement interventions for groups of and individual children and their families. Examples for this area of opportunity include specific programs for parents on topics related to how family life influences school achievement, development of parent support groups for common educational concerns (e.g., completing schoolwork), collaborative intervention planning between parents and teachers for a student referral concern (see Weiss and Edwards, this volume), and coordination of individuals and services for children (see Apter, this volume).

There is an opportunity to assess the efficacy of home-school interventions. Interventions have most often been implemented at the microsystem level, home or school; individuals need to implement interventions at the mesosystem level, the linkage between home and school cultures (Bronfenbrenner, 1979; Rotheram, 1989). The effect of these interventions on families' and educators' attitudes and perceptions of each other, parents' and educators' roles and responsibilities, family life, school reform and restructuring, and student outcomes needs to be determined.

If educators—school psychologists, administrators, teachers, and other related support service professionals—and community-based professionals—psychologists, counselors, family therapists, and social workers—can address these opportunities in a systematic and deliberate fashion, much will be learned about interactions and simultaneous influence of home and school environments on children's learning and development. If these opportunities can be addressed, the quotes by Bradley, Seeley, Scott-Jones, and Zigler (at the beginning of this chapter) may have moved beyond rhetoric to reality for all students.

REFERENCES

Bauch, P. A. (1988). Is parent involvement different in private schools? *Educational Horizons, 66,* 78–82.

Baumrind, D. (1966). Effects of authoritative parental control on child behavior. *Child Development, 37,* 887–907.

Becher, R. M. (1983). *Problems and practices of parent-teacher school relationships and parent involvement.* Unpublished manuscript. University of Illinois, Urbana.

Becher, R. M. (1984). *Parent involvement: A review of research and principles of successful practice.* ERIC Clearinghouse on Elementary and Early Childhood Education. Urbana, IL. (ERIC Document Reproduction Service No. ED 247 032)

Becker, H. J., & Epstein, J. L. (1982). *Influences on teachers' use of parent involvement at home* (Report No. 324). Baltimore, MD: Center for Social Organization of Schools.

Blase, J. (1987). Politics of teaching: The teacher-parent relationship and the dynamics of diplomacy. *Journal of Teacher Education, 38,* 53–60.

Brandt, R. S. (Ed.). (1989). Strengthening partnerships with parents and community [Special issue]. *Educational Leadership, 47*(2).

Bronfenbrenner, U. (1974). *Is early intervention effective? A report on longitudinal evaluations of preschool programs, Vol. II.* Washington, DC: Department of Health, Education and Welfare.

Bronfenbrenner, U. (1979). *The ecology of human development.* Cambridge, MA: Harvard University Press.

Carnegie Council on Adolescent Development. (1989). *Turning points: Preparing American youth for the 21st century.* Report of the Task Force on Education of Young Adolescents. Washington, DC: Author.

Chavkin, N. F., & Williams, D. L., Jr. (1985). *Parent involvement in education project. Executive summary of the final report.* Austin, TX: Southwest Educational Development Lab. (ERIC Document Reproduction Services No. ED 266 874)

Chavkin, N. F., & Williams, D. L., Jr. (1988). Critical issues in teacher training for parent involvement. *Educational Horizons, 66*(2), 87–89.

Chrispeels, J. A. (1987). The family as an educational resource. *Community Educational Journal, 14,* 10–17.

Chrispeels, J. A. (1988). Building collaboration through parent-teacher conferencing. *Educational Horizons, 66*(2), 84–86.

Christenson, S. L., Rounds, T., Roschelle, K. J., & Anderson, R. (1991). *Parent and teacher attitudes about roles in the home-school partnership.* Unpublished manuscript. University of Minnesota, Minneapolis.

Clark, R. M. (1983). *Family life and school achievement.* Chicago: University of Chicago Press.

Cochran, M. (1987). The parental empowerment process: Building on family strengths. *Equity and Choice, 4*(1), 9–23.

Cohen, D. L. (1990, April). Parents as partners:

Helping families build a foundation for learning [Special issue]. *Education Week, 9*(29), 13–20.

Coleman, J. S. (1987, August–September). Families and schools. *Educational Researcher,* 32–38.

Coleman, J. S., Campbell, E. G., Hobson, C. J., McPartland, J., Mood, A. M., Weinfeld, F. D., & York, R. L. (1966). *Equality of educational opportunity.* Washington, DC: U.S. Government Printing Office.

Coleman, J. S., & Hoffer, T. (1987). *Public and private high schools: The impact of communities.* New York: Basic Books.

Collins, C. H., Moles, O., & Cross, M. (1982). *The home-school connection: Selected partnership programs in large cities.* Boston, MA: Institute for Responsive Education.

Comer, J. P. (1980). *School power: Implications of an intervention project.* New York: Free Press.

Comer, J. P. (1984). Home-school relationships as they affect the academic success of children. *Education and Urban Society, 16*(3), 323–337.

Comer, J. P., & Haynes, N. M. (1991). Parent involvement in schools: An ecological approach. *The Elementary School Journal, 91*(3), 271–278.

Cutright, M. (1984). How wide open the door to parent involvement in the schools? *PTA Today,* 10–11.

Dauber, S. L., & Epstein, J. L. (1989, April). *Parent attitudes and practices of involvement in inner-city elementary and middle schools.* Paper presented at the annual meeting of the American Educational Research Association, San Francisco.

Davies, D. (1987). Looking for an ecological solution. *Equity and Choice, 4,* 3–7.

Davies, D. (1989, April). *Poor parents, teachers, and the schools: Comments about practice, policy, and research.* Paper presented at the annual meeting of the American Educational Research Association, San Francisco.

Davies, D. (1991). Schools reaching out: Family, school, and community partnerships for student success. *Phi Delta Kappan, 72*(5), 376–382.

Epstein, J. L. (1982, March). *Student reactions to teachers' practices of parent involvement.* Paper presented at the annual meeting of the American Educational Research Association, New York.

Epstein, J. L. (1984). *Improving American education: Roles for parents.* Washington, DC: 98th Congress-Second Session. Hearing before the Select Committee on Children, Youth and Families.

Epstein, J. L. (1985, April). *When school and family partnerships work: Implications for changing the role of teachers.* Paper presented at the annual

meeting of the American Educational Research Association, San Francisco.

Epstein, J. L. (1986). Parents' reactions to teacher practices of parent involvement. *The Elementary School Journal, 86,* 277–294.

Epstein, J. L. (1987). Toward a theory of family-school connections: Teacher practices and parent involvement. In K. Hurrelmann, F. Kaufmann, & F. Losel (Eds.), *Social intervention: Potential and constraints* (pp. 121–136). New York: deGruyter.

Epstein, J. L. (1988a). Effects on student achievement of teachers' practices of parent involvement. In S. Silver (Ed.), *Literacy through family, community and school interaction* (pp. 1–20). Greenwich, CT: JAI Press.

Epstein, J. L. (1988b). Parents and schools [Special issue]. *Educational Horizons, 66*(2).

Epstein, J. L. (1989). Building parent-teacher partnerships in inner-city schools. *Family Resource Coalition, 8,* 7.

Epstein, J. L., & Becker, H. J. (1982). Teacher practices of parent involvement. *Elementary School Journal, 83,* 103–113.

Epstein, J. L., & Dauber, S. L. (1991). School programs and teacher practices of parent involvement in inner-city elementary and middle schools. *The Elementary School Journal, 91*(3), 289–306.

Fantini, M. D. (1983). From school system to educative system: Linking the school with community environments. In R. L. Sinclair (Ed.), *For every school a community* (pp. 39–56). Boston, MA: Institute for Responsive Education.

Friedson, E. (1970). *Professional dominance.* Chicago: Aldine.

Garfunkel, F. (1983). *Parents and schools: Partnerships or politics* (Report No. 11). Boston, MA: Institute for Responsive Education.

Gibson, S., & Dembo, M. H. (1984). Teacher efficacy: A construct validation. *Journal of Educational Psychology, 76,* 569–582.

Gillum, R. M. (1977). *The effects of parent involvement on student achievement in three Michigan performance contracting programs.* Paper presented at the annual meeting of the American Educational Research Association. (ERIC Document Reproduction Service No. ED 144 007)

Goldstein, S., Strickland, B., Turnbull, A. P., & Curry, L. (1980). An observational analysis of the IEP conference. *Exceptional Children, 46,* 278–286.

Goodson, B. D., & Hess, R. D. (1975). *Parents as teachers of very young children: An evaluative review of some contemporary concepts and programs.* Washington, DC: Bureau of Educational Personnel Development, Office of Education. (ERIC Document Reproduction Service No. ED 136 967)

Gordon, I. J. (1977). Parent education and parent involvement: Retrospect and prospect. *Childhood Education, 54*, 71–79.

Gordon, I. J. (1978, March). *What does research say about the effects of parent involvement on schooling?* Paper presented at the annual meeting of the Association for Supervision and Curriculum Development, San Francisco.

Gotts, E. E. (1979). A classification of parenting programs, supports, and resources. In E. E. Gotts, A. M. Spriggs, & B. D. Sattes (Eds.), *Review of major programs and activities in parenting* (pp. 1–27). Charleston, WV: Appalachia Educational Laboratory.

Gough, P. B. (Ed.). (1991). Tapping parent power [Special issue]. *Phi Delta Kappan, 72*(15).

Graue, M. E., Weinstein, T., & Walberg, H. J. (1983). School-based home instruction and learning: A quantitative analysis. *Journal of Educational Research, 76*(6), 351–360.

Gross, M. J., Ridgley, E. M., & Gross, A. E. (1974). *Combined human efforts in elevating achievement at the Wheatley School.* Washington, DC: Nova University. (ERIC Document Reproduction Service No. ED 102 666)

Guttmann, J. (1982). Pupils', teachers', and parents' causal attributions for problem behavior at school. *Journal of Special Education, 76*, 14–21.

Hansen, D. A. (1986). Family-school articulations: The effects of interaction rule mismatch. *American Educational Research Journal, 23*(4), 643–659.

Haynes, N. M., Comer, J. P., & Hamilton-Lee, M. (1989). School climate enhancement through parental involvement. *Journal of School Psychology, 27*, 87–90.

Heleen, O. (1989). Involving the "hard to reach" parent: A working model. *Equity and Choice, 4*, 60–63.

Henderson, A. T. (1988, October). Parents are a school's best friend. *Phi Delta Kappan*, 148–153.

Henderson, A. T. (1989). *The evidence continues to grow: Parent involvement improves student achievement.* Columbia, MD: National Committee for Citizens in Education.

Herman, J. L., & Yeh, J. P. (1980). *Some effects of parent involvement in schools.* Paper presented at the annual meeting of the American Educational Research Association. (ERIC Document Reproduction Service No. ED 206 963)

Hess, R. D., & Holloway, S. D. (1984). Family and school as educational institutions. In R. D. Parke, R. M. Emde, H. P. McAdoo, & G. P. Sackett (Eds.), *Review of child development research: Vol. 7. The family* (pp. 179–222). Chicago: University of Chicago Press.

Hobbs, N. (1979). Families, schools, and communities: An ecosystem for children. In H. Leichter (Ed.), *Families and communities as educators* (pp. 192–202). New York: Teachers College Press.

Hoffman, S. (Ed.). (1991). Educational partnerships: Home-school-community [Special issue]. *The Elementary School Journal, 91*(3).

Hoover-Dempsey, K. V., Bassler, O. C., & Brissie, J. S. (1987). Parent involvement: Contributions of teacher efficacy, school socioeconomic status, and other school characteristics. *American Educational Research Journal, 24*(3), 417–435.

Hulsebosch, P. L. (1989, April). *Significant others: Teachers' perspectives on relationships with parents.* Paper presented at the annual meeting of the American Educational Research Association, San Francisco.

Irvine, D. J. (1979). *Parent involvement affects children's cognitive growth.* New York State Education Department, Division of Research, Albany, New York. (ERIC Document Reproduction Service No. ED 176 893)

Jennings, L. (1990, August). Parents as partners: Reaching out to families to help students learn. *Education Week, 9*(40), 23–32.

Kagan, S. L. (1984). *Parent involvement research: A field in search of itself* (Report No. 8). Boston, MA: Institute for Responsive Education.

Kagan, S. L., & Schraft, C. M. (1982). *When parents and schools come together: Differential outcomes of parent involvement in urban schools.* Boston, MA: Institute for Responsive Education. (ERIC Document Reproduction Service No. ED 281 951)

Knitzer, J., & Yelton, S. (1989). Interagency collaboration. In A. Algarin (Ed.), *Update: Improving services for emotionally disturbed children* (pp. 12–14). Tampa, FL: University of Florida, Florida Mental Health Institute.

Kroft, R. (1989). School-based parent involvement programs. In M. J. Fine (Ed.), *The second handbook on parent education: Contemporary perspectives* (pp. 119–144). New York: Academic Press.

Lareau, A. (1987). Social class differences in family-school relationships: The importance of cultural capital. *Sociology of Education, 66*, 70–74.

Lazar, I. (1978). *Summary: Lasting effects after preschool.* Consortium for Longitudinal Studies, Cornell University. (ERIC Document Reproduction Service No. 175 523)

Leitch, L. M., & Tangri, S. S. (1988). Barriers to home-school collaboration. *Educational Horizons, 66*, 70–74.

Leler, H. (1983). Parent education and involvement in relation to the schools and to parents of school-aged children. In R. Hoskins & D. Adamson (Eds.), *Parent education and public policy* (pp. 141–180). Norwood, NJ: Ablex.

Leyser, Y. (1985). Parent involvement in the school: A survey of handicapped students. *Contemporary Education, 57,* 38–43.

Lightfoot, S. L. (1975). Families and schools: Creative conflict or negative dissonance? *Journal of Research and Development in Education, 9,* 34–44.

Lightfoot, S. L. (1978). *Worlds apart: Relationships between families and schools.* New York: Basic Books.

Lindle, J. C. (1989). What do parents want from principals and teachers? *Educational Leadership, 47*(2), 8–10.

Litwak, E., & Meyer, H. J. (1974). The school and the family: Linking organizations and external primary groups. In S. P. Sieber & D. E. Wilder (Eds.), *The school in society: Studies in the sociology of education* (pp. 522–543). New York: Free Press.

Lusthaus, C. S., Lusthaus, E. W., & Gibbs, H. (1981). Parents' role in the decision process. *Exceptional Children, 48,* 256–257.

Lynch, E. W., & Stein, R. (1982). Perspectives on parent participation in special education. *Educational Leadership, 32,* 56–63.

Mayeske, G. W., Okada, T., Cohen, W. M., Beaton, A., Jr., & Wisler, C. E. (1973). *A study of the achievement of our nation's students.* Washington, DC: U.S. Government Printing Office.

McConnell, B. (1979). *Individualized bilingual instruction.* Final evaluation, 1977–78 Program Year. Report to the U.S. Office of Education, Division of Bilingual Education. Pullman, WA: Evaluation Office.

McDill, E. L., Rigsby, L., & Meyers, E. (1969). *Educational climates of high schools: Their effects and sources.* Baltimore, MD: Johns Hopkins University, Center for the Study of Social Organization of Schools. (ERIC Document Reproduction Service No. ED 030 205)

McKinney, J. D., & Horcutt, A. M. (1982). Public school involvement of parents of learning disabled children and average achievers. *Exceptional Education Quarterly, 3,* 64–73.

Merriam-Webster, Inc. (1985). *Webster's ninth new collegiate dictionary.* Springfield, MA: Merriam-Webster.

Miller, J. D. (1986, April). *Parental involvement in the schools: Causes and effects.* Paper presented at the annual meeting of the American Educational Research Association, San Francisco.

Moles, O. (1982). Synthesis of recent research on parent participation in children's education. *Educational Leadership, 40,* 44–47.

Moses, D., & Croll, P. (1987). Parents as partners or problems? *Disability, Handicap, and Society, 2,* 75–84.

Nardine, F. E., & Morris, R. D. (1991). Parent involvement in the states: How firm is the commitment? *Phi Delta Kappan, 72*(5), 363–366.

National Commission on Children. (1991). *Beyond rhetoric: A new American agenda for children and families.* Washington, DC: U.S. Government Printing Office.

National Commission on Excellence in Education. (1983). *A nation at risk.* U.S. Department of Education. Washington, DC: U.S. Government Printing Office.

Olmsted, P. P. (1991). Parent involvement in elementary education: Findings and suggestions from the Follow Through Program. *The Elementary School Journal, 91*(3), 221–232.

Olson, L. (1990, April). Parents as partners: Redefining the social contract between parents and schools [Special issue]. *Education Week, 9*(28), 17–24.

Palmer, F. H. (1977, October). *The effects of early childhood intervention.* Paper presented at the annual meeting of the American Association for the Advancement of Science, Denver.

Peterson, N. L., & Cooper, C. S. (1989). Parent education and involvement in early intervention programs for handicapped children: A different perspective on parent needs and the parent-professional relationship. In M. J. Fine (Ed.), *The second handbook on parent education: Contemporary perspectives* (pp. 197–236). New York: Academic Press.

Power, T. J. (1985). Perceptions of competence: How parents and teachers view each other. *Psychology in the Schools, 22,* 68–78.

Rankin, P. T. (1967). *The relationship between parent behavior and achievements of inner-city elementary school children.* Paper presented at the annual meeting of the American Educational Research Association, Washington, DC. (ERIC Document Reproduction Service No. ED 017 550)

Revicki, D. A. (1981). *The relationship among socioeconomic status, home environment, parent involvement, child self-concept, and child achievement.* (ERIC Document Reproduction Service No. ED 206 645)

Rich, D. (1987). *Schools and families: Issues and actions.* Washington, DC: National Education Association.

Rotheram, M. J. (1989). The family and the school. In L. Combrinck-Graham (Ed.), *Children in family contexts* (pp. 347–368). New York: Guilford.

Sattes, B. (1985). *Parent involvement: A review of the literature* (Report No. 21). Charleston, WV: Appalachia Educational Laboratory.

Scott-Jones, D. (1988). Families as educators. *Educational Horizons, 66,* 66–69.

Seeley, D. S. (1984). Educational partnership and the dilemma of school reform. *Phi Delta Kappan, 65,* 383–388.

Seeley, D. S. (1985). *Education through partnership.* Washington, DC: American Enterprise Institute for Public Policy Research.

Seeley, D. S. (1989). A new paradigm for parent involvement. *Educational Leadership, 47*(2), 21–23.

Seeley, D. S. (1991). The major new case for choice is only half right. *Equity and Choice, 7*(1), 28–33.

Seligman, M., & Darling, R. B. (1989). *Ordinary families, special children.* New York: Guilford Press.

Smith, M. B. (1968). School and home: Focus on achievement. In A. H. Passow (Ed.), *Developing programs for the educationally disadvantaged* (pp. 79–101). New York: Teachers College Press.

Smrekar, C. (1989, April). *The voices of parents: Rethinking the intersection of family and school.* Paper presented at the annual meeting of the American Educational Research Association, San Francisco.

Snider, W. (1990, November). Parents as partners: Adding their voices to decisions on how schools are run. *Education Week, 9*(44), 11–15.

Stevenson, D. L., & Baker, D. P. (1987). The family-school relation and the child's school performance. *Child Development, 58,* 1348–1357.

Swap, S. M. (1987). *Enhancing parent involvement in schools.* New York: Teachers College Press.

Swap, S. M. (1990). Comparing three philosophies of home-school collaboration. *Equity and Choice, 6*(3), 9–19.

Tangri, S. S., & Leitch, M. L. (1982). *Barriers to home-school collaboration: Two case studies in junior high schools.* Final Report, NIE Grant G-81–0033. Washington, DC: National Institute of Education.

Vaughn, S., Bos, C. S., Harrell, J. E., & Lasky, B. A. (1988). Parent participation in the initial placement/IEP conference ten years after mandated involvement. *Journal of Learning Disabilities, 21,* 82–87.

Vernberg, E. M., & Medway, F. J. (1981). Teacher and parent causal perceptions of school problems. *American Educational Research Journal, 18,* 29–37.

Vosler-Hunter, R. W. (1989). Families and professionals working together: Issues and opportunities. *Focal Point, 4*(1), 1–4.

Wagenaar, T. C. (1977, September). *School achievement level vis-à-vis community involvement and support: An empirical assessment.* Paper presented at the annual meeting of the American Sociological Association, Chicago.

Walberg, H. J. (1984, February). Families as partners in educational productivity. *Phi Delta Kappan, 65,* 397–400.

Walberg, H. J., Bole, R. J., & Waxman, H. C. (1980). School-based socialization and reading achievement in the inner city. *Psychology in the Schools, 17,* 509–514.

Whittaker, B. I. (1977). Citizen participation in educational decision making in an urban school district as perceived by parents and administrators (Doctoral dissertation, Georgia State University School of Education). *Dissertation Abstracts International, 38,* 3893A–3894A. (University Microfilms No. 77–29, 322)

Williams, D. L., & Stallworth, J. T. (1984). *Parent involvement in education: What a survey reveals.* Austin, TX: Southwest Regional Educational Development Lab: Parent Involvement in Education Project. (ERIC Document Reproduction Service No. ED 253 327)

Part II:

Programs and Models for the 90s

3

PARENT INVOLVEMENT AND SUCCESS FOR ALL CHILDREN: WHAT WE KNOW NOW*

Susan McAllister Swap

INTRODUCTION

Improving school achievement for all our children must be a national priority. Too many children are doing poorly in school. Levin (1987) estimates that currently about 30% of the children in this country are educationally disadvantaged. He emphasizes the association between poverty, cultural or linguistic differences, and low academic achievement and high dropout rates. He concludes that: "These educational deficiencies later translate into poor life chances for employment, income, and political and social participation" (1988b, p. 2).

The moral, educational, social, and financial burden of such pervasive school failure is unacceptable. Yet the numbers of children who are at risk for school failure are increasing. There are more children coming to our schools, particularly in urban centers, who are poor or from cultural or language minorities. Specifically, according to a recent Children's Defense Fund report (1989), the rate of poverty among young families with children almost doubled between 1973 and 1986. By the year 2000, the Census

Bureau projects that the total number of minority children will have increased by 25.5% from 1985 levels and that the proportion of all children who are minority will have increased from 28.0% to 32.7% (p. 116). A recent study of immigrant students in U.S. public schools (McCarty & Carrera, 1988), highlights not only the historic size of the current migration to the U.S. (about 2.7 million children of school age), but also the shift from traditional lands of origin. Our millions of newcomers are coming primarily from Mexico, Asia, Central and South America, and the Caribbean.

Public schools, and particularly our inner city schools, are being challenged to develop approaches to education that reverse this educational disadvantage. In addition to learning how to respond to the educational needs of the children arriving at our shores, we must find new ways to support success for all the children who currently populate our cities, regardless of race, class, ethnicity, or income level of their families. The problem of educational disadvantage is not a new one, nor is it confined to a single group or age level. But Jay MacLeod's ethnographic study of one group of urban youth (1987) provides a compelling view of the peril our society is facing. His investigation led him to the conclusion that we are developing a "static, nearly permanent

* Originally published by the Institute for Responsive Education, 605 Commonwealth Avenue, Boston, MA 02215.

element in the working class, whose members consider the chances for mobility remote and thus despair of all hope" (pp. 1–2). He insists that: "The problem is not that lower class children are inferior in some way; the problem is that *by the definitions and standards of the school,* they consistently are evaluated as deficient" (p. 99).

It is still possible to forge connections among quality education, hard work, academic achievement, and economic success in those populations that have been educationally disadvantaged. In this paper, we will explore how parent involvement can contribute to these connections by exploring the links between student achievement and parent involvement, the importance of continuity between home and school, three different philosophies underlying parent programs, and effective practices in parent involvement.

THE LINK BETWEEN PARENT INVOLVEMENT AND SCHOOL ACHIEVEMENT

The evidence that parent involvement activities enhance children's school success is overwhelming. Anne Henderson, who has done the most extensive literature review on the subject (1981; 1987) concludes: "The evidence is now beyond dispute: parent involvement improves student achievement. When parents are involved, children do better in school, and they go to better schools" (1987, p. 1). She explains that there is no one best way to involve parents, but "what works is for parents to be involved in a variety of roles over a period of time. The intensity of contact is important: public-relations campaigns, one-way communications devices, or dog-and-pony shows are not effective" (p. 6). "The form of parent involvement does not seem to be as important as that it is reasonably well-planned, comprehensive, and long-lasting" (1987, p. 2).

These positive effects of parent involvement on student achievement are sustained across grade levels (preschool through high school) in programs that are home-based or school-based, and for low-income as well as middle-income families. There is a caveat about programs in low-income settings, however. Although studies demonstrate that parent involvement activities work to the extent that students achieve better than matched controls, the programs do not seem to demonstrate levels of achievement that are comparable to those of middle-class children (see Cochran, 1988; Gillium, 1977; Tizard, Schofield, & Hewison, 1982; and Walberg, 1980).

There are some interesting exceptions to this pattern. For example, students in Comer's project in two public schools in New Haven have reached national achievement norms (Comer, 1980, 1988; Schorr, 1988). Begun in 1968 in two very troubled low-income schools, by 1988, children who had been in the program for 5 years significantly surpassed controls in other New Haven Title I schools on Metropolitan Achievement Tests in reading and math, approached national norms in reading, and attained the national norm in math (Comer, 1980). Fourth grade children were scoring at median grade level by 1980 on the Iowa Test of Basic Skills (Comer, 1988).

The program is still in operation and has spawned several adaptations in other sites. Special features of the program were and are the mental health team, the School Planning and Management team, and the involvement of parents in all levels of school activities. In the original schools, parents were involved in many roles over a long period of time, which included:

- working with teachers to share their goals for their children in school, and the experiences and skills they felt would help children attain those goals;

- working with teachers in the planning and execution of the social skills curriculum (an effort to teach children social skills that would be useful in the classroom and the larger community);

- functioning as paid aides in the classroom;

- volunteering for a variety of projects (e.g., accompanying the gospel choir);

- participating in social activities and events;

- being members of the School Planning and Management Team, the representative governance and management group in the school.

Comer explains: "We worked carefully with parents to make certain that their first projects were successful. Success breeds success and confidence, and as a result they were motivated to participate even more. When parents have a positive relationship with school staff, they can help children accept these people. This is important. When we ask low-income, minority-group children to achieve well in school—an instrument of mainstream society—we are often asking them to be different than their parents. With parents involved, there is no conflict" (1988, p. 219).

Henderson (1987) concludes that we still need to know what types and intensity of parent involvement are needed to raise the achievement level of low-income and minority children to that expected for middle-class students. I would suggest that Comer's project provides important clues about what the differentiating characteristics may be. In the next two sections, I will develop a hypothesis about how different approaches to parent involvement may affect the level of children's school success.

THE IMPORTANCE OF HOME-SCHOOL CONNECTIONS FOR CHILDREN AT RISK

The first question we must try to answer is why parent involvement programs that are reasonably well planned, comprehensive, and long lasting have important effects on the academic achievement of children at risk for school failure.

Regardless of the philosophy of the program, continuity in values between home and school reduces conflict for children, reinforces learning, and eases the transitions between the two environments. In more homogeneous communities, where teachers are drawn from the same culture and live in the same community as the parents, this continuity is taken for granted. However, in many communities today and especially in our major cities, teachers and parents often have different cultural and class backgrounds which lead to discontinuities for the children.

The usefulness of home-school continuity as a support for children's learning makes sense when we reflect on how children learn. Each child constructs knowledge anew, assimilating information that is gained through direct experience with people and objects into existing mental structures. A desire to make sense of the world propels the child toward new learning.

Although we do not know what the optimum conditions for new learning are for each child across the several areas of intelligence, Piaget provided us with a useful insight about how cognitive growth occurs with his concept of disequilibrium. Children move to the next stage in their construction of knowledge about the world when they recognize that there is a discrepancy or conflict between what they are experiencing and how they are making sense of it. But the degree of discrepancy must be "just right." As Kegan (1982) puts it, children who are "ripe for evolution" experience the kind of intellectual crisis that leads to new learning when presented with a particular problem "that is precisely suited" to informing the child *that something is fundamentally wrong* about the way one is being in the world" (p. 41). Then with repeated and varied encounters with the problem, the child will construct a new organization of the physical world that accommodates to this new experience.

Thus, one of the discoveries about disequilibrium is the need for the experience or problem to be appropriate to the child's developmental readiness. If the problem is too advanced or the child is not "ripe for evolution," he/she may ignore or reject the information or solve the problem incorrectly with no anxiety. If suitable opportunities for interaction with the environment are not provided, the child will not be catapulted into transition. These truths may provide a metaphor for helping us to understand what may happen to a child when there are significant discontinuities between ways of learning and knowing at home and at school. Because the population in our schools is becoming so diverse, it is imperative that we seek to understand the implications of these discontinuities.

Surface differences of language, skin color, use of touch and proximity, and even unspoken rules governing eye contact between teacher and child may make it more difficult for a child to draw on his or her past experiences and apply them to the new ways of learning at school. Other differences in ways of teaching and learning may be more subtle and perhaps even more disorienting for a child. Consider, for example, differences between the focus on individual achievement in Anglo culture versus the importance and centrality of learning through and because of relationships that is a part of Hispanic culture (Irujo, 1989); the experiences of rural children in the Carolina Piedmonts when they came to school in the city and were frustrated by different and unarticulated rules and expectations that linked particular classroom activities to a particular time and place (Heath, 1983); the differences between the focus on linear lessons in Anglo culture versus the focus on wholeness and the relationship of every part to the whole that is characteristic of Native American culture (Locust, 1988).

Confronted with significant discontinuities between home and school, failing to find a piece of themselves in school, failing to see how their past experiences of learning are reflected in school, failing to find confirmation of their construction of meaning in the world, these children may reject or ignore the new information they are receiving and continue to exclusively use their "old" processing schemas.

Because in these circumstances the match between developmental ripeness and environmental stimulation is not optimal, children's growth may be slowed.

Because we are aware that home-school connections are important to school achievement and that continuity in expectations and values are particularly important for educationally disadvantaged children, why are good parent involvement programs so rare, particularly in our inner-city schools? In the next sections, we will examine the barriers to home-school partnership and three different approaches to overcoming these barriers.

BARRIERS TO EFFECTIVE PARENT INVOLVEMENT PROGRAMS

Most of us are deeply familiar with the barriers that inhibit effective home-school collaboration. These barriers of tradition, attitude, and changing times are not trivial and must be directly acknowledged to be overcome. They include:

1. *A tradition of separation between home and school.* Williams and Stallworth (1983–84), for example, in extensive interviews, discovered that while parents were eager to play all roles at school, educators were more comfortable in relegating parents to insubstantial bake-sale roles, leaving them feeling frustrated, belittled, and left out. Even when educators see parent involvement as desirable, they may not see it as essential to achieving common goals. And even active parents may see their involvement as part of an adversarial process; that is, as a necessary step in achieving equal or optimum treatment for their children.

2. *A tradition of blaming parents for children's difficulties, particularly when parents are poor and not consistently involved in school.* Teachers may feel that parents who do not come to school "don't care" and that they have inadequate skills. The essence of this orientation is summarized (though not endorsed) by Heath and McLaughlin (1987). They assert that by the mid-1980s, parents were brought to the fore as

an important contributor to the inadequate preparation of children. According to this analysis, "Deficiencies in parenting and in families . . . lie at the core of students' identified inadequacies as future workers, citizens, and parents. . . . The inability or unwillingness of American families to socialize, support, stimulate, and encourage their children in the ways and objectives of schools lies at the root of the disappointing educational attainments cited by blue-ribbon commissions, special panels, and public officials" (p. 577).

Davies's (1988) sample of 150 teachers and administrators working with poor children in Boston, Liverpool, and Portugal echoed this deficiency orientation. In interviews, they revealed that they *did* "think of low-income/low-status families as being 'deficient,'" and many dwelled on family problems while ignoring family strengths (p. 53).

Interestingly, the educators' convictions about the apathy of "hard-to-reach" parents were not supported by data. Davies (1988) found that despite teachers' negative attitudes toward parents, parents in all three cultures expressed active interest in their child's progress at school and in getting involved in school. They just did not know how to get involved. Epstein's (1987) research adds another interesting wrinkle to this tradition. In her survey of 3,700 teachers in 16 districts in Maryland, she discovered that: "Teachers who used parent involvement frequently rated all parents higher in helpfulness and follow-through with learning activities at home, including parents with more or less education and single and married parents" (p. 128).

3. *Changing demographic conditions.* Seventy percent of mothers of school-aged children are now in the workforce compared to 30% in 1960. Many more female teachers combine teaching and child-raising (now 73%, a gain of about 20% since 1960). Poverty is rising (almost one in four children now lives below the poverty line), as is the number of homes headed by single parents (now 25%, double the figure in

1970). In some communities, teacher unions are becoming stronger and limiting the availability of teachers for assignments outside of school hours. About one million immigrants enter the U.S. each year, many of whom do not speak English fluently. These changes in availability and background often make it difficult for teachers and parents to work together, even though these very changes make the necessity for partnership even more compelling. (For more data and a fuller discussion, see Braun and Swap, 1987; and Children's Defense Fund, 1989).

4. *Persistent structures.* Despite changing conditions, schools typically maintain traditional patterns of interacting with "outsiders." Short conferences, large open houses, parent association meetings in the morning, fund-raising activities, and children's performances are ritualistic events, comfortable in their familiarity if not their effectiveness in building involvement between home and school. It is often a breakthrough just to realize that traditional structures may not be meeting current needs and that they could be adapted or changed.

Many schools have overcome these traditional barriers to parent involvement. In the section to follow, I will outline three different approaches to parent involvement, each of which leads to improved school achievement.

THREE PHILOSOPHIES UNDERLYING PARENT INVOLVEMENT PROGRAMS

In this section, I suggest that parent involvement programs are organized according to three different philosophies and hypothesize that the third approach leads to the highest gains in student achievement. The school-to-home transmission philosophy encourages parents to adopt and actively support the values and "ways of being" that have traditionally led to children's success in school. The second model is an interactive philosophy which assumes that there are important and valuable differences between the cultures of home and school. Parent involvement programs built upon this philosophical framework encourage dialogue and reciprocal influence in order to create continuity in children's learning. The third philosophy embraces a partnership between educators and parents that is based on mutual respect and an explicit, shared commitment to supporting success for all children. Although parent involvement programs in the real world sometimes blur these distinctions, the philosophies deserve careful analysis because they reflect different assumptions, values, and goals that affect program directions and content.

A Philosophy of School-to-Home Transmission

In this model, educators specify what parents should do to support their children's learning at home. Educators hope that parents will participate in two ways. The primary expectation is that parents will aid their child's learning by endorsing the importance of schooling and making sure that the child meets the minimum academic and behavioral requirements. For example, educators expect parents to make sure that a child completes homework. Or, if a child is getting into trouble at school, educators hope that the parent will work with them to reinforce expectations and create conditions at home that support a change in behavior (such as monitoring the amount of television watching or responding appropriately to a daily record of the child's satisfactory or unsatisfactory behavior in school).

A secondary hope (not quite an expectation) is that parents will spend enough time with their children to transfer to them what has come to be known as "cultural capital," that is, the ways of being, knowing, writing, talking, and thinking that characterize those who succeed in this culture. (For further discussion of the concept of cultural capital, see Delpit, 1988 or Heath and McLaughlin, 1987). A minimum version of this hope/expectation is that parents will read to their children and listen to their children read to them. Parents

might also contribute to their child's cultural capital through such activities as helping their child with a science project or visiting a museum. Ideally, by spending time with their parents, children will extend and enrich what they learn at school: Children will learn how to work hard, will gain knowledge and experience about the world, and will discover how to share this knowledge with others.

Epstein underscores the effectiveness of parent involvement programs based on a philosophy of school-to-home transmission, in which parents of children at risk are asked to reinforce at home those behaviors, values, and attitudes which educators believe will lead to school achievement:

> The evidence is clear that parental encouragement, activities, and interest at home and participation in schools and classrooms affect children's achievements, attitudes and aspirations, even after student ability and family socioeconomic status are taken into account. Students gain in personal and academic development if their families emphasize schooling, let the children know they do, and do so continually over the school years. (Epstein, 1987, p. 120)

Comer is explicit about the importance of parents supporting the growth of children's social skills:

> Children whose parents feel that they can and should be a part of the social mainstream have the best chance to acquire the social skills that will lead to school and life success. Children whose parents are not a part of the social mainstream can acquire such skills if they are taught in school and there is parental support for their acquisition and use. Regardless of the background of the parents, the climate and operation of a school must be reasonably good to constructively enhance children's social skills. (1980, p. 192)

Comer's conviction about the importance of parents' attention to their children's school achievement and social skills emerged in part from his own experience in his family. As he explains in *Maggie's American Dream,* his mother was a domestic with almost no formal education. Now a prominent child psychiatrist and educator, Comer explains how his mother supported his achievement by going to school functions, advocating for him with teachers, insisting on fine work, and taking him to the library. She learned the lexicon of how to be an effective parent and what it took for a black child to be successful in predominantly white schools by carefully listening to the women for whom she worked. She says: "So many people would just work and pay no attention to what's going on. I didn't just cook and clean. I worked with my eyes and ears open. I watched and listened to them and the way they lived. For me it was like going to school" (1988, p. 69).

It is important to explicitly state that the values and behaviors which are hypothesized to undergird school success are not confined to parents of a particular class, racial, or ethnic background. For example, middle-class parents may not support the "social mainstream" values of hard work, self-discipline, self-motivation, and respectful manners; poor families may teach those skills and attitudes very successfully.

Clark's (1983) research, for example, illustrates differences in commitment to transmitting these values and behaviors within a sample of poor black parents living in the inner city. He visited the homes of 10 poor black families and their high school children for at least 2 days each. He found that differences in achievement between the five children who were in the top 20% of the class and the five who were in the bottom 20% of the class were not attributable to poverty, family structure, mother's educational background, or other demographic variables. Rather, the differences were in the family culture and the nature of the parent-child and parent-school interactions. Parents of achieving students strongly encouraged academic pursuits, expected their children to continue their education, set clear and consistent limits, had frequent conversations and nurturant interactions with their child, and monitored the student's use of time. Moreover, the parents of achieving stu-

dents were involved with the school and visited the school periodically. In contrast, parents of the children who were doing poorly in school were not involved in school except when there was a negative incident. The students were less closely supervised and less explicitly encouraged to succeed.

The school-to-home philosophy could be summarized as follows: Educators hope that parents will adopt an orientation that explicitly supports schooling and school personnel, and that they will either teach their children the social skills required for success at school and in life, and/or be responsive to the school's attempts to educate parents and children about these values and skills. It follows that as the strength of the parent involvement program is enhanced, more and more children will be equipped to succeed in school.

This orientation strikes a responsive chord in many families who hope that educational achievement will be the route to economic success for their children. The glitter of the American dream of rags to riches continues to inspire many of America's poor citizens and to attract immigrants from around the world. Thus, clear direction from the school about the social and academic skills that are needed for success and the parents' role in supporting those skills can be a welcome offering.

Within this philosophy, parents are seen as a crucially important resource for children's success. However, as I have visited programs and reviewed published and unpublished literature based on programs of this type, I have noticed that parent programs based on school-to-home transmission often contain components that reflect an unwillingness to consider parents as equal partners having important strengths. Relationships may be defined through a contract, and parents may be reinforced for meeting their contractual obligations. For example, parents may be asked to sign an agreement indicating their commitment to providing a quiet space and protected time for their child to complete homework, or sign an agreement to read to or be read to by his/her child on a regular basis. Contracts rarely specify educators' obligations, and parents are seldom included in the negotiations about what should be done at home or how it will be done. Materials sent home to support educational enrichment are often in the form of recipes, presumably mistake-proof opportunities for parent-child involvement. Finally, parent education programs are often explicitly developed to help parents be "more effective parents" and to instruct them in the values and skills that will help them to be so. Each of these strategies suggests an unequal distribution of power and a conviction that school personnel know more about what parents should do to support their children than the parents do. However, if parents perceive that educators do not respect them or that they blame them for their children's difficulties, they may hesitate to become involved or become disillusioned over time.

Although research has shown that the cooperation of parents in supporting children's academic and social competence can have significant positive effects on the achievement of educationally disadvantaged students, the philosophy has four limitations that need to be considered:

1. Parents may not be able to devote sufficient time and energy to parent involvement activities. As Bronfenbrenner (1975) articulated, "[Many] families live under such oppressive circumstances that they are neither willing nor able to participate in the activities required by a parent intervention program. Inadequate health care, poor housing, lack of education, low income, and the necessity for full-time work . . . rob parents of time and energy to spend with their children" (pp. 465–466). If success for all children *depends* on parent involvement, then many children without this support will continue to fail.

2. A related limitation of the philosophy is the possibility that the promise of equal opportunity through education and hard work is false. Suppose parents and children do learn the ways of

thinking and being of the social mainstream, devoting much time, struggle, energy, and faith to the task. Then suppose, as is now increasingly the case, that *despite* success at school, young adults from impoverished or nonmainstream backgrounds are not able to find a decent job and economic success. As mentioned above, Jay MacLeod's book *Ain't No Makin' It* (1987) is an ethnographic study which documents just this breakdown of the connection between educational achievement and economic opportunity for poor white high school students from the projects in a major urban center. Generations of experience watching peers and family members struggle, only to find that there "ain't no makin' it" has confirmed for these students that the effort to conform is both demeaning and ridiculous. For the children and parents who have tried and feel betrayed, and for those who are teaching them and feel despair, this outcome is insidious and dangerous.

William Julius Wilson's book *The Truly Disadvantaged* (1987) alerts us that the social condition of poor urban blacks is steadily deteriorating, that today's ghetto neighborhoods are populated almost exclusively by the most disadvantaged segments of the black urban community, and that long-term unemployment, high rates of street crime, and long-term poverty are characteristic of this "underclass" (p. 8).

Both analyses suggest that parent and school partnership, though critical, may not always be sufficiently powerful to counteract the complex factors that lead to poverty and family dislocation. One antidote to the disadvantage to children created by parents whose lives are a struggle for survival is to secure for these children the support of a network of individuals, agencies, and businesses within the community. Such a network would not only benefit children, but perhaps secure for families the resources and skills to break the cycle of disadvantage. A closer and more intense collaboration between the school and these community groups and institutions on behalf of children at risk is a rich resource for families, and will be more fully discussed in a later section on family-school-community partnerships.

3. A third limitation of the school-to-home transmission philosophy is that it may be difficult to draw clear boundaries between the roles of school and home in formal education. In its most exaggerated form, parents would be asked to teach whatever skills or values the child was not acquiring, regardless of the financial or emotional cost to families. Parents who did not participate would be responsible for the failure of their child.

From my point of view, a study conducted by Mehran and White (1988) provides an example of a program which poses hard questions about appropriate boundaries. Parents of kindergarten children in Title I schools who were at risk for having difficulty learning to read were invited to participate in an experimental tutoring program. Of the 80 parents invited, 76 agreed to join, and 38 mothers were assigned to the experimental group. Parents were asked to come to two 4-hour training sessions in July, follow-up meetings twice a week during the summer, and additional meetings once a month during the school year. Parents were asked to tutor children in sounds and letters, basic sight words, blending of sounds, and other pre-reading skills for 15 minutes three times a week from August to April. Parents were asked to submit tutoring logs every 2 weeks. Any parents who had not mastered the tutoring techniques were offered additional assistance until mastery was achieved.

Of the original 38 parents, two left the district; four did not submit logs; 12 tutored their child 0–1 times per month; 12 tutored 2–4 times per month; and only eight had 8–11 tutoring sessions per month (12 were expected). When the results were analyzed, only children in this last group made significant and lasting gains.

One could look at these results and conclude that the eight mothers who continued with the program contributed importantly to their children's success in reading. One might also conclude that the other 28–30 mothers were not sufficiently responsible or that the experimenters were not sufficiently attentive to the mothers' level of motivation. A third view might be that the intensity and types of interventions required were inappropriate within most family contexts and that this effort did not effectively capitalize on the willingness of 76 out of 80 mothers to support their child's learning at home. Within the school-to-home transmission model, questions remain to be answered about what roles parents should play to support children's learning, what the curriculum should look like, and how and by whom these decisions will be made.

4. A fourth limitation is the danger of demeaning the value or importance of the child's culture in the effort to transmit the values and goals of the social mainstream. Locust (1988) describes this discrimination very clearly:

> Discrimination against persons because of their beliefs is the most insidious kind of injustice. Ridicule of one's spiritual beliefs or cultural teaching wounds the spirit, leaving anger and hurt that may be masked by a proud silence. American Indians experience this discrimination in abundance for the sake of their traditional beliefs, especially when such beliefs conflict with those of the dominant culture's educational systems. (p. 315)

A Philosophy of Interactive Learning

A philosophy of interactive learning undergirds some parent involvement programs. Such programs are built on an explicit premise of mutual respect between parents and educators, and they stress mutual learning and mutually developed objectives. Within this model, there is not a single mission, but two valued outcomes that justify parent involvement: students' successful achievement in the mainstream and the valuing of the goals and beliefs of the non-mainstream culture. This model may or may not permeate the structure and mission of the whole school. Sometimes only certain classrooms or programs within a school or district embrace this philosophy. The literature on such programs highlights parent involvement in classroom curriculum development as well as more standard activities, and parents are seen as the experts in their cultures with many strengths for the school to draw upon.

There seem to be several sources of inspiration for this model, though different sites may not share all of them. One source is the recognition by parents and/or educators of the importance of continuity in learning between home and school. School personnel may initiate an interactive learning approach because they value the richness and disparateness of the cultures of their pupils and the importance of understanding these cultures if they wish to support their students' learning. Finally, parents may initiate an interactive learning approach because political awareness and pride in their culture prompt them to insist on information about and appreciation of their culture in the school. Lightfoot (1978) articulates the importance of a *home-to-school* connection:

> If one recognizes the initial social and cultural task assumed by *all* families and their primary educative function, then it becomes clear that in order for schools to be productive and comfortable environments for children, they will have to meaningfully incorporate the familial and cultural skills and values learned in homes and communities. . . . When schools and families support dissonant values and goals, and when families and communities are perceived as inadequate and chaotic environments by arrogant and threatened school personnel, then education within families is devalued and systematically excluded from the school culture. Children experience the cultural dissonance between home and school, recognize the sharp contrasts and the forced choice they must make for successful accommodation in both worlds, and develop more or less functional strategies for relieving the environmental tensions. (pp. 170–171)

We seem suddenly to be in a world where these sharp contrasts and forced choices based on cultural differences are more dramatic and frequent. The reasons have already been suggested: increasing poverty and generations of individuals in poverty, many new immigrants from non-Western cultures, and a decreasing number of minorities in the teaching professions, a problem that has now reached a crisis point (Hawley, 1989; Plata & Chinn, 1989).

One solution to this discontinuity is to recruit more teachers into the school who reflect and value the child's culture (e.g., MacLeod, 1987). This goal must be a national priority in teacher preparation institutions. Another solution is to bring more parents into the school. When parents and teachers get to know each other through frequent informal communication, through shared projects, or through volunteering in the classroom, children's behavior and learning problems tend to diminish. Lightfoot (1978) explains:

> It is important to recognize that the presence of parents in the school not only provides more adults to teach reading or offer help and support to children but also transforms the culture of the school. With these black mothers present, there is no way that the curriculum and environment could remain unchanged. Even if the content of the lesson appears the same on paper, the transmission of the lesson takes on a different quality and character when presented by the mothers. Even if the concepts are unfamiliar and alien to the child's experience, the mother-teacher's style of interaction, her face, and her character are not strange. It feels like home. (p. 173)

A third solution is for parents or teachers to learn the points of difference in their cultures and to provide a lexicon for the children that would allow the children to become fluent in and appreciative of both cultures. We have already described the expectation that parents outside the social mainstream should learn the culture of the school. Proponents of this model would argue that educators who do not share the culture(s) of their students are also responsible for learning the ways of knowing of the children and families that they teach.

Lisa Delpit (1988) makes it very clear that teachers of "other people's children" have an obligation to create a lexicon for children that gives them access to the social mainstream. Starting with assumptions that "If you are not already a participant in the culture of power, being told explicitly the rules of that culture makes acquiring power easier. . . . Those with power are frequently least aware of—or least willing to acknowledge—its existence" (p. 282). Delpit explains how to teach students the culture of power while valuing the language, meaning-making, and culture that students bring to the classroom.

Heath (1983) provides another very compelling example of how white city teachers learned how to understand the culture of their newly integrated poor black students. In a focused staff development effort, teachers reflected on the insights Heath gained during her observations of the children's rural communities, supplemented these observations with their own experiences in the classroom, articulated the points of conflict and their reactions to them, discovered ways of valuing and making explicit their different ways of talking and working, and, perhaps most important, discovered ways of teaching that resulted in the academic success of those first grade children who had already been labelled as "potential failures."

In North Barrow, Alaska, Inupiat Eskimos came to resist education for their children that reflected only Western values. Okakok (1989) explained that after local control of public schooling was granted to the natives in the mid-70s, the community insisted that "although Western education would serve its purpose, it would now be a purpose determined by our own people" (p. 407). She continued: "While seeking to produce students with academic achievements comparable to those of other areas of the United States, the Board has also sought to bring into our schools certain elements of historical and contemporary Inupiat Eskimo culture and knowledge of our natural environment. We have found that the attainment of academic skills in our students is directly related to our ability to successfully introduce Inupiat Eskimo concepts and educational practices into our schools" (p. 408). Local efforts by parents and the community to seek a form of schooling that incorporated and respected the worldviews of two disparate cultures led this school system to educational strategies that included a low teacher-student ratio, bilingual education, the selection of skills taught, a program of parent involvement, and the introduction of elements of historical and contemporary Inupiat culture into the curriculum.

Despite its attractiveness as a way of enhancing school success for more children at risk, this interactive philosophy also presents problems when used as the underpinning of parent involvement programs.

1. It is a very difficult task to tease out the important elements of another's culture. At the very least, study of ethnographers' writings and the literature and history of the culture is required; ideally, educators would spend time in parents' homes and in the community learning firsthand about the strengths and values of the parents in the community. Such study requires time, administrative and faculty support, and an openness to deciphering and appreciating other worldviews.

2. Classrooms are now often filled with children from several different backgrounds, particularly in our cities. Teachers may need to be responsive to children and families from several different cultures and traditions. Without consultation and widespread staff commitment, attempts to respond to this diversity may result in fragmentation of teachers and the instructional program.

3. Some educators and families may believe that it is in the best interests of all for the American melting pot to be homogenized. They may feel that it is unrealistic and ultimately unethical for cultural differences to be maintained and celebrated. This perspective is reflected in the debate at Stanford over "non-Western" curriculum and in the controversy

about the appropriateness of bilingual instruction for children. In my view, three conditions should encourage us to examine the merits of the interactive perspective anew: our shrinking world, the transformation of the "minority" culture to the "majority" culture in our cities, and, as Levin (1988a) warns us, the specter of the educationally disadvantaged making up the underclass of a dual society, engendering "great political conflict and social upheaval" (p. 211).

A Philosophy of Partnership for School Success

There is an emerging model that draws on some elements of the two already described. It is a model which appears to meet Henderson's (1987) challenge of demonstrating levels of achievement in schools serving educationally disadvantaged children that are comparable to levels achieved in schools serving middle-class students. Schools which have adopted this model view parent-school partnership as a fundamental component of children's school success, and educators welcome parents as assets and resources in the search for strategies that will achieve success for all children. In this model, attitudinal and political shifts toward mutual respect and shared power are prerequisites to true partnership. The language used to describe this model is radical and visionary: "paradigm shift" (Seeley, 1989a) connotes a fundamental reorganization of the ways of thinking about a problem; "empowerment process" (Cochran, 1989) is defined as an ongoing process involving mutual respect, critical reflection, caring, and group participation which leads to a redistribution of valued resources. The most important precepts of this model are described below.

1. *Clarity and consensus about goals* (e.g., Chubb, 1989; Levin, 1987; Seeley, 1986, 1988, 1989a, 1989b). The school, parents, and community must have a shared sense of mission about creating success for all children. Such a commitment represents a significant

change in how school failure is conceptualized. David Seeley (1989a) terms this change in thinking and attitude a "paradigm shift" in which blaming children and families for failure is replaced by an expectation of success for *all* children, not just the "bright" ones; the establishment of specific and often ambitious yardsticks of success; and an active search for teaching strategies that will lead to success. In successful schools, the mission becomes embedded in a culture of collegiality, caring, and experimentation, in which "what must remain stable in the life of the school is the emotional and intellectual dispositions toward improvement on the part of Responsible Parties" (i.e., teachers, parents, administrators, and community representatives; Joyce, Hersh, & McKibbin, 1983, p. 6).

One of the key ingredients in developing a shared mission of success for all children is agreement on the standards by which success will be judged. School personnel must replace a generalized interest in "students reaching their potential" and "feeling good about themselves" with a commitment to specific standards. The standards may include indicators of student attendance, dropout or suspension rates, student retention, and self-esteem; they consistently include measures of proficiency in basic skills and reading, writing, and mathematics. In a paper describing the correlates of school effectiveness, Edmonds and Lezotte (1982) recommended that the ideal measures of pupil performance be locally generated, nationally validated, curriculum based, criterion referenced, and standardized. Moreover, the school or district should have a description of the level of mastery required for satisfactory progress. It seems that school-based discussion and agreement on goals and indicators of success are crucial because they add direction and zest to the teaching and learning efforts, increase the accountability of all participants, and provide a basis by which to include or reject educational programs or instructional strategies.

2. *A revised curriculum* (e.g., Comer,

1980, 1988; Cuban, 1989; Levin, 1987; Moses, Kamii, Swap, & Howard, 1989; Slavin & Madden, 1989). A remedial approach to educating at-risk students is replaced by an accelerated approach. A comprehensive, intensive curriculum is used which assesses children's progress frequently, and provides individual support through peer or teacher instruction. Teaching is based on an enriched curriculum that builds on connections with the life experiences of students in their families, communities, and cultures; that stresses active learning; and that builds critical thinking skills along with basic skills.

3. *Local autonomy and control* (e.g., Carnegie, 1988; Chubb, 1989; Goodlad, 1984). It is very important for teachers and principals to have the flexibility to respond to changing needs and discoveries within the building. Control over major decisions about budget, incentives, resources, curriculum, schedule, and teacher assignments builds commitment, ownership, and professionalism among the staff. Local control should be supplemented by central administrative support (financial, intellectual, and emotional) for experimentation.

4. *Partnership among educators, parents, and community members* (e.g., Comer, 1988; Henderson, 1987; Moses et al., 1989; Schorr, 1988). In the summary of what she learned in investigating 20–30 programs that were successful in breaking the cycle of disadvantage, Schorr states: "Successful programs *see the child in the context of family and the family in the context of its surroundings*" (1988, p. 257). Successful schools draw on parents for help and advice; they seek from parents confirmation of the schools' high expectations for the children; they clarify how parents can help support their children's achievement. Successful programs also draw on other resources within the community, creating business, agency, and medical partnerships so that services can be offered to children and families in a nonbureaucratic way and needed materials and funding can be obtained.

Recognition of the necessity of collaboration among educators, parents, and community representatives in meeting the goal of success for all children is an essential part of the "paradigm shift" as articulated by Seeley (1989a). If the school community honestly commits to the goal of success for all children, then the community also recognizes that the challenge is so great that it cannot be met by parents or teachers or agency personnel working in isolation. The combined resources of the community are essential to discovering and implementing effective solutions to improving public education.

The focus on intellectual activity and inquiry remains front and center in this model. Collaboration among adults does not highlight relationship building for its own sake, but rather problem solving to support school success. Ideally, adults model for children the excitement and productivity of sustained intellectual activity in the context of improving the school.

Model programs. Comer's project and its replications, Levin's accelerated schools in California, and Moses's program in Cambridge, Massachusetts are programs which illustrate partnership for school success. Comer's model (Comer 1980, 1988; Schorr, 1988) has already been highlighted. The original pilot schools in New Haven and the schools throughout the country which have adopted the model share the features of a common mission and public review of children's academic progress; enriched, integrated curriculum and a collaborative, preventive approach to handling children's behavior and academic problems through the mental health team; intensive, respectful partnership with parents in all aspects of the program, and local control as demonstrated through a School Planning Management Team. As described above, these schools are successful in supporting students in reaching mainstream levels of academic achievement.

Levin (1987, 1988a, 1988b; Freedberg, 1989) has initiated a vision of an "Accelerated School" in two pilot sites in California. The mission of these schools is

to move every student into the educational mainstream by the end of the sixth
grade. The development of objectives for
each child and periodic assessment of
each child's progress are components of
the model. The curriculum, which is still
evolving, rejects a remedial approach to
education and "emphasizes language—
reading and writing for meaning—in all
disciplines, even in mathematics. The
curriculum also applies learning to everyday problems and events. Instructional
strategies also include peer tutoring and
cooperative learning" (Levin, 1987, p. 20).

Local control of the program in each
school is ensured by a school-based
governance model, a steering committee,
and small groups or "cadres" of teachers
who are given time and resources to focus
on potential obstacles to fulfilling the
vision and plans for overcoming them.
Parent involvement is seen as integral to
the vision, and parents are involved in
the steering committee, in setting high
expectations for children, in affirming an
agreement which specifies the obligations
of parents, students, and school staff in
reaching the goals, and in providing
academic assistance to their children.
Although it is too soon to tell whether
this approach will be successful in
launching each child into the educational
mainstream by the sixth grade, energy,
commitment, and excitement are high
among students, educators, and parents.

Robert Moses (Moses, Kamii, Swap, &
Howard, 1989) is a parent with rich
experience as a community activist in the
civil rights movement, whose charismatic
intervention in a school led to significant
improvement in students' achievement in
mathematics. The focus of the project
became finding a way for all children to
have access to the college preparatory
mathematics curriculum of the high
school through transformation of the
middle and elementary school curricula.
A cornerstone of the "Algebra Project"
became:

> The expectation that every child in the
> Open Program could achieve math liter-
> acy, an ethos powerful enough to suffuse
> both peer and adult culture. The compo-

nents of this effort included changing the
content and methods of teaching math,
involving parents in activities that would
better enable them to support their
children's learning, teaching students to
set goals and motivating them to achieve,
and reaching out to Black college graduates in the Boston area who would serve
as tutors and role models of academic
success. (p. 428)

The project produced its first full
graduating class in the spring of 1986.
Not a single student was placed in lower
level math courses in the high school,
and 39% of the graduates were placed in
honors courses. Through a collaborative
governance model that involved all components of the school community, the
math tracking system was eliminated in
this school, and *all* children, including
the females and minority students who
had previously been excluded, gained
access to the upper-level mathematics
courses.

There are three challenges to widespread adoption of the partnership model
in inner-city schools. The first is a
requirement that there be a strong leader
who is able to articulate a vision of
success for all children, inspire belief in
the vision, and eagerly seek involvement
and ownership of the vision by teachers,
administrators, parents, and community
members. The leader may come from
outside the school (e.g., university profes-
sors or a parent) or from inside the school
(e.g., Deborah Meier as principal of New
York's Central Park East School; Schorr,
1988), but a strong leader must emerge
who can lead the school forward.

Another challenge is the energy required of all responsible parties for
initiating and maintaining the school
transformation. In schools which have
adopted the partnership model, the transformation appears to be invigorating and
renewing. Yet the commitment to do
more than is required, initially and over
time, may threaten the culture of most of
our inner-city schools.

A final challenge is the need to
maintain local control of governance and
resources in the schools which initiate
partnership models. In the bureaucracies

of large city schools, it is often extremely difficult to hold on to key personnel and resources long enough to allow an ambitious model to show results. Despite the obstacles, a model for success for all children now seems to be available to us. In the final section of this paper, we will take a closer look at how parent involvement programs are organized, analyzing six components of these programs and outlining effective practices in each area.

EFFECTIVE PRACTICES IN PARENT INVOLVEMENT

Joyce Epstein (1988) has outlined five areas of parent involvement: education programs for parents; communications with parents about school programs and children's progress; parent involvement at school; parent involvement in learning activities at home; and parent involvement in governance and advocacy. Effective programs and practices will be outlined in each of these areas and in a sixth: community linkages.

Education Programs for Parents

Definition and goals. Epstein (1988) suggests that schools can support parents in meeting their basic obligations as parents by offering information about children's health and safety, identifying medical or social service resources in the community as needed, and offering educational programs for parents on child-rearing issues. In addition, some schools provide programs that are designed to meet parents' needs not directly related to their parenting role (e.g., classes in English as a Second Language, workshops on getting a job, excursions to get to know the city).

As one element of a parent involvement program, parent education programs can provide a mechanism for getting parents into the school and can add to parents' knowledge about the complex role of parenting. When programs are effective, parents feel connected to the school in a common effort to support the growth and learning of their children.

Pitfalls. In designing an effective program, there are some very common pitfalls to avoid. The first is for educators to develop activities based on what they think parents should know or be interested in. As described in the section on school-to-home transmission, activities may be selected based on a deficit model of parent education rather than a model that builds on family strengths. (See Cochran, 1988; and Rich, Mattox, and Van Dien, 1979 for a fuller discussion of building on family strengths). If parents' interests are not tapped and they do not come to activities, educators who have taken the trouble to plan them often feel rejected and angry.

A second pitfall is to plan many single session activities on different topics. Although this strategy seems to be the best way to meet everybody's needs, it often has the opposite effect. The approach is very time consuming, because each activity requires different leaders, outreach, and organization. Often these activities are attended by different groups, so that parent involvement is not enhanced over time. Moreover, the organizers tend to burn out, because there is no sense of momentum and little reward.

A third common pitfall is to provide activities which permit little or no opportunity for parent interaction, feedback, or trial and adaptation of new ideas over time. Activities without these components may still be stimulating, but they seldom lead to changes in attitude or behavior.

A fourth pitfall, if a primary goal is to enhance parent involvement, is that parent education programs may function totally outside the ordinary life of the school. That is, parents may come to school for activities, but see only other parents, an outside "expert," and one school-based organizer. To enhance parent involvement with the school, it is useful to include some education activities of interest to both parents and educators.

Effective practices. The most critical dimension in providing educational programs for parents is to make sure that the programs offered are responsive to parents' needs and interests as they perceive them. Some form of needs assessment is critical, whether it be through interviews, questionnaires, group meetings, or some combination of these activities. All parents should have an opportunity to respond, and every effort should be made to ascertain that any sample of respondents is representative of the whole parent body. This may mean translating questionnaires into relevant languages, sending a school representative out into the community to speak to parents on their turf, or using a team of parents to contact one another. Although this may seem obvious, gathering information from parents is important because it demonstrates that parents' concerns and needs are of interest to school personnel. The process of gathering data may be as significant as the information collected.

Once data are gathered, programs should reflect the parents' priorities. If possible, an advisory committee of parents and educators should get together to review priorities, develop programs, and evaluate programs that were presented. Identifying a chair or co-chairs of a parent education committee is a useful step, because someone needs to take responsibility for calling and leading advisory board meetings, and for coordinating tasks such as finding out what parents want, identifying and securing resources, discussing programs with potential speakers or group leaders, and publicizing and evaluating the programs. In different schools, the leadership role may be assumed by a parent, teacher, administrator, or some combination of these. The job is usually performed better if it is not a "freebie." A stipend for a parent or teacher coordinator or release time for a teacher intensifies their commitment.

When presenting activities, parents' concerns about transportation, scheduling, and childcare should be noted and taken into account. In general, parents appreciate formal and informal opportunities to express their reactions to programs and to ask questions. Inviting parents to evaluate activities demonstrates an interest in program improvement and may support parents in feeling

that they have some ownership of the activities. A range of activities is usually most effective in drawing from a cross-section of the parent population. For example, some may prefer small discussion groups that meet over several weeks, whereas others may prefer a visit by an outside expert, or workshops to make and take toys. Ideally, resources will be available to offer programs over several years, so that different priorities can be addressed over time, and some issues can be explored in depth. In general, it is better to offer a few high-quality, well-planned activities than to provide a lot of mediocre events. Success breeds success, and excellent programs are the best way to recruit parents for future activities. (See Swap, 1987, for an extended discussion of these issues.)

The answer to the question, "Which parent education activities are most directly related to school achievement for educationally disadvantaged students?" continues to be somewhat ambiguous. As summarized by a digest of the ERIC Clearinghouse on Urban Education (1986), parent participation in at-home learning activities was generally effective in improving students' intellectual functioning and achievement, and parent education activities to prepare parents for home learning were often important. In addition, parent participation in a wide-ranging group of other activities (e.g., fundraising, attendance at school meetings) appeared to have some effect on student achievement if the activities were oriented to the needs of the community. If time and resources are limited and student achievement is the primary goal, it seems clear that some of the parent education activities should explicitly involve parents in supporting this goal.

COMMUNICATION WITH PARENTS

Definition and goals. Epstein includes in this category a range of communications initiated by the school about children's progress and school programs. Communication strategies might include standard activities such as conferences, report cards, notices, and open-house programs, as well as more innovative strategies developed by each school. From my perspective, this category should also include communication from home to school. Parents should be encouraged to share information that might help teachers understand their child's learning style, special strengths, or crises that might impede the child's responsiveness.

Good communication between home and school is the key to parent involvement, and the key to good communication is an attitude that welcomes parents as adult peers in a context of mutual respect. Effective communication is based on relationships between parents and educators in which each respects the other's contributions and expertise; boundaries are clear (e.g., teachers are not expected to be therapists and parents are not expected to be certified teachers); conflicts are dealt with openly and respectfully; and contacts are rewarding.

The most obvious reason for parents and teachers to communicate is to nurture the growth and learning of individual children by sharing information, insights, and concerns. However, if parents and educators are in a partnership to support school success for all children, then parent communication and collaboration must be viewed as a necessity and not an extra; sustained interest in modeling, monitoring, and enriching children's intellectual and social growth should be primary goals of adult communication; and the school must become a responsive community institution rather than an outpost of a distant and hostile bureaucracy.

General strategies for promoting effective communication. The principal of the school can set the tone. For example, Hauser-Cram (1983) discovered that there was significantly more parent involvement in schools where principals had established an explicit policy encouraging such involvement.

Once the expectation for involvement has been set, relatively frequent and informal contacts work best to develop relationships (e.g., a few words when dropping off a child, parent and teacher sitting together at a breakfast before school, sending brief notes back and forth). Informal relationships based on mutual respect provide the structure for more focused collaborative activities. Ideally, teachers or teachers and parents together could brainstorm about the most effective and efficient ways to communicate. They would discuss what parents and teachers want to know and what strategies are currently working well and not so well.

There is no single best solution: The best route to effective communication is one that is adapted to local conditions and the preferences and needs of the teachers and parents. In my experience, it is best to take advantage of the special interests and skills of particular teachers and parents: A teacher with artistic and journalistic skills might enjoy organizing a newsletter; a parent with youngsters at home might volunteer for a telephone chain; teachers might coordinate with students in the high school art department to develop a video illustrating an ordinary classroom day; a bilingual parent might contribute to a translation service; a parent living in a project might be willing to hold an information meeting there for other parents who find it hard to get to school. For ideas of what others have done to promote good communication, see Chrispeels, Boruta, and Daugherty, 1988; Henderson, Marburger, and Ooms, 1986; Office of Community Education, 1989a and 1989b. In-service programs for parents and teachers designed to promote good communication in schools are also available. (See, e.g., Braun & Swap, 1987; Cochran et al., no date).

Improving Conferences

For most schools, the child-centered conference is the focal point for communication with parents. A state-wide survey of working parents in California, for example, found that parents preferred the individual conference to other types of information programs offered by the schools (Hobbs, 1984). Despite its importance, many parents do not attend scheduled conferences. Epstein's survey of

Maryland school districts (1987), for example, revealed that "more than one-third of the parents had no conference with the teacher during the year" (p. 124).

There are several practices that may make conferences more productive and more widely attended. These practices are designed to overcome the built-in problems of the traditional conference format, in which two strangers attempt to share a great deal of information about a subject of deep mutual concern in 15 minutes. In many instances, the conference is also the primary mechanism for identifying and solving problems that the child may be experiencing and for resolving conflicts between parent and teacher. When differences of language, class, or background are added, problems of communicating comfortably and unambiguously are usually intensified. With conferences carrying such a heavy burden, it is not surprising that both parents and teachers come to them with trepidation as well as hope. These suggestions, directed to the teacher (adapted from Braun & Swap, 1987), can help.

1. *Relationship Building.* Conferences are easier to prepare for when you have a relationship with the parent(s) or guardian. Social events, classroom observations, notes, telephone call-in times, can help create a context for greeting the parent(s) and discussing complex information.

2. *Purpose.* Despite the fact that Epstein places conferences under the category of communication with parents about school programs and children's progress, conferences are likely to go better if they are reframed as opportunities for information sharing (teacher to parent and parent to teacher) and joint decision making.

3. *Preparation.* If this is a regularly scheduled conference, send early notification (2–3 weeks). If possible, add a personal note to a formal notice and offer some flexibility in appointment schedules. Don't wait if a problem emerges several weeks or months before the regularly scheduled conference, but try to get together as soon as possible. Plan for an appointment time that will be sufficient to discuss the anticipated content. For example, if a problem needs to be discussed, a half hour will probably be needed. Assemble relevant materials (papers, pens) if appropriate. Some teachers invite parents to bring in relevant materials or a list of questions or issues they want to discuss. Plan an agenda in which you allow at least half the time for parent concerns and ideas. Set priorities for discussing your own concerns and ideas, expecting that you will have time to deal with only one or two issues.

4. *Practice in Anticipation of Difficult Moments.* Most teachers have excellent communication skills. However, even sensitive communicators have difficulty giving negative feedback, resolving conflicts, and listening when they feel threatened, angry, or impatient. In-service training which identifies key skills and provides opportunities to practice difficult situations is essential. Having a colleague who will give you feedback when you try out ideas and language can be very useful.

5. *Setting the Stage.* Try to provide a physical environment which comes as close as possible to the setting you would create for a friendly, formal adult interaction. Two adult-size chairs are a minimum requirement (or three if both parents come), and privacy is important. Something to eat or drink that is traditional within the parents' culture is a nice touch if it can be managed.

6. *During the Conference.* Clarify the agenda, identifying issues or questions parents want to discuss. (Because of cultural differences, not all parents will feel comfortable in doing this.) Seek the parents' expertise about their child. Appreciate the child's unique qualities in a sincere, nontrivial way. Avoid jargon. If shortage of time is pressuring you into an ill-considered decision, arrange another meeting. If the conference results in plans for teacher or parent action, decide

how you will follow up to exchange results.

Administrators can:

1. Initiate a review of conference scheduling policy with central administration, teachers, parents, and union representatives. The goal would be to provide adequate teacher release time for conferences while continuing to offer flexibility in scheduling for educational and parental needs.

2. Model a welcoming attitude toward parents in formal and informal settings, and provide a written policy which supports parent involvement.

3. Make available a small budget for coffee, snacks, and duplication costs during conference times.

4. Create partnerships with media to publicize scheduled conference days and with businesses to support parent participation. In Houston, Texas, for example, Operation Fail-Safe focused on increasing parent participation in conferences. A local advertising agency designed a total public awareness campaign and the logo and theme appeared on 100 billboards throughout the city. Approximately $1,700,000 in public service advertising was donated by radio, television, and outdoor media to promote teacher-parent conference days. After the first year of operation, parent participation was up 47%; 75% of parents of elementary students participated in conferences. The Indianapolis school system has expanded on this model in their "Parents in Touch" program (Collins, Moles, & Cross, 1982).

Parent Involvement at School

According to Epstein, this category of parent involvement includes parent volunteers who assist teachers, administrators, and children in classrooms or in other areas of the school or who work as paid aides. "It also refers to parents who come to school to support student performances, sports, or other events" (1988, p. 2).

Definition and goals. The participation of parents in children's school events is one of the most obvious and direct ways to help children feel that their lives at home and at school are connected. No parent can deny the importance of this connection who has seen his/her child's pride when pointing out a composition or painting prominently displayed on the wall of the classroom, or has experienced their child's disappointment if the band solo, the caught pass, or the three lines in the school play were missed. Despite some nervousness, teachers also appreciate the support of parents during these events, and find adult acknowledgment of their hard work rewarding.

Parent involvement as school or classroom volunteers or paid aides can have a major impact on the school, on parents, and on children. Schools benefit from a well-run volunteer program because it extends what schools can accomplish. For example, the library can be open for more hours and children can receive individual attention in selecting books or using references; teachers can work with individual children while volunteers listen to groups of children read or assemble art materials for a project; parent expertise in computers can extend students' understanding and experience with computers; a paid aide in a bilingual classroom who shares the children's first language can help make connections between curricula and culture for teachers and students. In some inner city schools (as in Head Start programs), parent volunteers or aides with limited education and job experience discover their potential and receive the support they need to go back to school and find good jobs. As mentioned earlier, children, particularly those from minority cultures, learn more easily when they are helped by volunteers or aides who look and speak as they do.

Promising practices. Effective volunteer programs contain predictable components. These include:

1. A coordinator to identify needs, arrange training, and monitor the program.

2. A method to ascertain the interests and skills of potential volunteers and the needs of teachers, administrators, and specialists for volunteers. For example, teachers can develop one-page questionnaires that outline curriculum themes, one-time or ongoing needs, and opportunities for parents to list special interests, hobbies, or talents. As explained in *Focus on Parents: Successful Strategies for Parent Involvement* (Office for Community Education, 1989a) a volunteer job description can provide a standard format for providing information that includes the title of the position, a description of the work needed (skills, time commitment), and a contact person. Job descriptions could be disseminated by mail, in newsletters, in the local newspaper, by posting in the school or at community centers, or by broadcasting openings on local radio and television stations.

3. A method to match volunteers or aides and their supervisors.

4. A method to orient and train volunteers. Training may include a general orientation session led by the coordinator, but must include more detailed information from the supervisor about what is expected, opportunities to learn specific skills, and information about common questions or concerns (e.g., setting limits for children, procedures in case of illness, what to do if personality conflicts arise). Some schools or districts have published manuals for volunteers which summarize useful information and help to orient new volunteers. (For example, see National School Volunteer Program, 1979; South Carolina State Department of Education, 1985).

5. A procedure for monitoring the program. The coordinator should be a trouble-shooter who stays in touch with both school personnel and volunteers or aides to identify problem areas, significant accomplishments, and further needs.

6. A procedure for celebrating contributions and communicating them to others. When parents give their time and expertise to the school, it is important that their gifts be publicly acknowledged. A school might choose to offer certificates, a celebration dinner, a school assembly where children express their appreciation, and/or an article in the local newspaper or a program on local television explaining what individuals have done.

Parents Assisting their Children in Learning Activities at Home

Epstein (1988) includes in this category requests and guidance from teachers for parents to assist their children in home learning activities coordinated with their classwork. Teachers can offer information about skills needed to pass each grade. Parents may request information on how to monitor, discuss, and assist with homework and to make decisions about other activities that will help their children be successful in school.

Definition and goals. There are several different models that have been suggested for home-based learning activities. These include parent support for supplementary reading activities, parent involvement in generic enrichment activities, parent activities specifically tied to the school curriculum, and school activities that are generated from events and incidents in the community. All models are designed to support the child's success in school, and some are part of experimental programs to increase students' achievement test scores.

Promising practices. Perhaps the most commonly used model for home learning is a request from school for parents to support their child in supplementary reading activities, either by reading to the child, having the child read to them, or monitoring the child's silent reading for specified periods per day or week. The importance of these activities was highlighted by a remarkable study by Tizard, Schofield, and Hewison (1982). They discovered that elementary-age children in a working-class area of London who read aloud to their parents 2–4 times a week using books sent home from school showed highly significant gains in reading achievement compared to students with no intervention and to students who were provided with a special teacher who listened to them read and offered tutorial assistance in school. Other studies also support the connection between parent involvement and reading achievement. For example, Cummins (1986) learned that reading achievement scores improved when children read stories to their non-English-speaking parents and then explained the story in their native language. Epstein (1987) conducted a survey of parent involvement practices in inner-city schools and discovered:

> A story builds from all of the sources in the survey: Principals actively support parent involvement, especially in reading activities; teachers request more parent involvement on reading activities at home; parents conduct more learning activities in reading than in other subjects; and the students' reading achievement is improved. These results suggest the importance of subject-specific connections. (p. 128)

Student achievement also seems to increase when parents are more generally involved in supporting children's schoolwork at home. For example, Walberg, Bole, and Waxman (1980) discovered that when Chicago parents of elementary students participated intensively in a program to create academic support conditions in the home, the students gained .5 to .6 grade equivalents more on the Iowa Test of Basic Skills than did students who were less intensively exposed. Academic support conditions included a contract for home study, parent agreement to provide a study space for the child, daily discussion about school, parental enthusiasm about the child's achievements, and willingness to cooperate with the teacher. Several school systems have developed calendars of activities, suggestions for using the newspaper or TV, family math games, or reading charts. For an excellent sampler of such materials, see Chrispeels, Boruta, and Daugherty (1988). Other sources of home learning activities marketed more directly to parents are Dorothy Rich's

MegaSkills (1988), and Baron, Barn, and MacDonald's *What Did You Learn in School Today?* (1983). *MegaSkills* (1988) has been widely used, perhaps because it is organized according to skills required for achievement in school (e.g., motivation, perseverance, confidence, teamwork) and provides inexpensive and easy to follow suggestions of activities to do at home which support the development of these skills.

Several school systems have experimented with the third model of home-based learning activities in which home activities are specifically integrated with the classroom curriculum. For example, Epstein (undated) has developed a research-based process to involve parents in children's homework. "Teachers Involve Parents in Schoolwork" (TIPS) offers programs to support students' learning in math, science, social studies, and art. A Title I program in Chicago enrolled parents in a tutorial program one day a week so that they could help their children with their homework for one hour a week. Parent training included instruction related to the homework, discussions on topics related to child-rearing, crafts, and field trips. Children's achievement scores were slightly above expected levels. The Parent Partnership program in Philadelphia provides reading and mathematics booklets to parents as well as a Dial-A-Teacher-Assistance project for help with homework in all basic subjects. The San Diego Unified School District offers materials in English and Spanish that cover homework assignments in reading and mathematics through grade 6. Each of these projects and many others are described in Collins, Moles, and Cross (1982).

The fourth model seeks to create more opportunities for connecting home and community content to the school curriculum. Teachers and parents at the King School in New Haven (Comer, 1988) illustrated this model when they developed a politics and government unit as part of their social skills curriculum. The unit included many activities for parents, students, and staff around the mayoral election, culminating in an evening when students hosted a candidates' night for the parents, staff, and candidates.

Auerbach (1989) at the University of Massachusetts Family Literacy Project is searching for a way to draw on parents' knowledge and experience to inform school- and home-based instruction. She has formulated a "social-contextual approach to family literacy" which critically analyzes the assumptions and practices of programs which encourage parents to do school-based activities at home. Drawing upon the philosophy of other effective literacy programs among Hispanic, Piedmont, and Navajo families, Auerbach explains that in their program:

> The goal . . . is to increase the social significance of literacy in family life by incorporating community cultural forms and social issues into the content of literacy activities. The model is built on the particular conditions, concerns, and cultural expertise of specific communities, and, as such, does not involve a predetermined curriculum. Instead, the curriculum development process is participatory and is based on a collaborative investigation of critical issues in family or community life. . . . This approach fosters a new formulation of what counts as family literacy. This broadened definition includes, but is not limited to, direct parent-child interactions around literacy tasks; reading with and/or listening to children; talking about and giving and receiving support for homework and school concerns; and engaging in other activities with children that involve literacy. (p. 177)

Other activities include exploring family literacy practices, modeling whole language activities, validating culture-specific literacy forms, exploring parenting issues, practicing advocacy in dealing with the schools, and using literacy to explore issues of learning and teaching.

There is little evidence currently available about the effectiveness of connecting home and community content to classroom curriculum. Heath (1983), however, catalogues the success of one white teacher who changed her curriculum after participating in a seminar (with Heath and other teachers) whose purpose was to aid them in learning about the

traditions, values, and "ways of knowing" of children at the school who came from surrounding small communities. Mrs. Gardner, a first grade teacher, elected to teach 19 African-American students from "Trackton" who had been labelled as "potential failures" based on reading readiness tests administered in kindergarten. She designed a curriculum which resulted in all but one of the 19 children reading at or above grade level: eight were at the third grade level; six at second grade level; and four at grade level (p. 287).

From my perspective, it is clear that all four of these program types can be successful in raising the achievement of middle- and low-income students. The fourth model has special promise when parents do not feel comfortable in trying to implement school-based activities at home, and/or when a significant discrepancy between home and school cultures and learning styles suggests that teacher adaptation of curriculum to bridge these differences might be a critical first step in enhancing parent involvement and student achievement.

Parent Involvement in Governance and Advocacy

Epstein's (1988) final category includes parents as advocates and as decision makers in the PTO, Advisory Councils, Chapter 1 programs, or other committees or groups at the school, district, or state level. She indicates that schools can help parents perform in these roles by offering information and training in decision making and communication skills.

A brief history. The limited research that is available suggests that parental involvement in decision making, whether in policy or curriculum, is not particularly related to student achievement (ERIC Clearinghouse on Urban Education, 1986). One reason for this lack of effect is that although there are important and encouraging exceptions, parent involvement in school decision making is often just window-dressing. We will look briefly at three types of parent involvement in decision making: federally-mandated advisory councils at the school or district level, Individual Educational Plan meetings, and locally initiated school-community planning or management councils.

Williams (1989) reviewed the history of citizen advisory councils resulting from federal initiatives and concluded:

> In summary, parent advisory councils, even where there was disproportionate representation by middle-class parents, have tended to be dominated by principals, who set the agendas and decided what would be done with the councils' recommendations. School systems, having established these councils under federal or state mandate, too often have employed them as foils to allay public fears about the quality of their children's education rather than as channels for problem solving. (p. 92)

Malen and Ogawa (1988) also make the point that program-specific committees such as Title I, Chapter 1, or vocational education where the principal is granted final authority to make decisions, frequently limit the contribution of parents and teachers to policy making and have little impact on altering routines, standard operating procedures, or traditions.

Another format for parent involvement in decision making is the federally mandated participation of parents of children with special needs in meeting with educators to develop their child's Individual Educational Plan (IEP). Despite the language of Public Law 94-142 which specifies that parents be active, equal participants in making decisions about their child's placement and educational program, retrospective and observational studies document that this is not usually the case (e.g., see Brinckerhoff & Vincent, 1986). Unfamiliarity with testing and teaching jargon, dismay at the numbers of school personnel attending the meeting, and an ambiguous role during the meeting contribute to parental passivity. However, it is possible to raise parent participation. Brinckerhoff and Vincent measured significant increases in parent decision making in IEP meetings when

parents were assigned a liaison from school, when parents compiled information about their child at home, when a summary of this information was presented to school personnel in advance of the meeting, and when parents were asked to present their issues and goals first.

Parents have also been involved in many types of locally initiated school-community planning or management councils whose purpose is to improve schools and democratize decision making. Williams (1989), Davies (1979), and Malen and Ogawa (1988) describe many experiments. Often the experiment does not last or parents play a minimal role in decision making. Malen and Ogawa, for example, described an experiment which confounded their expectations. They saw the site-based governance councils in Salt Lake City as a "critical test" of the viability of structures for shared policy because these councils incorporated four highly favorable arrangements: The councils were located within each school; councils were given broad jurisdiction and formal policy-making authority; parents, teachers, and the principal all had equal voting power, and the principal had no veto power; and council members received training in group dynamics and information about the composition and operation of school-site councils. Nonetheless, the investigators discovered that the councils did not alter the pattern of decision making and principal-professional control traditionally found in schools.

It is certainly possible to find exceptions to the litany of failed experiments (e.g., Comer, 1980; Levin, 1988; Swap, 1987; Williams, 1989). Williams extracts the features that he has found lead to successful parent involvement in decision making: "In conclusion, astute and adroit political maneuvering that does not threaten the power of the establishment, coupled with a climate amenable to change and a militant organizational base, will go far toward ensuring success" (p. 96). If parents have not established an independent power base, a minimal requirement seems to be that school personnel share a framework that values parent participation as advocates and decision makers, and that some skill and background in running such groups is available to the members.

Framework for involving parents as advocates and decision makers. If one believes that it is the *school's* job to set policy and educate children, then including parents as advocates or decision makers is seen as annoying at best and counter-productive at worst. Seeley (1989b) calls this orientation the "delegation model" (parents delegate the job of education to the schools), and finds that "the model has become institutionalized in the roles and relationships of all the participants, and indeed deeply embedded in the assumptions and attitudes not only of school staffs, but of parents, students, and citizens as well" (p. 5). Within this model, parents have just two roles: to provide support for the schools and "to hold officials accountable for the delivery of services through the political process" (p. 5).

If, on the other hand, one believes that reform of schools is linked to the partnership model described above, then school personnel *need* the advice, strengths, perspective, and resources that parents can provide to pursue their common vision. In fact, school personnel cannot achieve their goals without the partnership of parents, students, and community representatives. Moreover, within this framework, parents and community representatives are accountable for school success, too. Thus, parental advocacy is part of a "we" rather than an "us vs. them" orientation, and parents cannot afford to be narrowly focused as passive observers or critics.

Often it is difficult to get parents to come in for IEP conferences or to volunteer for an advisory board. Often educators are not eager to learn about parents' goals and concerns (see Kidder, 1989, for an observational study which confirms these common experiences in one school in Holyoke, Massachusetts). When these attitudes exist, they cannot be permanently changed by tinkering with conference formats or adding a few special programs led by energetic outsiders or insiders. These attitudes are common because they are a reflection of the overall context of parent and teacher expectation and communication in this country. For parental advocacy and decision making to have real influence in improving schools, a re-visioning of the purpose and meaning of home-school collaboration must occur.

School-Community Linkages

As we have seen, parent involvement in schools has an important effect on the school achievement of educationally disadvantaged children. However, Heath and McLaughlin (1987) argue that family participation as the new key to school achievement is likely to fall short because some parents will not become involved. They urge schools to see the child as a member of a broader social network of community institutions, volunteer agencies, businesses, and resources present in the larger environment. They believe that it is possible for children from non-mainstream backgrounds to acquire cultural capital by participating in "such community offerings as work experience, athletics, scouting, and any of a host of others" (p. 579). They urge us to "think of the school in a new way, as a nexus of institutions within this environment. In this view, the school moves from the role of 'deliverer' of educational services to the role of 'broker' of the multiple services that can be used to achieve the functions previously filled by families or by families and schools acting together" (p. 579).

The notion of the school as a community nexus is a very powerful one that is beginning to receive wide support. Kagan (1989) explains:

> As schools embrace a more comprehensive vision of the nature of the child and of their own role in society, the schoolhouse doors swing open ever wider. To meet the comprehensive needs of children, contacts with agencies rendering health, welfare, and social services have become routine. Special education legislation has propelled interagency collaboration to a new level, and the need to meet the before- and after-school child-

care needs of children has fostered many connections between schools and communities. Collaborations between university scholars and school personnel have also helped mend town-gown schisms. And the existence of 40,000 partnerships between businesses and schools clearly indicates that the conventional vision of schools as isolated entities is outdated. (p. 110)

Schools can be brokers in two ways: promoting closer linkages between the family and the community and also closer linkages between the school and the wider community. Jackson and Cooper (1989) and Jackson, Davies, Cooper, and Page (1988) provide many examples of family-community linkages that not only help parents to help their children, but also to help themselves, such as GED (high school diploma) classes, English-as-a-Second-Language classes, or group trips to cultural activities. Schools' outreach to the community can provide important resources for stretched budgets and reduced personnel by bringing volunteers and donated resources (such as computers) into the school or by extending the school campus out into the community, through collaborative arrangements with community agencies, work sites, and cultural institutions.

Although the scope of this paper does not permit a full discussion of this concept, a richly collaborative home-school-community model that recognizes the potential of a child's multiple connections to his environment promises to contribute a critically important dimension to the effort to realize success for all children.

SUMMARY AND CONCLUSIONS

In this paper, we have examined the need for a renewed dedication to success for all children, particularly those at risk for academic failure and economic disadvantage. The strong, positive connection between student achievement and parent involvement was highlighted, and we speculated about why that might be so. Given that parent involvement programs can be so critical to improving children's

achievement, we considered why parent involvement programs were still not widespread in inner-city schools and what the barriers to parent involvement might be. A look at the philosophies that undergird parent involvement programs revealed that the dominant approach used to enhance student achievement was school-to-home transmission of values and skills. In addition, an interactive transmission approach was identified as having particular promise when the discontinuities between home and school disrupted student learning. Finally, the home-school partnership model seemed to offer the most promise for bringing school achievement levels of low-income and minority children to those expected for middle-class students. Epstein's typology of types of parent involvement was used to outline examples of effective current practice in each area and a sixth promising area, community linkages, was briefly identified as a promising direction for expanding resources to children, families, schools, and community organizations.

Current literature clearly demonstrates that for children at risk, the participation of parents in supporting their school success is not a frill. A timely, revised framework for parent involvement sees parent partnership as a necessary component of a vigorous school-based commitment to school improvement. For the new framework to succeed, parents and school personnel must give up some of their autonomy and reciprocal frustration and work together toward mutually defined goals. Commitment from community members and students is also essential to achieving these joint goals.

Parents can play many roles in schools, from recipients of information, to audiences and volunteers, to problem solvers and decision makers. For parent involvement to be transformed into meaningful support for student achievement and continuous school improvement, parent programs need to be carefully planned, implemented, and monitored with the goal of educational excellence constantly in the forefront.

Although there are many creative and successful ideas and programs upon which to draw, there is no single recipe for effective home-school collaboration. However, when the overall goals shape the philosophy and the programs, when joint planning and mutual respect are the norms for communication, and when effective leadership continues over time, there is little doubt that this new vision can become a reality.

REFERENCES

Auerbach, E. R. (1989). Toward a social-contextual approach to family literacy. *Harvard Educational Review, 59*(2), 165–181.

Baron, B., Barn, C., & MacDonald, B. (1983). *What did you learn in school today?* New York: Warner Books.

Braun L., & Swap, S. (1987). *Building home-school partnerships with America's changing families.* Boston: Wheelock College.

Brinckerhoff, J., & Vincent, L. (1986). Increasing parental decision-making at the Individualized Educational Program meeting. *Journal of the Division for Early Childhood, 11*(1), 46–58.

Bronfenbrenner, U. (1975). Is early intervention effective? In B. Friedlander, G. Sterritt, & G. Kirk (Eds.), *Exceptional infant: Vol. 3, Assessment and intervention.* (pp. 449–475). New York: Brunner/Mazel.

Carnegie Foundation for the Advancement of Teaching. (1988). *The imperiled generation.* New York: Carnegie Foundation for the Advancement of Teaching.

Children's Defense Fund. (1989). *A vision for America's future.* Washington, DC: Children's Defense Fund.

Chrispeels, J., Boruta, M., & Daugherty, M. (1988). *Communicating with parents.* San Diego County Office of Education, 6401 Linda Vista Road, San Diego, CA 92111.

Chubb, J. (1989). Making schools better: Choice and educational improvement. *Equity and Choice, 5*(3), 5–10.

Clark, R. (1983). *Family life and school achievement: Why poor black children succeed or fail.* Chicago: University of Chicago Press.

Cochran, M. (1988). The parental empowerment process: Building on family strengths. *Equity and Choice, 4*(1), 9–23.

Cochran, M. (1989). Empowerment through family support. *Networking Bulletin, 1*(1), 2–3.

Cochran, M. et al. (undated). *Cooperative communication between home and school.* A program of workshops for parents and teachers available from The Family Matters Project at Cornell University, G19A Martha Rensselaer Hall, Ithaca, NY, 14855.

Collins, C., Moles, O., & Cross, M. (1982). *The home-school connection: Selected partnership programs in large cities.* Boston: Institute for Responsive Education.

Comer, J. (1980). *School power.* New York: Free Press.

Comer, J. (1988). *Maggie's American dream.* New York: New American Library.

Cuban, L. (1989). At-risk students: What teachers and principals can do. *Educational Leadership, 46*(5), 29–32.

Cummins, J. (1986). Empowering minority students: A framework for intervention. *Harvard Educational Review, 56*(1), 18–36.

Davies, D. et al. (1979). *Patterns of citizen participation in educational decision making (Vol. II): Grassroots perspectives: Diverse forms of participation.* Boston: Institute for Responsive Education.

Davies, D. (1988). Low-income parents and the schools: A research report and a plan for action. *Equity and Choice, 4*(3), 51–59.

Delpit, L. (1988). The silenced dialogue: Power and pedagogy in educating other people's children. *Harvard Educational Review, 58*(3), 280–298.

Edmonds, R., & Lezotte, L. (1982). *The correlates of school effectiveness.* Unpublished paper.

Epstein, J. (1987). Parent involvement: What research says to administrators. *Education and Urban Society, 19*(2), 119–136.

Epstein, J. (1988). *Teacher attitudes and practices of parent involvement in inner-city elementary and middle schools.* Paper presented at the annual meeting of the American Sociological Association. Atlanta, GA; Session 79.

Epstein, J. (undated). *Teachers involve parents in schoolwork (TIPS).* Center for Research on Elementary and Middle Schools, Johns Hopkins University, 3505 North Charles Street, Baltimore, MD 21218.

ERIC Clearinghouse on Urban Education (1986). Parent participation and the achievement of disadvantaged students. *Equity and Choice, 2*(3), 73–78.

Freedberg, L. (1989). Don't remediate, accelerate: Can disadvantaged students benefit from fast-forwarded instruction? *Equity and Choice, 5*(2), 40–43.

Gillium, R. (1977). *The effects of parent involvement on school achievement in three Michigan performance contracting programs.* Paper presented at the annual meeting of the American Educational Research Association, New York.

Goodlad, J. (1984). *A place called school.* New York: McGraw Hill.

Hauser-Cram, J. P. (1983). *A question of balance: Relationships between teachers and parents.* Doctoral dissertation: Harvard Graduate School of Education.

Hawley, W. (1989). The importance of minority teachers to the racial and ethnic integration of American society. *Equity and Choice, 5*(2), 31–36.

Heath, S. B. (1983). *Ways with words: language, life, and work in communities and classrooms.* Cambridge, England: Cambridge University Press.

Heath, S. B., & McLaughlin, M. W. (1987). A child resource policy: Moving beyond dependence on school and family. *Phi Delta Kappan, 68*(8), 576–580.

Henderson, A. (1981). *Parent participation and student achievement: The evidence grows.* Columbia, MD: National Committee for Citizens in Education.

Henderson, A. (1987). *The evidence continues to grow: Parent involvement improves student achievement.* Columbia, MD: National Committee for Citizens in Education.

Henderson, A., Marburger, C., & Ooms, T. (1986). *Beyond the bake sale: An educator's guide to working with parents.* Columbia, MD: National Committee for Citizens in Education.

Hobbs, N. (1984). *Strengthening families.* San Francisco: Jossey-Bass.

Irujo, S. (1989). Do you know why they all talk at once? Thoughts on cultural differences between Hispanics and Anglos. *Equity and Choice, 5*(3), 14–18.

Jackson, B., & Cooper, B. (1989). Parent choice and empowerment: New roles for parents. *Urban Education, 24*(3), 263–286.

Jackson, B., Davies, D., Cooper, B., & Page, J. (1988). *Parents make a difference: An evaluation of the New York City Schools' 1987–88 parent involvement program.* Report to the New York City Public Schools.

Joyce, B., Hersh, R., & McKibbin, M. (1983). *The structure of school improvement.* New York: Longman.

Kagan, S. (1989). Early care and education: Beyond the schoolhouse doors. *Phi Delta Kappan, 71*(2), 107–112.

Kegan, R. (1982). *The evolving self: Problem and process in human development.* Cambridge, MA: Harvard University Press.

Kidder, T. (1989). *Among school children.* Boston: Houghton Mifflin.

Levin, H. (1987). Accelerated schools for disadvantaged students. *Educational Leadership, 44*(6), 19–21.

Levin, H. (1988a). Accelerating elementary education for disadvantaged students. In Council of Chief State Officers, *School success for students at risk* (pp. 209–226). San Diego, CA: Harcourt Brace Jovanovich.

Levin, H. (1988b, November). Don't remediate: Accelerate. In *Conference Papers* prepared for the Stanford University Centennial Conference.

Lightfoot, S. L. (1978). *Worlds apart: Relationships between families and schools.* New York: Basic Books.

Locust, C. (1988). Wounding the spirit: Discrimination and traditional American Indian belief systems. *Harvard Educational Review, 58*(3), 315–330.

MacLeod, J. (1987). *Ain't no makin' it: Leveled aspirations in a low-income neighborhood.* Boulder: Westview Press.

Malen, B., & Ogawa, R. (1988). Professional-patron influence on site-based governance councils: A confounding case study. *Educational Evaluation and Policy Analysis, 10*(4), 251–270.

McCarty J., & Carrera, J. (1988). *New voices: Immigrant students in the U.S. public schools.* Boston: National Coalition of Advocates for Students.

Mehran, M., & White, K. (1988). Parent tutoring as a supplement to compensatory education for first-grade children. *Remedial and Special Education. 9*(3), 35–41.

Moses, R., Kamii, M., Swap, S., & Howard, J. (1989). The Algebra Project: Organizing in the spirit of Ella. *Harvard Educational Review, 59*(4), 423–443.

National School Volunteer Program. (1979). *Handbook for Teachers—Effective involvement of school volunteers.* Alexandria, VA: The author.

Office of Community Education. (1989a). *Focus on parents: successful strategies for parent involvement.* Quincy, MA: Massachusetts Department of Education.

Office of Community Education. (1989b). *Focus on parents: successful strategies for involving hard-to-reach parents.* Quincy, MA: Massachusetts Department of Education.

Okakok, L. (1989). Serving the purpose of education. *Harvard Educational Review, 59*(4), 405–422.

Plata M., & Chinn, P. (1989). Students with handicaps who have cultural and language differences. In R. Gaylord Ross (Ed.), *Integration strategies for students with handicaps.* (pp. 149–174). Baltimore, MD: Brooke.

Rich, D. (1988). *MegaSkills.* Boston: Houghton Mifflin.

Rich, D., Mattox, B., & Van Dien, J. (1979). Building on family strengths: The "nondeficit" model for teaming home and school. *Educational Leadership, 40,* 506–510.

Schorr, L. (1988). *Within our reach: Breaking the cycle of disadvantage.* New York: Anchor Press/ Doubleday.

Seeley, D. (1986). Partnership's time has come. *Educational Leadership, 9,* 82–85.

Seeley, D. (1988). A new vision for public education. *Youth Policy, 2,* 34–36.

Seeley, D. (1989a). A new paradigm for parent involvement. *Educational Leadership, 47*(2), 46–48.

Seeley, D. (1989b). *A new paradigm for parent involvement: Moving parent participation to the next level.* Unpublished manuscript.

Slavin, R., & Madden, N. (1989). What works for students at risk: A research synthesis. *Educational Leadership, 46*(5), 4–13.

South Carolina State Department of Education. (1985). *Setting up the school volunteer program.* Columbia, SC. (ERIC Document Reproduction Service No. ED232 887)

Swap, S. (1987). *Enhancing parent involvement in schools.* New York: Teachers College Press.

Tizard, J., Schofield, W., & Hewison, J. (1982). Collaboration between teachers and parents in assisting children's reading. *British Journal of Educational Psychology, 52*(1), 1–11.

Walberg, H., Bole, R., & Waxman, H. (1980). School-based family socialization and reading achievement in the inner-city. *Psychology in the Schools, 17,* 509–514.

Williams, D., & Stallworth, J. (1983–84). *Parent involvement in education project,* Executive Summary of the Final Report. Austin, TX: Southwest Educational Development Laboratory.

Williams, M. (1989). *Neighborhood organizing for urban school reform.* New York: Teachers College Press.

4

PARTNERS OR ADVERSARIES? HOME-SCHOOL COLLABORATION ACROSS CULTURE, RACE, AND ETHNICITY

Larke Nahme Huang and
Jewelle Taylor Gibbs

The changing demographic tapestry in the United States will have significant impact on all arenas of American society. Demographers predict that non-White and Spanish-speaking youth under age 18 will constitute 30% of the nation's youth population in the year 2000 and 38% by 2020 (U.S. Bureau of the Census, 1987). The White majority, which currently accounts for nearly 80% of the total population in the U.S., will drop to 70% in 2020, and 60% in 2050, totalling 162 million as compared to 198 million in 1980. Currently, one in every five Americans is from one of the four ethnic minority groups (Suinn, 1987); in 60 years, it is predicted that more than one in three Americans will be non-White. By 2050, the African American population will expand slightly to about 16% of the total. Hispanics and Asians will be the most rapidly growing populations with the former increasing from 6.4% to 15% and the latter increasing from 1.6% to as much as 10% of the population (Bouvier & Agresta, 1987). These population changes and projected trends arise primarily from (a) increased immigration from Latin America, Asia, and the Caribbean, (b) higher birthrates of these immigrant and resident minority groups, (c) increased longevity of the minority population, and (d) lower birthrates of the resident White population.

These population trends have created a "demographic imperative" for social institutions that serve youth. Schools, in particular, will be dramatically affected by these changes. There are currently more than 44 million students in the nation's public schools and 40% of these are minorities (Vobejda, 1987). Hodgkinson (1986) projects that in the Class of 2001, minority enrollment levels will range from 70% to 96% in the nation's 15 largest school systems. Already in 1988, over 50% of the public school population in California was non-White.

The Task Panel on Infants, Children, and Adolescents of the President's Commission on Mental Health (1978a) estimated that 15% of the children aged 3 to 15 have mental problems that impair their functioning. Other recent epidemiological studies have concluded that 12% of the population under age 18, or 7.5 million children in the U.S., need professional mental health services (Gould, Wunsch-Hitzig, & Dohrenwend, 1981; Links, 1983). A disproportionate number of low-income families, more often African American and Hispanic, have had difficulties benefitting from school because of adjustment problems and are overrepresented among children with psychological problems (Comer, 1985; Rickel & Allen, 1987). Hodgkinson (1986) suggests that the Class of 2001 represents unique challenges with its high proportion of students "at-risk" for school failure, ascribing this to the following combination of factors: increasing minority enrollment levels in the larger and poorer urban school systems, one of four children living below the poverty level, 15% physically or mentally handicapped, 14% children of teenage mothers, 14% children of unmarried parents, 10% children of poorly educated, sometimes illiterate parents, and 40% coming from broken homes by the time they are 18 years old. In 1978, the President's Commission on Mental Health (1978b) noted that low-income minority children and adolescents were especially at risk for psychological disorders and behavioral problems due to their low socioeconomic status, their often stressful environments, and their lack of access to mental health services. A decade later, this situation has not measurably improved and children of color are still triply disadvantaged by their ethnicity, their poverty, and their social isolation (Children's Defense Fund, 1987).

Given these shifts in population and the projected risks for psychological and behavioral problems, what are the implications for the nation's school systems? And, more specifically, what are the implications for developing home-school collaboration? Schools are often the first point of recognition of adjustment problems. As they handle increasingly more youth from diverse ethnic, cultural, and racial backgrounds, it is essential that schools become familiar with the various sociocultural backgrounds of these students and their families. Research has demonstrated that children whose family backgrounds and primary social networks are consistent with the expectations and styles of the schools they attend perform better scholastically (Comer, 1984; National Coalition of Advocates for Students, 1988). Home-school continuity is associated with a greater advantage for these youth. The U.S. public schools are usually based on White, middle-class values and norms, thus ethnic and racial minority students often enter school at a distinct disadvantage. Before they can even begin

to achieve academically, they must make sense of relatively unfamiliar styles of communication, behavior, and expectations in the school environment.

Given these circumstances, home-school collaboration is a particularly challenging concept. Potentially, this interaction may facilitate the exchange of knowledge across cultures, races, and ethnicities and bridge the gap between home and school cultures. The resulting parental involvement may help to ensure a culturally sensitive and appropriate school program, academically and socially. Research has documented multiple benefits of active parent involvement (see Christenson, Rounds, and Franklin, this volume), including higher student achievement, improved behavior, increased attendance, more positive student attitudes toward school, and better homework habits (Comer, 1984; Hess & Holloway, 1984; Hoover-Dempsey, Bassler, & Brissie, 1987). On the other hand, home-school interaction across different ethnic and racial groups is vulnerable to misunderstanding and miscommunication. In order to facilitate home-school collaboration, one must be cognizant of the cultural differences and similarities among the various minority populations. Cultural and family attitudes toward school, the history and experiences of cultural minorities with mainstream institutions, and perceptions of economic opportunities and social mobility have implications for the success or failure of the home-school connection and the development of a working partnership or an adversarial stalemate.

The objective of this chapter is to provide a conceptual framework and sociocultural information pertinent to the development of home-school collaboration across cultures. This chapter will focus on four ethnic and racial minorities in the U.S.: Asian Americans, American Indians, African Americans, and Hispanic Americans. Sociocultural values and relevant historical and migration experiences of each group are presented with an attempt to highlight how these facilitate or hinder effective home-school interaction. An ecological model for home-school collaboration across culture, race, and ethnicity is presented in conjunction with the need to develop multicultural competence at all levels of the educational system and particularly in home-school collaboration.

A CONCEPTUAL FRAMEWORK

An ecological, multicultural perspective provides the underlying framework for this chapter. The ecological perspective, as proposed by Bronfenbrenner (1979), views the developing youth as an active agent in a series of interlocking concentric systems: *Microsystems* are those systems that have direct contact with and immediate daily effects on the child (for example, family, peers, school); *mesosystems* consist of the relationships between and among the microsystems (for example, the interaction between family and school and the effect of this interaction on the child); *exosystems* are settings which do not have direct contact with the child but in which decisions are made that directly influence the child (for example, school boards, PTAs, parents' employers); and the *macrosystem,* which represents the values and mores of the society or the "consistencies" or "blueprints" (Bronfenbrenner, 1979, p. 26) underlying the various systems. Each of these systems presents risks and opportunities for youth and development is viewed as a function of the reciprocal interaction of the individual with these systems.

The ecological perspective is particularly relevant in examining the impact of poverty, discrimination, immigration, and social isolation on the psychosocial development and adjustment of minority youth. Poverty has a negative impact on nearly all aspects of children's lives, including nutrition, health care, housing, education, and recreation (American Public Welfare Association, 1986; Rodgers, 1986; Schorr, 1986). For children who are both poor and members of ethnic minorities, there is a significant increase in the negative and long-term impact of poverty (Committee for Economic Development, 1987; Edelman, 1987; Wilson & Aponte,

1985). Newcomer status and language problems are additional sources of stress for children of immigrants and refugees, who must cope not only with the adjustment to a strange new culture but also with the loss of their native land and indigenous culture (Huang, 1989; Nidorf, 1985; Sluzki, 1979; Williams & Westermeyer, 1983).

The macrosystem of minority youth is shaped by historical, economic, and political realities. For example, the more recent Asian and Hispanic immigrants are often compared to European immigrants of the late 19th and 20th centuries; however, these contemporary non-White immigrants and their children encounter a very different set of attitudes and experiences from the dominant society than the earlier waves of primarily White immigrants. Second, structural changes in the economy, movement from a manufacturing to a service economy, and associated technological advances in the work force have resulted in high unemployment among minority adults, many of whom lack the education or skills to compete (Wilson & Aponte, 1985). Third, since the demise of the War on Poverty, political attitudes have become more conservative, resulting in a nationwide backlash against affirmative action programs in employment and higher education. In combination, these trends have hit low-income minority families particularly hard, acting as chronic stressors that diminish their ability to provide a stable and nurturant environment for their children (Edelman, 1987). In spite of these ecological stressors, many of these families have shown remarkable resilience and competence in handling the tasks of socializing their children in an often hostile and alien environment (Gibbs & Huang, 1989).

The ecological perspective provides a multidimensional view of a child as it assesses psychosocial functioning in the family, the school, the peer group, and the community. The impact of these systems on minority youth is critical in the socialization of children. For example, for families who have recently immigrated, children and adolescents are often in conflict between two competing sets of values and norms, which require them to develop one set of behaviors in the family setting and another set in school and community settings. Often these behaviors are diametrically opposed, leading to intergenerational and intercultural stress.

The multicultural perspective underscores the value of cultural diversity and strives toward a balance of universalism and pluralism. Diversity has been a difficult concept to accept, and in most fields, including psychology and education, attempts were made to fit people of different races and cultures into previously existing schemata. In the past, this homogenization of races and cultures has been a predominant American ethic (de-Anda, 1984; Green, 1982). Now, however, with the evolving demographics in the U.S., the predominant Western European traditions of this society are being challenged by new belief systems and cultures emanating from different parts of the world. Ethnicity is a key concept in this perspective. The term is used here to mean membership in a group of people "who share a unique social and cultural heritage that is passed on from generation to generation" (Mindel & Habenstein, 1981, p. 5) and who believe themselves to be "distinctive from others in some significant way" (Green, 1982, p. 9). Although race and ethnicity are not identical, they often overlap, as with Chinese Americans or African Americans. In contrast, Hispanics are defined by their common cultural heritage (Latin American) and their language (Spanish); however, they may be White, Black, or Indian, or a mixture of the three.

Ethnicity provides a cultural identity and a set of prescribed values, norms, and social behaviors for an individual or family. It also provides a significant framework through which the growing child views the self, the world, and future opportunities, while giving meaning to the child's subjective experiences, structure to interpersonal relationships, and form to behaviors and activities. For example, ethnicity may determine what kind of family a child grows up in, what language she will speak in the home,

what kind of neighborhood she lives in, what church she attends (if any), what school she attends, and what role models are available (Gibbs & Huang, 1989).

Ethnic identity, when combined with membership in a minority race, creates a dual challenge for an individual. In the U.S., where the dominant majority is Caucasian, there are many White ethnic groups, such as the Jews, the Poles, the Irish, and the Italians (Mindel & Habenstein, 1981). Members of these groups are able to practice their cultural customs in their homes and their places of worship, while blending into the mainstream social institutions, such as schools, businesses, government, and professional organizations. However, ethnic minority groups of color are readily identified by physical or linguistic differences. Minority groups are "those groups that have unequal access to power, that are considered in some way unworthy of sharing power equally, and that are stigmatized in terms of assumed inferior traits or characteristics" (Mindel & Habenstein, 1981, p. 8). Historically, minority status has been associated with a more restricted range of options in education and employment, as well as reduced opportunities for mobility and success in the wider society (Omi & Winant, 1986). Consequently, children of minority families are not only exposed to different family dynamics, school experiences, and community responses than children from White families, but they are also confronted with social and economic barriers that profoundly influence their opportunities (Gibbs & Huang, 1989).

Social class, another dimension that defines the child's world by ascribing a particular position and value to his family's socioeconomic status (SES), will largely determine the child's social environment, level of education, occupational aspirations, and lifestyle. For children and adolescents, social class may influence selection of friends, activities, and social roles. Membership in a social class often delineates the boundaries within which the growing individual will experience a restricted range of opportunities, choices, and challenges in particular social contexts.

In contemporary American society, there is an important interrelationship between ethnicity, race, and social class. Generally, high status is associated with membership in White, Anglo-Saxon, middle-class families, whereas low status is associated with membership in non-White, ethnic minority, lower-class families. Accordingly, youth in many Asian, Black, Hispanic, and Indian families are triply stigmatized in American society because they differ from the ideal norm in three major respects: They are non-White by race (except for Spanish-speaking Whites), non-Anglo-Saxon by ethnicity, and predominantly non-middle-class by socioeconomic status.

Ethnicity is, thus, an overarching dimension that provides the child with a framework for perceiving and behaving in the world. It shapes the child's personal and social identity; establishes values, norms, and expectations for appropriate behaviors; and defines parameters for choices and opportunities for the child's social, educational, and occupational experiences. Ethnicity influences the child's socialization in the family and provides the structures through which developmental tasks are mediated. In addition, it has a significant impact on the way the child is perceived and treated in the school, by peers, and in the broader community.

Ethnicity influences family processes and child-rearing practices. Parents from different ethnic groups may use different criteria to measure independence, competence, and interpersonal skills, and they may differentially value these behaviors as relevant or irrelevant to the child's successful adaptation to the social environment. Child-rearing practices reflect wide diversity in the techniques used to socialize youth according to the belief system, values, and norms of their ethnic group. Similarly, ethnicity influences the family's attitudes toward education and scholarly achievement and, in combination with historical experiences, shapes the style of interaction with educational institutions and their representatives.

The importance of ethnicity and cultural democracy in educational philosophy and policy is only recently coming to the forefront, displacing previous philosophies based on a melting pot or deficit model of cultural difference. This concept implies that an individual has a right to maintain a bicultural identity—to retain identification with the ethnic group while simultaneously learning to adopt mainstream American values and lifestyles (Rodriquez, 1983). Educational leaders are challenging the implicit mission of American schools to promote and transmit the culture and values that coincide with that of the majority culture. Rather they promote the right of American children to remain identified with their home and community ethnicity and suggest that the schools should actively contribute to the positive development and strengthening of these unique socialization experiences as valuable in their own right (Ramirez & Castaneda, 1974). A current example of this movement is the adaptation of new history textbooks for the California public school system, which give greater attention to the historical experiences, roles, and contributions of America's ethnic minorities.

SOCIOCULTURAL VALUES

In this section, important sociocultural information about Asian Americans, American Indians, African Americans, and Hispanics will be presented. This is a task "easier said than done." Within each minority group there is rich diversity and much heterogeneity. Simple generalizations and static descriptions about each group do a disservice to the complexities of their respective cultures and ways of life. Level of acculturation and social class are further complicating factors. Attitudes, behaviors, and values of individual members are strongly influenced by their degree of acculturation, their socioeconomic status, and their ties with ethnic institutions and communities. Oftentimes, highly acculturated ethnic minorities may share more in common with White mainstream groups than with each other. For example, first- and third-generation Japanese Americans may be less alike than middle-class Japanese Americans and White Americans. Two different minority group members in the same socioeconomic class may have more shared values than two similar minorities in different social classes. Thus, a third-generation Hispanic family may have more in common with a White or Black middle-class family than with an His-panic immigrant. Or, a Black upper-middle-class suburban family may share little in common with a Black urban-ghetto family. Thus, although the follow-ing discussion on traditional sociocul-tural values will be organized by race and ethnicity, it is important to keep in mind the limitations of this approach. Although it is expedient, it has the potential to obscure the wide diversity and finer distinctions within each group.

The Asian Americans

Demographic data. Asian Americans, the second fastest growing minority group in the U.S., currently number nearly 4 million and comprise over 30 distinct ethnic and cultural groups (U.S. Bureau of the Census, 1988; Wong, 1982). This is a young population with more than a third being school-age youth under 17 years of age (Powell, 1983). Growth for these various groups has been quite variable. For example, the overall rate of growth for Japanese Americans is nomi-nal due to a low fertility rate, minimal immigration, and high rates of outmar-riage. In contrast, the Southeast Asian American population is rapidly expand-ing over a short and concentrated period of time. The largest Asian American groups, except for Japanese Americans, are composed mainly of immigrants: 60% of Chinese Americans, 70% of Filipino Americans, and 98% of Southeast Asian Americans are immigrants (Wong, 1982). In general, this suggests a population where for many the migration process is still a fresh experience and integration of the "old" with the "new" is still ongoing.

Culture and family values. Asian American families show much diversity and variation. Regional differences, even within countries, the time of migration to the U.S., subsequent acculturation expe-riences, and socioeconomic status all contribute to this diversity. Asian Ameri-cans come from countries with different ideologies and cultures, often with a history of political antagonism, and their reasons for and patterns of immigration are numerous. They enter the United States with a wide range of educational and occupational backgrounds. The com-munities they establish in the U.S. are traditionally disparate and self-contained, representing unique blends of their coun-try of origin and the new, host society.

Although the differences in these groups abound, there are some shared values and experiences. For most Asian groups, a critical value is the primacy of the family system, particularly the ex-tended family. Traditionally, the nature and structure of many Asian family systems derived from Confucian philoso-phy, which dictated a sense of order and a prescription for role relationships within society. Guidelines for family relation-ships, patterns of communication, and negotiations with the outside world were delineated with the goal of harmonious existence in society and survival of the group as primary (Lin, 1938). Although it is impossible to predict the degree to which family structure and values brought to the United States by Asian immigrants have been retained, neverthe-less, it is quite likely that the traditional values have, albeit indirectly, shaped important characteristics of present-day Asian American families. Therefore, a brief overview may be useful.

The family is the basic reference group for the individual, exerting control over its members through a well-defined structure of hierarchical roles and a clear code of interpersonal conduct. Filial piety is of paramount importance and the individual's behavior is a direct reflection on the family (Ishisaka & Takagi, 1982). Obligations, responsibilities, and privi-leges of each family role are clearly delineated according to a hierarchal role structure with the father as the undis-puted head. Although some of these role arrangements have been disrupted with immigration and accommodation to a new country, derivatives of these rigidly defined roles remain. For example, fathers are often the figurative heads of families, especially when dealing with the public, whereas the mother may actually be the driving force in the family and the decision maker behind the scene.

In a comparison of the family structure in Japan and the United States, Yamamoto and Kubota (1983) describe the former as emphasizing the priority of the family group over the individual, vertical relationships, conformity to societal norms, and social control based on shame, guilt, and an appeal to duty and responsibility. Mainstream American families, in contrast, emphasize individualism, equalitarian relationships, independent behavior in society, and social control based on love and punishment. Japanese and other Asian families emphasize prolonged dependence, encouragement of obedience and conformity in children, and an emphasis on indirect, nonconfrontational techniques of parenting that rely on nonverbal communication (Kitano & Kikumura, 1976).

Congruent with a rigid system of role relationships in Asian families, patterns of communication are governed by the attributes of the parties involved. Gender and age determine the degree of open expression allowed, the initiator of conversation, the structure of the language used, and the topics to be addressed. Communication is often indirect, and outright confrontation is avoided. The rules for communication diverge sharply from American values of expression and the tendency to "speak your mind" or "let it all hang out" (Shon & Ja, 1982).

Expression of emotion is generally avoided and suppression of undesirable thoughts or emotions, such as anger or hostility, is highly valued. Internalizing rather than externalizing emotions, modesty, and withholding one's wishes or preferences is important. This is often demonstrated in the family's reluctance to praise achievements, a hesitancy to speak out, or a reluctance to ask questions (Nagata, 1989). For Vietnamese, harmony in interpersonal relationships is attained through tact, delicacy, and politeness, even at the cost of honesty and forthrightness (Le, 1983). The ideal child in many Asian families is expected to be reticent with adults and respectful and submissive toward those in authority and in superior statuses, including siblings (Bulatao, 1962 cited in Green, 1982).

Avoidance of shame and loss of face are guiding principles of behavior and powerful motivating forces for conforming to societal and familial expectations. Given that interdependence is the foundation of much of Asian family culture, everything an individual does is viewed as a reflection on the family as a whole. Therefore, bringing shame upon one's family is avoided at all costs.

Immigration and acculturation. Another shared dimension in Asian American families is the experience of acculturation and immigration. Level of acculturation is an extremely important concept in understanding Asian American families. A recent immigrant family may be very unfamiliar with American customs and values and may possess a distinctly Asian worldview. Asian values, traditions, and behavior may be the standards for this family. For a family that is third generation and very Westernized, however, ethnic differences may be minimal. English may be spoken in the home and values, attitudes, and behavior may be very Americanized. Excessive attention to cultural explanations may be inappropriate for this family. Somewhere in the middle range is the bicultural family that incorporates both Asian and American values and behaviors. For some, biculturalism may engender stress when the values come into conflict, whereas others may competently negotiate between the two cultures, mastering both and skillfully employing situation-appropriate behaviors (Huang, 1989).

In addition to the typical "generation gap" within families, Asian American families may experience "acculturation gaps" due to individual differences in rate of adaptation to a new environment. In recent immigrant families and even some second-generation families, parents and elders are more reluctant to accept the values and behaviors of the American society than their children, who readily become "Americanized" in dress and behavior and, subsequently, in values and attitudes. These varying rates of acculturation are often a source of family tension and disharmony. The traditional hierarchy of roles within the family is often in disarray as children and adolescents more readily acculturate to the host country and become emissaries for the parents with the outside world (Huang, 1989). In addition, wives are often forced to work for economic reasons. These age-role and sex-role reversals upset the prescribed distribution of power within the family, sometimes resulting in chronic stress and conflict and a breakdown of the family system.

The family's developmental stage at the time of immigration and resettlement and the climate of reception in the new host country may influence the process of acculturation and socialization to American society. In general, younger family members adjust more rapidly to the new society as they often have more facility in acquiring the new language. The reasons for migration from the country of origin, socioeconomic status in that country, process of actual migration, and degree of intactness of the family influence the ease of the family's transition and adjustment. Although many families migrate with the complete family, many others have individual members sponsored by relatives in the U.S. and consequently undergo long periods of separation from each other. Some children migrate with older siblings, leaving the parents behind. Readjustment to extended family life or to parents or family members who are recent immigrants and unacculturated may be a source of disharmony in the newly reunited family. For the Southeast Asian refugees, many families were separated during the process of escape and migration, and over half of all Cambodian refugee families experienced the death of a family member.

Immigration history may not seem as pertinent to Asian American youth or families born in the U.S.; however, it is important to understand the sacrifices made by previous generations in order to come to America. Many Asians immigrate to America for the futures of their children; thus, this becomes a powerful dynamic in the family and the sense of burden and responsibility placed on the children to justify parents' sacrifices plays an important role in child and family development.

Asian Americans in the public schools. In most Asian cultures, the scholar is held in highest esteem and the value of education is paramount. Although there is some variation across social class, in general, most Asian families strive for academic excellence in their children. To a certain extent, this value has been transported to the U.S. where Asian Americans perceive and have experienced restrictions in upward mobility in jobs and settings that are unrelated to education (Sue & Okazaki, 1990). Immigrants often expect that success for the child, and subsequently the family, will be achieved through education. Thus, there is strong pressure to attain a good education. Interestingly, this pressure and the intensity of this value seems to dissipate through the generations. Recent studies have indicated that more recent generations or less acculturated Asian American students do better on academic measures than their more acculturated peers (Dornbusch, Prescott, & Ritter, 1987).

The stereotype of the Asian American student as bright, conscientious, and quiet is extremely pervasive and tends to be perpetuated by periodic media stories heralding Asian American superachievers in education. Although stereotypes may contain seeds of reality, they are nevertheless unidimensional, harmful, and limiting to individual growth and reality. Many teachers have expectations of their students based on these stereotypes, thus obscuring the vast range of individual differences, abilities, and motivation. The majority of these youth are not "whiz kids" or "superachievers."

With the recent influx of immigrants and refugees, many Asian American students are entering school with limited English skills. Teachers in port-of-entry areas are becoming frustrated, over-whelmed, and annoyed with the difficul-ties in, and the lack of support services for, dealing with these students. In this era of cutbacks and limited resources, many teachers have tired of teaching "foreigners." Other teachers minimize cultural differences and expect Asian American students to mirror White, ma-jority students. They expect assertive, active participants in class, unaware that this expectation may contrast with the child's home environment, where quiet, obedient behavior is expected. The Asian American student in this situation must carefully negotiate between the conflict-ing expectations of the two settings (Huang & Ying, 1989).

The American Indians

Demographic data. The American Indian population, approximately 1.5 to 1.8 million, has doubled since the 1970 census and is currently characterized as mobile, urban, and young (U.S. Bureau of the Census, 1983). About 400,000 Indian people are under age 15, with the median age for American Indians being 20 years and for Alaska Natives, 18 years, both significantly lower than the national average of 30 years (U.S. Congress, Office of Technology Assessment, 1986). Cur-rently, there are more than 400 Indian tribes in the United States and about 200 reservations (Miller, 1982). Each tribe maintains unique customs, traditions, and social organizations; currently, there are 200 distinct tribal languages (Leap, 1981).

The survival of Indian tribal cultures and identity despite forced dispossession of their traditional homelands, govern-ment sponsored uprooting and relocation, and attempts to assimilate them into the dominant culture, thereby extinguishing tribal identity, attests to the strength and flexibility of this population. Rural pov-erty and federal reductions in tribal budgets have forced reservation Indians into urban areas for employment, scatter-ing families and diluting native traditions (LaFromboise & Low, 1989). According to the U.S. Bureau of the Census (1983),

24% of American Indians resided on reservations, 8% in the historically Indian areas of Oklahoma, 3% in Alaska Native villages, 2% on tribal trust lands, and 63% elsewhere in the U.S. Socioeconomically, the American Indian population is poor, with a median family income of $13,678 (U.S. Congress, Office of Technology As-sessment, 1986) compared to $17,604 for African American families, and $30,809 for White families (U.S. Bureau of the Census, 1989). For families on reserva-tions, median income is $9,942 and, for the 23% of Indian households headed by women, $9,320, both figures falling sig-nificantly below the U.S. poverty guide-lines.

Cultural and family values. The American Indian population is so com-plex and diverse that generalizations about cultural traits give rise to countless exceptions. Some Indians are highly tra-ditional, live in isolated rural areas on reservations, and speak little English; others have been raised in urban areas and have little contact with their Indian heritage. Although some have established a bicultural existence integrating values of the dominant society with values from their Indian background, others experi-ence continual conflict in the attempt to balance Indian and mainstream values and behaviors. American Indian family patterns are difficult to describe because the roles of specific family members and the structure of extended families vary across tribes and even among families within tribes. However, some obvious contrasts emerge when Indian families are compared with White, mainstream families.

Traditionally, Indian people live in a system of collective interdependence where family members are responsible not only to one another but also to the clan and tribe to which they belong. These relational networks serve to sup-port and nurture strong bonds of mutual assistance and affection (LaFromboise & Low, 1989). The individual's well-being remains the responsibility of the ex-tended family and when individual prob-lems arise, they become the problems of the community as well.

Relationships between family members and the community can be complex and often vary by tribe. Usually, in patriarchal tribes, the role of the male is to make important decisions and the female functions as the central "core" of the family, maintaining primary responsibility for the welfare of the children. In some tribes, however, child care is shared by the men. For example, Mescalero Apache men share responsibility for the children when not working away from the family (Ryan, 1980). Elders, such as aunts, uncles, and grandparents are important teachers and role models reinforcing tribal traditions. They are the safekeepers of tribal stories and songs and often spend time with children sharing their "oral tradition" (LaFromboise & Low, 1989).

Traditionally, tribal spirituality and tribal life are inseparable (Hungry Wolf & Hungry Wolf, 1987). Early in life, children are introduced to the spiritual life of the tribe which fosters a loving respect for nature as well as independence and self-discipline.

Indian worldviews regard children as beloved gifts (Hill Witt, 1979). This is manifest in child-rearing practices in which childhood is often marked by a variety of celebrations honoring an infant's developmental milestones, such as the first smile, first laugh, first steps, or first attempts at using language. American Indian families celebrate these developments but feel little pressure over the timing of such events. Their beliefs are based on acceptance of a child's own readiness and restraint from pressuring a child to perform (Dell, 1980; Everett, Proctor, & Cartmell, 1983). Indian children are rarely physically punished in their families (LaFromboise & Low, 1989).

Although communication patterns in Indian families vary from tribe to tribe, generally, these patterns might be characterized as hierarchal and diffuse. For example, information about a youth's misbehavior might be passed from the mother to extended family members or a relative designated as responsible for guiding the youth's character development. Restitution for the wrongdoing on the part of the youth may involve an apology to each of the family members who has been concerned or embarrassed by the youth's behavior. This indirect communication serves to protect the bonds between parents and youth and maintains the involvement of the extended family in preserving standards of behavior. Similarly, when a family member is worthy of praise for a significant accomplishment, this might be passed to an individual in the community who will inform other members of the community. This "camp crier" conveys good news about members of the community while maintaining each family's humility (LaFromboise & Low, 1989).

Autonomy is highly valued among American Indians, thus children are expected to make their own decisions and operate semi-independently at an early age. Family members allow children choices and the freedom to experience the natural consequences of those choices, while also emphasizing the impact of a child's behavior on others (LaFromboise & Low, 1989). This approach to child rearing has often been labeled as permissive or negligent by social service providers as it appears to them that Indian parents exercise minimal observable control over their children (Gray & Cosgrove, 1985).

In recent years, increased movement to urban areas has disrupted traditional Indian extended family functioning. Indians who have relocated to cities from reservations and other traditional Indian areas have often felt isolated from their families and Indian social support networks. In response to this sense of alienation, many Indian people in urban areas seek support from other Indians, neighbors, and nonfamily members and eventually reconstitute their extended family network. Those without the support of extended family life often experience greater stress in daily living than their more traditional relatives (LaFromboise & Low, 1989).

Indian youth from extended family networks in either reservations or urban areas encounter unique problems. Family responsibilities and expectations may be problematic for all youth; however, because tribal spirituality remains paramount among Indian people, families encourage and expect their children and adolescents to participate in various ceremonies. Unfortunately, their participation in these ceremonies sometimes violates attendance policies of White-operated mainstream schools and work sites, thus leading to negative consequences for Indian youth who opt to attend these ceremonies. Frequently these ceremonies are long distances from their school or work sites.

American Indians in the public schools. As with other ethnic minorities, when American Indian youth first enter school, they are confronted with the clash of cultures. Many of them feel stranded between two cultures as they speak an entirely different first language, practice an entirely different religion, and hold different cultural values and attitudes than the dominant culture. Yet, they are expected to perform successfully according to conventional, mainstream educational criteria.

This dilemma was highlighted in a study of nonverbal differences in communication styles of American Indian and Anglo elementary classrooms (Greenbaum, 1985). The study quantified differences in nonverbal behaviors of students in reservation and public school classrooms and found significant differences between the Choctaw Indian students and the Anglo students. Specifically, there was reduced duration and frequency of individual speaking by the Choctaw students, increased choral responding, and higher rates of peer-directed listener gaze during times when the teacher was speaking. These behaviors are characteristic of the Indian affinity for group rather than individually oriented behavior. Thus, although this is culturally appropriate behavior, it may be functionally disadvantageous in the classroom and may obstruct learning. For example, the greater peer-directed gaze while the teacher is speaking may negatively influence the teacher's judgment concerning the students' attention.

In addition to cultural clashes in the classroom, Indian students are confronted with their parents' often hopeless attitudes resulting from overwhelming impoverishment and discrimination, and are continually reminded of economic, experiential, and social discrepancies that exist between Indians and mainstream society. Frequent relocation, substandard living conditions, family unemployment, and overwhelming poverty also combine to make school adjustment particularly difficult for Indian youth. Academic functioning may be severely impaired and lags in performance of 1 to 2 years in elementary school and 2 to 4 years in secondary school are not uncommon (LaFromboise & Low, 1989). Indians 25 years of age or older average only 10 years of schooling, compared with a national average of 12 years (Development Associates, 1983). Academic performance is also hindered by developmental disabilities, neurosensory disorders, and other handicapping conditions that go undiagnosed and untreated, such as otitis media, or middle-ear disease, which occurs in over half of Indian children. Of American Indian adults, approximately one-third are illiterate, and only one male in five has a high school education (Brod & McQuiston, 1983). In urban high schools, dropout rates range as high as 85%; in reservation schools and boarding schools, which together educate about 80% of Indian youth, about 50% drop out (Coladarci, 1983; Giles, 1985). These trends result in a dearth of college-bound students as evidenced by the U.S. Bureau of the Census (1984) report that only 8% of American Indians are college educated.

The high premium placed on individual achievement and success in academic institutions frequently leads to conflict for Indian students and their families (LaFromboise & Low, 1989). For example, Indian students receiving scholarships from universities may feel they should share their financial awards with family members. Or, some students discover that the academic success for which they receive praise on campus may yield further estrangement from their own people. Still others encounter community members who actively discourage ambitions that involve leaving the reservation or the family (Lefley, 1975). Some Indian elders place little investment in schooling as they view it as taking their children away from tradition and into a destructive and alien world (Berlin, 1987).

A study of perceived problems of American Indian high school students found that they experienced depression, apathy, concerns about the future and decisions that needed to be made, difficulty finding ways of maintaining good grades, class scheduling problems, and questions of whether to stay in school (Dauphinais, LaFromboise, & Rowe, 1980). Students directly and indirectly experienced culture clashes in the classroom. For example, the Anglo values of individualism, competitiveness, and social status, so predominant in the classroom, are in direct conflict with Indian values of reciprocity, kindness, interdependence, and self-control over cultivation of social skills (Plas & Bellet, 1983; Trimble, 1981). Indian students handle these problems by talking with friends and parents rather than with school counselors or other support personnel.

The African Americans

Demographic data. African American youth are one of the most vulnerable and victimized groups in contemporary American society. Until very recently, they have been perpetually mislabeled and miseducated by the schools, mishandled by the juvenile justice system, mistreated by mental health agencies, and neglected by the social welfare bureaucracy (Gibbs, 1989). In 1986, according to the U.S. Bureau of the Census (1987), Black youth constituted nearly half of the total Black population of 29,306,000 (11.5% of the total U.S. population). Of these youth, 42.7% lived in families below the poverty line, and over 67.1% of those in female-headed families were poor (U.S. Bureau of the Census, 1987). Two of every five Black children live in female-headed households. These families are five times as likely to be welfare-dependent as two-parent families

(Children's Defense Fund, 1987). For African Americans 25 years of age and older, the median educational level completed was 12.3 years in 1985. From 1960 to 1985, the proportion of African Americans completing 4 years of high school or more increased from 20.1% to 59.8%. Simultaneously, high school dropout rates declined from 22% in 1970 to 12.4% in 1983 (U.S. Bureau of the Census, 1986).

The current status of African Americans in the United States has often been attributed to four major historical and social factors: slavery, segregation and discrimination, poverty, and urbanization (Franklin, 1967; Omi & Winant, 1986; Wilson, 1987). These factors, embedded in a backdrop of racism, significantly weakened the functioning of the African American family and major institutions of their community, thus indirectly creating a hospitable environment for the development of social, psychological, and behavioral problems among Black youth (Gibbs, 1989).

Psychosocial problems. African American youth are more likely than White youth to live in deteriorating inner-city neighborhoods, in substandard housing with poor sanitation, located in urban areas with depressed economies and high crime rates and less access to adequate health and educational resources (Children's Defense Fund, 1986a; Kasarda, 1985; Schorr, 1986). The social and economic characteristics of these neighborhoods generate chronic levels of stress for these youth and their families and contribute to the dismal statistics on four social indicators: school dropout rates, juvenile delinquency, substance abuse, and teenage pregnancy and parenthood.

In spite of the overall improvement in school dropout rates among African American youth since 1960, the rates in some urban areas currently range from 40% to 60% with some students leaving school as early as the seventh grade (Reed, 1988). Several surveys have found high rates of functional illiteracy among Black male adolescents (College Entrance Examination Board, 1985; Reed, 1988). In

1980, almost one-fourth of all 18–21-year-old Black youth neither had completed nor were currently enrolled in high school (U.S. Bureau of the Census, 1981). These educational deficiencies often result in a high unemployment rate and few opportunities for legitimate income for this population.

Official juvenile delinquency rates indicate that African American youth are more likely to be arrested than White youth for status offenses and index offenses. In 1985, Black youth accounted for 23.2% of all juvenile arrests. Black juvenile delinquents have higher rates than White juvenile delinquents of depression and of psychological and neurological symptoms, which are often undetected and undiagnosed, thus making the juvenile justice system the channel for handling Black youth with behavioral disorders (Dembo, 1988; Gibbs, 1982; Lewis & Balla, 1976). Clearly, the system of entry will determine the nature and quality of the services offered, the assessment and diagnosis of the problem behaviors, and the appropriateness and effectiveness of the intervention used.

Community surveys of drug and alcohol use have consistently reported that Black youth have lower rates of alcohol use than Whites, equal rates of marijuana use (Dembo, 1988; National Institute of Drug Abuse, 1979) and among older Black youth, higher rates of cocaine and heroin use. Drug use for many low-income African American youth is often linked to a life-style that includes delinquency and selling drugs. Whether these youth are identified in the school system, the juvenile justice system, or by social services, they are usually multiple-problem individuals with social and psychological problems including low self-esteem, impulsivity, high levels of anger and hostility, depression, and suicidal behaviors (Beschner & Friedman, 1986; Halikas, Darvish, & Rimmer, 1976; Lee, 1983). Currently, young Black intravenous drug users face the growing threat of infection with the AIDS virus. As of May 1988, non-Hispanic Black youth constituted 50% of the 1,212 persons under age 20 identified as having AIDS in the United States ("AIDS: A Complex New Threat," 1988).

Teen pregnancy continues to be a major psychosocial problem for African American teenagers, not only because they are often ill equipped to meet the developmental needs of their infants and children but because teen pregnancy and parenthood is associated with such negative sequelae as high rates of school dropout, welfare dependency, and unemployment (Children's Defense Fund, 1986b). In 1983, the birthrate for unmarried Black females aged 15–19 was 86.4 per 1,000. The rate for a comparable group of White females was 18.5 per 1,000. Of all Black females aged 10–19, nearly 10% gave birth (Gibbs, 1989).

Cultural and family values. The bleak picture of social problems among Black youth has been presented above; however, it is far from being the complete picture. On the contrary, this population has demonstrated incredible strength and resilience in response to their tragic and humiliating historical and social experiences in American society. From their adaptive responses to American society, four major values have been identified: the importance of religion and the church, the importance of the extended family and kinship networks, the importance of flexible family roles, and the importance of education (Allen, 1978; Billingsley, 1968; Leigh & Green, 1982; McAdoo, 1981; Staples, 1981).

In many African American communities, the church is the main focus of social and civic activity. Historically, the church has been a major support system for Black families, providing nurturance and social services particularly in times of crisis. Hill (1972) suggests that it was through the church that Blacks learned to use religion as a means to survive. Black ministers often serve as gatekeepers or spokespersons for their community and enable the church to provide such diverse resources as senior citizen services, daycare services, credit unions, housing developments, and education groups. The church also serves a function of promoting family solidarity, leadership development, and release of emotional and social tensions. In addition, it has provided an arena for social and community activity as well as for Black social and political protests (Staples, 1976). The Black church has been a strong force in leadership and a provider of multiple resources for the Black community, and it remains one of the few indigenous institutions that has not become externally controlled (Boyd, 1982).

For decades, the Black family had been maligned as a "culture of poverty" or a "tangle of pathology" (Billingsley, 1968). In the 1970s this deficit view of Black family life was challenged and important strengths of the family were identified. These included strong kinship bonds, adaptability of family roles, strong religious orientation, strong educational and work orientations, and strong survival and coping skills in the face of harsh socioeconomic realities (Boyd, 1982). As a result of strong kinship bonds, many Black families have evolved into extended families in which blood relatives and fictive kin are absorbed into a coherent network of mutual emotional and economic support. These patterns of kinship networks are especially functional for low-income Black families, who exchange resources, services, and emotional support. Stack (1975) describes this as a co-residence, kinship-based exchange network linking multiple domestic units, and generating lifelong bonds of three-generation households which are embedded in cooperative domestic exchange. A variety of adults and older children may participate in the rearing of any one Black child. Or, a neighbor may care for a close friend's children in times of economic stress or illness.

The flexibility of family roles and boundaries, a consistently important aspect of Black family functioning, developed in response to economic pressure. Role responsibilities and duties are not distributed according to traditional gender-based roles, but rather according to necessity at any given time. For example, in families where the mothers are working, an older sibling might act as a substitute "parent" or "parental child" for the younger siblings. Role flexibility may similarly extend to husband-wife roles; the wife may act as the "breadwinner" and the husband may assume responsibility for domestic duties and child rearing when the husband is unemployed or disabled. Traditional child-rearing patterns also tend to foster early independence in children as well as less differentiation in roles and family tasks (Peters, 1981). Recent empirical studies support the descriptive accounts of greater role flexibility and less gender-specific role functioning in Black families (Staples & Mirande, 1980), although these patterns vary according to socioeconomic status and rural/urban residence. The significant aspect of this family flexibility is that the sharing of decisions and tasks has been an important survival mechanism for Black families (Boyd, 1982).

Historically, African American families have valued education, hard work, and social mobility (Billingsley, 1968; Bowman & Howard, 1985; Gurin & Epps, 1975). It was these values which prompted mass migrations from the rural, agrarian South to the urban industrial North, which offered greater educational and economic opportunities for Blacks. In spite of widespread discrimination and poverty, many African American families have sacrificed to send their children to college and prepare them for professional careers. Unfortunately, in recent years, the impetus for higher education has slowed due, in part, to the social isolation of poor, inner-city Blacks and their lack of middle-class role models, the changing nature of the economy, and the increasingly hostile environment toward people of color (Gibbs, 1989).

African Americans in the public schools. As an instrument of education and socialization, the school has continually been a source of conflict and controversy for many African American youth (Gibbs, 1989). These students are frequently referred for school-related academic or behavioral problems and are overrepresented in special educational programs and nonacademic tracks. Many Black students drop out or are "pushed out" of high school after experiencing years of academic frustration and failure, low teacher expectations, high rates of suspension, and oftentimes chaotic or noneducationally oriented custodial school environments (Committee for Economic Development, 1987; Reed, 1988). Peer influences are also instrumental in shaping school experiences of Black adolescents (Cauce, Felner, & Primavera, 1982; Gibbs, 1985; Ogbu, 1985). In situations where the prevailing norms are anti-intellectual and college is not viewed as a viable option, African American teenagers have an especially difficult time if they are perceived as high achievers (Hare, 1988). These students are often rejected by their peers and derogatorily labeled "Whitey." Thus, these students not only have to negotiate two different cultures, but must simultaneously handle the conflict of academic success versus peer acceptance. In many inner-city neighborhoods, there is much peer pressure toward early involvement in sexual activity and experimentation with drugs (Brown, 1985; Hare, 1988; Ladner, 1971). Again, when students resist conforming to peer pressures, they may experience social isolation and ridicule.

The Hispanic Americans

Demographic data. Hispanics are the fastest growing minority in the United States. In 1985 the approximately 16.9 million Hispanics in the U.S., excluding Puerto Rico, represented 7.2% of the U.S. population. The largest subgroup of Hispanics is Mexican Americans (11.8 million), who tend to reside in the West and Southwest, followed by Puerto Ricans (2.6 million), who tend to concentrate in New York and New Jersey and primarily urban areas (Inclan & Herron, 1989). Hispanics also include other Spanish-speaking people primarily from Central and South America.

The Hispanic population, with a median age of 24 years, is younger than the non-Hispanic population. The proportion of children and adolescents in this population is 39.1% for Mexican Americans, 37.1% for Puerto Ricans, 19.8% for Cuban Americans, in contrast to 26% for the non-Hispanic population. In terms of education, Mexican Americans and Puerto Ricans have completed fewer years of formal education than non-Hispanics. In a 1985 census report, only 42% of Mexican Americans and 46% of Puerto Ricans aged 25 and older had completed high school compared to 74% in the total U.S. population (U.S. Bureau of the Census, 1985). This same report indicated that the proportion of Hispanic families whose income fell below the poverty level was more than double that of non-Hispanic families. Within the Hispanic group, 42% of Puerto Rican families, 13% of Cuban American families, and 24% of Mexican American families had family incomes below the poverty level. Thus, recent demographic data indicate an Hispanic population that, in general, tends to be disproportionately poor, to have less than a high school education, to be unemployed and underemployed, and to confront problems of illiteracy and lack of facility in the English language. Because over one-third of this ethnic group are presently children or adolescents, it is clear that the educational system will be confronted with increasing areas of need.

Although Hispanic families are quite diverse, an attempt will be made to outline some characteristic cultural patterns and values which differentiate them from the mainstream population. Socioeconomic differences, patterns of immigration, and level of acculturation also contribute to the diversity within these families.

Cultural and family values. The contemporary Hispanic family is undergoing substantial changes. Ramirez and Arce (1981), in their study of the Mexican American family, found a mixture of traditional and more contemporary patterns. Traditional values as the primacy of the family and extended kinship ties remained strongly entrenched. The traditional family is a tightly knit, hierarchical structure, with ascribed sex and status roles. Children have primary value and parents often "live for their children" (Gallegos & Valdez, 1979). An extended family system including compadres (godparents) is a highly valued source of emotional and social support, child rearing, financial support, and problem solving (Keefe, Padilla, & Carlos, 1978, 1979; Mindel, 1980). The functioning of this kinship network is characterized by affiliation and cooperation, whereas confrontation and competition are discouraged (Ramirez, 1989). This reflects the traditional Hispanic value of "personalismo," which stresses the goodness and quality of personal relationships and the deep respect for interpersonal affiliation, affection, and reciprocity. The concept of harmony through cooperation is more highly valued than achievement through competition. This contrasts sharply with the typical American values of individual achievement and interpersonal competition.

In contrast to these more traditional values, there seem to be some new variations in the area of male and female roles and conjugal decision making (Ramirez & Arce, 1981). Traditionally, the male assumed the instrumental role of provider and protector of the family. The concept of machismo and the patriarchal ideology in Hispanic families required men to be forceful and strong and to withhold tender or affectionate emotions. It encompassed a strong sense of honor, family, loyalty, and care for the children, while also connoting exaggerated masculinity and sexual virility and aggressiveness (Trankina, 1983). In contrast, the female assumed the expressive role of homemaker and caretaker of the children. Her role entailed self-denial and abnegation, and her personal needs were considered subordinate to those of other family members. Although residuals of these traditions remain in varying degrees, the concepts of machismo and absolute patriarchy have diminishing influence on the dynamics and structure of the Hispanic family. Rather, joint decision making and greater equality of roles and opportunities are increasingly more apparent. A major change is the increased frequency of women's employment outside the home which enhances a wife's status within the family and in decision-making processes (BacaZinn, 1980; Cromwell & Rutz, 1979).

In the family's early years, the home is usually child-centered with both parents tending to be permissive and indulgent with the younger children (Ramirez, 1989). Although emphasizing good behavior, parents nevertheless give a great amount of nurturance and protection to young children and adopt a relaxed attitude toward the achievement of developmental milestones or the attainment of self-reliance. Generally, Hispanic parents display a basic acceptance of the child's individuality and seem less pressured than Anglo-American parents to see that a child achieves developmental goals or to correct minor deviations from the norm (Ramirez, 1989). Following this relatively permissive and indulgent phase, parents begin to expect more responsible behavior from their children as they approach latency and adolescence, often assigning tasks or responsibilities in accordance with their age and ability.

Differences in sex-role socialization are usually evident in families and become especially prominent at adolescence. The adolescent female remains much closer to the home and is protected and guarded in her contacts with others beyond the family, so as to preserve her femininity and innocence. In contrast, the adolescent male is given much more freedom and is encouraged to acquire worldly knowledge outside the home in preparation for the time when he will assume the role of husband and father. He is encouraged to join with other males of his age in informal social groups in order to gain knowledge and experience in holding his own with other males (Ramirez, 1989).

The degree to which these sociocultural values are evident in Hispanic families varies according to the level of acculturation. The process of acculturation for the two larger Hispanic groups, the Mexican Americans and Puerto Ricans, is particularly complicated by their unique patterns of migration. The ease and frequency of movement between their homeland and the U.S. mainland renders the acculturation process disjointed, often leaving the children in a state of flux, and disrupting the normal progression of adjustment to a new culture. The child's family, school, and community systems will also be periodically disrupted with these migrations necessitating rebuilding of important referent points and identifications.

Hispanic Americans in the public schools. Evelyn Davila of the National Hispanic Scholar Awards Program of the College Board in New York, in testimony to the National Coalition of Advocates for Students, further elaborated on the educationally disruptive pattern of movement among Hispanics, particularly Puerto Ricans. She described this as circular migration between the U.S. mainland and Puerto Rico, usually provoked by economic necessity (NCAS, 1988). (Puerto Ricans are U.S. citizens so technically they are not considered immigrants even though they arrive from a very different culture.) In the 1981–82 academic year in New York City public schools, 18% of students entering the schools at nonstandard times were from Puerto Rico and the largest percentage of students leaving the New York City public schools, or 17%, were students leaving for Puerto Rico. In total there were 9,927 reported cases of students transferring during one year between New York and Puerto Rico (NCAS, 1988). This migration, among other factors, contributes to an average completion rate of only 8.7 years of school for Puerto Ricans and a 60% dropout rate prior to high school graduation. Among those who do graduate from high school, about 25% are delayed by more than one year (NCAS, 1988).

Hispanic youth in the American school system are confronted not only with the normative educational and developmental tasks associated with their age cohort, but face the added stresses of negotiating two disparate cultures. Many of these youth daily encounter language problems, value clashes, and a sense of alienation from the basic infrastructure of the school. Social class influences the school experience and expectation of Hispanic students (Vega, Hough, & Romero, 1983). Lower income families are often mired in the struggle for survival. They tend to be more socially isolated and minimally acculturated;

thus, their attention to school issues is severely hampered. Working-class families demonstrate broader social perception and more outside community involvement. They are more likely to be bilingual and functionally bicultural. However, for these families, the dissonance between home and school structures may be substantial, resulting in poor communication and less effective schooling. Middle-class families are usually fluent in English, more physically removed from Spanish-speaking neighborhoods, and more acculturated, with less dissonance between family expectations and the surrounding social environment, including the schools. Although some of the basic survival and acculturation issues are mitigated by higher socioeconomic status, other conflicts and dilemmas are present for these youth. Middle-class neighborhoods, and consequently schools, tend to be more racially and culturally homogeneous. Adolescent subcultures often reflect this, thus the Hispanic youth may be a distinct minority in such a residential area. This residential segregation may provoke identity conflicts and foster a painful sense of personal and social alienation (Vega et al., 1983). This situation inevitably hinders the effectiveness of the school and reciprocally minimizes the youth's ability to take advantage of oftentimes well-meaning, albeit limited, educational resources.

In an interesting study examining high achievement among socioeconomically disadvantaged Hispanic youth, So (1987) found that the middle-class referent group of the public school and the Hispanic reference group orientation together have a positive impact on educational achievement. The high-achieving disadvantaged student identified with his or her own ethnic group while aspiring to middle-class values. Those students who maintained strong communicative skills within the Hispanic culture outperformed those who did not aspire to the middle class and did not maintain strong communicative skills with their parents and reference group. It was concluded that these high achievers identified with different groups for different purposes;

specifically, identification with the minority ethnic group served emotional needs, such as greater comfort and compatibility with Spanish-speaking parents, whereas identification with middle-class values served instrumental purposes such as educational achievement and potential upward mobility.

In summary, although there are many similarities among the various ethnic and racial groups, such as the value of interdependence over independence, the primacy of the group over the individual, the emphasis on extended family networks rather than nuclear family units, and the clashes of roles and values in relation to the mainstream society, there are still striking differences among the groups and vis-à-vis the White American middle-class majority.

AN ECOLOGICAL FRAMEWORK FOR HOME-SCHOOL COLLABORATION

The overall objective of this book is to increase understanding of the nature and development of effective home-school collaboration. Clearly this is a worthy goal as substantiated by the recent Carnegie Council report, which emphasizes the positive relationship between parental involvement and students' achievement and attitudes toward school (Carnegie Council on Adolescent Development, 1989). As mentioned earlier, other studies have underscored the importance of parental involvement (Comer, 1984; Hess & Holloway, 1984). A particularly dramatic example is the Haringey Project (Tizard, Schofield, & Hewison, 1982, cited in Cummins, 1986). This project focused on the effects of parental involvement in the teaching of reading. Elementary school children were requested to read to their parents at home on a regular basis; parents were to complete a record of what had been read. The schools studied were in multi-ethnic areas where many of the parents were non-English speaking or non-English literate; nevertheless, parents were enthusiastic about the project and agreed to hear their children read. The results were striking. Children who read to their parents made significantly

greater progress than those who did not, including children who were having difficulty learning to read. Additionally, those children in the group involving collaboration with parents showed more reading improvement than those children in small groups receiving instruction from a reading specialist.

Hoover-Dempsey, Bassler, and Brissie (1987), in a study supporting the value of teacher and parent collaboration, found that teacher efficacy was highly correlated with parent involvement. That is, teachers' beliefs that they are effective in teaching, that the children can learn from them, and that they have access to a specialized body of knowledge, was associated with higher levels of parent involvement. Higher teacher efficacy may increase role differentiation and complementarity of teachers' and parents' roles such that neither party is a threat to the other.

Educators and researchers argue for ongoing constructive relationships between parents and schools in order to ensure that schools, families, and communities are strengthened as effective promoters of children's development. In spite of this, however, parental involvement of all types declines progressively during the elementary school years, and by the middle school years, the home-school connection has been significantly reduced. By high school years, there is minimal, if any, contact (Carnegie Council on Adolescent Development, 1989). This widening gulf between families and schools during the middle grade years is often a reflection of the parents' belief that they should increasingly disengage from their young adolescents. Many parents assume that adolescents should be independent and, consequently, they view involvement in their child's education as unnecessary. Although adolescents do seek greater autonomy, they neither desire nor benefit from a complete break in parent-school relations and total absence of parental involvement. Schools also play a part in this diminished involvement as they do not encourage and sometimes even actively discourage parental involvement beginning in the middle grade schools.

This pattern of diminished involvement is even more evident among lower income and ethnic and racial minority families. In low-income and minority neighborhoods, parents are often considered to be part of the problem of educating young adolescents rather than an important educational resource. They are more often viewed as adversaries rather than as partners.

What contributes to this pattern, particularly for minority families and the schools? How can we begin to explain and therefore begin to correct this declining involvement between the schools and these families? If this pattern runs counter to effective educational development of children and adolescents, what interventions can begin to reverse this trend? With the ethnic population in the United States growing from 17% in 1970 to 23.3% in 1980 (U.S. Bureau of the Census, 1973, 1983), educators and schools can expect to see more students from these various groups. As discussed earlier in this chapter, each ethnic or racial group perceives the schools and their roles vis-à-vis the school differently; their history of relationships with the schools varies, as does their daily experience. Similarly, their sociocultural values, family structures, and cultural traditions are quite diverse.

A new approach. In view of these complexities, we are presenting a model for viewing home-school collaboration across cultures that delineates a process of inquiry and reasoning. This model, which we first presented in our book, *Children of Color* (Gibbs & Huang, 1989), draws heavily from Bronfenbrenner's (1979) model of the person in the environment. At the center of the model is the developing individual, in this case, the child or adolescent. This individual is embedded in an intricate array of systems dynamically interacting with the individual and simultaneously with one another. The individual and the environmental systems are mutually influential, each changing over time and adapting in response to changes in the other (Garbar-ino, 1982). The interaction is reciprocal and ongoing throughout development, and each reciprocal interaction is marked by key transition points, which may be viewed as developmental crises or opportunities for growth and change. The two levels of interaction are depicted in Figures 1 and 2. In Figure 1, a typical ecological network for a developing child or adolescent, the significant microsystems being the family, the school, the community (neighborhood and peers), and perhaps, the church, is displayed. The bidirectional arrows indicate that the direction of influence is two-way. Each system affects and is affected by the individual. The geometric shapes of each microsystem and the individual represent the different histories, origins, and cultures of the various systems. For each system, the culture represents a blend of the subculture of race, of ethnicity, of social class, and of institutionalism. Generally, with the exception of youth in foster families, the shape around the central individual and the family microsystem should be the same, reflecting a shared history and culture.

The various shapes symbolizing the individual and the microsystems are particularly significant, as they represent the basis for the functioning and values of the particular microsystems. These shapes are distinct in order to highlight the differences and, subsequently, the potential for conflict among the various systems. For example, in Figure 1, the individual negotiates among three distinct cultural systems on a daily basis: He or she comes from the "Culture of the Triangle," attends a school in the "Culture of the Rectangle," and participates in a community characterized by the "Culture of the Pentagon." The values and beliefs of the school system, unlike this child's family system, are based on a combination of a "Rectangle" culture and the concept of institutionalism, which emphasizes the "organization" at the expense of other factors, including individual characteristics. Thus, to be successful in school, the child must accommodate to the norms of the "Rectangle" culture; to maintain harmony in the family, the

Figure 1
An Ecological Network: First Level Interactions

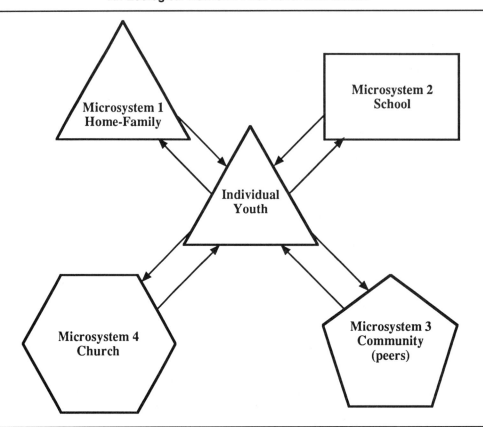

child must follow the values and norms of the "Triangle" culture; and to gain acceptance in the community, the child must abide by norms of the "Pentagon" culture. In order to develop a coherent sense of self, the child must gradually integrate these diverse cultural systems. The experience of this child would differ significantly from a child whose family, school, community, and peer systems all shared the same cultural basis. Although this geometric description of a child's ecology oversimplifies the reality, it is parsimonious, provides a starting point for assessment and intervention, and reflects our assumption that race, ethnicity, and the associated culture form the foundation for one's values and perceptions, and therefore, attitudes and behaviors in the world. Particularly in working with ethnic minority youth and families, delineating the ecological map and relevant cultural

systems is of paramount importance (Laosa, 1982; Lubeck, 1984).

More relevant to the focus of the current chapter is Figure 2, which highlights the second level of interactions, or what Bronfenbrenner (1979) calls the mesosystem. These are interactions between the various microsystems that have an impact on the individual and vice versa. For example, the interaction between the school and the family system, whether mutually supportive, absent, or actively hostile, will have an impact on the child, and reciprocally, the child will have an impact on this relationship. Similarly, the relationship between the family and the peer group or between the family and the church will affect the individual child or adolescent. As in the first level of interaction, the consonance or dissonance of cultures may affect the nature of these second level interactions.

Figure 2
The Mesosystems. Home-School Mesosystem (in bold lines): Second Level Interactions

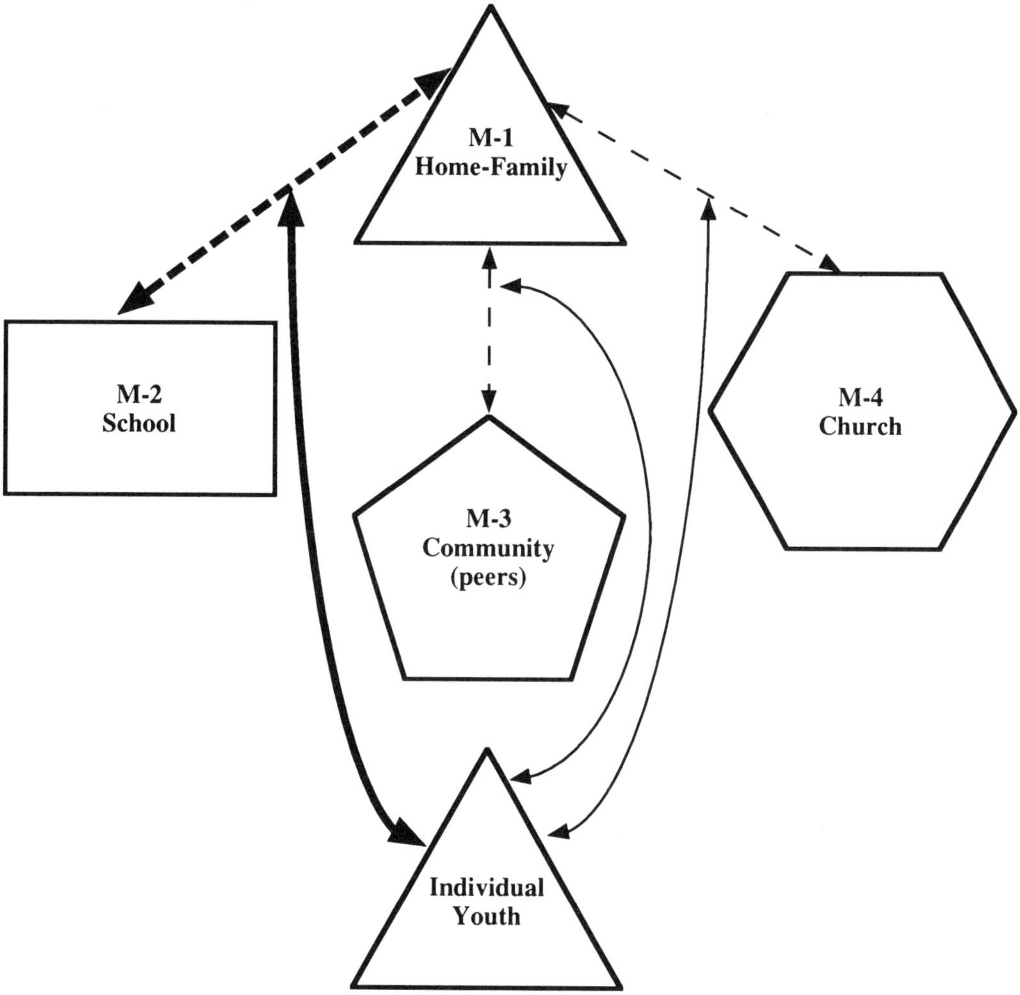

This is again represented by the various geometric shapes.

The home-school mesosystem is the particular focus of this chapter. Returning to Figure 2, the home system is represented by the Triangle and the school system by the Rectangle. For illustrative purposes, the individual will be an immigrant child, who has recently entered the mainstream school system. The Triangle culture, then, will be that of the immigrant. Besides the general sociocultural values of these immigrant families, they also bring a set of dynamics especially pertinent to home-school collaboration (NCAS, 1988).

School personnel, or third parties intervening in this mesosystem will have to consider the following:

1. Immigrant families have differing cultural expectations of schools based on the educational traditions in their homeland, which may range from total disengagement of parents to active involvement.

2. For some immigrants, in their homelands, teachers may have represented the ultimate authority for education and youth, therefore, parents have learned not to interfere or be involved.

3. For immigrants from rural, under-developed countries or those actively involved in civil or other wars, there may have been a total lack of experience with schools and the process of schooling.

4. Immigrant families often have limited ability to communicate with school personnel in English and, even if they have English comprehension, they may be reluctant to speak the language.

5. Immigrants often have limited time for school involvement due to heavy work schedules and efforts to "make it" in their new country.

6. Some immigrants may fear in-volvement with mainstream institutions in general, due to lack of appropriate documentation or wariness about their immigrant status.

7. Traditional school vehicles for promoting parent involvement, such as PTAs, Back-to-School nights, Adult Edu-cation, Parent Workshops, etc., may be totally alien and bewildering for immi-grant parents who are not necessarily apathetic or unwilling to participate, but are uninformed about the appropriate role.

Some parents do not understand that their involvement is both desirable and appropriate. These are just a few of the many issues that immigrant families may bring into the mesosystem relationship with the school.

The other component in this meso-system is the school. What are the issues that this system brings into the relation-ship? Of course, this will be determined on an individual basis as each school is unique with its own defining characteris-tics. Nevertheless, we offer some possibil-ities and a framework for assessing this system.

First, what is the school's history of dealing with immigrant students? Is this a new phenomenon for them, or do they have a track record of dealing with immigrant students? If the latter, what kinds of programs or resources have they developed for these newcomer students? Is their approach a proactive or reactive

one? That is, do they reach out with sensitivity and understanding to these new students and parents or are they more problem and crisis oriented? As this history and experience is assessed, it is important to see how this fits with the culture of the immigrant. In a study by NCAS (1988), immigrant parents ex-pressed a desire to be involved in their child's schooling, but found the school system unresponsive to them. Neither side was active in building a collaborative relationship but rather was waiting for the other to initiate contact. In this particular sample, there were shared expectations of willingness and desire for collaboration, but there was a misfit of approach.

Secondly, what is the composition of the school? Is the immigrant student the "solo" immigrant in the class? Are there a handful of immigrant students who may offer some support for each other, but place an extra burden on the classroom teacher? As with racial ethnic composi-tion, immigrant status has implications for the child's adjustment and accultura-tion. The presence of other ethnically similar immigrant children may ease the child's transition. However, it must be kept in mind that ethnic or racial sameness does not guarantee a support system. Earlier immigrants of the same ethnic or racial group, wishing to accul-turate to mainstream America and disre-gard memories of the past and hurtful incidents of rejection and "being differ-ent," may be reluctant to associate with newer immigrants. School-age children, often driven by the need to belong and to be accepted, tend to avoid the unusual or unfamiliar.

Third, what are the teachers' atti-tudes toward teaching immigrant stu-dents? Although many teachers find it challenging and desirable, many others resent the additional burden. Some may feel immigrant students and parents threaten their professional abilities and authority. Others may feel the lack of funds, resources, or time to assume the responsibility of reaching out to immi-grant parents. Some teachers may be reluctant to involve immigrant parents because of the time needed to develop productive parent participation and the lack of significant rewards for these efforts.

Fourth, what are the resources available to the school for working with this group of students and their families? Many schools attended by immigrant students are overcrowded, underfunded, understaffed, and housed in deteriorating buildings (NCAS, 1988). Observers may cite the ideal situations for immigrant students and home-school collaboration without realizing the limitations of the setting. Many school personnel are not responsive to change or to handling new situations because of tremendous lack of resources, in conjunction with a lack of motivation to change an ongoing system that is familiar even if ineffective. In this respect, schools are not different from other culturally distinct organizations (Sarason, 1971).

In developing home-school collaboration, particularly across cultures, it is critical to have, or begin to acquire, an intimate knowledge of the cultures of the two systems. Many people interested in educational planning or having a role in and concern for the educational setting have little knowledge of the culture of the school (Sarason, 1971). Similarly, many individuals interested in increasing parent participation have little understanding of the school backgrounds, historical experiences, attitudes, and values of the families they wish to involve. As a result, there is often more potential for clashes than for effective building of partnerships.

For the most part, schools are middle-class institutions, as reflected in their personnel and attitudes. Therefore, schools attended by low-income, low-status, and ethnic or racial minority families are inherently confronted by values, attitudes, and behavior clashes. This complicates the process of home-school collaboration and necessitates an ecological perspective incorporating the understanding of cultural and system diversity. Examination of the home-school mesosystem in terms of socioeconomic class and race factors and school staff and teacher attitudes may reveal critical points of disjuncture and conflict.

Influential factors in home-school interaction. Some minority parents may view the school as an instrument of oppression or as a racist institution. They may lack awareness of the importance of education in improving the lives of their children or may feel powerless and hopeless in regard to any possibilities of positive change for them. These negative views may be reinforced through contacts with teachers whose middle-class backgrounds have given them stereotypical views of minority children and their families (Brown, 1981).

Lower-class parents may also be unaware of their rights and obligations in demanding that the school provide their children with a quality education. So often when these parents visit a school or have contact with a child's teacher, they go as victims and powerless people. Communication between schools and low-income minority families is primarily negative and usually occurs when the child is having problems (Brown, 1981; NCAS, 1988; Reed, 1988).

School staff often feel that these parents are "hard-to-reach" and that the cause of this lies within the family and community, not with school policies and practices. Some educators believe that these parents do not have the time, interest, or competence to participate, and simply do not value education (NCAS, 1988). As a result, teachers and administrators often perceive these families, who deviate from the middle-class norm, as deficient and uncooperative and more a hindrance rather than a potential resource in the education of the children.

Fostering home-school collaboration across classes and cultures may start to change and hopefully improve these negative perceptions and expectations of the other. This mesosystem has the potential for major impact on the education and development of disenfranchised youth. Creating an atmosphere of mutual interest, understanding the stresses and strains of competing and diverse systems, and beginning to increase communication with and knowledge about the "unfamiliar other" may enhance the education of all participants. We suggest that this be undertaken within the framework of an ecological, culturally diverse perspective so that inquiry and investigation may supplant misperceptions, animosity, and subsequently, restricted educational opportunity.

MULTICULTURAL COMPETENCE IN HOME-SCHOOL COLLABORATION

In this chapter we provided sociocultural and demographic information about four distinct ethnic, racial minority groups in the United States, and delineated a model for conceptualizing home-school collaboration across cultures. This model, which focuses simultaneously on the individual and pertinent interacting social systems, is particularly relevant to ethnic minority youth, family, and institutions for a number of reasons. First, it emphasizes the subjective field of experience for the individual or the individual systems, which may generate important data not usually obtained by conventional, mainstream methods of inquiry. Second, it focuses attention on both the immediate and the more distant, deeply embedded, cultural environment (Garbarino, 1982). Third, by focusing on intersystem relationships and their impact on the individual and vice versa, it reveals connections that might otherwise be overlooked; in particular, it looks beyond immediate first level interactions (Huang & Gibbs, 1989).

This model has important implications for the roles of educators, psychologists, social workers, and others involved with the interface of home and school. The task for these providers working with ethnic minority youth is to identify the unique systems and cultural frameworks to be incorporated into a home-school connection. This requires a multicultural, multidimensional perspective. The provider must look at the individual student or family in their particular sociocultural context. Similarly, the provider must examine the sociocultural context of the provider and the school personnel involved in the collaboration. Finally, the provider must be attuned to the new culture generated by the collaboration, that is, the culture of the mesosystem.

In order to begin to do this, providers and teachers of these providers must broaden their perspective. Training programs need to adapt to the changing demographics of the United States and, subsequently, the school system, and assume a more culturally pluralistic approach. This does not imply total replacement of the current approach, but rather incorporation of ethnic minority cultures and consideration of the range of possibilities in a multicultural society. A balance between universalism and pluralism and the value of diversity must be attained on an individual level and on a larger societal level. This is a value that should be prominent in the foundations of an educational system and manifest throughout all levels of operation, including home-school collaboration. As this occurs, there is greater potential for the participants in home-school collaboration to be partners instead of opponents.

Culture-specific beliefs and practices must be understood along with conventional mainstream attitudes and behaviors. The precise blend of these two components needs to be tailored to the needs of the particular student and family. For example, for third-generation Japanese American families who are highly assimilated to American society and fluent only in English, conventional, mainstream approaches may be appropriate, whereas a different blend of approaches may be appropriate for a second-generation family. In contrast, the recent Hispanic immigrant may require a bicultural, bilingual provider or intercultural team who can develop a home-school connection to serve as a "bridge between the old and the new." Studies have demonstrated that high achievement among disadvantaged minorities may be enhanced by strengthening both the ethnic programs that are sensitive to cultural identification and the general academic programs that increase orientation toward the middle-class referent group (So, 1987). The significant point here is the availability of the different perspectives and approaches, which, in turn, reflects the provider's attitude toward diversity (Huang & Gibbs, 1989).

The study of cultural diversity has become increasingly accepted as a legitimate topic of scientific inquiry and training. Ethnicity is now recognized as an important independent and dependent variable, associated with different value systems, learning histories, philosophical outlooks, social structures, life experiences, and behaviors (Suinn, 1987). Content areas include, for example, topics such as values and practices of minority groups, historical experiences, the impact of ethnic minority status on child-rearing practices and psychosocial development of minority children and families, effects of discrimination and racism on the group, minority family structure and values, etc. The question remains, however, how best to incorporate ethnic minority content into the education and training of educational and social service providers. The debate focuses on single, specialized courses on minority content versus integration of minority content into the existing courses. Although the former option is easier to implement, the latter may be more effective in reaching a larger number of individuals and in socializing both ethnic minority and mainstream White professionals to the value of diversity and cultural pluralism. Proponents of the specialized-course approach contend that faculty members cannot be expected to offer other than superficial coverage of ethnic topics and that, under the auspices of academic freedom, they will continue to teach their courses as they so desire. However, faculty, like the curriculum, will have to evolve to meet the changing needs and demands of our society. Ethnicity, as a concept and as a topic of inquiry, is relevant to all instructors and all students, not just minority instructors and minority students. As this becomes increasingly apparent, and as a new generation of instructors emerges, one that has been socialized in our increasingly multicultural society with the value of cultural diversity, the level of multicultural competence among educational and service providers will be amplified and, accordingly, the children and families of ethnic and racial minorities will be better and more appropriately served.

REFERENCES

AIDS: A complex new threat to children's survival. (1988). *CDF* Children's Defense Fund *Reports, 91*(12), 1–8.

Allen, W. R. (1978). Black family research in the United States: A review, assessment and extension. *Journal of Comparative Family Studies, 9,* 167–189.

American Public Welfare Association. (1986). *One child in four.* New York: Author.

BacaZinn, M. (1980). Employment and education of Mexican-American women: The interplay of modernity and ethnicity in eight families. *Harvard Educational Review, 50* (1), 47–62 .

Berlin, I. N. (1987, July). Effects of changing Native American cultures on child development. *Journal of Community Psychology,* 299–305.

Beschner, G., & Friedman, A. (Eds.). (1986). *Teen drug use.* Lexington, MA: Lexington Books.

Billingsley, A. (1968). *Black families in White America.* Englewood Cliffs, NJ: Prentice-Hall.

Bouvier, L., & Agresta, A. (1987). The future Asian population of the United States. In J. Fawcett & B. Carino (Eds.), *Pacific bridges: The new immigration from Asia and the Pacific Islands* (pp. 285–301). New York: Center for Migration Studies.

Bowman, P., & Howard, C. (1985). Race-related socialization, motivation, and academic achievement: A study of Black youths in three generation families. *Journal of the American Academy of Child Psychiatry, 24,* 134–141.

Boyd, N. (1982). Family therapy with Black families. In E. Jones & S. Korchin (Eds.), *Minority mental health* (pp. 227–249). New York: Praeger.

Brod, R. L., & McQuiston, J. M. (1983). American Indian adult education and literacy: The first national survey. *Journal of American Indian Education, 1,* 1–16.

Bronfenbrenner, U. (1979). *The ecology of human development: Experiments by nature and design.* Cambridge, MA: Harvard University Press.

Brown, J. (1981). Parent education groups for Mexican-Americans. *Social Work in Education, 3*(4), 23–31.

Brown, S. (1985). Premarital sexual permissiveness among Black adolescent females. *Social Psychology Quarterly, 48,* 381–387.

Bulatao, J. C. (1962). Philippine values: The Manilenos mainsprings. *Philippine Studies, 10,* 51–86.

Carnegie Council on Adolescent Development. (1989). *Turning points: Preparing American youth for the 21st century.* Report of the Task Force on Education of Young Adolescents. Washington, DC: Author.

Cauce, A. M., Felner, R., & Primavera, J. (1982). Social support in high-risk adolescents: Structural components and adaptive impact. *American Journal of Community Psychology, 10,* 417–428.

Children's Defense Fund. (1986a). *Building health programs for teenagers.* Washington, DC: Author.

Children's Defense Fund. (1986b). *Welfare and pregnancy: What do we know? What do we do?* Washington, DC: Author.

Children's Defense Fund. (1987). *A children's defense budget.* Washington, DC: Author.

Coladarci, T. (1983). High school dropouts among Native Americans. *Journal of American Indian Education, 23,* 15–23.

College Entrance Examination Board. (1985). *Equality and excellence: The educational status of Black Americans.* New York: Author.

Comer, J. (1984). Home-school relationships and how they affect the academic success of children. *Education and Urban Society, 16*(3), 323–337.

Comer, J. (1985). The Yale-New Haven Primary Prevention Project: A follow-up. *Journal of the American Academy of Child Psychiatry, 24,* 154–160.

Committee for Economic Development. (1987). *Children in need: Investment strategies for the educationally disadvantaged.* New York: Author.

Cromwell, R., & Rutz, R. (1979). The myth of macho dominance in decision-making within Mexican and Chicano families. *Hispanic Journal of Behavioral Sciences, 1*(4), 355–373.

Cummins, J. (1986, February). Empowering minority students: A framework for intervention. *Harvard Educational Review, 56*(1), 18–36.

Dauphinais, P., LaFromboise, T. D., & Rowe, W. (1980). Perceived problems and sources of help for American Indian students. *Counselor Education and Supervision, 20,* 37–44.

deAnda, D. (1984). Bicultural socialization: Factors affecting the minority experience. *Social Work, 29,* 101–107.

Dell, P. F. (1980). The Hopi family therapist and the Aristotelian parents. *Journal of Marital and Family Therapy, 6,* 123–130.

Dembo, R. (1988). Delinquency among Black male youth. In J. T. Gibbs (Ed.), *Young, Black, and male in America: An endangered species* (pp. 129–165). Dover, MA: Auburn House.

Development Associates. (Ed.). (1983). *The evaluation of the impact of the Part A Entitlement Program funded under Title IV of the Indian Education Act* (Contract No. 380–80-0862). Washington, DC: U.S. Department of Education.

Dornbusch, S. M., Prescott, B. L., & Ritter, P. L. (1987, April). *The relation of high school academic performance and student effort to language use and recency of migration among Asian- and Pacific-Americans.* Paper presented at the meeting of the American Educational Research Association, Washington, DC.

Edelman, M. W. (1987). *Families in peril: An agenda for social change.* Cambridge, MA: Harvard University Press.

Everett, F., Proctor, N., & Cartmell, B. (1983). Providing psychological services to American Indian children and families. *Professional Psychology: Research and Practice, 14,* 588–603.

Franklin, J. H. (1967). *From slavery to freedom: A history of American Negroes.* New York: Knopf.

Gallegos, J., & Valdez, T. (1979). The Chicano familia. In J. Green & C. Tong (Eds.), *Cultural awareness in the human services: A training manual* (pp. 277–340). Seattle: University of Washington.

Garbarino, J. (1982). *Children and families in the social environment.* Hawthorne, NY: Aldine.

Gibbs, J. T. (1982). Personality patterns of delinquent females: Ethnic and sociocultural variations. *Journal of Clinical Psychology, 38,* 198–206.

Gibbs, J. T. (1985). City girls: Psychosocial adjustment of urban Black adolescent females. *SAGE: A Scholarly Journal on Black Women, 2,* 26–28.

Gibbs, J. T. (1989). Black American adolescents. In J. T. Gibbs & L. N. Huang (Eds.), *Children of color: Psychological interventions with minority youth* (pp. 179–223). San Francisco: Jossey-Bass.

Gibbs, J. T., & Huang, L. N. (1989). A conceptual framework for assessing and treating minority youth. In J. T. Gibbs & L. N. Huang (Eds.), *Children of color: Psychological interventions with minority youth* (pp. 1–29). San Francisco: Jossey-Bass.

Giles, K. N. (1985). *Indian high school dropouts: A perspective.* Milwaukee, WI: Midwest National Origin Desegregation Assistance Center.

Gould, M., Wunsch-Hitzig, R., & Dohrenwend, B. S. (1981). Estimating the prevalence of childhood psychopathology. *Journal of the American Academy of Child Psychiatry, 20,* 462–476.

Gray, E., & Cosgrove, J. (1985). Ethnocentric perception of childrearing practices in protective services. *Child Abuse and Neglect, 9,* 389–396.

Green, J. W. (1982). *Cultural awareness in the human services.* Englewood Cliffs, NJ: Prentice-Hall.

Greenbaum, P. E. (1985). Nonverbal differences in communication style between American Indian and Anglo elementary classrooms. *American Educational Research Journal, 22*(1), 101–115.

Gurin, P., & Epps, E. (1975). *Black consciousness, identity and achievement.* New York: Wiley.

Halikas, J., Darvish, H., & Rimmer, J. (1976). The Black addict: I. Methodology, chronology of addiction and overview of the population. *American Journal of Drug and Alcohol Abuse, 3,* 529–543.

Hare, B. (1988). Black youth at risk. In J. D. Williams (Ed.), *The state of Black America 1988* (pp. 81–93). New York: National Urban League.

Hess, R., & Holloway, S. (1984). Family and school as educational institutions. In R. Parke, R. Emde, N. McAdoo, & G. Sackett (Eds.), *Review of child development research: Vol. 7. The family* (pp. 179–222). Chicago: University of Chicago Press.

Hill, R. (1972). *The strengths of Black families.* New York: National Urban League.

Hill Witt, S. (1979, August). *Pressure points in growing up Indian.* Paper presented at the 87th Annual Meeting of the American Psychological Association, New York City.

Hodgkinson, H. (1986). *Future search.* Washington, DC: National Education Association.

Hoover-Dempsey, K., Bassler, O., & Brissie, J. (1987). Parent involvement: Contributions of teacher efficacy, school socioeconomic status, and other school characteristics. *American Educational Research Journal, 24*(3), 417–435.

Huang, L. N. (1989). Southeast Asian refugee children and adolescents. In J. T. Gibbs & L. N. Huang (Eds.), *Children of color: Psychological interventions with minority youth* (pp. 278–321). San Francisco: Jossey-Bass.

Huang, L. N., & Gibbs, J. T. (1989). Future directions. In J. T. Gibbs & L. N. Huang (Eds.), *Children of color: Psychological interventions with minority youth* (pp. 375–403). San Francisco: Jossey-Bass.

Huang, L. N., & Ying, Y. (1989). Chinese American children and adolescents. In J. T. Gibbs & L. N. Huang (Eds.), *Children of color: Psychological interventions with minority youth* (pp. 30–66). San Francisco: Jossey Bass.

Hungry Wolf, A., & Hungry Wolf, B. (1987). *Children of the sun.* New York: Morrow.

Inclan, J., & Herron, D. G. (1989). Puerto Rican adolescents. In J. T. Gibbs & L. N. Huang (Eds.), *Children of color: Psychological interventions with minority youth* (pp. 251–277). San Francisco: Jossey-Bass.

Ishisaka, H. A., & Takagi, C. Y. (1982). Social work with Asian- and Pacific-Americans. In J. Green (Ed.), *Cultural awareness in the human services* (pp. 122–156). Englewood Cliffs, NJ: Prentice-Hall.

Kasarda, J. (1985). Urban change and minority opportunities. In P. E. Peterson (Ed.), *The new urban reality* (pp. 33–67). Washington, DC: Brookings Institute.

Keefe, S., Padilla, A., & Carlos, M. (1978). *Emotional support systems in two cultures: A comparison of Mexican Americans and Anglo Americans* (Occasional Paper No. 7). Los Angeles: University of California at Los Angeles, Spanish Speaking Mental Health Research Center.

Keefe, S., Padilla, A., & Carlos, M. (1979). The Mexican-American extended family as an emotional support system. *Human Organization, 38,* 144–152.

Kitano, H., & Kikumura, A. (1976). The Japanese American family. In C. Mindel & R. Habenstein (Eds.), *Ethnic families in America* (pp. 41–60). New York: Elsevier.

Ladner, J. (1971). *Tomorrow's tomorrow.* New York: Doubleday.

LaFromboise, T. D., & Low, K. G. (1989). American Indian children and adolescents. In J. T. Gibbs & L. N. Huang (Eds.), *Children of color: Psychological interventions with minority youth* (pp. 114–147). San Francisco: Jossey-Bass.

Laosa, L. (1982). School, occupation, culture, and family: The impact of parental schooling on the parent-child relationship. *Journal of Educational Psychology, 74*(6), 791–827.

Le, D. (1983). Mental health and Vietnamese children. In G. J. Powell (Ed.), *The psychosocial development of minority group children* (pp. 373–384). New York: Brunner/Mazel.

Leap, W. L. (1981). American Indian language maintenance. *Annual Review of Anthropology, 10,* 271–280.

Lee, L. J. (1983). Reducing Black adolescents' drug use: Family revisited. *Child and Youth Services, 6,* 57–69.

Lefley, H. P. (1975). Differential self-concept in American Indian children as a function of language and examiner. *Journal of Personality and Social Psychology, 31,* 36–41.

Leigh, J. W., & Green, J. W. (1982). The structure of the Black community: The knowledge base for social services. In J. W. Green (Ed.), *Cultural awareness in the human services* (pp. 94–121). Englewood Cliffs, NJ: Prentice-Hall.

Lewis, D., & Balla, D. (1976). *Delinquency and psychopathology.* New York: Grune & Stratton.

Lin, Y. (1938). *The wisdom of Confucius.* New York: Random House.

Links, P. (1983). Community survey of the prevalence of childhood psychiatric disorders: A review. *Child Development, 54,* 531–548.

Lubeck, S. (1984, October). An ethnographic perspective on education as cultural transmission. *Sociology of Education, 57,* 219–232.

McAdoo, H. (1981). *Black families.* Newbury Park, CA: Sage.

Miller, N. B. (1982). Social work services to urban Indians. In J. Green (Ed.), *Cultural awareness in the human services* (pp. 157–183). Englewood Cliffs, NJ: Prentice-Hall.

Mindel, C. (1980). Extended familism among urban Mexican Americans, Anglos, and Blacks. *Hispanic Journal of Behavioral Sciences, 2*(1), 21–34.

Mindel, C., & Habenstein, R. W. (Eds.). (1981). *Ethnic families in America: Patterns and variations* (2nd ed.). New York: Elsevier.

Nagata, D. (1989). Japanese American children and adolescents. In J. T. Gibbs & L. N. Huang (Eds.), *Children of color: Psychological interventions with minority youth* (pp. 67–113). San Francisco: Jossey-Bass.

National Coalition of Advocates for Students. (1988). *New voices: Immigrant students in U.S. public schools.* Boston: Author.

National Institute of Drug Abuse. (1979). *National survey on drug abuse, 1979.* Washington, DC: Author.

Nidorf, J. (1985). Mental health and refugee youths: A model for diagnostic training. In T. Owan (Ed.), *Southeast Asian mental health: Treatment, prevention, services, training, and research* (pp. 391–429). Washington, DC: U.S. Department of Health and Human Services.

Ogbu, J. (1985). A cultural ecology of competence among inner-city Blacks. In M. Spencer, G. Brookins, & W. Allen (Eds.), *Beginnings: The social and affective development of Black children* (pp. 45–66). Hillsdale, NJ: Erlbaum.

Omi, M., & Winant, H. (1986). *Racial formation in the United States: From the 1960's to the 1980's.* Boston: Routledge & Kegan Paul.

Peters, M. F. (1981). Parenting in Black families with young children: A historical perspective. In H. McAdoo (Ed.), *Black families* (pp. 211–224). Newbury Park, CA: Sage.

Plas, J. M., & Bellet, W. (1983). Assessment of the value-attitude orientations of American Indian children. *Journal of School Psychology, 21,* 57–64.

Powell, G. J. (1983). America's minority group children: The underserved. In G. J. Powell, J.

Yamamoto, A. Romero, & A. Morales (Eds.), *The psychosocial development of minority group children* (pp. 3–9). New York: Brunner/Mazel.

President's Commission on Mental Health. (1978a). *Report to the President.* Washington, DC: U.S. Government Printing Office.

President's Commission on Mental Health. (1978b). *Mental health in America: 1978. Vol. 1.* Washington, DC: U.S. Government Printing Office.

Ramirez, O. (1989). Mexican American children and adolescents. In J. T. Gibbs & L. N. Huang (Eds.), *Children of color: Psychological interventions with minority youth* (pp. 224–250). San Francisco: Jossey-Bass.

Ramirez, M., & Castaneda, A. (1974). *Cultural democracy, bicognitive development, and education.* New York: Academic Press.

Ramirez, O., & Arce, C. (1981). The contemporary Chicano family: An empirically based review. In A. Baron, Jr. (Ed.), *Explorations in Chicano psychology* (pp. 3–28). New York: Praeger.

Reed, R. (1988). Education and achievement of young Black males. In J. T. Gibbs (Ed.), *Young, Black, and male in America: An endangered species* (pp. 37–96). Dover, MA: Auburn House.

Rickel, A., & Allen, L. (1987). Preventing maladjustment from infancy through adolescence. In A. E. Kazdin (Ed.), *Developmental clinical psychology and psychiatry* (No. 11, pp. 1–159). Newbury Park, CA: Sage.

Rodgers, H. R. (1986). *Poor women, poor families.* Armonk, NY: M. E. Sharpe.

Rodriguez, A. (1983). Education policy and cultural plurality. In G. J. Powell (Ed.), *The psychosocial development of minority group children* (pp. 499–512). New York: Brunner/Mazel.

Ryan, R. A. (1980). Strengths of the American Indian family: State of the art. In F. Hoffman (Ed.), *The American Indian family: Strengths and stresses* (pp. 25–43). Isleta, NM: American Indian Social Research and Development Associates.

Sarason, S. (1971). *The culture of the school and the problem of change.* Boston: Allyn & Bacon.

Schorr, A. (1986). *Common decency: Domestic policies after Reagan.* New Haven, CT: Yale University Press.

Shon, S., & Ja, D. (1982). Asian families. In M. McGoldrick, J. Pearce, & J. Giordano (Eds.), *Ethnicity and family therapy* (pp. 208–228). New York: Guilford Press.

Sluzki, C. (1979). Migration and family conflict. *Family Process, 18*(4), 379–390.

So, A. (1987, April). High-achieving disadvantaged

students: A study of low SES Hispanic language minority youth. *Urban Education, 22*(1), 19–35.

Stack, C. (1975). *All our kin: Strategies for survival in the Black community.* New York: Harper & Row.

Staples, R. (1976). *Introduction to Black sociology.* New York: McGraw-Hill.

Staples, R. (1981). The Black American family. In C. Mindel & R. Habenstein (Eds.), *Ethnic families in America: Patterns and variations* (2nd ed., pp. 217–244). New York: Elsevier.

Staples, R., & Mirande, A. (1980). Racial and cultural variations among American families: A decennial review of the literature on minority families. *Journal of Marriage and the Family, 42,* 887–903.

Sue, S., & Okazaki, S. (1990, August). Asian-American educational achievements: A phenomenon in search of an explanation. *American Psychologist, 45*(8), 913–920.

Suinn, R. M. (1987, March). Minority issues cut across courses. *APA Monitor,* 3.

Tizard, J., Schofield, W., & Hewison, J. (1982). Collaboration between teachers and parents in assisting children's reading. *British Journal of Educational Psychology, 52,* 1–15.

Trankina, F. (1983). Clinical issues and techniques in working with Hispanic children and their families. In G. J. Powell (Ed.), *The psychosocial development of minority group children* (pp. 307–329). New York: Brunner/Mazel.

Trimble, J. E. (1981). Value differentials and their importance in counseling American Indians. In P. Pedersen, J. Draguns, W. Lonner, & J. Trimble (Eds.), *Counseling across cultures* (pp. 203–226). Honolulu: University Press of Hawaii.

U.S. Bureau of the Census. (1973). *1970 census of population: Characteristics of the population.* Washington, DC: U.S. Department of Commerce.

U.S. Bureau of the Census. (1981). *School enrollment: Social and economic characteristics of students* (Current Population Reports, Series P-20). Washington, DC: U.S. Government Printing Office.

U.S. Bureau of the Census. (1983). *1980 census of population: Characteristics of the population*

(U.S. Summary, PC 80-1-B1). Washington, DC: U.S. Department of Commerce.

U.S. Bureau of the Census. (1984). *A statistical profile of the American Indian population: 1980 census.* Washington, DC: U.S. Government Printing Office.

U.S. Bureau of the Census. (1985). *Persons of Spanish origin in the United States: March 1985 (Advance Report)* (Current Population Reports, Population Characteristics, Series P-20, No. 403). Washington, DC: U.S. Government Printing Office.

U.S. Bureau of the Census. (1986). *Statistical abstract of the United States: 1987* (107th ed.). Washington, DC: U.S. Department of Commerce.

U.S. Bureau of the Census. (1987). *Statistical abstract of the United States: 1988* (108th ed.). Washington, DC: U.S. Department of Commerce.

U.S. Bureau of the Census. (1989). *Statistical abstract of the United States: 1989* (109th ed.). Washington, DC: U.S. Department of Commerce.

U.S. Congress, Office of Technology Assessment. (1986). *Indian health care* (OTA-H-290). Washington, DC: U.S. Government Printing Office.

Vega, W., Hough, R., & Romero, A. (1983). Family life patterns of Mexican-Americans. In G. Powell (Ed.), *The psychosocial development of minority group children* (pp. 194–215). New York: Brunner/Mazel.

Vobejda, B. (1987, June 2). Education leaders warn of crisis for U.S. youth. *Washington Post,* p. A-16.

Williams, D., & Westermeyer, J. (1983). Psychiatric problems among adolescent Southeast Asian refugees: A descriptive study. *Journal of Nervous and Mental Disease, 171,* 79–85.

Wilson, W. J. (1987). *The truly disadvantaged.* Chicago: University of Chicago Press.

Wilson, W. J., & Aponte, R. (1985). Urban poverty. *Annual Review of Sociology,* 11, 231–258.

Wong, H. Z. (1982). Asian and Pacific Americans. In L. R. Snowden (Ed.), *Reaching the underserved: Mental health needs of neglected populations* (pp. 185–204). Newbury Park, CA: Sage.

Yamamoto, J., & Kubota, M. (1983). The Japanese-American family. In G. J. Powell (Ed.), *The psychosocial development of minority group children* (pp. 237–247). New York: Brunner/Mazel.

5

HOME-SCHOOL PROCESSES IN DIVERSE ETHNIC GROUPS, SOCIAL CLASSES, AND FAMILY STRUCTURES

Sanford M. Dornbusch and
Philip L. Ritter

This chapter is a brief report on a lengthy series of studies of family-school relations in six northern California high schools and three Wisconsin high schools. These studies were initiated to help us understand the relative contributions of family structure and social status versus behaviors and interactions among students, their families, and peer groups. The size of the sample, ranging from 1,250 to 10,000 depending upon the variables to be studied, and the diversity of the population of high school students permitted an examination of ethnic, social class, and family structure differences. Group differences in the frequency of certain family behaviors and the relation of those behaviors to school outcomes were examined. Our hope was that similar family behaviors would have similar results across group boundaries, enabling school psychologists to develop interventions that can apply to diverse types of students and their families. These hopes were not completely realized; we will often report on group differences that demand differential interventions from school psychologists.

The authors of this paper are a sociologist and an anthropologist. Therefore, we believe our readers will trust us when we say that we have neither the desire nor the ability to specify appropriate treatments for students and their families. Our goal, daunting in itself, is to present the results of our studies in a way that encourages school psychologists, educators, and other mental health professionals to think realistically about the role of the school in dealing with adolescents and their families.

We studied high school students, but we believe that some of our findings apply to younger children. We are struck, for example, by the similarity of findings on parenting styles in early childhood and in adolescence. Often, there is a theoretical basis for our belief that these findings are broadly applicable, as in our discussion of attribution processes and parental reactions to grades. So, without making the claim that all our results apply across the age range, we urge our readers to consider their potential applicability to students in elementary, middle, and junior high schools.

Family Process and Statuses

We have studied the relation of family processes and family statuses to educational outcomes. Family processes refer to behaviors by family members and interactions within families, such as family decision making and parental involvement in schooling. Examples of family statuses include parent education level and family structure (e.g., single-parent, two-natural-parent, and step-parent families). A major goal of our approach is to show how the relation of various statuses to educational outcomes is mediated by family behaviors or processes that shape those outcomes.

The extensive literature that relates school performance to various statuses of the parents—parental education, family income, race and ethnic background, and family structure—produces a careful statistical portrait of education in our society, showing how educational performance is correlated with background variables such as ethnicity, family income, parental education (Jencks, Smith, Acland, Bane, Chen, Gintis, Heyns, & Michelson, 1972), or family structure (Hetherington, Featherman, & Camara, 1982). But what should we do with this knowledge?

Bronfenbrenner (1986) notes that these studies of social addresses (social statuses, such as parental education) should point to other lines of research. The status-attainment literature has revitalized the study of social mobility (Blau & Duncan, 1967), but more work is needed to identify the processes in family, school, and society that produce differences in status attainment.

When policymakers rely on a social-address perspective, there can be substantial negative consequences. We, as parents, educators, and members of our society, are selling short the majority of our children when we assume incorrectly that acquired and irrevocable intellectual advantages and disadvantages fall within lines demarcated by class, ethnicity, and household structure. An emphasis on social addresses is likely to perpetuate social inequality.

An alternative approach is to emphasize the role of family processes and behaviors, not family structure or social status. We believe knowledge about family processes and behavior, as well as information about how schools and families deal with each other, is needed. An understanding of which family behaviors are associated with better school performance is critical because this knowledge may provide suggestions of alternative

ways for families, children, and schools to relate to each other. With this knowledge base, less well-educated parents, single parents, stepparents, minority parents, and poorer parents could at least be aware of behaviors that more advantaged families, as well as the more successful among the less advantaged families, use more often with greater school success. The aim of this chapter is to diffuse knowledge of these behaviors to school psychologists, who are in a key position to influence both schools and families.

Samples

In 1985 data were collected from 7,836 students and 2,996 parents on processes in the family that related directly or indirectly to the level of high school performance by adolescents. Eighty-nine percent of the students in the six high schools participated in this study. This was not a random sample of individuals or schools. The sample should be considered the entire population of nonabsent students enrolled in the six schools. It is reasonable to argue that some of the students who are absent have characteristics not represented by that 89%. Some of those students may be nonrecorded dropouts, working, or in some other distinct group. Obtaining responses from these students warrants a more extensive and expensive methodology than was available for this work. Data were also collected from a sample of 307 teachers at the six schools.

The structural variables that we use include ethnicity, family structure, gender, and parental education (see Table 1). For most purposes, we grouped the various ethnic groups into Asian, Black, Hispanic, and non-Hispanic White, and Other. The family structures included two natural parents, single mother, single father, mother and stepfather, and father with stepmother. Socioeconomic status was measured by years of parental education, asked in eight categories ranging from 1, less than eighth grade, to 8, graduate or professional degree. The mean parental education, based on both parents when available, was 5.2, with the

TABLE 1
Characteristics of the 1985 Sample: Number of Cases

	Males		Females		Total	
	n	%	n	%	n	%
Ethnicity						
Asian	682	16.9	606	16.0	1288	16.4
Black	228	5.6	196	5.2	424	5.4
Hispanic	548	13.5	523	13.8	1071	13.7
Non-Hispanic White	2297	56.8	2232	58.9	4529	57.8
Other	233	5.8	141	3.7	373	4.8
TOTAL	4047		3789		7836	
Family Structure						
Two Natural Parents	2432	60.1	2241	59.1	4673	59.6
Single Mother	635	15.7	716	19.0	1351	17.2
Mother and Stepfather	321	7.9	367	9.7	688	8.8
Single Father	158	3.9	101	2.7	259	3.3
Father and Stepmother	158	3.9	114	3.1	272	3.4
Other	110	2.7	109	2.9	219	2.8
TOTAL	4047		3789		7836	

Note: Percentages add to less than 100% because the TOTAL rows include cases missing on Ethnicity or Family Structure

category 5 equal to some college beyond high school but not a 4-year degree. The ages of these high school students were mainly between 14 and 17 years, with a mean of 15.9.

In 1987, we began a new study using the same six schools plus three additional schools in Wisconsin (see Table 2). The new study included a longitudinal design, but for this chapter we only utilize the first year of data. The data were collected using the same ethnic, family-structure, gender, and social class variables as in 1985. With the addition of the Wisconsin

TABLE 2
Characteristics of the 1987 Sample: Number of Cases

	Males		Females		Total	
	n	%	n	%	n	%
Ethnicity						
Asian	805	16.0	739	14.6	1544	15.3
Black	425	8.5	521	10.3	945	9.4
Hispanic	852	17.0	847	16.8	1699	16.9
Non-Hispanic White	2616	52.2	2709	53.6	5325	52.9
Other	187	3.7	156	3.1	343	3.4
TOTAL	5016		5052		10068	
Family Structure						
Two Natural Parents	3010	60.0	2995	59.3	6005	59.6
Single Mother	829	16.5	961	19.0	1790	17.8
Mother and Stepfather	407	8.1	516	10.2	923	9.2
Single Father	176	3.5	124	2.5	300	3.0
Father and Stepmother	178	3.5	114	2.3	292	2.9
Other	333	6.6	288	5.7	621	6.2
TOTAL	5016		5052		10068	

Note: Percentages add to less than 100% because the TOTAL rows include cases missing on Ethnicity or Family Structure

schools, the number of cases was expanded to over 10,000.

In addition, in the section on Family Decision Making, we refer to an earlier study using the National Health Examination Survey (NHES). The NHES Cycle III was a national probability study of youths aged 12 to 18.

The research on which we base this chapter was not a product of our work alone. Our collaborators are too numerous to mention in detail. But we must note the signal contributions of Bradford Brown at the University of Wisconsin, Laurence Steinberg at Temple University, and P. Herbert Leiderman at Stanford. The collegial atmosphere they shaped has markedly assisted our own work, and their work itself is reflected in the findings below.

FAMILY PROCESS VARIABLES

In this chapter, four family process variables: parental reactions to grades, family decision making, parenting styles, and parental participation in school activities will be discussed, followed by a sociological and anthropological perspective on the improvement of home-school relationships. It is not our intent here to present the relevant statistical analyses supporting our findings, but to summarize those findings in a general way for practitioners and educators. The more technically oriented reader may wish to consult our journal articles (Dornbusch, Carlsmith, Bushwall, Ritter, Leiderman, Hastorf, & Gross, 1985; Dornbusch, Ritter, Leiderman, Roberts, & Fraleigh, 1987; Dornbusch, Ritter, Mont-Reynaud, & Chen, 1990).

Parental Reaction to Grades

Attributional analysis. Extrinsic reinforcement is defined as satisfaction that is provided independently of the satisfaction derived from engaging in the task itself. Bem (1967, 1972), Kelley (1967), and Kelley and Michela (1980) explain that a person's motivation to engage in a task is determined by whether they perceive the source of the motivation to

participate in the task is the self or is extrinsic to the self. As Ross (1976) points out, it is the person's own view of the source of the motivation, rather than the true source, that is critical.

Experimental research on preschoolers, school-age children, and adults has indicated that expected extrinsic rewards diminish subsequent interest in a task. This is in contrast to unrewarded activities, which do not decrease later interest (Lepper, 1983). These experimental results are best explained using attribution theory. Extrinsic reinforcement takes the place of reinforcement that is inherent in the task itself. An individual who finds a task rewarding in itself is already rewarded for participation in the activity. The actor is responding to the source of the stimuli. In situations where the actor is already interested in the task and there is no other source of the stimuli, the actor will internally attribute the source of the stimuli. If, however, the individual must respond to an outside or extrinsic source, then the individual's self-reinforcement is replaced or discounted by the extrinsic reinforcement. This use of extrinsic reinforcement is termed over-justification (Lepper, Greene, & Nisbett, 1973).

Do school children respond to extrinsic reinforcement in a fashion similar to that predicted by experimental research, or do other factors override the predicted effects of extrinsic rewards and punishment? The study presented here uses the 1985 data to field test the effects of extrinsic reinforcements by parents of high school students in response to their children's grades.

Measurement. Each student was given a list of 25 possible parental reactions to good grades and poor grades, and asked in which ways his or her parents responded (see Table 3). The possible responses were scored 1 = "never"; 2 = "sometimes"; and 3 = "usually." The items were combined into scores representing five parental reactions: Extrinsic Punishment, Extrinsic Rewards, Encouragement, Uninvolvement, and Negative Emotion. For each set of parents, five scores, one for each parental reaction, were calculated by

TABLE 3
Parental Reactions to Grades

When you get a GOOD grade, which of the following reactions do you get from your parents or guardians? (Darken one choice for each line.)

	Never	Sometimes	Usually
They praise me	O	O	O
They give me a gift	O	O	O
They increase my allowance	O	O	O
They give me more freedom to make my own decisions	O	O	O
They let me stay out later at night	O	O	O
They give me fewer restrictions	O	O	O
They tell me I should do even better	O	O	O
They say my other grades should be as good	O	O	O
They consider it natural and do nothing special	O	O	O
They don't know about it	O	O	O
They don't care	O	O	O

When you get a POOR grade, which of the following reactions do you get from your parents or guardians? (Darken one choice for each line.)

	Never	Sometimes	Usually
They get upset with me	O	O	O
They reduce my allowance	O	O	O
They take away my freedom to make my own decisions	O	O	O
They say I can't stay out as late at night	O	O	O
I have more restrictions	O	O	O
I am grounded	O	O	O
I lose the use of the car	O	O	O
They make my life miserable	O	O	O
They make me feel guilty	O	O	O
They encourage me to try harder	O	O	O
They offer to help me	O	O	O
They do nothing special	O	O	O
They don't know about it	O	O	O
They don't care	O	O	O

taking the mean in each category. Definitions for the five parental reactions are:

Extrinsic Punishment included six possible responses to poor grades: reducing the allowance, giving the student less decision-making freedom, not letting the student stay out late, increasing restrictions, losing use of the car, and grounding.

Extrinsic Rewards for good grades consisted of giving gifts, increasing the allowance, giving more freedom to make decisions, allowing the student to stay out later at night, and fewer restrictions.

Encouragement consisted of three parental responses: praise for good grades, the use of encouragement to try harder, and offers to help in response to poor grades.

Expression of *Negative Emotions*

included making the child miserable, getting upset, and making the child feel guilty; and for good grades included: other grades should be as good and the student should do even better. The score's emphasis on expressing negative emotions derives from our belief that almost all parents are bothered by poor performance, but only some parents overtly express their displeasure.

Uninvolvement included: not knowing and not caring about good or poor grades.

Results. Parental reactions to good grades and to poor grades fit into a simple pattern. In general, parental encouragement, as measured by the use of encouragement, praise, and offers to help, was associated with higher grades. The other forms of parental reaction tend uniformly to be associated with lower grades: the use of extrinsic rewards and extrinsic punishments, the expression of negative emotion, and lack of parental involvement. The strength of the relation between the parental reaction and grades differed from group to group. For example, non-Hispanic Whites had stronger correlations between grades and parental reactions than did Blacks.

Although this is a cross-sectional study, we do have grades over a 2-year span for a subset of the entire sample. Changes in grades are negatively associated with the use of extrinsic rewards and punishments, although more strongly negatively associated with extrinsic punishments. Thus, students whose parents used extrinsic rewards and, especially punishments, tended to have lower grades 2 years later than students whose parents did not use such reactions to grades.

In addition, when effort is the dependent variable, we find a similar though weaker relationship between parental use of extrinsic rewards and punishments and lower levels of student effort. For example, the mean amount of time spent on homework goes down for both male and female students as parents use higher levels of extrinsic reinforcers.

The only parental reaction that is associated with improved academic performance is encouragement—praise for good grades, encouragement to try harder, and offers to help with poor grades. Thus, the use of encouragement is consistent with over-justification's emphasis on internal motivation. Encouragement supports internal motivation because it assigns responsibility for further actions to the student. For those students whose grades are below C on the average, there is bad news. No parental response to grades appears to be associated with an increase in grades.

It is particularly noteworthy that "offers to help" is associated with an improvement in grades, whereas in separate analyses we found that actually "helping" with homework is associated with lower grades. Many parents respond to poor grades by enthusiastically assist-ing in the performance of homework by the student. That well-meant behavior may have, as a secondary result, the removal of control from the student. If, on the other hand, the student is the one who decides whether and when the parent is to assist in homework, responsibility is assigned, once again, to the student. To the extent that encouragement offers the child support and guidance, there is an increased probability of the child internalizing the goal of the parent.

Finally, the relationship between time spent on homework and grades is lower for students whose parents use either extrinsic reward or punishment than for students whose parents do not use such reactions. This suggests a lower level of internal motivation, an apparently lower investment of attention and energy while doing homework, as predicted by the over-justification approach.

Discussion. We find that for both sexes the expected relations between grades and parental reactions are generally present in each ethnic group, type of family, and parental-education group. It appears that within every social group the over-justification approach correctly predicts that giving extrinsic rewards and punishments does not lead to increased motivation. As predicted, extrinsic rewards and punishments are associated with low grades and with a decline in grades over a 2-year period. The only parental response that works to improve grades is a low-key one (e.g., encouragement, praise, and offers to help). That low-key response helps the student to internalize the values of the parents without exercising sufficient constraint or pressure to reduce internal motivation.

There are some important qualifications associated with these results. This study is not longitudinal. A more accurate test of the over-justification approach would include an initial measure of intrinsic interest, followed by some measure of parental response to grades, and finally followed by a later measure of interest. Experimental work has focused on some measure of intrinsic interest or motivation to participate in the selected activity. This study lacks any objective behavioral measure of such interest.

We did not attempt a direct measurement of parental reactions to grades. Students were asked to report what their parents do in response to poor and good grades. The students, of course, may be making observations that are highly subjective. However, this subjectivity may be an advantage. It may be more important to measure the student's perception of the parental reaction rather than measuring the objective parental reaction.

Our study does have the advantage of a very large and differentiated sample. Findings from numerous subgroups of that heterogeneous sample provide general support for our conclusions. In particular, these findings suggest the presence of an underlying set of relationships as predicted by the over-justification approach. It is reassuring that the results of laboratory experimentation by psychologists can be directly linked to real-life processes of considerable importance.

Our data suggest that for students who are doing very poorly in high school, encouragement by parents is not enough. Our best advice to parents faced with such low grades would be to accept the view that parental behaviors alone are not likely to make a positive difference. This is a point of possible intervention by school psychologists. The school psychologist could either participate in person or perhaps find a friendly teacher, administrator, or counselor to join the parents in a partnership to improve the academic performance of the troubled student.

Family Decision Making

Previous studies. A second family process variable of interest is family decision making, which Dornbusch and colleagues (Dornbusch et al., 1985) have shown to be related to adolescent deviance. They found a powerful tendency for single-parent families to permit adolescent youths earlier control over their own behavior in such decision-making areas as choice of friends and clothes, spending money, and hour to be home at night.

Permitting such early decision making by the youth alone is an understandable response by an overloaded single parent. However, despite its expediency, too early autonomy has an unfortunate consequence—an increased probability that the youth will engage in deviant acts (e.g., run away from home or be arrested).

This study, which predates the two family and school surveys, came from the National Health Examination Survey, a nationwide probability sample of youths aged 12 to 18 which included some information on school performance. In this sample of American youth, there was a higher rate of deviance among children in single-parent families than in two-parent families. Children in single-parent families also averaged lower performance on a number of tests of cognitive performance, including teacher judgments of the intellectual ability and achievement level of the student. Within each of the three levels of social class, children in single-parent households and children in stepparent households were not doing worse than children in two-parent families on IQ tests or achievement tests; yet, these students showed a tendency to be rated lower by their teachers on intellectual ability and performance than were students from two-natural-parent households. Further analysis of this surprising difference showed that the lower ratings from their teachers received by adolescents from single-parent homes were associated with the level of adolescent deviance in those single-parent households. Following that lead, we examined whether the form of family decision making for adolescents was related to school performance as measured by grades.

The current study. In 1987, we examined adolescent and parental participation in decision making, and the relation of forms of decision making to adolescent school performance and deviant behavior. Previous research suggested that the process of family decision making is related to adolescent deviance (Dornbusch et al., 1985) and grades in high school (Dornbusch et al., 1990). The present study investigates whether there are differences in the frequency of each form of decision making among youth from different backgrounds, ethnic groups, and family structures. Second, we examine the differential associations of these forms of decision making with two adolescent outcomes (school grades and deviant behavior) among youth from diverse backgrounds. Third, we ask whether the granting of autonomy to youth has more negative consequences in domains that are typically controlled by parents, such as curfew. Fourth, we relate forms of decision making to the extent to which adolescents believe they would emulate their parents. This provides an indirect measure of the extent to which adolescents find admirable the granting of early autonomy by their parents. Finally, forms of family decision making are related to other family processes, such as parenting styles, parental involvement in schooling, monitoring, and family organization. Thus, decision making is put into context with other processes that potentially affect adolescent outcomes.

Measurement. Forms of family decision making can be conceptualized as varying along a dimension of parental control and youth autonomy. During adolescence, family decision making concerns such issues as curfew, school program, and style of dress. By adolescence, youth may have considerable autonomy and make decisions on such matters by themselves, or parents may make the decisions without youth having any input. Alternatively, both the parents and the adolescent may discuss the choices. When there is discussion of issues, youths may have the last word, or parents may retain final authority.

In addition to the four decision-making arenas (choice of friends, how to spend money, choice of clothes, and how late to stay out) studied in our earlier work (Dornbusch et al., 1985, 1990), we expanded the scope of this study to include nine additional arenas: (a) what classes I take in school, (b) what I watch on TV, (c) how much time I spend with friends, (d) whether I have a part-time job, (e) at what age I can leave school, (f) whether I can drink alcohol, (g) when I

can start dating, (h) whether I should go out for a school sport, and (i) whether I should be in other school activities.

We measured the frequency of three mutually exclusive types of decision making: Discuss (regardless of who decides), Youth Alone (decision making in the absence of discussion), and Parent Alone (decision making without discussion). Each variable was first calculated as the number of decisions of a certain type (e.g., Discuss, Youth Alone, Parent Alone) in the 13 decision-making arenas. This number was then converted to a percentage of all the decisions reported. For example, a particular youth might answer for 13 arenas and report 54% as Youth Alone, 31% as Discuss, and 15% as Parent Alone.

In our previous study, the age of the adolescent was strongly associated with the forms of adolescent decision making (Dornbusch et al., 1985). The number of decisions made by Parent Alone decreased, and those made by the Youth Alone increased, with the increasing age of the adolescent. Discussion between parents and adolescent in decision making displays a different pattern, serving as a transitional style prior to the youth's assuming complete autonomy. To control for differences in age and make comparisons among social groups, we used the residual score after fitting a regression line based on age. The residuals reported represented the amount in percentage of decisions made that a youth differs from his or her expected score based on age. Thus the age of the youth is controlled. A negative score means fewer decisions of that form than expected, and a positive score means more decisions of that form than expected.

It is important that the school psychologist realize the relative nature of the variables we have used to measure family decision making. A 12-year-old may make many fewer autonomous decisions than a 17-year-old, and yet the 12-year-old may get a higher score on Youth Alone decision making. The score for each adolescent reflects the level of decision making compared to the mean for individuals of exactly the same age. Thus, it is the community context and the age of the adolescent that permits calculation of the residual for a specific student.

Results. After controlling for gender, ethnicity, level of parental education, and family structure we found:

1. Unilateral adolescent decision making (i.e., Youth Alone Decision Making) was associated with poor school grades.

2. Bilateral decision making by parents and youth (i.e., Joint Decision Making) was consistently associated with higher grades.

3. There was no consistent association between unilateral parent decision making (i.e., Parent Alone) and students' grades.

4. Gender differences were consistent in all ethnic groups: Female adolescents had less autonomy, participated more in discussions, and were subject to greater parental control than males.

5. There were social class differences in the frequency of forms of decision making. Youths from lower social class backgrounds reported more autonomy, more parental control, and less discussion than did youths from higher social class backgrounds. Better educated parents are far more likely to explain, discuss, and encourage dialogue with their adolescent children than are less educated parents.

6. The several analyses further revealed that, for both male and female adolescents, regardless of ethnicity, family type, or class background, early autonomy in decision making tended to be associated with increased adolescent deviance and poor school performance. Discussion in family decision making was associated with better grades and less deviance.

The relations between Parent Alone decision making and our outcome variables showed unexpected complexity. Although the positive association of Discussion and the negative relation of autonomy are evident in virtually all

subgroups of adolescents (gender, parent education, ethnicity, and family structure), the relations of unilateral parent decision making are not as clear. That is, Parent Alone decision making seemed to confer a slight advantage to particular subgroups in controlling deviance. In particular, Parent Alone decision making showed a tendency among males to be associated with lower rates of adolescent deviance. The findings are less clear for deviance among females.

Discussion. We cannot discount the social and cultural context in recommending particular forms of decision making for optimal adolescent development. It does appear, however, that too early autonomy clearly has more negative results in terms of school performance and deviance than does parental control. Discussion, which is associated with authoritative parenting, is clearly the best course. In choosing between the remaining forms of decision making, parents are advised not to abdicate their control in favor of youth autonomy—it is best to err on the side of parent control.

When we asked adolescents whether they would act like their parents when the adolescents, in turn, became parents, it was Discuss, not Youth Alone decision making, that was associated with adolescents' desiring to emulate their parents. These data suggest that, contrary to popular belief, youth do not truly want autonomy in the early adolescent years. What they do want is fairness, respect, and parental involvement in choices affecting their lives.

Parenting Style

Another central family process variable, drawn from developmental psychology, is parenting style. We tested a reformulation of the early work of Baumrind (1973) in the context of adolescent school performance. Baumrind's conceptualization focused on parenting practices for young children. Our study is unusual in that it extends Baumrind's typology of parenting styles (authoritarian, permissive, authoritative) to a large and diverse sample of adolescents, and it uses high school grades as the criterion variable (Dornbusch et al., 1987).

Baumrind's conceptualization. The authoritarian style of parenting is characterized by parents' attempts to shape, control, and evaluate the behavior and attitudes of their children in accordance with an absolute set of standards. Parents emphasize obedience, respect for authority, work tradition, and the preservation of order. Verbal give-and-take between parent and child is discouraged. Baumrind's studies found that such a mode of family interaction was associated with low levels of independence and social responsibility for children. Baumrind described the authoritarian pattern, somewhat more formally, as being high in demandingness on the part of the parents and low in parental responsiveness to the child.

A second pattern is permissive parenting, in which parents are tolerant and accepting toward the child's impulses, use as little punishment as possible, make few demands for mature behavior, and allow considerable self-regulation by the child. Baumrind found that preschool children of permissive parents were immature, lacked impulse control and self-reliance, and evidenced a lack of social responsibility and independence. In our current studies, permissive parenting is broken down into two subcategories: neglectful parenting and ideologically permissive parenting. Ideologically permissive parents are high in warmth and low in demandingness, whereas neglectful parents are low in both. In general, the pattern of findings for these two kinds of permissive parents is similar, but there is a slight tendency for neglectful parenting to result in more negative outcomes.

Authoritative parenting, the third type described by Baumrind, contains the following elements: an expectation of mature behavior from the child and clear setting of standards by the parents; firm enforcement of rules and standards, using commands and sanctions when necessary; encouragement of the child's independence and individuality; open communication between parents and children, with encouragement of verbal give-and-take, and recognition of the rights of both parents and children. Children of authoritative parents tend to be more socially responsible, more independent than other children, and higher in social and cognitive competence (Baumrind, 1983).

Results. In our study of the relationship between parenting style and school performance as measured by high school grades, we found:

1. For both boys and girls, grades were negatively related to both authoritarian and permissive parenting, whereas authoritative parenting was associated with higher grades.

2. The negative relation of authoritarian parenting to grades was the strongest of the three relations.

3. There were no important fluctuations among age groups in the associations between parenting style and grades. All 30 correlations (three measures for five age groups and two sexes) were in the expected direction. The parenting styles consistently relate to grades across different social groups.

4. There were ethnic differences in the strength of the correlations between parenting styles and grades. For Asians, the correlations of grades with both the authoritative and the permissive styles were near zero. For Hispanic males, authoritarian parenting showed almost no relation to grades, even though the relation was strongly negative among Hispanic females. Among Non-Hispanic Whites, our largest ethnic group, and Blacks, our smallest, all correlations were as expected. Asians appear to be the ethnic groups for whom our topology applies least well. Although our approach does not seem to be limited in application to only a single ethnic group, data from Asians appear to offer clear support only for the relation of authoritarian parenting to grades.

5. We sought to determine whether the forms of decision making were associated with the general styles of parenting covered in the previous section. The data

were exactly as hypothesized. Discuss was most positively correlated with an authoritative parenting style, Youth Alone was most positively correlated with the permissive style, and Parent Alone was most positively correlated with an authoritarian style.

6. Within the smaller sample of students for whom we know the education for their parents, the data support the view that the parenting-style typology applies fairly well across the social classes. Across four ethnic groups, three parental-education groups, two sexes, and three styles of parenting, the data supported the hypothesized relations between parenting style and grades.

7. We also found that diverse family structures did not limit the applicability of the relation between grades and parenting style.

Discussion. The Baumrind typology was developed from the intensive analysis of parenting in largely middle-class, White families. In our diverse sample, the data indicate that, across ethnic groups and social classes, authoritarian and permissive styles were associated with lower grades, and an authoritative style was associated with higher grades. Although the predictive power of Baumrind's typology differs from group to group, the conceptualization she developed from a largely middle-class, White sample does appear to have broad applicability within American society.

Nevertheless, our data show clearly that the success of Asian children in our public schools cannot be explained adequately in terms of the parenting styles we have studied. Compared to Whites, Asian high school students of both sexes reported that their families were higher in the index of authoritarian parenting and lower in the index of authoritative parenting. Yet, counter to the general association of such parenting patterns to grades, the Asians as a group were receiving high grades in school. In addition, although authoritarian parenting was significantly associated with lower grades among Asians, there was no signif-

icant relation between grades and the other two parenting styles. We end with more questions than answers in examining Asian parenting practices and school performance.

It is impressive that the diverse measures of parenting styles were associated with grades across a wide variety of social groups. The two sexes, the five age groups, the five types of family structure, and the three parental-education groups all exhibited the same predicted pattern. The families that were high in authoritarian or permissive parenting tended to have students who did less well in high school, and the families that were high in authoritative parenting had children who got higher grades in school. There were major differences between the sexes, among the age groups, among the family structures, and among the parental-education groups in the extent to which the different styles of parenting were employed. Yet, regardless of each group's mean scores on the parenting styles, the relation of each style to school performance exhibited the predicted pattern within each group.

Clark's (1983) study of successful parenting practices among poor Black families produced findings that are consonant with our results on the relation of authoritative parenting to school performance. In the family experience of successful poor Black children, Clark found more frequent dialogues between parents and children, parental encouragement of academic pursuits, clear and consistent limits for children's behavior, warm and nurturing interactions with parents, and consistent monitoring of how children spend their time.

In their review of parenting styles and school success, Steinberg, Elmen, and Mounts (1989) state that various studies converge in finding that parental authoritativeness is associated with school success among adolescents (e.g., Dornbusch et al., 1987; Hill, 1980). Indeed, authoritativeness is a correlate of competence during adolescence more generally and of adolescent achievement in school more specifically (Maccoby & Martin, 1983). They note that the benefits

of various components of parental authoritativeness have been demonstrated
across a wide variety of samples, including minority and nonminority youngsters
from affluent as well as disadvantaged
backgrounds (e.g., Clark, 1983; Dornbusch et al., 1987).

Parental Participation in School Activities

We examined the relationship between parental participation and school
performance of high school students
using two sets of questions. The questions
were: "How often does each of your
parents participate in the programs
planned by your high school for parents
or adults?" and "How often does each of
your parents attend high school activities
in which you participate (sports, music,
clubs, etc.)?" The mean response to each
question was related to school performance and differences among social
groups.

Results of student survey. We found:

1. As expected, participation by parents in school activities is associated with
higher grades.

2. Both non-Hispanic Whites and
Blacks have a higher level of participation
than Hispanics (perhaps because of language problems).

3. Asians have levels of participation
comparable to Whites, but attendance at
school functions is lower.

4. For both scores, parents of Asian
females participate more than parents of
Asian males.

5. Within family types, the results are
clear. Low-education parents are much
less likely to participate in school functions than are mid- or higher-education
parents.

6. Two-parent families have the highest level of participation.

Results of teacher survey. We surveyed 307 teachers at six northern California schools. We asked teachers ques-

tions about their contact with parents,
both actual and desired. We found:

1. Teachers believed that they initiated more contacts with parents than
parents initiated with them. Yet, 63% of
high school teachers in the study reported initiating contact with "almost
none" or "a few" parents. There is,
however, a substantial minority of teachers, 15%, who report initiating contact
with "most" or "almost all" parents.

2. Almost 80% of teachers agree that
many parents are uncomfortable or feel
out of place at school. A few interviews
with teachers and parents suggest that
minority parents are most likely to feel
hesitant and uncomfortable about interacting with teachers and the school. This
produces a situation that requires
thoughtful remedial action. Minority parents of average students are not likely to
interact with school personnel, nor are
they encouraged to do so. Although the
need may be great, minority parents of
average students are unlikely to initiate
contact with teachers.

3. A high proportion of teachers
indicated that they would prefer more
contact with parents of children with
learning difficulties and with parents of
children making little effort. Fewer teachers want more contact with parents active
in school affairs, parents of children
doing outstanding work, parents interested in helping their children, and
parents of average students; about half
the teachers would prefer more contact
with parents of children with disciplinary
problems.

4. Most alarming is that teachers
report little contact with parents of
average students, and, in fact, do not
prefer more contact with these parents.
This largest group of parents has little
contact with teachers; and teachers, who
operate under the present system, do not
want to increase their commitment to
such contact.

Discussion. Fewer than 29% of all
high school parents believed that it was
no longer appropriate for them to be

involved in the education of their children. It is obvious that a reservoir of parental energy and commitment exists that has not been tapped by American high schools. However, it is not likely that dramatic changes will occur with respect to parental involvement or parent-teacher contact. Results of our survey suggest that teachers and schools are not yet ready for a massive change in family-school relations. But the difficulty of the task in the short term should not inhibit the beginning of a reorientation of educational policy.

It should not be expected that overburdened teachers will change their practices. The present organization of schools does not encourage a high level of parent-school relations. It is up to educational theorists, researchers, and administrators to consider ways to bring more parents into the active school community.

SUMMARY: ANTHROPOLOGICAL AND SOCIOLOGICAL PERSPECTIVES

Much of differential school success and failure is blamed on socioeconomic, ethnic, and other social differences. Even if they were to try, there is not much that schools and practitioners could do to change their students' ethnicity, family income, parental marital status, or parental education level. However, our studies have suggested that family processes are more important than social statuses in influencing school success. In other words, what parents and families do is even more important than what families and parents are. For each of the four examples of family behaviors discussed in this chapter, there is some possibility of schools in partnership with the parents influencing changes in desirable directions. Many parents are eager for advice and will be influenced by information, whether given to them through newsletters or in direct communication by individuals associated with the school.

Our study of parental response to grades suggested that the only responses that tended to improve grades were low-key ones: encouragement, praise, and offers to help. Such responses help the student to internalize the values of the parents without exercising sufficient constraint or pressure to reduce internal motivation. For high school students whose grades are below C on the average, no simple parental response to grades appears to be associated with an increase in grades. Our best advice to parents faced with such low grades would be to work with the school psychologist, a friendly teacher, administration, or counselor to join in a partnership to try to improve the academic performance of the troubled student.

Decision making was another behavior that related to school performance. As noted by Margaret Mead (1928), making decisions is the major challenge for youth in American society. Youth in modern societies confront more choices than their adolescent counterparts of other times and places. For the adolescent, how choices come to be made is as important as what the choices are. Research should continue to address the implications of parenting processes, including family decision making, for optimal adolescent development in today's world. The relations we have found between decision making and educational performance are consistent with an earlier study by Epstein and McPartland (1977), who found that greater participation by the student in family decision making was associated with more positive personality development and better coping skills in school.

Closely related to decision making and also associated with school performance was parenting style. A major difficulty of much of the previous research including our own studies is their lack of longitudinal follow-up. As Steinberg and colleagues (Steinberg, Brown, Cazmarek, Cider, & Lazarro, 1988) put it, the combination of warmth, psychological autonomy, and behavioral restrictiveness are strongly linked to adolescent competence. Steinberg, Elmen, and Mounts (1989) did a longitudinal study and corroborated the previous cross-sectional findings with longitudinal data. Their results call into question the notion that parental authoritativeness merely follows from, rather than precedes, the development of competence in children (e.g., Lewis, 1981). It appears that parents of adolescents are constantly shifting their style of behavior, and that an adventitious movement toward authoritative parenting is correlated with positive school outcomes. Thus, rather than viewing parenting style as a given, school psychologists should consider measures to encourage authoritative parenting of children.

We also found that parental participation in school activities was associated with higher achievement. However, our teacher survey suggested that the present organization of schools does not encourage a high level of parent-school relations. Schools and school personnel need to work harder to bring more parents into the active school community. For example, schools involved in our study tried innovations such as offering day care for younger siblings so that parents could attend programs in the evenings, and special programs were offered in other languages for parents who could not speak English.

If nothing is done, who will be harmed? Our data indicate that the lowest level of family involvement in school programs and processes is among the parents of average students, minority parents, and in stepfamilies and single-parent families. Given these findings, failure to change parent-school relations will perpetuate inequality.

REFERENCES

Baumrind, D. (1973). The development of instrumental competence through socialization. In A. Pick (Ed.), *Child psychology: Minnesota symposium on child psychology* (Vol. 7, pp. 3–46). Hillsdale, NJ: Lawrence Erlbaum and Associates.

Baumrind, D. (1983). Rejoinder to Lewis's reinterpretation of parental firm control effects: Are authoritative families really harmonious? *Psychological Bulletin, 94,* 132–142.

Bem, D. J. (1967). An alternative interpretation of cognitive dissonance phenomena. *Psychological Review, 74,* 183–200.

Bem, D. J. (1972). Self-perception theory. In L. Berkowitz (Ed.), *Advances in experimental social psychology* (pp. 1–62). New York: Academic Press.

Blau, P., & Duncan, O. D. (1967). *The American occupational structure.* New York: Wiley and Sons.

Bronfenbrenner, U. (1986). Ecology of the family as a context for human development: Research perspectives. *Developmental Psychology, 22,* 723–742.

Clark, R. M. (1983). *Family life and school achievement: Why poor Black children succeed or fail.* Chicago: University of Chicago Press.

Dornbusch, S. M., Carlsmith, J. M., Bushwall, S. J., Ritter, P. L., Leiderman, H., Hastorf, A. H., & Gross, R. T. (1985, April). Single parents, extended households, and the control of adolescents. *Child Development, 56,* 326–341.

Dornbusch, S. M., Ritter, P. L., Leiderman, P. H., Roberts, D. F., & Fraleigh, M. J. (1987). The relation of parenting style of adolescent school performance. *Child Development, 58,* 1244–1257.

Dornbusch, S. M., Ritter, P. L., Mont-Reynaud, R., & Chen, Z. (1990). Family decision-making and academic performance in a diverse high school population. *Journal of Adolescent Research, 5*(2), 143–160.

Epstein, J. L., & McPartland, J. M. (1977). *Family and school interactions and main effects of affective outcomes* (Report No. 235). Baltimore, MD: Johns Hopkins University, Center for the Study of Social Organization of Schools. (ERIC Document Reproduction Service No. ED 151 713)

Hetherington, E. M., Featherman, D. L., & Camara, K. A. (1982). *Cognitive performance, school behavior, and achievement of children from one-parent households.* Washington, DC: National Institute of Education.

Hill, J. P. (1980). The family. In M. Johnson (Ed.), *Toward adolescence, the middle school years* (pp. 32–55). Chicago: University of Chicago Press.

Jencks, C., Smith, M., Acland, H., Bane, M. J., Chen, D., Gintis, H., Heyns, B., & Michelson, S. (1972). *Inequality: A reassessment of the effect of family and schooling in America.* New York: Basic Books.

Kelley, H. H. (1967). Attribution theory in social psychology. In D. Levine (Ed.), *Nebraska Symposium on Motivation* (Vol. 15, pp. 192–238). Lincoln, NE: University of Nebraska Press.

Kelley, H. H., & Michela, J. L. (1980). Attribution theory and research. *Annual Review of Psychology, 31,* 457–501.

Lepper, M. R. (1983). Extrinsic reward and intrinsic motivation. Implications for the classroom. In J. M. Levine & M. C. Wang (Eds.), *Teacher and student perceptions: Implications for learning* (pp. 281–317). Hillsdale, NJ: Lawrence Erlbaum and Associates.

Lepper, M. R., Greene, D., & Nisbett, R. E. (1973).

Undermining children's intrinsic interest with extrinsic reward: A test of the "over-justification" hypothesis. *Journal of Personality and Social Psychology, 28,* 129–137.

Lewis, C. (1981). The effects of parental firm control: A reinterpretation of findings. *Psychological Bulletin, 90,* 547–563.

Maccoby, E. E., & Martin, J. M. (1983). Socialization in the context of the family: Parent-child interaction. In E. M. Hetherington & P. H. Mussen (Eds.), Handbook of child psychology: Vol. 4. *Socialization, personality, and social development* (pp. 1–101). New York: John Wiley and Sons.

Mead, M. (1928). *Coming of age in Samoa.* New York: William Morrow.

Ross, M. (1976). The self-perception of intrinsic motivation. In J. H. Harvey, W. J. Ickes, & R. F. Kidd (Eds.), *New directions in attribution research* (Vol. 1, pp. 121–142). Hillsdale, NJ: Lawrence Erlbaum and Associates.

Steinberg, L., Brown, B., Cazmarek, N., Cider, M., & Lazarro, C. (1988). *Noninstructional influences on high school student achievement.* Madison, WI: National Center on Effective Secondary Schools, University of Wisconsin.

Steinberg, L., Elmen, J., & Mounts, N. (1989). *Authoritative parenting, psychosocial maturity, and academic success among adolescents.* Unpublished manuscript.

6

PARENT EDUCATION AS A MEANS FOR IMPROVING THE SCHOOL ACHIEVEMENT OF LOW-INCOME AFRICAN-AMERICAN CHILDREN

Craig L. Frisby

Any serious attempt to draw general principles from research on educational practices related to low-income African-American children and their parents must first address some difficult fundamental questions. Why not simply discuss parent education as a means for improving the school achievement of children in general, without regard to ethnic group or economic status? What are the salient issues surrounding African-American children and families that deserve special consideration? Are cultural differences between African-American children and other groups so wide as to require separate principles for understanding the effects of parent education on school achievement?

Throughout this chapter, these questions will be addressed by: (a) presenting some general information relevant to African-American children, with particular emphasis on research related to their school achievement; (b) discussing different interpretations of and issues involved in this research; and (c) discussing various findings within the parent education literature that attempt to address these concerns. For the purposes of this discussion, the group designated as "African-American" does not include Haitian immigrants (Jorge, 1982) or black Cubans (Dixon, 1986).

AFRICAN-AMERICAN CHILDREN AND SCHOOL ACHIEVEMENT

According to the U.S. Bureau of the Census, roughly 14–20% of American children under age 18 belonged to families receiving annual incomes below official poverty levels between the years 1970 to 1987. Although between 9–17% of white children existed below official poverty levels during these years, the figures for African-American children range from 39–47% (U.S. Bureau of the Census, 1990). A large percentage of the African-American poor in the United States are concentrated in large urban areas (e.g., New York, Los Angeles, Chicago, Detroit, and Philadelphia).

Although whites constitute a majority of the poor population in absolute numbers, many of the poverty-related problems are disproportionately distributed between whites and blacks. For example, blacks are more likely than whites to be arrested and imprisoned for various crimes (murder, manslaughter, robbery, rape) as well as to become victims of such crimes (Wilson, 1987). The most recent national statistics indicate that blacks have an unemployment rate that is more than twice as high as that of whites. Black children are three times more likely than white children to grow up in female-headed households with no spouse, and are nearly four times more likely than whites to be born to an unmarried mother (U.S. Bureau of the Census, 1990). In addition, a higher proportion of black families relative to white families exist on welfare (Wilson, 1987).

The subset of African-American families whose lives are most victimized by these problems is represented by a cohesive group that is clearly distinguishable from the lifestyles of mainstream black and white Americans. Wilson (1987) uses the term "black underclass" to describe this group, whose conditions are most sharply defined when contrasted with black urban communities prior to 1960:

> [I]nner-city communities prior to 1960 exhibited the features of social organization-including a sense of community, positive neighborhood identification, and explicit norms and sanctions against aberrant behavior. . . . In the earlier years, the black middle and working classes were confined by restrictive covenants to communities also inhabited by the lower class; [however] their very presence provided stability to inner-city neighborhoods and reinforced and perpetuated mainstream patterns of norms and behavior. . . . Today's ghetto neighborhoods are populated almost exclusively by the most disadvantaged segments of the black urban community. . . . Included in this group are individuals who lack training and skills and either experience longterm unemployment or are not members of the labor force, individuals who are engaged in street crime and other forms of aberrant behavior, and families that experience long-term spells of poverty and/or welfare dependency. These are the populations to which I refer when I speak of the *underclass* [emphasis added]. (pp. 3, 7–8)

Within the field of education, there has been much concern over the relatively poorer school achievement of African-American children, particularly those from the black underclass as described by Wilson. For the purposes of this chapter, the term "achievement" includes a number of domains relevant to school performance: standardized achievement test performance, promotion and graduation rates, mastery of specific academic material, educational aspirations, achievement motivation, academic self-esteem, and school attendance.

Achievement test performance. Recent figures compiled by the National Assessment of Educational Progress (a national education research group mandated by Congress to develop curriculum objectives and report data on student performance across various learning areas) show that blacks underperform national averages in all academic areas (e.g., science, mathematics, reading, writing) across all years for which data are available. For each age group tested, the gap between the performance of blacks and the national average tends to widen as the skills within each academic area become more complex (National Center for Education Statistics, 1989). In addition, recent figures for the annual Scholastic Aptitude Test (SAT) averages in years 1975–1988 show that blacks have consistently scored below national averages by about 100 points in both Verbal and Mathematics subtests (National Center for Education Statistics, 1989). For an overview of large scale studies chronicling racial differences in tests of achievement, information, and educational attainment, interested readers are encouraged to consult Humphreys (1988).

Other achievement problems. African-American children are overrepresented in vocational and general tracks, as well as in compensatory education programs (Oakes, 1985). In one survey of blacks in high school, 51% reported being registered in vocational tracks as compared to 34% of white students. Rowan (1989) conducted an extensive review of the research literature on the school achievement of black males, which uncovered the following major trends: (a) black males have a greater tendency to avoid intellectual engagement and competition; (b) young black males display negative attitudes and behavior toward school as early as fourth grade; (c) low academic achievement among black students quickly results in nonpromotion to the next grade followed by dropping out of school; and (d) at each grade level, black males are retained at significantly higher rates than black females (Rowan, 1989).

Fordham and Ogbu (1986) interviewed black high school students in a predominantly black school. They found that underachievers knowingly undermined their own achievement by not studying and cutting classes. High achievers were committed to doing well in school, but reported they had developed strategies for coping with academic success that included acting out, being the class clown, keeping their efforts a secret, and generally maintaining a low profile. These students were quite concerned about being labelled as "brainiacs" and being accused of "acting white" (Fordham & Ogbu, 1986).

INTERPRETATIONS OF UNDERPERFORMANCE

Three somewhat overlapping yet distinct theoretical frameworks have been used to interpret or explain the underperformance of African-American students relative to whites. These "schools of thought" can be identified as: (a) the "cultural relativist" perspective, (b) the "environmentalist" perspective, and (c) the "true deficit" perspective.

The "Cultural Relativist" Perspective

Social science research from the cultural relativist perspective tends to reflect the following characteristics:

Belief in the noncomparability of the races. Writers who adopt this perspective argue that children who are descendants of African parentage are so different from children who descend from European parentage as to require separate psychological principles for interpreting behavior. Therefore, to compare children's cognitive styles, IQ test performance, school-related behaviors, and parental child-rearing styles across racial groups is tantamount to comparing apples and oranges. An example of this viewpoint is offered by Boykin (1986), who writes:

The African perspective emphasizes spir-

itualism, whereas the Euro-American one emphasizes materialism. The former stresses harmony with nature; the latter stresses mastery over nature. The first relies on organic metaphors, the second on mechanistic ones. An orientation toward expressive movement contrasts with a compressive orientation toward impulse control. One culture emphasizes interconnectedness, whereas the other puts a premium on separateness; one values affect, and the other places reason above all else. . . . The former has a person-to-person emphasis, with a personal orientation toward objects; the second has a person-to-object orientation toward people. (p. 63)

Although not supported by current data (e.g., Troutman & Falk, 1982), one position that was popular for a time argued that black dialect represents a different but legitimate linguistic style that puts African-American children at an unfair disadvantage in standard reading and language tasks (Labov, 1972).

In summary, cultural relativist writers conclude that American schools by and large reflect European cultural values, which in effect penalizes African-American children educationally for their different cultural attributes (Akbar, 1981; Boykin, 1986; Hale-Benson, 1990; Kunjufu, 1984).

Sensitivity to unflattering labels. Cultural relativist writers take offense to the use of certain terms in referring to the black underclass that could be construed as pejorative or condescending (e.g., "culturally disadvantaged," "culturally deprived"). Because all groups have a viable and legitimate culture, these labels are viewed with suspicion by cultural relativists as implying an inherent superiority of white middle-class norms and culture (Boykin, 1986).

Emphasis on cultural strengths. "Deficit" models for explaining differences are criticized by cultural relativists (e.g., Wilson, 1978) as being motivated by thinking that is uninformed at best or racist at worst. Neutral "cultural difference" interpretations that emphasize either the adaptive nature of African-American behavior or the cultural strengths of African-American communities, are preferred (e.g., Cole & Bruner, 1971; Shade, 1982).

Interventions. Within the cultural relativist framework, intervention is broadly defined as providing opportunities or experiences for black children to be educated in an environment that is maximally sensitive to black culture. This can be accomplished through several means, which include multicultural curriculum materials, school/teacher racial sensitivity training, or black nationalist cultural training in an all-black environment (Hale-Benson, 1986; Hollins, 1982a, 1982b; Kunjufu, 1984; Lomotey, 1981).

The "Environmentalist" Perspective

Although some cultural relativists also promote hypotheses that are consistent with the "environmentalist" perspective, the latter perspective is clearly distinguishable by the following characteristics:

Emphasis on external causation. Environmentalists differ from cultural relativists in holding to a common set of psychological principles in understanding the behavior of both black and white children. Here, environmentalists assume that traditional academic expectations held by the majority of schools is a reasonable standard against which to evaluate all children regardless of culture. However, environmentalists argue that various forces *external* to black children are responsible for hindering their academic achievement. Here, low achievement orientation, aberrant patterns of school behavior, or academic problems presently found in children of the black underclass are viewed as being ultimately caused by either a legacy of past oppression (slavery) or current problems inherent in the larger society (e.g., job/housing discrimination, racism, social class subordination, poor economic conditions, deficient home environments). Hence, children of the African-American underclass are seen as *victims* of external forces, the removal of which will help in promoting equality with whites in academic achievement.

For example, the early work of Bernstein (1961), Hess and Shipman (1968), and Bee, Van Egeren, Streissguth, Nyman, and Leckie (1969) was influential in promoting the idea that a cognitively impoverished home-language environment and ineffectual mother-to-child teaching strategies were primarily responsible for black children's poor orientation to the academic demands of schools. More recently, Ogbu (1986) argued that a perceived "job ceiling" caused by generations of barriers to desirable employment causes black children to become disillusioned with school and develop negative attitudes toward cognitive tests. Gougis (1986) advances the argument that the low achievement in black children can be traced to emotional stress caused by racism.

Interventions. Within the environmentalist framework, intervention is broadly defined as providing opportunities or experiences to which black children are entitled, but for whatever reason, to which they have been denied access. Examples of denied opportunities and their related interventions are: (a) the right to equal access to education facilities, which is addressed by school desegregation efforts or special/regular educational litigation; (b) the right to political participation in the governing of school affairs, which is addressed by schools' efforts to increase black parent involvement and participation; and (c) the right to early experiences that promote school readiness and learning, which is addressed by early childhood education and/or parent training programs.

The "True Deficit" Perspective

Social science research from the "true deficit" perspective tends to reflect the following characteristics:

Emphasis on deficit models. Like the environmentalists, "true deficit" writers also hold to a common set of psychological principles in understanding the achievement-related behavior of both black and white children. Within this framework, discrepancies from a clearly articulated standard are seen as deficiencies that can hinder the extent to which African-Americans can fully benefit from opportunities in the larger society. Unlike the environmentalists, however, "true deficit" writers tend to attribute low achievement motivation, aberrant patterns of school behavior, or academic problems presently found in children of the black underclass to a self-perpetuating "culture of poverty" handed down and socially transmitted throughout successive generations. Here, the nonproductive attitudes, values, and behaviors of children from the black underclass are viewed as being so internalized (psychologically, socially, or constitutionally) that attributing causality to current external forces (e.g., racism, poverty, inadequate home conditions, etc.) appears superficial and irrelevant.

One school of thought, dominated by differential psychologists, explains black-white differences in school achievement as due in large part to the effects of more fundamental differences in general intelligence (psychometric g) distributions between racial groups (e.g., Jensen, 1973). Humphreys (1988) employs a medical model analogy to argue that (with the exception of Asians) American-born people of color in general, and African-Americans in particular, possess a higher proportion of genuine deficits in basic academic skills. According to Humphreys, these deficits warrant the diagnosis of an "inadequate learning syndrome."

Low confidence in traditional remedial efforts. Within the "true deficit" perspective, environmental factors (postnatal care, cultural practices, parental child-rearing behavior, home environment, etc.) are viewed as being responsible for a minimal proportion of variance in intelligence relative to genetic factors (Jensen, 1981). Therefore, the modest results from large-scale efforts to manipulate the environments of low-achieving young black children (e.g., see Jensen, 1988) are interpreted as having little or no effect on the most influential factor in scholastic achievement, which is psychometric g. Following this reasoning, Nichols (1987) argued that traditional environmental explanations (e.g., educa-

tional inequalities, poor motivation, malnutrition, verbal deprivation, teacher expectancies, prenatal disadvantages, styles of child rearing) are inadequate in explaining average racial group differences in intelligence. In a similar vein, Humphreys (1988) argued that traditional remedies for reducing black-white differences in scholastic achievement at the college level (e.g., affirmative action, improvement of test-taking skills, student financial aid, black faculty role models, encouraging attendance at all-black institutions) are destined to be ineffective (Humphreys, 1988).

Interventions. "True deficit" writers, like their environmentalist counterparts, value equal educational opportunities for African-American children. However, the feature that distinguishes "true deficit" theorists on this issue is the suggested strategy for achieving this goal. Because these writers tend to view black-white intelligence differences as pervasive, enduring, and intractable to environmental manipulation (Nichols, 1987), it is suggested that intervention efforts for facilitating scholastic achievement should focus on maximizing the instructional match for students of varying abilities (Havender, 1987). Here, students who have limited aptitudes for traditional forms of academic achievement are exposed to forms of instruction that maximize achievement by reducing the g loading of instructional methods (Bereiter, 1987).

STRUCTURAL FEATURES INFLUENCING THE NATURE OF PARENT EDUCATION FOR LOW-INCOME BLACKS

The belief in parent education as a means of significantly influencing the achievement of low-income black children is perhaps most consistent with the assumptions that underlie the "environmentalist" perspective. Much of the literature on parent education tends to be subsumed within the broader area of "parent involvement" in schools. For the purposes of this discussion, the term "parent involvement" refers to *all the ways in which parents interact with schools in building home-school-community partnerships for the purpose of benefiting the overall education of children.* The term "parent involvement" has been subdivided into the following five manifestations (Haley & Berry, 1988): (a) home-school communication, (b) parents as supporters of school activities, (c) parents as learners, (d) parents as teachers, and (e) parents as advocates and decision makers. However, Greenwood and Hickman (1991) provide a more comprehensive literature review of different schemes for classifying parent involvement.

Generally, the term "parent education" is included within parent involvement, and is typically used in referring to all activities included under the "parents as teachers (of their own children)" and "parent as learner" subdivisions. Nevertheless, the term "parent education" needs to be clearly defined, because the term can have different meanings to different writers. For the purposes of this discussion, a modification of Schlossman's (1983) definition of parent education will be used in referring to *all intentional efforts by a public or private agency to change attitudes and values or upgrade the knowledge and skills of parents in promoting improved child care or child rearing.*

Figure 1 is an illustration of various structural factors that influence the nature of parent education services to low-income black families. The influence of each of these factors is briefly discussed.

Figure 1
Structural Factors Influencing the Nature of Parent Education

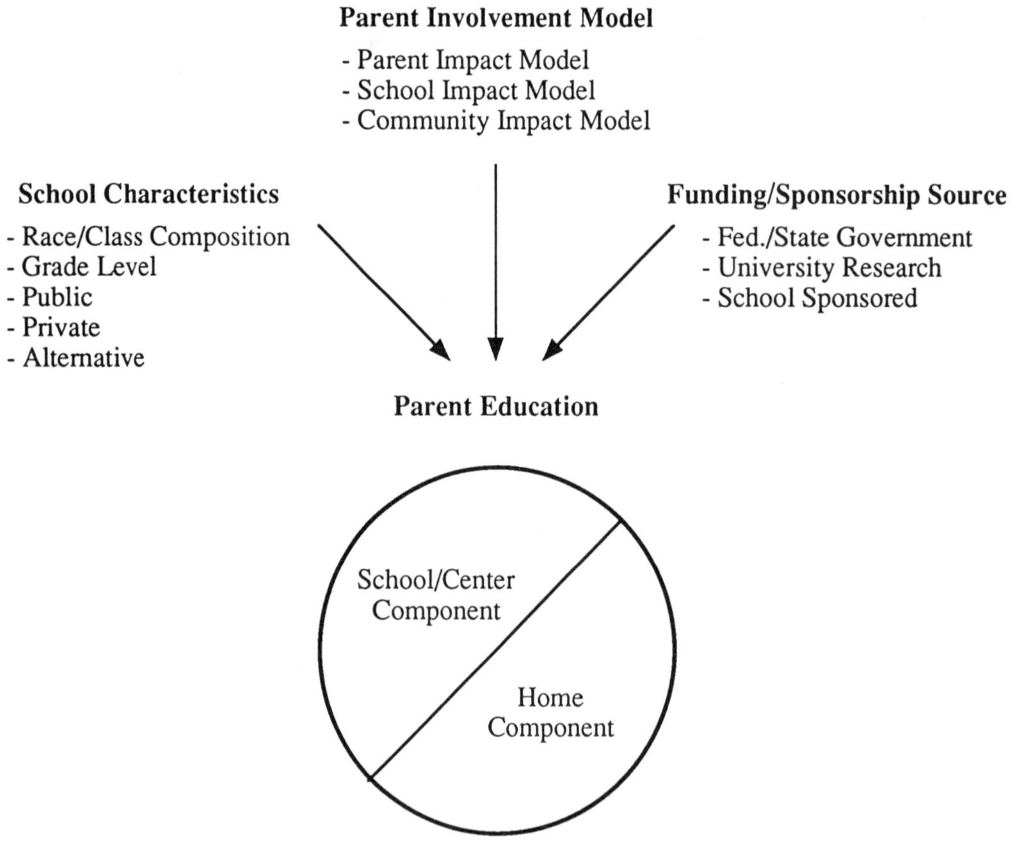

School Characteristics

The racial/class composition served by a school district influences the nature of parent education. Leler (1983) observes that parent education groups serving middle-class (predominantly white) parents are often voluntary, self-selective, and group self-directed, with the content often based upon the parents' perceptions of need. There are a variety of parent training packages designed to enable the "average" parent (i.e., functional middle-class families) to develop general "parenting skills." Included in this category are programs designed to help parents be more knowledgeable about general principles of child development and various methods for relating to and disciplining children. Examples of theoretical approaches to educating parents of "ordinary" children are Driekurs' Adlerian model, Ginott's sensitivity training, Gordon's Parent Effectiveness Training, and Transactional Analysis (summarized by Fine, 1980; Topping, 1986).

In contrast, parent education serving low-income black parents tends to be funded or connected with a government agency or research grant, and is usually based upon "expert" perception of parents' needs. This model may include comprehensive services to families, such as health, dental, and mental health services, and counseling/guidance services. Thus, in addition to programs oriented to improving children's academic success directly, the school may attempt to provide nonacademic services and information to low-income black families, which will enable the child to come to school more able to learn (Leler, 1983).

Parent involvement in education generally, and parent education specifically, is qualitatively different depending upon the grade level targeted. Parents of children in preschool and elementary school tend to have more of an inclination for school involvement than parents of children in the secondary grades (Hart, 1988; Ziegler, 1987). Preschool and elementary school parent involvement is characterized by regular and more frequent school visits in the interest of the child's basic skill acquisition, emotional adjustment, and social integration. In contrast, secondary school parent involvement tends to be more distant, and is characterized by visits to the school only when necessary (e.g., graduation, discipline problems) (Gotts & Purnell, 1987). Hence, the school's efforts to involve secondary parents (particularly when a child's problems have become more deeply entrenched) may be more difficult.

Whether or not a school can be classified as public, private, or alternative makes a big difference in the nature of parent education for black families. Although an overwhelming majority of black children attend the public schools, there is growing support among black parents for desegregated parochial schooling (Slaughter & Schneider, 1987). According to Slaughter and Schneider (1987), the following reasons account for why families of any color send their children to private schools: (a) a higher level of academic achievement for the child, (b) greater control and authority of the family in the child's education, and (c) greater value congruence between themselves and the school.

Coleman and Hoffer (1987) suggest that when the school community forms around particular ideas (e.g., religion), a "functional community" in the school is created. Here, the family, community, and school share the same idea as to what constitutes success in school. As a result, the school is more likely to develop an atmosphere that encourages students to higher achievements and educational aspirations (McDill, Rigsby, & Meyers, 1969). Private Catholic schools are also characterized by structured instruction, strong discipline, a decentralized bureaucratic structure, and a safe, orderly school climate (Frechtling, Raber, & Ebert, 1984). According to Slaughter and Schneider (1987), additional reasons why black parents in particular choose private (parochial) schools include: (a) familial disaffection with public schools in urban neighborhoods in which the families reside, and (b) the new availability of the necessary familial resources.

Although most black parents who send their children to private schools can be characterized as "middle-class" economically, private (particularly Catholic) schools in metropolitan areas are now serving children from all income categories and racial/ethnic backgrounds (Cibulka, O'Brien, & Zewe, 1982). Organizations like A Better Chance (ABC) and the Black Student Fund are set up specifically to locate, recruit, fund, and facilitate the adjustment of talented but economically disadvantaged black students attending private schools (Slaughter & Schneider, 1987). Whether or not black students achieve better in Catholic as opposed to public schools is a question of intense debate (Frechtling et al., 1984).

Alternative schools are community-based nonparochial private schools for black children that are also characterized by high expectations, high motivation, strong discipline, structured instruction, and a match between the culture of the student and the school environment (Frechtling et al., 1984). These alternative schools serve low-income black parents in urban communities who were disenchanted with the public schools yet are unable to afford expensive private schools. No substantial evaluation data as yet exist on the effectiveness of these schools in educating black children. In summary, it is reasonable to suggest that black parents who would make a substantial financial sacrifice to pay for private schools, or who are simply dissatisfied with public schools, may have a higher investment in the quality of their child's schooling than the average public school parent. These differences in turn may substantially alter the climate for parent involvement (and parent education) at these schools.

Parent Involvement Model

Gordon (1977, 1978) advanced a useful model for articulating qualitative differences between schools with respect to the nature of parental involvement. The form, content, and goals of any school's parent education efforts are inevitably influenced by these qualitative differences. In the "Parent Impact Model," most of the influence goes from the school to the home. This model assumes that parent educators or agencies can influence roles and relationships within the family. Underlying this model are assumptions that there is a body of information (derived from books or experts) that is essential for effective living, that teachers know and teach it, and that parents learn and apply it. Issues and concerns that arise from this model pertain to questions of how to reconcile differing opinions of experts, doubts as to whether or not alien values are being imposed on parents, and whether or not education efforts address superficial symptoms rather than root problems (Leler, 1983).

In the "School (Agency) Impact Model," most of the influence goes from the home to the school. This model attempts to make schools and other agencies more responsive to parents, and as a result parents may try to change the schools. The assumption is that if educators and other agency workers become more attuned to the family and the culture of the home, then a better working relationship with parents will lead to greater effectiveness in educating children. Many programs for low-income black children (e.g., Head Start, Follow Through, and Chapter I) require parents to serve on policy councils, committees, and boards. Here, low-income black parents are "educated" by developing "on-the-job" skills in group decision making and dealing with school/agency power structures. Issues and concerns that arise from this model pertain to whether or not school personnel can accept parents in this new role, and concerns as to whether or not parents' new found power will be used in constructive ways. For example, some parents may not see the need for parent education that professionals design, but instead they may desire that the professionals themselves change their behavior (Leler, 1983).

In the "Community Impact Model," the influence goes to and from home, school, and the larger community. This model works on the assumption that factors in the home, school, and community are all interrelated. Although some of these programs may no longer be in existence, examples of "community impact" programs described in the literature for low-income blacks have included Rev. Jesse Jackson's PUSH-EXCEL program (Murray, 1980), Dr. James Comer's New Haven Project (Comer, 1980; Comer, Haynes, & Hamilton-Lee, 1989; Webb & Parkay, 1989), Dr. Carolyn Tucker's Model Partnership Education Project (Tucker & Chennault, 1990), and the "Beethoven Project" of the Robert Taylor Homes in Chicago (briefly described in Bempechat & Ginsburg, 1989). The primary advantage of the Community Impact Model is that parent education efforts are not "piecemeal" and sporadic, but are placed within a broader social systems context. The primary disadvantage of this model is that the resources necessary to carry out a community impact model may well seem overwhelming (Gordon, 1977).

Funding/Sponsorship Source

Parent education programs for low-income blacks are shaped by the philosophy/regulations of the funding source. Some parent education programs are funded through grants from the federal/state level or private foundations. These funded programs can be primarily service oriented or part of a university research project. School-based programs that operate without benefit of outside funds must rely on either local school budgets or nonpaid volunteer support (Berger, 1987).

Federal level. The largest number of parent education programs for low-income blacks have traditionally been funded through the federal government. As a result of the Economic Opportunity Act of 1964, for example, Head Start began as a school-based program designed to provide comprehensive compensatory education, health, and social services to low-income preschool-aged children (Fine, 1980). Currently, there are over 1,400 Head Start programs

throughout the nation. The policy manuals for Head Start programs mandated parent participation as reflected in a variety of roles, one of which included teaching parents methods of stimulating the preschool child's intellectual growth at home.

Under an amendment to the Economic Opportunity Act of 1964, the national "Follow Through" program provided funds for sponsors (a group of persons at a university or institute who had developed a particular approach to early childhood education) to implement programs in over 150 communities serving low-income children (Olmsted, 1991; Olmsted & Rubin, 1983). Follow Through was a community involvement concept designed to assist Head Start children after they entered the public schools (kindergarten through third grade).

Whereas Follow Through was designed to function as an upward extension of Head Start, the Parent-Child Center (PCC) and Parent Child Development Center (PCDC) concept was designed to function as a downward extension of Head Start by providing comprehensive services to families with children within ages 0 to 3. PCCs are designed to provide education, health care, and social services to the entire family system. Intellectual stimulation activities begin with prenatal education of the mother, a program of stimulation in infancy, day care, and an education program for the parents in child development, family management, job skills, personality development, and husband-wife relationships (Gordon, 1968). Thirty-six PCCs across the country were initially funded in 1967 (Berger, 1987). The mission behind the creation of Parent Child Development Centers (PCDCs) was to develop a theory-based service delivery system that, unlike PCCs, would be amenable to controlled experimentation, rigorous evaluation, and replication (Dokecki, Hargrove, & Sandler, 1983). Within the PCDC concept, parents may participate in classes and support groups designed to increase their knowledge and skills related to the stimulation of infant development.

Title I of the Elementary and Secondary Education Act (ESEA) of 1965 (Chapter I) provides financial assistance to local educational agencies serving areas with concentrations of children from low-income families. Its goal is to raise student achievement (in the areas of reading, language arts, and math) of targeted groups of students who are entitled to receive its services (Keesling & Melaragno, 1983). These programs generally focus on providing extra instruction in reading or math. This extra instruction is frequently provided outside the regular classroom with aides often being employed to assist in teaching. Depending upon the needs of the local school district, Chapter I funds may be used to hire parent coordinators, school psychologists, or other support personnel who may function as parent educators.

Finally, Public Law 99–457 (the Education of the Handicapped Act Amendments of 1986) provides federal monies for states to develop comprehensive and coordinated early intervention systems for infants, toddlers, and preschoolers. This law allows for the development of parent education efforts as preventative measures for young children who are defined by individual states as biologically or environmentally "at risk" for developmental delays (Gallagher, Trohanis, & Clifford, 1989). Many of the criteria that states may use for determining "at risk" status (e.g., poverty status, drug dependent caregivers) impact a large number of African-American families.

State level. An example of an innovative state-funded parent education program with a plan for targeting low-income urban school districts is described by Winter (1988). Missouri's Parents as Teachers (PAT) program has provided funding for the training of over 1,500 parent educators who provide various early intervention services to parents in school districts throughout the state. Services provided for parents have included home visits, information sharing parent groups, formal screening services for toddlers, and a referral network for parents (Winter, 1988).

Independent studies. Walberg, Bole,

and Waxman (1980) and Rodick and Henggeler (1980) describe successful independent research studies for raising student achievement that have been conducted in low-income black schools. An example of a totally school-sponsored intervention program for low-income black elementary students is described by Gross (1974). The success of these independent programs depended in large part on parent education efforts.

Service Delivery Model

Parent education programs for student achievement can be delivered through either a "school(center)-based" or "home-based" model. Even though a program may be classified as "home-based" or "school(center)-based, "both types of programs may include both home and school components (see Fig. 1). In school(center)-based models, the local school functions as the center of a wheel, "with the spokes stretching out to the homes in the community through programs, resources, family centers, and support systems" that are housed within the local school (Berger, 1987, p. 195). Here, parents must come to the local school or center in order to take advantage of various services (e.g., workshops, classes, support groups, libraries). Examples of school-based models serving a high percentage of low-income black parents are the Head Start/Follow Through programs (Olmsted & Rubin, 1983) or Chapter I funded programs (Keesling & Melaragno). Examples of center-based models serving a similar population are Parent and Child Centers (PCCs) and Parent Child Development Centers (PCDCs) (Dokecki, Hargrove, & Sandler, 1983).

Home-based parent education programs differ from school(center)-based programs in the emphasis given to interaction with parents on their own turf (which is the home). Some programs are primarily school or center based, but include a significant home-base component (e.g., PCCs and PCDCs). Other programs are exclusively home based in focus (see Berger, 1987 for a brief description). Programs with a home-based component operate under the central assumption that the parent is the child's most important first teacher during the formative years (U.S. Department of Health, Education, & Welfare, 1976). Trained representatives (professionals, paraprofessionals, or volunteers) of a school or agency visit parents' homes and interact with the parent, child, or both together for the purpose of building parent competencies as teachers of their own children.

Various services that are likely to be found within the school(center) component of a parent education program are outlined in Table 1. "Low Resource"

services are those that can be delivered by school/center staff with minimal advanced training, additional curricular materials, or school/center resources. "Moderate Resource" services may include "low resource" activities; however, these services differ in that goals are more structured, and parent outcomes are more specified. Hence, a greater degree of parent-educator preparation is required. In addition, more of the school's resources are taxed and supplemental curricular materials begin to play a more important role. "High Resource" services may include both low and moderate resource services, but differ in that these services are delivered by staff with ad-

TABLE 1
Continuum of Activities and Services for School (Center)-Based
Parent Education Programs

Low Resources
- —Parents invited to school once or twice yearly to socialize informally with other parents and teachers. General information about the school and its activities, policies, curriculum, and the progress of individual children is shared by the school.
- —Parents attend monthly informal group discussion meetings with other parents to share self-selected problems/concerns. Discussions are facilitated by a parent educator.
- —Parents attend weekly lecture/discussion groups around topics selected by parent educator in areas of general child care, child development, family planning and nutrition. Parents may be notified of the topic to be discussed a few days before the meeting, or topics are outlined in a written guide or handbook that parents must bring with them from week to week.

Moderate Resources
- —Parents attend academic classes designed to help parents finish school or obtain a high school/college degree (e.g., alternative schools for pregnant teenagers).
- —Parents watch films or videotapes, observe real life demonstrations of optimal parent-child interaction techniques, or observe in classrooms on a weekly basis. Parents, led by a parent educator, discuss observations.
- —Parents attend classes with their infants/toddlers. Parent educator models techniques and parents practice techniques in classes on a weekly basis.
- —Parent attends "hands-on" workshops in which games, toys, and home learning activities are made from everyday household materials. Projects are taken home after sessions. Activity cards or "recipes" for home teaching may also be given to parents.

High Resources
- —Parents may check out materials from a toy-lending library, curriculum resource center, or reading library on the school/center site.
- —Parents receive individual mental health counseling; individual consultation services from pediatricians, psychologists, nutritionists, and nurses; referral services to other agencies.
- —Parents receive early and periodic medical screening and/or developmental assessments during pre-, peri- and postnatal phases of pregnancy (for both baby and mother).
- —Parent takes on a teaching role at the school/center, either in being a parent educator with other parents or tutoring children in classrooms.

vanced or specialized training. In addition, high demands are placed on the school or center's resources in order for these activities to be successful.

Various ways in which a school, center, or agency interacts with parents within the context of the home are outlined in Table 2. "Low Structure" activities are those that require nothing more than for parents to be passive receptacles of isolated bits of information. "Medium Structure" activities may include low structure activities, but differ due to the fact that parents are required to intervene more closely within the lives of their children at home. However, there is some room for flexibility as to how the parent chooses to implement suggested activities. "High Structure" activities may include both low and moderate structure activities, but are unique in involving

behaviors that are explicitly taught to parents by a home visitor. Here, there is little room for flexibility in how parent behaviors are implemented with their children.

GENERIC CORRELATES OF CHILDREN'S COGNITIVE DEVELOPMENT AND ACHIEVEMENT

There exists a body of empirical studies supporting the view that children's cognitive development and achievement are significantly associated with manipulable variables (for summaries of these studies, see Bloom, 1986; Broman, Nichols, & Kennedy, 1975; Clarke-Stewart, 1978; Epps & Smith, 1984; Friedman & Sigman, 1981; Gottfried, 1984; Hess & Holloway, 1985; Lareau, 1989; Scott-Jones, 1984; Seginer, 1983; Wallace, 1988). Specifically, these

TABLE 2
Continuum of Activities and Services for Home-Based Parent Education Programs

Low Structure

—Parents receive isolated bits of information from the school in the form of notes, notices, or newsletters sent by mail, or telephone calls from the school. The information received pertains to school activities, its discipline/homework policies, health regulations, progress reports concerning their child, and relevant telephone numbers to call in the event of questions or concerns.

Moderate Structure

—Activity cards or "recipes" are sent home to parents on a regular basis. Workbooks, reading materials, puzzles, games, and toys are lent to the parents from a home visitor with minimal explanation. Parents are encouraged by the school/center to use these materials with the child, but are not closely monitored.

—School sends progress reports about child home to the parent on a weekly, bi-weekly, or daily basis. Parent's responsibility is to reinforce (through rewards, privileges, etc.) acceptable school achievement and extinguish (through withdrawal of privileges) unacceptable school achievement within the context of the home.

—Parents are expected to monitor homework activities given to the child at school or provide opportunities for children to practice skills learned at school (e.g., reading to child, listening to child read, flash card drill on math facts).

High Structure

—On a weekly basis, a home visitor teaches specific parent-child interactive learning tasks to the parent using materials from either the home or school. The child is not present, so teaching takes the form of didactic one-way presentation or role-playing. Parents are closely monitored from week to week by the home visitor on the implementation of these activities.

—On a weekly basis, a home visitor teaches specific parent-child interactive learning tasks to the parent using materials from either the home or school. This is accomplished through verbal explanation and then demonstration of the activity with the child. The parent then practices the activity while the home visitor watches and provides feedback. Parents are closely monitored from week to week by the home visitor on the implementation of these activities.

studies usually take the form of multivariate investigations that are designed to uncover naturally occurring relationships between medical, environmental, or parental variables and children's developmental or achievement outcomes. This research, which relies heavily on correlational methods, does not inherently imply causality. However, program planners nevertheless use such data as fertile ground for designing effective interventions via parent education. This research is labeled as "generic," in the sense that questions unique to the cultural characteristics of low-income blacks were not the central concern of these investigations (although low-income blacks may have been included in the investigators' samples). Although there is a considerable degree of overlap, the independent variables from these types of studies fall into four main categories. These variables represent: (a) *general status or environmental* factors (e.g., broad SES indices; prenatal and perinatal risk factors; physical properties of the home such as crowding, personal space and excessive noise; structure and "predictability" of the home environment; provision of appropriate play and reading materials; family size; father absence; level of family discord and conflict); (b) factors related with parents' *knowledge or understanding* (i.e., knowledge of child development principles or milestones; parental reading skills; knowledge of school procedures; knowledge of social service and/or child care community resources); (c) factors related to parents' attitudes or values (i.e., value placed on educational achievement and intellectual endeavors; beliefs about child rearing; beliefs about parental role in educating children; attitudes toward the school system); and (d) factors related to parents' *behaviors or skills* (i.e., disciplinary techniques; quality and quantity of parent-child verbal interaction; parental teaching style; parental school participation). Variables within these four categories are interrelated and interdependent, which makes it difficult to isolate one factor to the exclusion of others.

It is interesting to note Wallace's (1988) observation that in these "generic" studies, SES is perhaps the most consistently powerful predictor of children's cognitive outcomes. However, race and SES are often confounded in American samples (i.e., non-white samples are disproportionately lower in SES), making it difficult to isolate the effects of racial status alone. Hence, *within* non-white samples, broad SES indices are less powerful predictors than more specific, proximal variables.

A SELECTED LITERATURE REVIEW ON SPECIFIC ISSUES RELATED TO BLACK PARENTING AND PARENT EDUCATION

At the beginning of this chapter, questions were raised as to whether or not there exist issues unique to low-income blacks that can facilitate the effectiveness of parent education efforts. Evidence that such issues do indeed exist is supported by two categories of research: (a) studies designed specifically to compare ethnic differences, and (b) studies using all-black samples.

Ethnic Difference Research

Child rearing. Strom (1979) used the Parent As A Teacher Inventory (PAAT) to identify similarities and differences among Anglo-, Black-, and Mexican-American mothers from upper-, middle-, and lower-class homes who had a child enrolled in the second grade. The PAAT provides information regarding what mothers expect of their child, how they respond to interaction with their child, and what actions they take in response to specific child behavior. PAAT responses can be grouped into five areas of strengths/weaknesses: Creativity, Frustration, Control, Play, and Teaching-Learning. Results indicated that the major source of variance among the three ethnic groups and class levels occurred between Anglo versus black mothers and upper-class versus lower-class mothers. Anglo and/or upper-class mothers had the highest scores on most or all PAAT areas whereas black and/or lower-class mothers obtained the lowest scores. With respect to main effects for race, black mothers exhibited more need to direct their children's behavior. Black mothers preferred playing games governed by rules with their children as opposed to make-believe play. Black mothers were less likely to approve of children dominating conversations and were more restrictive in the topics children were allowed to talk about. Black mothers were more likely to experience feelings of frustration when they could not answer their children's questions. The author concluded that the responses of Anglo mothers tended to be more consistent with the values promoted in child development research than those of black mothers.

Alvy, Harrison, Rosen, & Fuentes (1982) interviewed 100 black lower- and middle-class parents whose preschool children were enrolled in Head Start, 100 predominantly lower-class white parents, and 100 predominantly upper-middle-class white parents. In one component of the study, the researchers administered the Associative Group Analysis technique (Szalay, 1978). Here, parents give their word associations to various parenting concepts which in turn are combined into "meaning components." In regard to the concept of raising children, themes of love, difficulty, parental fulfillment, responsibility, and happiness were equally salient for whites. For the black parents, themes of love, teaching, and discipline predominate in their outlook on raising children (Alvy et al., 1982). Alvy (1985) reports interview data (on the same sample) on parental practices in response to their preschool child's obedience versus major defiance. In response to the child's obedience, the major ethnic differences were that a higher proportion of blacks (compared to whites) choose to do nothing, and that fewer black parents delivered global appreciative comments and praise that was more specific to the child's behavior. With respect to major disobedience, the researchers found that more white parents of both social classes reported using discussion, ordering, and removal of the child from the situation than did black parents. More black parents reported hitting their children with objects, though this difference was less

pronounced when comparing the black parents and the white low-income group. White parents tended to hit their children more out of anger and frustration, and to be ambivalent about hitting. In contrast, black parents justified hitting more in terms of being a useful technique for achieving a wide range of child-rearing objectives, and were more certain of its positive value.

Reis & Herz (1987) correlated parental race, age, parental depression, parenting attitudes, knowledge of development, and degree of social support with the Home Observation for Measurement of the Environment (HOME) subscale and total scores in a black and white adolescent female sample. The HOME scale is designed to measure such variables as parents' emotional and verbal responsivity, discipline style, organization of the environment, provision of play materials, variety in daily stimulation, and degree of parental involvement with their children. Results indicated that older (16 years or greater), white adolescent mothers with less punitive attitudes toward child rearing and discipline scored highest on parenting skills as measured by the HOME scale. Both this study and an earlier study (King & Fullard, 1982) found that racial minority mothers, on the average, had lower HOME scores than white mothers.

Stevens (1988) investigated whether ties to informal and formal support systems and a sense of personal control predicted parenting skill in each of three different groups of mothers. Results indicated that willingness to report child-rearing problems and seeking help from extended family members were important predictors for black teen mothers. The only important predictor for black adult mothers was locus of control. For white adult mothers, locus of control and seeking help from extended family members and professionals were all important predictors for parenting skill.

Dore and Dumois (1990) examined ethnic differences in responses to a self-image inventory completed by 134 black and Hispanic pregnant and parenting 11–20-year-old adolescents. They found that Hispanic subjects were reluctant to trust others with knowledge of their problems, whereas black subjects shared their problems readily. In addition, black females had plans for resuming schooling, whereas Hispanic females had less cultural support for career achievement.

For a review of literature on ethnic differences in child rearing with a specific emphasis on the role of black fathers, readers are encouraged to consult McAdoo (1986).

School and parent education attitudes. In a recent publication, Chavkin (1989) reports findings from two surveys. The first survey compared the attitudes of 1,188 black and Hispanic parents across six states with the attitudes of white suburban parents. Chavkin cites Williams and Chavkin's (1985) finding that most parents, regardless of minority status, expressed strong interest in helping their children with schoolwork at home and supporting schools in a variety of ways. In the second study described by Chavkin, 2,000 parents of public school children were surveyed. Findings from this survey showed that minority parents: (a) were less satisfied than suburban parents with the frequency of their contacts with teachers, (b) wanted to talk more often with teachers, and (c) felt intimidated by and awkward about approaching school personnel.

Rowland and Wampler (1983) surveyed black and white middle- and working-class mothers on their knowledge of, attendance at, interest in, and preferences for parent education programs (PEPs). They found that knowledge of, attendance in, and positive attitudes toward parent education were more prevalent among blacks. Those with less than a college education indicated the most willingness to attend a PEP if it were offered. Blacks and those with less than a college education preferred PEPs offered in schools and churches, rather than in mental health centers, and preferred larger groups in which they knew few people.

Although this brief review of studies is far from exhaustive, two consistent findings are suggested with respect to comparisons across racial groups: (a) the child-rearing attitudes and behaviors of white samples tend to reflect more closely principles advanced in traditional child development literature, and (b) black parents are similar to, and in some cases exceed, white parents in their desire to promote the academic development of their children (i.e., through working more closely with schools or through their willingness to receive parent education).

Research With Black Samples

Correlates of student achievement. Rankin (1967) conducted extensive interviews of parents of high- and low-achieving third and fourth graders from a black inner-city Detroit school. The following types of parental behavior were found to be significantly related to school achievement: providing experiences for children (e.g., playing games, attending church, talking); showing interest in the children's school activities (e.g., requiring children to make high marks, talking about school activities, helping with difficult homework); developing the children's interest in reading, and taking the initiative in contacting school personnel (e.g., conferring with the principal).

From the intensive case study of 10 low-income black families, Clark (1983) found that more parental visits to the school were associated with increased parental knowledge about the child's school life. He found that parents of the high-achieving black teenagers held common attitudes toward education. They are willing to put their children's growth and development before their own, and they feel responsible for helping their children gain a general fund of knowledge and basic literacy skills. These parents feel that pursuing knowledge is their children's responsibility and expect them to participate in some form of secondary school training. In addition, parents of children who do well showed great concern about the school's success with its students and believed that only with parent input will the school provide sound training. Families of high-achieving black teenagers were characterized by frequent dialogues between parents and children, strong parent encouragement of academic pursuits, clear and consistent limits for children, warm and nurturing interactions, and consistent monitoring of how time is used. Clark terms this style of parenting "sponsored independence," which is similar to the "authoritative" style described by Dornbusch, Ritter, Leiderman, Roberts, and Fraleigh (1987).

For a more thorough overview of empirical relationships between home environmental variables and the academic achievement of black students, readers are encouraged to consult Slaughter and Epps (1987).

Cultural characteristics. Many writers have attempted to identify unique cultural characteristics that have relevance for parent education efforts with low-income blacks. Turner (1987) observed that such cultural characteristics are easy to identify, simply because low-income blacks "have less contact with the middle and upper income classes, fewer resources, and less indoctrination into the ways of mainstream society" (p. 2). Some of these characteristics arise out of ancillary problems that disproportionately affect any persons of poverty status. Such problems are not "race-specific" per se. Other characteristics, however, are directly related to the effects of being black in a predominantly white society. A sample of characteristics that have been identified in the literature appears below:

1. *Diversity in black "consciousness."* Alvy (1985) discusses the diversity in racial attitudes held by low-income black parents, as observed throughout his years of experience leading parent education programs in the mental health field. For example, black parents share different degrees of ethnic identification/pride or ethnic denial/self-disparagement. This has implications for individual differences in parents' trust of whites or the "racial education" that black children receive from their parents. Religious convictions also can play a role in black parents' racial attitudes. In some communities, religion-based themes of black nationalism (e.g., Black Muslim faith) are

powerful forces. In other communities, themes and attitudes connected with the traditional black Christian church are more prominent.

2. *Problems associated with single and/or teenage parenthood.* A greater proportion of black mothers (compared to whites) are likely to be teenagers (Ladner, 1987) and single (Fine & Schwebel, 1988). Problems associated with teenage status include emotional immaturity, unrealistic beliefs about parenthood, lack of child development knowledge, frustration with a lack of leisure time, difficulties with financial responsibility, and strained relationships with either parents or partners (Brown, 1983). Problems associated with single parent status include increased financial pressures, emotional adjustment problems, loneliness, and dissatisfaction with their social lives (Fine & Schwebel, 1988).

3. *Greater extended family support.* In low-income black communities, grandparents, brothers, sisters, cousins, aunts, uncles, and informally "adopted" friends often live in close proximity (Turner, 1987). Fine and Schwebel (1988) documented that a higher proportion of black single-mother homes (compared to matched white homes) contained adults and/or children from outside the nuclear family. This extended family system and kinship network often functions as a source of support. For example, Stevens (1984) found that in black families in which a teenager has an infant, grandmothers (teenager's mother) facilitate the mother's parental socialization process. He concluded that in these situations, the infant is protected from the potentially detrimental effects of an immature, inexperienced parent.

4. *The value of children by the community.* Various writers (Nobles, 1978; King, 1976; Staples, 1976) maintain that black communities value children in unique ways. Here, it is argued that single parents can gain status or recognition from children's community roles. In addition, the stigma of unwed "illegitimacy" is often nonexistent in many poorer black communities. This may be due in part to the fact that single

parenthood (which disproportionately affects black communities due to shortages of eligible black men) is seen as a viable family alternative (Peters & Deford, 1978).

5. *Mistrust of large social agencies.* Turner (1987) observes that many low-income black parents harbor real or imagined fears that involvement with social agencies (i.e., health care, protective services, welfare) will result in negative consequences (e.g., taking one's child away). Many black parents may hold the perception that all agencies (including the school) are part of a "gigantic information network" committed to ferreting out and reporting any instance of wrongdoing. As a result, many poor black parents may be more quick to become defensive when innocent questions asked by professionals are perceived as "too personal." This helps to explain why many poor blacks who have problems are more likely to seek help from family members before trusting outside agencies (Turner, 1987).

6. *Sense of powerlessness.* Boyd (1977) discussed various factors that can foster a sense of helplessness and powerlessness in poor urban black parents. First, many black parents may distrust their own common sense about child rearing and feel intimidated by the opinions of teachers, psychologists, pediatricians, and other "experts." Second, many black parents feel that they must compete for their child's attention from television, movies, popular music, sporting events, and other seductive recreational activities. Third, many poor blacks routinely face economic humiliations in the form of credit or identification checks in business establishments, harassment by collection agencies, and insensitive sales personnel. Fourth, large urban school districts, with whom many black parents must deal, are more susceptible to the tendency to be impersonal, bureaucratic, overwhelmed, underfinanced, and driven by intense partisan "politics." These factors converge in fostering a feeling within some parents that external forces are more powerful than parental

control in shaping their children's educational futures.

7. *The will to "overcome."* In contrast to a sense of helplessness, Alvy (1985) argues that many black families, as a result of the cumulative history of sociopsychological survival in the face of racism, possess a strong will to overcome tremendous odds against successful child rearing. Turner (1987) observes that a consistent theme in traditional black Christian church worship is that "with enough faith, tough circumstances will get better."

PROBLEMS IN ASSESSING THE IMPACT OF PARENT EDUCATION ON SCHOOL ACHIEVEMENT

A clear picture of the relationship between parent education and the school achievement of low-income black children is fraught with a host of difficulties. First, the sheer volume of the database on this topic is overwhelming. Within the past 25 years, there have been literally thousands of intervention programs for low-income black children across the country that have included a parent education component to some degree. These various programs are discussed in numerous journal articles, books, government monographs, and ERIC documents. For summaries of the effects of a variety of parent education programs on school achievement (since the 1960s), readers are encouraged to consult literature reviews by Ascher and Flaxman (1987); Barth (1979); Becher (1984); Cotton and Savard (1982); Edwards (1987); Goodson and Hess (1975); Gordon (1979); Grau, Weinstein, and Walberg (1983); Henderson (1987); and Miller (1986).

Second, many parent education programs are service oriented and entail no rigorous evaluation component. Other programs may have an evaluation component; however, the lack of follow-up data leaves important questions about the effects of parent education to remain unanswered. Still other programs may have rigorous evaluation designs, yet some studies' failure to produce significant results makes it more likely that these programs are not published. This may create a biased sample of programs that are reported in the literature.

Third, the effects of many individual programs are reported as part of aggregate analyses of a number of programs. Parent education programs differ widely with respect to program duration, goals, content, and format. These factors determine what the dependent variables will be (e.g., intelligence, language performance, general school behavior, parents' teaching styles, parents' interactions with their children, parents' provision of more stimulating home environments), the kinds of measurement instruments used, and the research design. As a result, values obtained from meta-analyses of these programs may change as a function of the types of programs included within each analysis. Alvy (1985) perhaps best describes the essence of why it is difficult to compare different parent education programs:

> Further complicating factors are group composition and group dynamic factors. No two parent training groups are alike because no two groups have the exact same mix of parent and child characteristics. The dynamics of each group differ, and instructor and parent characteristics interact to make each group experience unique in its own right. (Alvy, 1985, p. 8)

Given this situation, conclusions from summaries of parent education research tend to be described in general, vague, and nonspecific language. Furthermore, many of these conclusions are intuitively self-evident. For example, Lazar (1981) concludes his analysis of early intervention programs with the following summary (Lazar, 1981, p. 305, as reported in Griffore & Boger, 1986):

1. Age of intervention—the earlier the better

2. Adult-child ratio—the fewer children the better

3. Number of home visits—the more the better

4. Direct participation of parents—the more the better

5. Services for families, not just the child—the more, the better

Becher (1982) offers more specific conclusions gleaned from her literature review of parent education programs for very young children:

1. Programs that use home visits by either professional or paraprofessionals, either alone or in combination with preschool classes for children, are more effective in bringing about cognitive gains in children than programs utilizing parent classes alone or in combination with preschool classes.

2. Programs that place a high emphasis on the parent-teaching component produce more stable, long-term gains in children.

3. No one type of program content (language development, sensorimotor development, cognitive development, child development principles, etc.) appears more effective than another.

4. A one-to-one parent-teacher relationship produces greater effects than a group instructional relationship.

5. Highly structured, prescriptive, concrete tasks for parents produce more stable gains than less structured programs.

6. There is no difference in the effectiveness of programs that teach parents specific teaching techniques versus programs that encourage a general style of interaction.

7. Programs that are most effective in producing considerable changes in both children and parents involve long-term consultation for a minimum of 18 to 24 months.

8. Effective programs are both prescriptive (attempting quality control through clearly specified goals, objectives, activities, and careful monitoring) and personalized (emphasizing the modification of content to achieve a proper fit for each parent-child dyad). (p. 1381)

Fourth, parent education efforts designed

to increase student achievement are often offered concurrently with other general services to the parent (e.g., vocational/employment counseling; health/nutritional services), other parent involvement activities (e.g., serving on advisory councils; tutoring in classrooms; curriculum development), and other direct services to the child (e.g., preschool instruction; medical services). As a result, the unique effects of a specific parent education component (e.g., workshops) may be difficult to tease out from the the general effects of program involvement. Some evaluators do a better job at this than others. For example, some researchers use evaluation procedures that are tied directly and exclusively to the goals and objectives of the parent education component within a program. Other evaluators simply compare program participants against nonprogram participants.

Fifth, many schools have demonstrated achievement gains with innovative classroom-based instructional techniques without a substantial parent education component (e.g., Frechtling, Raber, & Ebert, 1984), or from the effects of changed parent behaviors that require mastery of only a few simple techniques (Barth, 1979).

PRINCIPLES FOR EFFECTIVE PARENT EDUCATION

For the reasons stated above, a thorough quantitative evaluation of parent education programs is beyond the scope of this chapter, and is probably of limited value to practitioners. The more helpful approach is to summarize general principles that seasoned researchers and parent educators have cultivated from their years of experience in working with low-income black families. In doing so, the temptation to offer packaged "recipes" on dealing with "prototypical" low-income black parents is consciously avoided. Such an approach would foster undifferentiated stereotyping, which undervalues the diversity of circumstances under which practitioners must operate professionally. Instead, readers are encouraged to examine critically which

principle(s) is/are most relevant or helpful in their own unique circumstances.

1. *Examine the assumptions that underlie the need for parent education.* Generally speaking, all parent education models and approaches (regardless of target group) imply that there are ideas, skills, and techniques that would be helpful to parents. However, this implication does not also lead to the conclusion that parents are inferior or "deficient" because they do not possess these skills. When parent education efforts are targeted toward low-income blacks (and particularly when parent educators do not share either the same racial and/or income status), special care must be taken to ensure that the program is not based on implicit attitudes or assumptions that low-income black parents are inferior or deficient (Alvy, 1985).

Rich, Van Dien, & Mattox (1979) articulate explicitly some major assumptions that must underlie a "nondeficit" approach to working with poor black families (adapted from Rich et al., 1979, p. 32):

a. All children have had meaningful experiences. However, the [low-income African-American] child's experiences have been different and fewer in number in contributing to preparation for success in school.

b. Home environments, no matter how poor, are a citadel of care and concern for children.

c. All parents intrinsically possess the abilities to help their child succeed in school.

d. Schools should start with what the family has, instead of worrying about what it doesn't have.

e. Schools, no matter how understaffed or equipped, have the capabilities of reaching out and effecting parent involvement by using easy, inexpensive materials, without waiting for what probably won't come: organizational change or massive government funding.

2. *Seek help, assistance, or consultation from colleagues who are most sensitive to the needs of the target parents.* There are various reasons why this principle is important. First, schools

differ widely with respect to the extent to which the staff as a whole is sensitive to racial issues. Alvy (1985) notes that this is of particular concern when the parent educator is white and there are other black professionals on the staff. Here, some of the black staff may harbor either legitimate or irrational feelings that non-black parent educators are inappropriate for low-income black parents. However, the same feelings can also reasonably be applied to middle-class black parent educators. According to Alvy (1985), a good practice for parent educators (regardless of racial background) to follow *before* designing such programs is to seek suggestions, input, and guidance from other key black staff.

The second reason this principle is important is more pragmatic in nature. In the process of gaining experience, many parent educators discover to their chagrin that the topics covered in workshops or group meetings are of little concern to parents relative to other problems. An illustration comes to mind from this author's previous experience working as a school psychologist at a preschool. At that time, part of my responsibilities involved leading parenting workshops attended by large numbers of poor black parents. After what I thought was an engaging session on an interesting topic related to child development, I invited parents to share their thoughts on the workshop. Many of their concerns had nothing to do with the workshop. For example, one young father wanted to know how he could get his wife out of a restrictive drug rehabilitation program, and another single mother later in the week tried to ask me out for a date!

These and other similar experiences taught me that many poor black parents have more pressing needs that can be perceived as more important than parenting issues. In order for parents to attend fully to the content of parent education efforts, the sponsoring school may need to explore ways to either (a) address these issues directly within parent education groups (even though they may not be directly related to child development issues), or (b) be able to refer parents to

appropriate professional help. Consultation with a parent or staff member who is intimately familiar with these hidden issues can be an invaluable resource to parent educators.

3. *Build rapport with parents.* Many low-income black parents may have had frustrating or negative prior interactions with school personnel. In these instances, black parents often come away from these experiences feeling that they have not been afforded the simple courtesy of being heard. If black parents are consistently given these courtesies, the rapport that results will go a long way toward contributing to the success of parent education efforts. Olion (1988) offers the following suggestions for establishing rapport:

> Relax physically and center attention on the parents. Use eye contact to help focus upon the parents and to communicate to them that they are being heard. Understand what the parents are saying. . . . If parents are not talkative, ask them what their views are about school. What do they feel you should be doing with their [child] with special needs? Ask the parents about their practices in rearing their [child]. What are their problem areas? Give them opportunities to express anxieties. These are some questions that may open up the discussion; however, remember. . . . Black parents stop listening and talking when they are not heard. (p. 98)

4. *Minimize demand on reading skills.* Parent educators cannot assume that all low-income black parents have sufficient reading skills. Therefore, practices that may be routinely used with other groups (e.g., school-to-home written notices, workshop handouts, reading lists, etc.) may be threatening to parents who have poor reading skills. Olion (1988) cites research in which prerecorded telephone messages are used to provide a nonthreatening way for parents to be informed of school activities. In addition, trusted community persons can be used as informal liaisons between the school and parents for relaying messages. Parent workshops can minimize the need for reading by putting a stronger emphasis

on role-playing and audio-visual teaching aids (films, videocassettes, etc.).

These suggestions should be taken with caution, however. Taylor and Dorsey-Gaines (1987) argue persuasively that the environments of low-income black families are as rich in opportunities for developing literacy (reading and writing) as middle-class environments. If the primary objective of the parent program is to develop children's reading skills, Edwards (1987) reviews a number of successful programs for this purpose that have been used with low-income (but not necessarily black) populations.

5. *Make a special attempt to involve black fathers.* Some writers take offense at the depiction of black family life as primarily matriarchal and of black fathers (particularly teenage fathers of children born out of wedlock) as distant, irresponsible, exploitive, and emasculated (see review by McAdoo, 1986). This depiction ignores a sizable literature on black fathers (including teenage, unwed fathers) who are quite involved with their children and partners or at least have an interest in becoming more involved (see reviews by Brown, 1983; Hendricks, Howard, & Ceasar, 1981; Smith, 1988). Because most parent education programs are attended by women, participation may increase both quantitatively and qualitatively if schools could create incentives for black fathers to participate. A program designed to meet the unique needs of teenage fathers is described by Klinman and Sander (1985).

6. *Involve black fraternities and/or sororities.* Olion (1988) argues persuasively that members of black Greek organizations can be enlisted to aid black parents in their efforts to improve the academic and achievement functioning of black students. This aid can be direct, as in volunteering to tutor black students on a regular basis. College Greeks can also tutor parents who are weak in reading or math skills. However, this aid may also be indirect. Here, black Greeks may also pay for or provide child care services to black parents, thereby freeing them to participate in parent education classes offered by schools.

7. *Involve black churches and ministers.* The black church plays a central role in many black communities. Community churches may have meeting areas that are less threatening to parents than meeting at schools. Because the lack of transportation can be a major deterrent to parent involvement, many churches have vans or buses that may help in transporting parents to meetings (Olion, 1988). Local churches can sponsor activities such as writing contests, black history programs, and public speaking contests. These activities can be a source of pride for parents, as well as provide opportunities for their children to practice communication skills (Tucker & Chennault, 1990). Local ministers should be the first contact persons in initiating church-school partnerships.

8. *Involve teachers.* Ascher (1987) describes the benefits to teachers as a result of being given opportunities to visit the homes of black children. Specifically, home visits by teachers have the potential to increase teachers' understanding of the types of learning that take place in the home, which may facilitate classroom-based instruction.

Tucker and Chennault (1990) describe an innovative intervention project for low-achieving black students that links parents with the teachers of their children. Public school teachers of project children are asked to complete a form detailing the project child's academic strengths/weaknesses and positive/negative social behaviors at school. These teachers regularly confer with parent educators (who themselves are teachers or college graduate students) to exchange information about progress gained in addressing the problems specified by the public school teachers. This provides an opportunity for parent educators to share with parents what does and does not work in addressing the academic or behavior problems of a particular child. In addition, teachers participate in a series of joint workshops with parents for the purpose of ironing out hindrances to a collaborative partnership between the two groups.

9. *Involve business/financial re-*

sources in the local community. Employers may be petitioned to allow flexible working hours for black parents, so that they can attend parent education meetings. Where a corporation or large business may employ a large number of parents, times can be arranged with employers for parents' attendance at school meetings (Ascher, 1987).

Tucker and Chennault (1990) describe how citizens and leaders in the local community have contributed financially to the success of an intervention program for low-income black children that is based on the education "partnership" concept (Seely, 1981). For example, prominent businesses and individual citizens have made donations to launch the project. The local branch of IBM donated $50,000 of computer software for student use, including special programs designed to assist children who have reading and math deficiencies. Local TV stations have done stories about the project to encourage community support. Local banks and restaurants provide tours and dinners respectively for project children who are rarely exposed to these establishments. If these opportunities are contingent upon parent participation in parent education activities, then some parents who might not otherwise attend will be served.

10. *Specific parental skills taught.* The number of specific skills parents can learn in order to facilitate child growth and achievement is virtually limitless. Readers interested in names and addresses of professional organizations or curriculum developers (for information on parent education packages and programs) are encouraged to consult Berger (1987).

Most parenting skills are not "race- or class-specific," in the sense that they are equally applicable to all parents. However, the following suggestions come directly from research or projects involving only low-income black parents.

Tucker and Chennault (1990) describe a program for parents of low-achieving black fourth graders that includes a parent education component in addition to other interventions. These monthly parent education workshops fo-

cus on the following issues: (a) managing family stress to create a home environment that is conducive to studying and academic success; (b) identifying and verbally acknowledging children's positive qualities to elevate self-esteem; (c) managing anger and frustration to avoid child abuse; (d) expressing positive and negative feelings appropriately and encouraging and teaching children to do this; (e) helping children prepare for exams by structuring study time, and (f) knowing parental rights and responsibilities with regard to involvement with their children's teachers, principals, and the School Board.

Workshops typically include experiential exercises, role-plays demonstrating approaches and techniques, and the sharing of parenting strategies and techniques that participants have found to facilitate the academic achievement, adaptive functioning, and self-esteem of their children. Parent workshops, like the interventions with children, are research based. For example, in a 2-year study conducted by the program director and her research team (which involved 266 black families and 414 white families), specific parent behaviors that were statistically associated with academic achievement in the black group were identified (Tucker, Harris, & Brady, 1990). This information, in part, determines the issues focussed on in parent workshops. Other workshop content is based on responses to questionnaires periodically sent to parents as to the issues they would like to have addressed in upcoming workshops (Tucker & Chennault, 1990). In addition, project parents accompany their children on field trips, so that they can have common significant experiences about which to converse at home.

After conducting an in-depth case study of families of low- and high-achieving black adolescents, Clark (1983) offers the following suggestions for parents (adapted from Clark, 1983, pp. 215–216):

a. It is important that parents clearly define and fully accept their responsibilities for "parenting."

b. Help the adolescent establish relationships with other achievement-oriented persons.

c. Establish rules for every conceivable social situation by openly discussing "appropriate" behavior for that situation.

d. Parents should use their influence to establish educational activities in the household and routinely monitor the adolescent's use of time and space, while providing the adolescent with consistently enforced rules for behavior.

e. Family members should work to uncover and accentuate the positive characteristics of one another.

f. Parents should emphasize the importance of dedication to tasks for achieving goals. This may be done by providing the adolescent with regular leadership opportunities as part of many everyday family activities. Constructive part-time work in local institutions is also beneficial. Encourage the adolescent to interact in community institutions (e.g., schools, churches, business establishments, etc.).

g. Parents should encourage the adolescent to be reasonably ambitious in school and to pursue higher education. Enroll the young child in supplementary reading, math, and science programs—especially in grades 1–8. At least one evening a week take the child or adolescent to the library.

h. Insist that homework and other educational activities be regularly performed in the home. Play home games together, especially word games. Conduct family discussions centering on school concerns. Build the adolescent's vocabulary as part of everyday family life by discussing different subjects every day and writing notes to one another.

i. Students should be taught (by example) to love and respect parents and, as a result, other authority figures. They should also learn how to interact with other adults outside the family clan.

j. Parents should organize the siblings into a cooperative unit of persons who play, work, and learn together. This will give children more opportunities for intellectual stimulation and growth.

11. *Cultural adaptations.* Although there are large individual differences in many psychosocial characteristics of African-Americans, black people nevertheless share a special consciousness about what it means to be black in a predominantly white society. Therefore, it can be argued that parent education programs for low-income blacks must go beyond the teaching of generic skills to include material adapted exclusively for African-American parents. However, not all parent educators may be personally comfortable with some cultural adaptations suggested in the literature. In addition, not all cultural adaptations are appropriate for all low-income black groups. Therefore, each parent educator must examine himself or herself to determine which kinds of cultural adaptations are most congruent with their own unique personal style and situation.

Alvy (1985) describes a parenting program that is based on the theme "Pyramid of Success (POS) for Black Children." During the first session, the instructor uses a call-and-response teaching technique that is similar to the minister-congregation exchanges that characterize traditional black Christian worship. This technique is designed to identify for parents five life goals that characterize the POS: (a) achieving loving relationships, (b) obtaining good jobs, (c) getting a good education, (d) helping the black community, and (e) resisting the pressures of the "street." The parents are then taught that the successful achievement of these goals requires that children possess high self-esteem, self-discipline, pride in blackness, good school and study habits, and good physical health habits.

Every time a new skill or idea is taught, the instructor purposely draws the parents' attention to the associated goal within the POS. This teaching technique helps reinforce parents' mental link between what they are learning and how it will benefit their children.

The parenting program, in addition to teaching POS skills, includes special units that are particularly relevant to African-Americans. Examples of some unit titles are: The Meaning of Disciplining Children (Traditional Black Discipline vs. Modern Black Self-Discipline), Developing Self-Esteem and Pride in Blackness, Drugs and Our Children, Developing Sexually Responsible Children, and Single Parenting. The unit on discipline, for example, discusses concepts about discipline that were characteristic of the slavery era and contrasts this with concepts related to self-discipline that were derived from the civil rights era (Alvy, 1985).

Many writers stress the importance of fostering positive self-images in black children via intentional and systematic teaching of African culture and African-American history by their parents (Hale-Benson, 1986; Kunjufu, 1984). Arguments for such training are supported by perceptions of many writers that African-based culture is systematically denigrated by literature and the mass media (e.g., Mathis, 1974; Lee, 1987). Promoting a sense of positive identification with one's racial heritage is assumed to enable black children to withstand potential threats to self-esteem when competing academically in a white environment. Topics to be included in parent-to-child training are (adapted from Hale-Benson, 1986; Tucker & Chennault, 1990):

a. African cultural arts, which includes music, creative movement, sculpture, painting, arts and crafts, woodworking, dramatics and poetry. This can be accomplished through field trips or visits to museums, theaters, or art exhibits.

b. Aesthetic training to broaden acceptance of individual differences in general and African aesthetics in particular. This can be accomplished through explicit teaching and candid discussions of differences in skin color, complexion, physical features, and hair texture.

c. Teaching the "politics" of American holidays, particularly as they have influenced the history of African-Americans and other people of color (e.g., Thanksgiving from the point of view of Native Americans). This should include the celebration of holidays and role models that are pivotal in African-American history (e.g., Emancipation Proclamation, Martin Luther King, Jr. Day, Malcolm X's birthday, Kwanzaa, 14th Amendment to the Constitution).

Summary

The scholastic underperformance of African-American children, particularly those from low-income backgrounds, is well documented. Interpretations of this underperformance tend to be built on either "cultural relativist," "environmentalist," or "true deficit" assumptive frameworks. The belief in parent education as a means of significantly improving the scholastic achievement of low-income African-American children is most closely tied to "environmentalist" assumptions.

Parent education for low-income blacks is not a homogeneous concept, as its nature is shown to be influenced by a number of structural features (e.g., school characteristics, parent involvement model, and funding/sponsorship source). The need for parent education is supported by a large research literature that documents the generic correlates of optimal cognitive development and achievement in children and adolescents. In addition, research findings that are particularly relevant to the parenting needs of low-income blacks can be extracted from ethnic difference research and research involving predominantly black samples.

Problems in evaluating parent education programs are discussed. The chapter concludes with general principles gleaned from the literature that may be helpful for schools in their efforts to provide parent education for low-income African-American families.

ACKNOWLEDGEMENTS

This author gratefully acknowledges Ms. Jodi Cohen for her assistance in reviewing literature for this chapter. Special thanks is extended to Dr. Carolyn M. Tucker, Dr. Shirley Chennault, and Ms. Beverly Brady (University of Florida) for supplying helpful manuscripts on the Model Partnership Education Program.

REFERENCES

Akbar, N. (1981). Cultural expressions of the African American child. *Black Child Journal, 2*(2).

Alvy, K. T. (1985). *Parenting programs for black parents.* Studio City, CA: Center for the Improvement of Child Caring, Inc. (ERIC Document Reproduction Service No. 274 414)

Alvy, K. T., Harrison, D. S., Rosen, L. D. & Fuentes, E. G. (1982). *Black parent training programs: Adapted versions of standard programs for black parents and pilot test of adapted versions.* Studio City, CA: Center for the Improvement of Child Caring.

Ascher, C., & Flaxman, E. (1987). Parent participation and the achievement of disadvantaged students. In D. S. Strickland & E. J. Cooper (Eds.), *Educating black children: America's challenge* (pp. 70–76). Washington, DC: Howard University.

Ascher, C. (1987). *Improving the school-home connection for poor and minority urban students.* New York: Institute for Minority Education.

Barth, R. (1979). Home-based reinforcement of school behavior: A review and analysis. *Review of Educational Research, 49*(3), 436–458.

Becher, R. (1982). Parent education. In H. E. Mitzel (Ed.), *Encyclopedia of educational research* (5th ed) (pp. 1379–1382). New York: The Free Press.

Becher, R. (1984). *Parent involvement: A review of research and principles of successful practice.* Washington, DC: National Institute of Education.

Bee, L., Van Egeren, L. R., Streissguth, P., Nyman, B. A., & Leckie, S. (1969). Social class differences in maternal teaching strategies and speech patterns. *Developmental Psychology, 1,* 726–734.

Bempechat, J., & Ginsburg, H. (1989). *Underachievement and educational disadvantage: The home and school experience of at-risk youth.* Washington, DC: Office of Educational Research and Improvement. (ERIC Document Reproduction Service No. 315 485)

Bereiter, C. (1987). Jensen and educational differences. In S. Modgil and C. Modgil (Eds.), *Arthur Jensen: Consensus and controversy* (pp. 329–338). London: Falmer Press.

Berger, E. (1987). *Parents as partners in education.* Columbus, OH: Merrill Publishing Company.

Bernstein, B. (1961). Social class and linguistic development: A theory of social learning. In A. H. Halsey, J. Floud, & C. A. Anderson (Eds.), *Education economy and society* (pp. 288–314). New York: Free Press.

Bloom, B. (1986). *The home environment and school learning.* Chicago, IL: Study Group on the National Assessment of Student Achievement. (ERIC Document Reproduction Service No. 279 663)

Boyd, C. R. (1977). *"You don't have to be a star. . .": The natural role of parents as teachers.* Chicago, IL: Center for New Schools, Inc. (ERIC Document Reproduction Service No. 228 372)

Boykin, A. (1986). The triple quandary and the schooling of Afro-American children. In U. Neisser (Ed.), *The school achievement of minority children: New perspectives* (pp. 57–92). Hillsdale, NJ: Lawrence Erlbaum.

Broman, S. H., Nichols, P. L., & Kennedy, W. A. (1975). *Preschool IQ: Prenatal and early developmental correlates.* Hillsdale, NJ: Lawrence Erlbaum.

Brown, S. V. (1983). The commitment and concerns of black adolescent parents. *Social Work Research and Abstracts, 19*(4), 27–34 .

Chavkin, N. (1989). Debunking the myth about minority parents. *Educational Horizons, 67*(4), 119–123.

Cibulka, J., O'Brien, T., & Zewe, D. (1982). *Inner-city private elementary schools: A study.* Milwaukee, WI: Marquette University Press.

Clark, R. (1983). *Family life and school achievement: Why poor black children succeed or fail.* Chicago, IL: University of Chicago Press.

Clarke-Stewart, A. (1978). Evaluating parental effects on child development. In L. Shulman (Ed.), *Review of research in education* (pp. 47–119). Itasca, IL: Peacock.

Cole, M., & Bruner, J. S. (1971). Cultural differences and inferences about psychological processes. *American Psychologist, 26,* 866–76.

Coleman, J., & Hoffer, T. (1987). *Public and private high schools: The impact of communities.* New York: Basic Books, Inc.

Comer, J. (1980). *School power: Implications of an intervention project.* New York: The Free Press.

Comer, J., Haynes, N. M., & Hamilton-Lee, M. (1989). School power: A model for improving black student achievement. In W. D. Smith & E. W. Chunn (Eds.), *Black education: A quest for equity and excellence* (pp. 187–200). New Brunswick: Transaction Publishers.

Cotton, K., & Savard, W. G. (1982). *Parent involvement in instruction, K–12: Research synthesis.* St. Ann, MO: Comrel, Inc.

Dixon, H. (1986, March). *The Cuban-American counterpoint: Black Cubans in the United States.* Paper presented at the International Symposium on the Cultural Expression of Hispanics in the United States, Paris, France. (ERIC Document Reproduction Service No. 273 697)

Dokecki, P., Hargrove, E., & Sandler, H. (1983). An overview of the parent child development center social experiment. In R. Haskins & D. Adams (Eds.), *Parent education and public policy* (pp. 80–111). Norwood, NJ: Ablex.

Dore, M. M., & Dumois, A. O. (1990). Cultural differences in the meaning of adolescent pregnancy. *Families in Society, 71*(2), 93–101.

Dornbusch, S., Ritter, P., Leiderman, P., Roberts, D., & Fraleigh, M. (1987). The relation of parenting style to adolescent school performance. *Child Development, 58*(5), 1244–1257 .

Edwards, P. A. (1987). Working with families from diverse backgrounds. In D. S. Strickland & E. J. Cooper (Eds.), *Educating black children: America's challenge* (pp. 92–104). Washington, DC: Howard University.

Epps, E., & Smith, S. (1984). School and children: The middle childhood years. In A. Collins (Ed.), *Development during middle childhood: The years from six to twelve* (pp. 283–334). Washington, DC: National Academy Press.

Fine, M. (1980). *Handbook on parent education* (1st ed.). New York: Academic Press.

Fine, M. A., & Schwebel, A. I. (1988). An emergent explanation of differing racial reactions to single parenthood. *Journal of Divorce, 11*(2), 1–15.

Fordham, S., & Ogbu, J. (1986). Black students' school success: Coping with the burden of "acting white." *The Urban Review, 18,* 176–206.

Frechtling, J., Raber, S., & Ebert, M. (1984). *A review of programs and strategies used in other American school systems for improving student achievement.* Rockville, MD: Montgomery County Public Schools Dept. of Educational Accountability. (ERIC Document Reproduction Service No. 255 584)

Friedman, S. L., & Sigman, M. (Eds.). (1981). *Preterm birth and psychological development.* New York: Academic Press.

Gallagher, J., Trohanis, P., & Clifford, R. (Eds.). (1989). *Policy implementation & PL 99–457.* Baltimore, MD: Paul H. Brookes.

Goodson, B. D., & Hess, R. D. (1975). *Parents as teachers of very young children: An evaluative review of some contemporary concepts and programs.* Washington, DC: Bureau of Educational Personnel Development, Office of Education (ERIC Document Reproduction Service No. 136 967)

Gordon, I. (1968). *Parent involvement in compensatory education.* Chicago IL: University of Illinois Press.

Gordon, I. (1977). Parent education and parent involvement: Retrospect and prospect. *Childhood Education, 54,* 71–79.

Gordon, I. (1978). *What does research say about the effects of parent involvement on schooling?* Chapel Hill, NC: Occasional papers, School of Education, University of North Carolina, Chapel Hill.

Gordon, I. (1979). The effects of parent involvement on schooling. In R. S. Brandt (Ed.), *Partners: Parents and schools* (pp. 4–25). Alexandria, VA: Association for Supervision and Curriculum Development.

Gottfried, A. (Ed.) (1984). *Home environment and early cognitive development: Longitudinal research.* Orlando, FL: Academic Press.

Gotts, E., & Purnell, R. (1987). Practicing school-family relations in urban settings. *Education and Urban Society, 19*(2), 212–218.

Gougis, R. (1986). The effects of prejudice and stress on the academic performance of Black-Americans. In U. Neisser (Ed.), *The school achievement of minority children: New perspectives* (pp. 145–158). Hillsdale, NJ: Lawrence Erlbaum.

Grau, M. E., Weinstein, T., & Walberg, H. J. (1983). School-based home instruction and learning: A quantitative synthesis. *Journal of Educational Research, 76*(6), 351–360.

Greenwood, G., & Hickman, C. (1991). Research and practice in parent involvement: Implications for teacher education. *The Elementary School Journal, 91*(3), 279–288.

Griffore, R., & Boger, R. (Eds.). (1986). *Child rearing in the home and school.* New York, NY: Plenum Press.

Gross, M. (1974). *Combined human efforts in elevating achievement at the Wheatley School. Washington. DC.* Washington, DC: Nova University. (ERIC Document Reproduction Service No. 102 666)

Hale-Benson, J. (1986). *Visions for children: African American early childhood education program.* (ERIC Document Reproduction Service No. 303 269)

Hale-Benson, J. (1990). Visions for children: Educating black children in the context of their culture. In K. Lomotey (Ed.), *Going to school: The African-American experience* (pp. 209–222). Albany, NY: State University of New York Press.

Haley, P., & Berry, K. (1988). *Home and school as partners: Helping parents help their children. A resource packet.* Andover, MA: Regional Laboratory for Educational Improvement of the Northeast & Islands. (ERIC Document Reproduction Service No. 293 622)

Hart, T. (1988). *Involving parents in the education of their children.* Eugene, OR: Oregon School Study Council. (ERIC Document Reproduction Service No. 300 930)

Havender, W. (1987). Educational and social implications. In S. Modgil & C. Modgil (Eds.), *Arthur Jensen: Consensus and controversy* (pp. 339–351). London: Falmer Press.

Henderson, A. (Ed.). (1987). *The evidence continues to grow: Parent involvement improves student achievement.* Columbia, MD: National Committee for Citizens in Education.

Hendricks, L., Howard, C., & Caesar, P. (1981).

Help-seeking behavior among selected populations of black unmarried adolescent fathers: Implications for human service agencies. *American Journal of Public Health, 71,* 733–735.

Hess, R. D., & Holloway, S. (1985). Family and school as educational institutions. In R. Parke (Ed.), *Review of Child Development Research,* (Vol. 7, pp. 179–122). Chicago: University of Chicago Press.

Hess, R. D., & Shipman, V. C. (1968). Maternal influences upon early learning: The cognitive environments of urban pre-school children. In R. D. Hess & R. M. Bear (Eds.), *Early education: Current theory, research, and action* (pp. 91–104). Chicago: Aldine.

Hollins, E. R. (1982a). Beyond multicultural education. *The Negro Educational Review, 33*(3–4), 140–145.

Hollins, E. R. (1982b). The Marva Collins story revisited: Implications for regular classroom instruction. *Journal of Teacher Education, 33*(1), 37–40.

Humphreys, L. (1988). Trends in levels of academic achievement of blacks and other minorities. *Intelligence, 12,* 231–260.

Jensen, A. R. (1973). *Educability and group differences.* New York: Harper & Row.

Jensen, A. R. (1981). *Straight talk about mental tests.* New York: Free Press

Jensen, A. R. (1988). Raising IQ without increasing *g? Developmental Review, 9,* 234–258.

Jorge, A. (1982). *Perspectives on recent refugees and immigrant waves into South Florida. Occasional Papers Series, Dialogues No. 6.* Miami, FL: Florida International University Latin American and Caribbean Center. (ERIC Document Reproduction Service No. 263 280)

Keesling, J., & Melaragno, R. (1983). Parent participation in federal education programs: Findings from the federal programs survey phase of the study of parental involvement. In R. Haskins & D. Adams (Eds.), *Parent education and public policy* (pp. 230–256). Norwood, NJ: Ablex.

King, J. R. (1976). African survivals in the black American family: Key factors in stability. *Journal of Afro-American Issues, 4,* 153–167.

King, T., & Fullard, W. (1982). Teenage mothers and their infants: New findings on the home environment. *Journal of Adolescence, 5*(4), 333–346.

Klinman, D. G., & Sander, J. H. (1985). *Reaching and serving the teenage father.* New York, NY: Bank Street College of Education.

Kunjufu, J. (1984). *Developing positive self-images & discipline in black children.* Chicago, IL: African-American Images.

Labov, W. (1972). *Language in the inner city.* Philadelphia: University of Pennsylvania Press.

Ladner, J. A. (1987). Black teenage pregnancy: A challenge for educators. *Journal of Negro Education, 56*(1), 53–63.

Lareau, A. (1989). *Home advantage: Social class and parental intervention in elementary education.* London: Falmer Press.

Lazar, I. (1981). Early intervention is effective. *Educational Leadership, 38*(4), 303–305.

Lee, R. (1987, October). *Is black history a partial answer?* Paper presented at the Annual Conference of the National Black Child Development Institute, Detroit, MI. (ERIC Document Reproduction Service No. 287 953)

Leler, H. (1983). Parent education and involvement in relation to the schools and to parents of school-aged children. In R. Haskins & D. Adams (Eds.), *Parent education and public policy* (pp. 114–180). Norwood, NJ: Ablex.

Lomotey, K. (1981). *Nation building in the Afrikan community: It's time to build solutions to the education problem.* California: Sunshine Printers, CIBI Publication.

Mathis, S. (1974). True/false messages for the black child. *Black Books Bulletin, 2,* p. 19.

McAdoo, J. L. (1986). A black perspective on the father's role in child development. *Marriage and Family Review, 9*(3–4), 117–133.

McDill, E., Rigsby, L., & Meyers, E. (1969). *Educational climates of high schools: Their effects and sources.* Baltimore: Johns Hopkins University. (ERIC Document Reproduction Service No. 030 205)

Miller, B. I. (1986). *Parental involvement affects reading achievement of first, second, and third graders.* South Bend, IN: Indiana University. (ERIC Document Reproduction Service No. 279 997)

Murray, S. (1980). *The national evaluation of the PUSH for excellence project. Technical report 1: The evaluation of a program.* Washington, DC: American Institutes for Research. (ERIC Document Reproduction Service No. 185 693)

National Center for Education Statistics. (1989). *Digest of education statistics* (25th ed.). Washington, DC: U.S. Department of Education Office of Educational Research and Improvement.

Nichols, R. (1987). Racial differences in intelligence. In S. Modgil & C. Modgil (Eds.), *Arthur Jensen: Consensus and controversy* (pp. 213–220). London: Falmer Press.

Nobles, W. (1978). Toward an empirical and theoretical framework for defining black families. *Journal of Marriage and the Family, 40,* 679–688.

Oakes, J. (1985). *Keeping track: How schools structure inequality.* New Haven: Yale University Press. (ERIC Document Reproduction Service No. 274 749)

Ogbu, J. (1986). The consequences of the American caste system. In U. Neisser (Ed.), *The school achievement of minority children: New perspectives* (pp. 19–56). Hillsdale, NJ: Lawrence Erlbaum.

Ogbu, J. (1989, April). *Academic socialization of black children: An inoculation against future failure.* Paper presented at the Biennial Conference of the Society for Research in Child Development, Kansas City.

Olion, L. (1988). *Enhancing the involvement of black parents of adolescents with handicaps.* Paper presented at the Ethnic and Multicultural Symposia, Dallas, TX. (ERIC Document Reproduction Service No. 298 709)

Olmsted, P. (1991). Parent involvement in elementary education: Findings and suggestions from the Follow Through program. *Elementary School Journal, 91*(3), 221–232.

Olmsted, P., & Rubin, R. (1983). Parent involvement: Perspectives from the Follow Through experience. In R. Haskins & D. Adams (Eds.), *Parent education and public policy* (pp. 112–140). Norwood, NJ: Ablex.

Peters, M., & Deford, C. (1978). The solo mother. In R. Staples (Ed.), *The black family: Essays and studies,* Belmont, CA: Wadsworth.

Rankin, P. (1967, February). *The relationship between parent behavior and achievement of inner-city elementary school children.* Paper presented at American Educational Research Association Convention, New York.

Reis, J. S., & Herz, E. J. (1987). Correlates of adolescent parenting. *Adolescence, 22,* 599–609.

Rich, D., Van Dien, J., Mattox, B. (1979). Families as educators of their own children. In R.S. Brandt (Ed.), *Partners: Parents and schools* (pp. 26–40). Alexandria, VA.: Association for Supervision and Curriculum Development.

Rodick, J., & Henggeler, S. (1980). The short-term and long-term amelioration of academic and motivational deficiencies among low-achieving inner-city adolescents. *Child Development, 51,* 1126–1132.

Rowan, J. (1989). *The effect of gender on the non-promotion of black males.* Chicago, IL. (ERIC Document Reproduction Service No. 313 456)

Rowland, S. G., & Wampler, K. S. (1983). Black and white mothers' preferences for parenting programs. *Family Relations Journal of Applied Family and Child Studies, 32*(3), 323–330.

Schlossman, S. (1983). The formative era in Ameri-can parent education: Overview and interpretation. In R. Haskins & D. Adams (Eds.), *Parent education and public policy* (pp. 7–39). Norwood, NJ: Ablex.

Scott-Jones, D. (1984). Family influences on cognitive development and school achievement. In E. Gordon (Ed.), *Review of Research in Education* (Vol. 11, pp. 259–304). Itasca, IL: Peacock.

Seely, D. (1981). *Education for partnership.* New York: Ballinger.

Seginer, R. (1983). Parents' educational expectations and children's academic achievements: A literature review. *Merrill-Palmer Quarterly, 29,* 1–23.

Shade, B. (1982). Afro-American cognitive style: A variable in school success? *Review of Educational Research, 52*(3), 219–244.

Slaughter, D. T., & Epps, E. G. (1987). The home environment and academic achievement of black American children and youth: An overview. *Journal of Negro Education, 56*(1), 3–20.

Slaughter, D., & Schneider, B. (1987). *Newcomers: Blacks in private schools.* Evanston, IL: Northwestern University School of Education. (ERIC Document Reproduction Service No. 274 769)

Smith, L. (1988). Black adolescent fathers: Issues for service provision. *Social Work, 33*(3), 269–271.

Staples, R. (1976). *Introduction to black sociology.* New York: McGraw-Hill.

Stevens, J. (1984). Black grandmother's and black adolescent mothers' knowledge about parenting. *Developmental Psychology, 20*(6), 1017–25.

Stevens, J. H. (1988). Social support, locus of control, and parenting in three low-income groups of mothers: Black teenagers, black adults, and white adults. *Child Development, 59*(3), 635–642.

Strom, R. (1979). *Parental background: Does it matter in parent education?* Tempe, AZ: Arizona State University Parent-Child Laboratory. (ERIC Document Reproduction Service No. 241 154)

Szalay, L. B. (1978). *The Hispanic American cultural frame of reference: A communication guide for use in mental health education and training.* Washington, DC: Institute of Comparative Social and Cultural Studies.

Taylor, D., & Dorsey-Gaines, C. (1987). Growing up literate: Learning from inner-city families. In D. S. Strickland & E. J. Cooper (Eds.), *Educating black children: America's challenge* (pp. 85–92). (ERIC Document Reproduction Service No. 298 188)

Topping, K. (1986). *Parents as educators: Training parents to teach their children.* Cambridge, MA: Brookline Books.

Troutman, D., & Falk, J. (1982). Speaking black English and reading: Is there a problem of interference? *Journal of Negro Education, 51*(2), 123–133.

Tucker, C., & Chennault, S. (1990). *A research-based model partnership in education program for facilitating academic achievement self-esteem and adaptive functioning of low-achieving black children.* Unpublished manuscript.

Tucker, C., Harris, Y., & Brady, B. (1990). *The association of selected parent behaviors with academic achievement, adaptive functioning, and maladaptive functioning of second, fourth, and eighth grade black children and white children.* Unpublished manuscript.

Turner, A. (1987, February). *Multicultural considerations: Working with families of developmentally disabled and high-risk children.* Paper presented at Infant Development Association Conference, Los Angeles, CA. (ERIC Document Reproduction Service No. 285 360)

U.S. Bureau of the Census. (1990). *Statistical abstract of the United States 1990* (110th ed.). Washington, DC: U.S. Government Printing Office.

U.S. Department of Health, Education, and Welfare. (1976). *Home Start and other programs for parents and children.* Washington, DC: U.S. Government Printing Office.

Walberg, H., Bole, R., & Waxman, H. (1980). School-based family socialization and reading achievement in the inner-city. *Psychology in the Schools, 17,* 509–514.

Wallace, I. F. (1988). Socioenvironmental issues in longitudinal research of high-risk infants. In P. M. Vietze & H. G. Vaughan (Eds.), *Early identification of infants with developmental disabilities* (pp. 356–382). Philadelphia: Grune & Stratton.

Webb, R., & Parkay, F. (Eds.) (1989). *Children can: An address on school improvement.* A Joint Publication of the Alachua County Mental Health Association, Alachua County Public Schools, Gainesville/Alachua County Center of Excellence, Research and Development Center on School Improvement at the University of Florida. Gainesville, FL: University of Florida.

Williams, D., & Chavkin, N. (1985). *Final report of the parent involvement in education project.* Contract No. 400–83-0007, Project P-2. Washington, DC: National Institute of Education.

Wilson, A. (1978). *The developmental psychology of the black child.* New York: Africana Research Publications.

Wilson, J. (1987). *The truly disadvantaged: The inner city, the underclass, and public policy.* Chicago, IL: The University of Chicago Press.

Winter, M. (1988, November). *Parents as teachers: Beginning at the beginning.* Missouri State Dept. of Elementary and Secondary Education, Jefferson City. Paper presented at the National Conference on Early Childhood Issues: Policy Options in Support of Children and Families. (ERIC Document Reproduction Service No. 303 254)

Ziegler, S. (1987). *The effects of parent involvement on children's achievement: The significance of Home/school links.* Toronto: Toronto Board of Education. (ERIC Document Reproduction Service No. 304 234)

7

CHARACTERISTICS OF PARENT-PROFESSIONAL PARTNERSHIPS

Carl J. Dunst, Charlie Johanson,
Theresa Rounds, Carol M. Trivette,
and Debbie Hamby

The adage "two heads are better than one" fundamentally explains the benefits of cooperative arrangements. Cooperative endeavors are the joint efforts of a number of people that are mutually beneficial to all involved parties. The benefits that result from such endeavors are assumed to be greater than those accrued if efforts are carried out by one party or person alone.

It has long been believed that coordination and cooperation between parents and professionals are mutually beneficial and are advantageous not only to both groups but also to the children who are reared and educated by parents and professionals, respectively (see Kagan, 1987; Lombana, 1983, Chapter 1). For example, home-school communication has been advanced as a fundamental ingredient necessary for educational efforts to have maximum positive impact

Appreciation is extended to Pat Condrey for assistance in preparation of this chapter. Special thanks is extended to the parents and professionals who contributed information and shared their experiences for the research and case studies reported in the chapter. This chapter is based upon a presentation made at the Sixth Annual International Conference on Children with Special Needs, Division for Early Childhood, Council for Exceptional Children, Albuquerque, NM.

on child achievement (Smith, 1968). Similarly, Mittler, Mittler, and McConachie (1987) noted that collaboration between parents and professionals contributes to improved educational programs and social services for families and their children. According to Bronfenbrenner (1979), such parent-professional linkages form the basis for interconnecting home and school settings in ways that promote the exchange of ideas, information, and skills, which in turn build positive attitudes toward "educating" children in both parents and professionals.

The terms *collaboration* and *partnership* are now used most frequently to describe parent-professional relationships that aim to promote cooperation between parents and professionals (e.g., Buswell & Martz, 1988; Dunst & Paget, 1991; Jones, 1989; Lipsky, 1989; Lombana, 1983; National Center for Clinical Infant Programs, 1985; Powell, 1990; Schulz, 1987; Shelton, Jeppson, & Johnson, 1987; Weissbourd, 1987). Both terms have implicit meaning and presumed characteristics that make these types of relationships different from other cooperative endeavors. The purpose of this chapter is to examine the major characteristics of parent-professional partnerships and draw implications from the material for both policy and practice.

The chapter is divided into four

major sections. In the first section an operational definition of partnerships is provided together with a preliminary list of characteristics that define the "key elements" of partnerships. In the second section we examine the relationship between partnerships and both effective helping and empowerment. The point is made that partnerships are forms of effective helping that enable and empower both parents and professionals as part of collaborative efforts. In the third section we present the findings from both a parent-professional survey and case studies that provide empirical evidence regarding the major characteristics and processes involved in the development of partnerships. In the fourth section we present a parent-professional partnership model that helps explain the ways in which cooperative arrangements evolve into partnerships. We conclude with a brief description of the implications of the material for policy and practice. Collectively, the information presented in this chapter advances our knowledge of the meaning of partnerships and of the advantages adoption of partnerships has for both parents and professionals.

DEFINITION OF PARTNERSHIPS

Dunst and Paget (1991) recently reviewed and integrated the literature on parent-professional relationships and found no *operational* definition of either collaboration or partnership. An operational definition of a construct such as partnership is a necessary (though not sufficient) condition for being able to recognize a partnership when one observes its manifestation. Additionally, knowledge of the characteristics of partnerships is necessary for informing practitioners about the behaviors that need to be adopted if one chooses to use partnerships as a *collaborative helping style*.

Borrowing from the business literature (Clifford & Warner, 1987; Phillips & Rasberry, 1981; Uniform Partnership Act, 1941), Dunst and Paget (1991) defined a parent-professional partnership as "An association between a family and one or more professionals who function collabo-

ratively using agreed upon roles in pursuit of a joint interest or common goal" (p. 29). This definition provides a starting point from which to begin disentangling the characteristics that uniquely make a relationship between people a *partnership*.

Also borrowing from the business literature, Dunst and Paget (1991) proposed that partnership relationships are characterized by at least the following features: (a) mutual contributions and agreed upon roles; (b) desire to work together in pursuit of agreed upon goals; (c) shared responsibility in taking actions to achieve such goals; (d) loyalty, trust, and honesty in all "dealings" involving the partnership; (e) full disclosure of pertinent information between partners; and (f) parental locus of decision making in exercising their rightful role to decide what is in the best interest of their family and its members, particularly a developing child. Although not as exacting as the "rules" of business partnerships, this list of characteristics nonetheless provides guideposts for both knowing when relationships are partnerships as opposed to other types of collaborative arrangements, and structuring how one can behave in a way that shows a *presumption toward* adoption of partnership characteristics as a helping style.

In addition to the Dunst and Paget (1991) review a number of other recent articles provide additional insights about the major characteristics of parent-professional partnerships (e.g., Collins & Collins, 1990; Jones, 1989; Lipsky, 1989; Powell, 1990; Thornton, 1990; Vosler-Hunter, 1988). Vosler-Hunter (1988), for example, proposed that parent-professional collaboration is characterized by the following elements: (a) mutual respect for skills and knowledge, (b) honesty and clear communication, (c) understanding and empathy, (d) mutually agreed upon goals, (e) shared planning and decision making, (f) open and two-way sharing of information, (g) accessibility and responsiveness, (h) joint evaluation of progress, and (i) absence of labeling and blame. These elements are used by Vosler-Hunter and his colleagues as part of parent and professional collaborative training efforts aimed at improving cooperative relationships between the respective partners. The emphasis and benefits of this training were stated in the following way:

> If, as parents and professionals, we strive for open and honest communication, mutual respect for our skills and knowledge, and shared planning and decision making, [any] conflicts will not necessarily go away, but a working relationship will be established that can only serve to *improve services for our children* [italics added]. (Vosler-Hunter, 1988, pp. 2–3)

Both the Dunst and Paget (1991) and Vosler-Hunter (1988) descriptions of parent-professional partnerships, as well as complementary perspectives offered by others (e.g., Buswell & Martz, 1988; Lipsky, 1989; Lombana, 1983; Miller, Lynch, & Campbell, 1990; Schulz, 1987; Walker, 1989), provide a preliminary framework for (a) defining the meaning of partnerships and (b) operationally establishing the characteristics that make partnerships unique forms of cooperative relationships. The extent to which the proposed characteristics of partnerships could be empirically established was the major focus of the work reported in this chapter. However, whether or not partnerships can be recommended as a "best practice" depends upon the relative efficacy of partnerships as a "helping style" compared to other, more traditional ways of influencing behavior change in parents or children, or both. The relationship between partnerships and both effective helping and empowerment is briefly discussed next in order to place the material presented in the following and subsequent sections in proper perspective.

PARTNERSHIPS, EFFECTIVE HELPING, AND EMPOWERMENT

A number of investigators have noted the relationship between partnerships and both effective helping (Dunst, 1987; Maple, 1977) and empowerment (Collins & Collins, 1990; Whaley & Swadener,

1990). Others have also noted the relative advantage of partnerships over more traditional client-professional relationships as a way of influencing the behavior of help seekers (Dunst & Paget, 1991; Rappaport, 1981, 1987; Weissbourd, 1987). Maple (1977), for example, argued that participatory and equal involvement of help seekers in the helping process promotes the capabilities of help seekers in ways that allow them to "take control" over important parts of their lives so as to achieve desired outcomes. Participatory involvement, as used by Maple, is very much like partnerships as defined above.

Collins and Collins (1990), as well as others (e.g., Whaley & Swadener, 1990; Rappaport, 1981), specifically noted the relationship between partnerships and empowerment. Empowerment is an interactive process that builds upon and enhances people's acquisition of knowledge and competencies as part of partnership arrangements. Partnerships are at least one mechanism for promoting the types of give-and-take between partners that make the "whole greater than the sum of the parts" with respect to competency enhancing influences. According to Dunst and Paget (1991), partnerships are *enabling experiences* that (a) create opportunities for persons to work together in pursuit of a goal or interest and that (b) build upon and promote each partner's capabilities and capacities. Thus, professionals who attempt to work together with parents as partners are more likely to employ helping behaviors that have competency enhancing effects. Partnerships, by definition, enable people by creating opportunities to become competent in areas of life that partners deem important. Partnerships would therefore be expected to strengthen the functioning of partners as a result of collaborative experiences. Thus, to the extent that partnerships create opportunities (i.e., are enabling) for partners to collaboratively pursue agreed upon goals in ways that achieve desired intentions, the efforts should have empowering consequences.

There is now a corroborative body of evidence which indicates that a helping style that embodies the major characteristics of partnerships, particularly one that emphasizes *active involvement of help seekers that is competency enhancing,* has greater positive impact compared to other types of helping acts in which help seekers passively respond to help-giver advice (see Brickman, Kidder, Coates, Rabinowitz, Cohn, & Karuza, 1983; Brickman, Rabinowitz, Karuza, Coates, Cohn, & Kidder, 1982; Coates, Renzaglia, & Embree, 1983; Dunst & Trivette, 1988; Dunst, Trivette, & Deal, 1988; Dunst, Trivette, Davis, & Cornwell, 1988; Karuza, Zevon, Rabinowitz, & Brickman, 1982; O'Leary, 1985). Abstracting from available conceptual and empirical evidence, the case can be made that partnerships are an effective helping style that creates opportunities which are competency enhancing and in turn have empowering consequences.

CHARACTERISTICS OF PARTNERSHIPS

Two different but complementary lines of investigation were undertaken in order to obtain information necessary to either validate or invalidate the contentions reported above regarding (a) the characteristics of partnerships and (b) the relationship between partnerships and competency enhancement. The first was a parent-professional survey designed to obtain information about the specific characteristics that make parent-professional relationships partnerships. The second was a series of case studies designed to "unravel" how these characteristics get played out in practice in ways that reflect an emerging sense of parental control over important aspects of their lives. Data from both sources were expected to advance our knowledge about the specific meaning and impact of parent-professional partnerships.

PARENT-PROFESSIONAL SURVEY

Subjects

The survey was conducted with 69 parents and 102 professionals in two states (Alaska and North Carolina). The sample of parents included families with special needs children or children at-risk for poor developmental outcomes. The average age of the children was 4.1 years ($SD = 3.97$). The sample of professionals were all human service practitioners or administrators. The respondents were asked to list the behavioral and attitudinal characteristics they believed were important for parent-professional relationships to be *partnerships*. The results were expected to yield information about the major elements and characteristics of parent-professional partnership.

Method

Data summary and synthesis were carried out in several major steps. First, the various characteristics listed by the individual respondents were tabulated. A total of 94 separate descriptors were elicited. Second, the 94 descriptors were reduced to 26 characteristics by combining terms that had the same or very similar meaning. For example, the terms *reliable, consistent,* and *dependable* were combined and collectively labeled "dependability." Third, the 26 characteristics were rank ordered for the combined sample and for the parents and professionals separately, by computing the percentage of individuals who listed each element as a defining characteristic of partnerships. Fourth, chi-square analyses were used to discern whether the percentage of parents and professionals who listed each characteristic differed significantly between the two groups of respondents. Differences were tested at the .01 level in order to avoid spurious results given the fact that 26 separate analyses were performed on the data. Fifth, a Spearman correlation was computed between the rankings of the parents and professionals to establish whether there was agreement between the subsamples regarding the *relative importance* of the different characteristics. Sixth, the 26 characteristics were organized in four, nonmutually exclusive categories using an *a priori* categorization scheme that divided the 26 descriptions into two groups of behavioral *states* (beliefs and attitudes) and *traits* (communication style and behavioral actions). Operational definitions of beliefs, attitudes, communication style, and behavioral actions were used to assign individual characteristics to the categories (see Table 1). Seventh, summary scores were computed for each respondent in each state and trait category, and correlations were computed between these scores and several other descriptive indices (e.g., parent vs. professional) to establish the relationship among the measures.

Results

Table 2 shows the percentage for the combined sample and parents and professionals who indicated that certain characteristics were essential elements of partnerships. Trust, mutual respect, open communication, honesty, active listening, openness and flexibility, caring and understanding, shared responsibility, full disclosure of information, and information sharing, as well as a number of other characteristics, were listed as the major elements of parent-professional partnerships. A comparison of the characteristics listed in Table 2 with those described above (Dunst & Paget, 1991; Vosler-Hunter, 1988) finds considerable overlap between what has been proposed as the elements of partnerships with the actual characteristics listed by both parents and

professionals. There is, however, some difference in the relative importance attributed to different characteristics. For example, whereas Vosler-Hunter (1988) listed "mutually agreed upon goals" as an essential element of parent-professional collaboration, our findings indicated that this was a less important feature compared to other characteristics (e.g., shared responsibility and full disclosure of information).

The series of 26 chi-square analyses yielded significant differences between groups for six of the characteristics. A larger percentage of professionals (compared to the parents) indicated that mutual respect, flexibility, mutual support, empathy, reciprocity, and humor were major elements of partnerships. These results reflect the fact that certain partnership characteristics were deemed more important by the professional respondents.

A Spearman correlation computed between the rank ordering of characteristics for the parents and professional yielded an $r_s = .69$, $p < .001$. This finding showed that the ordering of the characteristics considered the most important, second most important, and so on by the parents and professionals was quite similar. This may be taken as evidence that both parents and professionals were in general agreement regarding the *relative*

TABLE 1
Operational Definitions of Four Behavioral States and Traits

Category	Definition
Beliefs	Cognitive attributions about how one should act or ought to behave toward other people. Beliefs are cognitive constructions or representations about objects (e.g., people) that reflect "truth" in how such objects ought to be treated.
Attitudes	Particular (emotional) feelings about a person, situation, or relationship. Attitudes refer to affective dispositions toward objects (e.g., people) that reflect favorable-unfavorable, desirable-undesirable, etc., evaluations of such objects.
Communicative Style	Methods and approaches for information sharing between partners. Communicative style refers to how information is given and received during interactions between people.
Behavioral Actions	Behaviors that reflect translation of attitudes and beliefs into actions. Behavioral actions include any implicit or explicit ways of acting toward others that are reciprocal in manifestation.

TABLE 2
Percentage of Parents and Professionals Listing Each Characteristic of Partnerships

Characteristic	Both Groups Combined ($N = 171$)	Parents ($N = 69$)	Professionals ($N = 102$)
Trust	51	45	55
Mutual Respect	51	39	59
Open Communication	46	44	47
Honesty	40	30	47
Active Listening	39	38	39
Openness	30	28	31
Flexibility	27	12	37
Caring	26	23	28
Understanding	25	20	28
Shared Responsibility	24	23	25
Full Disclosure of Information	23	29	20
Information Sharing	23	28	21
Acceptance	22	17	26
Mutual Support	21	10	28
Commitment to the Relationship	20	15	24
Reciprocity Between Partners	19	09	27
Mutually Agreed Upon Goals	18	10	23
Empathy	17	06	25
Dependability of Partner	15	15	15
Equality	15	12	17
Nonjudgmental	15	09	19
Positive Stance Toward Partner	14	10	16
Presumed Parental Capabilities	14	07	18
Humor	12	04	17
Confidence	09	09	10
Mutual Problem Solving	07	07	07

importance of the characteristics that define partnerships.

Further examination of the 26 characteristics listed most frequently as elements of parent-professional partnerships indicated that they could be organized into a number of sets of behavioral *states* and *traits*. Closer inspection suggested that the state characteristics could be subgrouped into beliefs and attitudes and that the trait characteristics could be subgrouped into two behavioral sets (communication style and behavioral actions). An independent classification of the 26 individual characteristics into one or more state or trait categories was undertaken by four raters. Using *a priori* operational definitions of the four state and trait categories (see Table 1 above), the four raters agreed at least 85% of the time (Range = 85% to

89%) as to which behaviors belonged to which state and trait categories.

Table 3 shows the results of the categorization. The majority ($N = 20$) of the 26 characteristics (77%) were assigned to a single category. Six of the characteristics were assigned to two different categories: respect, humor, active listening, openness, mutual support, and understanding. The latter indicated that the raters believed that these particular elements represented either states or traits depending upon how, and in which manner, the characteristic might be manifested in interactions between parents and professionals.

Table 4 shows the correlations between the four partnership measures as well as the correlations between the partnership and descriptive measures. All six correlations between the partnership

TABLE 3
A Categorization Scheme for Organizing the Major Characteristics of
Parent-Professional Partnerships

Category	Definition	Characteristics
Beliefs	Cognitive attributions about how one should act or ought to behave toward other people	Trust, mutual respect, honesty, acceptance, mutually supportive, nonjudgmental, presumed capabilities
Attitudes	Particular (emotional) feelings about a person, situation, or relationship	Caring, understanding, commitment, empathy, positive stance, humor, confidence
Communicative Style	Methods and approaches for information sharing between partners	Open communication, active listening, openness, understanding, full disclosure of information, information sharing
Behavioral Actions	Behaviors that reflect translation of attitudes and beliefs into actions	Mutual respect, openness, flexibility, understanding, shared responsibility, mutual support, reciprocity, mutual agreement about goals, dependability, equality, humor, problem solving

measures were statistically significant, indicating that the different dimensions of partnerships are interrelated rather than mutually exclusive. This was as expected, and may be taken as an indication of the related nature of the four behavioral dimensions of partnerships. The magnitudes of the correlations, however, were not so high as to reflect considerable overlap among the four measures. This was somewhat unexpected, and may be taken as evidence for the *multidimensional* nature of partnerships, at least as represented by our state and trait framework.

The set of three significant correlations between the partnership measures and the professional status measure simply reflects, as already noted, the fact that professionals (compared to parents) listed more characteristics as being essential elements of partnerships. Child chronological age was also significantly correlated with three of the four partnership measures. This presumably reflects the fact that the parents of older children had more experience with parent-professional relationships and were better able to articulate those characteristics that made

such relationships partnerships. None of the other descriptive measures were significantly related to any of the partnership measures.

Discussion

Collectively, the data from the parent and professional survey add to our knowledge about the meaning and characteristics of partnership relationships. On one hand, the results provide empirical evidence to support the contentions made by others regarding the essential elements of partnerships (e.g., Dunst & Paget, 1990; Jones, 1989; Lipsky, 1989; Vosler-Hunter, 1988; Walker, 1989). On the other hand, the findings extend our knowledge about the defining characteristics of partnerships, particularly those that are deemed most important by both parents and professionals. What the survey results do not establish are the particular characteristics that *uniquely* define partnerships and differentiate partnerships from other types of relationships. For example, a comparison of the characteristics listed in Table 2 shows that many overlap with those considered essential elements of

TABLE 4
Correlations Between the Partnership and Descriptive Measures

Measures	Partnership Measures				Descriptive Measures				
	BL	AT	CS	BA	LO	PS	PD	CA	DX
Partnership Categories:									
Beliefs	—	.320*** (N=171)	.198** (N=171)	.476*** (N=171)	.135 (N=171)	.466*** (N=171)	.118 (N=95)	.411*** (N=68)	.090 (N=68)
Attitudes		—	.382*** (N=171)	.599*** (N=171)	-.058 (N=171)	.253** (N=171)	-.053 (N=95)	.104 (N=68)	.011 (N=68)
Communication Style			—	.452*** (N=171)	-.080 (N=171)	.037 (N=171)	-.009 (N=95)	.224* (N=68)	.038 (N=68)
Behavioral Actions				—	-.016 (N=171)	.376*** (N=171)	.016 (N=95)	.217* (N=68)	.007 (N=68)
Descriptive Measures:									
Location (LO)[a]					—	.494*** (N=171)	.080 (N=95)	.524*** (N=68)	-.057 (N=68)
Professional Status (PS)[b]						—	.000 (N=95)	—[e]	—[e]
Professional Discipline (PD)[c]							—	—[e]	—[e]
Child Age (CA)								—	-.017 (N=68)
Child Diagnosis (DX)[d]									—

[a] Alaska = 1 vs. North Carolina = 2.
[b] Parent = 1 vs. Professional = 2.
[c] Education Background = 1 vs. Other = 2 (Therapy, Psychology, Social Work).
[d] At-Risk = 1 vs. Handicapped = 2.
[e] Not computed.
*p<.05, **p<.01, ***p<.001.

both effective interpersonal communication (e.g., DeVito, 1989) and various counseling techniques (e.g., Brammer & Shostrom, 1968; Ehly, Conoley, & Rosenthal, 1985). DeVito (1989) noted, for instance, that active listening, acceptance, trust, understanding, and respect, as well as other behaviors, are characteristics of individuals who communicate effectively with others. Similarly, Brammer and Shostrom (1968) noted that honesty, acceptance, flexibility, understanding, and caring are defining characteristics of effective counselors. What appears to *operationally differentiate* these various characteristics in partnerships compared to other relationships is the operative "mutual." Mutual trust, respect, honesty, flexibility, etc., denote the *complementary, joint,* and *reciprocal* efforts of partners as compared to the single-sided manifestation of these characteristics by, for example, counselors. In partnerships, both parties simultaneously display the defining characteristics, whereas in other types of relationships this may not necessarily be the case.

Other characteristics that uniquely define partnerships are also listed in Table 2. These include open (two-way) communication, shared responsibility, full disclosure of information, mutual support, reciprocity between partners, (mutual) dependability of partners, and equality in the relationship. These particular behaviors, more than any others, reflect differing forms of *reciprocity* between partners. These behavioral characteristics, together with the *mutual* display of the other states and traits described above, may at least tentatively be considered a "working" list of empirically and operationally defined elements that make partnerships different from other types of "helping" relationships.

Case Studies

The survey results presented above, although illustrative and elucidating, nonetheless depict a static view of the characteristics of partnerships. The display of the essential elements of partnerships would, however, be expected to be

dynamic rather than static. Partnership characteristics would be expected to differ in a number of ways among partners depending upon at least three factors. First, the particular characteristics that assume precedence in any given relationship would be expected to differ depending upon the focus of the "work" of the parent-professional partnership relationship at any given point in time. Second, the particular characteristics that uniquely define a partnership would be expected to change over time as a function of the evolving interactions between partners. Third, the ways in which evolving partnerships influence parents' sense of control over the "business" of the partnership would also be expected to change depending upon which partnership characteristics characterize the relationship between partners, and how successful the partners are in achieving desired outcomes. The case examples presented next were selected to illustrate these dynamic aspects of partnerships.

The case material comes from the experiences of parents of special needs and at-risk children participating in either center- or home-based early intervention and preschool programs. We present material on parent-professional relationships at different junctures in the development of partnerships to illustrate how the characteristics of partnerships evolve within the context of real life situations.

Abbott Family

"Jan and Bob Abbott" live in a small, rural logging community in the western United States. Bob works full-time as an independent logger and part-time as a school janitor. Jan works as a cashier at a community grocery market. The Abbotts have two children, "Dianne" who is 10 years old, and "Mark" who is 2 months of age. Jan and Bob both suspected something was wrong with Mark from the moment he was born. He acted very different than Dianne had as an infant. Mark was a very fussy baby who cried and screamed nearly all the time. No matter what Jan or Bob tried, Mark was constantly upset and irritable.

Mark's aversive behavior took its toll on the Abbotts in a number of ways. Jan and Bob's parents repeatedly said that Mark was "spoiled" and Jan "wasn't feeding him enough." Other family members and friends visited the Abbotts less and less. Neighbors started to complain about Mark's excessive crying and screaming. The Abbotts were reported to local authorities for child abuse by a neighbor. Attempts to obtain professional input and advice about the cause of Mark's problem were unsuccessful. More and more, Jan and Bob felt isolated and "at their wits end." Even their daughter Dianne began to spend more time alone in her room.

When Mark was about 3 years old, Jan became aware of a newly established early childhood—special education program operated by the public schools. Although she was reluctant to become involved with yet other professionals, she nonetheless decided to contact the staff to see "what could be done to help her and her child."

Jan scheduled a meeting with the preschool teacher to find out what the program had to offer. Jan's meeting with the teacher was initially a very uncomfortable encounter. She feared that the teacher might judge her adequacy as a parent. She was also hesitant to share "too much information" because she wasn't sure the teacher could be trusted. On top of all this, Jan was very emotionally upset and obviously "physically drained" from Mark's care.

The teacher initially attempted to do two things in her meeting with Jan. First, she simply listened to what Jan wanted to share with her, and clearly assumed a nonjudgmental, acceptance stance toward the mother and her situation. Second, the teacher noted a negative "tone" in Jan's descriptions of herself, Mark, and her situation, and therefore emphasized the positive aspects of what Jan said while acknowledging the difficulties Jan was facing. Because of the proactive and nonjudgmental stance the teacher took throughout the meeting with Jan, she

became much more relaxed and at ease as the teacher listened and attempted to understand her concerns. Jan later reported that the teacher's respect and sincere interest in what she was feeling and had to say was instrumental in establishing initial rapport between the two parties.

The first meeting between Jan and the teacher lasted 3 hours. At the end of this initial encounter, the teacher and mother made an "appointment" for the teacher to visit Jan once or twice weekly on the teacher's way home from school. Jan made arrangements with her employer so that she could be home to meet with the teacher. The respective flexibility on the part of Jan and the teacher made their home visiting arrangement convenient for both partners. Home visits were made by the teacher over the course of the next several years.

A considerable amount of time was spent discussing Mark's behavior and options for dealing effectively with his crying and screaming as well as other uncontrolled outbursts. Both the mother and father and the teacher talked repeatedly over the course of many months about the causes, consequences, and solutions to Mark's behavior problems. These discussions, characterized by openness, honesty, frank interchange of ideas, and mutual understanding, created a supportive situation that allowed all parties to share their feelings, knowledge, and expertise. These discussions alone proved very helpful as a way of relieving the Abbotts of much of their guilt and fear about Mark's behavior. As Jan and Bob became more at ease and relaxed, noticeable changes occurred in Mark's responsiveness to his parents and sibling. Together, the teacher and parents found different activities and interests that Mark responded to in a positive, favorable manner. The ability to enjoy Mark and take him on outings was described by Jan as a "new found freedom." It was discovered that Mark was particularly fond of horses, and horseback rides became a favorite activity of the family.

The development of a warm, trusting, and open relationship between the Abbotts and the teacher was a slow, evolving process. The building of a partnership between the family and teacher nonetheless was at least one major determinant of the small but noticeable positive changes that occurred in the Abbott's life. Both Jan and the teacher subsequently noted that the 2 years they worked together were very "labor intensive" and very "emotionally draining." Both agreed that their "work together" was well worth the effort. The sense of purpose and direction, as well as the parents' sense of control over Mark's behavior, gave the family a "new found" feeling of self-confidence that proved beneficial to all parties.

Baine Family

"Marie Baine" is an 18-year-old single mother of a 2-year-old daughter "Ashley." Marie has been labeled "mentally retarded" and is considered by many people, including her mother, to be incompetent as a parent. She lives with her mother and 7-year-old brother. Her mother has repeatedly urged Marie to "give Ashley up" for adoption, and she places unusual demands on Marie in an effort to "wear her down" so that she will "give in" to her mother's wishes. Marie, however, has very strong feelings about her capacity to be a "good mother" and her desire to become more independent and live on her own.

Since her child's birth, Marie has had frequent contact with a nurse at the local Public Health Department. On several occasions, Marie indicated to the nurse that she felt information about child development and ways to help Ashley learn would make her a better parent. The nurse suggested that Marie call the local early intervention program and inquire about available services for herself and Ashley.

Marie was very excited about the information provided by the early intervention program staff, but became concerned when she was told that the program used home visits to work with families. Marie, not knowing any of the program staff, felt that if someone came into her home, her mother might "sway them over" to her side about giving the child up for adoption, or worse yet, report her for child neglect. Sensing the reluctance on the part of Marie to have home visits, the early intervention practitioner assigned to work with the family suggested they meet at an agreed upon location outside the home.

During the initial contacts with Marie and Ashley, the interventionist spent considerable time trying to understand the mother's situation and concerns. The sincere interest, compassion, empathy, and respect shown for Marie by the interventionist became the "building blocks" for the subsequent development of a mutually trusting, open, honest, and collaborative relationship.

The evolving partnership between Marie and the interventionist was uniquely characterized by information sharing, shared responsibility, reciprocity, and cooperative problem solving. As trust developed between partners, Marie shared many of her concerns and frustrations regarding her mother and home life. A considerable amount of time was spent by Marie sharing her desires and aspirations for herself and Ashley. One major focus of the joint efforts of Marie and the interventionist was finding housing for herself and Ashley. Marie has often mentioned to the interventionist that she felt that this would give her more independence and a greater sense of control over her family's life.

One of the first things Marie and the interventionist did when Marie decided to "move out on her own" was for them to talk about "what it would take" to independently manage a household. This included discussions of household chores, meal preparation, bill paying, and other related matters. After these matters were discussed and key issues resolved (e.g., having enough money to pay the rent), both parties began developing steps that needed to be taken in order to identify housing options. Marie began by looking in the classified section of the local newspaper. Several "leads" were identified this way. The mother shared with the interventionist her feelings of inadequacy regarding her ability to actually contact someone and inquire about the availability of a house or apartment. Both partners worked together to "task analyze" what should be done and said as part of responding to a newspaper ad. Marie and the interventionist "role played" the techniques and strategies that would be used to "make contact" with potential landlords. Marie gained a tremendous amount of self-confidence as a result of the mutual problem solving and competency enhancing efforts between partners. The efforts paid off. After several contacts, she successfully found an apartment and now lives on her own with Ashley. Many of her other concerns and worries are still present, but she now feels much more confident in her own abilities.

Cranz Family

"Alice Cranz" was stunned with shock and disbelief when the doctors of NICU told her that her newborn daughter, "Heather," had contracted a severe strep-infection during delivery or possibly shortly before. When Alice and her husband, "Nick," first saw their infant daughter, they found her completely immersed in wires, tubes, and fighting for every breath of life. They were nearly paralyzed by what they saw. Heather remained in the hospital the first 9 months of her life. Both Alice and Nick Cranz were "up and coming" professionals whose career goals and aspirations were shattered by Heather's special need for intensive medical care and 24-hour-a-day supervision. Over the course of Heather's hospitalization, Alice and Nick discussed the matter of financial responsibility for Heather's care as well as day-to-day responsibility of her care following discharge from the hospital. A number of pragmatic considerations led to the decision that Alice would continue working full-time and Nick would "take a leave of absence" and assume primary responsibility for Heather.

Heather's discharge plan from the hospital included recommendations for early intervention and therapeutic services and for Nick to receive training in the use of the medical equipment to sustain Heather's breathing as well as other "medical interventions" necessary for the day-to-day care of his child. Nick quickly found "all the demands and expectations" placed upon him by the more than 10 professionals and agencies who began involvement with the family "too much to handle."

One of the professionals who visited Nick and Heather in their home quickly noticed the "pile-up effect" of all the things Nick was attempting to do, and how the excessive time demands placed upon him by others was becoming stressful and "out of control." The professional sensitively and empathetically "approached" Nick in a way that did not undermine any sense of confidence he did have as a parent. The home visitor was able to get Nick to share his concerns, and together they were able to translate this into a series of "action steps" to obtain resources and supports in response to Nick's needs and desires. The mutual problem solving, reciprocity between partners, and shared responsibility in "exploring options and evaluating choices" proved important in strengthening and promoting Nick's sense of competence as Heather's primary caregiver.

The major concerns identified by Nick included his sense of inadequacy in using Heather's medical equipment, the 24-hour-a-day care of Heather, the "excessive" number of therapy and clinic appointments recommended for Heather, and his wife's "judgment" of his particular "parenting style." Together, Nick, Alice, and the home visitor "tackled" each of these areas over a 4- to 6-month period of time. They began by scheduling "work time" together where all three could meet at least on a weekly basis. These meetings were characterized by openness, mutual sharing of concerns and information, and a joint commitment to "solving problems" for all family members. As a result of these "problem-solving sessions," Nick and Alice were able to determine and each make a personal commitment to mutually agreed upon goals. One major "element" of the contributions made by the home visitor to the partnership was sensitivity to each parent's need to "feel confident" as a caregiver. The home visitor, for example, was careful to note each parent's unique "caregiver strengths" and commented about how these different capabilities, taken together, contributed to the "best care possible" for Heather.

All in all, the systematic efforts of the parents and home visitor contributed to an increase in the parents' sense of both control and "meaningful" improvement in Heather's care as well as their own quality of life. As Nick put it, he felt his family was now "batting a thousand" as their life began to fall back into place.

Collectively, the selected material from the three case studies illustrates the processes involved in the development and manifestation of different partnership characteristics. On one hand, the case studies illustrate that different "elements" of partnerships assume primacy at particular points in time and vary according to both family and system influences. On the other hand, the case studies illustrate how partnerships can be an "effective helping style." Additionally, the case studies provide evidence regarding the empowering consequences of competency enhancement and active help-seeker involvement as a primary focus of working relationships between parents and professionals.

A MODEL OF PARENT-PROFESSIONAL PARTNERSHIPS

The results and findings from both the survey and case studies have led us to develop a parent-professional partnership model that attempts to explain how partnerships evolve between parents and professionals during the course of their work together. The model postulates that partnerships evolve as a result of both *interactive time* between people and the display of the different *behavioral states and traits* that characterize partnerships. This evolution is depicted in Figure 1. As can be seen, the nature of relationships changes from coordination to cooperation to collaboration to partnership as a function of the development of trust,

honesty, shared responsibility, disclosure of information, etc., between parents and professionals as they jointly work together in pursuit of agreed upon goals. At the most basic level, partnerships are assumed to be the consequence of the mutual display of partnership characteristics resulting from effective reciprocal interactions. Therefore, it may be appropriate to describe relationships between people as partnerships when and only when the relationship is characterized by certain operationally defined and behaviorally established states and traits. Given this perspective, it may be somewhat misleading for professionals to say to parents "up front" that they employ partnerships as a helping style.

An important and potentially illuminating feature of our model is the way in which the behavioral states and traits that characterize partnerships unfold over the course of interactive time (encounters) and converge and uniquely define particular collaborative relationships. Figure 2 shows how this *unfolding* and *convergence* can be conceptualized. Interactive encounters between parents and professional (or any potential partners) are seen as a necessary condition for certain states and traits to be manifested. This is represented by the time (t) dimension of the model. Over the course of interactive time, opportunities exist for different attitudes, beliefs, communicative behaviors, and behavioral actions to be displayed by both parties as a result of cooperative endeavors. To the extent that the particular states and traits displayed are consistent with those listed in Tables 2 and 3, the relationship may be appropriately described as a partnership.

The representation of the model may be taken one step further by specifying the particular states and traits that uniquely define particular partnerships. One such set of states and traits is shown in Figure 3. (Many others exist and most certainly define other partnership arrangements.) This particular partnership is characterized by the unfolding of different states and traits during two periods of *time* (t_1 and t_2), the development of *interdependencies* among the

Figure 1
**Emergence of different parent-professional relationships as a function of interactive
time between parents and professionals and the manifestation of different
behavioral states and traits.**

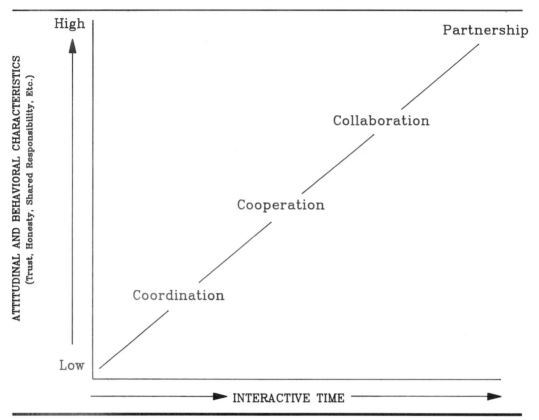

partnership characteristics both within
(e.g., trust and honesty) and across (e.g.,
open communication and empathy) categories of behavior, and the *convergence* of
multiple elements of behaviors that
uniquely define an interactive relationship. No doubt the model is complicated
by the fact that for a given relationship
between two persons, the particular characteristics that "define" the relationship
will differ depending upon the focus of
the work between partners.[1] Nonetheless,

our model tentatively provides a framework for conceptualizing and operationally defining the key element and characteristics that make collaborative
relationships between people *partnerships.*

CONCLUSION

We conclude our discussion of partnerships with a brief description of the
implications of the material presented in
our chapter for both policy and practice.
The implications for policy are both
radical and far reaching (see especially
Maple, 1977; Rappaport, 1981, 1984,
1987; Weissbourd, 1987). Striving to
employ partnerships between parents and
professionals as a way of influencing
parenting competencies and affecting

[1] This point was brought to our attention
by Patrick Bartholomew, a practitioner in our
program, who has extensive experience with
and commitment to parent-professional partnerships. His insights illuminated our understanding of partnerships and effective helping
processes.

Figure 2
Four major dimensions of parent-professional partnerships and their convergence across time (t).

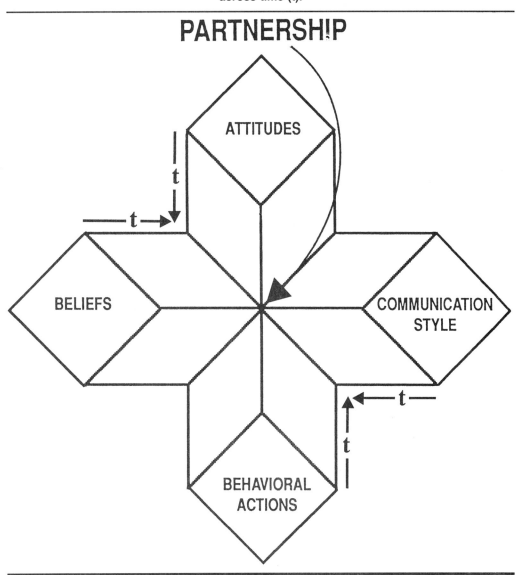

positive changes in children's behavior and development "requires a major breakdown of the typical role relationships between professionals" and parents (Rappaport, 1984, p. 19). Such a shift requires abdication of paternalistic approaches to helping relationships and adoption of empowerment, participatory involvement, and competency enhancement approaches to helping (e.g., Hobbs, Dokecki, Hoover-Dempsey, Moroney, Shayne, & Weeks, 1984; Maple, 1977; Rappaport, 1981). This is no small task. It will require major policy changes in how social programs view, interact, and treat families.

The implications for practice are somewhat more straightforward. Dunst and Paget (1991) reviewed and summarized much of what is known about working with practitioners who choose to employ partnerships as a helping style

Figure 3
Example of the evolution and convergence of different characteristics of parent-professional partnerships across two periods of interactive time (t_1 & t_2).

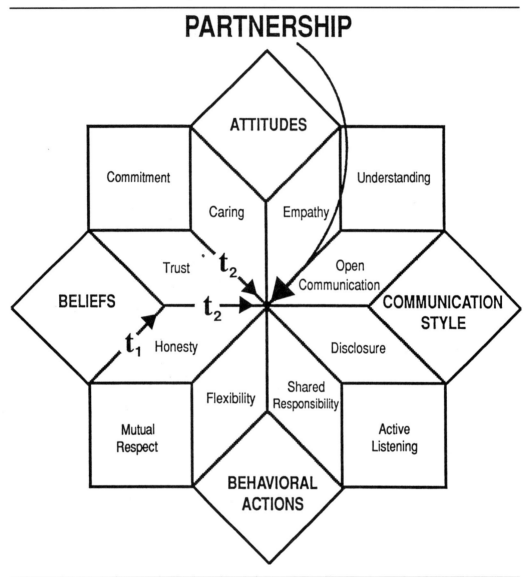

(see also Vosler-Hunter, 1988). Additionally, the findings reported in this chapter have several other implications for practice. First, the list of characteristics found to be the major elements of partnerships may be used as a "checklist" for assessing whether or not professionals assume certain attitudes and beliefs and manifest particular behaviors as part of interactions with parents. Second, the same list may be used to ask parents whether or not they believe the states and traits are behaviors particular professionals display in interactions with themselves. This information would be of particular value as a "validity check" for practitioners because it would provide a "second perspective" on the nature of their relationships between themselves and the parents with whom they work. Third, a "blank version" of the framework shown in Figure 3 could be used by both a parent and a professional to assess jointly the characteristics that uniquely define their working relationship. This would be useful as a way of promoting dialogue between partners, which in turn should strengthen their partnership arrangement.

In summary, the material presented in this chapter extends and expands our knowledge about parent-professional partnerships. We highlighted major concerns and considerations as an attempt to more fully explicate the meaning and characteristics of partnership relationships. We hope that our perspective on partnerships contributes to the understanding of partnerships as an effective helping process.

REFERENCES

Brammer, L., & Shostrom, E. (1968). *Therapeutic psychology* (2nd ed.). Englewood Cliffs, NJ: Prentice-Hall.

Brickman, P., Kidder, L. H., Coates, D., Rabinowitz, V., Cohn, E., & Karuza, J. (1983). The dilemmas of helping: Making aid fair and effective. In J. D. Fisher, A. Nadler, & B. M. DePaulo (Eds.), *New directions in helping: Vol. 1. Recipient reactions to aid* (pp. 18–51). New York: Academic Press.

Brickman, P., Rabinowitz, V., Karuza, J., Coates, D., Cohn, E., & Kidder, L. (1982). Models of helping and coping. *American Psychologist, 37,* 368–384.

Bronfenbrenner, U. (1979). *Ecology of human development.* Cambridge, MA: Harvard University Press.

Buswell, B., & Martz, J. (1988). The meaning of partnerships: Parents' perspectives. *Early Childhood Facilitator,* 4(2), 6–7. (Newsletter of the Colorado Division for Early Childhood.)

Clifford, D., & Warner, R. (1987). *The partnership book* (3rd ed.). Berkeley, CA: Nolo Press.

Coates, D., Renzaglia, G. J., & Embree, M. C. (1983). When helping backfires: Help and helplessness. In J. D. Fisher, A. Nadler, & B. M. DePaulo (Eds.), *New directions in helping: Vol. 1. Recipient reactions to aid* (pp. 251–279). New York: Academic Press.

Collins, B., & Collins, T. (1990). Parent-professional relationships in the treatment of seriously emotionally disturbed children and adolescents. *Social Work, 35,* 522–527.

DeVito, J. (1989). *The interpersonal communication book* (5th ed.). New York: Harper & Row.

Dunst, C. J. (1987, December). *What is effective helping?* Paper presented at the biennial meeting of the National Clinical Infants Program Conference, Washington, DC.

Dunst, C. J., & Paget, K. (1991). Parent-professional partnerships and family empowerment. In M. Fine (Ed.), *Collaboration with parents of exceptional children* (pp. 25–44). Brandon, VT: Clinical Psychology Publishing Co.

Dunst, C. J., & Trivette, C. M. (1988). Helping, helplessness, and harm. In J. Witt, S. Elliott, & F. Gresham (Eds.), *Handbook of behavior therapy in education* (pp. 343–376). New York: Plenum Press.

Dunst, C. J., Trivette, C. M., Davis, M., & Cornwell, J. (1988). Enabling and empowering families of children with health impairments. *Children's Health Care Journal, 17,* 71–81.

Dunst, C. J., Trivette, C. M., & Deal, A. G. (1988). *Enabling and empowering families: Principles and guidelines for practice.* Cambridge, MA: Brookline Books.

Ehly, S., Conoley, J., & Rosenthal, D. (1985). *Working with parents of exceptional children.* St. Louis, MO: C. V. Mosby.

Hobbs, N., Dokecki, P. R., Hoover-Dempsey, K. V., Moroney, R. M., Shayne, M. W., & Weeks, K. H. (1984). *Strengthening families.* San Francisco: Jossey Bass.

Jones, B. (1989, Winter). Parents as partners. *New Ways,* 16.

Kagan, S. (1987). Home-school linkages: History's legacy and the family resource movement. In S. Kagan, D. Powell, B. Weissbourd, & E. Zigler (Eds.), *America's family support programs* (pp. 161–181). New Haven: Yale University Press.

Karuza, J., Jr., Zevon, M. A., Rabinowitz, V. C., & Brickman, P. (1982). Attribution of responsibility by helpers and recipients. In T. A. Wills (Ed.), *Basic processes in helping relationships* (pp. 107–129). New York: Academic Press.

Lipsky, D. K. 1989). The role of parents. In D. K. Lipsky & A. Gartner (Eds.), *Beyond separate education: Quality education for all* (pp. 159–179). Baltimore: Brookes Publishing Co.

Lombana, J. (1983). *Home-school partnerships.* New York: Grune & Stratton.

Maple, F. (1977). *Shared decision making.* Beverly Hills, CA: Sage.

Miller, L., Lynch, E., & Campbell, J. (1990). Parents as partners: A new paradigm for collaboration. In W. Second (Ed.), *Best practices in school speech— language pathology: Vol. 1. Collaborative pro-*

grams in the schools (pp. 49–56). New York: Psychological Corporation.

Mittler, P., Mittler, H., & McConachie, H. (1987). Family supports in England. In D. Lipsky (Ed.), Family supports for families with a disabled member (pp. 15–36). New York: World Rehabilitation Fund.

National Center for Clinical Infant Programs. (1985). Equals in this partnership: Parents of disabled and at-risk infants and toddlers speak to professionals. Washington, DC: Author.

O'Leary, A. (1985). Self-efficacy and health. Behavior Research and Therapy, 23, 437–451.

Phillips, M., & Rasberry, S. (1981). Honest business. New York: Random House.

Powell, D. (1990). Home visiting in the early years: Policy and program design decisions. Young Children, 45(6), 65–73.

Rappaport, J. (1981). In praise of paradox: A social policy of empowerment over prevention. American Journal of Community Psychology, 9, 1–25.

Rappaport, J. (1984). Studies in empowerment: Introduction to the issues. In J. Rappaport, C. Swift, & R. Hess (Eds.), Studies in empowerment: Steps toward understanding and action (pp. 1–7). New York: Haworth Press.

Rappaport, J. (1987). Terms of empowerment/ Exemplars of prevention: Toward a theory of community psychology. American Journal of Community Psychology, 15(2), 121–128.

Schulz, J. (1987). Parents and professionals in special education. Boston: Allyn & Bacon.

Shelton, T. L., Jeppson, E. S., & Johnson, B. H. (1987). Family-centered care for children with special health care needs. Washington, DC: Association for the Care of Children's Health.

Smith, M. (1968). Schools and home: Focus on achievement. In A. Passow (Ed.), Developing programs for the educationally disadvantaged (pp. 87–107). New York: Teachers College Press.

Thornton, J. (1990). Team teaching: A relationship based on trust and communication. Young Children, 45(5), 40–43.

Uniform Partnership Act. (1941). Reprinted in Martindalu-Hubbell Law Digests, 1990, (pp. 177–181). Chicago: National Conference of Commissioners.

Vosler-Hunter, R. (1988). Elements of parent/ professional collaboration. Focal Point, 2(2), 1–3. (Bulletin of the Research and Training Center, Portland State University.)

Walker, B. (1989). Strategies for improving parent-professional cooperation. In G. Singer & T. Irvin (Eds.), Support for caregiving families: Enabling positive adaptation to disability (pp. 103–119). Baltimore, MD: Brookes Publishing.

Weissbourd, B. (1987). Design, staffing, and funding of family support programs. In S. Kagan, D. Powell, B. Weissbourd, & E. Zigler (Eds.), America's family support programs (pp. 245–268). New Haven: Yale University Press.

Whaley, K., & Swadener, E. (1990). Multicultural education in infant and toddler settings. Childhood Education, 66, 238–240.

8

COMPETENCE ENHANCEMENT TRAINING FOR CHILDREN: AN INTEGRATED CHILD, PARENT, AND SCHOOL APPROACH

Gerald J. August, Deborah Anderson, and
Michael L. Bloomquist

Currently there is both concern and alarm in our society about the proliferation of such public health problems as substance abuse, delinquency, suicide, and AIDS. These problems are no longer restricted to adults but are reported frequently in children and adolescents. To this growing list of childhood mental health problems can be added depression and anxiety disorders, attention deficit and learning disorders, as well as the potentially harmful effects that may arise when children are victimized by physical or sexual abuse, divorce, and inappropriate child care. Unfortunately, the prevailing system of mental health care has proven inadequate in reducing the prevalence of such maladies (Albee, 1982). The failure of the current mental health care system to adequately address these problems may be attributed, in part, to its acceptance of a victim-blaming mentality that contends that dysfunction resides primarily within the individual. Consistent with this perspective, treatment is primarily directed at the child with little if any attention given to the contexts or environments that children encounter. The majority of professional resources are allocated for individual assessment procedures aimed at identifying the pathognomonic "disease" agent and subsequent treatment within the context of hospitals, outpatient clinics, and private practice

settings. The considerable expense of such services, combined with their relative ineffectiveness, has resulted in an appeal for the development of preventive interventions that seek to modify antecedent conditions or emergent problems before they result in full-blown clinical disorders.

In recent years we have witnessed a gradual shift from the traditional clinical approach with its focus on risk and disorder, toward the development of community-based preventive intervention with its focus on adaptation and resilience. Such interventions typically begin early, are extended in time, consist of multiple components addressing risk or mediating factors, and are intensive in nature in order to maximize the chances for long-term and significant preventive effects. Central to many preventive intervention approaches is an emphasis on competence-building strategies that seek to foster the behavior effectiveness and positive self-perceptions of children regarding their functioning in the domains of school, interpersonal relations, and leisure activities (Ford, 1985). By means of strengthening children's personal and ecological resources, competence operates as a protective factor, buffering the individual against those forces that cause or contribute to psychopathology (Rutter, 1987; Garmezy, 1987). It is our contention that improving children's competence is a highly desirable goal statement for programs that seek to provide effective mental health care for children.

We recommend that interventionists adopt a competence enhancement perspective. This approach would broaden the therapeutic scope of mental health service beyond that focused solely on operant techniques for managing behavior or the teaching of cognitive skills to mediate behavior to include methods directed at environmental contexts that provide opportunities for children's real-life application, generalization, and maintenance of adaptive skills. Such interventions would recognize the importance of designing strategies within the context of two of the primary systems in which children and adolescents spend most of their early developmental years: the family and the school. These interventions would include multiple training components that would include specific training programs for children as well as training programs that would focus on the enhancement of parents, teachers, and peers as resources for children. Training strategies might vary from those that seek to alter dysfunctional communication patterns that exist within families and classrooms to those that teach parents and teachers how to prompt and reinforce newly learned skills within the context of real-life settings.

In this chapter, we present a multi-component competence enhancement model for conceptualizing and implementing programs that are aimed at children with behavioral and emotional disturbance. Although the model and subsequent program evolving from the model were developed for children identified at the early stages of problem development (i.e., secondary prevention), it can be easily adapted for large numbers of children whose current and future psychosocial functioning is of concern (i.e., primary prevention). This chapter begins with a discussion of competence as a critical construct underlying the development of mental health programs that seek to promote positive mental health outcomes. Next, we present a conceptual

model that has guided the development and delivery of our competence enhancement program for children with disruptive behavioral disorders. We follow with a review of past and existing competence enhancement programs. Finally, we present a description of a specific program for children with Attention Deficit Hyperactivity Disorder (ADHD) to serve as an example of a multicomponent competence enhancement intervention.

THE COMPETENCE PERSPECTIVE FOR PROMOTING MENTAL HEALTH

The construct of competence has its earliest roots in the writing of White (1959), who referred to competence as an "organism's capacity to interact effectively with its environment" (p. 297). Implicit in this conceptualization of competence is an inherent motivation on the part of individuals to actively explore, influence, and master their environment. More recently, Waters and Sroufe (1983) defined the competent individual as "one who is able to make use of environmental and personal resources to achieve a good developmental outcome" (p. 81). In a similar vein, Ford (1982) has identified competence in terms of two sets of outcomes: behavioral effectiveness in accomplishing personally and socially important goals and a sense of personal well-being. Each of these definitions views competence as an outcome variable that summarizes the quality of an individual's functioning in a given situation. Others have utilized competence as a process variable to refer to a hypothetical pattern of skills, beliefs, and/or behaviors that are useful in responding to specific situations (Strayhorn, 1988). In this sense, the terms competencies and skills are often used interchangeably.

Although we acknowledge the distinction between process and outcome, we prefer that the term competence be used in reference to behavioral outcomes, and that terms such as skills, strategies, and beliefs be retained to describe hypothetical processes mediating the acquisition of competence. In Figure 1 we provide a general model that illustrates

Figure 1

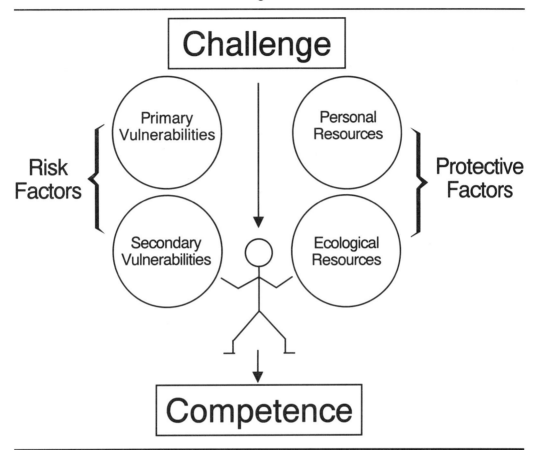

the various factors involved in the attainment of competence.

This model assumes that an individual's response to a specific situation or challenge (e.g., stressor) will be determined by a set of potential strengths and weaknesses that the child brings to meet the challenge, referred to here as risk factors and protective factors. Risk factors can include biological and genetic deficiencies of the child (i.e., primary vulnerabilities) as well as family and community environmental factors and life events (i.e., secondary vulnerabilities) that adversely affect development. Both primary and secondary vulnerabilities constitute major threats to adaptive functioning in the sense that they weaken the child's capacity to cope with various crises and transitions, referred to as developmental perturbations. Protec-

tive factors, in contrast, function to enhance adaptability by providing the child with needed resources that may be used to mitigate the effects of the developmental challenge. Protective factors include personal resources, which are assumed to be intrinsic attributes of the individual, and ecological resources, which refer to important people, organizational policies and rules, formal and informal activities, and other setting-related variables. Examples of personal resources are cognitive, affective, and social problem-solving skills, self-management of behavior (self-regulation), acquired information and tacit knowledge about the world, as well as self-perceptions of responsibility and performance efficacy. Ecological resources include environmental supports such as family cohesiveness, adequate rule setting, facilitative interpersonal interactions, responsive educational settings, and favorable friendship groups. Competence, within this scheme, represents an outcome of the interaction of risk and protective factors in the face of challenge. These factors may interact in a host of complex ways (see Rutter, 1983; Garmezy, Masten, & Tellegen, 1984) to yield competent or incompetent functioning. Werner and Smith (1982) have suggested that the interaction of risk and protective factors is a balance between the power of the person and the power of his or her social and physical environment. This balance is necessary throughout life, although different factors assume different degrees of importance at different developmental stages.

Although it is generally assumed that certain types of competence can be enhanced through educational efforts, attempts to assess and promote competence hinge on our ability to identify salient characteristics or specific personal/ecological resources that are available to competent children during different developmental periods. Moreover, once these characteristics and/or resources have been identified, it is necessary to identify the processes or mechanisms that affect their acquisition. One important domain in which competence can be acquired is social interactions and interpersonal relationships (i.e., social competence). Indeed, many interventionists over the past 15 years have viewed the enhancement of social competence as the primary focus of their prevention programs (Spivack & Shure, 1974; Allen, Chinsky, Larcen, Lochman, & Selinger, 1976; Weissberg, Gesten, Carnrike, Toro, Rapkin, Davidson, & Cowen, 1981). However, identification of specific processes underlying socially competent behavior has been elusive. Historically, most studies have emphasized individual component skills such as alternative solution thinking and have employed interventions that target such isolated skills for change (e.g., Spivack & Shure, 1974). More recently, investigators have begun to apply an information-processing approach to explain the acquisition of social competence (Ford, 1982; Dodge,

Pettit, McClaskey, & Brown, 1986). This approach has been incorporated in cognitive-behavioral interventions, which train children to use a framework of sequential processing strategies for mediating socially competent responding. This framework assumes that multiple processes are involved in behavioral and emotional responding, and thus training children to use a processing framework will be more effective than focusing on isolated component skills.

Rather than be conceptualized solely as an index of social adaptation, competence may be extended to children's adaptive functioning in academic and behavioral domains. For example, we define behavioral competence as the degree to which an individual demonstrates cognitions/behaviors that conform to accepted standards of conduct as determined by society. Examples of behavioral competence would include exhibiting rule-governed behavior in structured situations, complying with disciplinary requests in the home, inhibiting aggressive and impulsive behavior when frustrated or angered, and providing sufficient effort to reach a goal. Academic competence is defined as the degree to which an individual demonstrates cognitions/behaviors that mediate successful work-study habits and academic performance in educational settings. Although intelligence is a very powerful attribute of academically competent children, more modifiable attributes might include attending to and persisting at tasks, organizing time efficiently, and working on assignments in a reflective manner.

Adopting a competence perspective suggests that efforts be undertaken to provide children with the personal and environmental resources they will need to confront the various challenges imposed on them during development. As we learn more about the processes and/or mechanisms that mediate competence, we will be better able to mount specific interventions at appropriate points in time when such processes can be most effectively modified.

MODELS FOR COMPETENCE ENHANCEMENT INTERVENTIONS

Several conceptual models have been offered to guide the development and delivery of competence enhancement programs for children and adolescents. These models vary in terms of the primacy accorded to specific processes and mechanisms that are related to the development of adaptive behavior. Many intervention efforts target for change processes intrinsic to children themselves. Such person-focused programs are based on models that view the child as the primary source of risk in the sense that the child lacks certain knowledge, skills, or abilities and as a consequence is more vulnerable to various developmental challenges including stressful life experiences. Therapeutic activities are typically designed to teach the hypothesized deficient skills and abilities or to provide pertinent information to children at risk (Felner & Felner, 1989). Aspects of the child's social ecology that may be involved in shaping problematic developmental outcomes are generally ignored or given little attention by such models. On the other extreme are intervention models that place both the locus of risk and the primary point of intervention on elements in the child's social and physical environment. Such ecological-focused interventions attempt to facilitate adaptive behavior by providing "protective" resources in the person's environment or modifying existing conditions that are believed to be hazardous or stressful. Although both the person-focused and ecological-focused models address critical aspects of risk, neither by itself is sufficient to address the multifactorial etiology of most behavioral and emotional disorders of childhood.

A third type of model from which competence enhancement interventions can be mounted is the transactional model proposed by Sameroff and his colleagues (Sameroff & Fiese, 1988). This model emphasizes the reciprocal effects of children on their environmental contexts and contexts on children. The locus of risk does not rest solely within

the individual nor exclusively within the environment, but rather in the dynamic interactions occurring between children and their environment. Such interactions are influenced by personal attributes of the individual as well as by the nature of contextual settings encountered. It follows from this model that a pathologic outcome is the result of a specific vulnerability present within the individual coupled with a specific environmental hazard experienced at a developmentally sensitive point in time. Transactionally focused interventions may vary in terms of the processes and/or mechanisms targeted for change and thus may address several components. For example, coercive behavioral interactions often characteristic of conduct disorder children and their parents may be the primary transactional target for intervention. Intervention strategies may emphasize the ecological side of the risk equation by directing remediation efforts at modifying parents' child-management skills. An alternative type of transactional program, aimed at adolescent substance abuse, may target problematic peer relations with a focus on teaching adolescents specific skills to deal with elements of the peer culture that may influence the probability of a desired outcome. This approach focuses its change efforts on the personal side of the risk equation.

A synthesis or integration of the various intervention models may be particularly useful for prevention and promotion efforts in the mental health area where multifactorial causation is the rule rather than the exception (Felner & Felner, 1989). The findings from basic and epidemiological studies in this area of developmental psychopathology suggest the existence of complex etiologies involving a range of risk factors and mediators that span several ecological domains (individual, family, peer, school, and community). Interventions aimed at single risk factors that utilize narrowly defined treatment approaches may yield positive effects over the short term, but these effects may likely dissipate over time. Instead, what is called for are interventions with multiple components that address multiple risk factors and mediators. Such interventions will blend together relevant perspectives from personal-, transactional-, and ecological-focused models in creative ways to address the specific goals of the prevention program. For certain prevention goals, such as teenage pregnancy or drug abuse, an integration of the transactional and ecological perspectives may be productive. If peer influences, for example, are assumed to be the primary source of risk, then the focus of prevention strategies may be expanded to include a more extensive consideration of the peer culture including its organizational structure, rites of passage, and value system. Ecologically based prevention strategies may include the introduction of athletic and recreational programs within a community setting to provide constructive opportunities to foster peer-group acceptance and cohesiveness. In sum, the integration of the personal, transactional, and ecological perspectives reduces the degree to which we need to assume the presence of pathology within the individual, and allows us to look to the environment as both a source of risk and of protection in our understanding of developmental psychopathology and prevention.

REVIEW OF SCHOOL-BASED COMPETENCE ENHANCEMENT INTERVENTION PROGRAMS

Although the majority of prevention programs share the common goal of enhancing developmental outcome through promoting adaptive behavior, they vary in terms of their theoretical underpinnings and hence their targets for change. As discussed above, these interventions can be either single- or multifaceted in nature. Single-faceted programs are typically of the person-focused type which emphasize remediation of skill deficits in a given child. More recently, interventions have taken on a transactional or ecological orientation with a focus on modifying aspects of the children's social interactions or social environments such as the home and school settings. Multifaceted preventive interventions may draw from both perspectives. A review of previous and current school-based prevention programs suggests that intervention has evolved from limiting itself to a single target of change, whether person or environment, to addressing multiple targets that affect a child's behavioral and emotional responding.

Single-Faceted Interventions

The earliest prevention programs in the child mental health field sought to enhance social competence and were based on the person-focused model. The basic strategies targeted by these programs were interpersonal cognitive problem-solving skills (ICPS) such as alternative and consequential thinking, considered to be important to the resolution of many different kinds of interpersonal conflicts and thus, ultimately to behavioral adjustment (D'Zurilla & Goldfried, 1971). For example, Spivack and Shure (1974) at the Hahnemann Medical College taught ICPS to disadvantaged kindergarten children in a classroom setting via discussion, games, and activities. Children participated in daily 20-minute sessions for a period of 3 months. Compared to a group of control children, children receiving interpersonal cognitive problem-solving (ICPS) training demonstrated significant gains in alternative and consequential thinking and in overall behavioral adjustment as rated by their teachers. Such benefits were found whether the program had been implemented by teachers (Spivack & Shure, 1974) or by mothers (Shure & Spivack, 1978). Moreover, treatment gains remained stable at 1- and 2-year follow-ups. A program focused on building ICPS skills with middle class third and fourth grade children was subsequently evaluated by researchers at the University of Connecticut (Allen, Chinsky, Larcen, Lochman, & Selinger, 1976). Training consisted of biweekly 30-minute sessions delivered by the teacher over a 12-week period. In addition to the games and discussion employed by Spivack and Shure, the Connecticut program had children watch videotapes of children using ICPS strategies to solve problems. Although program children generated significantly more alternative solutions and provided more elaborate means-end thinking when posed with either hypothetical or real problems, they demonstrated no improvement on self-esteem or teacher-rated adjustment. Furthermore, program children did not maintain their initial gains beyond a 4-month time period. Project AWARE (Elardo & Caldwell, 1979) at the University of Arkansas incorporated ICPS and social role taking into a 7-month, 72-session program delivered to fourth and fifth graders. Program children demonstrated improved alternative thinking on one of six problems and showed greater improvement in self-reliance and respect for others than did controls.

A number of subsequent programs utilized a person-focused intervention similar to that of the Hahnemann and Connecticut groups, but augmented their programs to include a variety of teaching methods in order to enhance generalization of ICPS skills to real-life settings. McClure, Chinsky, and Larcen (1978) worked with the Connecticut group in their investigation of the effects of various teaching methods on ICPS acquisition. They evaluated the differential impact of employing three training methods: videotapes only, videotapes with discussion, and videotapes and role-playing exercises. The only significant effect observed was on a simulated peer-problem exercise with the highest score obtained by the group using both videotapes and role-playing. Dramatic results have been obtained by programs that offered children more diversified opportunities to practice their skills via additional teaching methods. For example, a group at the University of Rochester (Gesten, Rains, Rapkin, Weissberg, Flores de Apodaca, Cowen, & Bowen, 1982) compared the effects of incorporating role-playing, videotape modeling, discussion, and a variety of games in the delivery of ICPS to using videotapes only. The program consisted of seventeen 30-minute sessions delivered

to second and third grade students. When presented with a simulated peer-related problem task, children who received all variations of delivery showed more improvement than both videotape-only children and control children on measures assessing alternative and consequential thinking. In contrast, at immediate post-test the teachers rated controls as better adjusted than either group of trained children. At a 4-month follow-up, both full-training and videotape-only children were rated higher than controls on 7 of 10 teacher ratings of competence as well as on two peer sociometric measures. This study points to the importance of including long-term follow-up assessment of cognitive and behavioral skills as benefits attained from the program may be delayed. Additionally, the investigators suggested the efficacy of "booster" sessions that provide a review of previously learned skills as a means of further enhancing the maintenance of competence.

Multifaceted Interventions

Although the person-focused model provides a framework for a number of interventions, other prevention programs have been guided by an amalgamation of the person-, transactional-, and ecological-focused models. As home and school settings often constitute major sources of environmental influence in a child's life, multifaceted programs have typically augmented skill training by also addressing processes inherent to specific child-setting interactions. For example, PREP (Preparation through Responsive Educational Program) (Wodarski, Filipczak, McCombs, Koustenis, & Rusilko, 1979) assessed the academic and behavioral effects of an intervention that modified the child's home environment as well as providing the child with skills training. Thirty students with academic and/or social deficits participated in this year-long program. Each child was provided with training in social and academic skills, and the parents received training in family management in the home. In comparison to a control group, the experimental group improved in both academic and social areas immediately following intervention. At a 1-year follow-up, the trained group was found to have fewer suspensions, fewer disciplinary referrals, better attendance, and a higher rate of overall grade point average. However, these gains were not maintained by the experimental group at a 4-year follow-up.

In lieu of targeting the child's home environment as a supplement to child-focused training, a number of studies have addressed training the teacher to apply program concepts to daily class instruction to promote treatment-related competence in the classroom. A large scale prevention program that has served as a prototype for school-based intervention is Rochester's Primary Mental Health Project (PMHP) (Cowen, Gesten, & Weissberg, 1980). Implemented in over 20 schools in the greater Rochester area, this program was designed to identify high-risk children and to place them in a program to prevent the development of maladjustment. The intervention was based on an interpersonal cognitive problem-solving paradigm and consisted of training children in recognition of feelings, problem sensing and identification, generation of alternative solutions, consideration of consequences, and generalization to real-life problems. The classroom teachers conducted the program with the help of undergraduate students. In a series of program evaluations, program children improved significantly more than controls on several tests of cognitive and behavioral problem-solving skills. However, results on competence measures were equivocal. Gesten, Flores de Apodaca, Rains, Weissberg, and Cowen (1979) provided students with a 17-lesson program and found that program children improved significantly more than controls on measures of cognitive and behavioral problem-solving skills. In contrast, program children showed no improvement on post-program adjustment measures and teacher ratings of competencies. In a subsequent intervention trial the number of lessons was increased from 17 to 52, and Weissberg, Gesten, Rapkin, Cowen, Davidson, Flores de Apo-

daca, and McKim (1981) found that suburban, but not inner-city youngsters improved on skill-learning measures as well as measures of competence and problem behavior. Upon finding that suburban but not inner-city children improved on measures of competence and problem behavior following participation in the intervention, Weissberg, Gesten, Carnrike, Toro, Rapkin, Davidson, and Cowen (1981) modified the program by incorporating environmental remediation via the school. Teachers were trained to model cognitive, affective, and behavioral skills learned in the program. They were further encouraged to provide students with opportunities and prompts to use problem-solving skills in the classroom and to reinforce them for doing so. Results indicated that trained children improved relative to controls on teacher ratings of competence and problem behaviors and on their own perceptions of their problem-solving abilities. Collectively, these findings suggest that a multicomponent intervention involving school-based training was successful in teaching suburban and inner-city children to apply problem-solving strategies. However, in order to produce meaningful improvements in children's competence, a more intensive and multifaceted intervention was required.

Elias, Gara, Ubriaco, Rothbaum, Clabby, and Schuyler (1986) also utilized strategies of both the child-focused and ecologically focused models in their ISA-SPA (Improving Social Awareness—Social Problem Solving Project). Their 20-session program was aimed at children coping with the stress of transition to middle school and included a discussion component followed by application. The latter component consisted of having each child complete a personal problem-solving notebook together with a collective classroom problem-solving chart. Similar to the Rochester PMPH program, teachers received intensive training in facilitation of student problem solving in the classroom. At posttest, teachers rated program children as demonstrating significant improvement in both adjustment and problem-solving skills in comparison to controls.

In sum, prevention programs have evolved from utilizing a single-faceted approach centering on child skills training to a more comprehensive approach including strategies for modifying environmental influences. Few programs, however, have been truly multimodal with respect to targeting child, school, and home. Kirschenbaum (1979) has come closest to developing a true multicomponent program with his Social Skills Development Program (SSDP) implemented with children exhibiting problem behavior. Similar to its Rochester predecessor, SSDP utilizes a school-based intervention setting. However, it differs from the Rochester program in the expanded and diversified roles it requires of its professional staff. For example, paraprofessionals are employed to conduct therapy groups that include group discussion, structured activity designed to improve goal-related social competencies, empathy training, etc. Teachers and parents are not involved in direct service delivery, but instead receive consultation. Consultation contacts range in scope and specificity from developing cooperative relationships to devising specific contingency management systems (e.g., Kirschenbaum, 1979). Evaluations of the SSDP have produced only modest improvements in the adaptive functioning of high-risk, inner-city children, and suggest that more powerful interventions may be required to produce meaningful effects with such children.

Child, Home, and School Focused Competence Enhancement Intervention

The present literature review, which traces the evolution of mental health prevention programming from its early focus on remedial skill-building methods to its present community-based focus involving home-school collaboration, reveals that we are still a long way from producing the ideal multicomponent intervention. The merger of cognitive-behavioral technology and community psychology has led to a new generation of prevention programs with its focus on competence-building strategies and its utilization of children as well as their parents and teachers as resources.

In the development of competence enhancement interventions for young children with behavioral and emotional problems we advocate consideration of a multicomponent model. Our proposed model acknowledges the potential risks emanating from within the child, from the child's interactions with significant others, and from environmental settings encountered by the child. In accordance with this model, we posit three types of protective factors presumed necessary for children to develop competence: (a) children must possess and utilize executive-type information-processing strategies to direct, monitor, and regulate their behavioral and emotional responses (person-focused component); (b) those with whom children interact must consistently prompt and reinforce this information-processing approach (transactionally focused component); and (c) the contexts and/or environments which children encounter must make accommodations for conditions a and b (ecologically focused perspective). Although we present the components as independent categories to emphasize their primary orientations, we recognize that each component itself represents an integration of several components. For example, the effective utilization of processing strategies requires an integration of the person-focused and transactionally focused perspectives. A major focus is on training children to use specific information-processing strategies, but the efficacy of such strategies relies on feedback received from important contextual resources such as parents, peers, and teachers. The need for individuals to prompt and reinforce children's processing strategies involves the integration of the transactional and ecological perspectives. Thus, although change efforts are directed at interactions between children and parents/teachers, the ultimate success of such transactions is dependent on the availability of key environmental settings that may function as resources to reinforce children's real-life application, generalization, and maintenance of information-processing strategies.

This multicomponent scheme as applied to young children with disruptive behavioral disorders is illustrated in Figure 2.

As illustrated, the child-focused component of the intervention addresses training in the use of problem-solving and self-instructional strategies. The emphasis is on training children in five specific processing strategies: problem recognition, solution generation, consequential thinking, anticipation of obstacles, and execution of behavior. Children learn to apply these skills across five domains: interpersonal problem solving, anger/frustration management, negative thought and feeling management, poor effort management, and behavioral social skills training. The parent/teacher components of the intervention are conceptualized in three distinct ways. First, it is presumed that both parents and teachers

of disruptive children hold beliefs, attributions, biases, or expectancies that may adversely affect a child's behavior. If parents and teachers are to become positive resources in the pursuit of competence, they must first modify their cognitive sets. To this end, one of the initial goals of intervention training is to help parents and teachers come to a more realistic and accurate understanding of the child. Cognitive restructuring is a therapeutic concept that can be used to modify these types of faulty cognitions. In cognitive restructuring, parent/teacher training focuses on the identification of maladaptive thoughts, with the intent to replace them with more functional and adaptive thoughts. Parents and teachers learn to "reframe" or change the perceived meaning of a cognition from negative to positive.

Second, if children are to acquire, maintain, and generalize problem-solving strategies to regulate their behavior and emotions, both their parents and teachers

Figure 2

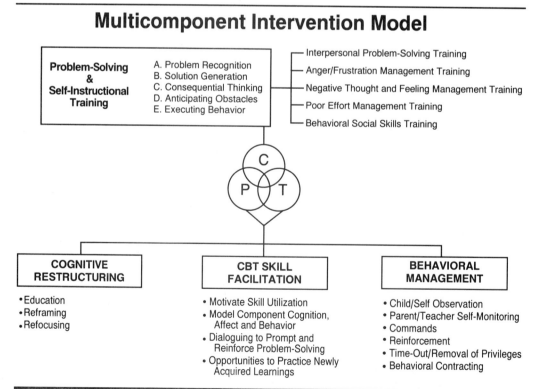

Multicomponent Intervention Model

need to learn strategies to facilitate children using their new skills at home and at school. To accomplish this goal, it is necessary for parents and teachers to (a) modify their environments to accommodate the child's skill usage; (b) adopt a more supportive interaction style with the child; (c) learn specific techniques (e.g., dialoguing) of how to prompt and reinforce children for using processing strategies; and (d) create opportunities for children to practice newly acquired learnings.

The third, and final element of the home-school collaboration involves training parents and teachers in the use of specific techniques for managing deviant behavior. Despite the best intentions of parents and teachers to espouse the competence enhancement approach, children may continue to exhibit undesirable behaviors that interfere with program learning. It is unrealistic to think that children with severe behavioral disorders could be completely habilitated by virtue of applying problem-solving strategies. Thus, in order to maximize the potency and comprehensiveness of the intervention, both parents and teachers need to supplement their role as problem-solving facilitators with their role as behavioral managers. In the latter role, parents and teachers learn skills related to improving commands, administering reinforcements for prosocial behaviors, ignoring inappropriate behaviors, and administering consequences for inappropriate behavior.

A MULTICOMPONENT COMPETENCE ENHANCEMENT INTERVENTION FOR ADHD CHILDREN

Attention Deficit Hyperactivity Disorder (ADHD) is characterized by developmentally inappropriate levels of inattention, impulsivity, and overactivity, which are typically manifested prior to 7 years of age (Barkley, 1989). In addition to these incipient symptoms, many children with ADHD go on to develop serious problems with peer relationships, academic difficulties, low self-esteem/demoralization, and verbal/

physical aggression. A significant number of these children with ADHD develop problems related to delinquent and antisocial behavior, substance use and abuse, depression, and a variety of other adjustment problems during adolescence and young adulthood (August, Stewart, & Holmes, 1983; Cantwell, 1985; Gittelman, Mannuzza, Schenker, & Bonagura, 1985). In light of the high prevalence of ADHD in the school-aged population and the documented associations between ADHD and later psychological maladjustment, there is clear rationale for the development of interventions that promote healthier childhood adaptation and decrease the likelihood of emergent psychopathology.

The most widely used intervention for children with ADHD continues to be psychostimulant medication. Despite the short-term efficacy of stimulants in improving these children's performance on laboratory tasks measuring sustained attention, impulsivity, and distractibility (Douglas, Barr, O'Neill, & Britton, 1986), long-term benefits have not been demonstrated (Charles & Schain, 1981). Given the limitations of stimulant treatment, alternative or adjunctive interventions have been recommended, particularly those that aim to provide skills that enable children with ADHD to adapt more effectively in their environment (i.e., competence). Cognitive-behavioral training approaches have been offered as procedures for promoting skill development in children (Braswell & Kendall, 1988). Central to these approaches is the development of executive control skills and reflective problem-solving strategies that provide children with a means to regulate their own behavior and emotion. A spate of treatment studies have assessed the effects of cognitive-behavioral training with ADHD children (see reviews by Abikoff, 1985; Kendall & Braswell, 1985). The training goals of these programs have been successfully achieved in the sense that children have evidenced significant changes on laboratory measures of impulsivity and observational measures of behavior. On a less encouraging note, cognitive-behavioral training methods have failed to produce significant transfer of training effects or long-term maintenance effects (Abikoff, 1979, 1985; Kendall & Braswell, 1985). If maintenance and generalization effects are to be obtained with such technology, the intervention program will require more direct targeting of transactional/ ecological processes with the goal of promoting the development of specific competencies.

The present intervention is for school-aged children with ADHD. The program was developed from a multicomponent model of competence enhancement that includes children, parents, and teachers as targets for training. We followed three steps in the development of this intervention, which we recommend for future intervention designers. The three steps are:

1. Perform a functional analysis of the perceived problem or disorder.

2. Design specific intervention strategies which will directly target those processes uncovered by the functional analysis.

3. Deliver the intervention within the child's social ecology.

In sum, the intervention seeks to modify cognitive processes intrinsic to the child, cognitive processes underlying the child's social interactions, as well as interaction patterns within the child's home, school, and community life. The intervention is conducted in such a manner as to make changes at the child, transactional, and ecological levels.

In the following sections we attempt to provide a brief overview of the various components of our competence enhancement intervention applied to children with ADHD. Because of space limitations, it is impossible to describe the program in detail. Detailed step-by-step description and procedures for conducting the intervention are provided in Braswell and Bloomquist (1991) and Bloomquist and Braswell (1990).

Functional Analysis of ADHD

A number of functional characteristics of children with ADHD have been described. These children have significant problems sustaining attention and inhibiting impulsive responding (Douglas, 1983). Many children with ADHD also have deficits in the spontaneous and strategic use of problem-solving strategies such as recognizing problems, generating alternatives and solutions, thinking of consequences, evaluating the effectiveness of strategies, and actually implementing strategies they choose (Douglas, 1983; Kendall & Braswell, 1985). These children also may be deficient in means-end problem-solving skills (Asarnow & Callan, 1985; Lochman & Lampron, 1986; Spivack, Platt, & Shure, 1976), which means they have difficulty setting goals and articulating the steps necessary to achieve goals. In addition, children with ADHD may have difficulty with perspective taking (Chandler, 1973; Gurucharri, Phelps, & Selman, 1984) so they are not adept at understanding the thoughts and feelings of others with whom they interact. Children with ADHD who are also aggressive may erroneously attribute hostile intent to the benign social behavior of others (Dodge, 1986) and exhibit difficulties modulating impulsive anger and frustration (Lochman, Nelson, & Sims, 1981).

Characteristics of parent and/or family relations as they covary with child behavior problems including ADHD have been identified. Parents, for example, are likely to make internal negative dispositional attributions toward their child in an attempt to infer causation about the child's problem behavior (Dix & Grusec, 1985; Sobol, Ashbourne, Earn, & Cunningham, 1989). Parents are also prone to maintain unrealistic beliefs and expectations about their child (Sobol et al., 1989; Vincent Roehling, & Robin, 1986) and/or exhibit an external locus-of-control cognitive style concerning their perceived ability to control their child (Campis, Lyman, & Prentice-Dunn, 1986; Morton & Tuma, 1988). From a behavioral perspective, a "coercive family process" is often characteristic of the interactions between children with behavioral problems and their parents (Gard & Berry, 1986; Patterson, 1982). The coercive family process is characterized by high levels of negative reinforcement for noncompliant behavior, low rates of positive reinforcement for appropriate behavior, inadequate discipline of the child's disruptive/inappropriate behavior, and poor parental monitoring of the child's behavior. A variety of family skill deficits have also been identified for families with a child exhibiting behavioral difficulties including deficits in family problem solving, communication, and conflict management (Foster & Robin, 1989; Ramsey & Walker, 1988; Ramsey, Walker, Shinn, O'Neill, & Stieber, 1989).

The authors do not know of any research that has specifically described the cognitive and behavioral characteristics of school personnel who frequently interact with children who have been diagnosed as ADHD. We hypothesize as do others (Braswell & Bloomquist, in press), that many of the cognitive and behavioral characteristics descriptive of parents and parent-child interaction, may also be operative in teachers and teacher-child interaction.

Specific Interventions for Children with ADHD

The present multicomponent competence enhancement intervention focuses directly on those cognitive and behavioral processes descriptive of children, parents/families, and school environments as detailed above. The child, parent, and teacher components are delivered in a coordinated and sequential manner over 18 weeks. Table 1 provides a description of how the three components are intermixed.

The child component. This component focuses on the acquisition of executive-type information-processing strategies that are useful in the regulation of behavior and emotion. Children are trained to utilize a five-step problem-solving sequence (D'Zurilla & Goldfried, 1971). Through the use of self-instruc-

tional training, children learn to state the five problem-solving steps to themselves when confronted with specific problem situations (Meichenbaum & Goodman, 1971). The steps guide children to recognize problems, generate alternative solutions, anticipate consequences and obstacles, and execute specific behaviors to solve problems.

After the children learn the five-step problem-solving/self-instruction process, they should theoretically be able to apply the skills to a variety of problem situations. To illustrate this point, an example will be given where a child is confronted with a problem of another child pushing him/her on the playground. The child may self-instruct in the following manner:

> *Stop! What's the problem?* (Step 1)—He shoved me and I'm feeling really mad. *What are some plans?* (Step 2)—Well, I suppose I could shove him back, or I could tell the teacher, or I could try to ignore him and walk away. *What is the best plan?* (Step 3)—Well if I push him back, we may get into a fight or I might really get in trouble. If I tell the teacher, that might work, but he may call me a tattletale. If I walk away, he might stop pushing me. I think this time I will try walking away and see if that works. *Do the plan.* (Step 4)—(the child walks away). *Did the plan work?* (Step 5)—Well I tried walking away and he stopped bugging me. The plan worked!

Once the children have mastered the generic problem-solving scheme, they learn how to apply these steps (strategies) to specific content areas. When applying it to different content areas, they still try to recognize the problem, generate alternatives, anticipate consequences and obstacles, and execute necessary behaviors. The most important domain for these children to focus on is interpersonal problem solving. Through interpersonal problem-solving training, children learn to apply problem-solving skills to better cope with interpersonal difficulties. To facilitate interpersonal problem solving, children are also trained in perspective-taking skills so they are better able to understand others' thoughts and feelings.

TABLE 1
Content and Sequence of Sessions for School-Based Competence Enhancement Training for ADHD Children

Week	Child Component	Parent Component	Teacher Component
1	Introduction		
2	Problem-Recognition I	Introduction	Introduction
3	Problem-Recognition II		
	Alternatives,	Group Process/Support,	Group Process/Support,
	Consequential Thinking,	Examine Parents'	Examine Teachers'
4	and Evaluation	Expectations for Program	Expectations for Program
	Executing Specific		
5	Behavior		
	Interpersonal	Examine Parent	Examine Teacher
6	Problem-Solving I	Cognitions and Behavior	Cognitions and Behavior
	Interpersonal		
7	Problem-Solving II		
8	Review	Child-Focused CBT I	Child-Focused CBT I
	Anger/Frustration		
9	Management I		
	Anger/Frustration		
10	Management II	Child-Focused CBT II	Child-Focused CBT II
11	Review		
12	Poor Effort Management I	Collaborative CBT I	Collaborative CBT I
13	Poor Effort Management II		
14	Review	Collaborative CBT II	Collaborative CBT II
	Negative Thoughts and		
15	Feelings Management I		
	Negative Thoughts and	Behavioral Child	Behavioral Child
16	Feelings Management II	Management I	Management I
17	Program Review I		
		Behavioral Child	Behavioral Child
		Management II, Program	Management II, Program
18	Program Review II	Review	Review

From Braswell and Bloomquist (1991).

Another relevant content area for these children is the management of anger and frustration. Children learn to utilize problem-solving steps, along with relaxation techniques and coping self-statements (e.g., "I'm not going to lose my cool," "I won't let him bug me," etc.) to control their anger and frustration. Because off-task behavior is a common problem for children with ADHD, they also receive training in applying the skills in effort management. Through effort-management training, children learn to use problem-solving steps and coping self-statements to enhance self-monitoring (e.g., "Oops, I'm staring out the window") and ability to stay on task (e.g., "I need to focus on my work").

To buttress the cognitive components described above, children are also trained in behavioral social skills. This is accomplished by training exercises directed at improving children's execution and maintenance of specific social behaviors (e.g., assertiveness, eye contact, initiating conversation, sharing, etc.). The therapist explains and models the social behaviors, engages the children in role-play exercises, and prompts children to apply these new social behaviors in their interactions with peers in group.

The parent/teacher component. Although parents and teachers do not participate in the intervention at the same time, the content of their training is very similar and therefore will be discussed together. There are four major areas of focus in the parent/teacher training. The first area focuses on modifying parents' and teachers' cognitions about these children. Educative and cognitive restructuring exercises are employed to help parents and teachers become aware of, and ultimately confront, the dysfunctional cognitions they hold toward these children. Parents and teachers learn to recognize maladaptive cognitions (e.g., "He is a brat"), and how to modify them in a more adaptive manner (e.g., "We both have a role in these problems"). The second, and most important, focus of the training is on what we refer to as "cognitive-behavioral child management." Parents and teachers are trained to prompt and reinforce children for using the cognitive strategies in the home and in the classroom. In this regard, parents learn to monitor the children and ask them to use "plans" (e.g., five-step problem-solving sequence) when the child is having a problem (e.g., noncompliance, fighting with sister/classmate, etc.). If the child successfully uses the plan, he or she eventually earns a tangible reward. The third area focus is "collaborative problem solving." This involves teaching parents and teachers to negotiate and solve problems *with* children (e.g., negotiate what time to go to bed using a plan). The fourth area focus is on improving parents' and teachers' behavioral management methods. Specifically, this involves teaching parents and teachers effective discipline techniques for reinforcing appropriate behavior and consequating inappropriate behavior of these children.

Ecological Delivery of Intervention

To this point we have mapped out the functional attributes of children with ADHD and their parents and teachers as well as the specific training content areas that focus on changing these functional attributes. In this section we will describe the implementation of training procedures.

Child training is conducted within the context of 18 group therapy sessions over a 9-week period in the school. Groups typically comprise 4 to 8 children and are led by two therapists. The therapist employs behavioral procedures, such as didactic instruction, modeling, role-play exercises, homework assignments, and behavioral contingencies. Group process is emphasized as a training task. This is achieved by encouraging children to use skills that they have learned to solve real-life problems that may emerge during group activities. For example, several children may get in an argument and the therapist prompts these children to use their skills (e.g., self-instruction, anger management, etc.) to solve the problems in group. Information from school and home regarding use of training skills in those environments is brought back to group sessions via structured homework exercises. This information is critically discussed and reinforced during each session.

The procedures for working with parents and teachers are quite similar. Parents meet as a small group with one therapist for nine weekly 90-minute meetings at the school, typically during evening hours. Teachers meet with one consultant for nine weekly 60-minute meetings during school hours. During these meetings, the therapist/consultant presents information through didactic instruction, but also attempts to facilitate group process whereby parents and teachers, in their respective groups, can support and reinforce each other. Modeling via videotaped and role-play examples of the specific techniques is also utilized to enhance training. Parents and teachers are given homework assignments that encourage them to prompt and reinforce children to apply the skills at home and school.

An important note to emphasize regarding the teacher component is that the entire school is involved in the intervention. That is, all teachers from the school participate in the training. The teachers are trained to prompt and reinforce problem-solving and self-instructional strategies used by *all* children in their classroom. Only those children identified as ADHD, however, receive the child- and parent-training components. By involving the entire student body in the school component, the children with ADHD are not singled out or labeled, and they have further opportunity to learn by observing their peers.

SUMMARY

The major objective of this chapter has been to propose a new conceptual framework for the design and implementation of school-based interventions for children with mental health problems. This approach represents a shift away from the traditional clinical approach with its focus on disorder and symptom reduction, toward a preventive orientation with its focus on adaptation and resilience. Central to the proposed framework is an emphasis on competence enhancement strategies that seek to strengthen children's personal and social resources while engineering environmental systems to accommodate skill learning. To facilitate adjustment gains that are both durable and generalizable, the proposed competence enhancement intervention is mounted on a transactional-ecological model of service delivery. The model calls for multiple training components that target for change those cognitive and behavioral deficits descriptive of "impaired" children, their parents, and their school teachers. Child training focuses on the acquisition and utilization of information-processing strategies that serve to direct, monitor, and regulate children's behavior and emotional responses. Educative and cognitive restructuring exercises are employed to help parents and teachers become aware of, and ultimately confront, dysfunctional cognitions that they may hold toward their children. In addition, parents and teachers work in collaboration to prompt and reinforce children for using new skill learning in home and school settings. The home and school are offered as ideal sites for collaborative-based intervention, as these contexts provide multiple opportunities for children to learn, practice, and evaluate new skills and knowledge in settings where they can be readily prompted and reinforced.

REFERENCES

Abikoff, H. (1979). Cognitive-training interventions in children: Review of two new approaches. *Journal of Learning Disabilities, 12,* 123–135.

Abikoff, H. (1985). Efficacy of cognitive training interventions in hyperactive children: A critical review. *Clinical Psychology Review, 5,* 479–512.

Albee, G. W. (1982). Preventing psychopathology and promoting human potential. *American Psychologist, 37,* 1043–1050.

Allen, G. J., Chinsky, J. M., Larcen, S. W., Lochman, J. E., & Selinger, H. V. (1976). *Community psychology and the schools: A behaviorally oriented multilevel preventative approach.* Hillsdale, NJ: Lawrence Erlbaum Associates.

Asarnow, J. R., & Callan, J. W. (1985). Boys with peer adjustment problems: Social cognitive processes. *Journal of Consulting and Clinical Psychology, 53,* 80–87.

August, G. J., Stewart, M. A., & Holmes, C. S. (1983). A four-year follow-up of hyperactive boys with and without conduct disorder. *British Journal of Psychiatry, 143,* 192–198.

Barkley, R. A. (1989). Attention deficit hyperactivity disorder. In E. Mash & R. A. Barkley (Eds.), *Treatment of childhood disorders* (pp. 39–72). New York: Guilford Press.

Bloomquist, M. L., & Braswell, L. (1990). *Multicomponent school-based cognitive-behavioral therapy for children with attention-deficit hyperactivity disorder.* Unpublished treatment manual, University of Minnesota, Minneapolis, MN. (Available from authors.)

Braswell, L., & Bloomquist, M. L. (1991). *Cognitive-behavioral therapy with ADHD children: Child, family, and school interventions.* New York: Guilford Press.

Braswell, L., & Kendall, P. C. (1988). Cognitive behavioral methods with children. In K. Dobson (Ed.), *Handbook of cognitive-behavioral therapies* (pp. 167–213). New York: Guilford Press.

Campis, L. K., Lyman, R. D., & Prentice-Dunn, A. (1986). The parent locus of control scale: Developmental validation. *Journal of Clinical Child Psychology, 15,* 260–267.

Cantwell, D. P. (1985). Hyperactive children grown up: What have we learned about what happened to them? *Archives of General Psychiatry, 42,* 1026–1028.

Chandler, M. J. (1973). Egocentrism and antisocial behavior: The assessment and training of social perspective-taking skills. *Developmental Psychology, 9,* 326–332.

Charles, L., & Schain, R. (1981). A four-year follow-up study of the effects of methylphenidate on the behavior and academic achievement of hyperactive children. *Journal of Abnormal Child Psychology, 9,* 495–505.

Cowen, E. L., Gesten, E. L., & Weissberg, R. P. (1980). An integrated network of preventatively oriented school-based mental health approaches. In R. H. Price & P. Politzer (Eds.), *Evaluation and action in the community context* (pp. 173–210). New York: Academic Press.

Dix, T. H., & Grusec, J. E. (1985). Parent attribution processes in the socialization of children. In I. Sigel (Ed.), *Parental belief systems: The psychological consequences for children* (pp. 34–67). Hillsdale, NJ: Lawrence Erlbaum Associates.

Dodge, K. A. (1986). A social information processing model of social competence in children. In M. Perlmetter (Ed.), *Cognitive perspective on children's social and behavioral development* (pp. 77–125). Hillsdale, NJ: Lawrence Erlbaum Associates.

Dodge, K. A., Pettit, G. S., McClaskey, C. L., & Brown, M. M. (1986). Social competence in children. *Monographs of the Society for Research in Child Development, 51,* (2, Serial No. 213).

Douglas, V. I. (1983). Attentional and cognitive problems. In M. Rutter (Ed.), *Developmental neuropsychiatry* (pp. 280–328). New York: Guilford Press.

Douglas, V. I., Barr, R. G., O'Neill, M. E., & Britton, B. G. (1986). Short-term effects of methylphenidate on the cognitive, learning, and academic performance of children with attention deficit disorder in the laboratory and the classroom. *Journal of Child Psychology and Psychiatry, 29,* 191–211.

D'Zurilla, T. J., & Goldfried, M. R. (1971). Problem solving and behavior modification. *Journal of Abnormal Psychology, 78,* 107–126.

Elardo, P. T., & Caldwell, B. M. (1979). The effects of an experimental social development program on children in the middle childhood period. *Psychology in the Schools, 16,* 93–100.

Elias, M. J., Gara, M., Ubriaco, M., Rothbaum, P. A., Clabby, J. F., & Schuyler, T. (1986). Impact of a preventative social problem-solving intervention on children's coping with middle school stressors. *American Journal of Community Psychology, 15,* 539–554.

Felner, R. D., & Felner, T. Y. (1989). Primary prevention programs in the educational context: A transactional-ecological framework and analysis. In L. A. Bond & B. E. Compas (Eds.), *Primary prevention and promotion in the schools* (pp. 13–49). Newbury Park: Sage Publications.

Ford, M. E. (1982). Social cognition and social competence in adolescence. *Developmental Psychology, 18,* 323–340.

Ford, M. E. (1985). Primary prevention: Key issues and a competence perspective. *Journal of Primary Prevention, 5*(4), 264–266.

Foster, S. L., & Robin, A. L. (1989). Parent-adolescent conflict. In E. Mash and R. A. Barkley (Eds.), *Treatment of childhood disorders* (pp. 493–528). New York: Guilford Press.

Gard, G. C., & Berry, K. K. (1986). Oppositional children: Training tyrants. *Journal of Clinical Child Psychology, 15,* 148–158.

Garmezy, N. (1987). Stress, competence, and development: Continuities in the study of schizophrenic adults, children vulnerable to psychopathology and the search for stress-resistant children. *American Journal of Orthopsychiatry, 57,* 159–174.

Garmezy, N., Masten, A. S., & Tellegen, A. (1984). The study of stress and competence in children: A building block for developmental psychopathology. *Child Development, 55,* 97–111.

Gesten, E. L., Flores de Apodaca, R., Rains, M., Weissberg, R. P., & Cowen, E. L. (1979). Promoting peer related social competence in schools. In M. W. Kent & J. E. Rolf (Eds.), *Primary prevention of psychopathology social competence in children* (Vol. 3, pp. 220–247). Hanover, NH: University Press of New England.

Gesten, E. L., Rains, M., Rapkin, B. D., Weissberg, R. P., Flores de Apodaca, R., Cowen, E. L., & Bowen, R. (1982). Training children in social problem-solving skills: A competence building approach, first and second look. *American Journal of Community Psychology, 10,* 95–115.

Gittelman, R., Mannuzza, S., Schenker, R., & Bonagura, N. (1985). Hyperactive boys almost grown up: I. Psychiatric status. *Archives of General Psychiatry, 42,* 937–947.

Gurucharri, C., Phelps, E., & Selman, R. (1984). Development of interpersonal understanding: A longitudinal and comparative study of normal and disturbed youths. *Journal of Consulting and Clinical Psychology, 52,* 26–36.

Kendall, P. C., & Braswell, L. (1985). *Cognitive-behavioral therapy for impulsive children.* New York: Guilford Press.

Kirschenbaum, D. S. (1979). Social competence intervention and evaluation in the inner city: Cincinnati's social skills development program. *Journal of Consulting and Clinical Psychology, 47,* 778–780.

Lochman, J. E., & Lampron, L. B. (1986). Situational social problem-solving skills and self-esteem of aggressive and nonaggressive boys. *Journal of Abnormal Child Psychology, 14,* 605–617.

Lochman, J. E., Nelson, W. M., III, & Sims, J. P. (1981). A cognitive behavioral program for use with aggressive children. *Journal of Clinical Child Psychology, 10,* 146–148.

McClure, L. D., Chinsky, J. M., & Larcen, S. W. (1978). Enhancing social problem-solving performance in an elementary school setting. *Journal of Educational Psychology, 70,* 504–513.

Meichenbaum, D. H., & Goodman, J. (1971). Training impulsive children to talk to themselves: A means of developing self-control. *Journal of Abnormal Psychology, 77,* 115–126.

Morton, P. Y., & Tuma, J. M. (1988). Stress, locus of control, and role satisfaction in clinic and control mothers. *Journal of Clinical Child Psychology, 17,* 217–224.

Patterson, G. R. (1982). *Coercive family process.* Eugene, OR: Castalia.

Ramsey, E., & Walker, H. M. (1988). Family management correlates of antisocial behavior among middle school boys. *Behavioral Disorders, 13,* 187–201.

Ramsey, E., Walker, H. M., Shinn, M., O'Neill, R. E., & Stieber, S. (1989). Parent management practices and school adjustment. *School Psychology Review, 18,* 513–525.

Rutter, M. (1983). Stress, coping and development: Some issues and some questions. In N. Garmezy & M. Rutter (Eds.), *Stress, coping and development in children* (pp. 1–41). New York, McGraw-Hill.

Rutter, M. (1987). Psychosocial resilience and protective mechanisms. *American Journal of Orthopsychiatry, 57,* 316–331.

Sameroff, A. J., & Fiese, B. (1988). Conceptual issues in prevention. In D. Shaffer, I. Philips, & N. B. Enzer (Eds.), *Prevention of mental disorders, alcohol, and other drug use in children and adolescents* (pp. 23–53). Rockville, MD: U.S. Department of Health and Human Services.

Shure, M. B., & Spivack, G. (1978). *Problem-solving techniques in childrearing.* San Francisco: Jossey-Bass.

Sobol, M. P., Ashbourne, D. R., Earn, B. M., & Cunningham, C. E. (1989). Parents' attributions for achieving compliance from attention-deficit disordered children. *Journal of Abnormal Child Psychology, 17,* 359–369.

Spivack, G., Platt, J. J., & Shure, M. B. (1976). *The problem-solving approach to adjustment.* San Francisco: Jossey-Bass.

Spivack, G., & Shure, M. B. (1974). *Social adjustment of young children.* San Francisco: Jossey-Bass.

Strayhorn, J. M. (1988). *The competent child.* New York: Guilford Press.

Vincent Roehling, P., & Robin, A. L. (1986). Development and validation of the Family Beliefs Inventory: A measure of unrealistic beliefs among parents and adolescents. *Journal of Consulting and Clinical Psychology, 54,* 693–697.

Waters, E., & Sroufe, L. A. (1983). Social competence as a developmental construct. *Developmental Review, 3,* 79–97.

Weissberg, R. P., Gesten, E. L., Carnrike, C. L., Toro, P. A., Rapkin, B. D., Davidson, E., & Cowen, E. L. (1981). Social problem-solving skills training: A competence-building intervention with second-to-fourth grade children. *American Journal of Community Psychology, 9,* 411–423.

Weissberg, R. P., Gesten, E. L., Rapkin, B. D., Cowen, E. L., Davidson, E., Flores de Apodaca, R., & McKim, B. J. (1981). The evaluation of a social-problem-solving training program for suburban and inner-city third-grade children. *Journal of Consulting and Clinical Psychology, 49,* 251–261.

Werner, E. E., & Smith, R. S. (1982). *Vulnerable but invincible: A longitudinal study of resilient children and youth.* New York: McGraw-Hill.

White, R. W. (1959). Motivation reconsidered: The concept of competence. *Psychological Review, 66,* 297–333.

Wodarski, J. S., Filipczak, J., McCombs, D., Koustenis, G., & Rusilko, S. (1979). Follow-up on behavioral intervention with troublesome adolescents. *Journal of Behavior Therapy and Experimental Psychiatry, 10,* 181–188.

9

FROM BLAME TO SOLUTIONS: SOLUTION-ORIENTED FAMILY-SCHOOL CONSULTATION

Cindy I. Carlson, Julia Hickman, and
Connie Burrows Horton

Research consistently finds that when families are involved in the educational process, children do better in school. Active parent involvement is related to numerous positive educational outcomes for schools, parents, and students (Comer, 1984). Alternatively, problems within the family frequently place children under significant emotional stress which, in turn, interferes with their school performance (Crombrinck-Graham, 1989; Doyle, Gold, & Moskowitz, 1984; Rutter, 1985). Numerous school-related problems of children and adolescents have been clinically and empirically related to dysfunctional family processes (see Graden & Christenson, 1987). Despite overwhelming evidence supporting the critical link between family and school, as well as the considerable overlap of home and school socialization roles, genuine collaboration between these social systems is infrequent. Moreover, when the home and school systems are required to engage one another, generally around a child problem, the relationship is frequently characterized by crisis, tension, defensiveness, blame, and miscommunication (Lightfoot, 1978).

Parents across the socioeconomic spectrum are often apprehensive about interactions with the school (Comer, 1984). Parents are typically called by the school only at times when their child is experiencing difficulty. Specifically, parents are most likely to be contacted by the school for behavior and attendance problems, academic problems, and monitoring children's progress, in that order (Leitch & Tangri, 1988). Parents may view the school problems their children experience as negative reflections on their parenting skills or as signs of future difficulty for their children over which they feel they have little or no control. Parents may also be experiencing stress in other areas of their life, and already feel like a failure, to which their child's difficulty in school represents yet another failure. In addition, some parents may have had bad school experiences themselves and may have mixed feelings about interactions with school officials (Comer, 1984).

The trepidation with which parents may approach the school appears to be warranted. Studies frequently find that teachers are more likely to blame parents for children's school-related problems than make attributions to either child-centered or school-centered causes (Leitch & Tangri, 1988). This is in contrast with parents, who are more likely to equally distribute attributions regarding the cause of their child's school problems among the child, the school environment, the child's friends, and themselves (Guttmann, 1982). The tendency of teachers to blame parents for children's inadequate functioning in school has most commonly been explained as an "ego defensive" attributional process (Beckman, 1973; Zuckerman, 1979). That is, although acknowledging certain individual differences (Muneno & Dembo, 1982), most teachers attribute student success to their teaching effort and skill, but attribute student failure to characteristics outside the school environment, most notably the parents or the students themselves. Such attributions protect a teacher's self-esteem from further damage in light of a failure experience. Therefore, when a student fails to perform as expected, if the teacher does not assume blame for the failure, their perceptions of self-efficacy will not suffer. One might hope that teachers were adequately trained as professionals such that attributional biases potentially harmful to students and parents were unnecessary. However, Comer (1984) reminds us that school staff, like parents, lack the degree of authority, respect, and autonomy that was characteristic of their position in earlier decades.

It has been noted that schools—more than parents—are in a position to create the conditions needed to overcome difficult relationship barriers (Comer, 1984). Comer has called for mechanisms to be placed in schools that permit teachers to work closely with parents while enhancing, not losing, their status or power. Equally important, given the oft sited stress and anxiety of parents of children experiencing school problems, is that home-school collaboration mechanisms also assure the empowerment, not blame, of parents (see Dunst, Johanson, Rounds, Trivette, & Hamby, this volume). The plea for home-school collaboration has seen a proliferation of parent-involvement programs that involve parents in the multiple roles of supporters, teachers, learners, and advisors/decision makers. Although the ongoing involvement of parents in the educational process of their children is clearly optimal as a primary prevention activity, school psychologists and educators are faced on a daily basis with facilitating home-school communication

when children are failing to adapt or to achieve in school. This chapter proposes that applying solution-oriented therapeutic approaches to the home-school interface provides an ideal intervention model for facilitating communication, reducing blame, building collaborative relationships, and empowering parents, teachers, and children who are experiencing difficulty in school.

In this chapter we will first provide the theoretical building blocks upon which our model of family-school collaboration is based. These include consultation and the indirect delivery model of services, systems theory, ecological theory, the enablement model of helping, the intervention technique of family-school meetings, and finally, and perhaps most important for our purposes, the solution-oriented brief therapy model. We will next demonstrate the application of solution-oriented therapy techniques to family-school collaborative problem-dissolving meetings. Finally, preliminary evaluation data on the effectiveness of this approach to family-school collaboration will be provided. It should be noted that, although we have outstanding predecessors in the conceptualization of solution-oriented brief therapy (de Shazer, 1982, 1985, 1988; Kral, 1986; O'Hanlon & Weiner-Davis, 1989; O'Hanlon & Wilk, 1987) and the practice of family-school meetings (Family-School Collaboration Project; Weiss & Edwards, this volume), an integrative model of solution-oriented family-school collaboration is in the formative stages.

FROM SYSTEMIC PROBLEMS TO SOLUTIONS: THEORETICAL FOUNDATIONS

Multiple theoretical frameworks have been used to guide our thinking about solution-oriented home-school collaboration. These conceptual frameworks will next be discussed, as they provide the foundation for our proposed model of solution-oriented family-school consultation practice.

Indirect Model of Psychological Services Delivery

Indirect delivery of mental health services to children refers to the practice of providing services, generally in the form of teaching, consulting, and enabling, to adults who have direct involvement with children. Recently, Gutkin and Conoley (1990) have argued the merits of the indirect service model for the practice and training of school psychologists pointing to the staggering proportions of children in need of services, the proven ability of paraprofessionals to provide services, and the recognition that it is the adults who control the environments in which children and their difficulties are embedded. Also noted by these authors, the primary environments of children are the home and school setting. Thus, in order to serve children effectively, school psychologists must first and foremost be expert in influencing parents and teachers.

Consultation

School-based consultation exemplifies the indirect model of mental health service delivery. School-based consultation with teachers, administrators, and, to a lesser extent, with parents, has been described, promoted, and empirically validated as the mental health practice of choice for school psychologists (e.g., Gutkin & Curtis, 1982). In the consultation model, school psychologists serve as consultants to adults who have daily interaction with the troubled child with a goal of not only resolving presenting problems (secondary or tertiary prevention), but also increasing the problem-solving ability of the consultee(s) (primary prevention). Consultation has generally been conceptualized as a dyadic process, with a work-related, problem-solving focus. Although the optimal form of the consultee-consultant relationship has been a topic of considerable debate (see, for example, Gallesich, 1982), many school psychologists prefer to adopt the perspective that consultation reflects a collaborative relationship. Successful consultation gener-

ally includes the following steps: (a) the establishment of a collaborative relationship, (b) clearly defining the problem, and (c) brainstorming multiple solutions from which the consultee may chose the solution most appropriate for their skills and setting. The long-term success of consultation is reflected in the empowerment of the consultee to resolve similar problems in the future without assistance.

Systems-Ecological Perspective

In general, from the systemic perspective, the problems of children are viewed within the context of their relationships and interactions with others, rather than being understood primarily as a reflection of individual psychological development (Fine, 1991). Systems, such as the family and school, represent purposeful entities comprising organized, interrelated parts (Conoley, 1987; Doherty & Peskay, this volume). The organization of the system, that is the norms and roles of the component parts, is evident in the repeated patterns of behavior that characterize members of the system. From a systemic perspective, the problem behavior of children is reciprocally determined through the interplay of their interactions with others in the system. Thus, causation from the systemic perspective is circular, not linear; neither the actions of the child nor the actions of significant others in the context can be viewed as causing the child's problem. Rather, it is the interplay of actions and related subjective evaluations over time that create a relationship, and it is the relationship that is viewed as maintaining difficulties experienced by the child and school. The child's relationships then become the focus of diagnosis and intervention. Based on the systemic premises of circularity and the interrelatedness of parts, a change in any part of a system is expected to influence or have a ripple effect on other persons within the system.

Ecology refers to the pattern of relationships between organisms and their environment. Ecological theory applied to human development proposes that individual development is the progressive, mutual accommodation between developing persons and the settings or systems in which they live (Bronfenbrenner, 1979). At the core of an ecological orientation are the following concepts: (a) Systems are nested hierarchically; (b) hierarchically lower system levels are autonomous, but also controlled to some degree by higher system levels; and (c) the quality of the interface or communication flow between systems is a key factor in the development of the members of the system (Bronfenbrenner, 1979). Thus, the reciprocal accommodation of the child to the school setting will be influenced not only by qualities of the child and qualities of the school, but also by the quality of the relationship between the multiple settings (home and school) in which the child exists, as well as the larger social context in which the multiple settings are embedded. Ecological theory underscores the importance of home-school communication.

Taken together, the systems perspective emphasizes the interrelatedness of the behavior of persons within an organized system such that no cause of behavior can be determined and a change in one element of the system is expected to reverberate to other related elements; ecological theory complements the systemic perspective by pointing to the interrelatedness of multiple hierarchical systems or settings within the child's ecological niche. The perspectives converge in viewing children's dysfunctional behavior as "blame-free" in that behavior is viewed as the adaptation of individual characteristics to the constraints of the system or setting in which the person resides.

Family-School Meetings

School principals, teachers, and school psychologists have long been meeting with parents, usually the mother, when children are experiencing difficulties in school. In addition, current legislation for specialized services to handicapped children requires that parents meet with school personnel annually to approve the child's Individualized Educational Plan. What is seldom observed, however, in meetings between the home and school is the presence of the child, the presence of other family members, or the presence of all school-related staff. In our model of family-school collaboration we propose that change in the child is more quickly accomplished and solutions to problems are more easily discovered when all the relevant persons in the child's system come together.

The idea of the family-school meeting was borrowed from the Ackerman Family Institute who initiated these meetings several years ago in the New York City public schools as a means of linking family therapy with school-based problems (see Weiss & Edwards, this volume). The family-school meeting concept was viewed as consistent with the systems theory premise that the whole is greater than the sum of the parts; therefore, an intervention that utilized the whole of the child's ecological world was likely to yield results distinct from interviews with one or more elements in the child's world. These meetings were notable for their task focus, blocking of blame, and involvement of all members of the family (including siblings) as persons who could contribute to resolving the child's problems.

ENABLEMENT MODEL

The enablement model of helping, developed by Dunst and Trivette (1987), is based on the premise that how we provide help to people strongly influences the outcomes that result. The enablement model shifts the focus of professional helping from the diagnosis and treatment of problems to the promotion of growth-producing behaviors and from the prevention of negative outcomes to the recognition of existing strengths. The enablement model rests on the assumption that the help seeker is capable of being competent when provided the opportunity to do so, and that it is the responsibility of the help giver to be positive and see the strengths of the client. The help giver may be of assistance in creating opportunities for competencies to be acquired or displayed by the help seeker, but the client is the essential agent of change and is expected to play a major role in deciding actions and solutions. The relationship between help giver and client then is one of a cooperative partnership that emphasizes joint responsibility.

Solution-Oriented Brief Therapy

Solution-oriented brief therapy is a model of treatment adapted from the brief psychotherapy models for working with individuals and families described by Watzlawick, Weakland, and Fisch (1974) and modified by de Shazer (1982, 1985), who has emphasized the categorization of solutions, and O'Hanlon (O'Hanlon & Wilks, 1987; O'Hanlon & Wiener-Davis, 1989), who has emphasized the use of language and suggestion. Brief therapists focus their intervention solely on a resolution of the presenting problem, with intervention strategies designed to disrupt the organized behavioral patterns surrounding the problem. The brief therapy approach to working with families is distinct from other popular family therapy models (e.g., structural), which require not only a resolution of the presenting problem but also a reorganization or "fixing" of the system in which the problem is embedded. Brief therapists, in contrast, have faith that systems will reorganize in whatever way necessary following a disruption of the dysfunctional behavior pattern linked with the presenting problem.

In the solution-oriented brief therapy approach there has been an important conceptual shift from problem resolution to solution identification. The role of the solution-oriented helper or therapist is to work in collaboration with the client to extract solutions from the client through the selective use of language and attention such that the focus of the helping conversation is on exceptions to the problem and strengths for dissolving the problem, which may be generalized from other areas of the consultee or client's life. The importance placed on language,

and language as a construction of social reality, is evident in the terminology of solution-oriented brief therapy. The term *difficulties* is used, for example in solution-oriented work, to replace the term *problems* (de Shazer, 1985). Difficulties are defined as normal situations that individuals experience in everyday life that frustrate our normal flow of existence. In response to recurring difficulties, persons come to develop a customary or repeated response. When the repeated response is not successful in alleviating the difficulty, persons are viewed as having a *complaint.* Solution-oriented therapists then direct their consultations with clients regarding their complaints toward a discussion of exceptions to the complaint pattern which point to the construction of solutions.

The major tenets of solution-oriented brief therapy, which have been elucidated by de Shazer (1985, 1987) and O'Hanlon and Wiener-Davis (1989), follow:

1. Change is constant and, in fact, inevitable.

2. Individuals have within themselves the resources to resolve complaints.

3. The therapist's role is to construct with the individual(s) solutions that "fit" with the constraints of the individual(s) situation.

4. It is not necessary to know all the details of the complaint in order to construct solutions.

5. It is not necessary to know the cause or function of the complaint, as viable solutions often are unrelated to the complaint.

6. Some or all complaints can be given new and at times creative meaning by shifting the individual's perspectives regarding the complaints.

7. Only small changes are necessary, therefore only small reasonable goals are necessary to set.

8. The individuals seeking help, not the therapist, determine what are the

goals they want to obtain. The therapist's role is to facilitate the individuals' being able to meet their goals.

9. Change in any part of the system will result in changes in the entire system and in other systems in which the complaint resides.

10. Rapid change is possible and highly likely.

The primary method for assessment, intervention, and evaluation in the solution-oriented approach is the interview. Through the use of solution-oriented interviewing (see Lipchik & de Shazer, 1988; O'Hanlon & Weiner-Davis, 1989), clients or consultees can experience significant shifts in their perceptions of difficulties or complaints during and after the course of the interview. These cognitive shifts permit persons to leave the interview situation free to act in accordance with more productive ways of behaving. Although clients are typically given simple task assignments at the end of an interview session, these are meant simply to reinforce a change that has already occurred either after the initial call for assistance with the difficulty and before the first interview or during the interview itself (O'Hanlon & Weiner-Davis, 1989). In keeping with this notion, and also with the idea of the ripple effect of small change, the interview can occur with any number of individuals related to the problem but should certainly include the major complaining persons.

Techniques of solution-oriented therapy. Brief therapists assume that difficulties often become complaints because individuals get stuck in the way in which they view the difficulty, and subsequently, in the way in which they behave regarding the difficulty. Solution-oriented brief therapists, therefore, co-construct with the client a resolution of the complaint by changing the client's "viewing" of the complaint and/or the client's "doing" or behavior surrounding the complaint.

Techniques for changing the viewing of a complaint are consistent with concepts based in cognitive psychology and social psychology, which argue that the subjective reality of individuals can be viewed as the construction of cognitive frames or "rules" regarding why things occur as they do. The frames that individuals use to define their states of being are at times very global and vague in nature. Nevertheless, people treat these global and vague frames as facts of life rather than subjective experiences or "stories" that are open to many other interpretations. A person's frame directly and indirectly influences their behavior. Brief therapists assume that one of the most significant reasons that difficulties become complaints is that individuals develop or use a frame for the complaint-related behavior that impedes the search for solutions thereby increasing the probability the difficulties become complaints.

The solution-oriented therapist employs many techniques designed to introduce uncertainty into the client's viewpoint, which will permit a shift in viewing of and behavior surrounding the complaint. In brief therapy, as in the family therapy literature and cognitive behavioral therapy literature, the technique referred to as "reframing" is used by the therapist to help the client transform or in some way modify their "rules" for developing meaning for particular difficulties in their life (de Shazer, 1988). Following is a brief discussion of some of the techniques of solution-oriented brief therapy for changing the viewing of the complaint. Unless otherwise indicated, this discussion is based on the book, *In Search for Solutions* (O'Hanlon & Weiner-Davis, 1989).

One technique used to introduce doubt into the client's frame for a complaint involves "normalizing" and "depathologizing" the behavior of concern (O'Hanlon & Weiner-Davis, 1989). The therapist, for example, might respond to the client's account of the problem with comments like "naturally," "of course," or "that doesn't surprise me," "sounds like a typical teenager." The therapist might even complete the client's story as a means of indicating that the pattern is normal and predictable. Describing the client's problem in behavioral rather than medical terminology also serves to depathologize the concern. A child who is labelled Attention Deficit Disorder, for example, can be described as a child who has difficulty staying seated in the classroom for longer than 5 minutes. The goal is not to refute an appropriate medical label but to refocus persons involved with the child toward aspects of the situation that are changeable and controllable.

A second technique for changing the viewing and increasing the controllability of a complaint is the technique of "deconstruction" (de Shazer, 1988). When persons give global frames for complaints, de Shazer recommends "deconstructing" the frame by first acknowledging it and then breaking it down into smaller parts that are more easily resolved.

The solution-oriented consultant can also change the participant's viewing of the complaint by summarizing what has been said thus far with a solution-oriented twist. Following a summarization by the consultant of the report by parents that their daughter is depressed, the consultant might add, for example, "How do you know it is depression and not normal teenage moodiness?" A similar technique involves expanding the scope of the complaint behaviors to other individuals and/or contexts. Expansion of the scope with the addition of the perspectives of other people who have noticed the complaint behavior, but who explain it differently, frequently points to solutions. For example, in a recent family-school meeting convened to discuss the behavior of an acting-out adolescent, the majority opinion of the child's teachers was that the child was bad; the addition of the perspective of a single teacher who was not having difficulty with this boy, and which pointed to the child's need for affection, refocused the problem-solving discussion of the group from punishment toward appropriate ways in which the child could receive attention from his teachers. Similarly, inquiring about other settings in which the identified problem child participates where the complaint behavior may be less evident or problematic may also point to solutions.

In addition to techniques to change "the viewing" of clients regarding their complaints, solution-oriented therapists also seek to change "the doing," or the behavior patterns, surrounding the problem. It should be noted that techniques that elicit new behaviors are also likely to shift the viewing of the problem by the client, and therefore, should not be viewed as unrelated to the techniques described above. One solution-oriented technique for changing the doing involves focusing initial interview questions on exceptions to the complaint. The therapist may ask questions such as the following: "What is happening when John remains in his seat?" "Tell me about the times John does complete his homework." If the client is able to respond with exceptions to the complaint, the consultant asks about how the client made that happen or what was happening that allowed the complaint to subside. In the behavioral exceptions to the complaint are found behavioral solutions which can then form the content for a task assignment as an experiment by the persons involved in the complaint to increase or decrease certain behaviors present in the exceptions to the problem. When exceptions to the problem cannot be identified by clients, solution-oriented therapists often have clients imagine and clearly describe the behaviors that would be characteristic of a future without the problem. This technique also suggests behaviors that need to increase or decrease surrounding the complaint.

In changing the doing of a problem, solution-oriented practitioners also borrow a number of behavioral pattern interruption techniques from the brief therapists. These include such strategies as changing the frequency, duration, time, intensity, or sequence of the behavior around the problem. In addition, behaviors in the sequence surrounding the complaint might be added or subtracted or the doing of the complaint attached to another pattern, usually an undesirable activity or ordeal (see Haley, 1984). A complaint pattern interruption successfully used by one of the authors involved the directive to a depressed adolescent to complete his homework in the dining room area rather than in his bedroom. This change in location of the complaint, which had been identified as depressive thinking that peaked in the evening hours, served to break a pattern of behavior associated with the complaint and to indirectly address an underlying cause of the complaint, social isolation within the family. Thus, it is helpful to change the doing of a complaint in a direction that facilitates continued growth and change.

A final focus of solution-oriented behavior change is attention to the abilities, resources, strengths, and solutions that are already evident in the consultee's life but which may not be recognized as valuable to the solution of the complaint. In a parent consultation with a mother who was having difficulty managing her adolescent daughter, for example, discussion of her managerial competence in the work setting, where she managed a large pool of secretaries, evoked both a sense of competence on the part of the mother and ideas for new behaviors she might try with her daughter.

In summary, the hallmark of the solution-oriented approach is the consultant's shift from a detailed analysis of the problem to an active search for solutions. In changing the viewing of problems, solution-oriented brief therapy employs techniques that introduce doubt into the existing perceptions of clients, reduce the uncontrollability of the behavior surrounding the complaint, and provide multiple solutions to the complaint, thus allowing the complainants to construct their own workable solutions. Changing the viewing of a problem often automatically results in the generation and initiation of new behavioral patterns; however, when solutions do not readily emerge from the consultee, solution-oriented therapists provide behavioral suggestions that disrupt the typical pattern of behavior surrounding the problem in such a way as to permit new possibilities of viewing and doing to emerge.

SOLUTION-ORIENTED FAMILY-SCHOOL MEETINGS

We believe that the interviewing techniques of solution-oriented brief therapy are well suited for family-school consultations (Carlson & Hickman, in press). Creating an expectation focused on change and solutions versus on diagnosis and problems appears particularly congruent with the goals of school-based family-school collaboration which we view to include: (a) cost effectiveness; (b) empowerment of all persons involved; (c) shifting attitudes from blame and defensiveness to shared responsibility and optimism; (d) changing behavior patterns from avoidance of failure and rigid adherence to previous solutions to collaboration and experimentation with solutions. Our adaptation of the solution-oriented framework assumes that the various social systems involved in the school-home relationship possess the resources to handle their own difficulties; however, they get stuck in their viewing of the child's problem and stuck in their efforts to change the child's behavior such that the child's difficulties appear stable, internal, and uncontrollable, the adults in the child's environment experience feelings of frustration and failure, often alleviated only by blaming another social system (e.g., the family is blamed by the school).

In our model when children experience school-related difficulties, a meeting is called with all of the family members of the identified problem child (unless siblings are too young to sit through a 1-hour meeting) and with all of the teachers of the identified problem child. In addition, at least one school administrator participates who will be able to maintain a coordinating role following the meeting. A meeting of this many people can be difficult to arrange, particularly at the middle or high school levels where the child experiencing difficulties has many teachers. The tendency on the part of the school will be to limit the meeting to those teachers who are experiencing problems with the child, and the tendency of the family will be to keep the less involved family members out of the meeting. We have found, however, that the effort to bring all of the persons involved with the child together is well worth it. Teachers who are not experiencing difficulty with the child and family members who are less concerned with the complaint are frequently the people who in their viewing of the child or their interactions with the child hold solutions to the complaint. A favorite example of the solutions that can be provided by unconcerned participants is provided by Carlson who was conducting a family-school meeting surrounding the delinquent behavior of an adolescent. When the adolescent's R.O.T.C. teacher was asked how he managed to avoid conflicts with this child, the drill sergeant indicated that he just tried to give him a hug every day. This was neither the expected response from a representative of the military nor a solution that had to this point been proposed in the meeting, and it served to point the participants toward the needs for warmth and affection that were underlying this teenager's disruptive behavior. Once all the participants have agreed to meet together, family-school meetings follow the suggested outline next described.

Phase 1: Introduction. The individual in charge of the meeting (usually a school psychologist, counselor, or principal) ensures that everyone at the meeting is formally introduced. It is surprising how often parents have not met key school personnel and vice versa. We next acknowledge the importance of each participant at the meeting in bringing about desired change, the advantage of having many perspectives, and the good fortune of the child who has so many persons interested in their growth. For example, parents may be introduced as the experts on the child in the informal setting of the home; the teachers may be introduced as the experts on the child's response to academic demands. The tone that is set very early is one of collaboration among persons of coequal status.

Phase 2: Explanation of the solution-oriented approach. Following introductions, participants in the meeting are given an introduction to the solution-oriented approach. Although this is not a necessary step in individual brief solution-oriented therapy (O'Hanlon & Weiner-Davis, 1989), we found that the norms for blaming and complaining within the school setting are so strong that some advance cognitive organizers are helpful. The idea is to establish early the expectation set that complaints are dissolvable and that viable solutions are possible to identify when everyone puts their heads together. Although everyone's perspective regarding parameters of the complaint will be elicited, attention will be focused on possible solutions to the complaint. A sample brief introductory explanation follows:

Today we are all going to put our heads together to find possible solutions to the concern that John is not completing his homework. We can assume that at least some of us are a little stuck in how to help John solve this problem or we wouldn't be here today. My philosophy about these meetings is that many heads are usually better than one head when it comes to solving problems; therefore, we are here for a kind of "meeting of the minds" to share ideas about things that seem to work for John.

Phase 3: Joining. As in most therapeutic modalities, joining is a necessary first step in building rapport with family-school meeting participants. Joining from the solution-oriented perspective involves (a) acknowledging each person's point of view and (b) matching the person's language (O'Hanlon & Weiner-Davis, 1989). Acknowledging each participant's point of view requires an indication to the individual that their perception of the problem has been heard by the group facilitator. Acknowledging behaviors are essentially consistent with good listening skills. Joining by matching the participants' language has three aspects. The first is to actually mirror the exact words and idiomatic expressions used by participants in their descriptions of the situation. For example, if parents are talking about their child's "attitude problem," the therapist would likely continue to use the word "attitude" in subsequent questions, such as what will be the first sign that the child's attitude is different. The second matching method is to use the participant's metaphors for the complaint either by continuing with one that they have already stated directly or creating one that is related to the individual's work or hobbies. For example, if a teacher mentions "the rocky road ahead," a later reference by the facilitator might include "now that you have the four-wheel drive to handle the rocky road ahead." A final aspect of matching language is matching sensory modalities. If a person uses visual expressions regarding "seeing clearly," for example, the therapist would continue to reference that modality commenting, for example, on "taking a closer look."

Phase 4: Negotiating a solvable complaint. The meeting leader next elicits each participant's complaint in as clear a description as possible. Asking participants to give a "video" description of their complaint really helps define the complaint in concrete behavioral terms. In providing a video description, the participant is asked to describe the complaint so that the other participants could see the complaint in action as on a video recording. This permits a translation of the complaint into behavioral terms for which solutions can more easily be identified.

Additional techniques for negotiating a solvable problem include searching for exceptions to the problem, identifying strengths of the child, or questioning parents and teachers about past solutions that have worked with the identified problem or problem child. Searching for exceptions highlights the times and ways in which the child's behavior is not a problem and often points to solutions for the problem. Similarly, identifying strengths of the child, parent, or teacher often points to skills that can be used to remediate the problem. Asking whether and how problems have been solved in the past often is effective because consultees or clients are frequently so focused on how "stuck" they are with the problem that they forget they may have solved the problem in the past and simply have

failed to continue implementation of the effective solution.

A third technique for negotiating a solvable problem is visualization of the future without the problem. This is often used when parents or teachers are unable to provide responses to the above questions. A frequently used question is, "If we had a magic wand, and the problem disappears, what will be happening?" It is important for the consultant to assure that the response to this question is one that provides a behavioral picture. A person's visualization of the future without the problem often points to behaviors that need to be increased, added, or deleted. It is interesting that future visualization often results in a picture that on face value bears little resemblance to the complaint. For example, a teacher may be complaining that a child is hopelessly disorganized. However, when asked to visualize the future without the problem, the teacher describes the child simply coming to class with a pencil. Clearly bringing a pencil to class is a more solvable problem than a disorganized personality.

The mental health specialist uses reflective listening and other therapeutic communication skills to negotiate a solvable complaint with each participant. Across participants, the therapist looks for commonalities and differences in the complaints and "viewing" of the problem. Commonalities point to agreement on a solvable complaint; differences may point to possible solutions.

Phase 5: Establish a solution goal. Once a solvable complaint has been agreed upon, the mental health specialist helps the participants decide on a mutually agreed upon initial goal for change. A positive versus negative goal is encouraged because it is much easier to increase a positive behavior than to decrease a negative behavior.

Phase 6: Gain agreement on the smallest change in the direction of the goal. Once a positive goal has been established, it is important in keeping with the solution-oriented model to gain agreement from the participants on what would be the smallest change possible in the direction of the desired goal. Working toward the smallest change is an important shift in both the viewing and doing of the complaint within the social contexts of the child such that lasting change, which generally occurs in small increments, can be rewarded. For example, the goal of losing 10 pounds is less easily accomplished and noticed than the goal of taking a 10-minute walk each day, a behavior that is pleasurable, will gradually move the overweight person toward weight loss, and can easily be noticed and reinforced by persons in the immediate environment. The following question may be asked of participants in order to elicit smallest change information: "On a scale from 1–10 with 10 being always completing homework and 1 being never completing homework, what will it take for you to know that John has moved from a 1 to a 3?"

Phase 7: Elicit multiple solutions toward accomplishing the smallest change. This step is quite similar to the brainstorming phase in problem-solving consultation. Here the mental health specialist elicits possible solutions to the complaint from the participants, as well as initiates possible solutions to the complaint which may have been exceptions to the complaint pattern that emerged during the early phase of the meeting. Again the meeting leader is charged with the responsibility of eliciting these exceptions and identifying resources or strengths within the complainant systems that will increase the probability that a viable solution will be found. A solution is more likely to be acceptable to the participants' systems if they have already noted them earlier in the interview.

Phase 8: Clarify individual responsibilities or task assignments. It is the role of the mental health specialist to elicit and clarify, if necessary, each participant's understanding of their role(s) in the solution plan. Not infrequently multiple members of the family-school meeting, not only the problem child, will be doing things differently as a result of decisions made at the meeting. It is also the role of the mental health specialist to

serve as a consultant to any and all participants as they implement the solutions agreed upon. Plans for follow-up should also be delineated at this time.

Phase 9: Follow-up. It is customary either for the meeting participants to agree to a subsequent follow-up meeting in which to assess progress toward the goal or for a designated coordinator to follow up individually with meeting participants or subsystems. In follow-up, as in assessment/intervention, the mental health specialist keeps the focus on what is different, what has already changed, and what do persons want to keep happening. It is not uncommon for the actual solution that emerges to bear little resemblance to the solution behaviors agreed upon in the initial meeting. In the event that the solution is working, but it is not what the group agreed upon, the mental health specialist simply congratulates them on a creative implementation of a new solution that obviously better fits their system. The concern in follow-up is substantiating that the members of the system did implement some small change in the agreed upon direction toward the goal. If no change has occurred, the solution-oriented process would be recycled. It deserves note that in practicing solution-oriented therapy we have not as yet encountered a situation in which no change has occurred between the family-school meeting and follow-up; participants who report no change are usually focused on a complete alleviation of the problem and need to be reminded of the initial goal of small change.

Phase 10: Evaluate and recycle if necessary. The solutions are all evaluated relative to the participants, the participants' goals, and their respective systems. In evaluation, the mental health consultant assists the participants to look at the advantages and disadvantages of the solution agreed upon with a focus on the advantages. As noted above, often participants have forgotten their agreed upon goal or have forgotten that the goal was to put into place the smallest change toward the goal. The consultant then serves to remind participants of the long-term advantages of gradual change and helps participants attend to small changes that have occurred. The consultant then capitalizes on this small change and encourages "more of the same" to build on the system's strengths and resources. As noted above, if the proposed solution(s) did not resolve the complaint, then the consultant would recycle through the solution-oriented interview process until a new set of solutions is identified.

PRELIMINARY EVALUATION OF EFFECTIVENESS

Program Evaluation Design

A preliminary, informal investigation of the usefulness of solution-oriented family-school meetings has been completed. The program evaluation sample consisted of seven student consultants and their family-school consultation cases. The student consultants were enrolled in an advanced family intervention practicum course in a doctorate-level training program in School Psychology. All student consultants had previously completed coursework in family psychology, family therapy, and school consultation. The remainder of the sample consisted of participants (parents, children, and teachers) in the family-school meetings. Data were collected from 7 teachers, 13 parents, 5 children, and the 7 consultants noted above.

In addition to the experimental group, data were collected on a control group of families and teachers who had been referred to the consultant but who had not yet experienced a family-school consultation meeting. However, there was an inadequate number of control subjects to permit comparisons.

Procedure. Student consultants were each assigned to a single public school setting across two suburban school districts. Two student consultants were placed in a high school, one in an alternative education setting, two in a middle school, and two in elementary schools. Student consultants were assigned cases primarily through the counselors in each of the schools, with the exception of the high school setting which had a counselor assigned to crisis

intervention work who directed appropriate referrals to the consultants. Schools were instructed to provide consultants with referrals in which the child or adolescent was experiencing school-related difficulties and these appeared to be related to family, as well as school factors.

Mid-semester, after consultants had mastered rudimentary skills in solution-oriented brief therapy techniques and in conducting family-school meetings within the school setting, data collection was initiated. Program evaluation data included both pre-post outcome evaluation data and process evaluation data.

For as many cases as was feasible, consultants and their family-school meeting participants (parent[s], children [age 11 & above], and teachers) completed a premeeting questionnaire which assessed their view of the problem, their view of the problem cause and solution, and their view of the family-school meeting as a means to solve problems. Premeeting questionnaires were completed 1–2 weeks prior to the scheduled meeting. A postmeeting questionnaire was completed 2 weeks following the family-school consultation meeting. The postmeeting questionnaire contained questions that paralleled the premeeting questionnaire, with only the wording of items changed to reflect pre-post meeting status.

In addition to the pre-post meeting qualitative data collected, consultants audiotaped, transcribed, and coded at least one of their family-school meetings using a code developed by the authors to reflect the solution-oriented process framework.

Measures. Measures included a self-report questionnaire, *Consultant's Questionnaire,* developed by the authors to evaluate the effectiveness of the family-school consultation meeting in changing the viewing and the behavior surrounding the child's problem within the school setting. The questionnaire included nine questions, which were rated on a 5-point Likert scale, designed to evaluate various criteria reflecting satisfaction with the family-school meeting. Several items were reverse scored to reduce response bias in ratings. Higher rating scores reflected a more positive evaluation of the family-school meeting. In addition to the Likert scale items, the pre-post meeting questionnaire included 10 open-ended questions regarding participants' view of the nature of the problem, the cause of the problem, and the problem solution. A parallel questionnaire was designed for completion in a 2-week follow-up of the family-school meeting in order to determine post-treatment outcomes.

A second measure was designed by the authors for process evaluation of treatment effectiveness. The authors constructed the *Solution-Oriented Process Evaluation Code,* which was designed to identify consultant behaviors within the family-school meeting that reflected the solution-oriented approach. The code included 16 therapist/consultant speech acts, which were organized within the solution-oriented therapeutic domains of *Joining, Negotiating a Solvable Problem, Changing Viewing, and Changing Doing.* In addition, the code included three categories of consultee responses: Positive, Negative, and Neutral. The code appears in Appendix A.

Coders were instructed to code each "turn-of-talk," defined as the entire speech of one person before another person speaks. It was permissible to provide each "turn" with multiple speech codes; however, consultee responses could only receive a single code. In addition to the coded speech acts, coders indicated the speaker. Speaker codes included the following: (1) therapist/consultant; (2) parent/guardian; (3) IP child; (4) sibling; (5) teacher; (6) other school personnel. Written transcripts were made from audiotapes of the family-school meeting. Coding was based on the written transcript in conjunction with the audiotape. All transcripts were coded by two student consultants in order to determine interrater reliability. Transcripts were also coded sequentially to permit analysis of the contingent behavior patterns within the family-school meetings in future studies.

Results

Changes in viewing and doing. The changes in the viewing of the problem as a result of the family-school meeting were evaluated with the open-ended questions on the Consultant Questionnaire. Results appear on Table 1. Regarding problem type, results indicated that the majority of respondents viewed the primary problem as behavioral prior to the meeting. Teachers, however, were somewhat more likely to see the problem as a mixture of behavioral, emotional, and learning problems. Following the meeting, teachers were more likely to view the problem as behavioral and parents more likely to view the problem as more complex, that is, having mixed features.

Regarding the primary locus of the problem, prior to the family-school meeting teachers viewed the problem as evident primarily within the school setting. Following the meeting, teachers were more likely to see the problem as existing both in the family and school settings.

Did the view of the problem change as a result of the family-school meeting? Results found that consultants were most likely to view the problem differently as a result of the meeting. Parents and teachers also evidenced some change in perceptions of the problem following the meeting. Adolescents were least likely to change their view of the problem.

When asked the cause of the problem, adolescents were most likely to view the school as the cause of the problem. Teachers and consultants were most likely to view the parent-child relationship as the source of the problem. Parents were quite differentiated in their view of the problem cause. Interestingly, neither teachers nor consultants identified the school as the cause of the problem.

It might be expected that attributions regarding the cause of the problem would be matched by expectations for resolution of the problem. In general, teachers and consultants, although they did not view the problem as caused by multiple systems, were likely to assert that multiple systems were responsible for resolving the problem. Consistent with their view that the school was not the cause of the problem, teachers never responded that the school alone should take responsibility for the problem solution. What is the degree of consistency between blame for the problem and expectations for solutions? Data showed that the adolescents were most likely to view blame and solution responsibility as residing within the same person or system. Parents and consultants, in contrast, were more likely to view cause and solution of the problem as distinct.

Participants were next asked to identify those persons involved in the plan to resolve the problem. Data in Table 1 indicate that adults tended to view multiple participants as involved in the solution plan, whereas adolescents were more likely to view the solution plan as involving a single person, system, or relationship. Inquiries about the clarity of the plan revealed that adolescents, teachers, and consultants tended to report clear action plans that were forthcoming from the family-school meetings. The plan reports of parents suffered from some ambiguity.

In summary, these data provide preliminary evidence that the family-school meeting exerted a moderate influence in changing the perceptions of participants in the meeting.

Family-school meeting satisfaction. Satisfaction with the family-school meeting was evaluated with the Consultant Questionnaire. Mean ratings, based on a 5-point Likert scale, as well as the results of paired comparison *t*-tests, appear on Table 2.

Data on Table 2 indicate that prior to the family-school meeting, adolescents experienced the greatest anxiety, whereas the adult participants noted a high degree of comfort with the meeting. Interestingly, following the meeting, adolescents indicated the highest levels of satisfaction. The authors view this as an important finding that suggests that the emphasis on solutions versus blame was a particularly positive experience for the identified problem child. Teachers were only moderately pleased with the experi-

ence, and, in fact, several expressed disappointment that problems were not emphasized to a greater extent.

Regarding involvement in the planning and implementation of the solution, all respondents reported higher than average participation ratings with parents most involved in the implementation of actions, and consultants reporting the least responsibility for implementation. The low solution implementation involvement of consultants would be appropriate for this model of consultation where the focus is on the empowerment of the complainants. Participants rated solution implementation as being moderately difficult. Although there were no statistically significant differences in perceptions of solution difficulty, teachers were most likely to view implementation as less easy.

Problem improvement was experienced to be the greatest by the adolescents who were the target of intervention. Parents and consultants also tended to view the problem as more resolved following the family-school meeting. Teachers, however, did not view the problem as improved. It is not clear from the data whether teachers simply responded to this item with a "wait and see" attitude or whether teachers viewed the meetings as ineffective in improving the problem.

Because a focus of the solution-oriented approach is to promote competence, participants were asked to rate their confidence in solving similar problems in the future. All participants except teachers indicated above average ratings in expected future problem-solving capability.

Overall satisfaction with the family-school meeting as an intervention strategy was assessed with two items, an overall rating and an indication of future use of the family-school meeting to resolve problems. All respondents except adolescents indicated that they were quite likely to use the family-school meeting in the future as a means to resolving child/school concerns. Moreover, all respondents including adolescents provided very positive overall rat-

TABLE 1
Respondents' Perceptions of the Problem and Problem Resolution

	Child (N=5)	Parent (N=13)	Teacher (N=7)	Consultant (N=18)
Pre-Meeting View of Problem Type				
Emotional	20	38	0	11
Behavioral	40	38	43	72
Learning	0	8	0	6
Mixed	20	15	57	11
None	20	0	0	0
Post-Meeting View of Problem Type				
Emotional	0	15	0	0
Behavioral	40	31	71	88
Learning	20	15	0	0
Mixed	20	31	29	13
None	20	8	0	0
Pre-Meeting View of Problem Locus				
School	40	46	71	44
Home	20	31	0	28
Mixed	20	23	29	28
None	20	0	0	0
Post-Meeting View of Problem Locus				
School	40	38	43	38
Home	20	31	0	44
Mixed	0	23	57	19
None	40	8	0	0
Pre-Post Meeting Change in Perception of Problem				
Change	20	46	43	63
No Change	80	54	57	31
Perceived Cause of the Problem				
Child	25	31	0	11
School	50	15	0	0
Parent or Family	0	15	14	11
Child-School Rel.	0	8	0	6
School-Family Rel.	0	8	0	6
Parent-Child Rel.	25	15	57	56
Multiple	0	8	29	6
Responsible for Solving the Problem				
Child	50	15	14	0
School	25	23	0	0
Parent or Family	25	8	14	6
Child-School Rel.	0	0	14	6
School-Family Rel.	0	15	14	18
Parent-Child Rel.	0	23	0	24
Multiple	0	15	43	47
Responsible for Cause vs. Solution				
Same Person(s)	57	38	57	33
Different Persons	25	62	43	61

Note: Entries are percentages.

ings regarding the family-school meeting as an intervention strategy.

In summary, although students experienced some distress in anticipation of the family-school meeting, and teachers expressed some negativity regarding aspects of the meeting, the overall ratings of this approach to resolving problems were quite favorable.

Family-school meeting interactive

TABLE 2
Participants' Perceived Satisfaction with the Family-School Meeting

	Child (N=5)	Parent (N=13)	Teacher (N=7)	Consultant (N=18)
Pre-Meeting Comfort Level	2.20 (1.30)	4.31 (.85)	4.29 (.76)	3.94 (.80)
Post-Meeting Satisfaction Level	4.00 (1.15)	3.75 (1.42)	3.0^t (1.53)	3.47^t (1.06)
Involvement in Planning the Solution	3.40 (1.81)	4.85* (.38)	3.57 (1.13)	3.67* (.48)
Involvement in the Solution	3.40 (1.52)	4.46** (.78)	3.86* (1.34)	2.25* ** (1.18)
Ease of Plan	3.50 (1.29)	3.50 (1.51)	2.71 (1.70)	3.21 (1.05)
Problem Improved	4.20 (.84)	3.50 (1.07)	2.00 (1.47)	3.29 (.69)
Confidence in Subsequent Problem Resolution	3.80 (.84)	3.67 (1.97)	2.83 (1.47)	4.0 (.69)
Would Use Family-School Meeting in the Future	2.20 (1.64)	4.50 (.67)	3.43 (1.81)	4.67 (.48)
Overall Rating of Effectiveness	3.80 (1.09)	4.30 (1.15)	4.0 (1.53)	4.22 (.65)

Note: Ratings are based on a 5-point Likert response format: 1 = lower satisfaction, 5 = highest satisfaction. Several items are reverse scored to reflect consistent directionality.

^{t} $p < .10$

* $p < .05$

** $p < .001$

process. The second part of the program evaluation examined the degree to which student consultants actually engaged in solution-oriented behavior within the family-school meeting. Proportions of total consultant talk appear on Table 3 along with the overall response quality of other participants. Examination of the means appearing on Table 3 indicates that consultants were most likely to use the strategies of Use Solution Language, Search for Exceptions to the problem, and Acknowledges the Viewpoint of others within the family-school meeting. Consultants were also quite likely to use a variety of techniques designed to alter the participants' "viewing" of the problem including the following: Obtain a Video Description of the problem, Reframes the problem, and Expanding the Frame of the problem.

Consultants were least likely to engage in the more strategically oriented intervention techniques of Action Interruption or Doing with a solution-oriented Twist directives. These strategies could be considered too directive or paradoxical for a family-school meeting. Student consultants, however, infrequently engaged in Identifying Past Solutions to problems or Identifying Smallest Change goals, both of which would be expected to be useful in these meetings.

Taken together the behavioral analysis of the consultants' speech indicated that they were quite successful in implementing a variety of solution-oriented techniques. Consultants were particularly likely to use behaviors that assisted in establishing rapport with the participants and that worked to change complainants' viewing of the problem. Consultants were least likely to use techniques that were highly directive or strategic, as would be

TABLE 3
Proportion of Consultant and Others Communication Behaviors in the
Family-School Meeting

Therapist Communication Behavior	Mean	Std. Dev.
Matches Language	4.23	2.99
Acknowledges View	14.86	8.61
Obtains Video Description	7.71	9.83
Searches for Exceptions	12.28	6.32
Future Visualization	4.57	6.16
Identifies Smallest Change	1.71	1.11
Uses Solution Language	11.28	4.75
Reframes Problem	7.00	6.11
Introduces Doubt	5.43	5.62
Expands Frame	8.00	9.76
Viewing with a Twist	4.28	2.63
Action Interruption	3.43	2.82
Provides Obvious Solution	2.28	1.89
Doing with a Twist	3.86	2.12
Identifying Past Solutions	3.43	4.16
Other	26.00	14.80
Participants' Responses		
Positive	41.87	16.48
Negative	30.14	21.51
Neutral	27.86	16.66

quite appropriate for an initial meeting of a time-limited duration. Consultants' failure to use techniques that would be expected to be helpful, such as identifying small changes, was interpreted by the investigators to be due to inexperience and lack of adequate training.

DISCUSSION

The purpose of this chapter was to introduce a model of family-school collaboration theoretically and practically embedded within the brief, solution-oriented psychotherapy literature. It was hypothesized that the emphasis on competence and strengths versus pathology and blame intrinsic to solution-oriented therapy would be a particularly useful model for communication at the home-school interface given the apprehensiveness with which parents have been noted to approach interactions with the school. Results of a preliminary investigation of the usefulness of solution-oriented family-school meetings for the resolution of school-related problems were promising,

particularly for parents and the identified problem child. Teachers, however, expressed less certainty that the family-school meetings would result in problem resolution.

The family-school meeting intervention strategy appeared to be a particularly positive experience for the identified problem children and their parents. It is likely that the unexpected focus on "what is working" within the meeting allowed the child and parent, both of whom were expecting to hear about blame and failure, to relax defenses and become involved in the collaboration. As noted by one of our student consultants, "I have observed that in using the solution-oriented approach, the participants' statements move from a negative nature to a more positive one, and participants will pick up on the types of questions asked and begin adopting the same line of questioning." Thus, the solution-oriented family-school meeting appears to address the call from Comer (1984) for schools to find mechanisms to foster communication with parents that enhance or maintain the parents' status and power. Given the plethora of literature that points to negative home-school relationships, an intervention strategy that leaves parents feeling more positive about themselves and their problematic child, and children feeling more hopeful, is clearly worth further investigation.

The solution-oriented family-school meeting, however, did not prove to be as effective with teachers. Although teachers were quite positive in their rating of the overall effectiveness of the intervention strategy, they were less favorable in their rating of problem resolution. The reason for the greater negativity of the teachers versus other participants is unclear from our data. It can be hypothesized, however, because teachers were favorable toward the concept of a family-school meeting but less favorable about the ability of such a meeting to produce meaningful changes in the child's behavior, that a solution orientation was inconsistent with the beliefs and experiences of teachers.

As noted earlier, research has consistently found that teachers tend to blame parents when children are experiencing difficulty in school. Sarason (1985) reminds us that teachers may be predisposed to blame parents, not only in service of their egos, but also because schools fail to establish positive relationships with parents before problems arise. Like parents, teachers most often wait until a problem is out of their control before they contact parents. Thus, parent-school collaboration most often occurs within the context of crisis, tension, frustration, and defensiveness, rather than within the context of a mutually supportive and respectful relationship. Teachers are not provided the training to establish strong working relationships with parents; thus, they remain reactive to crises (Sarason, 1985).

A second fact of the school culture is that teachers have little or no time to develop collaborative working relationships with parents (Sarason, 1985). Teachers today face not only limited time schedules but also increasing curriculum objectives. They also face increased pub-

lic demands for performance and accountability. When a teacher's merit evaluation is based on the academic performance of students, there is considerable pressure to narrow the scope of attention to curriculum and the classroom, and to provide records that prove accountability.

Schools, like families, have well-articulated belief systems that strongly influence staff functioning (Fisher, 1986). It has been documented that teachers are predisposed to have a belief system that places blame for student failure outside their classroom. Consistent with this belief, teachers who attended the family-school meetings were well prepared with clear documentation of the children's poor academic or behavioral performance. The verbal reporting of these records implicitly served a twofold function: (a) to convince parents that their child had a serious problem and (b) to convince all parties present that the teacher was competent and was not to blame. The focus of the solution-oriented meeting away from this documentation of problems to the child's successes appears inconsistent with a pervasive belief system held by school staff.

The incompatibility of school culture and teacher belief systems with solution-oriented family-school meetings suggests that a considerable amount of inservice teacher training may be necessary to shift teacher attitude from attention and documentation of a child's problems to a focus on strengths and possibilities. It also suggests that in conducting family-school meetings greater use of the intervention strategy of "Introducing Uncertainty" may be necessary, particularly in the school psychologist's interactions with teachers. Until teacher belief systems shift, it is also possible that family-school meetings require individual premeetings with teachers in which not only can the teacher's viewpoint of the child's problems be more strongly acknowledged, but also the seeds of uncertainty regarding the source of the problem can be planted.

There were numerous shortcomings in both our experimental implementation of the solution-oriented family-school meeting model and our preliminary investigation of effectiveness. First, the sample size was quite small preventing adequate statistical analyses of much of the data. Second, the student consultants were quite inexperienced with the brief solution-oriented approach. Thus, the effectiveness of the intervention approach was only weakly evaluated. In addition, the current evaluation lacked a control group and/or follow-up data on the effectiveness of this intervention. Finally, comments from our student consultants heightened our awareness to the dynamic tension between systems theory, solution-oriented therapy, and the realities of school schedules that is created by solution-oriented family-school meetings. A systems perspective promotes the participation of all relevant members of a system, and practical experience indicates that solutions most frequently emerge from the system members who are not "customers" for change. The solution-oriented model of therapy proposes that a change in one system element will ripple to other elements without their direct involvement. Schools, particularly the upper grade levels where each child has many teachers, all with different free periods, are particularly difficult settings in which to arrange meetings, making the ease of the ripple-effect approach quite desirable.

As is clearly evident from this discussion, the solution-oriented family-school meeting model requires further development and evaluation. We remain encouraged by the preliminary data which suggest that families and schools can join together in relatively brief meetings to resolve the school problems of children in a manner that enhances the positive affective experience of troubled children and their parents. It is clear, however, that modifications of the intervention are necessary to enhance its appeal to teachers and the ease of implementation, particularly in middle and high school settings. Moreover, it will be critical in adaptations of the solution-oriented family-school meeting model that critical elements of the model are not sacrificed for school adaptation simply because they

are difficult or inconvenient. It may be the very difficulty of organizing and conducting solution-oriented family-school meetings in the school setting that reflects an important focus of school culture change.

REFERENCES

Beckman, L. (1973). Effects of students' performance on teachers' and observers' attributions of causality. *Journal of Educational Psychology, 65,* 198–204.

Bronfenbrenner, U. (1979). *The ecology of human development.* Cambridge, MA: Harvard.

Carlson, C. I., & Hickman, J. (in press). Family consultation in schools in special services. In C. A. Maher & R. E. Greenberg (Eds.), Effective teams and groups: Vital contributions to special needs students [Special issue]. *Special Services in the School, 6*(3/4).

Comer, J. P. (1984). Home-school relationships as they affect the academic success of children. *Education and Urban Society, 16*(3), 323–337.

Conoley, J. C. (1987). Schools and families: Theoretical and practical bridges. *Professional School Psychology, 2,* 191–203.

Crombrinck-Graham, L. (Ed.). (1989). *Children in family contexts.* New York: Guilford.

de Shazer, S. (1982). *Patterns of brief family therapy.* New York: Guilford.

de Shazer, S. (1985). *Keys to solution.* New York: Norton.

de Shazer, S. (1988). *Clues: Investigating solutions in brief therapy.* New York: Norton.

Doyle, A. B., Gold, D., & Moskowitz, D. (Eds.). (1984). Children in families under stress. *New Directions for Child Development* (No. 24). San Francisco: Jossey Bass.

Dunst, C. J., & Trivette, C. M. (1987). Enabling and empowering families: Conceptual and intervention issues. In W. P. Erchul (Ed.), Family systems assessment and intervention [Special issue]. *School Psychology Review, 16*(4), 443–456.

Family-School Collaboration Project: Description. (no date). (Available from The Ackerman Family Institute for Family Therapy, 149 East 78th Street, New York, NY 10021)

Fine, M. J. (1991). A systems-ecological perspective on family-school intervention. In M. J. Fine & C. I. Carlson (Eds.), *Handbook of family-school intervention: A systems perspective.* Boston: Allyn & Bacon.

Fisher, L. (1986). Systems-based consultation with schools. In L. Wynne, S. H. McDaniel, & T. T. Weber (Eds.), *Systems consultation: A new perspective for family therapy* (pp. 342–356). New York: Guilford.

Gallesich, J. (1982). *The profession and practice of consultation.* San Francisco: Jossey-Bass.

Graden, J. L., & Christenson, S. L. (1987). Troubled families. In A. Thomas & J. Grimes (Eds.), *Children's needs: Psychological perspectives* (pp. 651–657). Washington, DC: National Association of School Psychologists.

Gutkin, T. B., & Conoley, J. C. (1990). Reconceptualizing school psychology from a service delivery perspective: Implications for practice, training, and research. *Journal of School Psychology, 28,* 203–223.

Gutkin, T. B., &, Curtis, M. J. (1982). School-based consultation: Theory and techniques. In C. R. Reynolds & T. B. Gutkin (Eds.), *Handbook of school psychology* (pp. 796–828). New York: Wiley.

Guttmann, J. (1982). Pupils', teachers' and parents' causal attributions for problem behavior at school. *Journal of Special Education, 76,* 14–21.

Haley, J. (1984). *Ordeal therapy: Unusual ways to create change.* San Francisco: Jossey-Bass.

Kral, R. (1986). *Strategies that work: Techniques for solution in the schools.* Milwaukee, WI: Brief Therapy Center.

Leitch, M. L., & Tangri, S. S. (1988). Barriers to home-school collaboration. *Educational Horizons, 70–74.*

Lightfoot, S. L. (1978). *Worlds apart: Relationships between families and schools.* New York: Basic Books.

Lipchik, E., & de Shazer (1988). Purposeful sequences for beginning the solution-oriented interview. In E. Lipchik (Ed.), *Interviewing* (pp. 105–117). Rockville, MD: Aspen.

Muneno, R., & Dembo, M. H. (1982). Causal attributions for student performance: Effect of teachers' conceptual complexity. *Personality and Social Psychology Bulletin, 8,* 201–207.

O'Hanlon, W. H., & Weiner-Davis, M. (1989). *In search of solutions: A new direction in psychotherapy.* New York: Norton.

O'Hanlon, W. H., & Wilk, J. (1987). *Shifting contexts: The generation of effective psychotherapy.* New York: Guilford.

Rutter, M. (1985). Family and school influences on behavior development. *Journal of Child Psychology and Psychiatry, 26,* 349–368.

Sarason, S. B. (1985). *Caring and compassion in clinical practice: Issues in the selection, training, and behavior of helping professionals.* San Francisco: Jossey-Bass.

Watzlawick, P., Weakland, J. H., & Fisch, R. (1974).

Change: Principles of problem formation and problem resolution. New York: Norton.

Zuckerman, M. (1979). Attribution of success and failure revisited, or: The motivational bias is alive and well in attribution theory. *Journal of Personality, 47,* 245–287.

Appendix A

Solution-Oriented Process Evaluation Code

THERAPIST/CONSULTANT SPEECH ACTS

I. JOINING
   1. Matching Client's Language (including sensory modality, language, & metaphors)
   2. Acknowledge Client's View

II. NEGOTIATING A SOLVABLE PROBLEM
   3. Request video description of the problem
   4. Search for exceptions, strengths, past solutions
   5. Request Visualization of future without the problem (includes magic wand, video picture of the future)
   6. Request smallest change (includes who would first notice the change, what would they notice)

III. CHANGING VIEWING
   7. Use of solution-oriented language (includes framing problem in past tense, when vs. if, will vs. would)
   8. Reframe (includes normalizing, depathologizing, transitional)
   9. Introduce Doubt/ Challenge Perceptions
   10. Expand/Broaden problem focused frame of who is involved (e.g., from individual to system)
   11. Summarize Viewing with a Twist (summarize existing viewpoints plus add a solution-oriented twist)

IV. CHANGING DOING
   12. Action/Pattern Interruption/ Prescription
   13. Provide Obvious Solutions
   14. Summarize Solutions (Doing) with a Twist
   15. Utilization of Past Solutions to Solve A Problem

16. Other (All therapist speech acts that cannot be coded by the above categories)

RESPONSES

17. Positive (indicates a change in the viewing or doing of the problem)

18. Negative (indicates no change in the viewing or doing of the problem, that is, a persistence of the initial viewpoint)

19. Neutral (speech not reflective of change; speech unrelated to the problem or problem child)

10

THE FAMILY-SCHOOL COLLABORATION PROJECT: SYSTEMIC INTERVENTIONS FOR SCHOOL IMPROVEMENT

Howard M. Weiss and
Martha E. Edwards

Research over the past 15 years has unequivocally demonstrated that when parents are involved in their children's education, these children have higher educational achievement, better attendance records, and more positive attitudes about education (Henderson, 1989). If the same results were obtained in research demonstrating the efficacy of a medical treatment, the demand for that treatment would be overwhelming. This has not been the case for family involvement in education. Nevertheless, establishing a genuine educational partnership, including school staff, students, parents, and significant others in the child's life, is crucial for renewing the quality of the American educational system. In this chapter we look at the barriers to family-school collaboration. Then we describe the program of intervention developed by the Family-School Collaboration Project at the Ackerman Institute to initiate and sustain positive working partnerships between families and schools.[1] In doing this, we delineate

the goals and history of the Project to illustrate the development of a model for organizational change in the family-school system. Then we describe the primary intervention strategies and give detailed and concrete examples of interventions in schools to encourage others to invest their professional energies in improving family-school relationships.

We define family-school collaboration as a cooperative process of planning and problem solving involving school staff, parents, children, and significant others used to maximize resources for students' academic achievement and social-emotional development. In our work with over 50 schools in New York City over the past 10 years, we have identified three major barriers to collaborative relationships between families and schools. First, schools and families rarely establish ongoing, routine vehicles for sharing information in a two-way dialogue, developing educational plans, and solving problems. One reason for this is that activities in which these types of communications could take place are not typically part of the school calendar. Another reason is that school staff often lack the

[1] The project was cofounded by Howard M. Weiss, Ph.D. and Arthur Maslow, M.S.W. Staff members who have added to our understanding of the family-school system and how to intervene in it include: Susan Bolitzer, M.S.W., Joel Comet, Ph.D., Egda Del Valle Delaney, M.S.W., Fran Schwartz, Ph.D., Ruth Seidenstein, M.S.W., Susan Shimmerlik, Ph.D., and Eileen Wasow, M.S.W.; and Mindy Zelen, B.A.

skills needed to elicit and constructively incorporate input from parents and children. Second, cultural, socioeconomic, and racial differences between school staff and families create either real or assumed barriers to communication and partnerships. Third, conceptions of the roles that parents could play in the school are unnecessarily limited. As a result, parents are often channeled into the roles of audience members or supporters but rarely looked upon as partners or co-decision makers.

To overcome these barriers and develop collaborative family-school relationships, we provide a program of staff training and consultation for schools and school districts. We have found that there are three prerequisites for success. First is the principal's commitment to family-school collaboration and use of every opportunity to convey this commitment to his or her staff, parent body, and students. Second is the selection of a coordinating committee composed of at least the principal, pupil personnel staff members (psychologist, social worker, and/or guidance counselor), teachers, and parents. It is this committee that will initiate efforts to assess the current family-school relationship and identify areas of need in the school for which family-school collaboration would serve as a resource. The committee is the conduit to the rest of the staff and parent body and takes responsibility for dissemination of the ideas and interventions into the school as a whole. We have found that this structure, rather than direct interventions with the entire staff or parent group, increases the ownership of the work and facilitates greater involvement and motivation. Third is the designation of a family-school coordinator in the school to take a major responsibility for initiating, organizing, and facilitating activities to enhance family-school relationships. In this chapter, we will focus on how the school psychologist can play this role. Nevertheless, other professionals such as the guidance counselor, social worker, or assistant principal, could also serve as the family-school coordinator. If these three preconditions are fulfilled, we have found that schools are able to restructure their existing activities and initiate other activities that will promote family-school partnerships to support the education of students.

To be more explicit about the kind of changes this effort entails, the following case example is provided. Analysis of the case and two alternative scenarios emphasize the ways in which schools might relate differently to families in order to be more helpful to the students. Consider the case of Ms. Nelson and her son, Philip:

Ms. Nelson is worried that her son, Philip, may have started school too early and comes to see Ms. Dooley, the assistant principal. Ms. Dooley tells Ms. Nelson that Philip's teacher thinks that he should be kept in kindergarten for another year. She notes that the school psychologist has talked to Philip and also finds him quite immature. Ms. Nelson rightly perceives that the decision has already been made and that the school is simply informing her as to what they are going to do. Ms. Nelson is angry that she was neither informed about the staff's initial concerns nor consulted in making their decision, even though she thinks that this is what Philip needs. She is also worried that when she tells her husband, he will accuse her of caving in to the school's pressures. Finally, she is concerned about Philip's reaction to his failure to move to first grade. She leaves the office frustrated and afraid of what will happen next.

This case is typical of encounters repeated with countless variations in our schools today and is a good illustration of the first barrier to family-school collaboration identified above. This barrier was the lack of routine vehicles that enable productive communication between families and schools in an atmosphere of cooperation. As a result, there is a certain degree of alienation between families and schools and some expectations that interactions will be adversarial. Another problem with the communication is that discussions about a problem often take place without the full participation of all concerned persons at the same time. The child is most frequently left out of these conferences. School psychologists may also be absent for initial exchanges about a problem. As a result, they are often asked to validate a position already taken by other staff members or to use their authority to make the case for the recommendation to the parent. A solution to these problems would be to find a way to come together to share information and devise a plan to improve the situation. In Philip's case, this did not happen. One might imagine the series of dyadic meetings that took place: The teacher spoke to the mother at the door of the classroom; the mother spoke to Philip on the way home; the mother spoke to the father at home; the father spoke to Philip; the teacher spoke to the assistant principal and the school psychologist; the mother spoke to the assistant principal. The decision was made, the actions were taken, and the alienation between family and school may further develop into an adversarial relationship. What a difference it would have made had the situation been handled in one of two ways. In scenario one, the school psychologist, as the family-school coordinator, works with teachers to develop orientation meetings in which the teacher, students, and parents participate. At the orientation for Philip's kindergarten class, the Nelsons have an opportunity to see Philip in the context of the other children. As a result, they realize that Philip was too young to start school. They speak to the teacher right there, who confirms their views on the basis of her own observations of Philip in the class. As a group, they decide to enroll Philip in the prekindergarten program. In scenario two, Philip has already started kindergarten and his parents and teacher are concerned about his progress. They seek an additional opinion from the school psychologist who observes the child in class. After doing the observation, the school psychologist leads a family-school problem-solving meeting with Philip, his parents, and the teacher to discuss everyone's concerns. After reviewing Philip's experience in kindergarten in this meeting, they jointly agree that he is not ready to move to first grade and that it is to his advantage to move to the prekindergarten class or to repeat kindergarten.

These latter ways of handling the situation reflect a collaborative relationship between families and schools. School staff develop activities that enable children, family members, and educators to interact together and experience elements of the educational program. Staff members, the child, family members, and significant others also meet together to hear each other's concerns, to reach consensus about primary issues, to decide where to focus, and to arrive at a specific plan of action.

BACKGROUND INFORMATION: THE FAMILY-SCHOOL COLLABORATION PROJECT

Project Goals and Objectives

The primary goal of the Project is for schools to use family-school collaboration as a resource for achieving the educational aims for the students. The significance of this goal is that family or parent involvement,[2] by itself, is not the primary aim of this work. Parent involvement needs to be inextricably tied to the educational aims of the school. Too often parent involvement programs merely seek to bring in family members without considering how they are linked to the education of the students. As a result, parent involvement programs are sometimes seen as competing for resources that would normally be given to other educational activities rather than using them to support these activities.

To accomplish this overall goal, a number of objectives must be achieved to overcome the barriers to collaboration that were articulated above. First, notions about the roles parents can play need to be expanded. Henderson, Marburger, and

---

[2] We recognize that individuals other than parents (e.g., grandparents, uncles and aunts, foster parents, guardians, siblings) are significant in students' lives. Thus, "family" or "parental" involvement could encompass all of these individuals.

Ooms (1986) identified at least five roles that parents could play in the school.

The first role they identified was *parents as partners* (e.g., getting children to school on time, getting vaccinations, checking that homework is done). Rich (1988) has expanded the role of parents as partners to include what they can do at home, in the course of daily activities such as cooking, shopping, or getting dressed, to build skills necessary for school achievement. Parents can build into these activities interactions that will help their children develop what Rich (1988) calls "megaskills" such as confidence, motivation, effort, responsibility, initiative, perseverance, caring, teamwork, common sense, and problem solving. Thus, parents can play significant roles as partners without physically coming to the school on a regular basis. What is needed, however, is for families and schools to communicate with one another so that they recognize that they are working in the same direction to support the children's education.

The second role Henderson et al. (1986) listed was *parents as collaborators and problem solvers*. Parents are needed to play these roles typically when their children are having difficulty. We have developed a format for meetings in which parents can work together with their child, teacher, and other school staff as problem solvers. These family-school problem-solving meetings are discussed in more detail later in this chapter.

The third role that Henderson et al. (1986) identified was *parents as audience*. This is the more typical role that parents have played in the past in which the parents attend and appreciate performances and productions given by the children in the school. The fourth role was *parents as supporters*. This role includes assistance given to teachers (e.g., as aides in the classroom, chaperons for class trips), to the school as a whole (e.g., as lunchroom supervisors, as parent organization participant), or to other parents (e.g., as mentors, participants in communication network). The fifth role that Henderson et al. (1986) listed was *parents as advisors and/or co-decision makers*. This includes parent representation on advisory committees or governance bodies to set policy for the school. It would include participation in school-based management programs being implemented in a number of schools throughout the country.

Although we have found expanding the roles that parents can play in schools to be important, the goal is not necessarily for parents to be in the school as much as possible. The reality of today is that many parents work in jobs outside the home and that it is very difficult for them to come to the school for events. This makes it especially important to be thoughtful about the choice of events and how they are conducted to give the message that families, students, and school staff need to work together to support and enhance the education of the students. If parents come to the school only twice in the year, yet hear this message, they may be able to be very effective in supporting the efforts of the school by what they do at home (e.g., monitoring homework, making sure children get to school on time, helping children learn organizational skills).

Consequently, the second objective is to establish a general climate of family-school collaboration in the school and design a series of activities to reflect this climate. A key element of these activities is the inclusion of the child in virtually all family-school interactions directly related to his or her education. If children are present, they have the opportunity to observe their parents and teachers cooperating on their behalf. They hear the same messages at the same time which clarifies expectations for them, their parents, and their teachers. The children are taken out of the difficult position of being the primary message bearer between home and school. The adults tend to focus more clearly on educational concerns and needs rather than ascribing blame for the existence of a problem. In addition, when children are included in the collaborative process, it actually becomes part of the school's curriculum for them. They learn skills of communication, problem solving, and teamwork and develop self-confidence and poise in so-cial situations.

Through these collaborative activi-ties, individuals who may initially seem different because of diverse educational backgrounds, cultures, races, and/or so-cioeconomic status can get to know one another. They develop an alliance based on the shared vested interest the family and school have in each child's educa-tional progress and social-emotional de-velopment. As a result, they begin to communicate more regularly and recipro-cally, develop trust in one another, and find ways to cooperate in educating the children. In this way they can overcome the legacy of previously alienated and/or adversarial relationships experienced by parents and school personnel either in the current school or in their own school history.

A third objective of the Project is for each school and district to assume *own-ership* for their efforts to establish a collaborative climate for family-school relations. A commitment to build a family-school partnership must be sus-tained over a number of years and activities that contribute to establishing a collaborative climate must touch the work of all school personnel throughout the year. Once achieved, this new school climate must be maintained as part of the ongoing educational program.

The Project staff are careful to ini-tiate this work by modeling the formation of a collaborative relationship in their interactions with school staff. After all, staff members must learn to work collab-oratively with each other if they are to be successful at establishing cooperative re-lationships with families. Project staff work with existing staff to implement and maintain family-school collaboration. No new staff are necessary to implement the program. After 2 to 3 years the existing staff can continue the program as part of their everyday work with little or no consultant support. They then continue to make new applications of the approach to suit their own needs. Family-school collaboration becomes a primary vehicle for accomplishing educational goals.

If schools can accomplish the goal of using family-school collaboration as a resource for achieving educational aims for students, it will also serve as an important preventive mental health pro-gram. Participation in collaborative fam-ily-school activities builds strong, con-structive bonds between children and the central adults in their lives at home and school. As a result, significant resources and procedures are available for identify-ing concerns and addressing them before they become protracted problems. Schools have found, for example, that before they refer a child to special education, they first hold a family-school problem-solving meeting to discuss the child's difficulties and develop a plan to help solve them. If the plan works, the child experiences being involved in solv-ing his or her own problems. Further-more, the child does not needlessly enter the special education program, thus free-ing resources for children in most need. If the problem persists, the child and family have already met to discuss their concerns and the referral to special education is more likely to be perceived as helpful to the student.

The focus and strategy of the Family-School Collaboration Project developed over time. Its history is important as a description of the development of a fundamental approach. Understanding the history allows others to learn from our cumulative experience and avoid some of our mistakes.

History of the Project

The Family-School Collaboration Project began in 1981 as a response to problems in the school referrals for family therapy coming to the Ackerman Institute. School staff understood that difficulties experienced by children in school were the result of larger influences on their life and would refer the family to therapy. Unfortunately, this referral for "help" was perceived by family members as implicitly or explicitly blaming them for the child's difficulties. As a result, the family either did not show up for therapy or terminated after one or two sessions. This is similar to the problems faced by school psychologists who receive referrals from classroom teachers of students having difficulties. The implicit message is often, "Deal with this child and then send him back to me." School staff often forget to include themselves as part of the system in which the student operates when they define a problem. As a result, they look for the solution in the family system. It was important to help school personnel conceptualize and deal with problems in the larger context of the family-school system rather than with a focus on the family system alone, the school alone, or the students as individuals.

Howard Weiss, Ph.D. and Arthur Maslow, M.S.W., the cofounders of the Project, began taking these cases back to the schools with the message that the child can be helped only when everyone works together. Instead of doing therapy sessions, they conducted a *family-school problem-solving meeting* at which all participants developed a concrete plan for the family and school to follow in order to help the child. Although the plan usually helped the child significantly, the more important outcome was the change in the relationships among the student, school staff, and family members. In interviews with parents about the effectiveness of these meetings, over half the parents spontaneously made remarks such as, "I really got a chance to see that the school cared about *my* child." It was this message that enabled the parents to join with the teacher, psychologist, guidance counselor, and/or principal to do what was needed in the long run to help the student.

Despite the Project's initial success, changing relationships between families and schools one family at a time through family-school problem-solving meetings was not an efficient way to effect significant change. Furthermore, waiting until students had problems severe enough to warrant such a meeting was counterproductive. It was much more difficult to shift a relationship that already had problems than it was to change the way the school and families developed their relationships from the beginning. Thus,

the Project staff began to develop a wider repertoire of school-wide activities called *climate-building activities.*

The specific climate-building activities implemented in any school depend on the particular needs of the students, families, and staff in that school. One major focus for intervention in many schools became the regularly held parent-teacher conference. These meetings were restructured to include children as active participants. Workshops were given to increase staff skills in collaborative planning and problem-solving skills so that they could facilitate cooperative interactions with parents and children together. Consequently, these meetings were renamed *family-teacher conferences.* Some additional activities that the Project has jointly developed with schools in order to address particular needs include: orientations of families to the school; orientations of particular groups of families (e.g., English-as-a-Second-Language programs, special education, students who had difficulties the previous year); planning and problem-solving meetings about possible holdovers; discussion forums about adult-student relationships focused around issues of trust, autonomy, drugs, and other issues of interest to students, parents, and school staff; parent groups planning school-yard activities to ensure a safe playground; and problem-solving meetings with groups of parents, children, school staff, and bus drivers to resolve issues of concern about bus travel.

Most clear in our development throughout the 10 years of the Project's work has been the importance of using a collaborative approach when working with school staff and parents. In so many staff development programs, the "professionals" come in and attempt to change the ways teachers and other school staff do their jobs. We have found that, in general, this way of intervening is ineffective. This is because it undermines the ownership of the work to build productive family-school relationships. Furthermore, it fosters dependence on outside consultants to carry the efforts and jeopardizes their continuation when the consultants are no longer present. Thus, the issue of ownership is critical. From our first encounter with school staffs, we aim to make the Project's work relevant to their needs and shaped by their efforts. Therefore, we model a collaborative approach by initially doing an assessment with the staff and parents to hear what their needs, concerns, and goals are and to incorporate them into any intervention plan. In addition, a coordinating team is selected to be responsible for promoting the major part of the change effort in the rest of the school. In that way, it becomes an effort that is initiated, implemented, and maintained by existing school staff and parents and not seen as something for which outside agents are primarily responsible. This also stimulates the creativity of the family-school community to devise applications that fit with their unique needs and desires. We have learned much from schools as they develop their own activities to build collaborative family-school relationships.

We emphasize that a single climate-building activity does not by itself change the quality of the school environment, nor do any number of activities when they are experienced as "one-shot" events. The most powerful means for recycling messages of collaboration and family-school partnership is to make sure that all activities are continually tied to the ongoing curriculum. In this way, the teachers recognize the direct supports that the family-school partnership brings to the achievement of their curriculum goals, and the parents understand how their efforts with their own children directly support the teachers' goals for learning and skill building.

Our history of starting with family-school problem-solving meetings and adding family-teacher conferences and climate-building activities to our repertoire of interventions is reflected in the comments of a principal whose school has been involved in the project for 3 years. The principal said:

> You know, in the first year, I thought family-school collaboration was having meetings with the child, parents, and school staff when the child was having

trouble in school. In the second year, I revised that and thought that family-school collaboration was changing our parent-teacher conferences to include children. In the third year, I revised that and thought that family-school collaboration was about climate-building activities that involved the whole school. Now I realize it's none of these things. Family-school collaboration is a process, a philosophy, that pervades everything you do in the school.

Her conclusion is consistent with our overall goal of making family-school collaboration an integral part of a school's work. However, it is not necessary to follow this sequence when intervening in a school. In fact, we have found it much more effective to begin by developing climate-building activities, such as an orientation for families and students at the beginning of the school year. When needed, family-school problem-solving meetings can be used as an example of how to work collaboratively with others. The strategies and techniques used in these meetings can then be generalized to how classroom discussions, staff meetings, and/or parents' association meetings are conducted.

The above comments also illustrate the traps that many mental health professionals fall into when intervening in larger systems. They take the approach of pulling the identified unit (e.g., child, family) out of the system in which it resides rather than recognizing that the child's or family's patterns of behavior are integrally connected to that system. Thus, the *family-school system* is the unit of intervention. In the next section, a theoretical net is used to elucidate the factors involved in establishing a collaborative school climate and increasing social connectedness between families and schools.

Theoretical Foundation

The theoretical foundation for our family-school collaboration approach draws heavily on two sets of concepts developed by social psychologists and sociologists. These concepts serve as guides for understanding the family-school system as it currently exists and for planning change efforts. The first set of concepts was developed by Tagiuri (1968) to describe the elements of organizational climate. These concepts have been used to formulate the critical components of a collaborative school climate. Because cooperation between systems implies social connectedness, a second set of concepts synthesized by Seeman (1968) provides the Project with a framework for understanding the degree of social connectedness or alienation between families and schools.

Model of climate. A central focus of the Project's work is to build or enhance collaborative aspects of a school's climate. Our use of the concept of climate comes from the work of Tagiuri (1968) who conceived of climate as the total environmental quality within an organization. Anderson (1982) previously pointed to the applicability of Tagiuri's notions to the area of school climate in her review of that literature.

According to Tagiuri, climate is "a relatively enduring quality of the internal environment of an organization that (a) is experienced by its members, (b) influences their behavior, and (c) can be described in terms of the values of a particular set of characteristics (or attributes) of the organization" (Tagiuri, 1968, p. 27). He identified four dimensions of the environment that contribute to school climate: *culture, milieu, social system,* and *ecology.*

The climate of a school experienced by staff, children, parents, and others is a qualitative phenomenon that shapes how they relate to one another. The four dimensions of *climate* provide a framework for describing the characteristics of a school that either promote or serve as barriers to collaborative partnerships between families and schools. This framework is explicitly used with school personnel to analyze how a school's climate influences the degree of social connectedness and cooperation between families and school staff. With this perspective, they can then plan ways to change specific aspects of their school's physical

and social environment in order to establish a collaborative climate. Table 1 lists Tagiuri's definitions of the four elements of environment and the Project's applications of these concepts to the family-school community. Each one of these concepts is further discussed and illustrated as we first describe the elements of a collaborative climate and describe the barriers to achieving that goal.

The Family-School Collaboration Project works to develop a particular type of family-school relationship grounded in what Tagiuri would call a shared culture. When a school and the families of its students share a "school culture," they hold common sets of beliefs, expectations, values, and meanings about achieving a quality education for all the children. Basic to the family-school partnership is the shared belief that collaboration between home and school yields more resources and productive outcomes for students, families, and staff than can be generated separately. There is the expectation that families have a right and responsibility to be involved in the educational process (i.e., to know what is going on, be involved in decisions about their children's education, and have access to school personnel). In such a culture, both families and school staff believe that everyone, including the child, is doing the best he or she can given the circumstances. They expect that if they can work together, they will be able to develop solutions to the problems they encounter.

The greatest roadblocks to the establishment of such a culture are the lack of a collaborative professional spirit among staff and the overt and covert cycles of reciprocal blaming between families and the school. These interactions often derive from expectations that parents or teachers have that others are their adversaries. With such expectations, the meaning people attribute to specific events often emphasizes who is to blame rather than what has occurred, what concerns interested persons have, and what solutions would satisfy everyone in the interest of the child. Such blaming often

TABLE 1
Tagiuri's Definitions of the Elements of Organizational Climate and the Project's Applications to the Family-School Community

Culture	*Definition*: Aspects of the social environment such as belief systems, values, general cognitive structures, meaning.
	Application: Beliefs about how children learn, value of education in one's life, cognitive structures related to conception of problems and how to solve them, meaning attributed to language used.
Milieu	*Definition*: Characteristics of persons and groups.
	Application: School staff, student, and parent morale; racial and ethnic backgrounds; socioeconomic status; level of education; school staff's, family members', and students' previous experiences in schools; level of achievement in school.
Social System	*Definition*: Patterned relationships of persons and groups.
	Application: The nature of the interactions among school staff, family members, and students ranging from hierarchical to collaborative, from shared leadership to solitary leadership, from adversarial to allied, from alienated to close, from professional to personal, from task-focused to emotionally-focused. These interactions can be face-to-face, on the telephone, or by written letters or notes.
Ecology	*Definition*: Physical and material aspects of the environment.
	Application: Classrooms and other space designated for particular purposes; the design and condition of the school building; signs and bulletin boards; telephone and intercom systems; money; time; educational materials; allocation of resources such as the scheduling of classes; the nature of the surrounding neighborhood and transportation system.

derives from assumptions that parents do not really care about their children or that teachers do not care about educating students. When blaming is a significant part of the school's culture, energy and efforts are wasted in defensive behaviors rather than constructive problem solving.

The culture of the school is integrally connected to the characteristics of the members of the family-school community. Tagiuri's concept of *milieu* captures the attributes of the specific persons and groups that make up the family-school community. In many schools, the persons are a heterogenous group comprising wide-ranging ethnic heritages, socioeconomic status, and previous experiences with schools. In other schools, the milieu may be more homogenous. In either case, the Project starts with the premise that all parents are concerned about their children's success in school. Family-school relationships begin with the creation of a bond based on the common vested interest in each child. Understanding and respecting

the diversity of cultural heritages represented by families and staff is a precondition for using these differences as resources for broadening and deepening family-school relationships.

There are aspects of the milieu that sometimes block collaboration between families and schools. When different ethnic and racial groups have few opportunities to recognize or develop common interests, they often make assumptions about others' intentions as if they were adversaries. Moreover, when parents have had very different schooling experiences themselves, they often come to the school with different expectations and beliefs about what would be best for their own children. These hurdles can be overcome by creating opportunities for parents and teachers to express their diverse beliefs and by helping them to understand the educational approach and rationale of the school. Differences then can be addressed over time as subjects for a legitimate ongoing dialogue.

The *social system* of the family-school community is observable in the patterned interactions of students, family members, and school staff with one another. Such patterns can be described in terms of alliances, coalitions, role complementarities, and group norms. How individuals in each of these constituencies perceive the characteristics of these interaction patterns shapes their subsequent reactions. Thus, for example, when parents perceive themselves to be treated as hierarchically subordinate to teachers or when they are only contacted when their children are in trouble, they tend to assume defensive positions. They focus on their natural alliance with their own children and protect their interests *against* demands of the teachers. Such relationships can be shifted by activities that position school staff, parents, and students as partners in an ongoing educational endeavor. When teachers enlist parents and students as their collaborators in finding effective paths for learning, family members perceive them as seeking family-school connections that can foster greater academic achievement or person-social growth for their children. Teachers can then take a direct task-focused approach to problem solving rather than waste time on emotionally focused interactions aimed primarily at establishing or defending against blame.

In their training, intervention, and consultation work, Project staff work with school personnel to create opportunities for problem solving and climate building which place school staff, families, and students in a collaborative, educational context with one another. In these settings, new expectations for family-school interactions can be established which can guide subsequent joint efforts. Over time, families and school staff develop a new set of norms for their relationships with one another.

One of the arenas in which this new set of norms can be readily communicated is the physical or material aspects of the school environment, what Tagiuri termed the *ecology*. Project staff work with school personnel and families to assess whether aspects of the school ecology send messages of collaboration and partnership or messages of disconnection and distance. For example, do signs at points of entry welcome parents and seek their involvement, or do they emphasize the school's position of control? Does the school office divide staff and family members with a high physical barrier from behind which one must wait for acknowledgement or is the office physically open and accessible? Does the condition of the building show caring and educational purposefulness? One school principal recognized the importance of the many letters the school administration sends home over a school year as a critical ecological factor. He and the staff laid them out across a number of tables and asked, "Do these letters communicate that we want a collaborative relationship with the families of our students?" The answer was, "No." Many of the letters sent the message: "We regret to inform you." All letters were rewritten so that they purposefully contributed to the establishment of a climate of cooperative partnership with families.

When school staff carefully and continually attend to the ways in which each aspect of the school environment—culture, milieu, social system, and ecology—communicates the value of family-school partnership, they gradually establish an enduring climate of collaboration.

Increasing the degree of family-school connectedness. The specific operations necessary to establish a collaborative school climate involve developing educational activities including conjoint interaction among school staff, students, and members of their families (especially parents or guardians). The Project staff trains school personnel to create activities that are specifically designed to increase the degree of connectedness (or decrease the degree of alienation) between family and school.

To guide thinking about building connections among students, parents, and educators we added a set of five concepts to the model of climate. These concepts are: *power, meaning, norms, inclusion,* and *self-relatedness.* These concepts describe elements of social connectedness or alienation and were synthesized by Seeman (1968) from the work of such classical theorists in sociology, psychology, and political thought as Durkheim, Marx, Adorno, Merton, Nettler, and Mills. The definitions of these concepts are given in Table 2. Each of these concepts is used to conceptualize activities that will increase the appropriate connections between school and families.

The concept of *power* points to the expectations that participants in a system have that their own actions can determine the occurrence of desired outcomes. For example, parents need to envision how they can affect their own children's school success. They need to be clear about the relationship between what they do at home and its impact on school achievement for their children. Schools must clarify for parents how experiences at home translate into academic performance in the classroom. One way could be for parents to support organizational and scheduling skills that are emphasized in school by negotiating television, homework, and leisure reading time, and making available a quiet, well-lit place to study. Another could be the involvement of parents in the homework assignment itself. For example, in elementary school, children might be asked to interview parents for information about family life, culture, countries of origin, or types of employment. Children might discuss at home books read in class or themes and values discussed in class. A third way could be preparatory activities, which provide children with the requisite skills and attitudes for success in school and in life. Preparatory activities are what Rich (1988) called "megaskills" (confidence, motivation, effort, responsibility, initiative, perseverance, caring, teamwork, common sense, and problem solving).

As parents feel empowered, school staff will find parents to be effective allies in their efforts to help children succeed in school. Shared power becomes greater power. Parents and school staff are much more likely to achieve the educational outcomes toward which they are working if they form a solid partnership than if they work in isolation.

Meaning is the second factor that contributes to increased family-school connectedness. A situation, communication, or activity is meaningful for parents, students, and staff when it provides sufficient information for making clear decisions and when individuals believe

TABLE 2
Seeman's Concepts of Connectedness in a Social System

Power	Individuals can achieve by their own behavior the outcomes sought.
Meaning	Individuals have a sufficient amount of information to predict future outcomes and there are clear standards for decision making.
Norms	A high expectancy that there are adequate socially approved behaviors to achieve given goals.
Inclusion	The assignment of high reward value to goals or beliefs held by particular individuals or groups. This is contrasted with isolation in which a low reward value is assigned to goals or beliefs held by particular individuals or groups.
Self-relatedness	A high degree of connection between a given behavior and rewards associated with that behavior in contrast with rewards that are vague and anticipated only in the distant future.

Note: The concepts Seeman originally identified described the opposite end of the continuum of connectedness (i.e., powerlessness, meaninglessness, isolation, normlessness, and self-estrangement). The end of the continuum reflecting connectedness is stressed here as the concepts are used to identify the qualities that should be planned into interventions to increase connections between family and school. As a result, the definitions have been paraphrased to reflect the focus on this end of each continuum.

that they can predict satisfactorily what the future outcomes of their behavior will be. School staff and parents need to share enough information to derive appropriate *meaning* and predict outcomes about which they are concerned.

The Family-School Collaboration Project staff assess with school personnel the ways in which information is shared between schools and families. Parents typically receive rather truncated reports from their children and may receive direct communications from the teachers infrequently. This often does not enable them to understand the general and specific purposes of their children's school work and the teachers' methods of instruction. When they have a context for understanding their child's school experiences, they can make appropriate decisions and act in ways that help their children in their school efforts. Similarly, teachers and other school staff need information from parents in order to predict outcomes well. If children are going through a difficult transition (e.g., birth of a sibling, divorce, move), this information is helpful for the teacher to understand possible changes in the child's behavior and to plan how to respond appropriately. These communications usually take place when something is going wrong. Furthermore, parents sometimes receive mixed messages from the child and the teacher. As a result, parents may be unclear about what is actually happening and how to respond appropriately. This speaks to the need for frequent communication among staff, students, and parents. They need to communicate regularly about what is going well and what is going poorly.

Norms are a critical element for increasing the degree of connectedness between families and schools. Norms refer to the relatively widely shared expectations for behaviors to achieve specific goals. Because connections to families are not an integral part of the school curriculum, there often are few clear *norms* about how parents should or can communicate effectively and work with schools. As a result, parents develop their own idiosyncratic ways of interacting with the school and may adopt inappropriate methods for reaching their goals. Parents, for example, may want their children to succeed in any way possible. Consequently, they may help their children too much. When parents check and correct their child's homework, the teacher will not know whether a child is having a particular problem. When parents do the science fair project or drill the children on upcoming tests, the students do not learn to accept these responsibilities by themselves. On the other extreme, parents may feel frustrated at not knowing what to do to help their children and leave it all for the teacher to handle. If the child is having trouble in school, a concerned parent may feel that the only way to obtain help is to demand desired services. These parents would assume a more cooperative posture if they experienced that the school norm for dealing with such issues is to meet with staff, to share concerns, and to solve problems together.

Issues of *inclusion* and isolation are particularly salient as our school systems become increasingly diverse. Families will be isolated from the school if they believe that their goals and beliefs are given a low value by the school. By contrast, families experience themselves as included when they believe that they share goals and beliefs with the school. Parents who come from different cultures than those represented by mainstream education may not value the same goals and beliefs held by school staff. For example, some parents may value the goal of learning educational basics, but not value creative thinking, experiential learning, or other less traditional forms of educational activities. They may then be in conflict over the style and quality of education given to their children. Parents who are disenfranchised from society, especially when economically deprived and who may not have had a good education themselves, may not value education in the same way school staff do. They either may not believe that schooling will provide opportunities for advancement for their children or they may see the school as a competitor that creates distance between them and their children. The Project consultants work with school personnel to develop opportunities for families, students, and school staff to share their ideas about education and other important themes or issues. Such opportunities often result in the realization that parents, students, and staff do not hold such different basic values and goals for education or in the development of some common educational values and goals.

Finally, *self-relatedness* contributes to a sense of connection to others in that rewards from an activity are experienced as intrinsic to participation in that activity rather than in a vaguely anticipated future. For parents and teachers to experience a sense of *self-relatedness,* they need to perceive their activities with children as inherently rewarding and linked to the children's educational progress. Parents and teachers often feel estranged from one another because their interactions implicitly or explicitly emphasize blame. As a result, parents may agree to plans in which they help children with homework or teachers may agree to provide special attention primarily to reduce the experienced blaming. Rather than being done for their intrinsic reward, such as interacting with the child or helping the child master a skill, the activities are done in order to show others that one is not a "bad" parent, teacher, or student. It is the blaming that often estranges the blamer and the blamed person from the intrinsic rewards of the educational tasks and those associated with the task.

Summary of theoretical framework. When designing activities to change the relationship between families and schools, the two sets of concepts used to define factors that contribute to organizational climate and to increase social connectedness serve as a theoretical checklist. We need to ask whether these activities increase power, meaning, norms, inclusion, and self-relatedness for both family and school. Do they promote interactions in which families, students, and school staff share information, make plans, and solve problems together? Do the physical cues (ecology) consistently reinforce the messages of welcome and partnership? The frequent experience of curriculum-based and social activities throughout the school year by staff, students, and family members establishes a collaborative school *culture.* They come to share the beliefs that families are a critical educational resource and should be an integral part of the educational process. With the establishment of such basic shared values, parents, students, and staff consistently ascribe meanings to educational concerns or problems that are not based on blame. When school personnel, students, and family members interact with one another in ways and circumstances that send clear messages about the value of their collaborative partnership, the overall school climate fosters continued constructive family-school relations. These relationships provide continuity to long-term educational purposes over the course of the child's school career. The school climate is perceived as collaborative when school staff, parents, and children consistently ascribe meanings like openness, connectedness, cooperation, trust, respect, and inclusion to their experiences of the school environment.

CLIMATE-BUILDING ACTIVITIES

In this section, we describe the activities actually implemented in schools that helped establish collaborative family-school climates. As conceived by Tagiuri (1968) and applied in this chapter, a school's climate is the quality of the environment deriving from the characteristics of its ecology, culture, milieu, and social system. Change in any one of these components would not necessarily affect the others nor alter the climate. The configuration of all four is essential. As a change strategy, however, we begin with a focus on the external factors such as the ecology and social system. This decision is based on the work of social psychologists who studied attitude and behavior change (McGuire, 1968). They found that it is easier to change behavior, after which attitude change follows, than to change attitudes in order to change behavior. Accordingly, when intervening in schools, we have found that it is most effective to change the nature of the interactions among participants and to change the physical characteristics of the environment first. Once school staff and family members have had new experiences, they are more receptive to changing their ideas about the family-school relationship.

When intervening in schools, we look for opportunities to change the nature of the interactions between school staff and families, taking note of the ecological cues in the situation that will affect these interactions. These interactions are changed by restructuring or creating new activities in which school staff and families are engaged. We work with schools to think about, plan, and implement activities that will promote productive interactions between families and schools. Hence, these activities are called "climate-building activities." In this section, descriptions of actual climate-building activities that we have developed with school staffs and implemented in schools are presented. In addition to the description of the activity, an account of how the activity enhances the climate of the school as well as the ways the activity increases the connectedness between families and schools is also given. Also included are some notes about the difficulties experienced or additional components that could be added to the activities.

The Family-School Problem-Solving Meeting

The process of developing climate-building activities with schools is a collaborative one. The activities are based on the needs expressed by the school staff. What they often raise first are the difficulties they have with particular children and/or their parents. In these cases, we use the family-school problem-solving meeting as a vehicle for demonstrating to the school how they can change their relationship with an individual family. When staff see the effect of particular strategies and techniques used

in the meeting, they can begin to generalize these same strategies and techniques to improving their relationships with other families. Thus, although the meeting can be quite helpful to the particular child experiencing school difficulties, the power of the meeting as an intervention strategy for climate building comes in demonstrating to staff how to work collaboratively and in a nonblaming way with families. This then changes the *social system* of the school.

When a child experiences a school problem and a family-school problem-solving meeting is called, the meeting is always attended by the child, parents, and the child's teacher. When appropriate, other relevant school staff (e.g., social worker, school psychologist, resource room teacher, principal) or family members (e.g., siblings, grandmother), and significant others (e.g., friends, physician, babysitter) attend the meeting. These others may have a useful perspective to bring and/or may be an important resource for the problem's solution. An important principle of the family-school collaborative model is that *all* of these actors must be brought together to explore and solve the problem. They are important both as resources for understanding as well as resolving the problem.

Problems that have triggered these meetings include: truancy, severe behavioral problems, difficulties in learning to read or coping with class material, coping with presumed or identified learning disabilities, drug use, educational implications of physical handicaps and disease (e.g., epilepsy, diabetes), multiple external stresses of poverty (including food, shelter, clothing), suicide threats, concerns about child abuse, and manifestations in school behavior of family problems (e.g., marital conflict, separation/divorce, alcoholism, chronic illness, emotional disorders, family violence). In other words, the full range of problems faced by families and schools can be addressed in family-school meetings.

In the meeting, the child, family members, and school staff sit in a circle and share their concerns. The leader of the meeting blocks attempts to blame and helps the group develop a concrete plan of action. Sitting in a circle is an important *ecological* concern. The presence of a table, for example, tends to inhibit the child who often gets dwarfed by the table and the adults. The goal of the family-school meeting is not to solve the entire problem, which may not be possible in a 50-minute session. What is possible is to create a relationship among the participants that will enable them to continue to work on the problem and to develop and implement other solutions in both home and school contexts.

The meeting follows a structured set of steps that establish and maintain a collaborative problem-solving process. The sequence ensures that all participants have an opportunity to voice their concerns and to find ways they can work together to accomplish one or two agreed upon goals to improve the situation for the child. The meeting flow steps are: (a) introduction and overview, (b) finding facts, (c) blocking blame, (d) checking for consensus, (e) determining a decision, and (f) arriving at action (Hawkinshire, 1971).

Introduction. The *introduction* to the meeting occurs in two places. One is when the meeting is set up and participants are asked to attend. The other is at the beginning of the actual meeting. In both types of introductions, the facilitator sets a nonblaming, problem-solving tone for the meeting. This is done by communicating the following: (a) the purpose of the meeting is to discover what help the student, family members, and/or school personnel need to provide as good a school experience for the student as possible; (b) everyone will have the opportunity to share their concerns about how things are going; and (c) the outcome of the meeting will be a concrete plan of action to deal with one or two problems that all agree must be resolved. This introduction signals to all that their concerns are important and will be heard. It may be calming for the student as well as the parents to hear that the meeting is not a punishment for bad behavior but that it is meant to be helpful. It establishes the appropriate boundary between home and school by emphasizing that the primary focus is on school issues, not on family life. Parents may be relieved that school staff will not pry into their private affairs and may then be more forthcoming with relevant information and more willing to problem solve. Finally, the introduction signals to all that the meeting has a clear purpose, that of finding a set of actions that will begin to solve the problem. Thus, the problem will not just be "talked about," but something will be put in place to move forward and improve the situation.

Finding facts. In the second step, *finding facts,* the "facts" are the information, thoughts, and feelings reported by the participants as well as the behaviors they display in the meeting. It is important that each person has an opportunity to describe his or her concerns or version of a problem and the effect it may be having. Because the meeting is a time-limited activity, it is important to signal the participants to report one or two major concerns rather than a long list of worries or complaints. In this finding-facts phase, the facilitator will probe for the factors in the family-school relationship that maintain the problem. These factors may be part of the *historical context* of the problem, (e.g., the child began to behave differently in school when his brother left home). Or these factors may be a part of the *social* or *activity context* in which the child is located. For example, the behavior of concern may be displayed only with some peers and not with others or only in tasks done individually but not in group tasks. The facilitator should also find out when the problem does *not* occur in order to build on the student's positive school experiences. The leader may also probe to discover the meaning that participants give to behaviors they describe. For example, adults often label children as "lazy" or "not trying hard." These inferences or hypotheses about the intentions or purposes of others are clarified by hearing directly from these other persons. The behaviors that led to these labels may then be reframed, for example, as the child fears making mistakes. This way of looking at the problem gives the child more of an opportunity to try out new behaviors. Finally, the attempted solutions to the problem should be elicited so as not to repeat ineffective solutions.

Blocking blame. Throughout the meeting, it may be necessary for the facilitator or other participants to *block* the implicit or explicit *blame* of self or others. Solutions based on blame are doomed to failure and there are a number of techniques that can be used to deal with blame. The meeting leader may *reframe* a parent's anger as advocacy and deep concern for their child's education. The facilitator may *validate* a teacher by pointing out the natural tension between parents who have one child in the class and the teacher who is concerned for the welfare of 30 children. He or she may then *refocus* the discussion to what could be done for the child in the context of the large classroom. The leader could directly *block blame* by restating that the purpose of the meeting is to find solutions, not to point the finger of blame at anyone in particular. These are four strategies for dealing with blame. Others include: (a) agreeing, (b) probing, and (c) illustrating.

Checking for consensus. Throughout the finding-facts phase, the facilitator looks for areas of agreement around which parents, students, and school staff could work together. The facilitator *checks for consensus* by highlighting agreements that are explicit or implicit in what participants report. For example, the teacher may report that the student does not listen to instructions and therefore does not get the homework assignment written down. The parents may express concern that they do not know whether their child has homework or not and that they cannot follow up to make sure the child has done the assignment. The facilitator, at that point, might highlight the fact that both teacher and parents are concerned about the child's getting his homework done.

Decision and action. Although in any one meeting there may be a variety of concerns that participants agree on, it is necessary to decide which one to focus on first. This is what is meant by *determin-*

ing a decision. Out of all the things discussed, for which one will it be most helpful to develop a plan? After that decision is made, the participants *arrive at action* by specifying who will do what, when, where, and how. For example, the plan for the above problem involving homework might include the teacher checking that the child writes the assignment in a notebook with the teacher initialing it. The teacher might also pair up the students who could check each other. The initials at the bottom of the assignment would signal to the parents that the full homework assignment has been written down. They could put their initials at the end of the homework to signal the teacher that they are following up and monitoring that the assignments have been completed.

Follow-up meeting. A follow-up meeting may also be scheduled at this first meeting to increase the obligation to follow through with what everyone has agreed to do. When the follow-up meeting is held and some participants report that they did not do what the plan required, the facilitator may need to block blame at that point as well. This would be done by concluding that the plan made in the previous meeting was a *bad plan.* It did not account for the constraints that prevented participants from doing their tasks and therefore a different plan is needed to work on the problem. The group then explores what did and did not happen and develops a new, more workable plan.

These meetings are similar in structure to the types of meetings proposed by Aponte (1976) and Dowling and Pound (1985), where the primary purpose is to achieve a productive outcome for a specific child. That is certainly one of the purposes of the family-school meeting described above. However, a second purpose is that the problem-solving process and outcomes for dealing with the specific problem of a particular child contribute to a collaborative climate among school staff, parents, and students that carries over into other areas of the school. These meetings are designed to be implemented in the context of other changes so as to maximize the second-order change of how school personnel think about their goals and strategies to achieve those goals. School staff begin to see that the same collaborative strategies and techniques can be used to work with larger groups of parents in orientations, in group problem-solving meetings about children's progress in school, or in how children, parents, and bus drivers can work together to make the trips to and from school safe and pleasant. Furthermore, staff may find that these same behaviors can be generalized to how they work together in staff meetings or in establishing partnerships between teachers and paraprofessional staff.

Although family-school problem-solving meetings can be very helpful for individual children and their families and for staff to see in concrete terms how to work more collaboratively, their payoff is relatively small given the amount of time and effort invested. We have found that activities which include more staff, students, and family members have a greater benefit for the entire school. We have worked with schools to develop and implement a variety of activities which are described below. Examples of these activities include: (a) the family-teacher conference, (b) orientations of families to the school or to specific programs, (c) written communications from the school to families, (d) multicultural celebrations, and (e) group problem-solving meetings.

Family-Teacher Conferences

The family-teacher conference is a restructured version of the perennial parent-teacher conference in that teacher, parents, *and student* meet together. Because virtually all schools have a version of this activity and it is the primary vehicle for face-to-face communication between parents and teachers, it is a good one to start with in addressing family-school relationships. The goal of family-teacher conferences is to share information about the child's school progress (academic and behavior) and plan for how to help the child move forward. These conferences replace the parent-teacher conferences,

which are often the primary form of direct communication from school to home about how the child is doing in school. In some school districts (e.g., New York City), they are mandated to occur twice a year.

In the meeting, each of the participants expresses his or her perception of what is going well and not so well. On the basis of consensus, a plan is developed which helps the child continue doing what is going well and improve what is not going well.

Preparation prior to conferences for teachers, students, and parents is important to ensure that a collaborative process is used. *Teachers* might use role-plays or problem clinics to practice the skills needed to run a collaborative meeting or to anticipate and develop solutions to problems they might have. Before teachers do this, it is often helpful to do a role-play of a conference without the child present and then do a role-play of the same situation with the child present. Then they can see for themselves the difference between the two types of meetings.

Students can have class discussions, do role-plays, or do writing exercises to learn about how to collaborate in the meetings around their education. The first step is to help children see the connection between their own actions and the reports of their progress in school. They might, for example, fill out a mock report card and compare their own grades to those given to them by the teacher. This helps them learn to evaluate themselves and take responsibility for thinking about how they are doing. Alternatively, they might list two or three things they do well and two or three things with which they are having difficulty. They could then start the conference by talking about what goes well and what does not go well for them in school. Students can also do role-plays in the classroom to gain more clarity about their role in these conferences and to increase their ability to understand the positions of teachers and parents.

Parents can prepare for conferences by discussing them in meetings and doing the same role-play (with the child out and then with the child in) as the teachers do. They could also fill out a brief form a week or so before the conference to let the teacher know some of the concerns or questions they have. The teacher could be prepared to address these concerns at the conference.

Restructuring the conferences in these ways has an effect on the climate and degree of connection between the school and family. The milieu has changed by including the child because in any activity, it is important for all the relevant constituents to be present. If the conference is about the child, the child should be there to represent his or her concerns and to be involved in developing a plan for his or her education.

The changes affect the *culture* by reinforcing the belief that children ought to be involved in the discussions and planning around their own education. This helps to build the *norm* that a collaborative approach to education is most effective.

The conferences constitute a new *social system* in which adults are likely to behave better (are less defensive, less argumentative, more cooperative) because they are in the presence of children. Teachers, parents, and students communicate directly with one another. This increases the available information from which they each derive *meaning* about what will be helpful for the child. This also reduces the potential for miscommunications when parents go home and talk to their child about the conference. Participants are likely to have a greater level of investment in a plan that is developed out of a consensus of their concerns and that they had a hand in creating. This will also increase the *self-relatedness* for the participants, as each will be clearer about what their part in the plan is and can work to support its success.

It is important to attend to *ecological* factors and, consequently, the chairs are arranged in a circle so that physical barriers do not impede communication or suggest differential status. This also sig-

nals to the participants that the meeting is collaborative.

Orientations to the School or to Specific Programs

Many schools hold meetings at the beginning of the school year to introduce parents and students to the school and its staff. There are often two meetings—one for the parents and one for the children. These sessions typically consist of one-way communication from the school to parents or children about the curriculum, rules and routines, and typical operations of the school. Although it is necessary to impart information of this type, the way in which it is done sets up a hierarchical rather than a collaborative relationship between families and schools. A different format for an orientation meeting is needed for the school to send the message that they need the parents as partners in educating their children.

Such an orientation would include the teacher, parents, and students. The goal of the orientation is for the teacher parents, and students to get to know one another and to send a message that "We need to work as partners to achieve quality education." A variety of activities could be done as long as participants have enough time for meaningful discussion to take place. The teacher could use stimulus questions, which enable participants to engage in reciprocal dialogues about school. For example, parents and students might discuss their goals for the school year and then report them to the rest of the group. This could be followed by a group discussion. Parents and students might also discuss the students' strengths and ways they can continue to make progress. This will help to reinforce the child's competence.

Because the orientation occurs at the beginning of the school year the effects on *culture* can be powerful. The school staff have an opportunity to establish the *norm* of collaboration around educational goals early in their relationship with parents and students. It is especially important to do this when the children are first entering school (i.e., in kindergarten), and then reinforce that norm throughout the child's entire school career. The teacher also has an opportunity to model *sequences of problem solving* (obtaining information, checking for the level of consensus, blocking implicit or explicit blame). The *belief* in the importance of all relevant members of the system participating in the activity is also demonstrated by inviting children to come with their parents.

Orientations of this type affect the *social system* by reducing the *isolation* of parents. They get to know the parents of other children and can see the children with whom their child will be in school. Parents have been known to set up their own network to organize volunteer projects for the school and to pass on communications from the school. In that way, they can serve as important supports to the teachers who will not have to take on these extra tasks.

A meeting of this type allows the teacher to get to know the different parents and children in the class and vice versa, thus addressing the *milieu* of the classroom. In this way, they can get past the superficial differences of age, race, socioeconomic status, culture, language, or gender, to hear about the beliefs, expectations, and ideas that parents, students, and teachers have about education.

As in other activities, attention to *ecology* is important. Teachers may engage the students in the preparation of invitations for the orientation meeting. Letters sent to parents communicate the expectation of a family-school partnership and welcome questions from parents. Orientation activities may include the writing of family-school contracts spelling out their mutual obligations. All of these written documents are physical reminders of the school staff's desire for a collaborative family-school relationship. The orientation could also include a tour of the school.

Orientations for special groups in the school. Sometimes there are special programs in the school (e.g., special education, English as a Second Language [ESL], or a remedial reading program)

that may require a separate orientation. There may also be groups that are isolated from the rest of the school and may require an orientation. We found this to be the case with the parents of children in an English-as-a-Second-Language program. In this particular school, 150 children spoke 26 different languages. At the school orientation held at the beginning of the year, parents of only four of these children attended. In December a special orientation for these families was held which was attended by 125 parents.

The goal of orientations for special groups is the same as for general orientations, which is to provide an opportunity for parents, students, and school staff to get to know one another and for the school to send a message that "We need to work as partners to achieve quality education." However, special modifications are needed. First, the *milieu* factor of different languages was addressed by having a parent who spoke both English and one of the five main language groups (Spanish, Urdu, Chinese, Haitian Creole, and Russian) serve as interpreter and main recruiter for the parents. These volunteers created communication networks among parents speaking the same language and thereby encouraged each other to come to the orientation at the school. This greatly decreased the *isolation* of parents who had been segregated from the rest of the school community by virtue of language and culture differences. The teachers decided not to include children in the milieu of the orientation. However, afterwards they concluded that having the children there would have improved the meeting. Second, ecological concerns were met by scheduling the orientation in the morning as a breakfast so that parents who dropped their children off at school could stay for an extra hour and a half and not miss too much work or other activities. After a general welcome in the cafeteria by the principal along with breakfast foods and coffee, the parents broke into five smaller language groups.

The purpose of the discussion in these groups was to get to know each other, thus creating a different *social system*. In the planning of this activity, the teachers were very concerned that parents did not understand what they were trying to do for the students. This resulted in their planning presentations about the ESL program in order to give parents this important information. However, each time they went back to the goal of their orientation—to get to know one another—they decided that giving this information could wait until they knew one another better. It was clear that if they had made these presentations, it would have changed the climate of the meetings considerably and would have impeded the progress toward the goal of getting to know one another.

The discussion was stimulated with questions such as, "What was school like in your home country?" "How is that different from what you've encountered in this country?" The answers were enlightening to the teachers and other school staff. Some parents explained that in their country, parents were discouraged from being involved in their child's school experience—from helping with homework, from even coming into the school building. They assumed that it was the same in this country. School staff had assumed that these parents who did not come to the school simply did not care about the education of their children. Other parents expressed concern over the things in the school they had most access to observing (e.g., they saw that some children did not have the same dress for performing in concerts). They thought that the children should all be dressed the same and volunteered to sew uniforms. Some parents volunteered to teach others how to sew. From this came a host of proposed volunteer contributions from parents—to each other and to the classroom. By the end of the meeting, the blackboard was full of names and ways in which parents were willing to contribute to the school.

Structuring the activity as they did also enabled the school staff to address *culture*. They were able to elicit the parents' previous experiences in their countries of origin and the expectations and beliefs about education that shaped the way they interacted with the school. In this way, they changed their view of parents as not interested to that of caring and concerned. Their discussions of education in this country provided important *meaning* for understanding their children's educational experiences here.

Written Communications

A fourth type of climate-building intervention involves the written communications sent from the school to the parents. The way in which these memos or letters are written sends a powerful message to the parents about the relationship that the school wants to have with them. An underlying goal of written communications is to provide consistent messages to families that the school will work with them in a collaborative way to promote the educational success of the student.

To achieve consistent, positive messages, school staff write and revise existing letters, so that they send the following messages: (a) We want to develop a working partnership with parents; (b) parents' input is critical to the educational achievement of their child; and (c) if there is a problem, we will work together to find a solution.

These messages are different from the ones conveyed by letters which have phrases such as: "We regret to inform you that your son/daughter may not be graduating to the next grade"; "You are required to meet with us to discuss your son/daughter's progress"; "Please come to a meeting on ____ where the team will present their findings to you and make recommendations for your child." A different message about the same types of situations might be: "We share your concern for your child's education. We are holding a group meeting for parents, children, and teachers to discuss ideas and suggestions about how to help children improve their school performance. Teachers will also be available for individual family conferences following the meeting."

One *ecological* constraint is around making sure the letters or flyers that go home with students actually get to the parents. To help solve this problem, schools can send home written communications on the same day of every week. If parents know to expect communications on this day, they can get into a routine to check with their children to see if they have any messages from school.

Letters from school are often authoritarian in tone, which contradicts the collaborative *social system* that schools wish to develop. Rather than emphasizing the *power* of the school, the message needs to convey the notion that all the resources of the school, parents, and students (i.e., shared power) are needed to help students do as well as they can in school.

With regard to *milieu*, if there are groups of parents in the school who do not speak English, efforts to send letters in their languages would be needed. Letters and newsletters from the school play an important part in establishing a shared *culture*. Informative articles about how children learn and how this relates to the teaching methods used in the classroom can be used to develop common values and expectations about education.

Multicultural Celebration

Each school decides on the activities that meet the particular needs of the family-school community. Therefore, it is critical to talk with the school staff, parents, and students to identify their concerns. Staff and parents in an elementary school to which many new immigrants had sent their children were concerned about the diversity of the population and the potential for divisiveness in this type of milieu. They reasoned that if they knew one another better, they could work together better. As a result, they planned a Multicultural Night.

The goal of the multicultural night was to celebrate the school's ethnic and cultural diversity, to learn more about the members of the family-school community, and to affirm common goals of educational quality. This addressed issues of both *culture* and *milieu*. Individuals

who are from different cultures or ethnic heritages often assume that they are different in other ways (e.g., that they have a different set of values or beliefs). Although this may be true to some extent, the assumed differences are often greater than the real differences. Furthermore, the differences often carry with them the idea that one culture is better than another. This is often the case when school staff tend to be of one culture and a relatively high socioeconomic class and parents and students tend to be of different cultures and lower socioeconomic class. Family-school activities, such as the multicultural night, provide opportunities for all members of the family-school community to demonstrate their shared commitment to the children's education and their willingness to work together.

For this climate-building activity teachers incorporated preparations for the event into their class curriculum. Some emphasized social skills (e.g., that it is polite to taste a little of everything when people cook for you). Others did units on family history and decorated their rooms with family tree diagrams. Others did geography lessons about the countries from which their students' families came and decorated their rooms with flags from these different countries.

Ecology was addressed in several ways. The event was scheduled in the evening so that parents who worked during the day could attend. When parents and students entered the building, student ushers greeted them and welcoming signs directed them to the proper place. In each classroom, teachers and parents had organized a pot-luck dinner to which parents brought foods that reflected their ethnic heritage. Some students and their families dressed in native costumes. The decorations in the rooms and the foods contributed by the families served as physical reminders of the respect for and celebration of the cultural diversity in the school. The teacher, parents, and children ate their dinners in the rooms and engaged in discussions, games, or other activities. The evening ended with an assembly in the auditorium. Song sheets had been sent home with the children several days earlier so that parents could learn the words to the songs. Then the entire group of parents, teachers, and students joined together singing. A Korean family, in traditional Korean dress, led the group in singing one verse of "It's a Small World" in the Korean language.

The original idea for the multicultural night came from the Parents' Association. The parents' contributions triggered a significant shift in the family-school *social system.* In the implementation of this event, teachers and parents worked closely together to make and carry out many decisions. In this way, the parents and teachers functioned as equal partners, collaborating to carry out an activity that was proposed by the parents.

Group Problem-Solving Meetings

In another school, staff were looking for ways to help children who might not be promoted to the next grade. The school was mandated by state law to send out a letter in January to the parents of children who had not scored well on the achievement tests or who were not doing well in class, informing them of the possibility of their child being held over. This letter also requested that parents come to a school meeting to see what could be done. In this school, similar letters were also sent out to children who were in danger of being taken out of the "gifted" program. Rather than having many individual meetings, we planned a community meeting for each grade to develop plans to help these children. Children in both the regular and "gifted" programs attended the same meeting.

The goal of these meetings was to problem solve in groups so strategies that will help children who were having difficulties in school could be implemented. These included children who might be held back at the end of the year as well as children who might be taken out of the "gifted" program. This was an important *milieu* factor. Although some

might assume that these two groups of children are very different, we wanted to emphasize the similarities among children who have trouble in school. A common theme for children in both of these groups was the fear of failure. For some children this might look like laziness and a refusal to try because failure was so likely. For others, this might look like disorganization and forgetfulness. We helped participants to refrain from labeling the behavior and to understand its origins in order to develop strategies for children to overcome their fears.

Letters sent in the past were rewritten to emphasize the importance of parents working in partnership with the school to help their children. Because this was a new activity, parents were given the option of attending this group meeting or having a private meeting with the teacher. Over half the parents elected to attend the group meeting.

The participants in the meeting were: the children, parents, teachers, principal and assistant principal, guidance counselor, and social worker. Attention was paid to *ecology* in several ways. The discussions were held in the library where participants sat in a large circle, reflecting the collaborative nature of the meeting. In addition, refreshments were available as participants entered the library where the meetings were held.

Each meeting began with participants reporting on the children's strengths, which were listed on the board. This was an important influence on the *social system* as it signalled both parents and children that they were not there to be blamed for having difficulties in school. Then the discussion moved to the difficulties the children experienced, which were also listed on the board. Then school staff, parents, and children proposed strategies that would help the children remediate the difficulties. The discussions included issues of how much parents should help students with homework and the importance of children developing the courage to make mistakes. They also helped to shape the *culture* by clarifying the *beliefs* about how children learn. For example, teachers emphasized the importance of letting children make mistakes on homework, rather than correcting it for them, so that the teachers could see where the children needed help. Furthermore, the whole format of the meeting reduced the *isolation* experienced by parents, students, and teachers, who sometimes think they are the only ones having problems.

At the end of the meeting, parents were given a packet of written materials, which contained strategies to use at home to help children develop behaviors like responsibility-taking and perseverance. After the group meetings, the teacher met with each child and his or her parents individually to make a concrete plan for what they could do to help the student. In a debriefing with the school staff, they remarked that these types of meetings should be held for *all* parents and students in the classroom, not just for those who are having difficulties.

These brief descriptions are meant to provide only a sampling of activities that could be used to build a collaborative family-school climate. The range of activities is limited only by the creativity of the school staff and families to think of and implement them. The identification of activities emerges out of a discussion with staff and families of their concerns about the education of their children. Once the educational concerns are clear, activities that use the combined energy and resources of families, students, and school staff can be designed and implemented. Below, the intervention strategies and techniques that Project staff use are described.

INTERVENTION STRATEGIES AND TECHNIQUES

Interventions are tailored to the needs of the group that is requesting help in developing more collaborative family-school relationships. In the past, we have contracted with individual schools and trained the entire staff. The benefit is that the staff has a high level of familiarity with the concepts and techniques. The side effect is that the level of ownership in the school may be low.

A different model, aimed at increasing staff ownership of the change process, is to train a small team of educators and parents in each school who take responsibility for disseminating the approach throughout the rest of the school. In this way, the team, rather than the Project consultant, becomes the central catalyst for school change. The consultant supports the team's efforts to apply the concepts, strategies, and techniques they learn as they involve the rest of the staff in improving family-school relationships.

The team approach is especially effective when several schools are starting family-school programs as a part of a district-wide initiative for improving family-school relationships. Teams from these several schools attend the same central training workshops and have the additional benefit of hearing and learning from each other. Teams consist of representatives of the major constituencies of the school: principal, family-school coordinator, teachers, and parents. Teams could also include other staff members (e.g., assistant principal, and mental health professionals not serving as the family-school coordinator, such as social worker, psychologist, guidance counselor). Consultations and demonstrations on-site at each school by the Project staff are combined with the group training so as to engage the entire staff. Regardless of which overall strategy for training school staff is used, it takes at least 2 to 3 years for significant changes to be effected in the school climate. In addition to these long-term change efforts, we have provided 1- or 2-day workshops for groups of professionals (e.g., school psychologists, social workers, guidance counselors, principals, or entire school staffs).

Interventions basically consist of three types of activities: (a) training sessions, (b) consultation sessions, and (c) modeling by providing direct service in the form of family-school problem-solving meetings. We ensure that these activities themselves are implemented in a collaborative way. For example, in training sessions the participants apply concepts and techniques in their designs for actual activities which will be imple-

mented in the school. The consultation
sessions provide the opportunity for staff
members who have not been formally
trained to be active participants in the
planning and implementation of climate-
building activities. In family-school problem-solving meetings, team members and
other staff learn to become more effective
participants and some core staff gradually
take over leadership of these meetings.
Each of the activities implemented in the
Family-School Collaboration Program are
described.

Training Sessions

Training workshops provide participants with a conceptual framework and
specific sets of techniques for working
collaboratively with families. The content
of the workshops is focused on the
following seven areas:

1. Concepts that help participants to
view the family and school as part of one
system in which each affects the other
and how this mutual influence could be
used to support the educational goals of
students.

2. Plans for school activities aimed at
developing a general climate of collaboration and mutual support between the
school and families of school children.

3. Strategies for restructuring relationships between families and schools
and among members of each system in
order to change alienated or adversarial
interactions to collaborative interactions.

4. Identification of relevant systems
and individuals as targets for interventions.

5. Steps for establishing a collaborative process: overview and purpose statement, finding facts, blocking blame,
checking for consensus, determining a
decision, arriving at action.

6. Techniques for interviewing.

7. Procedures for follow-up from
family-school meetings.

Teaching techniques used in training
include:

1. Brief lectures, using diagrams to
illustrate the theoretical foundations of
the approach.

2. Detailed applications of the theoretical model to actual examples of families and schools in specific activities.

3. Learning exercises to demonstrate
experientially the dilemmas of change
viewed from a systems perspective. For
example:

—Role plays of teacher-parent meetings and teacher-family meetings
(with the child present) are juxta-
posed to compare their relative
effectiveness for defining and solving problems;

—Simulations of family-school meetings are used to explore the reciprocal attitudes of family members
and school personnel regarding
specific educational problems.
Stop-action techniques are employed to build skill in participating and conducting family-school
meetings.

—Blocking blame exercise in which
typical blaming statements are examined and ways in which participants could block the blame in
these statements and refocus onto
problem solving are developed.
This is done with the entire group
and then participants break into
dyads to practice the technique.
Participants are also encouraged to
identify their "Achilles' heel" of
blame (i.e., the area in which they
are most vulnerable to attack) and
develop productive ways to handle
blame that would be directed at
them in this area.

—Videotapes of actual family-school
activities are used as learning aids
to illustrate the techniques and
strategies and their effects on family-school relationships. These illustrations help to build the participants' skills in systemic thinking,
meeting flow strategies, and collaborative problem solving.

Consultations

The purpose of consultations is to help school staff clarify their own goals and develop plans for specific activities that will enable them to achieve these goals. There are six steps to this process: (a) Define concerns, (b) set priorities, (c) determine target, (d) identify constituencies within the target, (e) select goal, and (f) plan activity. Each of these steps is discussed.

Define concerns. Although we focus on family-school collaboration, the goal of our work in schools is not these relationships, per se. The goal is quality education for children. An important *means* to achieving quality education for all children is collaboration between family and school. Thus, if schools identify parental involvement as a goal for the year, it is likely that this must compete with other programs that are also important to the school. Rather than setting up this type of situation, we ask school professionals to identify their educational goals and help them develop ways that family and school can work together as partners to realize these goals. Thus, the family-school partnership becomes a piece of *every* program that is implemented in the school, rather than competing for attention with these programs. Educators may identify concerns such as low reading scores, high holdover rate, racial tensions, or drugs as priorities on which they need to focus. The critical issue is to determine how parents and educators can work together to address these concerns.

Set priorities. Professionals in each school must determine the priorities of their concerns and assess their own resources for achieving change in each area.

Determine target. After priorities are set, the target for intervention is determined. It may be possible for the entire school to be the target. On the other hand, it may make sense to limit it to a smaller group (e.g., the incoming kindergarten class), with the idea that over several years the intervention will spread to other grades. If the concern is about a particular population (e.g., students in special education or in English-as-a-Second-Language programs), then these groups would become the targets for the intervention.

Identify constituencies within the target. In order for the intervention to be successful, all relevant members of the system must be included. This *always* means including the child, parents, and teacher(s). Others in the school who are involved with the target individuals should also be included in the planning, implementation, and follow-up in some way. These might include the assistant principal, social worker, guidance counselor, psychologist, and special education personnel. Others in the system that could be important resources, but who are often overlooked, should also be considered. These might be siblings or other members of the family (e.g., grandparents, aunts, uncles), babysitters, office staff, lunchroom staff, custodial staff, school guards, and individuals from the neighborhood or community.

Select goal. On the basis of the identified concern and the characteristics of the target individuals, the specific goals of the intervention activity are selected. The goal may be to get to know one another, as would be the case in the initial phases of the change process. A different goal might be to implement an activity that would address a specific problem such as the coordination of services between regular education and special education.

Plan activity. Preliminary work provides the foundation of consensus for the purpose of the actual home-school activity. Three phases of the activity need to be addressed in planning. The first is the *pre-activity* events, such as invitations and publicity. If, for example, parents were invited to the school for a special activity in the way that they are always invited, it is likely that the activity will not have the desired impact. Therefore, in addition to sending home flyers about the activity with children, a group of parents may serve as networkers who call a certain number of parents and ask them to call one or two friends. In this way, the invitation comes not only from the school but also from parents, which is likely to provide a stronger message to other parents.

Second, the actual *activity* is planned, including a step-by-step flow of events with time estimates specified and a clear division of labor among participants. This might look like the following:

5:00–6:00	Teachers set up classrooms Parent and student volunteers pick up food and drinks from the Parent Activity Room and deliver to classrooms
5:45	Children greeters assemble in the front hallway for meeting
6:00	Doors open Children greeters are in front hall and on every floor Assistant principal is at front door Teachers and parent volunteers stay in rooms to greet guests
6:00–7:20	Teachers, children, parents eat dinner in rooms and do their group activities
7:20–7:30	Teachers, children, and parents clean up in rooms Program participants go to the auditorium
7:30–7:35	First floor goes to the auditorium
7:35–7:40	Second floor goes to the auditorium
7:40–8:15	Assembly in the auditorium
8:15–8:45	Clean-up crews go back to the rooms and finish clean-up
8:45–	Food donation committee takes leftover food to the local shelter for homeless families

Follow-up. Finally, plans are made for *follow-up.* Follow-up should include at least three components: (a) evaluating the event, (b) disseminating information about the event to others, and (c) following up on what was started in the event. Evaluation could be done informally by having dis-

cussions in the classrooms with children, in the Parents Association meetings, and in the staff meeting to see what went well, what did not go so well, and what they would like to do in the future. The evaluation could also be done more formally by calling parents to interview them, by interviewing children, or by distributing a very short questionnaire at the end of the activity for participants to complete before leaving. Information dissemination could be done verbally in the classroom, Parents Association meetings, or staff meetings, or in written form. An article in the school newspaper, written by a student, teacher, and parent, might summarize the activity and present thoughts on how the event went. Finally, whatever occurred at the activity needs to be followed up so that momentum toward reaching the goal of collaborative family-school relationships to address educational objectives continues.

Modeling Collaboration Through Direct Service

Experience is often the best teacher. Therefore, Ackerman staff lead family-school problem-solving meetings or conduct other types of collaborative activities to enable school staff to experience a different type of relationship with families without the burden of full responsibility for the activity. In this way, school staff, parents, and children are able to observe different approaches for handling diverse school problems. This is often an important catalyst for the shift in perceptions of school staff and families. An important shift needed in many schools is to see, as one principal put it, that "us and them are we." Once this initial change takes place, school staff and parents are often quite able to develop their own ideas, strategies, and techniques for using the family-school partnership to address school concerns and achieve school goals.

THE SCHOOL PSYCHOLOGIST AS FAMILY-SCHOOL COORDINATOR

Staff members of the Family-School Collaboration Project at the Ackerman

Institute occupy the outside position of systems consultant with schools and school districts. Although the position of outside consultant often appears to insiders to have special advantages, we believe that such advantages are short-lived if they exist at all. Professionals such as school psychologists, who take on the position of the family-school coordinator, operate within the system. As a result, they have the benefit of knowing the staff and parent group with whom they work. They also have a fuller understanding of the unique needs of the family-school system. Therefore, they can help to identify a core group of interested staff members and coordinate the implementation of small changes that will gradually extend to the rest of the school. Nevertheless, whether initiating a change process as an outside or inside consultant, the support and commitment of the principal and key staff are still essential.

For school psychologists to take over the role of family-school coordinator, their current roles must change. Typically, psychologists work with students and families who have been referred to them by others and whose problems have been defined by others. This usually means that they are more peripheral to what goes on throughout the school and would not be in a position to institute significant change efforts. As family-school coordinators, psychologists would take on the roles of consultant and facilitator. Rather than working with students or parents alone, they would work conjointly with students, parents, teachers, and other school staff. They would consult with teachers to identify cases in which family-school meetings would be helpful in order to intervene before problems became too protracted. They would also meet with students, parents, and staff to identify needs, to develop and implement plans for climate-building activities, and do follow-up from these activities. The family-school coordinator might, for example, do informal interviews in the lunchroom to determine how teachers thought the family-teacher conferences went. The family-school coordinator might develop a questionnaire for parents to fill out after family-school conferences to get feedback about aspects of the school.

These activities put the family-school coordinator in a more central position within the school. In that way, psychologists can do more preventive mental health work that is targeted to a larger number of children rather than spending so much time in one-to-one counseling with individual children. If psychologists do individual counseling, it would always be after a family-school meeting in which the psychologist would have the opportunity to understand the larger context in which the child is located. Counseling under these circumstances is more likely to be effective than if the psychologist works in a vacuum.

SUMMARY AND CONCLUSIONS

The renewal of American education requires a genuine partnership between schools and families, one in which families become an integral part of the educational process. Psychologists can play an essential role in this effort by using their skills to help schools overcome a history of relations often structured by mutual blaming. They can facilitate the establishment of a collaborative family-school climate by helping the professional staff recognize the ways in which families can be resources for the schools. The approach described here can serve as a model for school psychologists to define a new role for themselves as family-school coordinators. They can apply their psychological training and knowledge of child development to promote cooperation between families and schools. This position offers them a means for implementing many of the same functions they have now but from a family systems perspective.

Although research has shown that parental involvement is directly related to success in school, school staff often express reluctance to work more with parents and parents do not often involve themselves in the school's activities. We have found at least three reasons for this reluctance: (a) there are few mechanisms for family-school collaboration built into the school routine and, thus, what is done is perceived as taking away from teaching; (b) diversity of culture, language, race, socioeconomic status, across families and between families and school staff create real or imagined differences that lead to alienation; and (c) the conception of roles that parents might play is limited.

This chapter describes the ways in which the Family-School Collaboration Project of the Ackerman Institute for Family Therapy has worked with New York City schools and school districts to build family-school partnerships. The Project aims to help schools use the resources of family-school collaboration to achieve their educational goals. We define family-school collaboration as a cooperative process of planning and problem solving involving school staff, parents, children, and significant others used to maximize resources for students' academic achievement and social-emotional development. The Project has developed a program of assessment, consultation, and training to help schools to work systematically at the task of connecting family and school for the benefit of children's education. This approach includes strategies for organizational change and specific activities which serve both preventive and direct intervention mental health functions.

On the basis of an assessment conducted collaboratively with school staff and parents, the following are identified: (a) the state of family-school relationships, (b) goals for improving these relationships, and (c) identification of specific activities schools could use to build collaborative family-school relationships. The purpose of these activities is to improve the climate of the school and, thus, are called climate-building activities.

In consultation sessions and planning meetings, Ackerman Project staff work with school staff and parents to develop detailed plans for these activities. In the planning, they identify the types of pre-activity work that must be done (invitations, publicity), specify the division of labor for the activity, and include

follow-up (evaluation, information dissemination). Two types of activities that are implemented in almost every school include the family-school problem-solving meeting and family-teacher conferences (a restructured version of the parent-teacher conference). Other activities that are implemented depend on the unique needs of particular schools and creativity of school personnel for devising ways families and schools can work together. Activities that the Project has jointly developed and implemented with schools include: orientations of families to the school; orientations of particular groups of families (e.g., English-as-a-Second-Language programs, special education, students who had difficulties the previous year); planning and problem-solving meetings about possible holdovers; discussion forums about adult-student relationships focused around issues of trust, autonomy, drugs, and other issues of interest to students, parents, and school staff; parent work groups planning school-yard activities to ensure a safe playground; and problem-solving meetings with groups of parents, children, school staff, and bus drivers to resolve bus travel issues.

When needed, training workshops are conducted for the entire staff or for a smaller committee of committed school staff and parents. These workshops include: (a) concepts to think about school climate, social connectedness, and systems; (b) strategies for designing and implementing family-school activities; (c) techniques for participating in and conducting collaborative problem-solving meetings; (d) tactics for blocking blame and refocusing self and others to engage in more productive interactions; (e) interviewing techniques; and (f) contextual and thematic analysis. In the workshops we combine didactic presentations with experiential exercises to help participants understand and practice collaborative ideas and skills.

The model proposed in this chapter emphasizes the shared vested interest that schools and families have in the academic success and psychosocial development of children. Children are included in virtually all family-school inter-actions in ways that enhance their own self-image and problem-solving skills. The work assumes that school personnel, parents, and significant others are doing the best they can in their work with children. When problems develop, chil-dren, parents, and school personnel can collaborate to find solutions without being sidetracked by concerns about implicit or explicit blame ascribed by others.

Creating a collaborative climate be-tween families and schools requires that school staff recognize students' families as a major resource for improving educa-tional outcomes. The benefits of this resource will become available when family-school relations is addressed as a major factor in the educational achieve-ment of children.

REFERENCES

Anderson, C. (1982). The search for school climate: A review of the research. *Review of Educational Research, 52*(3), 368–420.

Aponte, H. J. (1976). The family-school interview: An eco-structural approach. *Family Process, 15*(3), 303–311.

Dowling, J., & Pound, A. (1985). Joint interventions with teachers, children and parents in the school setting. In J. Dowling & A. E. Osborne (Eds.), *The family and the school: A joint systems approach to problems with children* (pp. 91–111). London, England: Routledge & Kegan Paul.

Hawkinshire, F. B. W. (1971). *Clinical interviewing techniques.* Unpublished lecture. New York: New York University, Department of Human Relations and Social Policy.

Henderson, A. (1989). *The evidence continues to grow: Parent involvement improves school achievement.* Columbia, MD: National Committee for Citizens in Education.

Henderson, A. T., Marburger, C. L., & Ooms, T. (1986). *Beyond the bake sale: An educator's guide to working with parents.* Columbia, MD: The National Committee for Citizens in Education.

McGuire, W. J. (1968). The nature of attitudes and attitude change. In G. Lindzey & E. Aronson (Eds.), *The handbook of social psychology* (2nd ed., Vol. 3, pp. 136–214). Reading, MA: Addison-Wesley.

Rich, D. (1988). *Megaskills: How families can help children succeed in school and beyond.* Boston, MA: Houghton Mifflin.

Seeman, M. (1968). Alienation and social learning in a reformatory. *American Journal of Sociology, 69*, 270–284.

Tagiuri, R. (1968). The concept of organizational climate. In R. Tagiuri & G. H. Litwin (Eds.), *Organizational climate: Exploration of a concept* (pp. 10–32). Cambridge, MA: Harvard University Press.

Part III:

Approaches for Enhancing Home-School Collaboration

11

SCHOOL-BASED INTERVENTIONS FOR INFANTS AND TODDLERS IN A FAMILY SETTING

Martha Farrell Erickson

In recent years educators have faced a new array of demands and issues as schools in many states have expanded the scope of their work to include service to infants and toddlers and their families. Recognizing their lack of training in this area and the inappropriateness of many of their typical assessment and intervention strategies for application with this younger population, school psychologists and other school-based professionals often are intimidated and overwhelmed by the thought of working with babies. Certainly, the lack of training and experience in working with infants and toddlers is a real concern—and one that must be addressed promptly and aggressively by training programs. But, in the meantime, there are young children and families to be served, and school psychologists and other professionals in the education system must define their role in this challenging new arena. Early intervention presents a rich opportunity for school psychologists to continue the role expansion that began over the last two decades and, most important, to unite with other educators to build strong partnerships with families from the very beginning of a child's life.

In this chapter I propose a framework for school-based interventions with infants and toddlers in a family setting. First, I discuss briefly the potential role of the school psychologist in early intervention efforts, with an emphasis on the scope that I believe "early intervention" can and should encompass within our school systems. Then, drawing from existing knowledge about the factors that promote good developmental outcomes for young children, I outline and discuss some issues that need to be addressed when working with infants and toddlers within a family context, illustrating points with specific intervention strategies when possible. Finally, I present a brief annotated bibliography of practical resources for school-based professionals working with families and their young children (Appendix A).

THE ROLE OF SCHOOL PSYCHOLOGISTS: RECOGNIZING OPPORTUNITY IN THE CHALLENGE

Some school psychologists seem to dwell on their lack of preparation for working with very young children and to overlook or underestimate what they already have to offer to this new venture. Despite the lack of professional experience with infants and toddlers, school psychologists nevertheless do bring special skills to the early intervention effort. Those skills can be grouped into four general areas, as follows:

1. School psychologists are particularly skilled in *measurement and assessment,* including behavioral observation and interview techniques that are of great value in assessing young children for whom standard testing procedures are often inappropriate. Of all professions involved in early intervention, school psychologists probably are best prepared to evaluate and select appropriate assessment procedures for young children and their families.

2. School psychologists are especially skilled in *evaluating the effectiveness* of intervention efforts with children and families, something far too seldom done in the early childhood field. Whether monitoring the effectiveness of intervention with a particular family or designing large scale program evaluations, school psychologists offer much to this process.

3. School psychologists provide an understanding of the *integration of the various domains of development* (i.e., intellectual, language, social-emotional, motor), as well as a broad view of development over the lifespan. This perspective is helpful in considering the developmental needs and issues of the parent, as well as the young child.

4. The *counseling skills* of the school psychologist are useful with the parents of infants and toddlers, whereas *consultation processes* can be helpful in collaborative problem solving with other professionals who serve the young child and family.

Although other professionals, such as early childhood educators, are experts in early development, their knowledge and experience is complemented by these four areas of special expertise that psychologists bring. If assessment and intervention for young children and their families are to be carried out effectively, the contribution of school psychologists should not be overlooked.

For school psychologists, the early intervention challenge presents an opportunity to redefine their role in ways that are consistent with directions set by the Spring Hill and Olympia Conferences in the early 1980s (Cardon, 1982; Meyers, Brown, & Coulter, 1982; Ysseldyke & Weinberg, 1981). In several specific ways, early intervention presents an opportunity to move well beyond a traditional "gatekeeping" role, an opportunity to do things "right" from the very beginning:

1. First—and especially germane to the topic of this volume—is the opportunity to *work with families*. As this book attests, working with families is important for children of any age. With infants and toddlers we have no choice—it is mandatory. Within the early education/ special education system, of course, working with families is mandated by Public Law 99–457. I recall hearing an official from the Minnesota Department of Education say, "Every time you say infants or toddlers, you also will say 'and their families.'" But, with any infant or toddler, there also is a *developmental* mandate to assess and intervene within a family context, for it is within the context of relationships with caregivers that early development unfolds (Sameroff, 1987; Sameroff & Fiese, 1990). It is in relation to significant others that we see the most important aspects of an infant's development, and it is there that the most important interventions occur.

2. Early intervention is a unique opportunity for *interdisciplinary, interagency collaboration.* Required by law, but also necessary because of the usual points of access to infants (e.g., the health care system) and the reality that infant development takes place in the context of family and community, collaboration is essential for serving infants and toddlers. School psychologists with an ecosystems perspective on behavior (see Doherty & Peskay, this volume) and with skills in consultation and group process, can and should assume an active role in linking professionals within the school system and in serving as liaisons among schools and other agencies serving young children and families.

3. Working with infants and toddlers and their families is an opportunity to *work proactively and preventively* rather

than reactively. Service may be strictly preventive, as in the case of infants who present no identifiable disability but are at risk for later difficulties because of some condition within the child (e.g., low birthweight, extreme irritability, low muscle tone), the family (e.g., adolescent parenthood, history of victimization, chemical abuse), or the broader social environment (e.g., extreme poverty, homelessness, inadequate social support). Or service may be preventive in terms of promoting optimal development, and thus preventing secondary learning and adjustment problems, for infants who do have an identified primary disability (e.g., Down syndrome, vision impairment, hearing impairment). In either case, there is a rich opportunity for proactive work with families, to support them in the early months and years of their children's lives and to build a partnership to nurture children's development from infancy through the school years.

4. Finally, the option of serving not only infants with identifiable disabilities but also those who are "at-risk" presents an opportunity for school psychologists to *expand their involvement beyond the arena of special education.* Already accessible through our school systems are infants and toddlers who are not identified for special education services, but who can benefit from family-focused services: children of teen parents in secondary schools; younger siblings of school-age children; participants in early childhood family education classes, usually offered to the general public through community education (see, for example, Early Childhood Family Education Statutes Sec. 121.882, 124.2711, & 275.125, July, 1989, regarding the Minnesota Early Childhood Family Education Model that now is being adopted in other states). Currently, school psychologists are conspicuously absent from existing school-based efforts to serve these populations. They could and should bring valuable expertise to such programs through consultation, assessment, program evaluation, or co-teaching with a parent educator or early childhood teacher.

KNOWLEDGE BASES TO INFORM PRACTICE

As schools rise to the challenge of serving infants and toddlers and their families, there is no need to start from scratch in developing assessment and intervention strategies appropriate for this population. Educators need not reinvent the wheel. Other professionals, particularly in health care, early childhood education, and infant mental health, worked with babies and parents long before public education entered the field, and those professions offer much on which to build. Likewise, infant development and family adaptation has been the focus of major research efforts in recent decades, and that body of research knowledge (as discussed in later sections of this chapter) has important implications for serving young children and their families. Whatever role school psychologists define for themselves in early intervention, it will be important to be familiar with these knowledge bases and to be aware of resources for staying abreast of new developments in this rapidly growing field.

Basically, there are three broad bodies of knowledge that can and should inform our practice. The first is *basic developmental research, which examines factors that account for different developmental outcomes.* Research in this area asks the questions: What factors are associated with competence and healthy adaptation, and which factors predict or are associated with poor adjustment and lack of competence in different domains of the child's development? Knowledge of these factors helps professionals identify targets for prevention and intervention. We need to look for ways to build and strengthen factors associated with good outcomes and ways that we can eliminate or ameliorate factors associated with poor outcomes. As reflected in later sections of this chapter, examination of recent developmental studies reveals that factors most critical to a child's healthy development often are aspects of parental thoughts, feelings, and behavior; family functioning; and the broader social system in which the child and family operate.

A second body of knowledge, and that most directly applicable to intervention, derives from *prevention and intervention research that evaluates the effectiveness of specific approaches* for working with infants and toddlers and their families. At this point, this body of research is relatively limited, with modest, mixed, and sometimes contradictory findings (e.g., Meisels & Shonkoff, 1990). Careful, controlled studies of early intervention are costly and complicated. Interpretation of findings is never simple; questions about the general effectiveness of interventions and about for whom and under what conditions such interventions will be effective must be addressed. Effects of intervention may not be apparent immediately and/or may be manifest in surprising, indirect ways. Such was the case, for example, with Head Start. Initial evaluations revealed only a minimal and short-lived impact on the school performance of Head Start participants (Cicirelli, 1969). However, in independent long-term follow-up studies that focused on attitudes and behavior, as well as academic performance, Head Start participants were doing significantly better than other low-income children who did not participate in Head Start. They were more likely to remain in school, were less likely to be held back or placed in remedial classes, and they had fewer social difficulties (Lazar & Darlington, 1982; Schweinhart & Weikart, 1980). Thus, long-term follow-up studies with comprehensive, far-reaching measures are required. Some rigorous, major studies are currently in progress and it is hoped they will provide clearer direction for practice.

Clinical evidence of effective intervention comprises a third body of knowledge that can inform practice. Although less systematic and rigorous than large studies, such evidence nevertheless can lead to useful hypotheses that help to set direction for our work with individual families (always to be evaluated for that particular family in any case). Themes that appear repeatedly among clinical reports warrant attention and consideration as possible directions when intervening with families. (*Zero to Three* and the *Family Resource Coalition Report,* described in the annotated list of resources, are excellent sources of clinical information about interventions with young children and their families.)

Examination of these three knowledge bases reveals basic themes, threads that appear repeatedly throughout the research literature and the testimony of professionals who have worked with infants, toddlers, and their families. These themes provide a starting point for determining how to address the needs of families with young children. In the section that follows, I describe some of these themes and discuss strategies for pursuing them with families of infants and toddlers. (Table 1 provides an outline of the themes and strategies discussed throughout this chapter.) Recognize that the field of early intervention is evolving rapidly, and this is *not* a static guide for service. Rather, it is a framework that can serve as a starting point. Any professional working with families and their young children has a responsibility to stay abreast of new information in the field. And, most important, we each have a responsibility to monitor constantly the development of children we are serving and the feelings of their families in response to our efforts with them. As with best practice with children of any age, what matters is what works for *this* child and *this* family.

A FRAMEWORK FOR INTERVENTION

Handicapping conditions and/or risk factors (i.e., variables that increase the likelihood that a child will have learning or adjustment difficulties) can be present in the child, in the family, and in the broader environment—or any combination thereof. Likewise, "protective factors," (i.e., variables that enhance development and can buffer against the effects of handicapping conditions or risk factors) exist in the child, the family, and the broader environment. The task of early intervention is to eliminate, ameliorate, or reduce the impact of risk factors and to

TABLE 1
Intervention Themes and Strategies

Themes	Related Strategies
Attachment; Parental sensitivity to infant cues and signals	Videotaping of parent-child interaction and guided viewing of tape
"Baby Talk"; Promoting language and building memories	Imitating baby Recalling with parents their own pet names, ways adults talked to them
Encouraging exploration of the environment	Babyproofing Creating opportunities
Facilitating mastery	Responding to baby's cues Cause and effect toys "Just enough" help Support and adaptations for children with disabilities
Parental knowledge and expectations of child behavior	Teaching developmental sequences Discovering competencies and developmental level of individual child "Reframing" developmental meaning of behaviors "Talking through" the baby Exercises in perspective-taking
Parental emotional issues	Exploring memories, developmental history Empowerment through collaborative problem solving Building trust and confidence through professional-parent relationship
Social support	Direct provision of support by professional Engagement of others from natural support network in intervention activities Role-playing to strengthen skills and confidence in seeking support Facilitating use of other formal resources

build and strengthen protective factors in an effort to facilitate optimal competence and well-being for children over the course of their development.

Regardless of whether we are working with an infant with an identifiable disability or one who is at-risk because of familial variables or environmental circumstances, there is little we can do directly to modify the characteristics of the infant, particularly in the earliest months of life. What we can influence are the ways in which caregivers respond to that child; and thus we can influence the parent-child relationship and, indirectly, the quality of that child's development. Recent literature covering the three knowledge bases described previously (basic developmental research, prevention/intervention studies, and clinical reports) identifies several salient aspects of parental behavior and points to underlying beliefs and attitudes and social and emotional contexts that may support or inhibit those parental behaviors. Although there are many unanswered questions about when, where, and how to influence these variables, the behaviors, attitudes, and social factors described below seem to be relatively accessible and amenable to change. As such, they provide a useful starting point for assessing and working with children and families served by school psychologists and other early childhood professionals.

A Firm Foundation: Infant-Caregiver Attachment

Many developmentalists believe that the central issue in the first year of life is the establishment of a sense of basic trust (Erikson, 1963). Trust is established primarily through experience with caregivers who are consistent and predictable in their care for their infants. Erikson's basic developmental notions of trust and security in infancy were explicated and expanded upon by various other theorists and researchers, including John Bowlby and Mary Ainsworth in their pioneering work on the importance of parent-infant attachment. Bowlby's theoretical and clinical work (1973, 1980, 1982) and research facilitated by Mary Ainsworth's method for assessing the quality of attachment (Ainsworth, Blehar, Waters, & Wall, 1978) have had a powerful influence on early intervention with infants and their parents. A detailed discussion of attachment is beyond the scope of this chapter; however, a brief overview of the importance of attachment and the factors that promote secure attachment provides a useful framework for thinking about early intervention strategies. Readers are referred to Bretherton and Waters (1985) for a more complete discussion of attachment theory, patterns of attachment identified with Ainsworth's measure, and the importance of quality of attachment in infancy for the child's subsequent development. For a discussion of clinical implications of attachment theory and research, readers are referred to Belsky and Nezworski (1988).

Attachment theory proposes that human infants are predisposed to form attachments to the adults who care for them in the first few months of life. Attachments develop over time, typically becoming firmly established by the time the child is about 1 year of age. Nearly all infants form attachments, the only likely exceptions being children who are so severely disabled that they cannot engage in reciprocal interactions with caregivers, or those children, perhaps in institutions, who have no opportunity for sustained interactions with a caregiver. Although caregiver-infant attachments are virtually universal, these relationships vary in quality and can be classified broadly as secure or anxious. In general, a secure attachment is reflected in the child's ability to use the caregiver as a secure base from which to explore the world and as a reliable source of comfort during times of distress. The child who is securely attached explores and plays with confidence and enthusiasm in the presence of the attachment figure, periodically sharing a look, vocalization, a smile, or showing the caregiver a toy. When tired, sick, or perhaps upset by a separation (as in the Strange Situation Procedures, Ainsworth's laboratory assessment of attachment), the securely attached child readily seeks and accepts comfort from the caregiver. Through months of experience with a caregiver who is sensitive and predictable, this child learns to trust that the caregiver will be there to meet her needs. And this child learns to trust in her own ability to solicit that care. That basic trust in caregivers and in self, or what sometimes is described as the child's "internal working model" of self and others, is carried forward, influencing the child's expectations and behavior in subsequent relationships with other adults and peers. Although not an inoculation against later problems, secure attachment in infancy does seem to lay the foundation for healthy resolution of subsequent development issues (Arend, Gove, & Sroufe, 1979; Erickson, Sroufe, & Egeland, 1985; Lewis, Feiring, McGuffog, & Jaskir, 1984).

In contrast, the anxiously attached child typically presents one of two patterns of behavior: anxious-resistant or anxious-avoidant. The "anxious-resistant" (sometimes called "anxious-ambivalent") child is preoccupied with maintaining contact with the attachment figure, apparently so unsure of the caregiver's availability and predictability that he dares not venture out to play and explore. Usually extremely upset by separation from the caregiver, this child nevertheless displays ambivalence upon reunion, often alternating between desperate clinginess and active resistance (sometimes even aggression) when the caregiver offers comfort. This pattern of attachment has been shown to be related to inconsistent, unpredictable care during the early months of the child's life (Ainsworth et al., 1978; Egeland & Farber, 1984).

A second pattern of anxious attachment is described as "anxious-avoidant," and has been shown to be related to interactions with a caregiver who is unresponsive to the infant's bids for care and attention. Anxious-avoidant children typically show no visible distress when separated from their caregiver and actively avoid interacting with their caregiver upon reunion. We might infer that with "internal working models" of others as unpredictable or unavailable, and self as powerless to solicit needed care, anxious-resistant and anxious-avoidant children move forward in development with little confidence that they will be successful in other relationships and ventures. Not surprisingly, anxiously attached 1-year-olds are likely to present significant behavior problems by the time they are 4 to 5 years of age, especially in cases where their caregiving environment does not improve during the intervening years (Erickson et al., 1985). (Recent attachment research describes a fourth pattern of attachment, often characterized as "disorganized." These children often present contradicting behaviors simultaneously, such as reaching out to the caregiver with a grimace on their face. Although less is known about the meaning of this pattern, it appears to be associated with traumatic abuse [Main & Hesse, 1990].)

The Path to Security and Competence: Parental Sensitivity

Sensitive care for children in the early months of life emerges as the most powerful predictor of the quality of the child's attachment (Ainsworth et al., 1978; Egeland & Farber, 1984). Parental sensitivity and responsiveness also are associated with a higher level of mastery motivation (Yarrow, Rubenstein, & Pederson, 1975) and higher intellectual functioning at subsequent ages (Beckwith, Cohen, Kopp, Parmelee, & Marcy, 1976; Bradley & Caldwell, 1984). Thus, promoting parental sensitivity becomes a logical target of early intervention efforts. Sensitivity encompasses: recognition that even the youngest infants can signal their needs and wishes; accurate reading and interpretation of infant cues and signals; a contingent response to infant signals (that is, letting the child's signals, rather than the parent's needs or wishes, set the agenda); and consistency or predictability over time. An excellent resource for parents who want to learn about the meaning of their baby's signals is *Born Dancing* by Thoman and Browder (1987), described in the annotated list of resources (Appendix A). Of course, no parent can or should jump at every little signal the baby gives, but the child's overall experience should be that his signals are effective in getting a response and that caregivers are available and willing to respond. A parent's capacity to respond sensitively requires an awareness of the meaning of cues and signals, a willingness to respond, and the emotional strength and social support necessary to sustain sensitivity over time (Dunst & Trivette, 1990).

Insensitivity may be manifest in various ways. It may be a persistent, chronic failure to respond to the infant's cries and other bids for attention—an especially pernicious form of insensitivity. The long-term effects of emotional unresponsiveness, well described by Egeland and Erickson (1987), include anxious-avoidant attachment, declining intellectual functioning, and serious behavior problems. Insensitivity also may be inconsistent, erratic patterns of responding. Or it may be intrusiveness, which is a failure to respect the child's signals that say, "I don't feel like playing (or eating or being tickled or kissed) right now" (Egeland, Pianta, & O'Brien, in press). Early intervention professionals sometimes are the worst offenders in terms of intrusiveness, persistently trying to engage the infant in developmentally stimulating activities even when the child's behavior clearly says that this is not the time. Insensitivity does *not* imply bad intentions on the part of the adult, but may result from inaccurate knowledge, erroneous beliefs (e.g., that responding consistently to a baby's cries will "spoil" the baby), stress and exhaustion, or emotional issues that render the caregiver unable to be available to the child. Insensitivity has been described as the common variable in various patterns of child maltreatment as well. Whether a child is physically abused, verbally abused, or physically or emotionally neglected, the underlying insensitivity appears to be the central factor accounting for long-term psychological consequences (Erickson & Egeland, 1987).

In the preventive intervention work that Byron Egeland and I have done with high-risk parents and their first-born children (Project STEEP, as described in Appendix B) we found guided viewing of videotapes to be a useful strategy for strengthening parents' skills in interpreting and responding sensitively to their infant's cues and signals. This strategy, consistent with a strength-focused, empowerment approach, facilitates the parents' awareness of their own skills rather than setting up the professional as the expert who teaches parents how to respond. This strategy is being adopted by staff in several early intervention programs in our state and reportedly is very helpful in interpreting the meaning of signals given by disabled or high-risk infants whose cues often are less vigorous or clear than those of a more robust baby.

As a permanent record of behavior, the tape is useful to staff and supervisors for identifying strengths in both parent and child and for monitoring progress.

We found the videotaping to be enjoyable for parents and, when used during home visits, an effective way to engage other family members and friends in supporting the baby's development. On their child's birthday, parents receive a copy of the cumulative tape covering the first year of the child's life—a powerful incentive for participation, according to many of the parents we serve.

BABY TALK: FACILITATING LANGUAGE DEVELOPMENT, BUILDING MEMORIES

The way parents talk to their babies is another theme to pursue through early intervention. Parents sometimes do not recognize the need to talk to a baby who is too young to understand. For example, several studies have shown that teen mothers talk less to their babies than older mothers (e.g., Epstein, 1980; Osofsky & Osofsky, 1970). Other parents may give up talking if their baby initially is unresponsive to their talk, as with many disabled infants. It may be necessary with some parents to help them develop a rationale for talking to their babies. The most obvious reason is that talking to babies—long before they can understand the words or talk back—has been shown to be a factor in promoting language development (Clarke-Stewart, 1973). When babies begin to babble and experiment with their own voice, parents can reinforce the babbling by imitating the baby's sounds and engaging in a reciprocal "conversation" with the baby—an important lesson for the baby in language, as well as in cause and effect. Secondly, the parent's voice is an important source of comfort for a baby (Nugent, 1985). What a relief for parents, struggling to stay on top of other tasks while still caring for a baby, to discover that their baby can be comforted just by the sound of a familiar voice rather than always needing to be picked up or fed!

Talking gently, playfully, and positively to babies is a way of establishing habits for when the child is older. In our work, we have found this "practice" time to be important for parents who have a coarse, rough way of talking with friends and family. For example, upon hearing herself on videotape with her new baby, one mother said, "Oh, no! Do I always talk in that 'whiskey baritone'?" Furthermore, what parents say to their babies is a way of building a storehouse of memories for later. Older children like to know what pet names their parents called them, what songs were sung to them, what stories they were told. Parents may recognize the importance of this if they are asked about what pet names their own parents called them, what songs and stories their parents sang or told them, and the manner in which their parents usually spoke to them. From the first day of a child's life, parents can begin to communicate their love and nurture their child's sense of self-esteem by the words they use and the tone of their voice.

Moving Out Into the World: Exploration, Mastery, and Autonomy

Critical to all aspects of the child's development is the opportunity to explore the object world. Studies have shown a relationship between school success and opportunities during infancy to play with a variety of materials in a relatively unrestricted physical environment (e.g., Bradley & Caldwell, 1984). This is an important issue for early intervention in some so-called "high-risk" families where opportunities for exploration may be impeded either by crowded, unsafe physical environments or by overly restrictive, authoritarian childrearing approaches that fail to recognize the importance of exploration for the child's development. Intervention may need to address how to babyproof the environment, ways to provide appropriate play things at little or no cost, and parental beliefs and attitudes about play and exploration. For children with disabilities, opportunity to explore is a critical issue for intervention. For example, children with motor impairment or low muscle tone may be motivated to explore, but unable to act on that motivation. Parents and professionals can engage in collaborative problem solving to

find ways to adapt the environment or to provide support and assistance that allows the child to explore. Williamson (1988) clearly describes, and illustrates with photographs, such a process in his case study of Allison, a 7-month-old infant with Down syndrome who exhibited passive behavior related to low muscle tone and lack of postural control. By providing various kinds of postural support to Allison, capitalizing on her visual and auditory interest in social interaction, and gradually increasing demands for motor control, Williamson and Allison's parents successfully facilitated her development of self-initiated exploratory play.

Children not only need to explore the environment, but to master it. Infants *need* experiences that allow them to feel some degree of control over the environment (e.g., MacTurk, McCarthy, Vietze, & Yarrow, 1987; MacTurk, Vietze, McCarthy, McQuiston, & Yarrow, 1985). Mastery of the environment begins with the child's experience in using a cry, a smile, or outstretched arms to actively solicit a response from caregivers. As infants develop cognitive and motor skills that enable them to purposefully explore objects, mastery becomes increasingly important. The task for parents is to create situations where a goal is attainable with some effort on the part of the child. For example, with a toy just out of reach a baby can scoot across the floor, grasp the toy, and begin to play with it. If the toy is too far out of reach, the baby will tire and give up out of frustration. On the other hand, if the parent places the toy in the baby's hand, the child is deprived of the experience of pursuing and reaching the goal. Cause and effect toys (e.g., squeak toys, busy boxes, Jack-in-the-box) are important in this period of development, certainly in terms of the child's cognitive understanding of concepts of cause and effect (Piaget, 1952), but also because of the opportunity for children to have the empowering experience of seeing their own actions bring about a consequence.

Striking a balance between giving too little help or too much help is a challenge that increases in importance as the child moves into the toddler phase when autonomy is the central developmental issue (Erikson, 1963). Given too little help and emotional support when faced with the many problem-solving tasks that toddlers encounter each day, children feel overwhelmed and learn that they are incompetent and others are unavailable to help. With too much help, children get the message that others have to solve the problem because they are incapable. Parent-child difficulties around autonomy issues at age 2 have been associated with behavior problems at age 5 (Erikson et al., 1985). A delicate balance is required for toddlers to experience their own competence and the reliability of help and support when they have exhausted their own resources. Interestingly, this parallels the experience between professional service providers and parents: Just as professionals want parents to provide just enough of a platform that children feel they have accomplished something independently, so should professionals offer only as much help or support as parents truly need. Empowerment is a central theme at all levels in family-focused intervention. Respecting and encouraging autonomy can be especially difficult for parents of a young child with disabilities. One mother, whose daughter has limited use of her legs, tells the poignant story of watching through tears as her little girl walked slowly, with braces and crutches, to get some cookies. This mother knew how much easier it would have been to get the cookies for her daughter, but she was wise enough to cheer her on as she did it herself.

Parental Knowledge, Attitudes, Beliefs, and Expectations

To a large extent, parental behavior is a function of what parents know and understand about how children develop and learn. Knowledge underlies the beliefs parents hold about childrearing and the expectations they have for their child's behavior. In working with families and infants, one of the first aspects of parental knowledge encountered is recognition of the capabilities of the infant. Some parents seem to have a view of the newborn as a little doll rather than a human being with remarkable capabilities. Actually, for years even physicians and child development professionals grossly underestimated the abilities of infants. For example, many parents have been told for years that newborns are unable to see. However, recent research has demonstrated the ability of newborns to recognize their mother by sight and sound (Nugent, 1985). Nugent has developed a useful guide for professionals to use to help parents discover their newborn infant's capabilities (see annotated list of resources at end of chapter), a brief strategy that has been shown to be effective in promoting positive parent-child interaction. Videotaping is a useful tool for parents and professionals to discover collaboratively the baby's competencies, and is especially helpful with babies whose handicapping conditions may tend to obscure their capabilities.

Developmental sequences. A related issue for intervention is parental knowledge of normal developmental sequences, knowledge that helps to determine the behavioral expectations that parents have for their children. For example, many parents expect their child to sit still and watch TV for long periods of time, long before children normally are capable of such sustained attention. Or parents expect a toddler to remember and generalize rules from one time and place to another. This can lead to unhappiness and frustration for both parent and child. Some parents become upset when their 10-month-old baby hits another baby's face while trying to explore it with her hands. They do not recognize that at 10 months of age their child is not yet able to learn the "no hitting" rule, and furthermore lacks both the impulse control and the motor control necessary to inhibit hitting.

Teaching parents normal developmental sequences can help them develop more appropriate expectations for their child's behavior. A useful reference for both parents and professionals is *The*

First Twelve Months of Life (Caplan, 1973), which presents month-by-month sequences of motor, language, mental, and social development. Not only is it important to familiarize parents with normal developmental timetables, but also to focus on individual differences and on what *this* individual child's own developmental timetable is. With any child, but especially with children with disabilities, the challenge for professionals is to help parents develop expectations that are appropriate to that child's abilities and developmental pace.

Developmental meaning. Possibly even more important than knowledge of developmental sequences is understanding the developmental meaning of a child's behavior. The misunderstanding of behavior can lead to attribution of negative characteristics either to the child or the parent, as in the case of two often-misinterpreted behaviors (e.g., Egeland & Breitenbucher, 1980; Newberger & Cook, 1983). The first is separation protest, which usually appears by 7 or 8 months of age. Some parents take that as a sign that the baby is spoiled, demanding, inappropriately dependent, and overly fussy. And/or they may feel that they are bad parents to have created such a difficult child. Many parents believe from the beginning that they will spoil their baby by responding consistently to his cries, so separation protest confirms their fears. Relief and reassurance come with the understanding that separation protest is a normal, healthy phenomenon that indicates that the baby now recognizes that the caregiver still exists even when out of sight (Piaget's notion of object permanence, 1952); that the caregiver appropriately has become important as a source of security for the child; and that as the child's needs for closeness continue to be satisfied, he gradually will become more able to separate and become increasingly independent (Ainsworth et al., 1978; Erickson et al., 1985; Sroufe, Fox, & Pancake, 1983).

A second commonly misunderstood behavior is toddler negativism, which parents again may take as a sign that their child is "nasty" or "spoiled" and that they

have failed as parents. It is helpful for parents to understand that the toddler's negativism is the tool that the child uses to begin to establish a separate sense of self and to exercise newfound autonomy—a major developmental accomplishment. During this period of development children need clear, consistent limits to protect them from an overwhelming sense of chaos, and they also need opportunities to make choices and act independently within those limits (see Breger, 1974, for an excellent discussion of this developmental period).

When child behaviors trigger negative attributions, one way to intervene is to verbally "reframe" the behaviors for parents, reinterpreting the behavior as reflecting a positive motive or characteristic in the child. Table 2 presents a brief list of behaviors that often trigger negative attributions, followed by the way they can be positively reframed for parents. Reframing behavior is one step toward perspective-taking; parents see things through the baby's eyes. In our work we also simulate exercises to help parents experience things as the baby does. For example, with a group of parents of toddlers we had them walk around holding their arm straight up in the air, to see what it felt like when they had their toddlers walk holding their hands. We also sometimes "talk through" the baby, saying for example, "Hey, Mom, I'm tired of this playpen. I need to get out and move around."

Emotional Issues, Past and Present

Even when some parents have accurate knowledge and understanding about their child's development, and have set realistic expectations for their child, their own emotional issues make it difficult for them to put that knowledge into practice. Research points to several aspects of parental emotional issues that may need to be addressed through intervention. These are intimate issues that should only be addressed within the context of a close, trusting relationship with the parent—a relationship that requires time

TABLE 2
Reframing Infant Behaviors

Behavior	Negative Attribution	Reframe
Crying	She's just trying to get at me.	She sure lets you know when she needs something.
	She's such a brat.	She's really able to tell you what she wants.
Thumbsucking	He's such a wimp. He's going to ruin his teeth.	Isn't it great that he's found a way to comfort himself?
Separation protest	She's so spoiled. I can't move without her hanging on my leg.	You sure are special to her. She really knows you'll take care of her.
Getting into things and making messes	What a pain in the neck! He won't ever stay out of my stuff.	He is so curious and eager to learn. He wants to see and touch everything. That must be exciting for him.
Saying "no!"	She's so defiant. She'd better learn some respect fast!	She's becoming so strong and independent. She needs to show you she has a mind of her own.

and patience to build (Egeland & Erickson, 1990; Erickson, 1989).

Recent studies demonstrate the importance of one's own childhood experience as an influence on current parenting. It has long been believed that parents who were abused or neglected as children are more likely to maltreat their own children. Retrospective studies show that a majority of abusive parents were victims of abuse in their own childhood (e.g., Herrenkohl, Herrenkohl, & Toedter, 1983; Steele & Pollock, 1968). Findings from prospective studies are less clear, with anywhere from 18% (e.g., Straus, 1979) to 70% (Egeland, Jacobvitz, & Papatola, 1987) of abused children going on to become perpetrators. The highest estimates are among low-income families where additional stressors are likely to increase the risk of ongoing abusive patterns. Even given the highest estimates, that still leaves 30% who apparently break the so-called intergenerational cycle of abuse. Recent research has focused on parents who break that cycle and factors that allow them to do so, findings with important implications for

preventive intervention (Egeland, 1988). Egeland's study indicates that one factor that enables abused parents to care well for their own children is having faced their past honestly and come to some resolution of those early relationship issues, often through formal counseling or therapy.

In a similar vein, Main and Goldwyn (1984) found that a mother's self-perception of early personal relationships strongly influences the quality of attachment with her infant. Mothers are likely to foster an anxious attachment with their child if they deny the pain of their own childhood, dismiss its potential effect on their own parenting, or, alternatively, are preoccupied with their past pain and still caught up in rage or shame. Regardless of the quality of the mother's childhood experiences and early relationships, if she has faced her pain and come to some healthy resolution of those early issues, she is likely to develop a secure attachment with her own child.

Thus, the challenge for early intervention is to support and encourage parents through a reexamination of their own past, to help them face the pain, to see that it was not their fault, and to help them recognize that they do not have to repeat the past with their own child. In her eloquent paper, "Ghosts in the Nursery," Fraiberg and her colleagues (Fraiberg, Adelson, & Shapiro, 1980) provide a helpful model for working with parents who were abused as children. For all parents, maltreated or not, it is a useful exercise to consider what they want to repeat from their own past and what they do not want to repeat. It is empowering for parents to recognize that they have a choice, while still remaining aware of the ongoing influence their own early experience has on their parenting.

The concept of "internal working models," discussed in the earlier section on parent-infant attachment, is relevant when considering the parent's emotional issues as well. For parents who have a history of being abused or neglected, their "working models" may lead them to expect and assume the worst of professionals who work with them. With expectations that others are uncaring and untrustworthy, and an image of self as unworthy of being cared for, they may be quick to feel judged or shamed or let down. The challenge to the professional is to behave in a way that contradicts those working models (see Egeland & Erickson, 1990). This takes time, patience, persistence, and a commitment to a nonjudgmental, empowering approach to intervention.

Of course, current circumstances and stresses also exert a powerful influence on parent-child relationships and child developmental outcomes. For many families, financial hardship, lack of adequate housing, relationship difficulties, and other stressors make it difficult to sustain the energy and sensitivity necessary to promote their child's healthy development (Pianta & Egeland, 1990). Early intervention needs to acknowledge those stressors, be certain that parents have an opportunity to deal openly with the feelings engendered by the stress, and engage in constructive problem solving to reduce the sources of stress. Building social support and linking families to appropriate resources is a critical role for professionals working with infants and toddlers and their families.

Learning that one's child has a disability is a special source of emotional stress, and perhaps one of the most important things to address through early intervention (Gallagher & Vietze, 1986; Marfo & Kysela, 1985). A mother of a child with Down syndrome described the deep depression she experienced during the first few months of her baby's life, how she could see only the disability and not the baby, and how she grieved for the loss of the normal baby that she had expected to have. Early intervention professionals and a support group of parents of children with Down syndrome helped her work through those painful feelings and begin to discover the child behind the disability. Some disabilities, of course, are not immediately diagnosable and leave parents only with vague feelings that something is not right with their child or that they are doing something wrong. As professionals work to diagnose and understand the child's difficulties, they also must keep a focus on the parents' perceptions and feelings.

Social Support

One of the most important themes in the literature on what accounts for good outcomes for children and families is social support (Kagan, Powell, Weissbourd, & Zigler, 1987; Powell, 1987). In several ways school-based early intervention can enhance the support available to families and young children. Of course, the professional service provider can and should be one source of support. However, most important is the strengthening of systems that will support the family long beyond their involvement in early intervention. One way to do that is to identify the existing natural support system of the family (e.g., Dunst & Trivette, 1988). Then, significant support people can be directly involved in early intervention, rather than focusing only on mother and child, as often happens. For example, home visits can be a time to engage fathers, grandparents, friends, or childcare providers in activities to promote the infant's development. This may mean that "home visits" are not always in the family's own home, but may be a trip to grandma's house, the park, or the childcare facility. And it may mean breaking free of the constraints of school hours in order to accommodate the work schedules of family members. In the STEEP program the videotaping strategies described earlier have proven an effective way of involving others. Also, special family events in the evening are effective, allowing parents to define "families" as broadly as they choose. To encourage participation we have held drawings for small door prizes, taken a Polaroid photo of each child and his or her family, set up tables where parents could make a toy to take home for their children, and set up video equipment for parents to show their children's videotapes to friends and relatives.

Some parents need to work on ways to solicit and accept support from others, both from their natural support networks and from formal resources in the community. They might benefit from role-playing to practice direct, assertive ways to ask for help from family and friends, and they may seek reassurance that they need not feel guilty for wanting extra help at this demanding time in their lives. To ensure that parents get the formal services they want and to which they are entitled (e.g., support groups, subsidized rent, respite care, home health aide, vocational counseling or training), it is often helpful to provide information about available resources, to familiarize them with how to access those services, encourage them to prepare a list of questions to ask, and even to practice what they will say when they phone the agency. The temptation sometimes is to make the phone call for the parent, to be a "broker of services." However, it is more empowering to support the parent as they do it on their own, strengthening skills that they surely will have a chance to use again in the future. Recognize that some services are not very user-friendly, providing no outreach and perhaps even creating administrative roadblocks for potential participants. You may want to take the initiative in your community to build networks with other agencies and look at ways that you can make services more accessible to the families that need them the most. In Minneapolis, such efforts are being coordinated by interdisciplinary committees through the United Way.

CONCLUSION

In working with infants and toddlers and their families, we must ensure that parents have the information, support, and encouragement that they need to facilitate their child's optimal development and maintain their own sense of well-being. The school system, as a public resource available to families throughout the growing-up years of their children, is a powerful source of such supportive intervention. School psychologists have much to offer to the domain of family-focused early intervention, and there is much from which all professionals can draw in the basic and applied research on what accounts for good outcomes for children and families. Working with families during the early months or years of a child's life provides an opportunity for proactive efforts to create strong partnerships with parents based on a shared desire for what is best for the child. It is an opportunity to build and strengthen protective mechanisms—in the child, the family, and the broader social environment—that can buffer the effects of whatever risk factors exist for the child and family.

REFERENCES

Ainsworth, M. D. S., Blehar, M. C., Waters, E., & Wall, S. (1978). *Patterns of attachment: A psychological study of the Strange Situation*. Hillsdale, NJ: Erlbaum.

Arend, R., Gove, F., & Sroufe, L. A. (1979). Continuity of individual adaptation from infancy to kindergarten: A predictive study of ego-resiliency and curiosity in preschoolers. *Child Development, 50*, 950–959.

Beckwith, L., Cohen, S. E., Kopp, C. B., Parmelee, A. H., & Marcy, T. G. (1976). Caregiver-infant interaction and early cognitive development in preterm infants. *Child Development, 47*, 579–587.

Belsky, J., & Nezworski, T. (Eds.). (1988). *Clinical implications of attachment.* Hillsdale, NJ: Erlbaum.

Bowlby, J. (1973). *Attachment and loss: Vol. 2. Separation.* New York: Basic Books.

Bowlby, J. (1980). *Attachment and loss: Vol 3. Loss, sadness and depression.* New York: Basic Books.

Bowlby, J. (1982). *Attachment and loss: Vol. 1. Attachment (2nd ed.).* New York: Basic Books (original work published 1969).

Bradley, R. H., & Caldwell, B. M. (1984). The relation of infants' home environment to achievement test performance in first grade: A follow-up study. *Child Development, 55,* 803–809.

Breger, L. (1974). *From instinct to identity: The development of personality.* Englewood Cliffs, NJ: Prentice-Hall, Inc.

Bretherton, I., & Waters, E. (Eds.). (1985). Growing points in attachment theory and research. *Monographs of the Society for Research in Child Development, 50*(1–2, Serial No. 209).

Bromwich, R. (1978). *Working with parents and infants: An interactional approach.* Baltimore: University Park Press.

Caplan, F. (1973). *The first twelve months of life: Your baby's growth month by month.* New York: Bantam Books.

Cardon, B. W. (1982). The future: A context for present planning. *School Psychology Review, 11*(2), 151–160.

Cicirelli, V. (1969, June). *The impact of Head Start: An evaluation of Head Start on children's cognitive and affective development. Report presented to the Office of Economic Opportunity* (OEO Report No. PB 184 328). Athens, OH: Westinghouse Learning Corporation for Federal and Scientific and Technical Information, U.S. Institute for Applied Technology.

Clarke-Stewart, K. A. (1973). Interactions between mothers and their young children. *Monographs of the Society for Research in Child Development, 38*(7, 8, 9, Serial No. 153).

Dunst, C. J., & Trivette, C. M. (1988). A family systems model of early intervention with handicapped and developmentally at-risk children. In D. R. Powell (Ed.), *Parent education as early childhood intervention: Emerging directions in theory, research and practice* (pp. 131–180). Norwood, NJ: Ablex.

Dunst, C. J., & Trivette, C. M. (1990). Assessment of social support in early intervention programs. In S. J. Meisels & J. P. Shonkoff (Eds.), *Handbook of early childhood intervention* (pp. 326–349). New York: Cambridge University Press.

Early Childhood Family Education Statutes. (July, 1989). Section 121.882: Early childhood family education programs, Section 124.2711: Early childhood family education aid, Section 275.125: Tax levy, school districts. St. Paul, MN: Minnesota Department of Education.

Egeland, B. (1988). Breaking the cycle of abuse: Implications for prediction and intervention. In K. D. Browne, C. Davies, & P. Stratton (Eds.), *Early prediction and prevention of child abuse* (pp. 87–99). J. Wiley & Sons, Inc.

Egeland, B., & Breitenbucher, M. (1980). *Final report: The effects of parental knowledge and expectations on the development of child competence.* (Grant No. 90-C-1259). Washington, DC: Administration for Children, Youth and Families, Office of Child Development, HEW.

Egeland, B., & Erickson, M. F. (1987). Psychologically unavailable caregiving. In M. R. Brassard, R. Germain, & S. N. Hart (Eds.), *Psychological maltreatment of children and youth* (pp. 110–120). New York: Pergamon.

Egeland, B., & Erickson, M. F. (1990, December). Rising above the past: Strategies for helping new mothers break the cycle of abuse and neglect. *Zero to Three, 11*(2), 29–35.

Egeland, B., & Farber, E. A. (1984). Infant-mother attachment: Factors related to its development and changes over time. *Child Development, 55*(3), 753–771.

Egeland, B., Jacobvitz, D., & Papatola, K. (1987). Intergenerational continuity of abuse. In R. Gelles & J. Lancaster (Eds.), *Child abuse and neglect: Biosocial dimensions* (pp. 255–276). New York: Aldine de Gruyter.

Egeland, B., Pianta, R. C., & O'Brien, M. A. (1990). *Maternal intrusiveness in infancy and child maladaptation in early school years.* Manuscript submitted for publication.

Epstein, A. S. (1980). *Assessing the child development information needed by adolescent parents with very young children.* Ypsilanti, MI: High/Scope Educational Research Foundation. (ERIC Document Reproduction Service No. ED 183 286)

Erickson, M. F. (1989). The STEEP program: Helping young families rise above "at-risk." *Family Resource Coalition Report, 8*(3), 14–15.

Erickson, M. F., & Egeland, B. (1987). A developmental view of the psychological consequences of maltreatment. *School Psychology Review, 16*(2), 156–168.

Erickson, M. F., Sroufe, L. A., & Egeland, B. (1985). The relationship between quality of attachment and behavior problems in preschool in a high-risk sample. In I. Bretherton & E. Waters (Eds.), *Monographs of the Society for Research in Child Development, 50*(1–2, 147–166, Serial No. 209).

Erikson, E. (1963). *Childhood and society* (2nd ed.). New York: Norton.

Fraiberg, L. (Ed.) (1987). *Selected writings of Selma Fraiberg*. Columbus: Ohio State University Press.

Fraiberg, S., Adelson, E., & Shapiro, V. (1980). Ghosts in the nursery: A psychoanalytic approach to the problems of impaired mother-infant relationships. In S. Fraiberg (Ed.), *Clinical studies in infant mental health: The first year of life* (pp. 164–196). New York: Basic Books.

Gallagher, J., & Vietze, P. (Eds.). (1986). *Families of handicapped persons*. Baltimore: P. H. Brookes.

Greenspan, S., & Greenspan, N. T. (1989). *The essential partnership: How parents and children can meet the emotional challenges of infancy and childhood*. New York: Viking Penguin, Inc.

Herrenkohl, E. C., Herrenkohl, R. C., & Toedter, L. J. (1983). Perspectives on the intergenerational transmission of abuse. In D. Finkelhor, R. J. Gelles, G. T. Hotaling, & M. A. Strauss (Eds.), *The dark side of families: Current family violence research* (pp. 305–316). Beverly Hills, CA: Sage Publications.

Kagan, S. L., Powell, D., Weissbourd, B., & Zigler, E. (Eds.). (1987). *America's family support programs*. New Haven: Yale University Press.

Lazar, I., & Darlington, R. (1982). Lasting effects of early education: A report from the Consortium for Longitudinal Studies. *Monographs of the Society for Research in Child Development, 47*(2–3, Serial No. 195).

Lewis, M., Feiring, C., McGuffog, C., & Jaskir, J. (1984). Predicting psychopathology in six-year-olds from early social relations. *Child Development, 55*, 123–136.

MacTurk, R. H., McCarthy, M. E., Vietze, P. M., & Yarrow, L. J. (1987). Sequential analysis of mastery behavior in 6- and 12-month old infants. *Developmental Psychology, 23*, 199–203.

MacTurk, R. H., Vietze, P. M., McCarthy, M. E., McQuiston, S., & Yarrow, L. J. (1985). The organization of exploratory behavior in Down Syndrome and non-delayed infants. *Child Development, 56*, 573–581.

Main, M., & Goldwyn, R. (1984). Predicting rejection of her infant from mother's representation of her own experiences: Implications for the abused-abusing intergenerational cycle. *Child Abuse and Neglect, 8*, 203–217.

Main, M., & Hesse, E. (1990). Parents' unresolved traumatic experiences are related to infant disorganized attachment status: Is frightened and/or frightening parental behavior the linking mechanism? In M. T. Greenberg, D. Cicchetti, & E. M. Cummings (Eds.), *Attachment in the preschool years* (pp. 161–182). Chicago: Chicago Press.

Marfo, K., & Kysela, G. (1985). Early intervention with mentally handicapped children: A critical appraisal of applied research. *Journal of Pediatric Psychology, 10*, 305–324.

Meisels, S. J., & Shonkoff, J. P. (Eds.). (1990). *Handbook of early childhood intervention*. New York: Cambridge University Press.

Meyers, J., Brown, D. T., & Coulter, W. A. (1982). Analysis of the action plans. *School Psychology Review, 11*(2), 161–185.

Newberger, C. M., & Cook, S. J. (1983). Parental awareness and child abuse: A cognitive-developmental analysis of urban and rural samples. *American Journal of Orthopsychiatry, 53*, 512–524.

Nugent, K. J. (1985). *Using the NBAS with infants and their families: Guidelines for intervention*. New York: March of Dimes.

Osofsky, H. J., & Osofsky, J. D. (1970). Adolescents as mothers: Results of a program for low-income pregnant teenagers with some emphasis upon infants' development. *American Journal of Orthopsychiatry, 40*, 825–834.

Piaget, J. (1952). *The origins of intelligence in children*. New York: International Universities Press.

Pianta, R. C., & Egeland, B. (1990). Life stress and parenting outcomes in a disadvantaged sample: Results of the Mother-Child Interaction Project. *Journal of Clinical Child Psychology, 19*(4), 329–336.

Powell, D. (Ed.). (1987). *Parent education and support programs: Consequences for children and families*. Norwood, NJ: Ablex Publishing.

Sameroff, A. J. (1987). The social context of development. In N. Eisenberg (Ed.), *Contemporary topics in developmental psychology* (pp. 273–291). New York: Wiley.

Sameroff, A. J., & Fiese, B. H. (1990). Transactional regulation and early intervention. In S. J. Meisels & J. P. Shonkoff (Eds.), *Handbook of early childhood intervention* (pp. 119–149). New York: Cambridge University Press.

Schweinhart, L. J., & Weikart, D. P. (1980). *Young children grow up: The effects of the Perry Preschool Program on youths through age 15*. (Monograph No. 3). Ypsilanti, MI: High-Scope Educational Research Foundation.

Sroufe, L. A., Fox, N., & Pancake, V. (1983). Attachment and dependency in developmental perspective. *Child Development, 54*, 1615–1627.

Steele, B. F., & Pollock, C. B. (1968). A psychiatric study of parents who abuse infants and small children. In K. E. Helfer & C. H. Kempe (Eds.), *The battered child* (pp. 89–133). Chicago: University of Chicago Press.

Straus, M. (1979). Family patterns and child abuse in a nationally representative sample. *Interna-*

tional Journal of Child Abuse and Neglect, 3, 213–225.

Thoman, E., & Browder, S. (1987). *Born dancing: How intuitive parents understand their baby's unspoken language and natural rhythms.* New York: Harper & Row.

Williamson, G. G. (1988, March). Motor control as a resource for adaptive coping. *Zero to Three, 9*(1), 1–7.

Yarrow, L. J., Rubenstein, J. L., & Pederson, F. A. (1975). *Infant and environment: Early cognitive and motivational development.* New York: Wiley.

Ysseldyke, J., & Weinberg, R. (Eds.). (1981). The future of psychology in the schools: Proceedings of the Spring Hill Symposium. *School Psychology Review, 10*(2).

APPENDIX A

Selected Resources for Early Intervention With Infants and Toddlers and Their Families

Belsky, J., & Nezworski, T. (Eds.). (1988). *Clinical implications of attachment.* Hillsdale, NJ: Erlbaum.

This 440-page volume presents a comprehensive discussion of attachment issues, research on antecedents and consequences of different patterns of attachment, and clinical applications of attachment theory and research. It is an important step toward bridging the gap between research and practice.

Bromwich, R. (1978). *Working with parents and infants: An interactional approach.* Baltimore: University Park Press.

This book describes intervention approaches used with families in the UCLA Infant Studies Project. A useful resource for anyone involved in intervention with infants and toddlers and their parents, it includes case studies, measures used to assess progress in parenting, and a nitty-gritty description of approaches used in specific problem situations.

Erickson, M. F., & Egeland, B. (1987). A developmental view of the psychological consequences of maltreatment. *School Psychology Review, 16*(2), 156–168.

This article summarizes some of the findings from the Minnesota Mother-Child Project, which provided the basis for the development of the STEEP preventive intervention program. Beginning with the conten-

tion that parental insensitivity is the central feature of all patterns of abuse and neglect, the authors discuss ways in which insensitivity is manifest toward infants and toddlers, the lasting impact of such insensitivity, and implications for intervention.

Family Resource Coalition. *Family Resource Coalition Report.* 230 North Michigan Avenue, Suite 1625, Chicago, IL 60601.

Published three times a year, this publication integrates information from research and practice in a style that is comfortable both for professionals and the general public. Content includes descriptions of innovative family support programs, research findings, publications and media resources on families and children, as well as practical advice for parents. Although the focus is not limited to families with infants and toddlers, there is much useful information for practitioners serving that population.

Fraiberg, L. (Ed.). (1987). *Selected writings of Selma Fraiberg.* Columbus: Ohio State University Press.

Selma Fraiberg was a pioneer of the infant mental health movement and her work continues to have a profound influence on early intervention. Edited by her husband following her death, this 688-page volume presents 29 of Fraiberg's most significant papers, including the eloquent, moving "Ghosts in the Nursery," which describes therapeutic strategies for helping parents break free of their own history of abuse and move toward healthy interaction with their own children. Also of particular interest to professionals who work with families with infants with disabilities are Fraiberg's writings about her research and clinical work with blind babies and their parents.

Greenspan, S., & Greenspan, N. T. (1989). *The essential partnership: How parents and children can meet the emotional challenges of infancy and childhood.* New York: Viking Penguin, Inc.

Within a framework of the six major stages of emotional growth from birth to five (initially described in Dr. Greenspan's earlier book, *First Feelings*), this book provides a practical guide for parents to explore their children's feelings and move toward a stronger emotional connection. Using a variety of case examples, the authors describe how simple "floor time" play can be used to help parents and children face challenges related to anger, sadness, fears, sexuality, competitiveness, self-esteem, and eating and sleeping patterns.

Meisels, S. J., & Shonkoff, J. P. (Eds.). (1990). *Handbook of early childhood intervention.* New York: Cambridge University Press.

This comprehensive, scholarly 760-page volume is a must for any early childhood professional. In 30 chapters by a wide range of early childhood experts, this book addresses developmental vulnerability and resilience, theoretical bases of early intervention, models for assessment and service delivery, research perspectives, and policy and programming. Many chapters focus specifically on strategies for serving families with young children.

Michigan Association for Infant Mental Health. *Infant Mental Health Journal.* IMHJ, 4 Conant Square, Brandon, VT 05733.

This is the official publication of the International Association for Infant Mental Health and the World Association for Infant Psychiatry and Allied Disciplines. Published four times per year, the journal includes literature reviews, research articles, program descriptions, and book reviews. This is an informative, useful journal for practitioners from varied disciplines.

National Center for Clinical Infant Programs. "Zero to Three" Bulletin. NCCIP, 15th St., N.W., Suite 912, Washington, DC 20005.

Published five times per year, this news-letter is a scholarly collection of articles on both research and practice, as well as up-to-date information on publications and relevant conferences. This is an excellent resource for staying abreast of new developments in the field of early intervention.

Nugent, K. J. (1985). *Using the NBAS with infants and their families: Guidelines for intervention.* New York: March of Dimes.

This small paperback provides directions for helping parents to recognize the capabilities of their newborn. Based on the Brazelton neonatal assessment, the intervention procedure focuses on the infant's adaptation to stimuli and self-comforting strategies.

Thoman, E., & Browder, S. (1987). *Born dancing: How intuitive parents understand their baby's unspoken language and natural rhythms.* New York: Harper & Row.

This is a remarkably affirming, refreshing, inspiring book. Although its target audience is expectant parents, this book is an invaluable resource for professionals working with parents of infants. Firmly grounded in recent research on infant development and parent-infant interaction, it nevertheless lifts you up and takes you dancing through the intricacies of parent-infant relationships.

APPENDIX B

The STEEP Program: Steps Toward Effective, Enjoyable Parenting

STEEP is a preventive-intervention program designed to promote healthy parent-infant interaction and prevent social and emotional problems among children born to mothers who are at risk for parenting problems (i.e., due to poverty, youth, lack of education, social isolation, and stressful life circumstances). Developed by Drs. Martha Farrell Erickson and Byron Egeland at the University of Minnesota, the program is based largely on findings from the Minnesota Mother-Child Interaction Project, a 16-year study of factors that account for good developmental outcomes among children born into high-risk circumstances.

The STEEP intervention program begins with home visits during the second trimester of pregnancy to help mothers deal with feelings about pregnancy and preparation for parenting. Home visits, done by "family life facilitators," continue every other week until the babies reach 2 years of age. Also, from the time babies are about 4 weeks old until they are 2, the facilitators conduct biweekly group sessions with each group of eight to ten mothers and babies. The facilitator provides basic information about infant development, helps the mothers learn to understand and respond to their infants' cues and signals, and guides the mothers in recognizing their own infants' special characteristics and needs. The format is not didactic teaching, but rather, demonstration and active involvement of mothers and babies. One goal of both the group and home visits is to help parents recognize how their own developmental history and current life events influence the way they interact with their children. The program focuses on empowering families to identify and build on their strengths and available resources. Although the group component of the STEEP program is aimed at mothers and infants, fathers and other family members participate in home visits and other special activities.

Since 1987 Drs. Egeland and Erickson have been conducting a 5-year longitudinal study of the effectiveness of the STEEP program, funded by the National Institute of Mental Health. Currently the STEEP program also is being implemented successfully in several community sites, with consultation and supervision provided by Dr. Erickson, and the STEEP model has been utilized in in-service training programs for early intervention professionals around the country.

12

HOME-SCHOOL PARTNERSHIPS AND PRESCHOOL SERVICES: FROM SELF-ASSESSMENT TO INNOVATION

Kathleen D. Paget and
Susan D. Chapman

In the winter of 333 B.C., the Macedonian general Alexander and his army arrive in the Asian city of Gordium to take up winter quarters. While there, Alexander hears about the legend surrounding the town's famous knot, the "Gordian Knot." A prophecy states that whoever is able to untie this strangely complicated knot will become king of Asia. This story intrigues Alexander, and he asks to be taken to the knot so that he can attempt to untie it. He studies it for several moments, but after fruitless attempts to find the rope-ends, he is stymied. "How can I unfasten the knot?" he asks himself. He gets an idea: "I'll just have to make up my own knot-untying rules." So he pulls out his sword and slices the knot in half. Asia is fated to him. (von Oech, 1983, pp. 47–48)

Through the fable quoted above, a noted consultant on innovation conveys several important messages of relevance to school psychologists interested in creating partnerships with parents of preschool-age children. First, a very complex problem may have a simpler solution than first appears to be the case. Secondly, arriving at this solution may require a departure from traditional rules or procedures. Thirdly, when stymied after examining a problem, we must engage in a process of explicit question asking in order to arrive at novel ideas, or our own "knot-untying rules."

Partnerships with parents of young children are important, and like the Gordian Knot, they are complex. They embody all the ambiguities of interpersonal relationships—communication styles, interactive behaviors, wants and needs, biases, attitudes, and expectations regarding change. Because of their complexity, partnerships deserve the most creative thinking school systems have to offer and an appreciation for the process of innovation.

Considerable momentum exists currently to implement partnerships with parents and to collaborate across disciplines in doing so. In fact, "partnership" and "collaboration," as concepts, are receiving so much attention that Kagan (1991) recently termed them the "buzzwords of the 1990's, just as 'prevention' was a buzzword of the 1980's." We believe there are risks involved when concepts become "buzzwords." First, the intricacies of the concept can become lost in the press to operationalize it through policy implementation and program development; and secondly, a concept may begin to be viewed as a monolithic entity or curative, capable of solving problems and enabling professionals to rest comfortably with the "solution." Given the importance of partnerships with parents of preschool-age children, we believe that *reflexive* action toward quick implementation of partnerships, as a buzzword, is ill-conceived, ill-fated, and premature; rather, participants in partnerships must engage in a *reflective* self-assessment process that examines one's own values and beliefs, expectations, desire for change, and patterns of interactive behaviors. Feedback from parents regarding their satisfaction with professional services (e.g., Crutcher, 1991; Kramer, 1991) challenges any temptation we may feel to remain complacent; and Roberts and Magrab (1991) go so far as to suggest that a new discipline of "family-centered child psychology" is necessary to adhere adequately to the many principles underlying professional-family interactions. Indeed, we have entered an era of family-centered intervention (Szanton, 1991).

Scholars in the fields of psychology and education write convincingly that partnerships with parents constitute an *ongoing* process of determining what works for a given situation, under certain circumstances, for any given program. As Sarason (1987) has noted,

> Schools are in a transactional relationship with a society that has changed and will continue to. change in significant ways, predictable and unpredictable. [There is no] way of structuring schools that will make future change unnecessary—[there is no] way of "solving" the problem so that we never have to solve it again. . . . Those of us in the educational arena deal with problems that must be "solved" again, and again, and again. (pp. 118–119)

Because partnerships constitute an ongoing process of problem solving, the primary aim of this chapter is to contribute to a self-assessment process for the reader, encouraging examination of individual and systemic attitudes toward partnerships. In attempting to attain this goal, we emphasize that one's own self-knowledge is a prerequisite to relationships with parents and that such assessment must take place at multiple levels within a school system. Too often, readers' reactions to ideas published in books and journals are along the lines of "That is all very well and good, but it won't work in my school system." We wish to reflect our understanding of this reaction and

encourage the reader to respond to information in this chapter with a critical eye toward examination of personal and systemic impediments within one's own circumstances that may block the formation of partnerships with parents of preschool-age children. We believe the clarity that emerges from a self-assessment process forms the backdrop for clearer and more simplified goals and innovations. Without such a process, professionals run the risk of bringing to relationships with parents ambivalence, ambiguity, and lack of direction, which can easily doom partnerships to failure. Stated differently, anything less than a serious attempt to understand our own attitudes, beliefs, and goals is akin to continually rearranging deck chairs on a sinking Titanic, and our activities never solve the real problem or reach the intended goal.

Secondary aims of the chapter are (a) to establish a rationale for partnerships with parents of preschool-age children; (b) to present a paradigm to guide thinking about these partnerships; (c) to discuss salient features of effective partnerships, including process, content, and outcome issues; and (d) to present information from illustrative programs. This information is intended to serve as a catalyst for the self-assessment process described above.

RATIONALE FOR PARTNERSHIPS AT PRESCHOOL LEVEL

Nationwide trends reveal that the proportion of children enrolled in prekindergarten and kindergarten programs has nearly doubled during the past 20 years (Rogoff, 1991). Most 5-year-old children are enrolled in public school kindergartens, and, as a result of recent education reform activities, public-school-based programs for at-risk and handicapped 3- and 4-year-olds are burgeoning (Duff, 1990). The rationale for partnerships between schools and the parents of these young children is multiply determined from theoretical, demographic, legal, empirical, and humanitarian vantage points. Thus, for many different reasons, compelling evidence supports parental-professional partnerships as an integral part of early childhood education.

Applied developmental theory underscores the primary importance of the family as a context for the development of young children (Bronfenbrenner, 1986; Silber, 1989) and of parent involvement in preschool education programs (Bredekamp, 1987). Outcomes of empirical research and program evaluation efforts (e.g., Head Start) support the need to promote continuity between home and preschool programs, and research efforts have verified a relationship between parent involvement, parental and child development, and the overall effectiveness of preschool education (Weikart, 1987). Powell (1989) provides a compelling and comprehensive review of efficacy research of parental involvement in early childhood programs, and the reader is referred to this source for detailed information. The essential point from both theory and research is that the ultimate objective of promoting healthy child development is more likely reached when there is a concern with healthy parent development (Weissbourd, 1991).

Demographic trends for children under the age of 6 years demand that school personnel consider carefully the resources available to families when establishing lines of communication with them. The earlier ages at which children are entering structured learning environments is related to demographic characteristics of American families. According to Rogoff (1991), the proportion of children younger than age 6 whose mothers are in the labor force has increased dramatically, from 29% in 1970 to 61% in 1988. Furthermore, statistics from the National Center for Children in Poverty (1990) reveal that children below the age of 6 years are more likely than any other age group to be poor, that minority children under 6 are more likely to be poor than white children under 6 and that children under 6 living with a single mother are more likely to be poor than children under 6 who are living in two-parent families (pp. 17–20). Moreover, the most alarming increases in the

prevalence of child maltreatment are occurring among the preschool population (American Humane Association, 1987). Specifically, children below age 6 represent about 43% of all abused and neglected children (Vadasy, 1989); and as younger children become more visible to school personnel, the incidence of reported maltreatment among preschool-age children is even likely to increase. Furthermore, because poor children are overrepresented in the foster care system and the overall number of foster care children is increasing (National Center for Children in Poverty, 1990), an increasing number of parents with whom school personnel interact will be foster parents. Because children in poverty are more at risk for health problems, developmental retardation, and developmental delays, they will comprise many of the referrals at the preschool level for psychological and speech/language services within public school systems. Partnerships with the parents of many of these children will require sensitivity to the pressures of single parenthood, combined with demographic variables, such as minority and socioeconomic status.

Concomitant trends reflect increasing ethnic diversity of the mainstream American population (Children's Defense Fund, 1989). In response to prevalence figures regarding this diversity, scholars and human service providers are calling for enhanced sensitivity to cultural factors when interacting with families of differing ethnic backgrounds (Harrison, Serafica, & McAdoo, 1984; Webb-Watson, 1989). Carter and McGoldrick (1989) advance the notion that cultural factors influence family life cycles; Hines (1989) emphasizes the need for professionals to interpret families' responses to intervention as a function of cultural factors; Hanson, Lynch, and Wayman (1990) suggest that the ethnic background of family members strongly influences their beliefs about childrearing, desire for change, and intervention practices; and Kaiser and Hemmeter (1989) emphasize the importance of designing intervention plans in a manner consistent with the cultural beliefs of families. Thus, when school personnel interact with parents of preschool-age children, we must bear in mind the impact of cultural variation on a host of behavioral variables, including childrearing practices and reactions to recommendations regarding their children.

Schorr (1989) synthesizes the impact of demographics on home-school relationships in the following way:

> Urbanization and increased mobility, greater family stress, and the sapping of family authority by television, have all widened the distance between home and school. That distance is of course greater still for children whose class, race, education, and family income differ most from those of the school staff. When the social network and style of the school are too dissonant from home and neighborhood, and the parents' alienation from the school is communicated to the children, the perception that school is the enemy can effectively destroy the chances that a child will learn. (p. 228)

Historically, low income and minority parents have been the hardest to reach by school systems. In response to the call for partnerships with parents, we have an even greater challenge than in the past. Some may say the situation is hopeless because these parents frequently do not show up for conferences and lack concern for their children. Schorr (1989) suggests an alternative perspective that challenges us to think differently:

> Poor and minority parents often have an especially high—*even passionate* regard for education, and view it as the most promising means to improve their children's futures. Parents may buy books and encyclopedias and now computers that they cannot afford, in the hope of supporting their children's education. But parents often need help in translating their yearning for their children's educational achievement into useful action. (p. 228)

Garbarino (1989) asserts that all children are *teachable* when teachers and other school personnel possess a desire to explore and discover teaching strategies that work and to discard those that do not work. We extend this notion to apply to parents of young children, by stating that all parents are *reachable* when school personnel are flexible and when they persist at finding communication strategies that work with particular parents. The behaviors exhibited by family members, which on the surface appear to be problematic, may be recast into a strengths-oriented form of communication. Thus, instead of expecting problems, a strengths orientation may be exactly what parents need in order to be reached by school personnel. In the words of Weissbourd (1991), instead of thinking "What is your problem?" we need to be thinking "What do you have going for you?" (p. 16).

We wish to advance the notion that failure to consider cultural factors is tantamount to ignoring the very essence of a family's worldview and their rules for understanding their experiences. Rather than explain cultural variation in terms of deviant, pathological, and nonnormative behaviors, much of the current literature argues cogently for recognition and appreciation of cultural difference as differences in individuals' subjective experiences (Nobles, 1978; Webb-Watson, 1989; Jipson, 1991). The operative issue here is that school systems begin to recognize, appreciate, and respect differences in subjective experience when parents first bring their children to school.

This process is likely to occur within a context where conflicting points of view already exist regarding the appropriateness of public school as a delivery system for services to "at-risk" and handicapped preschool-age children (Kagan, Powell, Weissbourd, & Zigler, 1987). On the one hand, the public school is viewed as available, safe, convenient, stable, and affordable. On the other hand, schools are viewed by some professionals as resistant to the modification of traditional elementary oriented programs to create developmentally sound programs for preschoolers (Duff, 1990). The beginning of developmentally sound programs in public schools is the recognition by all school personnel that the transition into public school is a major event for a family. This is the case whether a child is 6 years of age and enrolling in first grade or 4 years of age and enrolling in a public-school-sponsored preschool program. During this transition, parents are likely (a) to examine all aspects of the school in an effort to ensure that their child's needs will be met and (b) to feel anxiety over the eventual evaluation of their child's performance (and the concomitant evaluation of themselves as parents). As stated by Schorr (1989):

> Teachers often reach and display lasting judgments as early as the first few days of school. The first-grader who is called upon to count, recognize letters, shapes, or colors, or simply to sit still or not grab, and who is unable or unwilling to respond as expected—that child is in trouble. (p. 222)

Parents who have older children are not likely to be experiencing the public school for the first time when they enroll their preschooler; nevertheless, because most parents want the best for each of their children, it is reasonable to assume that they feel vulnerable, anxious, and hopeful that the educational experience will be a good one each time they enroll a child in school. Thus, the early nature of relationships between school and parent, school and child, and parent and child makes it imperative that these relationships be the best they can be.

Despite the philosophical debate regarding public-school sponsorship of preschool initiatives, The Preschool Program of Public Law 99-457 (The Education of the Handicapped Amendments of 1986) reflects the reality that public-school-sponsored preschool programs will not only be increasing in number but also extending to the 3-year-old population. Thus, the challenges facing public schools to implement sound programs for normally developing, "at-risk" and disabled preschoolers are very real.

The parent involvement provisions within the Preschool Program of the law reflect (a) more financial coverage of costs incurred in implementing parent involvement programs and (b) flexible programming to promote combinations of home,

school, center, and half-day/full day options. The spirit of the law was driven by the importance of the family to young children's development and is consistent with the notion of "parental partnership" (House Report 99–860, 1986); however, the letter of the law is a downward extension of the "parent involvement" provisions of Public Law 94–142 (U.S. Department of Education, 1986). Within the Preschool Program (Part B), for example, the language still speaks of Individualized Educational Plans (IEPs), in contrast to the Individualized Family Service Plans (IFSPs) of the Early Intervention Program for Handicapped Infants and Toddlers (Part H). It is important that readers recognize, however, that the spirit of both programs within the law was to reflect respect of the family. In this regard, Silverstein (1989) has stated "There is nothing more central to this legislation than respect for the family. . . . Congress was trying to say 'Do not have professionals come into a family situation and assume that the mom and dad don't know anything'" (pp. A-3 and A-4). Because the language of the Early Intervention Program (Part H) is more reflective of innovative thinking and more explicit regarding family strengths and needs, suggestions have arisen that educational systems turn to the spirit of family support within Part H when conceptualizing and implementing preschool programs.

It is not surprising that criticisms have arisen as to whether the law provides appropriate guidance for the creation of programs that are well matched to the needs of preschool-age children and their families. The essence of the criticism is that the developmental needs of children and parents, when children are between 3 and 5 years of age, were virtually overlooked and that Part B is too much of a downward extension of Public Law 94–142. To illustrate this point, a recent issue of the newsletter of CEC's Division for Early Childhood (Staff, 1991) contains the following call to professionals:

> It is time to accept the fact that Part B

was not written with 3–5-year-old children in mind, and now with the expansion of Part B to age three, to make the modifications necessary to ensure appropriate services for these very young children. (p. 2)

The prevailing controversy, stirred by hues and cries from professional organizations, scholars, and practitioners in the fields of education and psychology, consists of one essential message—that simple implementation of parent involvement at the preschool level in the form it has taken for school-age children would be a travesty. To implement developmentally sound preschool programs we must do much more than provide written notice to parents about the time and location of IEP meetings. To respect both the spirit and the letter of new legislation, Sarason (1987) reminds us to avoid mistakes made in the past:

> I have to ask how programming for four-year-olds fits in to an overarching vision of *family living*. Clearly, the size, structure, and stability of families have changed (and continue to change) rather dramatically. . . . Frankly, I bristle when I hear people uttering the pious generalization that families should be involved in these programs, because in my experience those transactional relationships are superficial and ritualistic in the extreme. I am reminded here of Public Law 94-142 which mandated a parental role in the education of a handicapped child. Practice has made a mockery of that mandate. (pp. 125–126)

We believe these fervent statements must be taken seriously by school systems, and we include them here to stimulate readers to assess their own beliefs regarding (a) how the parent involvement mandate of Public Law 94-142 has been implemented in their own school systems, (b) why it has been implemented in such a manner, and (c) how changes and/or improvements can be made in the implementation of Public Law 99-457.

School psychologists and other school personnel need to consider sources of appropriate information to guide the creation of partnerships with parents of young children. In this respect, Sarason (1987) has lamented the liabilities created when educational personnel do not have cohesive knowledge and tested principles to rely on when implementing new educational policy. He terms this "the engineering fallacy" (p. 125) because of the sharp contrast with engineers who, when given a task (e.g., building a new bridge), know the specific facts and principles that are requisite to accomplishing the task. The lack of basic knowledge or tested principles related to public-school-sponsored partnerships with parents of young children (a) corroborates the need for ongoing self-assessment of attitudes, values, and beliefs about partnerships as innovation rather than tradition and (b) leads us to propose that school psychology and related educational disciplines currently exist in "Wave 1" of an evolution that will consist of multiple waves. This conceptualization is similar to Bickel's (1990) description of the multiple waves of knowledge that guided the effective schools literature. It is also important to recognize that as school systems implement partnerships with parents of preschool children, the literature on "effective early childhood schooling," where effectiveness is viewed as a confluence of interrelated dimensions, such as knowledge, development, and culture (Jipson, 1991; Spodek, 1986), is burgeoning and is guided by a momentum all its own. We believe that this attitude of questioning traditional practice in early childhood education (e.g., Swadener & Kessler, 1991), combines with other knowledge bases (e.g., effective schools, effective communication, effective systems-level management) to serve as important departure points when accessed by school psychologists and other school personnel. This chapter represents a first attempt to derive relevant information from other knowledge bases in order to establish a conceptual framework within which to think about partnerships with parents of young children. The chapter is designed to be a stimulus for future research and discourse that move professional understanding of partnerships forward toward excellence.

THE NEED FOR SYSTEM-LEVEL
INNOVATION

Effective partnerships with parents of young children require a desire for innovation and departure from tradition at all levels of a school system. As stated by Sarason (1987):

> Creating programs for four-year-olds confronts educators with far more than theories of development and the organization of a curriculum. That task confronts them with all that is known about the cultures of the school and teacher training programs, and the changes in them the new programs may require. It forces them to pay attention to the organizational climate or ambience of the program setting—leadership, decision making, planning, problem solving, inservice education—especially if the program is embedded in a larger, bureaucratic system. . . . If the conditions whereby a staff learns, changes, and grows do not exist for them, can they create and sustain those conditions for the children? (p. 123)

Teachers, principals, superintendents, and support services personnel all need to be acting in concert, *guided* by effective decision making, problem solving, and ongoing training; and *rewarded* by a meaningful incentive system. With respect to innovation in management, Peters (1987) describes the need to communicate a "revolution in management" at multiple levels of a system (p. xi). This perspective warrants the serious attention of school systems when designing and implementing early childhood programs and partnerships with parents. Peters delineates the requisites of innovation diffusion as: (a) *achieving flexibility by empowering people* (e.g., using self-managing teams, providing incentives, simplifying structures/eliminating bureaucratic rules, spending time recruiting, training, and retraining); (b) *creating a corporate capacity for innovation* (e.g., modeling innovation, supporting innovative failures, supporting committed employees, encouraging pilot projects); (c) *learning to love change* (e.g., developing an inspiring vision, managing by example, creating symbols that reflect priori-

ties, evaluating employees on their love of change); and (d) *turning the system upside down to keep up with a turbulent world* (e.g., measuring what is *important* rather than what is *efficient*, decentralizing information, authority, and strategic planning; setting conservative goals). In short, he asserts that change in the metabolism of organizations is sometimes necessary for innovation to become possible.

Emphasizing the importance of the school building principal as the manager and instructional leader of a school, Duff (1990) recently raised the question whether principals are ready for early childhood programs in their schools. Related to this question is a recent endorsement for a developmental approach to early childhood programs from the National Association of Elementary School Principals. This group recently issued a guide entitled "Early Childhood Education and the Elementary School Principal: Standards for Quality Programs for Young Children," setting forth developmentally appropriate standards for early childhood programs. Included in the standards is to understand, value, and be comfortable working closely with parents, and encourage and support teachers in their work with families (Schweinhart, 1988). We view this endorsement as a major step forward in helping to set the overall managerial and professional tone of any given school toward quality early childhood programs. As a method for operationalizing standards such as these, Farkas (1981) provides self-assessment forms for principals to complete regarding their specific attitudes and beliefs toward partnerships with parents. Given the information presented above, we encourage readers to examine their school systems with an eye toward identifying areas where change is both necessary and possible in order to create effective early childhood programs and parent partnerships.

A PARADIGM OF EARLY
PARTNERSHIPS

Because of the early nature of the relationship between a school system and parents who are launching their preschool-age child into the school arena, we believe a special paradigm is necessary to illustrate the essential processes that should occur between family and school. We believe the processes of *nurturance and receptivity to feedback* are key to effective partnerships at the preschool level. Stated more specifically, the paradigm suggests that nurturance and feedback characterize three relationships: (a) the relationship between the parent(s) and young child, (b) the relationship between the school and the young child, and (c) the relationship between the school and the parents of the young child. Figure 1 illustrates these multiple, bidirectional relationships in more graphic

fashion, with the preschool-age child at the center as the reason the parent and school are communicating.

From the school to parents, nurturance should be expressed through such means as (a) constructive feedback, (b) emotional support, (c) appreciation for the stresses of parenting a young child, (d) helping parents understand their complex emotions when their child exhibits learning difficulties or disabilities, (e) being careful not to use language that quickly categorizes the child and the family, and (f) providing numerous opportunities to communicate about their child. From parents and school personnel to young children, nurturance should be

Figure 1
A paradigm of nurturance and feedback to guide the development of partnerships with parents of preschool-age children.

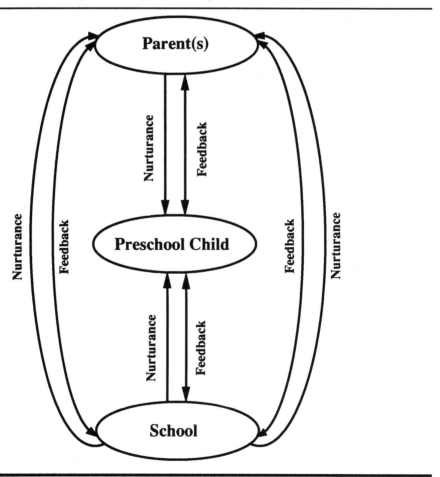

expressed through such means as providing opportunities for children to act responsibly, setting developmentally appropriate goals, creating meaningful reward systems, and fostering enthusiasm for learning and the development of social relationships. Through these efforts, we express concern for such concepts as self-esteem and well-being, for children and their parents. According to Beane (1991), "the idea of enhancing self-esteem in schools becomes part of the larger effort to create a more caring, just, and humane world" (p. 158).

Readers who have experience working with young children know that feedback from these children is given naturally to their parents and teachers through a multitude of verbal and nonverbal behaviors, manifested in their play, in their approach to and performance of tasks, and in their relationships with other children and adults. Indeed, this feedback is an ongoing stream of behavioral cues in need of recognition and appreciation by parents and professionals. Feedback provided from parents to the school should also be characterized as an ongoing stream of information, taking place in a context where discussion about young children, as well as endorsements and criticisms of school procedures are both expected and lively. We believe that the adoption of this posture by both parents and schools would help to alleviate the tendency to be defensive and protective of one's own point of view. We do not intend to imply that the principles of nurturance and feedback mean that school personnel provide unconditional positive regard for all behaviors of parents, or unconditional acceptance of the content of feedback. Rather, the paradigm suggests that *school personnel and parents interact within a context where both disagreement and agreement are possible and expected.* Thus, in the face of differences in points of view, school personnel attempt to strengthen and nurture relationships with parents, perceiving them as part of the solution rather than as part of the problem (Szanton, 1991). In doing so, school personnel interact with parents in

the spirit of family support (Kagan et al., 1987) and represent a system that nurtures the family system (Unger & Powell, 1991). Perhaps the best endorsement of what we are presenting through our model comes from Weissbourd's (1991) description of family resource programs:

> Trusting relationships are the essence of a family resource program. Just as we know relationships of trust lead to a child's developing a good sense of self, so it is through such relationships that families' strengths are enhanced. As professionals, we no longer see ourselves as "child savers" . . . saving the child from the parent, but rather as joining with them on behalf of their children. (p. 15)

FEATURES OF EFFECTIVE PARTNERSHIP

The conceptual paradigm of nurturance and feedback presented above provides a general heuristic within which to think about partnerships with parents of preschool children. Nevertheless, the need exists for complementary information regarding specific features of effective partnerships at the preschool level. Thus, the discussion that follows delineates salient features of effective partnerships within the context of process, content, and outcome issues.

Process Issues

Features related to the *process* of partnerships are presented below within a more specific context of relationship and communication issues, and the symbolic and functional design of a school environment to promote effective partnerships.

Partnerships as relationships. School personnel must remember that partnerships are, first and foremost, *relationships.* Although this appears on the surface to be a truism, a relational context is often ignored when scholars and researchers discuss ideas related to partnerships. The essential message we wish to convey is that a given partnership is only as good as the relationship between the individuals who are involved with each other (Weissbourd, 1991). Thus, we present in Table 1 our attempt to delineate features of effective relationships. Implied in this listing is the notion that such features intentionally and unintentionally influence the quality of interactions school personnel have with parents. We encourage readers to peruse Table 1, bearing in mind past experiences with parents of children referred for services and how the features listed in the table help to illuminate what was transpiring in those situations. Of most importance is that school personnel (a) do not give up on parents when they begin to exhibit negative behavioral and emotional reactions that are natural to any relationship, (b) monitor our own responses to events within the relationship, (c) avoid assuming a "we-they" attitude, and (d) evaluate how well we are creating opportunities for the relationship to flourish.

Partnerships as communication. In addition to conceptualizing partnerships within the framework of effective relationships, the literature on interpersonal communication has much to offer school personnel who communicate with parents of preschool-age children. According to Hamlin (1988), there is a natural set of responses created by simply being in an audience and listening to a speaker, that affect audience members, making their basic mental set quite predictable. Knowing what these givens are helps us understand what we have to do to prepare to communicate with an audience. Potential reactions shared by audience members include feelings of passivity, anonymity, and possible resistance.

Observational studies of parental behavior during conferences (e.g., Goldstein, Strickland, Turnbull, & Curry, 1980) and interviews with parents regarding their responses to school personnel (e.g., McKinney & Hocutt, 1982; Turnbull & Turnbull, 1986) parallel the above listing of responses from audience members. That is, parents historically have tended to verbalize less than professionals and assume a rather passive role vis-à-vis the professional. With parents of young children, we must avoid a reoccur-

TABLE 1
Partnerships as Effective Relationships

Individuals in effective relationships:
- often value shared power.
- sometimes need distance from each other.
- express differences of opinion and sometimes argue.
- feel vulnerable with each other.
- take risks when communicating with each other.
- often desire loyalty from each other.
- share a respect for the confidentiality of information.
- appreciate reciprocity, mutual sharing.
- share knowledge of multiple roles played by each other in other aspects of one's life.
- share a variety of activities and interests.
- share an appreciation for change and growth.
- share a desire to work toward a common goal, but deviate from that goal when other objectives become necessary to attain.
- allow each other freedom of choice.
- bring experiences with past relationships into current relationships, for better or for worse.
- try to be aware of the influence of past experiences on current relationships.
- share a normalizing perspective on problems.
- appreciate differences in style, pace, needs, and wants.
- appreciate informal communication, fun, recreation, humor.
- communicate in a context where creative criticism as well as positive feedback is expected.
- are not clairvoyant, but are empathetic and observant.
- actively seek opportunities to communicate, even when conditions are not optimal.
- recognize that it is sometimes difficult to ask for assistance or advice.

rence of this pattern; to do so, additional suggestions from the interpersonal communication literature warrant our attention. Hamlin (1988) notes that when audience members are given ways to become involved rather than remain passive, they feel an enhanced sense of control over what happens to them. The same principle applies to the responses felt by parents who enter an interaction with school personnel. Thus, school personnel are wise to consider ways in which the communication process can be structured to elicit responses from parents, to involve them actively in interactions, and to enhance their sense of control over what happens to them and their children. Of interest in this endeavor are inventories of attitudes and preferences for involvement (to be completed by parents, teachers, support service personnel, and administrators), which can be found in Turnbull and Turnbull (1986) and Farkas (1981).

To plan for specific interactions, Hamlin (1988) also suggests the use of a "Fore-Thought Chart" (p. 58), completed by both parties to an interaction, to anticipate each other's goals, needs, and expectations. The chart, which could be useful for school personnel and parents presents a simple structure for people to use to anticipate and make explicit some of the cognitive and emotional processes likely to influence an interaction. Although emphasizing the usefulness of entering interactions with semistructured responses to questions about goals, needs, and expectations, Hamlin (1988) also asserts the need to be flexible when the interaction demands a departure from planned goals. A sample chart is presented below:

School Psychologist	Parent
Goals	*Goals*
Needs	*Needs*
Expectations	*Expectations*

A synthesis of communication principles thus far suggests that school personnel plan and structure interactions so as to involve parents actively and to anticipate respective goals, needs, and expectations. Although this is true, an important caveat is in order. A trend emerging from recent research regarding parental preferences for involvement in early childhood programs (e.g., Able-Boone, Sandall, Loughry, & Frederick, 1990; Summers et al., 1990) strongly indicates that parents prefer informal methods of communication over formal methods. Powell and Eisenstadt (1988) coined the term "kitchen talk" (cited in Powell, 1989, p. 94) to describe the atmosphere in which such informal communication should take place. Thus, we caution school psychologists not to overstructure or overformalize interactions with parents. Weissbourd (1991) describes it this way:

> Family resource and support staff members strike a rare balance with parents by being informal and collegial while maintaining the professional advisory role. This style, combined with the flexibility and accessibility of the programs, creates an atmosphere where parents have time to develop trust and feel safe before risking too much personal information about themselves. As a result, they feel more in control and can take in information when they are able and ready, without feeling pressured to change. . . . This creates a contrast to their experiences in more traditional settings where professionals must maintain formalities, routines, and stricter agendas, where more time is spent in filling out forms than in building relationships. (pp. 15–16)

We believe that informal and spontaneous communication creates an important context within which more formal communication can effectively take place. School systems are wise to consider (a) mechanisms from family resource and support programs that can be adapted to promote informal and natural communication with parents (Kagan et al., 1987), (b) various formats for doing so (e.g., small support groups, recreational activities), and (c) strategies for increasing sensitivity to cultural variation through informal communication techniques. Careful consideration of informal communication strategies is especially relevant to minority families and families who may be in a position to experience negative consequences from asking for assistance or "help" from school personnel. (See Dunst, Trivette, and Deal, 1988, for a complete discussion of the negative consequences of help seeking.)

Partnerships as symbolism and functionalism. A third process issue related to partnerships involves the operationalization of relationship and communication skills through (a) the design and structure of classroom, school, and district buildings to reflect a priority on parents and (b) functional procedures for matching various mechanisms of parental involvement with resources available to the school and family.

In describing excellence in management, Peters (1987) emphasizes the role played by symbolism in the management environment. Simply put, there are symbolic and very important ways managers communicate their priorities and values. Applying this notion to partnerships with parents of young children, we strongly encourage school systems to consider ways in which the design, structure, and decoration of classrooms, hallways, and reception areas in various buildings currently do or do not reflect a value placed on young children and their parents. Are the classrooms designed in accordance with developmentally appropriate practice (e.g., play, social interaction, a variety of group seating arrangements)? Do pictures on the wall indicate to parents that they are valued as partners in the education of young children? Are there specific arrival and departure zones in the classroom and procedures to encourage communication between school staff and parents on a daily basis? Are there specific ways in which the school district as a whole could reflect a stronger emphasis on valuing parents?

Complementing a consideration of the symbolic messages school systems send to parents should be an emphasis on functional communication. Although a multitude of mechanisms exists for school systems to develop communication with parents (Paget, 1992), the real challenges exist when turning these mechanisms into functional action plans.

To become workable action plans, the various mechanisms must be matched to specific resources available to schools and families.

One of the most frequently used mechanisms for communication between school and home for school-age children has consisted of written notes in the child's book bag. Jennings (1990) notes that a book bag is much like a "black hole" because of the difficulty ensuring that the communication will reach home, and if it does, that it will rise to the top of the book bag. Especially with preschoolers, we suggest that school personnel avoid overdependence on the book bag as a communication device with parents and consider the multitude of other mechanisms, such as home visits, planned and unplanned conferences, telephone calls, PTA-organized group activities, membership on school advisory councils and in support groups, mechanisms for volunteering in classrooms, and creating resource centers containing information of interest to parents. Involving the parents of young children in shared assessment procedures and as members of multidisciplinary teams is another important mechanism that deserves serious consideration by school psychologists. For detailed information regarding pragmatic considerations when implementing this particular option for parents, the reader is encouraged to read Hicks, Bloch, and Friedman (1990), Linder (1990), and Roberts, Wasik, Casto, and Ramey (1991).

For any of these mechanisms to be functional, they must be matched to the resources available both to the school and to the family. Such resources include money, time, energy, space, health, transportation, child care, literacy, telephone, incentives for involvement, social support networks, and scheduling flexibility. Given that partnerships are likely to be developed within a context of limited resources, we suggest a role for school psychologists as "resource mobilizers" or "resource coordinators" between families and schools. It does not make sense to us, for example, for school systems to offer school-based conferences as the sole mechanism for parent communication if many of the families need child care during or transportation to the conference. In such a situation, as "resource mobilizer," a school psychologist could play a valuable role in assisting the school and family in the exploration of available resources for child care and transportation. In this fashion, it is possible to interpret limitations on resources in a manner that energizes rather than enervates, and to overcome vaguely articulated reasons why partnerships are not possible. We believe this notion is consistent with the parable quoted in the beginning of this chapter about the need to find our own knot-untying rules. We also suggest that effective partnerships do not necessarily require inordinate amounts of time, space, money, or energy when a given school system, as a whole, is committed to the ideals of partnership—as a set of ongoing processes composed of relationship building, exploration of effective communication skills, functional problem solving, and action.

Content Issues at the Preschool Level

A discussion of content issues is important here because what we discuss with parents of preschool-age children should be different from what is discussed with parents of school-age children. First and foremost, the content of what we communicate needs to be guided by applied developmental theory (Bredekamp, 1987; Katz, 1987), emphasizing the importance of nurturance, self-efficacy, effectance motivation, enthusiasm for learning, exploration, play, peer interaction, friendship formation, and freedom to experiment with language and communication. These principles should guide the education of young children and partnerships with their parents. Kagan (1989) puts it this way:

> No longer seen solely from a cognitive perspective, children's learning is now viewed by many as the synthesis of social, emotional, health, and cognitive factors. According to this new understanding, children influence—and are influenced by—a social network including family, school, and community. (p. 32)

Thus, principles of social-emotional health should guide the education of young children and partnerships with their parents. We recognize a striking similarity between applied developmental principles and certain Native American Indian values regarding childrearing. Brendtro, Brokenleg, and Van Bockern (1990) describe the values of *mastery, generosity, independence,* and *belonging* as the "seeds of encouragement" in individuals. Whereas healthy children reflect a balance of these qualities, their absence or distortion results in nonexistent or destructive relationships and the "seeds of discouragement." Indisputably, young children and their parents need to feel capable of mastering challenges, giving to others, achieving a sense of independence, and being an important part of groups. Thus, these are the values that need to be prioritized in early childhood programs *for the children themselves and nurtured in our partnerships with their parents.* An important implication of this is that there is much more to our relationships with parents of preschool-age children than providing them with written assignments to complete with their children. We label these relationships "no homework" partnerships to dissuade professionals from a sole emphasis on cognitive skills (e.g., number and letter recognition) as the basis of parent-child interactions. In this vein, we encourage readers to consider ways to encourage parents to prioritize activities that stimulate nurturance, play, enthusiasm for learning, and self-efficacy in their young children *and to model these values in our interactions with parents and children.*

Outcome Issues at the Preschool Level

Evaluating the effectiveness of partnerships is a complex process. The paradigm of nurturance and feedback presented earlier depicts multiple relationships (i.e., between parent and school, parent and child, child and school). If one takes seriously the notion that multiple relationships are involved in the process of partnership, then the same multiplicity must be captured through evaluation efforts. Lessons from Head Start are particularly relevant in discussions of outcome because the inadequacy of using one traditional measure of effectiveness (e.g., IQ) was clearly revealed. The unintended side effects of Head Start efforts (e.g., increased motivation from parents to be involved with their children's education) revealed that unplanned effects may reveal program efficacy more realistically than planned effects (Robinson & Choper, 1979). Although evaluation efforts need to be focused enough to establish clearly illuminated goals and specific objectives tied to activities and measurement devices (Alessi, 1989), they also need to be broad enough to capture unintended program effects. Thus, partnerships reflect a process of exploration, discovery, and creativity in determining what works for certain people under specific circumstances and what changes are necessary over time. The wisdom of Schorr (1989) again is relevant:

> Many of the most effective interventions with high-risk families are inherently unstandardized and idiosyncratic. Many agencies have found a mix of services, adaptable to different sites and responsive to particular family needs, to be an essential component of effective intervention. When a home visitor, for example, responds flexibly to a family's unique problems, the unique outcome may be just what the family needs but what the evaluator dreads. (p. 268)

Jacobs (1988) has developed a detailed plan for program evaluation which can be applied to the evaluation of partnerships and the multiple relationships therein. Her plan is characterized by multiple tiers that include (a) *needs assessment,* or demonstrating a need for the program in the community and the gathering of baseline data; (b) *accountability,* to account for who is using the program and at what cost; and (c) *clarification,* to give ongoing feedback to the staff and participants to make continuous improvements. Applied to our model of nurturance and feedback, the processes of assessing needs, measuring accountability, and clarifying when and in what

way changes are necessary, are integral to the formation and maintenance of multiple relationships among children, parents, and school systems.

Scholars in the field of program evaluation encourage the use of qualitative and quantitative data. Quantitative information helps to establish how a program (the independent variable) produces changes in intervening events, which in turn influence the behavior of program participants (dependent variable) while controlling for competing explanations for observed effects (Campbell & Stanley, 1966). Qualitative data reveal much more about the processes involved with relationships. Regarding the need for both types of information, Schorr (1989) states:

> Are program objectives like the acquisition of trust or the development of warm personal relationships, found to be essential attributes of virtually all programs serving high-risk families, to be sacrificed because they are so much harder to reduce to quantifiable terms than is performance on multiple-choice or IQ tests? For many services, how they are delivered is as important as that they are delivered. (p. 269)

Schorr (1989) also states that the rush to quantitative judgment can sometimes interfere with progress in the development of complex programs. To dissuade professionals from the practice of prematurely evaluating programs, she cites Donald Campbell's caution to "Evaluate no program until it is proud" (p. 269) and encourages program personnel to decide for themselves when something special is happening that works and when they want other people to know about and borrow it. Thus, qualitative information, carefully discovered, recorded, and consolidated from our experiences with parents will assist in the development of a cohesive knowledge base regarding what works, with particular parents, in particular circumstances.

We suggest that school psychologists explore the use of focus groups as a qualitative research and evaluation strategy. The focus group is a research or evaluation technique that relies on the interaction of a group around a topic supplied by the researchers or evaluators. Thus, it is useful for capturing the subjective experiences of individuals in relationships. "The hallmark of the focus group is the explicit use of the group interaction to produce data and insights that would be less accessible without the interaction found in the group" (Morgan, 1988, p. 12). Summers et al. (1990) demonstrated the effective use of focus groups as a research tool to capture the preferences of practitioners and parents regarding family-centered early intervention services. Such groups have much potential for gathering information from parents, educators, special educators, social workers, administrators, and school psychologists regarding the conceptualization, implementation, and ultimate value of partnerships at the preschool level. Questions designed to elicit information regarding such domains as parental satisfaction with services, specific areas of learning about child development and parenting, parental and child self-efficacy, as well as professionals' concerns and ideas for improvement would likely yield rich information for future program development efforts. For more information regarding the planning and implementation of focus groups as a qualitative research and program evaluation strategy, the reader is encouraged to read Morgan (1988).

Dunst (1991) recently synthesized what is necessary for future program evaluation efforts with family-based programs. He states that the direction of evaluation efforts should be guided by (a) the need for longitudinal perspectives to establish patterns and changes in different aspects of child, parent, and family functioning; (b) the need to use more positive behavior indicators (e.g., well-being) as outcome measures; (c) the need to examine the interactions between program variables and family variables, and how interactions influence outcomes; (d) the need to use alternative methodologies; and (e) the need for more case study research that illuminates the processes of program implementation. We would add to this list that the evaluation of relationships is a key issue for the present and the future, thus necessitating innovative conceptualization of strategies for capturing relational processes.

ILLUSTRATIVE PROGRAMS

In this section of the chapter, illustrative programs serving parents are presented. We do this to offer readers a point of departure for their own efforts when developing partnerships with the parents of young children. The programs listed were selected according to their apparent adherence to the principles of (a) nurturance and bidirectional feedback advanced as essential in this chapter, (b) respect for ethnic and socioeconomic diversity, (c) a functional match between program offerings and resources available to families, and (d) a priority placed on relationships between parents, children, and professionals. Not all the programs listed serve preschool-age children as their primary population, although exemplary aspects of all the programs should be considered when conceptualizing partnerships with parents of young children. Space limitations preclude the listing of all relevant programs in existence at the present time; of special significance, nevertheless, are programs reflecting sensitivity to the particular problem of illiteracy. For information on specific programs addressing this problem, the reader is referred to Edwards (1990), Schmidt (1990), and Fox (1990).

Schorr (1989) describes her visit to the New Haven School Development Program, which is listed in Table 2. Portions of her description bear repeating here because of their consistency with the basic messages of this chapter:

> Dr. Comer wanted to make sure I understood that the essence of his intervention is a process, not a package of materials, instructional methods, or techniques. "It is the creation of a sense of community and direction for parents, school staff, and students alike." . . . learning is initially a process of identification with emotionally important people—parents and teachers—that occurs in a supportive

TABLE 2
Programs Illustrating Parent Involvement

Program Name	Type Intervention	Target Pop	Timing of Intervention	Goal of Intervention	Focus of Intervention	Format of Intervention	Evaluation
Children's Playroom, Inc. Harrisburg, PA*	Education, support, and retraining for Parents & Children 0–6	All parents w/children under the age of 6	Ongoing Program. Parents usually attend one session a week	Prevent further child abuse & develop confidence and competence of parents	Identify families at risk for abuse or neglect; retrain parents identified as abusers; provide information about parenting & child development; provide resources	Supervised play; discussion, lending library, GED assistance	Parents submit an anonymous evaluation, which is reviewed by the board of directors, outside evaluation triannually. Recidivism referral currently ongoing
Building Parent to School Partnerships LaGrange, IL*	Training parents of handicapped children to interact effectively with professionals; and training parents to implement home-based programs	Parents of handicapped school children	Ten 2½ hr training sessions	1) Help schools & parents collaboratively plan, implement, and evaluate programs; 2) Train parents to become effective participants in their children's education 3) Train parents to implement programs at home, independent and with school personnel	Training of families with handicapped children	1) Training sessions 2) Trust-building problem-solving techniques; parents training parents	An evaluation has been completed showing that target skills have been successfully taught
MELD (Minnesota Early Learning Design) Minneapolis, MN*	Informal discussion, Formal discussion	Expectant parents & parents of 0–1½	Pregnancy to when child reaches 1½	Provide information and support to new parents in small long-term support groups	That there is no one right way to parent, and the peer self-help approach	Meetings every two weeks for 2 years. Included is informal and formal discussion	Knowledge increased in 24 or 36 areas of parenting. Parents indicated MELD was an important source of support. Outside evaluation is up—Teen pregnancy is down

TABLE 2 (continued)

Program Name	Type Intervention	Target Pop	Timing of Intervention	Goal of Intervention	Focus of Intervention	Format of Intervention	Evaluation
Parent-Child Centers (Dunn, 1988)**	Education & Support	Families needing services for children prebirth through 18; however, the focus is on prebirth through 3	Prebirth through 18	Coordinate services for all parents, including education, information and support	Local needs and concerns reflected in the community	Play groups, parent groups, home visits, family mediation, peer support groups	Not specified
New Futures School Albuquerque, NM*	Education, Counseling, Child Care	Teenage mothers community outreach/educ. on teen parenting	Pregnancy-mothers leave at the end of the semester they give birth	Assist teenage moms in experiencing a positive, enriching pregnancy through increasing ability, self-esteem, continuation in school, and health	Providing a school setting in which mothers can increase their parenting skills and continue high school education	School setting	Internal evaluations to obtain level of client satisfaction. Collection of information about health of mother and baby and continuation in school. External evaluation — future pregnancy rate, school attendance
The Family Center Clayton, MS*	Information & support, education counseling, newsletter and referral services	All families with children 0–5	Children 0–5 classes offered during day, dinner & lunch hours, evenings and weekends	(1) Provide information, support, improve children's success in school (2)increase parent & community knowledge of child & family development	Knowledge, support and other indicated resources	Guided workshops, support groups, home visits, classes, health	Questionnaires, Discussion

TABLE 2 (continued)

Program Name	Type Intervention	Target Pop	Timing of Intervention	Goal of Intervention	Focus of Intervention	Format of Intervention	Evaluation
Children with Teachers at Home Campobello, SC*	Contact, resource knowledge, early education, workshops, lending library	All parents of preschoolers	Anytime children age 0–kindergarten	(1) Improve relationship between school & home by working with parents before child is in school. (2) Also increase school participation	Improving knowledge of parenting	Workshops	No. of school functions attended, amount of involvement with PTA/class aids. School retention of SPED placement
Family Matters Project Cornell University*	Parent/school Education/support	All age groups. Suitable for all educational levels and SES groups	Teacher inservice, parent training. Ongoing program.	Empower parents and build on existing parent strengths and outside resources	Role and importance of parents. Parent responsibility	Teacher and parent workshops. Additional readings	Available from project
The School Development Program Yale University(Comer, 1989)**	Parent/School involvement	Parents and teachers of K-6 graders	Beginning involvement for parents of kindergartners and continuing on governance board	(1) Reduce parent/teacher conflict (2) Increase parent participation in planning and curriculum of school	—Importance of home/school collaboration —Importance of parent role models team building	Parent/teacher/ adminstrator management team. —Parent training/ involvement program	—Student achievement and interest increased. —School/home became unified —Parent self-esteem increased —Parents' level of responsibility increased

TABLE 2 (continued)

Program Name	Type Intervention	Target Pop	Timing of Intervention	Goal of Intervention	Focus of Intervention	Format of Intervention	Evaluation
Family Enhancement Program*	Community-based, prevention oriented family support service	Families of mixed ethnic and racial groups. Approx. 50% were low SES	Not specified	(1) Encourage healthy family living; provide parent education and support;(2) promote proactive or preventive strategies	Forming supportive relationships and information exchange. Development of personal resources	Parent education, support "special group" education (i.e., teenage parents)	Each discussion and training workshop is evaluated after each session. Evaluations are assessed to make programs more responsive
Parent Services Project Fairfax, CA*	Social events, family classes, workshops and alternative forms of child care	Families utilizing state funded child care programs	Parents seen on a daily basis when they pick up or drop off their child for care. This makes a natural entry point for services to be implemented in the preschool years.	Raise parents' sense of importance; diminish feelings of isolation; increase parenting skills; assist parents in securing needed resources for themselves; add a quality of enjoyment in family events	Family fun, interaction, parenting classes, adult activities for parents to nurture themselves, and additional services	Planned activities, family events, classes and workshops; peer support groups, interest groups, community service referrals	Annual reports

TABLE 2 *(continued)*

Program Name	Type Intervention	Target Pop	Timing of Intervention	Goal of Intervention	Focus of Intervention	Format of Intervention	Evaluation
Early Childhood Family Education Program Minneapolis, MN*	Education, and discussion contacts	Families. All parents of children birth to kindergarten and expectant mothers are eligible	Regularly 2 hours per week	(1) Build and support the confidence and competence of parents in providing good parent/child interactions. (2) Build partnerships between home, school, and community	Helping parents feel more competent and comfortable in their parenting role	Classes, parent-child interaction time, children's activities	Process and baseline data collected
Variety Preschoolers' Workshop Syosset, NY Parent-Professional Preschool Performance Profile (The Five P's) (Hicks, Bloch, & Friedman, 1990)**	Multidomain assessment for young children	Children ages 2–6 with learning, language, and/or behavior problems	Before, during, and after effectiveness intervention	Planning and tracking intervention	Involving parents in assessment and intervention planning	Assessment	Replication and validation studies

* Additional information can be found in *Programs to Strengthen Families* (Family Resource Coalition, 1988) which is cited in the reference list.

** Additional information can be obtained from indicated source in the reference list.

climate. He likens the school's impact on child development to the family's. "They don't have their effect through the specific skills they transmit alone, but through their values, climate, quality of relationships. Especially in the early years, the content is almost, *almost* incidental. Children learn by internalizing the attitudes, values, and ways of meaningful others. And then, whatever content you expose children to, they learn it" (p. 234).

CONCLUSIONS AND FUTURE DIRECTIONS

This chapter has presented information relative to (a) the rationale for partnerships with parents of preschool-age children; (b) a paradigm of specific principles to guide the creation of partnerships; (c) features of effective partnerships with respect to process, content, and outcome; and (d) illustrative programs that adhere to the basic principles and features endorsed as important for preschool-age children. The chapter represents a strong endorsement of innovation as a precursor to the development of partnerships with parents of preschool-age children. To implement innovative policy effectively, we have strongly urged educational personnel to engage in a process whereby they evaluate their own beliefs, attitudes, and values regarding a variety of topics related to partnerships with parents of preschool-age children. These topics include public-school-sponsored early childhood programs; the extent to which parents and families should be involved in these programs; the form that parent involvement has taken under P.L. 94–142; experiences from past relationships that will influence future relationships; methods for improving communication regarding the value of parents, both to their children and to the school district; and innovative, functional procedures for matching mechanisms of involvement to specific available resources. We have proposed that the school psychologist play an integral role as "resource mobilizer" for the school and the home. We also emphasized that the conceptualization and implementation of

innovative procedures is an ongoing process, characterized by (a) serious consideration of how traditional practices may be maintaining certain inequities between professionals and parents, and (b) appreciation for the results of program evaluation efforts that provide ongoing feedback about what works and what does not.

The importance of spending what Peters (1987) states as "lavish time on recruiting, training, and retraining" (p. 157) cannot be overemphasized. Administrators, teachers, and support services personnel who have questioned their own beliefs about working with parents and the processes, content, and outcomes involved in partnerships are those professionals who are aware of the necessity to continually train, retrain; educate, and reeducate. These professionals will be seeking out resources, such as literature on innovation (Peters, 1987; von Oech, 1983) and partnerships in disciplines other than education (Dunst & Paget, 1990); and joining organizations in early childhood education/special education (National Association for the Education of Young Children and The Division of Early Childhood—Council for Exceptional Children) as arenas in which to nurture ongoing accumulation of knowledge and collegial relationships with other professionals. These professionals will be synchronized with the momentum toward reconceptualization and improvement of current practice occurring within the fields of early childhood education and early childhood special education (e.g., Swadener & Kessler, 1991). These professionals will possess a mindset of discovery, exploration, creativity, and trial and error; willing to be stymied for a while yet able to persist and find their own "knot-untying rules" for effectively representing public schools through relationships with parents of young children. In short, these are the professionals who realize that to innovate and reconceptualize is, "in pale and halting strokes, to fill in what is missing and what could be. To reconceptualize is to be angry and to dream" (Lubeck, 1991, p. 168).

REFERENCES

Able-Boone, H., Sandall, S. R., Loughry, A., & Frederick, L. L. (1990). An informed, family-centered approach to Public Law 99-457: Parental views. *Topics in Early Childhood Special Education, 10,* 100–111.

Alessi, G. (1989). Ethical issues facing school psychologists in family therapy: A commentary. *Professional School Psychology, 4,* 265–272.

American Humane Association. (1987). *Highlights of official child abuse and neglect reporting.* Denver: Author.

Beane, J. A. (1991). Enhancing children's self-esteem: Illusion and possibility. *Early Education and Development, 2,* 153–160.

Bickel, W. E. (1990). The effective schools literature: Implications for research and practice. In T. B. Gutkin & C. R. Reynolds (Eds.), *The handbook of school psychology* (2nd ed., pp. 847–867). New York: Wiley.

Bredekamp, S. (Ed.). (1987). *Developmentally appropriate practice for children birth to age eight.* Washington, DC: National Association for the Education of Young Children.

Brendtro, L. K., Brokenleg, M., & Van Bockern, S. (1990). *Reclaiming youth at risk: Our hope for the future.* Bloomington, IN: National Educational Service.

Bronfenbrenner, U. (1986). The ecology of the family as a context for human development: Research perspectives. *Developmental Psychology, 22,* 723–742.

Campbell, D. T., & Stanley, J. (1966). *Experimental and quasi-experimental designs for research.* Chicago: Rand McNally.

Carter, B., & McGoldrick, M. (Eds.). (1989). *The changing family life cycle: A framework for family therapy* (2nd ed.). Boston: Allyn & Bacon.

Children's Defense Fund. (1989). *Vision for America's future.* Washington, DC: Author.

Comer, J. P. (1989). Parent participation in schools: The School Development Program as a model. *Family Resource Coalition Report, 8*(2), 4–5.

Crutcher, D. M. (1991). Family support in the home: Home visiting and Public Law 99-457. *American Psychologist, 46,* 138–140.

Duff, R. E. (1990, Fall). Is the school principal ready for the very young? *The Palmetto Administrator,* pp. 9–11.

Dunn, A. (1988). Parent-child centers: Bringing families and communities together. *Family Resource Coalition Report, 7*(3), 8–9.

Dunst, C. J. (1991). Evaluating family resource programs. *Ten years: Family Resource Coalition Report,* pp. 15–16.

Dunst, C. J., & Paget, K. D. (1990). Parent-professional partnerships and family empowerment. In M. J. Fine (Ed.), *Collaboration with parents of exceptional children.* Brandon, VT: Clinical Psychology Publishing Company.

Dunst, C. J., Trivette, C., & Deal, A. (1988). *Enabling and empowering families.* Cambridge, MA: Brookline Books.

Edwards, P. A. (1990). Strategies and techniques for establishing home-school partnerships with minority parents. In A. Barona & E. Garcia (Eds.), *Children at risk: Poverty, minority status, and other issues in educational equity* (pp. 217–236). Washington, DC: National Association of School Psychologists.

Family Resource Coalition. (1988). *Programs to strengthen families* (rev. ed.). Chicago: Author.

Farkas, S. C. (1981). *Taking a family perspective.* Washington, DC: Family Impact Seminar and Institute for Educational Leadership, Inc.

Fox, B. J. (1990). Antecedents of illiteracy. *Social Policy Report.* Society for Research in Child Development, 4(4), Winter.

Garbarino, J. A. (Ed.). (1989). *What children can tell us.* San Francisco: Jossey Bass.

Goldstein, S., Strickland, B., Turnbull, A. P., & Curry, L. (1980). An observational analysis of the IEP conference. *Exceptional Children, 46,* 278–286.

Hamlin, S. (1988). *How to talk so people listen: The real key to job success.* New York: Harper & Row.

Hanson, M. J., Lynch, E. W., & Wayman, K. I. (1990). Honoring the cultural diversity of families when gathering data. *Topics in Early Childhood Special Education, 10,* 112–131.

Harrison, A., Serafica, F., & McAdoo, H. (1984). Ethnic families of color. In R. D. Parke, R. N. Emde, H. P. McAdoo, & G. P. Sackett (Eds.), *Review of child development research: Volume 7: The family* (2nd ed., pp. 329–371). Chicago: The University of Chicago Press.

Hicks, J. S., Bloch, J. S., & Friedman, J. L. (1990). *Validation studies of the Five P's.* Syosset, NY: Variety Pre-Schooler's Workshop.

Hines, P. M. (1989). The family life cycle of poor black families. In B. Carter & M. McGoldrick (Eds.), *The changing family life cycle: A framework for family therapy* (2nd ed., pp. 513–544). Boston: Allyn and Bacon.

House of Representatives Report 99–860. (1986, September). *Education of the Handicapped Act Amendments of 1986.* Washington, DC: Author.

Jacobs, F. (1988). The five-tiered approach to evaluation: Context and implementation. In H. Weiss & F. Jacobs (Eds.), *Evaluating family programs* (pp. 37–68). New York: Aldine de Gruyter.

Jennings, L. (1990, August 1). Parents as partners: Reaching out to families to help students learn. *Education Week,* pp. 23–29.

Jipson, J. (1991). Developmentally appropriate practice: Culture, curriculum, connections. *Early Education and Development, 2,* 120–136.

Kagan, S. L. (1989, January 11). Family-support programs and the schools. *Education Week,* pp. 32–33.

Kagan, S. L. (1991, January). *Interdisciplinary collaboration.* Paper presented to the Center for Family in Society, University of South Carolina, Columbia, SC.

Kagan, S. L., Powell, D. R., Weissbourd, B., & Zigler, E. F. (1987). *America's family support programs: Perspectives and prospects.* New Haven, CT: Yale University Press.

Kaiser, A. P. & Hemmeter, M. L. (1989). Value-based approach to family intervention. *Topics in Early Childhood Special Education, 8,* 72–86.

Katz, L. (1987). Early education: What should young children be doing? In S. L. Kagan & E. F. Zigler (Eds.), *Early schooling: The national debate* (pp. 151–167). New Haven, CT: Yale University Press.

Kramer, S. (1991, May). *The day I slept on the bathroom rug.* Keynote address, 8th Annual Forum on Young Children and Their Families: Parents, professionals and interagency partnerships: Facilitating positive interactions. Morganton, NC.

Linder, T. (1990). *Transdisciplinary play-based assessment: A functional approach to working with young children.* Baltimore: Paul Brookes.

Lubeck, S. (1991). Reconceptualizing early childhood education: A response. *Early Education and Development, 2,* 168–174.

McKinney, J. D., & Hocutt, A. M. (1982). Public school involvement of parents of learning-disabled children and average achievers. *Exceptional Education Quarterly, 3,* 64–73.

Morgan, D. L. (1988). *Focus groups as qualitative research.* Newbury Park, CA: Sage.

National Center for Children in Poverty. (1990). *Five million children: A statistical profile of our poorest young citizens.* Washington, DC: Author.

Nobles, W. W. (1978). Toward an empirical and theoretical framework for defining black families. *Journal of Marriage and the Family, 40,* 679–688.

Paget, K. D. (1992). Proactive family-school partnerships in early intervention. In M. J. Fine & C. Carlson (Eds.), *The handbook of family-school*

intervention: A systems perspective (pp. 119–132). Boston: Allyn & Bacon.

Peters, T. (1987). *Thriving on chaos: Handbook for a management revolution.* New York: Alfred Knopf.

Powell, D. R. (1989). *Families and early childhood programs.* Washington, DC: National Association for the Education of Young Children.

Powell, D. R., & Eisenstadt, J. W. (1988). Informal and formal conversations in parent discussion groups: An observational study. *Family Relations, 37,* 166–170.

Roberts, R. N., & Magrab, P. R. (1991). Psychologists' role in a family-centered approach to practice, training, and research with young children. *American Psychologist, 46,* 144–148.

Roberts, R. N., Wasik, B. H., Casto, G., & Ramey, C. T. (1991). Family support in the home: Programs, policy, and social change. *American Psychologist, 46,* 131–137.

Robinson, J. L., & Choper, W. B. (1979). Another perspective on program evaluation: The parents speak. In E. Zigler & J. Valentine (Eds.), *Project Head Start: A legacy of the War on Poverty* (pp. 467–476). New York: Free Press.

Rogoff, B. (1991). U.S. children and their families: Current conditions and recent trends, 1989. Extracted from Nicholas Zill's summary report of the Select Committee on Children, Youth and Families, U.S. House of Representatives. *Newsletter of the Society for Research in Child Development,* Winter.

Sarason, S. B. (1987). Policy, implementation, and the problem of change. In S. L. Kagan & E. F. Zigler (Eds.), *Early schooling: The national debate* (pp.116–128). New Haven, CT: Yale University Press.

Schmidt, P. (1990, August). English-literacy classes help avert family rifts. *Education Week,* p. 29.

Schorr, L. B. (1989). *Within our reach: Breaking the cycle of disadvantage.* New York: Doubleday.

Schweinhart, L. J. (1988). *A school administrator's guide to early childhood education.* Ypsilanti, MI: High-Scope Press.

Silber, S. (1989). Family influences on early development. *Topics in Early Childhood Special Education, 8,* 1–23.

Silverstein, R. (1989). *The intent and spirit of P.L. 99–457: A sourcebook.* Washington, DC: National Center for Clinical Infant Programs.

Spodek, B. (1991). Reconceptualizing early childhood education: A commentary. *Early Education and Development, 2,* 161–167.

Staff. (1991, May/June). Developmental delay: Questions and answers. *Communicator,* pp. 1–2.

Summers, J. A., Dell'Oliver, C., Turnbull, A. P., Benson, H. A., Santelli, E., Campbell, M., & Siegel-Causey, E. (1990). Examining the Individualized Family Service Plan process: What are family and practitioner preferences? *Topics in Early Childhood Special Education, 10,* 78–99.

Swadener, B. B., & Kessler, S. (Eds.). (1991). Reconceptualizing early childhood education [Special issue]. *Early Education and Development, 2*(2).

Szanton, E. S. (1991). Services for children with special needs: Partnerships from the beginning between parents and practitioners. In D. G. Unger & D. R. Powell (Eds.), *Families as nurturing systems: Support across the life span* (pp. 87–97). New York: The Haworthy Press.

Turnbull, A., & Turnbull, H. R. (1986). Families, professionals, and exceptionality. Columbus, OH: Merrill.

Unger, D. G., & Powell, D. R. (Eds.). (1991). *Families as nurturing systems: Support across the life span.* New York: The Haworthy Press.

U.S. Department of Education. (1986). *Education of the Handicapped Amendments.* Washington, DC: Author.

Vadasy, P. (1989). Child maltreatment and the early childhood special educator. *Topics in Early Childhood Special Education, 9,* 56–72.

von Oech, R. (1983). *A whack on the side of the head: How to unlock your mind for innovation.* New York: Warner Books.

Webb-Watson, L. (1989). Ethnicity: An epistemology of child rearing. In L. Combrinck-Graham (Ed.), *Children in family contexts: Perspectives on treatment* (pp. 463–481). New York: Guilford.

Weikart, D. P. (1987). Curriculum quality in early education. In S. L. Kagan & E. F. Zigler (Eds), *Early schooling: The national debate* (pp. 168–189). New Haven, CT: Yale University Press.

Weissbourd, B. (1991, January). *Building family strengths through community support programs.* Paper presented to the Center for Family in Society, University of South Carolina, Columbia, SC.

13

AN EMBEDDED CURRICULUM APPROACH FOR TEACHING STUDENTS HOW TO LEARN

Kenneth A. Kiewra

Our educational system does not teach students how to learn. It teaches students content such as math and science, but not how to learn such content. Reflect on your own education. Did anyone teach you how to record lecture notes, read a textbook, or study for an exam? Did anyone teach you how to use your memory more effectively? Probably not. And yet, students are expected to know how to learn. Consider an analogy to baseball. Would a child be expected to play baseball adequately without training in fundamentals such as hitting, throwing, and catching? Of course not. Why then are students expected to learn without training in how to learn?

One argument is that a great many parents and teachers assume that the ability to learn progresses naturally as children develop biologically and in response to the environment. This assumption precludes parents and teachers from trying to increase a student's learning potential.

A second argument for why students are not taught how to learn is that most parents and teachers know little about learning and how to teach it. Thus, even when the learning process is viewed as modifiable, the techniques for improving it are unknown.

With respect to the first argument, recent advances in educational psychology suggest that acquiring the ability to learn is not a gradual and automatic process. Learning potential can be accelerated through certain means. In fact, John Bransford (1979, p. 259) suggests that there are two types of learners as depicted in Figure 1: Those who learn in a slow and gradual manner (let's call them the restricted learners), and those who learn in a rapid and exponential manner (let's call them autonomous learners). Learning curves in Figure 1 might represent learning in a single situation or learning over a lifetime. Bransford speculates that autonomous learners know how to learn. They understand the process of

Figure 1
Autonomous versus restricted learners: Hypothetical paths of development

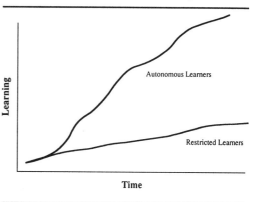

289

learning and use effective learning strategies. As a result they learn more. This increased knowledge, in turn, helps them to learn new knowledge.

Teachers and parents can be instrumental in producing autonomous learners if taught to do so. The field of educational psychology, however, has provided inadequate training for prospective teachers and parents. Most educational psychology classes and textbooks teach about learning and instruction rather than about how to teach learning. In fact, I have not found a single educational psychology textbook that describes how learning can be taught in the natural context of the home or the classroom. And yet, instruction in learning can be embedded into learning contexts throughout the school curriculum (e.g., Derry & Murphy, 1986; Palincsar & Brown, 1984; and Pressley & Levin, 1983).

This chapter deals with two ways that parents and teachers can help students succeed in school. First, effective parents and teachers should teach students in ways that are compatible with how students learn. In short, parents and teachers should provide learner-compatible instruction. For example, if students learn best when information is well organized, then information should be presented this way. Second, parents and teachers should teach students how to learn and thereby produce autonomous learners like those depicted in Figure 1. This can be accomplished within the context of any course and even in the home. In short, teaching students how to learn involves parents and teachers repeatedly modeling effective learning techniques in the context of content learning and making these techniques explicit to students. To meet the goals of learner-compatible instruction and teaching learners how to learn, parents and teachers must first understand several learning principles. The first section of this chapter describes three important principles of learning. The second section describes techniques for providing learner-compatible instruction based on these principles. The last section explains how to teach students how to learn based on the idea of embedding learning strategy instruction into various contexts.

PRINCIPLES OF LEARNING

In this section three learning principles are described. These principles have important implications for providing learner-compatible instruction and for teaching students how to learn.

Attention Is Selective

In any learning situation perhaps hundreds of stimuli (i.e., incidents, messages) compete for a student's attention. Human learning systems, however, are extremely limited in the number of stimuli they can process (e.g., Cherry, 1953; Sperling, 1960). Therefore, it is crucial that teachers and parents help students attend to the most important stimuli and ignore irrelevant stimuli.

The limited and selective nature of attention is easily understood in the context of a cocktail party. Imagine that you are trapped talking with a not-at-all-interesting person. As he explains the great gas mileage his Chevy Vega got when he traveled to Okachookee, you find that your attention shifts about the room selecting more interesting stimuli to process. You notice some "nut" with a lamp shade on his head. You see someone accidentally drop a potato chip, look around, and then deliberately squash it into the carpet with the heel of his shoe so that no one will notice it. You smell the host's dog who needs bathing. You hear that Bob is splitting from Carol; Ted is leaving Alice; Bob is now interested in Alice; Carol is intrigued by Ted; and Ted is interested in Bob. There are, however, many more conversations and observable incidents that you do not notice at this party including the fantastic gas mileage the Vega once got on a trip to Shreveport.

Whether at a party, at a ball game, in a classroom, or at home, people are confronted with many stimuli. Some stimuli are selected for processing such as the "nut" with the lamp shade in the example above, but most encountered stimuli are not selected for attention. Information that is selected can enjoy further processing or analysis and be committed to memory (i.e., learned). For example, you might think that the "nut" looks and acts like your Uncle Harvey. Making this connection helps you to remember the incident. Alternatively, information that is not selected for attention is forever lost and cannot be learned (McKay, 1973). Knowing that attention is selective is not sufficient. Instructors and parents should know what types of stimuli students are likely to select. Experiments (e.g., Treisman, 1964) have been conducted in which students listen to two different messages simultaneously via headphones. One message is played in each ear. Students are asked to shadow or repeat the message in a designated ear as it plays. This is a very demanding task requiring practically all of a student's selective attention. As a result, very little of the message in the nonshadowed ear is heard or remembered. It is interesting to note, however, what types of messages are heard in the nonshadowed ear. Students do recall hearing (a) gross physical changes such as a change in volume or pitch; (b) personally relevant information such as their own name; and (c) information relevant to the shadowed message, suggesting that information that relates to one's objective is captured.

Internal Connections and External Connections Facilitate Learning

Once students have selected information, it must be acted upon further to be retained permanently in memory. Most students believe that the appropriate strategy for long-term retention is rehearsal (i.e., repeating the information over and over). Rehearsal is actually an ineffective strategy for long-term retention (e.g., Craik & Watkins, 1973).

To demonstrate, study the two trigrams in Figure 2 for about 5 seconds, cover them with a piece of paper, wait about 10 seconds, and then try to recall them.

Now check your answers. Did you get

Figure 2
Trigrams

X G R   T C N

them both correct? How were you able to retain that information? You probably used a rehearsal strategy.

Now try the same task again. Examine the two trigrams in Figure 3 for about 5 seconds, cover them with a piece of paper, wait about 10 seconds, then read the instructions below before attempting to recall them.

Before recalling the trigrams, count out loud, backwards, from 60 to zero, by threes. Now try to recall them. You probably did not remember them correctly this time because the counting task prevented you from rehearsing further. Without continuous rehearsal information was lost from memory. In fact, try now to recall the initial trigrams in Figure 2. You probably failed to recall them this time, only moments after having both rehearsed and recalled them.

Rehearsal is an effective strategy for holding information for a short time such as when a new phone number is held in memory while dialing it. It is, however, an ineffective strategy for long-term retention.

The key to effective long-term retention and understanding is building internal and external connections (Mayer, 1984). Figure 4 illustrates a person who is reading a text. The Xs in the text represent ideas within the text. The triangles in the reader's memory represent previously acquired knowledge. The broken lines connecting the Xs represent the internal connections among the ideas to be learned. The solid lines connecting the to-be-learned information (the Xs) to prior knowledge (the triangles) represent the external connections. For example, this learner might be reading the passage

Figure 3
Trigrams

V S L   B T R

Figure 4
Internal and external connections

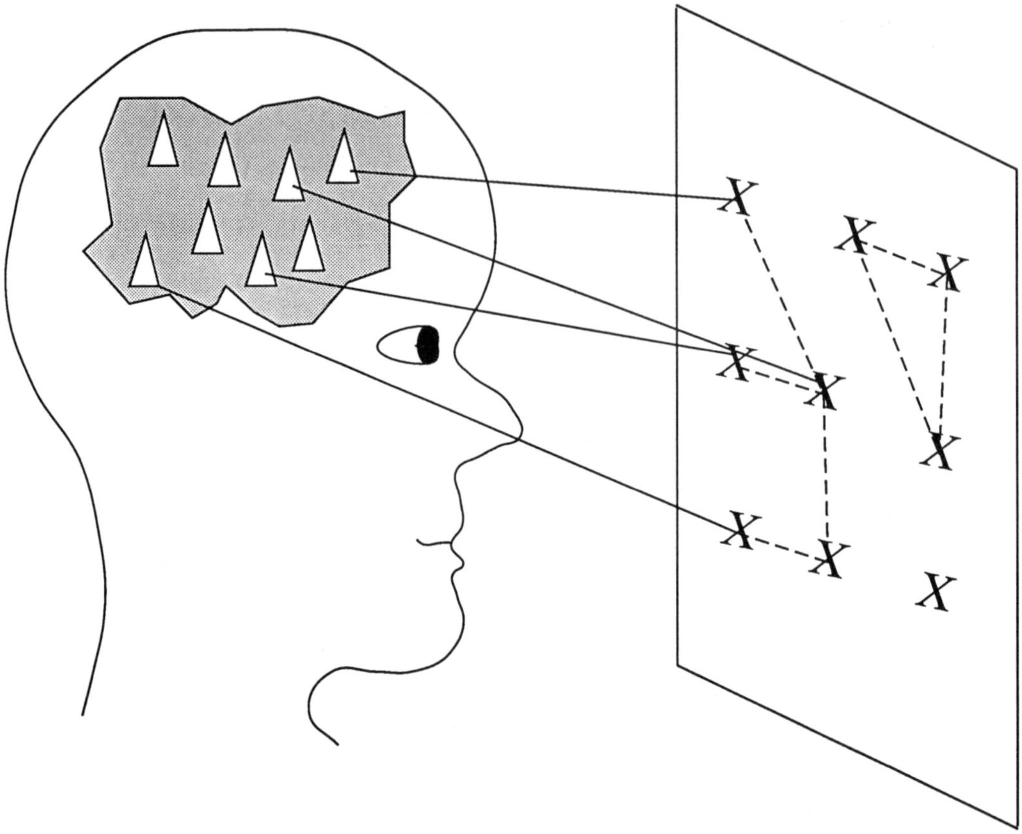

about moths and butterflies appearing in Figure 5. Connecting information about the moths and butterflies is building internal connections. For example, both have two sets of wings; during rest, wings

Figure 5
Moths and butterflies passage

Moths and Butterflies

A moth has two sets of wings. It folds the wings down over its body when it rests. The moth has feathery antennae and spins a fuzzy cocoon. The moth goes through four stages of development.

A butterfly also goes through four stages of development and has two sets of wings. Its antennae, however, are long and thin with knobs at the ends. When a butterfly rests, its wings are straight up like outstretched hands.

are outstretched for the butterfly but draped over the body for the moth. An example of an external connection is relating information about the moth to previous knowledge in memory about grasshoppers. It is through this interplay of internal and external connections that information is learned and understood.

When learners build internal connections they are organizing the information. There are at least three advantages to organizing information. One, the information can be stored more economically in memory (Mandler, 1967). It is much easier, for example, to store the 12 words organized into three groups in Figure 6 than it is to store them as a single list. Two, organized information is easier to retrieve from memory because there are multiple pathways for locating it (Tulving,

Figure 6
Twelve words organized into three groups

things in a closet	things in a kitchen
— tennis racket	— table
— coat	— stove
— shoes	— fork
— vacuum	— saucer

things in a shed
— lawnmower
— rake
— bicycle
— hose

1962). For example, the word "fork" in Figure 6 can be retrieved by recalling the category "Things in a kitchen" or by recalling one or two other items within that category. Three, the information is better understood and remembered (Bower, 1970). Returning to the moths and butterflies passage, we understand that both go through four stages of development and have two sets of wings, but differ with respect to how they rest and the appearance of their antennae.

External connections, as mentioned previously, involve relating the new, to-be-learned information to previous knowledge stored in memory. This process makes the new information more meaningful, makes its storage more economical, and also aids retrieval because additional pathways to the information are developed (see Mayer, 1984). For example, students in a health class who are learning about insulin shock might compare this new information to previous knowledge about diabetic coma. They would understand that too much insulin is the cause in the former case, whereas too little insulin is the cause in the latter case. This new information about insulin shock could then be stored along with information about diabetic coma. Recalling information about one of these is likely to trigger recall about the other.

From the brief discussion about external connections, it is apparent that students must possess background knowledge to make external connections. If students lack background knowledge, then external connections cannot be made and new information cannot be meaningfully learned (see Wittrock, 1974). For example, read the passage in Figure 7 and try to understand and retain it.

Although you had no difficulty reading this passage, chances are that you did not know what it was about. With respect to remembering it, you might be able to memorize it word-for-word, but still be unable to recall it in a meaningful fashion. For example, you would not know why a "deuce" would, just as well, serve the purpose of the day. If you have difficulty learning and remembering this passage about running it is because you do not have the background knowledge in memory necessary to form meaningful external connections.

To explain briefly, a log is a journal in which workout records are kept. LSD is the acronym for long, slow distance. Max VO_2 is one's maximum oxygen intake, which represents ability to transform oxygen into energy. Fartleking, a Swedish word meaning speed play, involves running portions of a longer course with high intensity. Polypropylene and Gore-tex are fabrics designed for winter running, and a deuce is an intense, consecutive 2-mile run. In sum, this particular runner was aware that she had been running too slowly and was perhaps losing physical efficiency. A fartlek workout with occasional hard running over a longer course was a possible solution for regaining some fitness. The fear that the winter clothing would hinder speed over the course of a long run forced her to consider running hard for a sustained 2 miles instead. Now that you understand what the words

Figure 7
A passage for which most students lack background knowledge

After checking the lot it was obvious that I had been doing far too much LSD. As a result my max VO_2 was bound to suffer. It was obviously a time to attempt some fartleking. I wondered if the Gore-tex and polypropylene would hinder my attempt at using speed. If so, perhaps a quick deuce would, just as well, serve the purpose of the day.

mean you have the background knowledge necessary to make external connections and thereby learn the passage. If you are yourself a runner, then you can make many more external connections relating the events of this passage to personal experiences.

Another example demonstrating the importance of background knowledge for making external connections comes in having to learn that Native Americans along the Northwest Coast lived in homes with slant roofs made with wood planks. This information appears arbitrary to most young learners unless they connect this new information to background knowledge about the timber resources and yearly rainfall of the Pacific Northwest.

Learning Must Be Self-Monitored

An autonomous learner does not depend on a parent or an instructor to monitor or guide her learning. She does it herself. Unfortunately, students rarely monitor their own learning adequately. Read the passage in Figure 8 about the worried man.

Did you understand it? Most people reply affirmatively. It is only when asked particular questions, like the following, that they realize that they do not understand: Why did the man take off his overcoat? Why did he roll down his window? Individuals finally gain complete understanding when told that the passage is about a submerged car.

In academic circles, the problem is that learners typically do not ask themselves whether or not they know. They wait for their instructors to ask them. As

Figure 8
Worried man passage

The man was worried. His car came to a halt and he was all alone. It was extremely dark and cold. The man took off his overcoat, rolled down the window, and got out of the car as quickly as possible. Then he used all his strength to move as fast as he could. He was relieved when he finally saw the lights of the city, even though they were far away.

a result, students do not know that they do not know until they are tested. Of course, then it is too late.

Research has shown that poor learners, relative to good learners, fail to check their current level of understanding relative to anticipated criteria, and also fail to engage and modify acquired strategies for selecting information or for forming internal and external connections. These learners are said to be deficient in *metacognition* (e.g., Flavell, 1981; Meichenbaum, 1976; and Ryan, 1981). Fortunately, just like any other memory strategy, metacognition can be taught and learned.

In order for metacognition to be effective, however, learners must have knowledge about principles of learning and their implications for learning. What good is it to know that you do not understand a reading passage, for example, unless you know why you do not understand it, and how to achieve understanding? Thus, in order for a student to be autonomous, he must understand the learning principles described in this section just as an instructor must understand them in order to teach in a learner-compatible way and teach students how to learn. In the next section, specific instructional strategies for facilitating selective attention, internal and external connections, and metacognition are described.

Learner-Compatible Instruction

Learning is maximized when students are helped to attend to relevant stimuli, build internal connections within the material, build external connections between new information and background knowledge, and monitor their own learning. In this section, instructional techniques for helping students carry out these activities are discussed.

Selective Attention

It was shown in the first section that students tend to pay attention to physical changes, personally relevant stimuli, and to things they are looking for (i.e., context-driven stimuli). Techniques for aiding selective attention based on these attributes are discussed in turn.

Physical properties. Why do you think that television commercials are louder than the programs they interrupt? Why is it more expensive to place a boldface advertisement in the newspaper? Why do you notice a bird flying past your window even when you are intently reading a book? In each case, the answer has to do with physical properties of the stimulus grabbing selective attention. Stimuli that are suddenly loud, bold, or moving command peoples' attention.

In academic settings the same principles apply. Teachers or parents can gain students' attention by varying the physical properties of the stimulus. Obvious techniques include varying the volume, pitch, or rate of words. Occasionally speaking very loud or very soft gains attention, as does speaking slowly and enunciating certain words or syllables for effect. When writing, information can be printed in bold letters, underlined, or written in an unusual color. The parent/instructor can command attention by using movement. Walking about the room and incorporating subtle hand and facial gestures can prove effective.

Movement, however, could force students to attend to irrelevant stimuli. I recall attending a graduate level psychology class when a student two rows in front of me frequently swung his leg. Each time he did, my selective attention was stolen from the instructor to the swinging leg. Students should sit in the front row of all classes so that potential distractions are less likely to occur.

Personally relevant stimuli. Familiar stimuli are likely to receive selective attention. Have you ever sat down in a crowded cafeteria in which there are dozens of conversations occurring? Very often your ears "perk up" when something familiar or interesting is discussed. If someone mentions Topeka, Kansas, your hometown, you are more likely to tune in than if they mention Frost Bite Falls, Minnesota (unless, of course, you were once a fan of the "Rocky and

Bullwinkle" show). If someone mentions a movie that you saw two nights ago, then you are likely to attend selectively. I remember attending a basketball game on the campus of Kansas State University. During this particular game several large pieces of paper were being passed around for signing. Each was a get well card for the coach who had become ill. When a card with perhaps 75 signatures reached me, I quickly signed it without reading it and began passing it along. As I began to pass it, I noticed a familiar name that seemed to jump off the list. I would have sworn that I did not look at a single name on the list, and yet that one familiar name was attended to selectively. Humans have a tremendous capacity to automatically scan all available information and then select only the most relevant.

Parents and instructors can take advantage of this tendency by incorporating personally relevant information in their teaching. When practicing story problems in math, for example, problems can be developed that relate to the purchase and maintenance of a new car if the students' interests pertain to cars. When discussing war in the Middle East, for example, personal implications of that war can be incorporated into the lesson.

Context-driven stimuli. Contextual stimuli, stimuli that we are looking for, also tend to gain selective attention. There is an old adage, "That when a thief meets a saint, all that he sees are his pockets." People notice what they are looking for often to the exclusion of other stimuli. Dentists notice teeth, not hands; mechanics notice fuel pumps, not car mats.

Oftentimes, students try hard to learn, but fail to select the most important ideas for further processing. There are several things that can be done to help students select relevant stimuli. Eight important techniques are described.

One, present students with objectives prior to instruction (Mager, 1962). Whether or not objectives are formally composed, students should be told prior to instruction what the expected outcomes are. Objectives should inform students what overt behaviors they must be able to do following instruction (e.g., find the hypotenuse of right triangles), under what conditions the behaviors must occur (e.g., given novel triangles with the length of two sides given), and how often or well the behaviors must be performed (e.g., eight of ten correct). If you are worried that objectives might limit learning for information not covered by objectives, then simply develop objectives for that material as well.

Two, present students with pre-questions or questions embedded within instruction. Questions serve an attention-focusing function, and can also encourage learners to think beyond the information if written for that purpose (see Anderson & Biddle, 1975).

Three, provide students with overviews prior to instruction (Mayer, 1979). These signal the major topics and topic organization. Overviews permit students to focus attention on subordinate information while learning, and to incorporate this information within the overall structure of the lecture or text.

Four, importance markers embedded within written or oral instruction aid learning (see Lorch, 1989). In text, certain physical cues, described previously, such as underlining, italics, and bold print draw attention. In addition, incorporating titles and headings in text signal important information.

In lecture contexts, instructors can cue student note taking by writing information on the board, or by providing verbal cues such as "this is critical." There is a high positive correlation between points recorded in students' notes and their subsequent recall of these points (e.g., Kiewra & Benton, 1988).

Five, note-taking frameworks facilitate learning (Kiewra, DuBois, Christian, McShane, Meyerhoffer, & Roskelley, 1991). A note-taking framework presents the major topics and subtopics from the lecture or text, with spaces between ideas for note taking. Frameworks help in three ways. One, they provide a structural overview of the material. Two, students attend to those topics while reading/listening and fill in necessary details that

would likely be missed without the framework. Three, students generate a more complete record of the lecture/text to review than without using the framework.

Six, teachers and parents can train students to identify certain "alert" words that signal the *structure* of the information. Students should select this structural information in order to help form internal connections among ideas. Basically, there are two knowledge structures into which all information can be organized initially: the hierarchy and the sequence. A hierarchy shows superordinate-subordinate relations among ideas, whereas a sequence shows sequential relations over time. An example of hierarchical information is types of saws. Saws would be the topic, and subtopics would include types of saws such as hack, rip, and cross. This information can be represented spatially as shown in Figure 9. Examples of sequential information are the events leading up to the Korean War, and the steps necessary for solving a problem. This latter example is spatially represented in Figure 10. Certain words can alert the reader to the structure of the information. Words like *types, parts, aspects,* and *kinds* indicate hierarchical relations. Words like *next, first, later,* and *before* signal sequential relations. For example, if you read the phrase "The process of photosynthesis . . . ," you know that the forthcoming information is organized sequentially given the alert word *process.* If you read the phrase "Substyles of Baroque music," you know that the forthcoming information is organized hierarchically given the alert word *substyles.*

All information within a hierarchy or sequence can ultimately be compared using a third knowledge structure: the matrix. The matrix is a downward extension of a hierarchy or sequence used to compare and contrast information. For example, the three types of saws appearing in Figure 9 can be compared along several dimensions such as function, appearance, and cost. The resulting matrix framework appears in Figure 11. Similarly, the sequential information

Figure 9
A hierarchical representation for types of saws

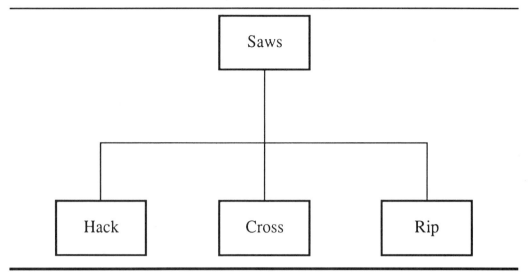

about problem solving in Figure 10 can be extended downward into a matrix showing the purpose, actions, and precautions for each step. Certain words and phrases can alert students to comparative information. Examples include *however, whereas, conversely, similarly,* and *different from.*

Students should not only be trained to search for alert words in text and lectures that signal the structure of information; they should also learn that all fields have structures for organizing information. Knowing this in advance permits the student to search for important information to instantiate the structure. For example, history is always a sequence of events. Cutting across all events in history are the dimensions who, what, when, where, why, how, and so what. There are no exceptions to this. A student in a history class should approach the class looking to complete the matrix framework presented in Figure 12. Students in a music class need to learn the primary structure in their field. All music has rhythm, melody, harmony, and style. In literature, all short stories contain a plot, setting, characters, and theme. Again, students must know the structure of knowledge so they can attend to both the organization of the knowledge and the relevant details.

Seven, repeating information commands students' attention. Studies have shown that when information is read several times or when a videotaped lecture is viewed repeatedly, students learn more information. Repeated instruction, though, does not simply result in more learning; it results in qualitatively different learning (Kiewra, Mayer, Christensen, Kim, & Risch, 1991). Upon the first presentation, students capture

Figure 10
Sequential representation of problem solving

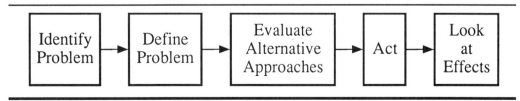

Figure 11
Matrix framework for types of saws

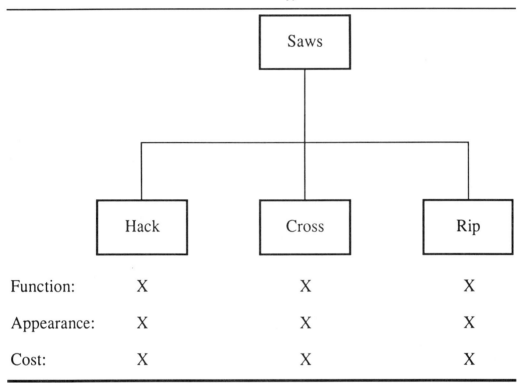

	Hack	Cross	Rip
Function:	X	X	X
Appearance:	X	X	X
Cost:	X	X	X

the main ideas and the structure of those ideas. With subsequent presentations, students capture more subordinate details to embellish the main ideas. Apparently, students actively shift their attention from main points to more subordinate material on subsequent presentations.

Eight, students' attention can also be directed following instruction. Instructors or parents can prepare study notes for students. Research has indicated that students attending a lecture will recall more lecture points if they listen to the lecture without recording notes and then review a set of notes provided by the instructor than if they record and review their own notes (Kiewra, 1985). This might occur for two reasons. One, during the lecture students' attention might be divided between listening and the activity of note taking. Students trying to record

Figure 12
Matrix framework for history

Historical Events

Revolutionary War → Civil War → World War I

When:
Who:
Where:
What:
How:
Why:
So What:

an adequate set of notes for review might miss some noteworthy information and might not think about the information they are recording. A second reason is because students are generally poor note takers — recording only a fraction of important ideas (see Kiewra, 1987). Notes provided by the instructor, therefore, serve a superior review function. If notes are not provided, students should be encouraged to record as many brief notes as possible. This keeps them actively involved in the lecture, and, most important, gives them a complete account of the lecture. This is crucial when students later build internal and external connections during the review process.

Building Internal Connections

Students who generate and/or review spatial representations like those illustrated in Figures 9–11 are more likely to form internal connections among to-be-learned information than those learning without representations. Kiewra and his colleagues (Kiewra, DuBois, Christian, & McShane, 1988) conducted a study in which students first watched a videotaped lecture without recording notes. Afterward, students were provided with either a complete text of the lecture, a complete outline of the lecture, or a complete set of matrix notes to review. Reviewing the matrix notes produced the highest recall of lecture ideas and also the greatest integration of ideas. A matrix is effective because it can be studied vertically, such that information within a topic is connected, and studied horizontally, such that information across topics is connected. Outline notes actually obscure cross-topical relations because comparative information is always separated by topic and separated physically when topic information appears over several pages.

Teachers and parents might be reluctant to provide students with completed matrices to review, believing that students are responsible for acquiring information. An alternative approach, then, involves providing students with a spatial framework for note taking (like that in Figure 12). This approach makes the

student attentive to both the content and structure of the information before acquiring it, and makes the student more active throughout the learning episode. Research by Kiewra and his colleagues (Kiewra, DuBois, et al., 1991) showed that students taking notes on a matrix framework recalled more ideas and better integrated those ideas than students learning without a matrix framework.

Of course, teachers and parents can help students to form internal connections by helping them to search for alert words and construct spatial representations thereafter. Receiving or generating spatial representations, however, does not ensure that students will actually make internal connections. Without instruction in how to review spatial representations, students are likely to review them as a collection of discrete ideas, rather than as potentially integrated ideas. Students need some instruction in forming both vertical and horizontal internal connectors.

In the matrix about personality theories presented in Figure 13, an important vertical connection about Behaviorism involves relating each part of the central idea with its corresponding portion in the example. In this case, the "person behaving" is a "student working." The "reward received" is "high grades." The "punishment avoided" is "failure." Another important vertical connection exists between the central idea and therapy. Therapy involves getting a person to work for a reward or to avoid a punishment, which is exactly the central idea of Behaviorism.

An important horizontal connection concerns where and when the theories were developed. Both were developed in the United States; Behaviorism preceded Humanism. Another horizontal connection concerns the central ideas. In Behaviorism, the person acts upon the environment, whereas with Humanism the person responds to the environment. More specifically, in Behaviorism, the person behaves to change the environment (get something or avoid something). In Humanism, the person is healthy only when treated with respect by others.

Figure 13
A matrix representation for personality theories

| | Personality Theories | |
	Behaviorism	**Humanism**
Where and When Developed:	United States, early 1900s	United States, mid 1900s
Founder:	J. B. Watson	Carl Rogers
Central Idea:	Person behaves to receive reward or avoid punishment	Person behaves in healthy ways when treated with respect and dignity
Examples:	Student working to get high grades or avoid failure	Someone in supportive family
Therapy:	Shape behavior by getting person to work for reward or avoid punishment	1. Help person to feel good about self 2. Treat self with respect

External Connections

External connections involve relating to-be-learned information with prior knowledge. Teachers and parents can facilitate this process by making explicit the connections for students in an ongoing fashion. When learning about the causes of World War II, for example, an instructor can relate the causes to the causes and/or the outcomes of World War I, if previously learned. The causes of World War II can also be related to the causes of more recent world conflicts. When learning about a new bird, such as the Redbilled Hornbill, a parent can point out how it is similar to more familiar birds with respect to origin, habitat, appearance, and mating rituals.

One of the most effective means for helping students develop external connections is by providing them with examples. In a study conducted by Pollchick (1975), college students read a text about seven psychological defense mechanisms such as denial, displacement, and sublimation. Students in one group read the standard text, which defined and described each defense mechanism. Students in a second group read the same passage with the addition of two examples for each defense mechanism. When later asked during testing to identify novel examples of the defense mechanisms, the group that had received examples in the text answered about 30%

more items correctly on the test. These results are important because they illustrate that examples help students to learn (i.e., identify) the concept, not just to state its definition.

When providing students with examples, it is important to provide a range of examples and to demonstrate how the examples relate to the definition. Providing a range of examples is crucial in order to prevent students from developing a restricted schema of the concept. For example, when teaching a child the concept of cup, it would be restrictive to show her a series of white cups only. She needs to see that cups can also be brown and green. Similarly, it would be restrictive to show her only plastic cups or only large cups. In order to fully learn the concept of cup, she needs to see a range of examples that vary along the features of size, material, color, etc.

As another example, consider a young doctor friend who was unable to diagnose his own case of shingles. Previously, he had observed the rash only on older patients and in its advanced stages. Without previous examples of the rash appearing on younger patients and in its initial stages, he was unable to make the diagnosis.

When providing an example, it is effective to match portions of the example to portions of the definition. For example, the definition of positive reinforcement is "the presentation of a stimulus, following a response, that leads to an increase in behavior." An example would be Johnny raking his Grandmother's leaves more often after she paid him $5 for doing it originally. Many students, however, do not fully understand why this is an example unless it is matched to the definition. The definition of positive reinforcement can be represented as a sequence of events with the example mapped onto it to illustrate their correspondence as seen in Figure 14. Now when a student confronts a new example, she can attempt to map it onto the definition for positive reinforcement or for one of the other behavioral terms (e.g., negative reinforcement) which can be represented in a similar fashion.

A more systematic means for facilitating external connections is the use of anchored instruction. This involves anchoring instruction to a particular context such that all learning is relevant to this context. Anchoring instruction to a particular context enables learners to understand the kinds of problems an expert in an area encounters and how she solves them. From the standpoint of external connections, all learning is tied to a familiar and relevant context.

An example of anchored instruction is the age-old activity of developing a play store within the classroom or home. This single context can become the anchor for learning about math, inflation, taxes, supply and demand, and even social courtesies. When I was a high school student, my entire course in Government and Law was anchored to a semester-long mock trial. This context was invaluable for making external connections when

learning about jury selection, inadmissable evidence, depositions, etc.

Another means for facilitating external connections is by supplying students with a framework of the to-be-learned information in advance of instruction. In this sense the overarching framework becomes the prior knowledge to which more detailed information is connected during the learning process. The framework appearing in Figure 15 is one that Mayer (1983) used in advance of instruction about the process of radar. It provided students with a simple model of how the radar process works. This permitted learners to tie detailed knowledge about the radar process to this framework while they read a text about radar. Having the advance framework produced a greater understanding of the passage than if the passage was read without the framework. Frameworks such as the one used by Mayer are effective for facilitating selective attention and internal connections as well as external connections.

Students can also be trained to use alert words to identify and then represent potential external connections. For example, when reading about *conservative* viewpoints on the economy, the student should be aware that there are potentially liberal and moderate viewpoints, too. When reading about *advantages* of *breast-feeding,* disadvantages need to be considered, as do alternative means of feeding such as by bottle.

The spatial representation system discussed earlier readily incorporates external connections. A passage on breast-feeding, for example, might describe three advantages of breast-feeding. They can be represented hierarchically as

Figure 14
Mapping corresponding parts of concept definitions and examples

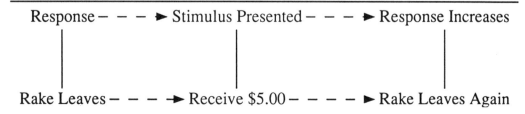

Figure 15
A conceptual model used by Mayer (1983) teaching about the radar process

---

1. **Transmission:** A pulse travels from an antenna.

2. **Reflection:** The pulse bounces off a remote object.

3. **Reception:** The pulse returns to the receiver.

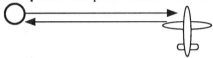

4. **Measurement:** The difference between the time out and the
   time back tells the total time traveled.

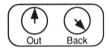

5. **Conversion:** The time can be converted to a measure of
   distance because the pulse travels at a constant speed.

☐ seconds = ☐ miles

---

shown in Figure 16. A serious reader, however, would pursue the potential external connection of *advantages* and seek out disadvantages, perhaps representing advantages and disadvantages as shown in Figure 17. A serious reader would also pursue the potential external connection of *breast-feeding* and consider bottle feeding, perhaps representing the problem as shown in Figure 18.

The matrix provides an effective structure for incorporating external con-

Figure 16
Hierarchy showing advantages of breast-feeding

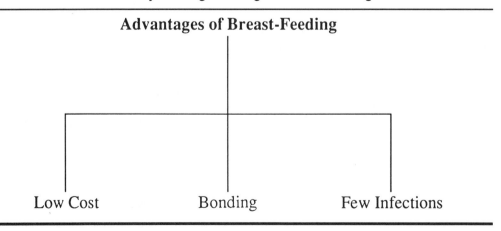

Figure 17
A hierarchy showing advantages and disadvantages of breast-feeding

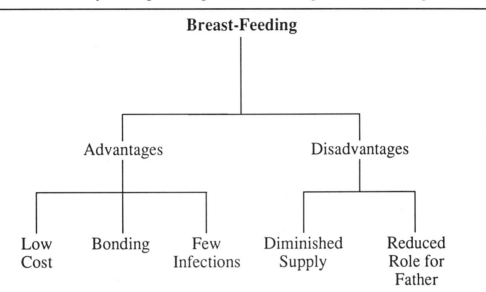

nections. A matrix can be extended horizontally by adding more topics. When representing a passage that compares two novels, for example, a student can add other familiar novels and compare these as well. A matrix can also be extended vertically by adding new repeatable categories such as novel examples and implications. In fact, I teach my students to always generate novel examples and specify the implications of any learned principle.

Monitoring Learning (Metacognition)

Effective instructors and parents, teaching in a learner-compatible way, monitor student learning by asking such questions as, "What did you record in your notes? How did you read your textbook? Why did you use that technique? What information did you select? How will you learn that information? Did you make effective internal and external connections? Do you have adequate background knowledge? Do you understand?" Ultimately, however, students must monitor their own learning to become autonomous. The problem is that learners typically do not ask themselves about their own learning. They wait for others

to ask them. As a result many students do not know that they do not know until they are tested.

The executive skill of self-monitoring can be taught to students through modeling its use whenever appropriate. When teaching students content through the use of a matrix, for example, the instructor can model self-monitoring by saying such things as: "Have I found all the topics and subtopics? Do I see how these topics are similar and different? Can I think of novel examples for these new concepts?" The instructor should explicitly draw students' attention to this self-monitoring behavior and explain how and why it is done.

Sometimes, however, students act metacognitively, but still perform poorly. One reason might be that students are not checking their knowledge in a manner commensurate with the type of situation in which they will ultimately be placed. (The cartoon that appears in Figure 19 makes this point.) This is partially the fault of an educational system that shrouds criterion knowledge in secrecy. I cannot think of another function in our society that does not readily tell people about the task for

Figure 18
A matrix representation of feeding

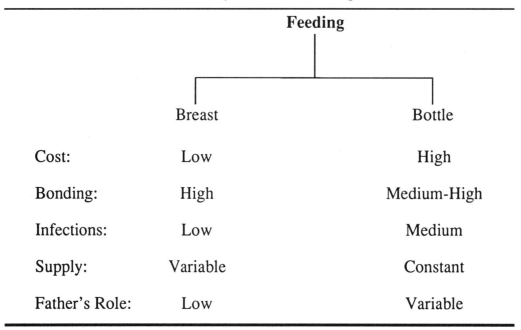

which they are preparing. Students need to know the expected performance when instruction begins so they can learn, and monitor their learning, in a manner appropriate for the task.

Perhaps the best way to help students develop internal criteria of expected performance is by placing them in test-like situations throughout the learning episode. Sagerman and Mayer (1987) did this in an experimental setting. They had students read several passages, answering strictly factual questions or conceptual questions after each. Following the last passage, all students took both a factual and conceptual test. Results indicated that students practicing strictly with conceptual questions outperformed those practicing strictly with factual questions on the conceptual test. The opposite occurred for the factual test questions.

In my own classes, I expect students to integrate information to solve novel problems. Many students, however, fail dismally when faced with these problems. Recently, I have provided practice problems on a weekly basis that simulate the type of problems students are later faced

with when tested. At first, performance on these test-like situations is poor. I therefore follow up their poor performance with explicit feedback on how performance can be improved. For example, I talk about how they should structure their answers or provide evidence to substantiate a point. Following several testing and feedback sessions performance increases substantially.

A few things probably occur as a result of test-like situations. First, students learn that their current performance is inadequate. This experience of mild failure then provides a framework or anchor for learning how to improve. With feedback, students can now determine what is necessary to improve performance. Thus, they develop more precise criteria for what they must do. This more precise criteria, in turn, helps them to learn in a manner commensurate with the types of problems they will ultimately face.

TEACHING LEARNERS TO LEARN

Up to this point, key aspects of learning have been discussed along with their

Figure 19
Faulty metacognition

implications for instruction and learning. The hope is that instructors and parents will teach students in a way that is compatible with how students learn. Although learner-compatible instruction aids student learning, it does not necessarily teach students how to learn — which is arguably the ultimate goal of education. In fact, a student provided with a matrix, for example, might do better on a forthcoming test, but not understand how the matrix helped nor be able to generate one subsequently. Fortunately, those who teach in learner-compatible ways are just a few simple steps from teaching learners how to learn.

Teaching students how to learn can occur simultaneously with learner-compatible instruction over a period of time. A person teaching in a learner-compatible way simply explains what he is doing, why he is doing it, and provides opportunities, in the context of content instruction, for students to gradually acquire the skill. For example, when presenting students with information about wars in a matrix form, the students are told explicitly about how the matrix was formed (i.e., where the topics, repeatable categories, and details were found) and why it is beneficial (i.e., for seeing relations both within and across the wars). In subsequent situations, the students might be given only the framework of the matrix (i.e., topics and repeatable categories) and asked to fill in the details. Later, students might be prompted to find topics, repeatable categories, and details for a given unit of information. Through these experiences the skill of generating matrices is gradually transferred from the instructor/ parent to the students until they can spontaneously and autonomously generate a matrix when it is appropriate. In summary, an effective instructor teaches learners how to learn by teaching in a learner-compatible manner and by making his techniques and rationales explicit through talking aloud. The effective instructor also provides multiple opportunities for students to learn and automatize the skills/principles gradually through successive exposure and practice.

This technique, which can be used in the teaching of any strategy (e.g., identifying alert words, spatially representing knowledge, building internal and external connections), is called the embedded curriculum because it involves embedding learning-strategy training into the context of any lesson. This approach is consistent with the way a plumber or an electrician might train an apprentice. While the tradesperson works, she speaks aloud so that her thoughts and actions become overt and explicit for the watchful apprentice.

This means of training is also compatible with how a parent teaches a young child. The child learns much about the world and about learning in ongoing interactions with his parents. While a parent and child roll out clay on the kitchen table, for example, the parent might use the opportunity to embed the teaching of color, shapes, and numbers in the context of their play. Perhaps more important, the parent can teach the child something about the learning process. For example, the parent who helps the child to compare a triangle and a rectangle is teaching the student to select relevant information and make internal connections. Helping the child to relate the clay shapes to similar shapes in the home helps the child to form external connections. Posing questions for the child about the activity helps the child to learn metacognitive skills. I think that John Bransford (1979) would agree that many people who are autonomous learners were placed on that path rather early by both parents and teachers who embedded the teaching of learning in the context of everyday learning.

REFERENCES

Anderson, R. C., & Biddle, W. B. (1975). On asking people questions about what they are reading. *Psychology of Learning and Motivation, 9,* 90–132.

Bower, G. H. (1970). Organizational factors in memory. *Cognitive Psychology, 1,* 18–46.

Bransford, J. D. (1979). *Human cognition.* Belmont, CA: Wadsworth Publishing.

Cherry, E. L. (1953). Some experiments on the recognition of speech with one or two ears. *Journal of the Acoustical Society of America, 25,* 975–979.

Craik, F. I. M., & Watkins, M. J. (1973). The role of rehearsal in short-term memory. *Journal of Verbal Learning and Verbal Behavior, 12,* 599–607.

Derry, S. J., & Murphy, D. A. (1986). Designing systems that train learning ability: From theory to practice. *Review of Educational Research, 56,* 1–39.

Flavell, J. H. (1981). Cognitive monitoring. In P. Dickson (Ed.), *Children's oral communication skills* (pp. 35–60). New York: Academic Press.

Kiewra, K. A. (1985). Learning from a lecture: An investigation of note taking, review, and attendance at a lecture. *Human Learning, 4,* 73–77.

Kiewra, K. A. (1987). Note taking and review: The

research and its implications. *Journal of Instructional Science, 16,* 233–249.

Kiewra, K. A., & Benton, S. L. (1988). The relationship between information-processing ability and note taking. *Contemporary Educational Psychology, 13,* 33–44.

Kiewra, K. A., DuBois, N. F., Christian, D., & McShane, A. (1988). Proving study notes: A comparison of three types of notes for review. *Journal of Educational Psychology, 80,* 595–597.

Kiewra, K. A., DuBois, N. F., Christian, D., McShane, A., Meyerhoffer, M., & Roskelley, D. (1991). Note taking functions and techniques. *Journal of Educational Psychology, 83,* 240–245.

Kiewra, K. A., Mayer, R. E., Christensen, M., Kim, S., & Risch, N. (1991). Effects of repetition on recall and note taking: Strategies for learning from lectures. *Journal of Educational Psychology, 83,* 120–123.

Lorch, R. F. (1989). Text-signaling devices and their effects on reading and memory processes. *Educational Psychology Review, 1,* 209–234.

Mager, R. F. (1962). *Preparing instructional objectives.* Belmont, CA: Fearon.

Mandler, G. (1967). Organization and memory. In K. W. Spence & J. T. Spence (Eds.), *The psychology of learning and motivation* (Vol. 1, pp. 327–372). New York: Academic Press.

Mayer, R. E. (1979). Twenty years of research on advance organizers: Assimilation Theory is still the best prediction of results. *Instructional Science, 8,* 133–167.

Mayer, R. E. (1983). Can you repeat that? Qualitative and quantitative effects of repetition and advance organizers on learning from science prose. *Journal of Educational Psychology, 75,* 40–49.

Mayer, R. E. (1984). Aids to text comprehension. *Educational Psychologist, 19,* 30–42.

McKay, D. G. (1973). Aspects of the theory of comprehension, memory and attention. *Quarterly Journal of Experimental Psychology, 25,* 22–40.

Meichenbaum, D. (1976). Cognitive factors as determinants of learning disabilities: A cognitive function approach. In R. Knights & D. Bakker (Eds.), *The neuropsychology of learning disorders: Theoretical approaches.* Baltimore: University Park Press.

Palincsar, A. M., & Brown, A. L. (1984). Reciprocal teaching of comprehension-fostering and monitoring activities. *Cognition and Instruction, 1,* 117–175.

Pollchick, A. (1975). *The use of embedded questions in the facilitation of productive learning.* Unpublished doctoral dissertation, Vanderbilt University, Nashville, TN.

Pressley, M., & Levin, J. R. (Eds.). (1983). *Cognition strategy training: Educational applications.* New York: Springer-Verlag.

Ryan, E. B. (1981). Identifying and remediating failures in reading comprehension: Toward an instructional approach for poor comprehension. In T. G. Waller & G. E. MacKinnon (Eds.), *Advances in reading research.* New York: Academic Press.

Sagerman, N., & Mayer, R. E. (1987). Forward transfer of different reading strategies evoked by adjunct questions in science text. *Journal of Educational Psychology, 79,* 189–191.

Sperling, G. (1960). The information available in brief visual presentations. *Psychological Monograph, 74,* 1–29.

Treisman, A. M. (1964). Verbal cues, language and meaning in selective attention. *American Journal of Psychology, 77,* 206–219.

Tulving, E. (1962). Subjective organization in free recall of "unrelated" words. *Psychology Review, 69,* 344–354.

Wittrock, M. C. (1974). Learning as a generative process. *Educational Psychologist, 11,* 87–95.

14

TRAINING PARENTS TO FACILITATE HOMEWORK COMPLETION: A MODEL FOR HOME-SCHOOL COLLABORATION

Daniel Olympia, William R. Jenson,
Elaine Clark, and Susan Sheridan

Introduction—Homework can be a controversial subject for both teachers and parents. Differing expectations, lack of consensus on homework responsibility, and the dearth of effective teaching practices fuels the differences between teachers and parents. The evidence is clear, the majority of parents value homework and want some type of homework assigned to their children (Friesen, 1978; Keith, 1986). Parents feel that homework helps their children develop a sense of responsibility, self-discipline, and prepares them for future study (Friesen, 1978). Parents also have the pragmatic view that homework will help their children perform better on examinations and improve their chances for promotion to the next grade (McDermott, Goldman, & Verenne, 1984). Clearly, parents value homework and want it assigned.

Results of polls conducted in several large school districts document that teachers also value homework and have many similar expectations (Cooper, 1989). For example, teachers believe homework teaches essential organizational skills. Teachers also view homework assignments as teaching students practical

skills about common learning resources such as libraries, reference books (i.e., dictionaries, encyclopedias), periodicals, and new computer resources (i.e., bulletin board services, CD-ROM reference sources). In addition, teachers understand the expectations for assigned homework that are held by parents and school administrators. Thus, teachers also value homework and feel that it should be assigned.

Definition: Homework is a term that many have used but few have defined in formal terms. Keith (1986) defines homework as that work which is typically assigned for completion outside the normal class period. Cooper (1989) further refines this definition as "tasks which are assigned to students by school teachers . . . meant to be carried out during non-school hours" and adds that students can have "options of completing homework during other times, such as study halls, library times or during subsequent classes" (p. 7). Although homework may be partially completed in school, it is assumed that the majority of assigned work is completed at home. Cooper excludes practices such as in-school guided study, lessons presented via home video, audiocassette, or TV and extracurricular activities such as team activities or debate clubs (Cooper, 1989). Lee and Pruitt (1979) further categorize home-

This project was supported in part by a grant from the Utah State Office of Education, Special Education Division, Salt Lake City, UT.

work to include practice, preparation, extension, and creative homework assignments. We suggest that these definitions be further refined to reflect the importance of generalizing academic skills to new, nonacademic settings. For purposes of this chapter, we define homework as academic work assigned in school designed to extend the practice of academic skills into other environments during nonschool hours.

Both parents and teachers value homework for its assumed self-discipline and academic benefits. However, with the high expectations for homework and its benefits, some research has shown that much of the homework assigned to students does not conform with stated definitions, best practice teaching techniques, or validated instructional practices (Keith, 1986; McDermott et al., 1984). To avoid problems, assignments should parallel classroom instruction and curriculum, include complete introductory explanations with adequate mastery of an instruction step, and provide immediate feedback. These essential components are frequently lacking, which creates a gap between homework assignments and effective instructional practices.

Parents expect teachers to assign meaningful homework tasks that are thoroughly explained in class. Teachers in turn expect parents to supervise home activities and act when necessary as an instructional tutor and consultant. However, parents are not usually trained to monitor and aid with academic assignments and few teachers are formally trained in designing practical homework assignments. High expectations and poor practices lead to disappointment. School personnel who provide parents and teachers with effective homework training programs and ways to improve basic homework skills can fill a valuable intervention need.

Homework and the Role of the School Psychologist

School psychologists face essentially the same problems as parents and teach-

ers. There are some training exceptions, but most graduate programs do not train school psychologists in basic instructional techniques. They are commonly trained in traditional academic assessment techniques of debatable instructional value (Reschly, 1988). Most practical instructional techniques that are used by school psychologists are acquired on the job in school settings.

Understanding our limitations is the first step in offering empirically validated services for homework difficulties. The purposes of this chapter are twofold. First, we want to briefly review the research literature on the value of homework, effectiveness variables, types of homework, and practical homework techniques. Second, we want to provide a systematic approach for improving homework practices that can be used by school psychologists or other school personnel to train parents. There are no "silver bullet" approaches to improving homework skills. Instead, there are a collection of best practice techniques that can be implemented, evaluated, and revised.

The "Do It Yourself" program was developed at the University of Utah and is based on a 5-week parent training/consultation model (Olympia, Jenson, & Neville, 1990). In this program parents are taught to implement, troubleshoot, and self-tailor a homework program over 5 weeks of training.

The first step in evaluating the value of homework is to ask whether it actually improves a student's academic ability or achievement. If it does, what maximizes its effectiveness?

What We've Learned about Homework Effectiveness

A great deal has been written about homework. Walberg, Paschal, and Weinstein (1985) found approximately 400 articles on homework. Some of these were research articles, but most were opinion pieces, and the opinions have not always been favorable to homework. In fact, some authors have expressed the view that assigning homework may be harmful or at least ineffective. As early as 1910, several articles in the *Ladies' Home Journal* and *School Review* (now the *American Journal of Education*) opposed homework on the grounds that it was unsupervised and allowed students to practice errors. More recent authors also question the value of basic homework programs. Some research reviews showed marginal gains or even negative results (Friesen, 1978; Knorr, 1981). Pendergrass (1985) suggests that the research findings on the value of homework based on improvements in grades and achievement test scores are inconclusive and stresses that instruction that occurs in the classroom is more important than the academic side benefits of homework.

Other studies and reviews, however, show a direct link between well-designed homework assignments and academic improvement (Keith, 1986; Otto, 1985; Paschal, Weinstein, & Walberg, 1984; Walberg et al., 1985). The differences in research results can be attributed to the type of study and the variables that constitute a good homework program. Walberg et al. (1985) point out that many negative findings in the research on homework are based on poorly designed correlation studies. They suggest that making a correlational inference of assigning homework and negative achievement to students experiencing difficulty is analogous to "attributing diseases to medicines because they are taken by sick people" (p. 77). Well-designed studies that employ randomized control groups and quantitative verification of completed homework assignments generally show positive academic improvements.

Parents and teachers who ask "Is homework really effective?" can be assured that the effects of a well-designed homework program are generally positive and can substantially help a student. Homework is a variable that can be altered by teachers and parents (Bloom, 1984). Parents and teachers can be proactive about homework assignments, whereas many factors are unmodifiable (e.g., poor family background, genetics, poverty, divorce). Basic cornerstone academic subjects such as reading, spelling, and mathematics show significant improvements with regular homework assignments (Keith, 1986; Paschal et al., 1984; Walberg et al., 1985). In fact, a good homework program may have a positive effect irrespective of the socioeconomic status of the parent. Students benefit equally whether they are from lower, middle, or upper socioeconomic groups. Research suggests that graded homework assignments produce an effect that is three times larger than the student's social class standing (Walberg et al., 1985). Parents can have an effect on their child's academic future that goes beyond social class standing.

VARIABLES THAT INFLUENCE HOMEWORK EFFECTIVENESS

The *grade level* at which students should first receive homework assignments has been the subject of much discussion. The issue has been complicated by variability in definitions of homework and qualitatively different practices used by teachers across grade levels. For example, kindergarten students may be assigned homework which consists of 15 minutes of paired or oral reading with a parent. The homework literature has also been compromised to some degree by biased samples that used students who were given homework for punitive or remedial purposes. Standardized achievement test outcomes associated with homework indicate only slightly positive effects for elementary students whereas junior and senior high school students show the greatest effects (Cooper, 1989). In his meta-analysis of the homework research, Cooper estimates that the average student completing homework over a 10-week period will perform better than 52% of students not doing homework at the elementary level, 60% better if the students are at the junior high school level, and 69% better if students are at the high school level. Stronger positive effects for elementary students are evident when comparisons use class grades and class tests as outcome measures.

A stronger case for the use of homework at the elementary level may be found in the training of student work habits for junior and secondary levels (Cooper, 1989). In the elementary grades, teachers give homework to promote positive attitudes and good study habits, to provide parents with opportunities to express their own educational values, and to facilitate the transition from elementary to later grade level expectations (Keith, 1986). Although there is no research available to determine if homework has these intended effects, these stated purposes enjoy a good deal of popular support.

Merely assigning work is not enough to ensure positive results. *Graded homework* in which a student is given rapid *feedback* is a critical variable in making homework effective (Walberg, 1984). If there are long feedback delays or assignments are not graded, the positive effects of assignments are generally lost. Walberg et al. (1985) has indicated that "this graded-homework effect is among the largest one discovered in education research literature" (p. 76). A rule for parents is that younger and academically delayed students cannot wait long for feedback. For instance, to wait a week for feedback on a spelling test is a common but contradictory example of ineffective homework feedback. The faster the feedback, the more potent the effect.

Another important effectiveness variable is a good in-class *explanatory introduction* to a homework assignment. If a student is not given the basic information about how to do the assignment, the task is frequently left to a parent. There is a common homework caricature of a bewildered parent sitting at a dining room table looking at a child's homework assignment while the child tries to help. Neither the parent nor the child in this picture understands the assignment. Good in-class explanations of homework and legible materials (e.g., not pale, copied work sheets) are essential. A good explanatory practice is to start the homework assignment in class with a quick teacher check to ensure the student understands the assignment (Keith, 1986).

A good homework assignment is a *relevant homework* assignment. This seems to make sense, but it is a frequently violated principle of good homework design. Teachers who feel the expectation to assign homework often give a large quantity of homework without considering its quality. These large volume assignments are often developed well beforehand and in an automated fashion. They typically fail to parallel the unique aspect of the day-to-day instruction and the academic pacing of a particular subject. These assignments are out of instructional synchronization. When this happens, there is no connection with what is taught in the classroom and homework becomes busy work. Teaching methods and homework practices can exert significant influences on student progress (Good & Grouws, 1979). Exemplary teachers tailor assignments to reflect day-to-day teaching and student options. For example, in a survey of 311 exemplary teachers (most winners of the Teacher of the Year award), the teachers tailored their homework assignments in two basic ways. Specifically they allowed optional assignments for current classroom topics and provided several alternative homework approaches for each subject of the day (Featherstone, 1985). Both practices require a close synchronization between daily instruction and homework options.

Good homework programs maximize *time on task* for a student. Next to relevant feedback, time on task is probably the most potent variable for improving a student's academic achievement through homework. According to Walberg (1985):

> If one thing is widely recognized about the effect of schooling, it is that *time on task* predicts how much is learned. Time is by no means the only ingredient of learning, but without it, little can be learned. Homework, of course, extends the school day. (p. 78)

Homework increases learning by increasing the length of time a student is working on academic subjects. This is particularly true for students that have achievement difficulties because they are distractible and frequently off-task. Regularly scheduled homework times are essential to improving a student's time on-task. If schedules are not set, then other pressing activities such as athletics and social and extracurricular activities reduce a student's regular homework study time and total time on academic tasks. Although other commitments are important for all students (and particularly those with academic difficulties) there is no substitute for time on-task based on a consistent homework schedule. Parents must choose which commitments are important and where homework fits into this value hierarchy. If academic achievement and homework are truly important to a parent, then other commitments and activities should come second to a structured homework schedule.

How much homework time should be assigned is a difficult question. However, comparisons of student and parent views of time actually spent completing homework are enlightening. In a recent census report, parents estimated that high school students spent a median of 6.9 hours per week and elementary students 5 hours per week engaged in homework (Bureau of Census, 1984). Several surveys of high school students actually showed that students estimate their homework study time to be 3 hours or less per week (National Center for Education Statistics, 1980, 1983). It is quite likely that elementary students probably spend less time on homework than high school students weekly. Parents overestimated their child's homework time by nearly 100%.

Another sobering statistic is that 57% of American high school students reported spending 2 or more hours and 37% reported spending 3 or more hours watching television each evening (as reviewed by Keith, 1986). Students may actually spend more time *each day* watching television than they spend doing homework the *entire week*. There is some evidence that merely reducing television time each evening can improve homework performance in some children (Wolf, Mendes, & Factor, 1984). For American students, television is a potent factor that detracts from homework and reduces time on-task. The cumulative negative effect of excessive television watching on reading ability has been reported by Searles, Mead, and Ward (1985). These researchers found that students who averaged 4 hours of television viewing each day were the poorest readers.

For students experiencing academic problems, mandatory scheduled homework times are important. This means that homework is scheduled for the same time each day, and the student should study for the full scheduled time. This is particularly true for students who report no homework or rush through their assignments. These students should fill scheduled homework times with independent reading, letter writing, or other activities instead of being allowed to reduce their instructional time on-task (e.g., by watching television, etc.).

What should be the length of time that a student spends doing homework each evening? This is a difficult question and clearly varies with the age of the student, ability, and the type of homework assignment. Exact time norms do not exist, but general guidelines have been formulated. Keith (1986) and Cooper (1989) provide some guidelines for homework times and amounts by grade level. These are presented in Table 1.

TYPES OF HOMEWORK ASSIGNMENTS

As homework times vary, so does the type of homework assignment. Not all assignments are of the same basic type. Assignments vary according to the student's age, ability, and the subject matter taught in class. The most frequently assigned homework task is *practice homework*. With this type of homework, students hone skills that are presented in class through drill and practice. This type of homework is necessary for basic skill development in which memorization is required (e.g., learning math facts, spelling, writing letters, memorization of anatomy terms). Practice homework extends

TABLE 1
Guidelines for Homework Time and Number of Assignments by Grade Level.

Grade	Time/Night	Number of Assignments/Week
1–3	10–45 minutes	One to three
4–6	45–90 minutes	two to four
7–9	1–2 hours	three to five
10–12	1.5–2.5 hours	four to five

the school instruction and gives a student the exposure needed to master a skill. In a sense, practice homework can be viewed as "more of the same" type work (La-Conte, 1981) and is most common in elementary grades.

Problems with practice homework occur when nonrelevant assignments are given or a student is required to practice an already mastered step ("busy work"). Good practice homework requires immediate grading and feedback and movement to the next skill level when mastery occurs. Practice homework is also particularly vulnerable to cheating by students when they are not well supervised (Lee & Pruitt, 1979).

The next type of frequently assigned homework is *preparation homework* that readies a student to gain maximum benefit from an upcoming topic (Lee & Pruitt, 1979). Preparation homework can be viewed as "read-to-get-ready" (LaConte, 1981). For example, assigning background reading in a topic, preparatory library work, becoming familiar with science terminology, or using a computer keyboard are all examples of preparation homework. A common problem with preparation homework is that it can be overly general. Specific assignments with a quick review for the entire class before introducing a new topic is a good practice with preparatory homework.

Extension homework is a generalization technique in which a student extends skills to new applications or situations (Keith, 1986). This type of homework may be closer to the actual goals of education, which is the transfer of learning from one context to another (Keith, 1986). Learning a computer language and then applying that language to a particular problem would be an exten-

sion homework assignment. Similarly, mastering a mathematical technique and then applying it to solve practical problems is another example of extension homework.

A basic difficulty with extension homework is that it is often complex and difficult to correct and grade. However, if extension assignments are made specific and simple, evaluating the attempts can be straightforward. The extra time needed to design and evaluate extension homework is worth the effort because of the valuable learning experience these assignments provide.

Creative homework assignments are frequently the combination of the three other types of homework assignments. A creative assignment assumes mastery of a skill that is extended to a new context with a unique result. Learning the complexities of a poetic rhyming style and producing a new poem could be considered a creative homework exercise. Learning the basic principles of conceptualizing, designing, and carrying out a psychological experiment might be another example. However, creative homework assignments are difficult to grade and often require a global assessment by the teacher.

It is also easy for a student to be shortchanged on a creative homework assignment in several ways. For example, mastery of a skill is necessary for many types of creative homework assignments. Although they may be attractive, this type of homework assignment is no substitute for practice or preparation homework. Good creative homework assignments also take effort to design on the part of teachers. To provide gifted students with a clothes hanger and ask them to construct an invention with it simply short-changes talented students. Good creative assignments require creative teachers. Parents may also become confused if the teacher does not provide clear communication regarding the intent of creative homework assignments. Students can develop resentments if parents have misguided expectations for the content or quality of these types of homework assignments.

Although the research on the effectiveness of different types of homework assignments is not clear, some type of homework appears more effective than no homework (Foyle, 1984; Foyle & Bailey, 1984). Most homework assignments follow a basic skill acquisition model that interfaces with the purpose of the assignment. In elementary grades where skill acquisition is based on memorization and practice (e.g., multiplication tables, writing letters, spelling), homework should involve primarily practice and preparation assignments. Although practice and preparation homework continues to be assigned in later grades, extension assignments are also relevant as transfer and application skills become important. Creative homework is a refinement technique and is useful for assignments where unique applications are prized. However, to assign only one type of homework is probably a mistake. Even a student struggling with mastering multiplication facts needs variation with extension and creative homework assignments. A balance is required so that a student makes adequate academic progress while maintaining an interest in assigned homework.

BEST PRACTICE TECHNIQUES

The research literature has several reports of successful techniques that have been used to improve homework compliance. These techniques are diverse and have been used on a range of students from elementary grades through high school. These are empirically proven approaches that should be incorporated into any parent/consultation program. A brief review of these techniques is helpful in establishing a rationale for the parent training program presented in this chapter. These include incentive/motivational systems, response cost procedures, homenotes, self-instructional methods, and parent training strategies.

Most homework assignments for students experiencing academic difficulties are unrewarding experiences. These students have frequently experienced failure and difficulty with other academic assignments and will not do homework out of a sense of responsibility. Yet, increasing on-task instructional time is essential to improving basic skills.

Incentive or Motivational Approach

Because homework is hard work for these students, an *incentive or motivational approach* has been successfully used in several research projects. Phillips (1968) used tokens with predelinquent students to increase the amount of homework completed. The tokens could be exchanged for an allowance, television time, snacks, and other backup reinforcers. Harris and Sherman (1974) used an ingenious tic-tac-toe game to reinforce homework completion. Homework teams were formed and questions from a social studies homework assignment were asked by the teacher. For each correct answer by a team, they were allowed to put an X or O on a blackboard tic-tac-toe game. The team that won the game was allowed to leave school 15 minutes early.

Malyn (1985) used a "spinner" and magic ink system to increase homework compliance in students with behavior disorders. A spinner is a cardboard circle divided into five wedges with an arrow attached to the center (see Figure 1). Each spinner wedge represents a backup reinforcer. The "magic ink" system involves two pens. The first pen is filled with invisible ink. The second pen is an illuminating pen that makes the invisible mark visible when touched to it.

The student's arithmetic homework was checked at the beginning of the school day. If the student had completed the assignment and 80% of the problems were correct, the student could touch the developing pen to one of a hundred boxes

Figure 1
Example of a spinner.

1. Sleep on couch
2. Friend over
3. Mom or Dad - slave for 5 min.
4. FREE CHOICE!
5. ~~1/2 cup marshmellows~~
6. sleep with flashlight
7. Play catch with Mom or Dad
5. chocolate milk

on a poster board. On average, one out of three boxes held an invisible star. If the selected box contained a star, the student was then allowed to spin the spinner for a reward. Using this system of random reinforcement, Malyn (1985) demonstrated significant increases in homework performance.

Related to incentive systems are basic *response cost* systems which penalizes a privilege if homework is not completed. Although some studies have shown that earning free time can improve academic performance (Johnston & McLaughlin, 1982), the loss of free time after school can also be an incentive. Lieberman (1983) devised a system in which students earned the right to do homework at home. Initially, all students were allowed to take their homework home for completion. However, students that repeatedly did not complete or return their homework were placed on probation for 5 days. During these 5 consecutive days, the students were required to report to the "homework room" after school to complete their assignments. A follow-up period then ensued in which homework completion alternated between home and school for 5 days. Lack of homework completion resulted in an additional 5 days of in-school probation. This system would appear to be promising given close collaboration between parents and teachers, however, there is currently a lack of empirical evidence for its effectiveness (Lieberman, 1983).

Homenotes

Feedback or *homenotes* have been used effectively to improve homework completion (Dougherty & Dougherty, 1977; Lordeman & Winett, 1980). Generally, homenotes are completed by the teacher. They include items such as assigned academic tasks, the grades given on assignments and tests, and homework items that have been turned in and those that have been missed. A major strength of homenotes is that they build a communication link between parents and teachers. In addition, a parent-based incentive system can be set up in-home dependent on the performance reported on the note. In the Lordeman and Winett (1980) study involving junior high school students, the note simply informed the parent of the rate of submission of homework reading assignments and a statement providing feedback about their child's work. The effects of the feedback note appeared to increase overall homework submission approximately 20%. Parents also had an opportunity to use an Answer Back recorded message containing the daily homework assignment and entire class results from the previous day. Interestingly, few parents used the Answer Service and the authors concluded that it was relatively ineffective in increasing homework performance.

Self-Instruction

Self-instructional procedures are attractive for improving homework completion because they teach basic self-management skills to students. This is especially important to some parents who may be reluctant to use incentive systems. Horner (1987) suggested a four-stage problem-solving model that could be used with parents to improve homework performance. The stages teach students to (a) set up a notebook for both in-class and homework assignments, (b) design a daily schedule for homework, (c) use verbal problem solving ("What is it I have to do?"; "How did I do?"), and (d) fade out the prompts used to teach independent work. Although these training stages seem practical, Horner offers no data on their effectiveness at increasing homework.

A similar self-instructional study that provides effectiveness data was presented by Fish and Mendola (1986). In this study, the authors used verbal self-instructional techniques with three children to improve homework completion in mathematics, reading, and language arts. The students were taught basic verbal problem-solving (Meichenbaum & Goodman, 1971) in eight, 30-minute training sessions over a 2-week period. The school psychologist used a five-step procedure where the first step consisted of the psychologist modeling aloud:

Task 1. Now what time is it? Oh! Time for me to do my homework.
Task 2. Where am I going to do it? I know, I'll do it in the ____ (whatever room subject usually does homework in).
Task 3. Now, what homework do I have

tonight? Okay, first I'll do ____ then ____ and then ____
Task 4. Good! It looks like I can.
Task 5. If my mind wanders, I'll tell myself, "Back to work!"
Task 6. After I'm finished I can play.
(Fish & Mendola, 1986, p. 270)

During the *second* step, the psychologist verbalized the steps while the student performed a task. Step *three* involved a transition in which the student both verbalized the steps and completed the task. In the *fourth* step, the verbalizations were faded to a whisper and finally were performed silently by the student in the *fifth* step. This procedure caused a marked increase in homework completed for the three experimental students with excellent follow-up results (i.e., approximate average increase of 40%). However, the authors provided homework completion data only, with no accuracy data for the assignments.

Parent Training

Parent training techniques and materials have been used in some limited reports to improve students' homework performance. However, most of these reports are non-data-based and present merely an outline of parent training for homework problems. For example, Harris (1983) has listed several steps for improving homework performance: (a) setting a basic schedule, (b) establishing a reward system based on a homework behavior chart, and (c) use of follow-up meetings with teachers and parents. The case study data presented by Harris involve a single case study of one student and showed that homework performance improved substantially over baseline rates using this approach.

Several commercial sets of materials are also available for parent training (see Table 2). These materials can be helpful to school psychologists when designing a specific training program for parents. Materials developed by Anesko and Levine (1987), *Winning the Homework War*, are excellent for basic assessment of homework difficulties and developing homework habits. The assessment home-

TABLE 2
Commercially Available Homework Programs for Parents and Teachers.

Anesko, K. M., & Levine, F. M. (1987). *Winning the homework war.* New York: Simon and
Schuster.
Canter, L. (1988). *Homework without tears for teachers.* Santa Monica, CA: Lee Canter and
Associates.
Canter, L. (1988). *Homework without tears for parents.* Santa Monica, CA: Lee Canter and
Associates.
Hart, D., & Rechif, M. (1986). *Mindmovers: Creative homework assignments for grades 3–12.* New
York: Addison Wesley.
Kuepper, J. E. (1987). *Homework helpers: A guide for parents offering assistance.* Minneapolis,
MN: Educational Media Corporation.

work checklist included in this program is well researched (Anesko, Schoiock, Ramirez, & Levine, 1987) and many of the techniques are based in best practices (i.e., daily homework record, setting appropriate goals, self-instructional training, etc.). The main limitation of this program is that the training book can be difficult for some parents to read and carry out the instructions. These materials may be more helpful to the school psychologist who consults with parents and is in a position to interpret various features of the program for them.

The *Homework Without Tears* series marketed through Canter and Associates are also good training materials (Canter & Hausner, 1987). Parents particularly like the materials because they are easy to read and filled with good illustrations and humorous cartoons. An added advantage is that these materials can be used with Assertive Discipline classroom techniques used by many teachers. The series includes a *Homework Organizer* for the student and a manual for the teacher. The basic approach is similar to others with an emphasis on time scheduling, basic incentives, communication techniques, and common sense tips. However, little information is available on the overall effectiveness of the materials.

Homework Helpers (Kuepper, 1987) and *Mindmovers: Creative Homework Assignments Grades 3–12* (Hart & Rechif, 1986) are two recent publications directed toward teachers and parents that provide many examples of homework contracts, various types of homework assignments, study skill sheets, and other aids to facilitate homework completion. Although these materials are easily adapted for classroom use, there is no systematic evaluation of their effectiveness.

In reviewing the literature, it is obvious that several techniques are available for improving homework performance. It is important to stress that these techniques do not work with every child. In addition, there are several types of training materials that combine several techniques into packages for parents. But not all packages cover all techniques nor are they all suited for group training purposes. There is a particular need for materials that can be used by school psychologists in a cost-effective group format. It is also important that these materials can be used to tailor an individual program for a student through a collaborative exchange between parents and school psychologists. Parents cannot be expected to implement effective homework compliance programs by simply reading a book or "interacting" with a workbook. Collaboration and interaction with school psychologists, teachers, and others appears to be a critical element in all of the interventions reviewed in earlier segments of this chapter.

UNIVERSITY OF UTAH'S HOMEWORK TRAINING PROGRAM

The *Do it Yourself Homework Manual: A Sanity Saver for Parents*[1] was

---

[1] Author Note: Requests for a printed copy

TABLE 3
Effects of Homework.

- Time spent on homework influences the achievement of students from elementary through high school.
- Time spent doing homework affects achievement in a variety of subject areas.
- Homework can have a strong impact on the achievement of low income students.
- Homework is one of the *few* variables affecting student achievement that we can exploit.
- The positive effects of homework exist for both high and low ability students.
- In grades 5 and 6, it has been shown that students who do homework outperform those who do not.

developed at the University of Utah (Olympia et al., 1990). It was designed as a group-based parent training program with an emphasis on parents designing their individual programs. The materials were primarily developed for late elementary level students. However, some aspects can be used with junior and high school students. The basic design of the program involves a 5-week group training sequence led by a school psychologist. The training includes group meetings devoted to assessing homework problems, interfacing with the school and structuring the home environment, motivation, self-instruction training, and parent tutoring.

Early in the program, parents are supplied with a manual that includes the instructions and materials for 5 weeks of training. Technical jargon is avoided and the manual is written at a level that is easily understood by most parents. In addition, the manual contains many illustrations and icons representing various skills and points that are emphasized in the program. Each weekly session is designed to teach a specific skill or task and parents are encouraged to try these skills at home with their child. It is critical that the parents try each skill between sessions and problem solve the difficulties at the next session with the psychologist and other parents. Frequently, parents learn more from the success and failure experiences of other

parents than simply from the information presented in the group. After the 5-week training most parents have developed, tried, and refined an individualized homework training program for their child. No two programs are exactly alike. However, there are essential components that are stressed for any good program. These components will be highlighted in the basic discussion of the 5-week training sequence.

Week 1: Introduction and Assessment of Homework Difficulties

The first week of training is critical because it sets the stage for later successful training. Parents will likely drop out after the first session unless they feel comfortable and expect to learn practical skills from future group meetings. Humor also helps parents feel at ease, particularly at the beginning of the first session. An amusing story, joke, or disclosure that shows the psychologist is not perfect helps in establishing a link with parents. It is also a good idea to have each parent describe their child, the child's assets, and what particular difficulties they are having with homework. It is important for parents to see that other parents have similar problems and that consistent effort will improve their child's homework performance.

After the opening remarks and information, the session moves to the importance of homework. A table is included in the manual that summarizes research literature on the positive effects of homework. This table is useful with some intact families or couples in which one

of The Do It Yourself Homework Manual—A Sanity Saver for Parents should be sent to Dr. William Jenson, 327 MBH, Department of Educational Psychology, University of Utah, Salt Lake City, UT 84112.

parent values homework while the other parent doubts its effectiveness. The findings should not be overpresented, but it is critical for the group leader to stress that consensus between parents is essential. Without parental agreement, the homework program probably will not work.

Following the introduction, parents are asked to respond to a series of typical homework problems or situations. Seven problems (Olympia et al., 1990) are listed in the parent manual, including such items as:

1. Your child comes home from school to begin what has become a daily battle over when he/she will start their homework.

    Yes No

2. You remind your child for the third time to start doing his homework as he/she continues to watch television, "Sure mom, right after the next show . . .

    Yes No

3. When your child arrives from school, they've forgotten or lost their homework assignments.

    Yes No

Parents are encouraged to add personal difficulties encountered with their child's homework. The strategy in reviewing problem situations is to sensitize and motivate parents to seek solutions to these problems.

The next task for the leader is to present how the information included in this training will give parents practical solutions for homework problems. A basic overview of the techniques and general structure of the parent training is given. For example, parents are told they will be given skills in assessing homework problems, developing a cooperative interface with their child's teachers, setting up a home-school information link, designing the homework environment, motivating the child, teaching self-management skills, and setting up a parent or sibling tutor program. Many parents have been disappointed in the past by vague approaches that leave them with little guidance. This overview is important to show what practical skills will be taught

that will help solve problems identified by the parents.

The last task of the first training session is to start parents on a basic self-assessment of their homework problems. A 20-item Homework Problems Checklist (adapted from Anesko, Schoiock, Ramirez, & Levine, 1987) is provided and parents are encouraged to complete it for the next meeting (see Figure 2). The checklist yields basic scores in five problem areas: "What Problems" (what homework is assigned and organizational problems); "Where Problems" (difficulties in homework environment); "When Problems" (difficulties in time schedules); "Why Problems" (difficulties in motivation, arguing); and "How Problems" (difficulties in understanding instructions and assignments). Scores above 2 in any area indicate a significant problem that parents should focus on during future training. The parents should be asked to bring their completed checklists for the next session for review.

It is important to conclude the first week's training on an optimistic note. Parents should be given the idea that practical solutions for homework problems do exist for their child's homework problems. Parents should understand that no "silver bullet" will cure all homework difficulties; each family unit is unique and requires individualized interventions. The group training will offer these solutions if parents work collaboratively and design a homework program slowly in a step-by-step fashion. The group leader should tell the parents that the following week will be dedicated to interfacing with the school and solving "What," "Where," and "When" problems. This skill preview at the end of each session helps bring parents back to the next week's training.

Week 2: Interfacing with the School and Designing a Homework Environment

In Week 2, parents accomplish three specific goals: (a) establishing appropriate communication with the classroom teacher, including the use of a homenote

Figure 2
Homework Problems Checklist.

Homework Problems Checklist

Check one for each statement.		0	1	2	3
For each statement, how often does your child:		Never	At Times	Often	Very Often
1.	Fail to bring home assignments?				
2.	Not know the exact assignment.				
3.	Deny having a homework assignment.				
4.	Refuse to do homework assignment.				
5.	Whine or complain about homework.				
6.	Need constant reminders to begin.				
7.	Put off doing homework to last minute.				
8.	Need constant supervision/assistance.				
9.	Daydream.				
10.	Is easily distracted.				
11.	Is easily frustrated.				
12.	Fail to complete homework.				
13.	Take excessive time to complete homework.				
14.	Does messy work.				
15.	Hurry and make careless mistakes.				
16.	Dissatisfied with work, perfectionist.				
17.	Forgets/deliberately fail to return assignments.				
18.	Complain that the work is boring.				
19.	Argue with parent about homework.				
20.	Report homework done at school, parent not sure.				

To determine approximate areas of homework difficulty for your child, you will need to use the SUMMARY sheet below. Under each area (WHAT, WHERE, . . .,etc.) specific items from the Homework Problems Checklist are given.

Add the scores for the items listed under each category. Divide by the number of items in each category and you will obtain an average rating for that area.

SUMMARY

WHAT		WHEN		WHERE		HOW		WHY	
item	score	item	score	item	score	item	score	item	score
1		6		8		2		3	
2		7		9		5		4	
17		8		10		6		11	
20		-		13		7		17	
TOTAL = /4		TOTAL = /3		TOTAL = /4		8		18	
						13		19	
						16		7	
						TOTAL = /7		14	
								15	
								TOTAL = /9	
AVERAGE		AVERAGE		AVERAGE		AVERAGE		AVERAGE	

If the average score is ABOVE 2.00 in any of the categories, you have identified general problem areas that interfere with your child's ability to be successful at homework.

system; (b) identifying and establishing good homework environments; and (c) organization of a homework schedule.

The second week of training begins with a review of basic points by the school psychologist from Week 1. Parents are asked about their Homework Checklist results and areas of specific difficulty. Parents who have completed the checklist are congratulated. Parents who have not completed the checklist are encouraged to complete it so they can design an individualized homework program. Parents need to do the weekly assignments if they are to design and troubleshoot a program.

The second week's training focuses on What, Where, and When problems that may have been identified by the checklist. The first part of the group focuses on interfacing with the school. Parents are given simple instructions and suggestions on talking with teachers and how to use the Homework Checklist in these conversations. Role-playing and modeling these skills with some parents helps reduce anxiety, normalizes homework problems, and often allows humorous exchanges. Parents are also taught the different types of homework (practice, preparation, extension, and creative types) and how to judge good and poor homework assignments. A list of good and poor communication techniques is also covered.

After making contact with the student's teacher, the parent(s) explains that their child's difficulty with homework is a concern. The school psychologist also suggests that parents bring a completed Homework Checklist to the first meeting with the teacher to point out specific areas of difficulty. Parents are then encouraged to establish a Homenote System with the teacher. Without a homenote, it is impossible for parents to determine *what* homework has been assigned and turned in. The homenote is simply a note initialed daily by the classroom teacher detailing the student's assignments (see Figure 3).

Although the Homenote System is requested and initiated by the parents, it remains the child's responsibility to carry out. The child must fill in the assign-

ments and hand it to the teacher for his or her initials. A list of *problem solvers* is also given to the parent if the child is resistive or loses the note. Parents are encouraged to link home privileges such as play time, television viewing, and extended bedtime to receiving an accurately filled out and initialed note. In addition, a list of ideas is provided to help overcome the objections of a teacher who is reluctant to fill out the note.

Once the parent has contacted the teacher and established a homenote program, the *home environment* has to be structured. Parents are given guidelines for setting up a good homework study area. These guidelines suggest that students do their homework in only one spot at a desk or table. This area should be well lit and free from distractions. Noise, music, television, toys, books, and food should be restricted and not allowed in the homework environment. The desk should be stocked with a *homework survival kit* that includes homework essentials such as pencils, paper, dictionary, and erasers. It is also a good idea to equip the homework environment with a "Keep Out" or "Do Not Disturb" sign to alert others not to disturb the students while they are doing homework.

A *structured time* is as important as a structured environment. A set time to do homework that takes precedence over other activities (i.e., play, television, sports, special activities) is essential in getting homework done. An established routine that develops into a habit is a goal of good homework training. A child should be allowed some free time after school. However, a time before and immediately after dinner are good times for most students. Clearly, homework time should occur *before* television watching even when special programs occur. Once homework assignments are completed, the child should be given free time. If a child does not have homework or rushes through it at school, the parent should use *mandatory homework time* which requires a student to use the entire scheduled homework time to do extra reading or review multiplication tables (i.e., practice homework).

Figure 3
Example of a homenote.

School Home Note

Name:_____		Date:_____

SUBJECT	HOMEWORK ASSIGNMENT	TEACHER/INITIAL

Comments:

Were assignments handed in?

Test Scores:

At the close of the second session, parents are given the homework assignments of establishing contact with the teacher, implementing a homenote, setting up a homework environment, and structuring a set homework time. Parents should also be given a preview of the third week (motivating reluctant students).

Week 3: Motivating Students to do Homework-Incentive Programs

The third session is planned to provide parents with skills to motivate their child to complete homework. Some parents have difficulty accepting the idea that their child needs some type of incentive or motivational system to get them to do their homework. Week 3 begins with a rationale about why students do not want to do their homework. In fact, this session is devoted to "Why" or motivational problems.

Parents are told that most students that have difficulty completing homework probably have a negative history with academics. Academics may be similar to going to the dentist or getting a shot from the doctor. First, in the past many of these students may have been punished by others for not performing, so there is a negative connection with academics. Second, many of these students are poorly skilled in basic academics (i.e., reading, arithmetic, spelling, and writing) and the tasks are difficult and seem insurmountable. Third, many of these students feel foolish or incapable when they do their academics so they invent excuses such as they are bored or the academic assignments have no practical use. Homework is truly work for these students and they need some type of temporary motivational system.

It is important to stress with parents that a motivational system is not a "bribe" but rather a reinforcement or reward

Figure 4
"Do Not Disturb" icon.

system. Bribes are defined as a payoff for (a) something illegal or illicit or (b) stopping a misbehavior (e.g., offering candy to a tantruming child in a grocery store to get him to stop). Motivational systems are used to increase appropriate behavior, such as homework. They clearly are not bribes but necessary techniques.

Effective motivational systems are characterized by several essential components. First, they should not take much time or be too expensive. Second, the system should be unique and attractive to the student. The system should be so valued by the students that they will work for the reward and even prompt the parent for it when homework is finished. Third, the system should be simple and not complex. Fourth, the motivational system should include a random or variable payoff contingency to maintain steady performance instead of a fixed system that occurs at a set time, such as at the end of the week. Fifth, the system should reward the child immediately and frequently. Long delays destroy most

incentive systems, particularly when a student is first starting a program. For example, delays of a week are too long for most students to wait for doing their homework.

Examples of several motivational systems are presented during this session. Basic rules on how to establish behavioral contracts are described for parents' use with older students. For instance, cumulative requirements (e.g., when you get five B assignments) instead of consecutive requirements (e.g., when you get five B assignments in a row) are suggested. In addition, explicit requirements, small steps, time limits, random bonus payoffs, and privilege loss are recommended for good basic contracts. Contract forms with several examples are offered to parents in the training manual.

The parent manual also contains several incentive systems that can be used with younger children. A "Wheel of Fortune Spinner" and "Mystery Motivator" system are included. These are high-interest, low-cost systems for students that frequently deliver variable reinforcements. For example, a Mystery Motivator is simply a reward written on a slip of paper that is put in a sealed envelope (i.e., rewards can be such items as staying up 30 minutes later, king or queen of the television set, or an edible treat). This envelope is taped to a piece of paper that has several squares with the days of the week printed in each square (see Figure 5).

The parent uses an invisible ink pen (i.e., PENTECH brand ERASABLE markers) and places one or two random, invisible stars in the day boxes (e.g., a star in Monday and Thursday). When the students complete their homework assignment, they are given the developer pen and they color the box for that particular day. If a star appears, they get the reward written on the paper in the envelope. If there is no star, they try again the next day following completion of their homework assignments. The materials for the Mystery Motivator system cost less than $2 to get started.

Motivational strategies that address specific problem areas are also reviewed. Another motivational system, "Beat the Buzzer" is explained for parents. This system, in which a student works to complete an assignment for a reward

Figure 5
Mystery Motivator example.

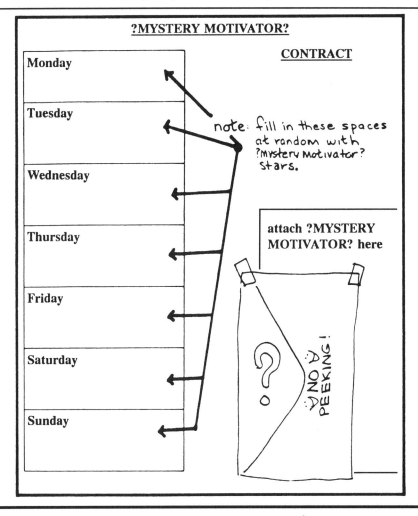

before a timer rings, is particularly useful for students who take an exceedingly long time to complete assignments. Also included are instructions for the system "My Parent, the Homework Consultant" in which a dish of candies is placed in clear view of the student. Each time the student asks for help from a parent, it costs one of the candies in the dish. This system is used for students who ask unnecessary questions or try to get the parent to do their assignments. The last motivation system is called "Chunking, or an Inch is Easier than a Mile." Some students have difficulty with long assignments such as a long spelling assignment. With chunking, the words are broken into groups or chunks of three. When the student can correctly spell and write three words they earn a small reward like an M&M or Skittle candy. Nonfood items can also be included by using additional minutes of TV privileges, Nintendo, or telephone time. This system is useful for overwhelmed students who feel they cannot do a whole assignment.

At the end of Session 3, parents are asked to develop a motivational system for their child for the next meeting. The importance of frequent success and making homework enjoyable and fun rather than boring or punishing should be emphasized. The best way to get the student to work is to pair homework with something enjoyable. Parents are asked to bring their motivation system to the next meeting for other parents to see, and to report on its effectiveness. In this way, parents are able to evaluate their own successes (or failures) and make any necessary adjustments in the context of a supportive group.

Week 4: Teaching Student Self-Management and a Home Tutoring Program

The specific goals for the fourth session include (a) providing parents with examples of several approaches for children to develop improved self-management, (b) tutoring skills for parents who wish to reinforce learning in reading, spelling, and mathematics, and (c) preparing for quizzes and tests.

Self-management. Self-management is a skill that most parents want students to acquire in all areas of living. They frequently refer to "responsibility" or "self-direction" as homework goals for their child and would like to see children internalize the drive to do their homework. However, internalized motivation does not happen spontaneously for many students. It must be learned, ingrained as a habit, and rewarded. At the beginning of Session 4, parents are asked to show their incentive systems from the previous week. The school psychologist discusses each parent's example and indicates that these systems are the beginning of developing an internalized habit. If students are successful, rewarded, and do a behavior long enough, it starts to become a habit with internalized value. Self-management also helps in the development of these habits.

Self-management skills taught in this session are derived from the research literature. Parents are taught the simple steps of helping a student develop "self-talk" skills around doing their homework. The school psychologist illustrates for parents how they can:

1. Model a "self talk" skill verbally for their child.
2. Shift the skill to the child who imitates the parent's verbalization.
3. Have the child whisper the instructions subvocally.
4. Have the child silently repeat the instructions alone. (see Figure 6)

Completing the steps for self-instructional training can be built into a homework contract, and a checklist for doing the steps can be developed by a parent.

Home tutoring. Many students who do not do their homework are substantially behind academically. This causes a downward spiral in that the further behind they are academically, the less they want to do their homework, and the less likely they are to get caught up. There is no substitute for increasing time on academic tasks to help students to catch up. Tutoring is an excellent catch-up tech-

Figure 6
Self-instruction training with icon.

"Now, what time is it? Ah-ha! Time for homework.

Well, where am I going to do it. I know...I'll do it in the (dining room, at my desk, etc.).

Now, what's first for tonight...OK...it looks like math is due tomorrow...then I'll do social studies. Good!

Looks like the work is pretty heavy tonight, but I've got to get started.

If I start to daydream, I'll just say, 'NO! Back to work.'

When I'm done I can enjoy a cookie (TV, playing, etc.)."

---

nique. However, extra tutoring is often difficult to arrange and many parents cannot afford the extra expense. Parent or sibling tutoring can be a practical low-cost solution but it can have real drawbacks. First, most home tutoring programs are too ambitious. Parents want to do too much too soon. Second, home tutoring programs can be extremely punishing to the students when parents or siblings get frustrated. If a sibling is used, the sibling must be older, mature, non-punishing, and receive some type of incentive for correctly and consistently running the tutoring program.

Home tutoring should be implemented in small steps. The parent manual outlines tutoring that is based on sessions that last no longer than 10 to 15 minutes, four times per week, and with the same daily schedule. Consistency, verbal reinforcement, and small steps are stressed for parents. Parents are taught to reinforce effectively using IFEED rules (i.e., immediately, frequently, eye contact, enthusiastically, describe what is right) with lists of verbal reinforcement examples (e.g., "that's performance plus," "this is the uncola of homework," "zykes, that's great work," "tubular work," "that's a great example of quintessential perfection"). In addition, parents are taught to relax, not to demand immediate perfection, and to control their anger.

Convenience and efficiency are emphasized with parents for home tutoring. The academic materials (i.e., book, flash card, paper, pencils) should be kept in a convenient container such as a coach's clipboard (e.g., a clipboard that has a container in the bottom for storage). A simple progress sheet is attached to the clipboard and the academic materials are kept in the bottom. Having to collect and assemble materials before a tutoring session can reduce on-task time and the overall probability of using the program.

Home tutoring stresses the basic academic skills of reading, arithmetic facts, and spelling. The home tutoring reading program is based on a program developed by Seaman (1989). This program was originally based on the use of common children's books and household materials and has been adapted for brief academic interventions supervised in the home. Parents are taught basic step-by-step procedures for reading-error correction following an outline in the parent manual. The arithmetic and spelling programs are based on a Cover, Copy, and Compare technique developed by Skinner, Turco, Beatty, and Rasavage (1989). This technique is based on a five-step sequence: looking, writing, covering, writing from memory, and comparing the results for arithmetic and spelling facts. All three approaches are empirically validated and if consistently used have been shown to significantly improve a child's performance over time.

In the last part of Session 4, parents learn how to prepare their children for classroom tests and quizzes. Parents are told that helping a child prepare for a test incorporates both self-management and parent tutoring. Assessing preparation difficulties such as cramming and late Sunday night study are reviewed. Organization, scheduling, and learning to study

for a test are taught. The basic study steps for preparing for a test involve the SQ3R technique (i.e., survey, question yourself, read the assignment, recite the material, and review the materials). Parents are taught to judge the general quality of their child's homework assignments and how quality can affect test performance. A Homework Quality Checklist is provided in the parent manual.

At the conclusion of Week 4, parents are encouraged to help their child with either a self-management program or to start a parent/sibling tutoring program. They are told that the last session is a wrap-up and will involve basic troubleshooting of homework difficulties.

Week 5: Troubleshooting Common Problems

There should be a 2- to 3-week period from the fourth to the last week of the group. This allows parents enough time to run a homework program and come back during Session 5 with issues to troubleshoot. Periodic telephone calls to parents during this period are helpful in maintaining contact, problem solving, and general treatment integrity. At the beginning of the last group, the school psychologist should solicit problems from parents and write them on a board to be solved. The parent manual also contains several examples of problems and solutions. For example, the problems and possible solutions for messy work, incomplete or missing work, arguing, and homework refusal are discussed in the manual. A special section contains information for the unsupervised child whose parents are at work. Techniques for supervision and controlling situations such as television usage are covered. For example, locking up the television power cord with a small tool chest lock and hiding the key until homework is completed is one technique reviewed for working parents (see Figure 7).

In the wrap-up session working out solutions and making necessary modifications are emphasized for the group. Nothing is perfect, nor will every technique work all the time. Some techniques

Figure 7
Tool chest lock for TV.

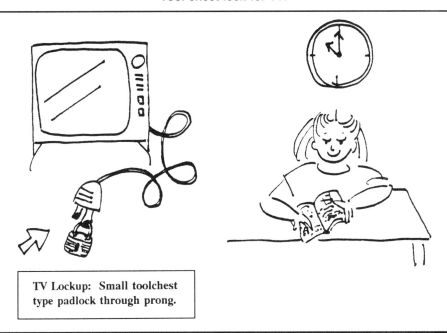

TV Lockup: Small toolchest
type padlock through prong.

will work for a while, and then as the child gets older other techniques may be required. Yet, homework should be as enjoyable and successful as possible.

SUMMARY

Home and school collaboration is possible for homework difficulties. A key to successful collaboration is a training program that offers practical solutions to homework difficulties and uses parents as full partners. In training parents to be effective home/school collaborators, a program has to be interesting and useful to parents, and successful and reinforcing to students. The program should have an established written curriculum based on validated, practical techniques. However, the program should not be so structured that it fails to allow parents the freedom to choose the techniques for the development of their individual program.

The process of training is critical to the parent/school collaboration process. Well-written materials are necessary but not sufficient for successful collaboration

with parents. A well-led group is also necessary. School psychologist group leaders should present themselves as facilitators with some but not all the answers. The group process should be geared to slowly develop a homework program by assessing problem areas, learning a technique for that problem, trying the technique, engaging in problem solving to overcome difficulties, and adjusting the technique. The development of a program requires many small steps and the school psychologist needs to be a facilitator for this process.

To date, the *Do It Yourself Homework Manual: A Sanity Saver For Parents* homework program presented in this chapter is being field tested and refined. Copies of the parent manual can be obtained by writing the primary authors at the Department of Educational Psychology, University of Utah, Salt Lake City, UT. Areas of related research include the development of a homework manual for teachers using a classroom-based, cooperative learning approach to homework. This work involves the development of three- and four-member homework teams that work cooperatively with the assigned roles of homework Coach, Manager, Referee, and Score Keeper (Wolfe, Fantuzzo, & Wolter, 1984). These teams work for group incentives and utilize peer tutoring, self-monitoring, and academic self-grading techniques to reduce academic failures particularly for slow learners and at-risk students.

In conclusion, homework appears to be an effective means of enhancing opportunities for home-school collaboration in our current educational environment. Research has established that the window of opportunity provided by homework can be used to maintain and increase educational achievement. Unfortunately, many families are trapped into a continual cycle of conflict when supervising their children's' homework. The school psychology practitioner can provide a valuable service to teachers, students, and parents who value homework but lack specific skills to make it an effective intervention strategy.

REFERENCES

Anesko, K. M., & Levine, F. M. (1987). *Winning the homework war.* New York: Simon and Schuster.

Anesko, K. M., Schoiock, G., Ramirez, R., & Levine, F. M. (1987). The homework problems checklist: Assessing children's homework difficulties. *Behavioral Assessment, 9,* 179–185.

Bureau of Census. (1984). *School enrollment—social and economic characteristics of students: October 1983* (advance report) (Series p-20, No. 394). Washington, DC: U.S. Government Printing Office.

Bloom, B. S. (1984). The search for methods of group instruction as effective as one-to-one tutoring. *Educational Leadership, 4,* 4–17.

Canter, L., & Hausner, D. (1987). *Homework without tears: A parent guide for motivating children to do homework and succeed in school.* New York: Harper and Row.

Cooper, H. (1989). *Homework.* White Plains, NY: Longman, Inc.

Dougherty, E. H., & Dougherty, A. (1977). The daily report card: A simplified and flexible package for classroom behavior management. *Psychology in the Schools, 14,* 191–195.

Featherstone, H. (1985, November). What does homework accomplish? *Principal, 65,* 6–7.

Fish, M. C., & Mendola, L. R. (1986). The effect of self-instruction training on homework completion in an elementary special education class. *School Psychology Review, 15,* 268–276.

Foyle, H. C. (1984). The effects of preparation and practice homework on student achievement in tenth grade American History (Doctoral dissertation, Kansas State University, 1984). *Dissertation Abstracts International, 45,* 2474A-2475A.

Foyle, H. C., & Bailey, G. D. (1988). Research homework experiments in social studies: Implications for teaching. *Social Education. 52,* 292–94, 296–98.

Friesen, C. D. (1978). *The results of surveys, questionnaires and polls regarding homework.* Iowa City, IA: University of Iowa. (ERIC Document Reproduction Service No. ED 159 174)

Good, T. L., & Grouws, D. A. (1979). Missouri mathematics effectiveness project: An experimental study in fourth grade classrooms. *Journal of Educational Psychology, 71,* 355–362.

Harris, J. R. (1983). Parent aided homework: A working model for school personnel. *School Counselor, 31,* 171–176.

Harris, V. W., & Sherman, J. A. (1974). Homework assignments, consequences, and class performance in social studies and mathematics. *Journal of Applied Behavior Analysis, 7,* 505–519.

Hart, D., & Rechif, M. (1986). *Mind movers: Creative homework assignments—Grades 3–12.* New York: Addison-Wesley.

Horner, C. M. (1987). Homework: A way to teach problem solving. *Academic Therapy, 22,* 239–244.

Johnston, R. J., & McLaughlin, T. F. (1982). The effects of free time on assignment completion and accuracy in arithmetic: a case study. *Education and Treatment of Children. 5,* 33–40.

Keith, T. Z. (1986). *Homework.* (Kappa Delta Phi Classroom Practice Series). West Lafayette, IN: Kappa Delta Phi.

Knorr, C. L. (1981). *A synthesis of homework research and related literature.* Bethlehem, PA: Lehigh Chapter of Phi Delta Kappa. (ERIC Document Reproduction Service No. ED 199 933)

Kuepper, J. E. (1987). *Homework helpers: A guide for parents offering assistance.* Minneapolis, MN: Educational Media Corporation.

LaConte, R. T. (1981). *Homework as a learning experience: What research says to the teacher* (Whole 1036–1-10). West Haven, CT: National Education Association, NEA Professional Library.

Lee, J. F., & Pruitt, K. W. (1979). Homework assignments: Classroom games or teaching tools. *The Clearing House, 53,* 31–35.

Lieberman, L. (1983). The homework solution. *Journal of Learning Disabilities, 16,* 435.

Lordeman, A. M., & Winett, R. A. (1980). The effects of written feedback to parents and a call-in service on student homework submission. *Education and Treatment of Children, 3,* 33–44.

Malyn, D. (1985). *Use of chart moves and spinners with homework compliance.* Unpublished masters thesis, University of Utah, Salt Lake City, UT.

Meichenbaum, D., & Goodman, J. (1971). Training impulsive children to talk to themselves: A means of developing self control. *Journal of Abnormal Psychology, 77,* 115–126.

McDermott, R. P., Goldman, S. V., & Verenne, H. (1984). When school goes home: Problems in the organization of homework. *Teachers College Record, 85,* 391–405.

National Center for Education Statistics. (1980). *High school and beyond: Base year (1980) data.* [Data file]. NCES, Washington, DC: U.S. Department of Education.

National Center for Education Statistics. (1983). *High school and beyond: Sophomore cohort: First follow-up (1982).* [Data file]. NCES, Washington, DC: U.S. Department of Education.

Olympia, D. E., Jenson, W. R., & Neville, M. R. (1990). *Do it yourself homework manual: A sanity saver for parents.* Manuscript submitted for publication.

Otto, W. (1985). Homework: A meta-analysis. *Journal of Reading Research. 5,* 764–766.

Paschal, R. A., Weinstein, T., & Walberg, H. J. (1984). The effects of homework on learning: A quantitative synthesis. *Journal of Educational Research, 78,* 97–104.

Pendergrass, R. A. (1985). Homework: Is it really basic. *The Clearing House, 58,* 310–314.

Phillips, E. L. (1968). Achievement place: Token reinforcement procedures in a home style rehabilitation setting for predelinquent boys. *Journal of Applied Behavior Analysis, 1,* 213–223.

Reschly, D. (1988). Special education reform: School psychology revolution. *School Psychology Review, 17,* 459–475.

Seaman, J. (1989). *Guidelines for parent tutors.* Unpublished manuscript.

Searles, D. T., Mead, N. A., & Ward, B. (1985). The relationship of students' reading skills to TV watching, leisure time reading and homework. *Journal of Reading, 11,* 158–162.

Skinner, C. H., Turco, T. L., Beatty, K. L., & Rasavage, C. (1989). Cover, copy and compare: a method for increasing multiplication performance. *School Psychology Review, 18*(3), 412–420.

Walberg, H. J. (1984). Families as partners in educational productivity. *Phi Delta Kappan, 65,* 397–400.

Walberg, H. J., Paschal, R. A., & Weinstein, T. (1985). Homework's powerful effects on learning. *Educational Leadership, 42,* 76–79.

Wolf, D. A., Mendes, M. G., & Factor, D. (1984). A parent administered program to reduce children's television viewing. *Journal of Applied Behavior Analysis, 17,* 267–272.

Wolfe, J. A., Fantuzzo, J., & Wolter, C. (1984). Student administered group-oriented contingencies: A method of combining group-oriented contingencies and self-directed behavior to increase academic productivity. *Child and Family Behavior Therapy, 6,* 45–59.

BEHAVIORAL INTERVENTION: A HOME AND SCHOOL APPROACH

Richard M. Wielkiewicz

The present chapter integrates behavior management techniques with a systems-based view of assessing and managing behavior problems. It begins with a discussion of assessment issues and presents a ten-step approach to assessment of behavioral problems. The second section presents a complimentary eight-step approach to intervention. The next section discusses strategies for promoting a cooperative approach to behavioral assessment and management and the fourth section discusses the design of behavior management programs from a home-school perspective.

A HOME-SCHOOL APPROACH TO THE ASSESSMENT PROCESS

Behavioral interventions can be categorized in a number of different ways, but I have found it useful to contrast informal and formal interventions. Informal interventions are usually done without collecting baseline data or conducting a detailed problem assessment. Because time in any educator's day is limited, many school-based behavior management efforts are informal. In contrast, formal programs address all the steps outlined below. The division between formal and informal procedures can be arbitrary because many behavior management efforts rep-

resent a compromise between the approaches.

A problem with informal methods is that the context of behavior may be ignored. Parents and school practitioners often see behavior problems differently (Achenbach, McConaughy, & Howell, 1987; Phares, Compas, & Howell, 1989; Victor, Halverson, & Wampler, 1988). When an intervention is based upon information from only one system, serious problems occurring in other systems may not be noticed. Complete assessment of any behavior problem requires data from all components of the child's system. Because assessment is such a complex process it is helpful to approach the task in a systematic manner. The following systematic description of the formal assessment process was first presented by Wielkiewicz (1986) who modified steps presented by Kanfer and Phillips (1970) to make them more applicable to school-related problems. The assessment procedure is summarized in Table 1 and described below. It should be emphasized that these procedures are presented as a series of steps for organizational purposes and to maintain clarity. In actual application, it will often be necessary to approach behavioral assessment and programming in a more flexible way depending upon the child's needs.

TABLE 1
A Home-School Approach to Formal Assessment

Step 1: General Analysis of the Problem and Its Impact upon Academic Learning and Performance
   A. State the problem in general terms, including its history.
   B. Is it a behavior excess or a skill deficit?
   C. What is the impact of the problem behavior upon academic performance?
   D. Describe the problem's frequency, intensity, and duration.
   E. What conditions precede and follow the behavior?

Step 2: Clarification of the Problem
   A. Consider causal relations that might exist among observations.
   B. Define the problem behavior in more detail.
   C. What evidence suggests that the problem behavior is maintained by circumstances in the environment?
   D. Determine the impact of the problem behavior upon others.
   E. Does the behavior occur in a number of different situations or is it generally restricted to a single situation?
   F. What does the child gain from the behavior that tends to maintain it over a long period of time?

Step 3: Motivational and Reinforcement Analysis
   A. What are the child's strengths?
   B. What does the child like in terms of activities, toys, or whatever else might be relevant to a behavior management program?

Step 4: Developmental Analysis of the Problem
   A. Are the child's skills age-appropriate?
   B. What is the history of the problem behavior's development?
   C. Obtain a brief medical history of the child.
   D. Obtain a detailed school attendance history and review the child's cumulative file.

Step 5: Analysis of the Child's Self-Control
   A. Evaluate the child's deficits and excesses in self-control.
   B. Does appropriate behavior appear in other environments?

Step 6: Analysis of the Child's Social Relationships in School
   A. What role does adult or peer attention play in maintaining the problem behavior?
   B. Does the child have friends?
   C. Does the child participate in group activities?

Step 7: Analysis of the Child's Sensory Capacity
   A. Are the child's hearing and vision okay?

Step 8: Analysis of the Child's Behavior at Home
   A. Does the behavior problem appear at home?
   B. How are behavior problems handled at home?
   C. What other problems are seen at home?

Step 9: Analysis of Interpersonal Relationships at Home
   A. What is the composition of the child's household?
   B. How do others in the family get along with the child?
   C. Do responsible adults respond consistently to the child's behavior?
   D. Is family conflict present?
   E. Are the child's biological parents divorced? Is the noncustodial parent involved with the child? To what extent?

Step 10: Initial Identification of the Problem Behavior and Potential Targets for a Behavior Management Program
   A. Integrate the information. Is intervention necessary?
   B. What will be the target of intervention?
   C. Are additional data needed?
   D. Reminders:
      1. Assessment is a continuous process.
      2. All conclusions remain subject to revision.
      3. Children behave consistently with respect to their perception of the environment.
      4. Resolving contradictions can help in understanding the child.

Source. Wielkiewicz, R. M. (1986). *Behavior management in the schools* (pp. 47–48). Needham Heights, MA: Allyn & Bacon.

Home-School Assessment Steps

Step 1: General analysis of the problem and its impact upon academic performance. When a behavior problem is first noticed, it is helpful to state the problem in general terms and reconstruct its history, documenting all previous and current interventions so a record is available for later reference. Then, classify the problem as either a skill deficit (the child fails to behave in a desired manner), a performance deficit (the child has the skill but fails to emit it appropriately), or a behavior excess (the child is doing too much of something undesirable).

Next, determine the problem's relation to academic performance. Appropriate sources of data include teacher records and results of group testing. If a learning problem is suspected, appropriate assessment should be conducted before beginning a behavior management program to avoid establishing goals beyond the child's present level of functioning. If the behavior problem reflects lack of motivation rather than lack of ability, it would be desirable to reward on-task behavior such as completing seat work, contributing to discussions, and doing homework, rather than focus on reducing the undesirable behavior.

Finally, analyze the frequency, intensity, and duration of the problem behavior. The goal is to learn when and where the behavior occurs, the situational variables and antecedents associated with the behavior, how adults and the child's peers react to the behavior, and whether consequences that might maintain the behavior are occurring.

Step 2: Clarification of the problem. The goal of Step 2 is to consider causal relations that might exist among the observations and define the problem behavior in more detail. This analysis should answer three questions: (a) Does the problem behavior occur in a wide range of situations or is it generally restricted to a single situation? (b) Does the child gain anything from the behavior that tends to maintain it over a long period of time? and (c) What is the impact of the behavior upon others in the child's school?

Step 3: Motivational and reinforcement analysis. Although the focus may be on problem behavior, it is important to learn about the child's strengths to plan incentives for the child and to assist in educational and vocational programming. Two questions should be answered: (a) What does the child do well? and (b) What does the child like that could be used as reinforcers in a behavior management program? Reporting the child's strengths also balances presentation of assessment results to the child's parents.

Step 4: Developmental analysis of the problem. It is desirable to know whether the child's social, academic, self-help, and physical skills are age-appropriate. This can be ascertained by ranking the child with respect to his or her peers in each of these areas. This analysis should establish expectations about the child's behavior and indicate whether the problem behavior represents a deviation from behavior expected of a child at that stage of development. A medical history and cumulative file review should also be completed because a major medical problem or frequent absences from school may be important in planning a behavior management program. In addition, the assessor should be aware of the possibility that a more in-depth assessment of intellectual, physical, social, and adaptive skills may be necessary.

Step 5: Analysis of the child's self-control. This analysis is directed at both the methods and degree of self-control shown by the child in daily life. It includes an evaluation of both deficits and excesses in self-control, either of which could become the focus of a behavior management program. It is important to determine whether the problem behavior is within the control of the child, which allows one to decide whether the problem is the result of not performing a known skill, or reflects a need to learn a new skill.

Step 6: Analysis of the child's social relationships in school. Social skills are an important component of school success and self-esteem. Children may be in trouble because they lack skills for successful social interactions. Careful observation of the child's interactions with peers is needed to determine whether the child is accepted or rejected, and what behaviors attract the attention of peers. Many desirable and undesirable behaviors are maintained by adult attention. Observe the child's interactions with adults, noting whether adult attention is used effectively to reward appropriate behavior and whether misbehavior leads to appropriate consequences or is ignored.

Step 7: Analysis of the child's sensory capacity. When a behavior management program is contemplated, it is important to consider whether sensory deficits are related to the problem. A child could appear to be ignoring or defying adult requests when the requests are not being heard. Likewise, a child who is unable to see clearly may appear disruptive while asking neighbors for help. In most cases, an informal assessment of the child's hearing and vision should be sufficient, but any suspicion of a sensory deficit warrants further investigation.

Step 8: Analysis of the child's behavior at home. An analysis of any child's behavior at home depends upon the willingness of the child's parents to share information. It takes diplomacy to elicit information from parents, who may feel threatened by any contact with their child's school (see Doherty & Peskay, this volume). Three questions should have priority: (a) Does the behavior problem identified in school also appear at home? (b) How are behavior problems handled at home? and (c) What problems are seen at home in addition to those identified at school? The Personality Inventory for Children (Lachar, 1984), the Behavior Rating Profile (Brown & Hammill, 1978), the Child Behavior Checklist (Achenbach & Edelbrock, 1983), or the Home Situations Questionnaire (Barkley, 1981) are just some of the instruments that can be helpful in answering these questions. Other useful assessment techniques are reviewed in Mash and Terdal (1988).

Step 9: Analysis of interpersonal relationships at home. A complete assessment of a child's family system is not likely to be performed by school personnel because of time constraints and lack of people trained in family assessment and therapy. However, a lot can be learned during family conferences, phone calls, or interviews. Fine and Holt (1983) suggest that an assessment of the family system should seek answers to a variety of questions including: (a) Who holds the power at home and school? (b) What roles does the child play in each setting? (c) What triangulation of relationships exists in each setting? (d) How rigid are the home and school systems? (e) How are different family members affected by the child's behavior? (f) How is the family system maintained? (g) What is lost and gained by family members if the child changes? See Doherty and Peskay, this volume, and Zimmerman and Sims (1983) for more discussion of family-systems assessment and treatment.

Step 10: Initial identification of the problem behavior and potential targets for a behavior management program. After collecting the information suggested in the previous nine steps, the practitioner should have a reasonably complete picture of the child. It would be appropriate at this stage to summarize the available information, identify a target behavior, or discuss the information at a team meeting. As one struggles to integrate the data obtained from an assessment, it helps to realize that assessment is a continuous process with no conclusions. Instead, they are hypotheses, subject to revision at any time. One can never eliminate the possibility that new data will change one's view of a problem behavior and lead to a new intervention strategy.

Child assessment data are often contradictory and confusing, particularly across multiple settings. For example, different test results may seem contradictory or the child's reported behavior may differ across environments. Remember that the data may be confusing, but the child is behaving consistently with respect to his or her perception of the environment. The assessor's task is to identify that consistency and determine what, if any, interventions are implicated. Contradictory assessment data can often point toward areas that the assessor most urgently needs to understand because they point to key variables associated with the behavior. For example, differences in behaviors at home and at school may suggest that effective interventions have already been developed in one setting. Resolving the contradictions that an assessment inevitably produces can make the greatest contribution to understanding a child's behavior.

A HOME-SCHOOL APPROACH TO INTERVENTION

The central characteristic of behavior management programs is that they should be sensitive to the information generated. A management program should be modified if new information indicates a different approach is needed or the program results in minimal behavior change. To simplify the presentation, both the assessment and behavior management processes have been presented in a stepwise manner. However, neither process is linear. Both need to be responsive to the information they generate. At any time it could be necessary to return to an earlier step in the process in order to try something else or gather more information. Administrators of behavior management programs must be flexible. This means being willing to revise hypotheses and change intervention strategies as necessary.

Steps in Intervention

A brief description of the eight steps in a formal behavior management program is presented below. For a more complete description, see Wielkiewicz (1986).

Step 1: Identify the problem. Once a problem has been identified, it is necessary to determine how to approach it. One option is to conduct a formal assessment as described in the previous section, and then develop an intervention plan. In other cases, the problem may not be regarded as serious enough to justify a full assessment, or an immediate response may be needed. Regardless of whether a full assessment is conducted immediately, it is crucial to remain flexible during the behavior management process. The response of children and the system as a whole to the intervention process may require reconsideration of the intervention strategy at any step in the process. The response of a child to intervention strategies also provides important assessment data (Christenson, Abery, & Weinberg, 1986; Wielkiewicz, 1986).

Step 2: Refine the definition of the problem. Refining the definition of the problem means to state the target behavior in a manner appropriate for a behavior management program. Personality traits and global behavioral labels such as disruptive, depressed, hyperactive, anxious, are replaced with definitions that specify *what* behavior occurring under *what* circumstances will be rewarded or punished. A good definition of a behavior to be managed or modified has three characteristics. First, it should not require any observer interpretation, such as a judgment of whether or not the behavior was provoked. Second, the behavior must be countable or measurable. Third, one should be able to explain the definition to another person.

In addition to defining behavior in terms that are concrete, measurable, and reliable, specify the problem in terms of a behavior to be increased. The presence of a behavior excess usually indicates that a more desirable behavior is absent.

Step 3: Assess the baseline rate. The baseline rate of a behavior refers to its frequency or rate of occurrence prior to the start of a behavior management program. Once the program is begun, data continue to be collected using the *same* technique. Baseline data provide the standard against which the success of the behavior management program is judged. If the frequency or duration of the target behavior changes sufficiently in the desired direction, the program is regarded as successful. Useful techniques for collecting baseline data include frequency counts, percentages, and time sampling.

Step 4: Identify the reinforcer and contingency. Finding a reward that can be easily delivered at school can be a problem. Christian (1983) suggested that rewards used in school be placed on a hierarchy ranging from the most concrete to the most abstract rewards. Categories of consequences, along with examples appear in Table 2.

Christian pointed out that most children are operating at the two highest levels of reinforcement: praise and internal self-reinforcement. When dealing with a child's problem behavior the goal should be to start at the highest level possible on the hierarchy and advance toward higher levels. Explaining this hierarchy to parents may reduce resistance of parents who do not wish to "bribe" their children to do what they are "supposed to be doing." It also helps to point out that the ultimate goal is to completely eliminate the behavior management program.

After a reward has been selected, state the contingency or rule for administering the reward. The contingency defines the relationship between behavior and the reward (or punishment). A contingency can specify that a stimulus is presented or removed when a behavior occurs or fails to occur. It is a good idea to put the contingency in writing and have someone else look at it before it is activated.

Step 5: Begin the program. Begin the behavior management program by announcing the rules to the child or by simply applying the contingency. The most effective programs will have the child's parents playing a key role and accurate communication among all parties will be essential to success. A handout describing the basic rules of the program and frequent phone contact are effective ways to ensure success. Once begun, it is important that the program be objectively administered. Its rules should provide the necessary guidance as to when rewards are delivered or taken away. If the program administrator finds himself or herself making subjective judgments regarding what should be done, the program should be revised to eliminate the subjectivity. Keep in mind that this is a common occurrence because children often will be curious about the limits of a particular program and attempt to establish limits that are in their favor.

Finally, it is important to be patient because the target behavior is not likely to change instantaneously.

Step 6: Observe the effects of the program and initiate steps to strengthen

TABLE 2
A Practical Reinforcement Hierarchy for Classroom Behavior Modification

Consequence Level	A Infantile Physical Contact	B Food	C Toys	D School Implements	E Privileges	F Praise	G Internal Self- Reinfrocement
Examples	Hugs	Milk	Balloon	Eraser	Free Time	Verbal Comments	"I did well"
	Pats	Raisins	Marble	Ruler	Errands	Grades	"My work's all complete"
	Physical Proximity	Crackers	Kite	Notepad	Collect Papers	Certificate	
		Gum	Clay	Crayon			
	←_____Concreteness				Abstractness_____→		

Source: Christian, B. (1983). A practical reinforcement hierarchy for classroom behavior modification. *Psychology in the Schools, 55,* 171–178. Reprinted with permission of Clinical Psychology Publishing Co.,Inc., 4 Conant Square, Brandon, VT 05733.

generalization. This is a continuation of Steps 4 and 5. If behavior changes in the desired direction, the program is continued until the appropriate behaviors are well established. At this point steps to obtain generalization of desired behavior to new environments or situations may be started.

Strengthening generalization from a training setting to a new setting can be accomplished by either bringing elements of the new setting into the training environment or taking elements from the training environment to the new setting. For instance, parents who have been providing home-based reinforcement for school behaviors may wish to apply similar techniques at home. This process has the best chance of success if the child's parents visit the classroom to learn more about the program and discuss how it could be applied at home. Similarly, the school-based portion of the program may include behaviors targeted by the parents at home. By fading out those elements the parents cannot implement (see Step 8), it is possible to construct a program that is similar to the home. More thorough discussions of generalization may be found in Rutherford and Nelson (1988), Stokes and Baer (1977), and Wielkiewicz (1986).

Step 7: Modify the program, if necessary. Behavior management programs frequently do not work the first time and the most successful applications of behavior management principles are accomplished by those who can successfully modify a failing program. When a program appears ineffective several explanations may be possible: It may need more time to take effect, the reward may be insufficient, the program may be inconsistently administered, the target behavior may be unclearly defined, other competing contingencies may be maintaining the behavior, or the program may have been faded too quickly.

Another reason for the apparent ineffectiveness of a behavior management program is that something important may have been overlooked when the original assessment was performed. Often an accurate picture of the child's family

system does not emerge until a behavior management program has been in effect for some time. Marital conflict, financial problems, serious illness, and alcoholism are examples of home situations that can affect school behavior. Both behavior management and additional family services may be needed in these situations.

Step 8: Fade out the program. The successful behavior management program eventually puts itself out of business. That is, the program is slowly faded out so the target behavior occurs at a normal rate without a formal behavior management program. Fading is accomplished by reducing the amount and frequency of reward. At the same time, praise and other rewards from significant adults (good grades from the teacher and positive attention from parents, for example) take the place of the structure of the behavior management program.

As suggested earlier, the steps in behavior assessment and management described above are not intended to represent a linear process. Instead, it is often necessary to approach behavior problems more creatively. However, the above steps should be useful in ensuring that the major questions are posed and that important child and family characteristics are not overlooked. If these procedures are applied in a flexible manner, the school practitioner should find the results rewarding.

Following the procedure outlined above does not guarantee consistent success in conducting assessments and developing cooperative behavior management programs, because the potential for home-school conflict always exists when sensitive issues surface. A sampling of strategies that can be valuable in enhancing cooperation and decreasing conflict are now discussed.

ENHANCING HOME-SCHOOL COOPERATION IN BEHAVIORAL ASSESSMENT AND MANAGEMENT

Essentially, a child's world consists of three subsystems: home, school, and community. When these subsystems are united in the pursuit of common goals, behavior management programming can be efficient and rewarding. When these subsystems have conflicting goals, the behavior management process can be difficult and frustrating. The role of the behavior management consultant is to be as sensitive as possible to the needs of each subsystem, while coaxing them to come together in support of the child's needs.

Communicating to Prevent Conflict

Schools routinely communicate a great deal with parents. Regular communications include report cards, conferences, meetings of the parent-teacher organization, and various notes that are sent home with students. When a special conference with the parent or parents is requested by the school, the proposed topic is usually "bad news" from the parents' perspective. Even if the news is positive, the initial reactions of parents to a request for a school conference are likely to be negative. Because the school represents a source of public authority, parents are likely to feel threatened by the prospect of having their competence as parents scrutinized. Thus, interactions with parents should be as nonthreatening as possible. A few strategies for communicating with parents are discussed.

Avoiding negative attributions. A helpful way to view school-home interactions is from the perspective of attribution theory, which is concerned with understanding how people infer causal relationships. The relevance of attribution research to school-parent relationships is based upon a very simple premise: *Parents will resist being regarded as responsible for their children's problems.* If parents are blamed or accused by school staff of being responsible for the problems of their children, they are likely to take a defensive stance that is almost certain to impede progress toward remediating the child's behavioral or academic problems.

People tend to take credit for positive outcomes and deny responsibility for negative outcomes (Harvey & Weary, 1984). Thus, one goal of a school confer-

ence should be to communicate something positive to the parents and to present negative information (i.e., the description of the problem) in a way that totally avoids pinning the responsibility upon the parents. It is particularly important to avoid forcing the parents into making what would be called "internal and stable" attributions. An internal attribution ascribes the cause of an event to some internal characteristic of the individual; a stable attribution is one that cannot be changed (Seligman, Abramson, Semmel, & Von Baeyer, 1979). If parents become convinced that they are incompetent and responsible for their child's behavior problems, the home-school relationship is likely to be characterized by hostility and discomfort. Although information must be communicated at a parent conference, it should not be presented in such a way as to place blame on anyone.

One approach is to emphasize problem solving. Instead of focussing upon defining the problem behavior and its causes, the team can be directed toward a mutually agreeable goal, focussing upon deficit skills and how to teach and reward them. When both teachers and parents are conjointly involved in the consultation process, stimulus variables related to the target behavior may be more readily identifiable. Furthermore, generalization of treatment effects to both the home and school settings may be more obtainable (Sheridan, Kratochwill, & Elliott, 1990). As noted earlier, a behavior excess almost always indicates that a desirable behavior is absent. By establishing mutually acceptable goals to increase desirable behavior, it is often possible to decrease behavior excesses. For more discussion of this approach see Carlson, Hickman, and Horton (this volume) and Christenson and Cleary (1990).

A complementary issue concerns the issue of "taking credit" for improvement in the child's behavior problems or general adjustment. Although parents are likely to respond defensively to any attempts to blame them or have them take direct responsibility for their child's misbehavior or failure to perform, they would like to be able to take credit for improvements or the positive accomplishments of their children. Dunst and Trivette (1987) and Dunst and Johanson (this volume) describe a way of thinking about helping relationships that emphasizes giving power to the client as opposed to taking credit for improvement that occurs. Their model states that parents need to attribute behavior change to their own actions in order to acquire a sense of control or competency. The idea is to "empower" parents so they are able to deal effectively with problems. By doing so, not only is the short-term referral problem solved, but future problems may be avoided.

Conducting cooperative parent meetings. Many factors contribute to the ease with which parents move toward accepting the reality of a child's problem behavior and the need to do something about it. These factors include the severity of the problem, the degree to which the problem is a part of the family system, the personalities of the parents, and the manner in which the parents are informed of the problem. Waterman (1982) recommends that parents be informed in a direct manner that accurately, realistically, and completely describes the problem without any false reassurances that the child will "grow out of it." In addition, she suggests that both sensitivity to the emotional needs of the parents and dealing with them as rational, mature persons eager to learn more about their child may be helpful.

School personnel should recognize that parents are likely to express a wide range of emotions when they hear the facts about their child's behavior and academic performance. Some of these emotions may be directed against the school and the people who work there. It would be most helpful to redirect the energies of the parents toward contributing to the resolution of the child's problem behavior. In many ways a meeting with a child's parents is similar to a counseling or therapy session. In their review of family therapy, Zimmerman and Sims (1983) noted that two therapist characteristics were consistently associated

with deterioration: first, therapists who had "poor relationship skills" and directly attacked "loaded issues" and family members' defenses very early in treatment; second, therapists who did little to support family members. The implication is that school personnel should be aware of the emotional issues likely to be revealed in a parent conference and avoid attacking the parents on sensitive issues. In addition, parents should leave the meeting feeling supported by school personnel rather than in conflict with them.

Reframing: Placing a positive perspective on problems. When a practitioner's hypothesis is that the child's misbehavior plays an important role in the system, how can the school bring about a change in behavior via a parent conference? Bowman and Goldberg (1983) have suggested "reframing" is a technique that can be valuable.

The essence of reframing is that an attempt is made to alter the current patterns by dealing with them in an indirect manner that avoids eliciting defensive behavior. LeClave and Brack (1989) describe reframing as finding a "more adaptive, and less painful, means of viewing the world" (p. 69). The idea of reframing is to attach new, less negative, even positive connotations to events so as to provide motivation for change and adaptation. For instance, suggesting that child misbehavior reflects a need to gain parental attention, can help parents to see their child's behavior in a different light leading to beneficial change when they begin attending to desirable behavior. A reframe for presenting behavior management techniques to parents is to suggest that what the parents are doing would work for most children, but the child's uniqueness suggests that a different approach is needed. LeClave and Brack also suggest the word "unique" has much better connotations than the word "abnormal."

Coyne and Biglan (1984) describe reframing strategy as focussing not so much on the problem behavior itself, but on altering patterns of coping with the problem. Reframing, then, is a technique of helping others to see the problem in a way that leads to more effective coping behavior. This approach can be especially helpful in breaking patterns of attending to undesirable behavior. By reframing the goal of the misbehavior from an attempt to annoy and irritate adults to an attempt to gain needed attention, it may be possible to modify patterns of attending to the child. The result is that the child receives attention for positive behavior and undesirable behavior disappears.

Reframing is a technique that allows school personnel to communicate with parents without implying that they are responsible for their child's misbehavior. This approach encourages a collaborative relationship between parents and school staff. Most parents are motivated to maintain a positive self-image of their parenting skills and will respond defensively to suggestions that they are at fault or need to change in order to improve the child's behavior. The mechanism of change in the reframing technique lies in placing the behavior in a frame that emphasizes the positive motivations of all concerned. The goal is to reveal previously unrecognized positive and caring feelings, which are frequently masked by angry and apparently uncaring ones. By reframing the problem in this manner, new options for change are opened up for the family. Placing a positive connotation upon a symptom and changing its meaning for the client is an important element in the success of reframing (Shoham-Salomon & Rosenthal, 1987).

Anticipating Problem Situations

Difficult problems occur that interfere with the harmonious functioning of the subsystems. However, my own experience indicates that most of these problems fall into one of three categories: marital conflict, child abuse, and child depression/suicide.

When a behavior management program is undertaken, the practitioner should be alert for signs of marital conflict. Children living in homes characterized by interparental conflict have the greatest risk of showing behavioral

problems (Emery, 1982). This finding has been documented by numerous researchers (Beattie & Maniscalo, 1985; Drake, 1981; Forehand, McCombs, Long, Brody, & Fauber, 1988; Guidubaldi, Cleminshaw, Perry, & McLoughlin, 1983; Guidubaldi & Perry, 1984; Hetherington, 1979; Jouriles, Murphy, & O'Leary, 1989; King & Kleemeier, 1983; Pfeffer, 1981; Slater & Haber, 1984). From the systems perspective, the school practitioner needs to look for situations where the child's behavior has a role in the marital (or post-marital) relationship. For example, behavior problems may be inadvertently rewarded by one parent who interprets such problems as a sign of the other parent's incompetence. On the other hand, marital conflict itself may be centered around child-rearing issues causing inconsistency in rules and discipline methods. If a behavior management program is in opposition to the role the child plays in the family system, it can be very difficult to bring about behavior change.

In contrast to marital conflict and divorce, child abuse is less prevalent. However, it has a profound impact (Barahal, Waterman, & Martin, 1981; Belsky, 1980; Williams, 1983; Wolfe, 1985). Wolfe (1985) found that abusive parents generally display symptoms of depression and health problems and are likely to be involved in stress-inducing family situations impairing their competence as parents. Their children come to reflect the qualities of this environment, behaving so as to present the parent with a high number of problem situations, which helps maintain a high level of conflict. The general pattern within an abusive family is one of disharmony, conflict, frustration, stress, and the relatively infrequent use of positive rewards. When this situation is encountered, the school practitioner is often working in cooperation with social agencies. However, the school can offer training and expertise in child behavior management that may be unavailable from other sources. The school may also provide a point of reference for the other subsystems so that communication remains

open and the child's needs gain promi-
nence.

The third major difficulty faced by
the school practitioner is whether the
child shows signs of depression or suicide. Internalizing behavior problems
(e.g., anxiety, depression) can be difficult
to recognize because the accompanying
behaviors are sometimes subtle and not
as attention-getting as externalizing behavior problems. However, because depression is one of the few mental disorders that can lead to fatal consequences,
it is prudent to look for associated signs
whenever an assessment is undertaken.
(See Guetzloe, 1989, for an overview.) If
evidence indicates that a suicide attempt
is possible, resources of the entire system
will need to be quickly mobilized to
protect the child against harm.

Marital conflict, child abuse, and
depression-suicide are three issues that
are sometimes associated with behavior
management or special education assessments. When these issues surface, the
school psychologist will typically find
that it is not *what* is communicated so
much as *how* it is communicated that
has the greatest influence on the success
of behavior management programs and
other interventions. The main goal is to
coax the subsystems into entering collaborative relationships. In a collaborative
relationship, clear boundaries exist between the two systems, with parents and
teachers each having clear authority
within their own domain. At the same
time, the relationship is characterized by
flexibility and open communication with
each party taking the initiative to solve
actual or potential problems as concerns
arise (Power & Bartholomew, 1987).
Although system interventions such as
family therapy are beyond the expertise
of many behavior management consultants, it is possible to have a favorable
influence on systems issues by applying
skillful communication strategies.

Another way of enhancing home-
school cooperation is to design behavior
management programs in which parents
play important roles. This aspect of
designing behavior management programs is described.

DESIGNING BEHAVIOR MANAGEMENT PROGRAMS TO ENCOURAGE PARENTAL PARTICIPATION

The use of home-based behavior
management programs can decrease the
burden upon school personnel (Atkeson
& Forehand, 1979), enhance home-school
cooperation, avoid problems associated
with in-school reinforcement, and directly assist parents with child management problems (Kelley & Carper, 1988). If
parents learn child management techniques via direct instruction or participation in school-based programs, they can
become empowered with problem-solving
skills that will enable them to cope more
effectively with future problems. Some
methods of increasing home-school cooperation and parent behavior management
skills are described.

Bibliotherapy, Workshops, and Parent Training

Harris and Fong (1985) argued that a
high priority should be placed upon
providing parents of developmentally disabled children with training in behavior
management techniques. It is easy to
extend this argument to any child problem with a behavioral component because improvement in behavior will be
most general and long lasting if home-
school cooperation and consistency are
encouraged. Harris and Fong also suggested that the school psychologist must
work closely with classroom personnel to
help maintain a healthy relationship
between home and school. Reframing any
failure of parents to follow through with
suggested programs in terms of the
intense sadness and stress that the
parents are likely to experience may
motivate school personnel to provide
more support rather than criticize the
parents. Because many parents can benefit from training in child management
techniques (Ramsey & Patterson, 1989;
Ramsey, Walker, Shinn, O'Neill, & Stieber,
1989; Sheridan, Kratochwill, & Elliott,
1990), parent training can be an important component of programs to interrupt

the chain of circumstances leading to problem behavior.

School practitioners have many resources from which to draw when working with parents to modify child behaviors. Numerous informative books about child problems and child management techniques are available. *Taking a Look at Discipline* (Garman, 1983), *A Parent's Guide to Child Discipline* (Dreikurs & Grey, 1970), *How to Help Children with Common Problems* (Schaefer & Millman, 1981), *Effective Parents/Responsible Children* (Eimers & Aitchison, 1977), *Training and Habilitating Developmentally Disabled People* (Wielkiewicz & Calvert, 1989), *How to Discipline Without Feeling Guilty* (Silberman & Wheelan, 1980), *Sign Here: A Contracting Book for Children and Their Parents* (Dardig & Heward, 1981), and *The Good Kid Book* (Sloane, 1988) are examples of such resources.

Other formats for conducting parent training include videotaped programs (Webster-Stratton, Kolpacoff, & Hollinsworth, 1988; Webster-Stratton, Hollinsworth, & Kolpacoff, 1989), combining parent training with family therapy (Brunk, Henggeler, & Whelan, 1987) and various workshops (e.g., Barkley, 1987a, 1987b). Making books, workshops, and other resources available to parents can meet the needs of some parents while enabling school psychologists to use their time more efficiently. For an excellent overview and history of parent training techniques see Schaefer and Briesmeister (1989).

Home Notes

A more direct way of encouraging parental involvement in behavior management programs is to use home notes. Using home notes, teachers provide feedback to parents regarding the child's behavior, and parents reward good or improved behavior. Home-school notes have many advantages over more traditional, entirely school-based, behavior management programs (Kelley, 1990). First, home-school notes may promote a collaborative relationship between home and school. Second, home-school notes allow the emphasis to be placed upon the positive accomplishments of the child. Third, this type of program can be done by a classroom teacher with a minimum time commitment. Fourth, giving the child's parents responsibility for providing rewards avoids problems associated with in-class reinforcement. Fifth, parents typically have access to a much wider range of reinforcers than school personnel. Sixth, home notes are an effective way to communicate basic behavior management principles to parents in a nonthreatening, concrete format. This knowledge can empower parents with problem-solving skills applicable to a wide range of problems (e.g., McMahon, Forehand, & Griest, 1981).

Because school performance is rewarded by parents, teachers are relieved of most tasks involved in conducting a behavior management program (e.g., Schumaker, Hovell, & Sherman, 1977). However, a potential problem with home-based programs is that parents may not be skilled in the application of behavior management techniques. Thus, parent behavior should be monitored to ensure that they follow the rules of the program. If problems develop as a consequence of parental inconsistency or lack of understanding, it may be necessary to provide training or consultation, or to recommend family counseling.

The mechanics of a home-note system are described below following the eight-step format discussed earlier. Briefly, a printed note (see Figures 1 and 2) is filled out once a day by the child's teacher. The child receives points according to the quality of academic and behavioral performance. The child takes the note home and uses the points to "purchase" from a menu of rewards provided by the child's parents. Kelley (1990) also has several examples of school-home notes along with a useful handout for parents and teachers describing the activities involved in a home-note program.

Steps 1 and 2: Identify and refine the problem definition. This type of program is most likely to succeed when the

FIGURE 1
Daily/Weekly Report Card

Student's Name: _____ Date: _____

The student's academic performance was (initial appropriate space)

_____ Excellent (25 points)

_____ Good (20 points)

_____ Acceptable (10 points)

_____ Unacceptable (0 points)

The student's general behavior was

_____ Excellent (25 points)

_____ Good (20 points)

_____ Acceptable (10 points)

_____ Unacceptable (0 points)

Teacher's comments: _____

_____

_____

_____

_____

Source: Wielkiewicz, R. M. (1986). *Behavior management in the schools* (pp. 209–210). Needham Heights, MA: Allyn & Bacon.

student shows inconsistent performance, and the underlying problem seems to be poor motivation. If the child lacks the skills necessary for academic and behavioral success, it may be necessary to provide direct training in the deficit skills.

Step 3: Assess the baseline rate. Baseline data can be obtained by completing the home note for a week without providing any feedback to the child. In this way, a reasonably objective record of the teacher's impressions can be obtained, and it will later be possible to determine whether the program leads to positive change. This record also provides an excellent basis for determining the number of points to be exchanged for the rewards.

Step 4: Identify the reinforcer and contingency. Implementing a home-note program is very simple. At the end of each

school day, the child's teacher fills out a note to the parents, such as shown in Figures 1 and 2. The child takes the note home, and the parents tabulate the points earned for that day. The points earned are then exchanged for rewards as negotiated between the child and parents. Given that the child can earn up to 50 or 60 points per day, a reasonable starting point might be about 300–400 points for a reward of moderate size, such as a movie or small toy. In order to get the program off to a good start, one or two small rewards that can be "purchased" with relatively few points should be available.

An important element of a home-note program is the role of the child's teacher in providing social reinforcement for good performance and feedback regarding unacceptable behavior. Because the target behaviors are not precisely specified and may vary from day to day,

FIGURE 2
Daily/Weekly Report Card

Student's Name: _____ Date: _____

The student's academic performance was (initial appropriate space)

_____ Outstanding (30 points)

_____ Good (25 points)

_____ Above Average (20 points)

_____ Acceptable (15 points)

_____ Improvement Shown (10 points)

_____ Improvement Needed (5 points)

_____ Not Acceptable (0 points)

Teacher's comments: _____

_____

_____

The student's general behavior was

_____ Outstanding (30 points)

_____ Good (25 points)

_____ Above Average (20 points)

_____ Improvement Shown (15 points)

_____ Improvement Needed (10 points)

_____ Acceptable (5 points)

_____ Not Acceptable (0 points)

Teacher's comments: _____

_____

_____

_____

_____
Source: Wielkiewicz, R. M. (1986).

the child's teacher should provide feedback regarding the reasons for each day's performance rating. For example, if the child did not complete an in-class assignment or failed a spelling test and received a low rating for the day's academic performance, this should be explained. If the child's behavior was rated as "unacceptable," the reasons for the rating should be given. Also, it would be helpful if the teacher helped the child to develop a plan, such as studying the spelling words, to gain a higher rating in the future. Similarly, if the child did well, the teacher should concretely describe the desirable behaviors.

Step 5: Begin the program. Several elements need to come together in order for a home-note program to begin. First, an appropriate format for the note must be determined. Figure 1 shows a simple home-note format, whereas Figure 2 is more detailed. The latter is most appropriate when the child's behavior is generally poor and much improvement is needed. The additional rating levels allow the child to earn some points for less than optimal performance. Note that both formats request a rating of behavior *and* academic performance. Because each affects the other, it is recommended that both ratings be used even when improvement in only one area is needed. This will allow the child to receive some positive feedback.

The next step is to meet with the child's parents to discuss the classroom situation and options for handling it. During the conference, the home-note system should be offered as one method of dealing with the child's behavior. If the parents are willing, a date to begin the program should be set, allowing for a 1-week baseline period. Alternately, the baseline data could be gathered prior to the conference to show the parents and provide an opportunity to set "prices" on the reward menu during the conference.

If the child's parents are reluctant or unwilling to cooperate with the home-note program, one option for the school is to conduct an entirely school-based behavior management program. Improved child behavior may stimulate parental interest in participation. On the other hand, it may be necessary to explore more deeply the nature of the home-school system to develop strategies to increase parental participation. Most of the chapters in the present volume address this issue either directly or indirectly.

A few days prior to the start of the program, both the parents and the teacher should explain the program to the child. At the end of the first day of the program, the teacher should have a brief conference with the child to present the note and provide feedback regarding the day's accomplishments. Under no circumstances should the teacher get into arguments with the child over the appropriate rating for the day, although the teacher must also make every effort to be fair and realistic in setting standards. At the start of the program, phone contact between the teacher and the child's parents may be needed to clarify the program rules. Children may want to collect rewards while keeping the points. A good way to clarify this issue is to explain that the points are like money; once spent, they are gone.

Step 6: Observe the effects of the program and take steps to strengthen generalization beyond the training environment. Once the program begins, the child's parents or other administrator of the program should keep a record of the number of points earned each day and the total number of points earned each week. As the number of points earned increases, subjective reports of classroom behavior should reflect the improvement represented by the points. If not, the purposes and goals of the program should be reviewed. Because the training environment is the classroom, it is not necessary to be concerned with generalization, although the child's parents may desire help in starting a similar program at home.

Step 7: Modify the program, if necessary. If the program fails to produce the expected changes, the first issue to examine is the child's and parents' understanding of the program. Parents will sometimes take away a reward that has been earned with good behavior in school when the child misbehaves at home. Such behavior on the part of the parents should be taken as a sign that they need additional help in learning to manage their child's behavior. Another possibility is that the child does not understand the connection between the points earned in school and the promised reward. This could be remedied by a careful explanation or by reducing the total number of points necessary to earn a smaller reward.

As in almost all behavior management programs, it is always possible that the rewards are not powerful enough to bring about behavior change. It is also possible that the material reward is not the issue from the child's point of view. When the child's behavior shows improvement, significant adults should respond with obvious pride in the child's accomplishment. If this element is missing, the program could fail. An examination of the motives of the parents and the function of the child's behavior in the family system may be in order.

A home-note program may not be

effective in every case. If either the child's ability or skill level was overestimated at the beginning of the program, the feedback provided by the home-note points may be insufficient to improve performance. In such cases, more thorough assessment and a new behavior management program might be needed.

Step 8: Fade out the program. Home-note programs are not meant to be completely faded, because periodic report cards and parent-teacher conferences are a regular occurrence as the child progresses through school. The goal is to fade out the daily notes from the teacher and the reliance upon the reward system to maintain good behavior. As noted previously, an important part of making the transition to a reward-free system is that the adults must provide the child with positive attention and praise for good performance. As the child begins to excel, the number of points required for a reward can be increased, while the frequency of home notes is decreased. If good performance can be maintained with a weekly home note, it would be reasonable to consider eliminating the point system. If both parents and teachers respond positively to the accomplishments of the child, it can be expected that the formal behavior management program can be replaced by natural contingencies such as attention and praise for good grades and behavior.

Monitoring School Performance of Older Children

By modifying its format, a home-note program can be adapted to the needs of older students. Practitioners working at the junior and senior high school level often face referrals involving students who lack motivation. Frequently, these youths come from families with parents who are aware of the value of a high school diploma but are not skilled in motivating their child to obtain it. Whether or not the student is placed in special education, the need is to motivate them to organize their schedule, attend classes, study regularly, behave appropriately in class, and produce high quality

work. A daily monitoring program can be used as a tool for teaching and rewarding academic survival skills.

The Daily Performance Record shown in Figure 3 is designed to be as flexible as possible. It allows for monitoring attendance, homework, preparation for class (having books, note-taking materials, pencil or pen, etc.), completion of in-class assignments, quality of completed work, and other behaviors relevant to successful performance. Each category of behavior is worth 1 to 5 points, with 1 point representing unacceptable performance and 5 points representing outstanding performance. The Daily Performance Record is meant to be the responsibility of the student, who should carry the record and present it to each teacher at the end of the academic period. Because the Daily Performance Record provides reminders and detailed criteria for acceptable behavior, the student can learn new skills, such as appropriate organizational habits. Monitoring performance and record keeping can be shared between the home and school in any manner that can be negotiated.

Baseline data can be collected by distributing a Daily Performance Record to each teacher and having them complete it every day for a week. At the end of the week the Daily Performance Records are collected by the consultant who performs the necessary computations (described below). These data can then be used to communicate the nature of the problem and a proposed solution to the youth's parents. Thus, it becomes the school's responsibility to monitor performance and the parents' responsibility to reward appropriate or improved performance.

The reward is based upon the percent of available points earned. As shown in Figure 3, each of the behaviors monitored in the program is given a rating of 1 to 5 points. A percentage is computed by dividing the total number of points earned by the total number of possible points for a given day. The total possible points is equal to five times the total number of behavior categories that were rated, summed across subjects or periods.

FIGURE 3
Daily Performance Record

Name: _____

Date: _____

Points
5 = Outstanding Performance
4 = Good Performance
3 = Acceptable
2 = Improvement Needed
1 = Unacceptable

Points Earned: _____

Total Possible: _____

Percent: _____

Period or Subject

	1	2	3	4	5	6	7
Attendance							
Homework Completed							
Has Needed Materials							
In-class Assignments Complete							
Quality of Completed Work							
Teacher's Initials							

Comments and Upcoming Assignments:

_____

_____

_____

_____

Note: Adapted from Wielkiewicz, R. M. (1986). *Behavior management in the schools* (p. 216). Needham Heights, MA: Allyn & Bacon.

This method is useful because the number of applicable behavior categories is likely to change from day to day, according to the instructional methods used by each teacher.

The most difficult part of making this program succeed is negotiation of rewards and privileges among the school-based consultant, the youth, and the youth's parents. For some students the process is relatively simple because the contract shifts attention from inappropriate to appropriate behavior. Soon after adults begin paying attention to the behaviors needed for school success, these behaviors increase and it seems that the particular reward is not crucial to the program's success. On the other hand, some students resist participation in the program. Often, negotiation of the behavior program needs to focus equally upon the student and the parents who are often not accustomed to providing positive consequences for behavior. However, putting the agreement in writing and having it signed by the student, the parent(s), and an administrative witness, helps to establish the trust needed to make such an agreement work. Reframing techniques and careful attention to the wording of the contract can help to keep the contract negotiations on a positive track.

Two issues seem to dominate the negotiation process. First, selection of back-up rewards needs to be worked out between the parents and the student with the school practitioner serving a mediating function. Sometimes parents express the belief that their children should perform in school because they are supposed to, not because they are rewarded. This issue can be approached in many ways, but many parents will accept a program when it is framed as analogous to working at a job.

A second issue that often needs to be discussed is potential embarrassment from carrying the Daily Performance Record to each teacher. There is an easy remedy for this problem. The negotiating team can determine criteria for improved performance that allows the student to avoid being placed on the full contract. For instance, teachers can be surveyed at the end of each week and asked to rate the student's performance for a whole week using the Daily Performance Record. If the student receives a given rating or higher as negotiated with the student and parents, they could avoid being placed on the daily monitoring program. Falling below the established criterion would mean the student would begin the full program the following week.

Some students may not be motivated by rewards that parents are able to provide. A backup contingency, instituted at many schools, is to use after-school detention on those days when the student fails to complete assigned work. If the detention is adequately supervised, it can provide students with an environment that rewards academic productivity and encourages greater academic responsibility.

Summary. Home-note programs such as those described above are extremely powerful techniques (Kelley, 1990). In addition to directly addressing a child's needs, they enhance home-school cooperation at a concrete and effective level. In a nonthreatening way these programs can also empower parents to solve other problems involving their children. In my experience, using home-note programs has encouraged parents to contact schools for help and represents the type of cooperative relationship that school systems should foster.

A Team Approach to Management of Attention Problems

Attention problems are a common referral issue in schools. Both teachers and parents may have questions about children who have difficulty following directions, fail to remain on task, fail to complete assigned tasks, frequently leave their seats, are easily distracted by extraneous stimuli, approach tasks in a disorganized manner, are very fidgety or overactive, talk excessively, or show signs of impulsivity. The syndrome characterized by these behaviors is often diagnosed as Attention-Deficit Hyperactivity Disorder (ADHD; American Psychiatric Association, 1987; Goldstein & Goldstein, 1990).

Whether or not ADHD has been formally diagnosed, school personnel are likely to be concerned when the associated behaviors interfere with adequate functioning in school. Behavior management techniques can be very helpful in improving functioning at home and at school. The most efficient way to address the complexities of managing attention problems is to employ a systems approach.

Open and accurate communication with the child's parents is necessary. School staff members must be aware that the coping skills of the child's parents may be exhausted and the parents may lack confidence in their ability to parent the hyperactive child, with or without a formal diagnosis of ADHD (Barkley, 1981, 1990). They may also have received numerous negative messages regarding their parenting skills from relatives, friends, and various professionals. Thus, it is critical for the school to approach the child's parent(s) in an empathetic manner.

School psychologists can be a resource for parents who want information about strategies for assisting children with attentional problems. If needed, parents can be referred to helpful resources such as *The ADD Hyperactivity Workbook for Parents, Teachers, and Kids* (Parker, 1988), *Your Hyperactive Child* (Ingersoll, 1988), or the pamphlet by Goldstein and Goldstein (1986), "Challenge: A Newsletter on Attention Deficit Hyperactivity Disorder" (Challenge, Inc., P.O. Box 2001, West Newbury, MA 01985). It is important to be thoroughly familiar with the parent education options available in the community and refer parents to them as needed. The training program described by Barkley (1987a, 1987b) is a popular model.

One behavior management program I have found particularly effective for children with attentional problems was named the "coupon program" by one of my colleagues. It is a response cost token program based upon writings of Kendall and Braswell (1985), Salend and Allen (1985), Rappaport, Murphy, and Bailey (1982), Wielkiewicz (1986), and Witt and Elliott (1982).

The coupon program. The best use of token programs is to reward a child's appropriate behavior. This is not always feasible, especially in a classroom situation where the teacher is busy with the needs of many other children. Also, for hyperactive children in a classroom, the main goal is to keep them focussed on assigned academic tasks. If the child is rewarded for "paying attention" to work, the reward itself is a distracting stimulus that may draw the child off-task. An alternate method of rewarding on-task behavior is to have the child begin a time period with several tokens. The contingency is that the child then *loses* a token each time a classroom rule is violated. This is called a response-cost contingency meaning that certain responses "cost" the child a token.

A disruptive or off-task child is usually violating classroom rules that other children in the classroom obey most of the time. Therefore, a reasonable goal is for the child to obey classroom rules. Three to five rules seems to work well with many children. Some examples of effective rules are:

1. Stay in your seat, unless you have permission to leave.
2. Stay on-task until all work is done.
3. No talking without permission during "WORK" time.
4. Obey the teacher.
5. Keep all four legs of your chair on the floor.

Rules 1, 2, and 3 are standard classroom rules that will differ according to the needs of the teacher and the classroom. Rule 4 is a general rule that can serve as a "catch-all" for unanticipated situations. If the child does something disruptive that is not covered by the rules, a warning can be given followed immediately by the response cost contingency if the behavior continues. Rule 5 is an example of how a rule can be directed at a particular problem behavior. In this example, a teacher was concerned that a child might be hurt because he frequently tilted his chair backwards.

Like all token programs, the coupon program depends upon a menu of reinforcers. The reinforcers on the menu can be "purchased" by the child using the coupons that remain at the end of each time period. Small reinforcers that can be "purchased" for just a few coupons such as candy, a sticker, or a pencil keep the child from becoming discouraged in the early part of the program. The reward menu should also include items that require the child to save coupons over a longer time period. The "cost" of such items might range from 25 coupons to several hundred coupons.

The coupon program will be most effective if the child's parents are active participants from the beginning. A daily home note can be used to communicate the child's performance for each day and parents can also provide the rewards. Careful monitoring by school personnel will be needed to be sure that the rules are being followed but this can represent an excellent opportunity for developing home-school cooperation and empowering the parents by helping them to learn problem-solving skills.

A more concrete description of the "coupon program" procedure is presented.

1. The child receives a predetermined number of coupons for the designated time period. Five to 10 coupons for a 30-minute seatwork period is a typical number. Use the baseline data to decide the number of coupons to begin with.

2. Each time the child disobeys one of the established rules, one of the coupons is taken away by the teacher without any negative comments. It would be appropriate to simply state the rule that was violated. Some program administrators will be more comfortable giving a warning before removing a coupon. As long as follow-through on the warning is consistent and predictable, the coupon program will be effective.

3. If the child runs out of coupons, then no more can be taken away. The child never goes into "debt" because this would lead to unnecessary discouragement. The best response to misbehavior after the child runs out of coupons is to ignore it.

4. At the end of the designated time period or as soon as convenient for the teacher, the child is allowed to deposit the remaining coupons into the "bank." These coupons, once earned, may not be lost regardless of the child's behavior.

5. Once the program begins to show positive effects during the designated time period, it is usually desirable to expand to other times during the school day. The child begins with a "fresh" set of coupons during each additional time period until acceptable behavior is well established. Later, when on-task behavior is well established the child can be given coupons that are expected to last a longer time. Allowing the child to start "fresh" during each time period at the beginning of the program will enable the child to make up for poor performance at one time with improved performance the next period.

6. To monitor the effects of the program, it is only necessary to keep an accurate count of the number of coupons lost by the child during each time period. The expectation is that this number will steadily decline.

Experience indicates that the best way to begin the coupon program is to limit the time period for the program to around one-half hour. Once the child becomes successful during this time period, expansion of the program to other times is usually accomplished easily. The next step, once the program is working throughout most of the day, is to begin to gradually increase the demands upon the child by giving him or her a larger number of coupons that are expected to last for a longer time period. Once coupons are expected to last the entire day and rule violations remain at a low but acceptable level, the number of coupons given to the child can also be decreased gradually.

At this point it may be possible to have the student "graduate" from the coupon program, perhaps by earning a party for the entire class. On the other hand some students may not be able to control their behavior without the benefit of the coupon program as a firm, consistent reminder to remain on task and inhibit disruptive behavior. An alternative approach is to switch to a home-note program.

A reason for the popularity of the coupon program with regular and special education teachers is that it gives teachers an effective, active way of responding to misbehavior. Taking away a coupon substitutes a very effective response for an ineffective verbal reprimand. The program also fits well into the daily routine of most teachers who can remove a coupon without interrupting the teaching process. A disadvantage of the program is that other children sometimes express a desire to be included.

Variations of the coupon program can be used by parents at home or out in public. It works especially well in public places such as a shopping mall, church, or any place where it is difficult to administer timeout. On a shopping trip, for instance, three rules could be established: (a) Stay right next to me unless you have permission to go somewhere else, (b) do not touch anything without permission, and (c) obey all commands of your parents. Then give the child eight coupons and say that each time a rule is broken they lose a coupon. But, if five coupons are left when it is time to leave, the child can have a valuable reward, and if only one coupon is left the child can have a much smaller reward. If all coupons are taken away, the trip is immediately ended and the child spends time in a timeout chair at home. Parents who use this program with their child need to be fairly strict and prepared to end a couple of shopping trips early. Later, a real improvement in the child's behavior in public should be noticeable.

CONCLUSION

Thinking about behavior management in terms of its implications for the entire system in which the child functions is one way to increase its effectiveness. Paget (1987) stated that "our field must keep pace with systems thinking because it holds potential for creating a gradual paradigm shift in the practice of psychology in educational settings" (p. 430). Virtually all problems encountered in the school system have implications for other components of the child's environment. Furthermore, characteristics of systems outside the school will influence the efficacy of interventions

conducted in the school. Behavior management techniques are no exception.

REFERENCES

Achenbach, T. M., & Edelbrock, C. (1983). *Manual for the child behavior checklist and revised child behavior profile.* Burlington, VT: University Associates in Psychiatry.

Achenbach, T. M., McConaughy, S. H., & Howell, C. T. (1987). Child/adolescent behavioral and emotional problems: Implications of cross-informant correlations for situational specificity. *Psychological Bulletin, 101,* 213–232.

American Psychiatric Association. (1987). *Diagnostic and statistical manual of mental disorders* (3rd ed., rev.). Washington, DC: Author.

Atkeson, B. M., & Forehand, R. (1979). Home-based reinforcement programs designed to modify classroom behavior: A review and methodological evaluation. *Psychological Bulletin, 86,* 1298–1308.

Barahal, R. M., Waterman, J., & Martin, H. P. (1981). The social cognitive development of abused children. *Journal of Consulting and Clinical Psychology, 49,* 508–516.

Barkley, R. A. (1981). *Hyperactive children: A handbook for diagnosis and treatment.* New York: The Guilford Press.

Barkley, R. A. (1987a). *Defiant children: A clinician's manual for parent training.* New York: The Guilford Press.

Barkley, R. A. (1987b). *Defiant children: Parent-teacher assignments.* New York: The Guilford Press.

Barkley, R. A. (1990). *Attention deficit hyperactivity disorder: A handbook for diagnosis and treatment.* New York: The Guilford Press.

Beattie, J. R., & Maniscalo, G. O. (1985). Special education and divorce: Is there a link? *Techniques: A Journal for Remedial Education and Counseling, 1,* 342–345.

Belsky, J. (1980). Child maltreatment: An ecological integration. *American Psychologist, 35,* 320–335.

Bowman, P., & Goldberg, M. (1983). "Reframing:" A tool for the school psychologist. *Psychology in the Schools, 20,* 210–214.

Brown, L. L., & Hammill, D. D. (1978). *Behavior Rating Profile: An ecological approach to behavioral assessment.* Austin, TX: PRO-ED.

Brunk, M., Henggeler, S. W., & Whelan, J. P. (1987). Comparison of multisystemic therapy and parent training in the brief treatment of child abuse and neglect. *Journal of Consulting and Clinical Psychology, 55,* 171–178.

Christenson, S., Abery, B., & Weinberg, R. A. (1986). An alternative model for the delivery of psychology in the school community. In S. N. Elliott & J. C. Witt (Eds.), *The delivery of psychological services in schools: Concepts, processes, and results* (pp. 349–392). Hillsdale, NJ: Lawrence Erlbaum.

Christenson, S., & Cleary, M. (1990). Consultation and the parent-educator partnership: A perspective. *Journal of Educational and Psychological Consultation, 1*(3), 219–241.

Christian, B. (1983). A practical reinforcement hierarchy for classroom behavior modification. *Psychology in the Schools, 20,* 83–84.

Coyne, J. C., & Biglan, A. (1984). Paradoxical techniques in strategic family therapy: A behavioral analysis. *Journal of Behavior Therapy and Experimental Psychiatry, 15,* 221–227.

Dardig, J. C., & Heward, W. L. (1981). *Sign here: A contracting book for children and their parents.* Bridgewater, NJ: F. Fournies & Associates.

Drake, E. A. (1981). Helping children cope with divorce: The role of the school. In I. R. Stuart & L. E. Abt (Eds.), *Children of separation and divorce: Management and treatment* (pp. 147–172). New York: Van Nostrand Reinhold.

Dreikurs, R., & Grey, L. (1970). *A parents' guide to child discipline.* New York: Hawthorn/Dutton.

Dunst, C. J., & Trivette, C. M. (1987). Enabling and empowering families: Conceptual and intervention issues. *School Psychology Review, 16,* 443–456.

Eimers, R., & Aitchison, R. (1977). *Effective parents/Responsible children.* New York: McGraw-Hill.

Emery, R. E. (1982). Interparental conflict and the children of discord and divorce. *Psychological Bulletin, 92,* 310–330.

Fine, M. J., & Holt, P. (1983). Intervening with school problems: A family systems perspective. *Psychology in the Schools, 20,* 59–66.

Forehand, R., McCombs, A., Long, N., Brody, G., & Fauber, R. (1988). Early adolescent adjustment to recent parental divorce: The role of interpersonal conflict and adolescent sex as mediating variables. *Journal of Consulting and Clinical Psychology, 56,* 624–627.

Garman, G. C. (1983). *Taking a look at discipline.* Elizabethtown, PA: The Continental Press.

Goldstein, S., & Goldstein, M. (1986). *A parents guide: Attention deficit disorders in children.* Salt Lake City, UT: The Neurology, Learning, & Behavior Center.

Goldstein S., & Goldstein, M. (1990). *Managing attention disorders in children: A guide for practitioners.* New York: John Wiley & Sons.

Guetzloe, E. C. (1989). *Youth suicide: What the educator should know.* Reston, VA: The Council for Exceptional Children.

Guidubaldi, J., Cleminshaw, H. K., Perry, J. D., & McLoughlin, C. S. (1983). The impact of parental divorce on children: Report of the nationwide NASP study. *School Psychology Review, 12,* 300–323.

Guidubaldi, J., & Perry, J. D. (1984). Divorce, socioeconomic status, and children's cognitive-social competence at school entry. *American Journal of Orthopsychiatry, 54,* 459–468.

Harris, S. L., & Fong, P. L. (1985). Developmental disabilities: The family and the school. *School Psychology Review, 14,* 162–165.

Harvey, J. H., & Weary, G. (1984). Current issues in attribution theory and research. *Annual Review of Psychology, 35,* 427–459.

Hetherington, E. M. (1979). Divorce: A child's perspective. *American Psychologist, 34,* 851–858.

Ingersoll, B. (1988). *Your hyperactive child: A parent's guide to coping with attention deficit disorder.* New York: Doubleday.

Jouriles, E. N., Murphy, C. M., & O'Leary, K. D. (1989). Interspousal aggression, marital discord, and child problems. *Journal of Consulting and Clinical Psychology, 57,* 453–455.

Kanfer, F. H., & Phillips, J. S. (1970). *Learning foundations of behavior therapy.* New York: John Wiley & Sons.

Kelley, M. L. (1990). *School-home notes: Promoting children's classroom success.* New York: The Guilford Press.

Kelley, M. L. & Carper, L. B. (1988). Home-based reinforcement procedures. In J. C. Witt, S. N. Elliott, & F. M. Gresham (Eds.), *Handbook of behavior therapy in education* (pp. 419–438). New York: Plenum Press.

Kendall, P. C., & Braswell, L. (1985). *Cognitive-behavioral therapy for impulsive children.* New York: The Guilford Press.

King, H. E., & Kleemeier, C. P. (1983). The effect of divorce on parents and children. In C. E. Walker & M. C. Roberts (Eds.), *Handbook of clinical child psychology* (pp. 1249–1272). New York: John Wiley & Sons.

Lachar, D. (1984). *Multidimensional description of child personality: A manual for the Personality Inventory for Children* (rev. ed.). Los Angeles: Western Psychological Services.

LeClave, L. J., & Brack, G. (1989). Reframing to deal with patient resistance: Practical application. *American Journal of Psychotherapy, 43,* 68–76.

Mash, E. J., & Terdal, L. G. (Eds.). (1988). *Behavioral*

assessment of childhood disorders. New York: The Guilford Press.

McMahon, R. J., Forehand, R., & Griest, D. L. (1981). Effects of knowledge of social learning principles on enhancing treatment outcome and generalization in a parent training program. *Journal of Consulting and Clinical Psychology, 49,* 526–532.

Paget, K. D. (1987). Systematic family assessment: Concepts and strategies for school psychologists. *School Psychology Review, 16,* 429–442.

Parker, H. C. (1988). *The ADD hyperactivity workbook for parents, teachers, and kids*. Plantation, FL: Impact Publications.

Pfeffer, C. R. (1981). Developmental issues among children of separation and divorce. In I. R. Stuart & L. E. Abt (Eds.), *Children of separation and divorce: Management and treatment* (pp. 20–32). New York: Van Nostrand Reinhold.

Phares, V., Compas, B. E., & Howell, D. C. (1989). Perspectives on child behavior problems: Comparisons of children's self-reports with parent and teacher reports. *Psychological Assessment: A Journal of Consulting and Clinical Psychology, 1,* 68–71.

Power, T. J., & Bartholomew, K. L. (1987). Family-school relationship patterns: An ecological assessment. *School Psychology Review, 16,* 498–512.

Ramsey, E., & Patterson, G. R. (1989, November). Coping with antisocial children. *Principal, 69,* 34–36.

Ramsey, E., Walker, H. M., Shinn, M., O'Neill, R. E., & Stieber, S. (1989). Parent management practices and school adjustment. *School Psychology Review, 18,* 513–525.

Rappaport, M. D., Murphy, H. A., & Bailey, J. S. (1982). Ritalin vs. response cost in the control of hyperactive children: A within-subject comparison. *Journal of Applied Behavior Analysis, 15,* 205–216.

Rutherford, R. B., Jr., & Nelson, C. M. (1988). Generalization and maintenance of treatment effects. In J. C. Witt, S. N. Elliott, & F. M. Gresham (Eds.), *Handbook of behavior therapy in education* (pp. 277–324). New York: Plenum Press.

Salend, S. J., & Allen, E. M. (1985). Comparative effects of externally managed and self-managed response-cost systems on inappropriate classroom behavior. *Journal of School Psychology, 23,* 59–67.

Schaefer, C. E., & Briesmeister, J. M. (Eds.). (1989). *Handbook of parent training: Parents as co-therapists for children's behavior problems*. New York: John Wiley & Sons.

Schaefer, C. E., & Millman, H. L. (1981). *How to help children with common problems*. New York: Litton Educational Publishing, Inc. (Paperback edition published by Plume Books, New American Library.)

Schumaker, J. B., Hovell, M. F., & Sherman, J. A. (1977). An analysis of daily report cards and parent-managed privileges in the improvement of adolescents' classroom performance. *Journal of Applied Behavior Analysis, 10,* 449–464.

Seligman, M. E. P., Abramson, L. Y., Semmel, A., & Von Baeyer, C. (1979). Depressive attribution style. *Journal of Abnormal Psychology, 88,* 242–247.

Sheridan, S. M., Kratochwill, T. R., & Elliott, S. N. (1990). Behavioral consultation with parents and teachers: Delivering treatment for socially withdrawn children at home and at school. *School Psychology Review, 19,* 33–52.

Shoham-Salomon, V., & Rosenthal, R. (1987). Paradoxical interventions: A meta-analysis. *Journal of Consulting and Clinical Psychology, 55,* 22–28.

Silberman, M. L., & Wheelan, S. A. (1980). *How to discipline without feeling guilty*. Champaign, IL: Research Press.

Slater, E. J., & Haber, J. D. (1984). Adolescent adjustment following divorce as a function of family conflict. *Journal of Consulting and Clinical Psychology, 52,* 920–921.

Sloane, H. N. (1988). *The good kid book*. Champaign, IL: Research Press.

Stokes, T. F., & Baer, D. M. (1977). An implicit technology of generalization. *Journal of Applied Behavior Analysis, 10,* 349–368.

Victor, J. B., Halverson, C. F., Jr., & Wampler, K. S. (1988). Family-school context: Parent and teacher agreement on child temperament. *Journal of Consulting and Clinical Psychology, 56,* 573–577.

Waterman, J. (1982). Assessment of the family system. In G. Ulrey & S. J. Rogers (Eds.), *Psychological assessment of handicapped infants and young children* (pp. 172–178). New York: Thiene-Stratton.

Webster-Stratton, C., Hollinsworth, T., & Kolpacoff, M. (1989). The long-term effectiveness and clinical significance of three cost-effective training programs for families with conduct-problem children. *Journal of Consulting and Clinical Psychology, 57,* 550–553.

Webster-Stratton, C., Kolpacoff, M., & Hollinsworth, T. (1988). Self-administered videotape therapy for families with conduct- problem children: Comparison with two cost-effective treatments and a control group. *Journal of Consulting and Clinical Psychology, 56,* 558–566.

Wielkiewicz, R. M. (1986). *Behavior management in the schools: Principles and procedures*. Needham Heights, MA: Allyn & Bacon.

Wielkiewicz, R. M., & Calvert, C. R. X. (1989). *Training and habilitating developmentally disabled people: An introduction.* Newbury Park, CA: Sage Publications.

Williams, G. J. R. (1983). Child abuse. In C. E. Walker & M. C. Roberts (Eds.), *Handbook of clinical child psychology* (pp. 1219–1248). New York: John Wiley & Sons.

Witt, J. C., & Elliott, S. N. (1982). The response-cost lottery: A time efficient and effective classroom intervention. *Journal of School Psychology, 20,* 155–161.

Wolfe, D. A. (1985). Child-abusive parents: An empirical review and analysis. *Psychological Bulletin, 97,* 462–482.

Zimmerman, J., & Sims, D. (1983). Family therapy. In C. E. Walker & M. C. Roberts (Eds.), *Handbook of clinical child psychology* (pp. 995–1025). New York: John Wiley & Sons.

16

HOW TO DEAL WITH DIFFICULT SCHOOL DISCIPLINE PROBLEMS: A FAMILY SYSTEMS APPROACH ADAPTED FOR SCHOOLS

Michael R. Valentine

Most educators believe that the family is the most significant *single* influence on the development of children, and that the school system is probably the second most important environmental influence. However, when a student is having difficulty adapting to the school system (e.g., poor grades, disruptive classroom behavior, truancy, or vandalism) the school system's intervention plans (e.g., time out, behavior modification, systematic suspension, detention, individual or group counseling) have traditionally tried to influence the individual student in isolation from the most significant influence in the child's life—the family (Petrie & Piersel, 1982).

From a family-systems perspective, many of these individually oriented intervention programs are doomed to failure, especially if the family's influence and value system are at variance with the school system's intended behavior changes. For example, consider the situation where school personnel may try to stop a student from fighting at school, yet the father's message to the child is, "Don't let anyone push you around . . . stand up for yourself, be a man." From the family-systems perspective, it is imperative for the family to be involved to achieve more effective and enduring school-related behavioral changes.

Until this point in time, there has not been an easily adapted family-systems approach that could be applied in the school system without requiring extensive training. In addition, many of the concepts used by family-systems theorists are not easily translated into concrete, specific intervention strategies for use at different intervention levels in the school by teachers, parents, counselors, psychologists, and administrators. Recently, however, a highly structured, short-term approach called "Brief Family Intervention" has been adapted to the school setting and can be used with ease at different levels of intervention: by parents experiencing difficulty in getting their children to do what they want, by teachers and administrators in the classroom or school dealing with discipline problems directly, and by counselors and school psychologists working with parents of children who are having difficulties (Valentine, 1987, 1988).

A flow chart that gives an overview of the total school-based intervention plan is presented in Table 1. The flow chart is divided into four levels. In Level One, a general philosophical orientation of the principles of the approach is given to three different target populations: parents, school personnel, and appropriate community resources.

In Level Two, based on the general philosophical orientation of Level One,

Table 1
School-based Intervention Plan

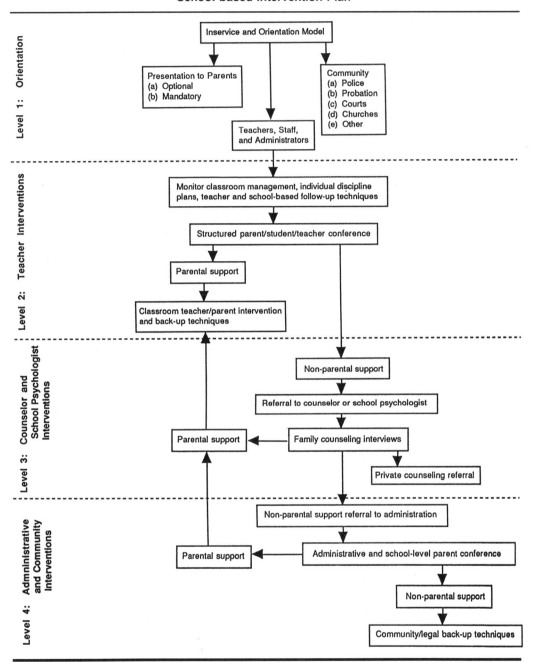

more specific classroom and school-based skills, interventions, and backup techniques are given to teachers and school personnel to increase the chances of successfully getting the students back on track behaviorally and academically. As part of Level Two interventions, if the teacher and school-based interventions do not seem to work, teachers are then also taught how to run a highly structured 10-minute solution-oriented teacher/parent/student conference. This Level

Two teacher-run parent conference is in its simplest form a task-oriented approach of asking parents to support the school, to give the student very clear specific messages to stop inappropriate behavior and start more desired behavior, and to cooperate in backing up the school and the student in a nonpunishing way to ensure success. The goal is for the student to get the message that both parents and the school mean business, will work together, and the student must do the desired behavior.

Level Three of this model deals with the relatively small percentage of students who are unresponsive to school-based teacher interventions. Here a referral is made to the counselor and/or the school psychologist to run a highly structured brief family counseling session designed to have parents see that—if they wish to do so—they can get their child to act appropriately and to do what they want the child to do.

If the counseling sessions do not seem to work and the parents are unable or unwilling to get the child under control, then Level Four of the model, involving administrative and community interventions, is implemented.

The intervention program is based on these underlying principles: (a) If your intervention works, it works; (b) if it does not work, keep trying something else until something does work; (c) never use more control or force than is necessary; and (d) start with simple and obvious explanations and interventions. If these do not work, move to the more complex and sophisticated interventions. The intervention structure of this approach is like a path analysis that branches into two possible outcomes. One, the intervention works, and the student is back on task being successful; or two, the intervention does not work, and the student is still acting inappropriately. If the intervention does not work at one particular level, the philosophy is to continue to use interventions within that level but add the structure and interventions of the next level until you get the student back on task. In this chapter, I describe the philosophical and historical basis for the approach, provide a brief overview of Level One—orientation of the principles of the approach, and provide a brief overview of Level Three—the counseling model. The focus of this chapter is not on Level Two, teacher-based interventions. For more information on Level Two readers are referred to Valentine (1987).

PHILOSOPHICAL AND HISTORICAL PERSPECTIVE

A general introduction to some of the philosophical and historical perspectives and to assumptions of family-systems theory that have influenced the development of the Brief Family Intervention (BFI) model is necessary. Historically, most psychologists have looked at inappropriate behavior in students from an intrapsychic, one-person, and/or medical model (Okun & Rappaport, 1980). They assumed that some process or intrapsychic phenomenon inside the child's brain caused him to act inappropriately. It was their belief that if they could get inside his head and change whatever was going on intrapsychically, they could change the child. They tried to work with the child, usually in individual counseling or therapy, to change his inappropriate behavior. Using a medical-model analogy, they tried to do some type of therapeutic surgery to fix these maladaptive, intrapsychic perceptions or beliefs. Even if the psychologist believed that the family had something to do with the child's behavior, they usually worked with the child individually. This orientation prevailed even in group counseling. In group, they dealt with one person at a time as if the problem were intrapsychic and in isolation from the family context. Even if some of the other group members' influence and experience were used to help change one person's perspective, they basically saw the individual as having the problem and dealt with him in isolation from the family context. The individual patient *had* the trait or symptom and it had to be changed.

Behaviorists, who generally reject the intrapsychic and medical models of human behavior, historically operated primarily from a one-person model, and typically saw the child as the one with the problem or symptom, even though often they saw the environmental context or specific reinforcers from the environment as a source of maintenance of the inappropriate behavior. Therefore, the child's behavior could not be understood as separate from the context in which it occurred, a context represented by a two-person model in which the child's behavior is the result of interactions between the child and responses from the child's environment. The focus, however, was still on the symptom bearer and the behaviorists brought all their research and behavioral technology to bear on this identified patient and tried to shape, extinguish, or reinforce certain targeted behaviors. Again, this attempt was usually done in isolation from the family context or dynamics.

Family-systems theory brought about a major theoretical shift from a one-person or intrapsychic model to a multi-person, interactional model. Psychologists using the family orientation no longer view the child in isolation as the targeted symptom bearer to be changed. Instead, they look at the total family configuration, and in some cases, even the environmental context (e.g., schools, school personnel), to see how these contexts affect the child's behavior (Petrie & Piersel, 1982). The child is no longer seen from a one-person model in which he is the problem, or even from a two-person model in which the child's problems are seen as an interactive effect between two people (teacher/student, mother/son). Instead, the family orientation model sees the child's behavior as a function of the interrelations and dynamics of at least three people and everyone is part of the problem and part of the solution (Haley, 1980). To illustrate the difference in the perspectives of the various models, I will paraphrase and adapt a story told by Jay Haley, a famous family therapist, to a school-related example. From a one-person model, a teacher talking to a student who was not doing well would say, "The student is stupid" (trait attribute). If the teacher operated

from a two-person model, she might say, "There must be something about my personality (e.g., I'm too domineering) in interaction with this student that inhibits him and makes him appear stupid." If the teacher operated from a three-person model, she might say, "The student is caught between two different approaches, ideas, orientations, or beliefs—mine and those of teacher X or the parents; not knowing which to adopt, and not wanting to offend either of us, he seems confused, uncertain, and inhibited" (Haley, personal communication, 1983).

Many times, from a family-systems perspective, the symptom bearer, or identified patient (I.P.) is seen as (a) being caught between two opposing positions, or (b) having to set up a very tenuous coalition with one of the two opposing positions—a process that often leads to rather unfortunate and destructive outcomes. Counselors need to look for various coalitions that might take place among any groups of three or more (e.g., mother/father/child, parents/child/school, family/school/hospital, and so on) (Haley, 1980). One of the working hypotheses that should be tested when a student does not seem to respond to individually oriented school-based interventions is, "Who in the system is in coalition with the child or is supporting the child in the continuation of this behavior?" The assumption is that the child does not have enough power on his own to continue to act inappropriately if significant others expect him to stop. Therefore, one must find with what power base the child is aligned to help maintain the behavior. Another way of expressing this is, "Whose shoulders is the child standing on?" (Minuchin & Fishman, 1981). Going back to the previously mentioned example of the student fighting, it becomes clear that the student is standing on the father's shoulders, and receives support with statements like, "Don't let anyone push you around. Stand up for yourself. Be a man." In school-related discipline problems there are two major systems—the school system and the family system. The assumption is, if everyone in these two systems is saying to the child, you cannot do a specific behavior, such as fighting, the behavior will stop.

As illustrated in Table 2, there are four major combinations and possible outcomes between school and family. One, the school and family are clear about what is expected—the behavior must stop or never begin. The result is that the behavior stops, and there is no problem. Two, the school is not clear and the parents are clear. The usual result is that the behavior stops or never started and there is no problem. For example, many parents will not let their children fail in school, be truant, or cuss at a teacher, and they are successful in achieving these goals even if the teacher is not clear, a good instructor, and/or the school is not a good educational institution. Three, the school is clear and the parents are not clear or supportive. The result is a problem. And four, both school and parents are not clear, which results in a difficult problem.

Understanding what a person does, or what his or her motives are, becomes quite different as one shifts from the individual to the broader context in which that person functions. From this new vantage point, psychopathology or dysfunctional behavior is seen more as the product of a struggle between persons than as between internal forces within a single person (Haley, 1980).

The movement away from an intrapsychic perspective to an interpersonal, family-systems perspective might appear to be a minor shift, but the implications are profound in the fields of psychology and education. Because of this shift, the child is no longer seen as crazy or emotionally ill. For all practical purposes, we have wiped out most psychological jargon, nomenclature, and diagnostic categories. We now simply say that the child is acting inappropriately, and we need to put a stop to such behavior. Rather than trying to analyze intrapsychic phenomena, we look at the interaction and communication patterns between the child and the parents and/or teachers. We analyze actual interactions that can be seen and changed. It is assumed that if you can change the interactions within the family system, you can change the child's behavior, and eventually, the subjective, phenomenological experience of that child. From the family-systems perspective, the child is no longer seen as the only one with whom to work. We want to look at the broader picture—the family system. In so doing, we are not looking for causation or for blame: We are looking for what is actually going on in the family's interactions and for how the family can change these interactions if they wish to do so. With this shift in orientation the assumption is that parents and teachers are already capable and have the skills needed to change children's behavior and have them act appropriately. Therefore, we do not need to put teachers and parents through elaborate training sessions to accomplish the desired behavioral change in children.

A corollary to this assumption is: We look for strengths, not weaknesses, in people and do not need to diagnostically label individuals, especially children, in some negative way to get behavioral change. The bottom line is that both parents and teachers are capable and if

TABLE 2
Outcomes Between School and Family

	School Role	
Parent Role	**School Clear**	**School Unclear**
Parents clear	No problem	Most likely no problem
Parents unclear or clear that they will not support the school	A problem	A difficult problem

both tell the child he cannot act inappro-priately, then it is a very, very rare child who will continue to act inappropriately. If the child continues to act inappropri-ately, examination of the school and/or the family system to see who is giving the child direct or indirect permission is needed. In most situations the plain and simple truth is that we, as adults, let most kids act inappropriately. We do not clearly communicate to children to stop inappro-priate behavior; we do not take a stand to stop it, nor do we clearly communicate what we really want children to do.

There is a wide range of philosophical and theoretical orientations in the field of family therapy (Levant, 1984). This par-ticular model, Brief Family Intervention, falls within the framework of what many systems theorists call "the communica-tion systems purist perspective" (Okun & Rappaport, 1980). In this model and perspective it is assumed that what people actually say is a reflection of what they mean, the way they see the world, and what they believe.

Brief Family Intervention is based on communications systems theory, which suggests that words reflect a concept. Most of us are familiar with the classic linguistic illustration of the word "snow." For most of us in our western culture, "snow" basically has one meaning and only one perceptual reality. Eskimos, however, have more than seven words for various types of snow, thereby creating over seven different perceptual realities. Therefore, the word helps to define the concept, the belief, and the reality.

Beliefs and concepts about the world are linked intrinsically to our choice of words, interactions, and communication patterns. For the most part, we act and communicate congruently with what we believe. Therefore, if we wish to change the way we act and communicate with children, we must examine and question our beliefs about the causes of students' inappropriate behavior. It is the conten-tion of this approach that if most of the popularly held beliefs of why students misbehave were objectively examined, little or no evidence would be found to support these beliefs. Success at objec-tively evaluating, challenging, and erod-ing these popular beliefs would then leave open the possibility of communicating and acting in a totally different manner. Such changes in beliefs and communica-tion patterns would then set the stage to quickly stop most students' inappropri-ate behavior.

The logic of this intervention ap-proach is simple: If you believe that the student is incapable of doing what you want him to do, then you will not directly and clearly tell him to do what you want him to do. If you actually videotaped or took anecdotal records of teacher-student or parent-child interactions while in the heat of battle, you would rarely hear the adult give clear direct messages to either stop the inappropriate behavior or start doing a more desired behavior. For exam-ple, if you believe that a student is hyperactive and unable to sit still, you will not tell him to sit still. Such a direct statement is incongruent with your belief that he is hyperactive and unable to sit still. However, if the belief system is challenged by objectively collecting evi-dence, and thereby proving that the student is in control of his behavior and is capable of sitting still, then it becomes reasonable and congruent with the new way of seeing things to tell the student in very specific and concrete terms to sit still. This new way of seeing the student as capable also enables the direct commu-nication patterns or statements to be backed up, if need be, with actions that convey to the student that he is to do the desired behavior.

The structural basis of this approach is: (a) If you do not believe a child is capable of doing what you want, you will not give clear direct messages to stop the behavior and instead you will use any of a variety of vague, abstract, indirect com-munication patterns; if, however, (b) you can erode the belief system that the child is incapable by using questioning tech-niques to show adults they actually have *observable evidence* that the child is capable (based on the child's past perfor-mance), then adults can change their indirect communication patterns and give clear direct messages to help insure that the child is successful. A corollary to this is: The "very highly complex" behaviors that we require of children, especially junior and senior high school students (e.g., no hitting, kicking, spitting, raise your hand and wait to be called on, no talking while the teacher is giving instructions) are all within the developmental and behavioral repertoire of students and there is no legitimate excuse for not requiring them to perform these tasks in schools. This approach makes a strong distinction between acquisition and maintenance of behaviors. If students do not know how to do a specific behavior, then teach them. But if they have demonstrated that they are capable of doing the behavior by the fact that they have done the behavior in the past, then set up a system that requires that they maintain "appropriate" behavior.

The first step in developing effective interventions is to understand how beliefs and communication patterns are intrinsically linked. It is imperative that consultants to teachers and counselors to families know how to analyze erroneous beliefs and vague, abstract, or indirect communications patterns well. Knowing how to analyze these popular erroneous beliefs and indirect, vague communication patterns (Level One Orientation) is the cornerstone of this approach and forms the basis of intervention strategies at the other three levels of the model. Additionally, understanding the process of analyzing erroneous beliefs and indirect communication patterns provides parents, teachers, school psychologists, and administrators the foundation for developing and implementing effective backup techniques and strategies to help solve a wide range of school-related problems.

LEVEL ONE:
BASIC COMPONENTS OF THE MODEL

Level One components include: (a) analyzing erroneous belief systems; (b) analyzing indirect, vague communication patterns; and (c) developing nonpunishing backup techniques. Each of these three Level One components are described.

Component One:
Analyzing Belief Systems

The intent of Component One, Analyzing Belief Systems, is to determine whether parents' and teachers' beliefs about why the referred child misbehaves are substantiated by observable evidence. Parents and teachers hold beliefs about the child's behavior, some of which are legitimate beliefs and some of which are erroneous beliefs. Sometimes parents' or teachers' beliefs suggest the child is incapable of behavioral control, which then becomes their excuse for not having and/or telling the child to behave. One of the tenets of Brief Family Intervention is to look for evidence to support or disprove beliefs held by parents and teachers or to see if their beliefs are in fact legitimate or erroneous.

Analysis of erroneous parental and teacher belief systems is an important first step in this approach because people usually act congruently with their beliefs about inappropriate behavior. This then sets in motion certain self-fulfilling behavioral and communication patterns that in essence say to the child: Continue the inappropriate behavior because I really do not believe you are capable of doing otherwise.

Consultants using this approach need to develop questioning techniques that allow teachers and parents to see whether their belief system is related to the inappropriate behavior. For example, the parents of a 17-year-old daughter, previously hospitalized and supposedly "emotionally handicapped," wanted her to wash her face and take a bath on her own. When questioned as to why they believed she had not been doing that, the father stated, in the mother's and daughter's presence, that the daughter had been brain damaged since birth. When asked if she had ever in her life washed her face or taken a bath on her own, the father said that she had on different occasions. When asked if she washed her face or took a bath when he made her, he replied, "Sure, but it is a knock-down, drag-out fight to get her to do it. She throws such a temper tantrum, you would not believe it." With the father's answers to these two questions, the evidence was clear. The daughter was capable of taking a bath and "brain damage" had nothing to do with that specific behavior.

In looking at popular belief systems of parents and educators about why children do what they do (e.g., hyperactivity, ADHD, phases or stages of development, emotional illness, socioeconomic status, inadequate role models, peers), the question becomes, "Is the child seen as capable of doing what is wanted, or does the belief system imply that the child is incapable of controlling the specific behavior?" The ultimate way to determine if the child is capable is by *observable evidence.* Has the child ever done once what is wanted? If so, then the child is capable, and all the previously entertained excuses (i.e., belief systems) need to be set aside for change to occur. Once this is clearly seen by parents and teachers, the real issue is changed from, "Can the child do or control the behavior?" to "What needs to be done to get the child to do the desired behavior?" With the hundreds of possible beliefs or excuses for children's inappropriate behavior, counselors need to prepare and develop both general and specific questioning techniques to help both parents and teachers realize that the child is capable of behavioral control. Suppose parents or teacher believe a child is hyperactive because of sugar or a biochemical process. First, have the parents or teacher describe and define in very specific behavioral terms exactly what the child is doing that leads them to believe the child is hyperactive. Then, using the specific behavior (i.e., will not sit still, gets out of seat, calls out, wanders around the room), ask questions to see under what circumstances the child controls these behaviors. Does he ever sit still? Does he act the same in all seven of his junior high school classes? Does he sit still when the teacher is in a "bad mood" or is right beside him? The mother? The father? The principal? Does he act the

same at school? At your home? On weekends and weekdays? At the dining room table? Watching TV? At the neighbors? At the grandparents? In church? In court? If he was given a million dollars to stop the inappropriate behavior and do what he was supposed to, could he do it? If his behavior changes under these different circumstances, how do the parents or teacher explain that in terms of biochemistry, blood-sugar level, or any other reason? Does he have two different biochemical systems, one to turn the sugar on and one to turn it off only when the principal is around? How does that work?

Again, when most popularly held beliefs and excuses for children's inappropriate behavior are systematically explored and questioned, evidence to support them is often not found. Instead evidence that children are capable of controlling their behavior is clearly shown and identified.

Component Two: Analyzing Communication Patterns

The intent of the second component of this approach is to illustrate to parents and teachers that adults who do not believe that a child is capable of performing the desired behavior usually use vague, indirect, and unclear communications and behavioral interventions which, unfortunately, say to the child, "Keep on doing the inappropriate behavior." Again, it is the contention of this approach that if actual parent-child/teacher-student communications were videotaped or recorded verbatim, it would be evident that in most incidents when children act inappropriately, adults do not give clear, direct, specific, and concrete messages to children to stop the inappropriate behavior and start doing what they wish them to do. A concomitant basic tenet of this approach is that if adults believed that children were capable and gave clear, direct messages, this alone would stop most of the typical discipline problems educators and parents deal with from day to day. Therefore, under Component Two I discuss both (a) vague and indirect communication patterns and (b) direct messages.

Vague and indirect communication patterns. Vague and indirect communication patterns are quite common. In order for psychologists to use this model with teachers or parents, it is critical for communication patterns to be committed to memory, because this is the basis of all intervention strategies. Twelve typical communication patterns, categories, or examples, and possible implications of these communication patterns are described:

1. *Ignoring Inappropriate Behavior:* Parents and teachers ignore inappropriate behavior in the hope that the disturbing behavior will stop, but in actuality this technique conveys to the child the message to keep on acting inappropriately. For example, if all policemen ignored everyone who drove at 70 mph, it would be a clear message to all drivers that it is okay to travel at 70 mph or more, until someone took a stand, set a limit, and then made people stay within that limit.

2. *Actually Encouraging Inappropriate Behavior:* Consider this statement from a frustrated mom: "That was real cute. Why don't you save that up and show that to your father when he gets home, so he can see what I've been putting up with all day?" This statement implies to the child that mom is not electing to stop the behavior, but is telling the child to do it someplace else or under different circumstances. In a sense, the behavior is okay to perform, just do it for others as well. The following statements also encourage inappropriate behavior: "I dare you . . .," "Go for it," "I would like to see you try it."

3. *Demanding Honesty About the Symptom:* Consider the parent who addresses stealing by demanding, "Tell me the truth. No kid of mine lies to me. Tell me what you did." The parent's approach may imply to the child that telling the truth is all that matters and that the parent is not demanding that the child

stop stealing, just that the truth be told about the fact that stealing is happening.

4. *Being Concerned About the Symptom:* In regard to children hitting each other, an adult may comment in despair, "Tell your sister you are sorry you hit her," or the parent or teacher might tell others, "He's not even sorry that he hit her." A possible implication is that it is better to be sorry about hitting than to stop hitting. So continue to hit her—just feel sorry about it and tell everyone "I'm sorry. I didn't mean it."

5. *Making an Effort to Change:* "Try to get to class on time" is a common refrain from parents or teachers. Unfortunately, the implication is just *try* to do it, not do it. Just make an effort sometime between now and the time you die.

6. *Think About the Behavior:* Parents and teachers often say, "Think twice before you do that again." Implication: It is okay to do that again but only after you have thought about it. By the way, all great thieves have thought it over.

7. *Don't Get Caught:* Adults say to children who have been in trouble, "Don't you ever let me catch you doing that again." Implication: It is okay to do it again, but don't let me catch you.

8. *Abstract Meaningless Directions:* When children misbehave, it is not uncommon for adults to respond in vague ways: "Grow up." "If you respected me, you wouldn't do that." "You're not working up to your potential." "If you loved your sister, you wouldn't hit her." This particular communication style is vague and does not tell children exactly and specifically what adults want. Furthermore, it really has nothing to do with the specific behavior in question (such as sitting still, hitting, etc.). Implication: Hitting your sister tells others you do not love her. It says nothing about stopping the behavior. The real trick here is to operationally define abstract terms in concrete, specific, behavioral terms. For example, ask the parent or teacher, "What does the student have to stop doing or start doing so that you will think he is

grown up, acting his age, mature, respectful, etc.?"

9. *Statements of Fact:* Some students are chronically unprepared for
class. Teachers respond by saying, "I see
you didn't bring your paper and pencils to
class today." Implication: You are very
observant about the obvious, but you
didn't tell him to bring his paper and
pencils to class every day.

10. *Questions:* When students misbehave, adults often ask questions to get
students to think about their behavior.
Examples include: "How many times do I
have to tell you to stop that?" and "Why
are you fighting?" One unintended implication of this technique is: I'm not telling
you to do anything, I'm just asking you to
give me a good reason "why" you are
doing what you are doing. The real
question is: If they tell you a good enough
reason "why" they are doing what they
are doing, is it a good enough reason to let
them continue to act in the inappropriate
way?

11. *Behavioral Contracts or Threats:*
Threats are common in adult communications to children. Examples such as "If
you do that again, I'm going to spank you"
and "If you don't do these 10 problems
now, you are staying after school" imply
to the child a degree of choice. The
potential message for the child is "It's
your choice, do x or y, either one is okay
with me. I'm not telling you to do
anything, but if you don't do what I really
want 'x' then I'm going to punish you
with 'y' if you like it or not."

12. *Wishes, Wants, and Shoulds:*
Parents and teachers may articulate their
preferences in a soft way: "I wish you
wouldn't do that." "You should sit still."
Implication: I'm not giving you a clear
message not to do it, I'm just telling you
what I prefer.

Even though at times these vague
communication patterns work with some
children, they rarely work with hard to
handle children. Vague, indirect communication patterns must be analyzed to
determine whether a clear message to
perform is present and whether they

reflect adults' beliefs that (a) they do not
have the power, influence, or right to
change the child's behavior (e.g., "This is
a democracy—children have a right to
make their own choices," "I don't want to
be authoritarian"); or (b) the child is
incapable in some way (e.g., hyperactive,
brain damaged, etc.).

Direct messages. Clear direct messages convey to the child in very specific
terms what is to be done. For example,
the statement, "John, sit in your seat
now, and stay there until I tell you to get
up. While you are there, do these 10
problems neatly and correctly. Have them
finished in 15 minutes. Start immediately, do absolutely nothing else but these
problems, and do not stop until you are
finished," is a clearer, more direct message than the typical vague teacher
message of, "Get to work."

Direct messages reflect an underlying
adult position, attitude, or belief system
that states: (a) It is reasonable, from the
adult's personal value system, to tell the
child and expect the child to do the
particular behavior; (b) the adult sees the
child as capable of doing what is asked;
and (c) the child has to do what is
requested—the child has no choice
whether or not to comply in this particular area. This is not a hostile, authoritarian, dogmatic position. Instead this is a
clear, objective statement of what is
expected, couched in a context of love
and caring, and it is hoped it is used only
in areas that are deemed by the adult as
"must" behaviors for the child's own
well-being.

Parents and teachers telling the child
what to do will not always get the child to
do what is desired. However, in most
situations, just telling the child what to
do in clear, direct messages, in and of
itself does work. The powerful and successful use of clear messages can be
illustrated to parents and teachers by
asking them questions like:

- When you got the child to do what
  you wanted on the 10th time,
  when he was completely out of

control, how did you get him to do it? Parents and teachers typically respond with a variation of "I told him to do it right now and I meant it."

- When you are successful at keeping your child on restriction, how do you do that? Common parental response is "I told her that she was on restriction and was not to see anyone, talk to anyone on the phone, or watch TV."

- When your child threw a temper tantrum and you could not take it anymore, what did you do? Parent's answer: "I sent him to his room." How did you do that? Answer: "I told him to go to his room now, and I meant it."

- When a teacher is successful at using behavior modification and time out, ask, "How did you get the child behind the time out screen the very first time?" Answer: "I told the student to go there." Did he want to do that? Answer: "No. The student had no choice. If he acts up, he has to go behind the screen." The first time the student went to time out, did he act appropriately? Answer: "No, the student kept sticking his head around the corner and making faces." What did you do? Answer: "I told the student to stop making faces and get behind that screen and stay there until I told him to come out." It is amazing how parents and teachers can almost always get "out of control" children to stop inappropriate behavior on the 10th time when they use clear messages.

Component Three: Backup Techniques

The intent of the third component is for parents and teachers to develop backup techniques that set the stage for the child to complete the required behavior with success. These techniques in essence say to the child: "Parents will be parents, teachers will be teachers, and you can count on them to give you guidance and structure to make sure you are successful when you don't do the desired behavior on your own." The choice is, "Would you like to be successful on your own?" or "Would you like us to help you be successful until you get the message you can be successful on your own?" It is not, "Would you like to be successful (i.e., go to school) or fail (i.e., drop out of school)?" Some children, especially those with long histories and habit patterns of being out of control, will test adults to see if they mean what is said. Even though a student who participated in a family counseling session heard his parents change their minds about the student's capabilities, and, consequently, now give clear messages to do a specific behavior, the student may not be convinced. When this occurs, the goal for adults is to back up what is wanted in a nonhostile, nonpunishing way and convince the child to do what is wanted. Although the number of backup techniques is limited only by the adults' imagination, the structure is always the same—an emphasis on success or success, *never* on success or failure.

Questions and principles to keep in mind while devising a backup intervention include:

- What is the behavior the child must do to be successful? What is the goal? What is the real problem to be solved? Focus on that and stick to that only. For example, if the student did not complete the math problems, devise interventions to make the student do the 10 math problems rather than writing 100 sentences or staying after school.

- Communicate verbally and nonverbally to the child: (a) You must do the goal behavior—there is no way out; (b) I love you and care about you so much that I will not hurt you, belittle you, or punish you, but you will do the goal behavior; and (c) I expect you to be successful and I will not allow you to do anything other than be successful.

When teachers or school personnel see students as being capable, expect students to behave and perform appropriately, and give clear, specific concrete communications, they will usually get most students to do what they want. However, if students do not respond and the teacher adds an effective backup technique that says you must do the goal behavior—there is no way out—an even larger percentage of students will comply. For the small percentage of students and families for which teacher, classroom, and school intervention-based measures do not work (Level One and Level Two) it is imperative for teachers to refer the family to counselors, social workers, or school psychologists to run a family counseling session (Level Three—family interventions) in the school. The same underlying structural components in the first two levels are used in the family session from a different role and perspective. At Levels One and Two the teacher and school personnel are trying to make the student and the parents go along with their clearly stated goals, rules, and standards. At Level Three, the counselor or school psychologist is not trying to make the parents do anything. They facilitate and clarify the parents' position in relation to the school's position, have the parents clearly set their own goals or rules for desired behavior, and have the parents understand that they as parents are very capable and can change almost any behavior if, in fact, they really wish to do so. To succeed at this third level of intervention, the counselor or school psychologist must: (a) Help the parents clarify their values and position in relation to the child's inappropriate school behavior, (b) erode the parents' erroneous beliefs about their child's inappropriate behavior, (c) clarify and differentiate the parents' successful versus unsuccessful communication patterns, and (d) help develop effective backup techniques from the parents'

perspective to accomplish the parents' stated goals.

After a family counseling session and if the parents adopt a firm stand, give clear messages, and back up their statements, the child's inappropriate behavior will, in most cases, stop immediately. However, if the parents choose not to take a firm stand, the behavior will continue. Then, at least at this point, it becomes very clear that the inappropriate behavior is valued and encouraged by the parents and the parents will have to take responsibility for it.

This approach is a comprehensive school-based program that integrates and coordinates the various roles of parents, teachers, counselors, psychologists, and administrators. The fundamental components of the model (Level One), however, are the basis for developing intervention strategies for the other three intervention levels. The remainder of this chapter focuses on the counselor's and school psychologist's role in working with parents (Level Three).

LEVEL THREE: FAMILY COUNSELING

In order for this part of the model to work, it is imperative to have the child and the significant adults engaged in parenting at the sessions. The child must be in the session to hear the parents change their belief systems about the child's inappropriate behavior. This process not only sets the stage for the parents to change their communication and interaction patterns with the child, but also sets the stage for the child to change self-perceptions and personal beliefs. Some educators believe the child should not be present when discussing the child's problems. Others believe there should be an initial session without the child present to clarify or set goals. Both these options are considered a mistake from the Brief Family Intervention Model. First, there are no secrets. The child, teacher, and parents know what the child is doing. Second, do not worry that the parents will not support the teacher or school in front of the child, or whether the parents disagree with each other. This is probably already happening and may be the reason the child is acting out in the first place. The child has to be present to see how the parents and the school deal with and resolve these problems. Remember, the child is probably acting out because the parents directly or indirectly are supporting the behavior in some way. Third, if the child is not present the child's sense of paranoia is increased, and unwittingly another triangulation process (parents-child-school) has been created. Everyone should be present to hear what is said. This reduces the chances of miscommunication and misunderstanding. As previously mentioned, the child needs to hear the erosion of the parents' belief systems. This is a Brief Family Intervention Model, which in the school setting is translated to one, maybe two, sessions. The problem must be discussed and resolved quickly because most parents are not contracting for 15–20 sessions. Operate from the position that the first session may be the last and any additional sessions become icing on the cake.

This approach operates from the perspective that both parents and children are capable and there is no excuse for inappropriate behavior. This is especially true for the "highly complex" behaviors we typically require of students: Raise your hand and wait to be called on, no talking while the teacher is giving directions, no fighting in school, etc. These tasks are within the behavioral repertoire of the child and of the parents' capabilities to make them happen. If educators believe parents are the most important people in the child's life and are capable, then they look for their strengths and capabilities not weaknesses and pathologies. Even popular terms used in family work today, such as "dysfunctional families," predispose a negative bias and suggest incapabilities. Stop looking for things wrong in the parents and start looking for strengths and capabilities and ways to improve on those strengths and capabilities to solve problems. The bottom line is: If you believe the parents are the most important people in the child's life, that parents and

child are capable and competent, and/or the child's behavior is a function of something else going on in the family, then the child must be present in the sessions so long-term solutions to these problems can be achieved.

As previously stated, counselors and school psychologists should memorize techniques to question and debate popular belief systems, and memorize how to analyze actual adult-child communication patterns. Most of the counseling steps and interventions are tied to a thorough knowledge of the underlying core conditions or major components of the model. Although space does not permit examination of all the techniques to analyze beliefs and communication patterns, some examples of each will be given in the description of the formal steps of the counseling model. Additional information is provided in *How to Deal with Discipline Problems in the Schools: A Practical Guide for Educators* (Valentine, 1987) and *How to Deal with Difficult Discipline Problems: A Family Systems Approach* (Valentine, 1988).

The Brief Family Intervention counseling model has five formal steps and two additional optional steps to help parents resolve school-based concerns. The seven steps of the model are summarized using the term, counselor, in a generic way to represent all mental health professionals.

Step One: Statement of the Problem and Setting Goals for Solution of the Problem

In Step One of the family counseling session parents, with the clarifying help of the counselor, set the goal for the counseling session. Setting the goal requires stating the problem and the desired behavior change in observable, behavioral terms. Because of the time constraints in school settings, this step is usually more difficult than it seems and requires a very active, directive role on the counselor's part. It requires the counselor to actively clarify parents' statements of the problem so that when the final goal is agreed upon, everyone in the room will know exactly what the problem is and what needs to be done to solve the problem. The counselor helps parents set their goals for the solution to the problem. The counselor's role is to be a family advocate and have the parents see their capabilities. Their role is not to manipulate or force the parents into doing what the school wants. The active directive role of the counselor is in terms of process, not content. The counselor's role is to clarify the goal in specific concrete behavioral terms (process) not what the goal is (content). Counselors work with the parents' rather than the school's perception of the problem.

Even when the parent begins with an observable behavior it is important to clarify the nature of the problem and solutions. Consider the exchange between the parents and counselor about Brian:

Parent: Brian is truant from school. I've gotten two calls at work in the last week.
Counselor: How is that a problem for you and what would you like done about it? (For some parents, truancy is not a problem. It is the fact that the school keeps calling them at work that is the problem.)

Consider the exchange between the parents and counselor about Susan:

Parent: I really feel Susan has a *poor self-concept*. She has a *bad attitude* toward school, and she is not working up to her *potential*. (The italicized abstract terms are too vague to be useful. Neither parent, student, nor counselor will know when the stated goal has been met under these communication patterns. Terms like these need to be actively clarified.)
Counselor: Let's take these ideas one at a time. What is Susan doing that leads you to believe that she has a poor self-concept? What behaviors must she do, so when she does them, you will think

she has a good attitude? What does she need to do, in concrete, specific terms to convince you that she is working up to her potential?

In this way, the counselor helps modify the parent's communication pattern and directs the parent to state the goal in observable, behavioral terms. Even at this point, if the parent begins with a fairly clear description the counselor may have to assist the parent in defining the desired behavior even more specifically. Consider this exchange between parent and counselor:

Parent: She's making mostly Ds in school and I know she is capable of doing better. I never see her doing her homework. If she would just try to get better grades, I'd think she was working up to her potential.
Counselor: If she really tries, and still gets Ds and Fs is this okay with you? Do you want her to *get* better grades, or just *try* to get better grades? What grades does she need to get before you are satisfied that she is working up to her "potential"?

These examples are intended to provide several ways of clarifying the desired behavior. The counselor will, of course, use his clinical skills and ask questions in an empathetic manner to clarify the issues and to understand exactly what the parents want their child to do. Three examples that might help illustrate how counselors explore and analyze specific communication categories or patterns to help parents set goals are:

A. Don't get caught—"Don't you ever let me catch you doing that again."
   Implication: Continue the behavior, but don't get caught doing it.
   Counselor's inquiry to parent: "I'm not sure what you meant by that statement. Are you telling your son to stop stealing and never steal again, or are you telling him it is okay to steal

as long as he does not get caught? Which did you mean to say to him?

B. Statement of facts—"I see you didn't bring your books and papers home again."

Implication: A statement of the obvious rather than a demand for change. This presumes that the student is unaware of his behavior and needs to be informed.

Counselor's inquiry to parent: Do you wish to make sure he knows that you *observed* that he didn't bring his books and papers home, or do you wish to give him a clear statement *to bring* his books and papers home? Which did you mean?

C. Questions—"I want to know why he is not going to school and doing his work?"

Implication: Giving a "good enough" answer why is more important than changing the behavior.

Counselor's inquiry to parent: If your son tells you a good enough reason why he is not going to school and is getting straight Fs, is it okay with you that he never goes to school again, never does any work, gets straight Fs, flunks out, and does not get a high school diploma? Would that be okay with you or would you like something else to happen?

In this first step, the counselor *actively* clarifies each parental statement so that the "how," "when," "where," "for how long," and "to what degree" becomes concrete, behavioral, and specific. If the parent states that the child has to do his school work, the counselor should inquire about specific standards: How long must he continue to do it? A week? A semester? Until he graduates? In all subjects? How much of it has to be correct? To what standards? And so forth.

Sometimes, parents try to push the decision making onto the counselor or onto the child. At times parents sound very convincing when they say things such as, "He is 16 years old; he should know better. He needs to be responsible for his own actions." At this point the counselor must be firm and insist that the parents reach an agreement regarding the desired behavior change. This decision must not be left to the student; it has

been left to the student in the past and it has not worked. If it had worked, they would not be seeking help.

In reply to the parents' contention that the child "should know better," the counselor might say, "Yes, I agree with you, he *should* know better, but he has demonstrated to you very clearly by his actions that he *does not* know better. He has not gone to school for the last 2 months, and he has gotten straight Fs; evidently, this is not a problem to him. Because it is no problem to him that he flunks out of school, and it appears that he is willing to be responsible for that, is this behavior a problem to you, the parents, and if so, are you willing to do something about it?"

The parents need to agree on the problem and on the behavioral standards for the solution of the problem. Sometimes the counselor gets the sense that the parents do not agree and they are not supporting each other (e.g., Mom says, "Straight As"; Dad says, "School's not that big of a deal"). At this juncture, the counselor must be very empathetic and nonblaming but very directive. Tell the parents that it is important that they get together as a team and come to some type of agreement on at least a minimum standard acceptable to both. Only by doing so will they be able to support each other to make the child successful at school.

Even if there are marital difficulties, the counselor needs to confront the parents empathetically, but directly. Are they willing to work together and support each other in this area of the child's educational welfare even though they have personal differences in their marriage? If they agree, this helps clarify the child's position in the family and enables rapid change to take place. If they disagree and will not work together to help the child, this, unfortunate as it is, also clarifies the child's position in the family and some of the family issues, and requires a referral to outside agencies for more extensive marital and family work. Setting the goal in very specific behavioral terms, reaching agreement, and being willing to work together is a large part of the problem. If counselors can get the parents to do that alone, many times this in and of itself solves the problem. Having made the goal very clear, and having reached agreement on the problem, the family and counselor are ready to begin Step Two in the Family Counseling Model.

Step Two: Analysis of Erroneous Parental Belief Systems

In Step Two of this model, the counselor explores parents' belief systems about why the child is not doing the desired goal behaviors set in Step One. The intent of this step is to have parents see whether their belief systems about the child's misbehavior are substantiated by actual observable evidence of the child's behavior and to develop therapeutic blocks so that neither the parents nor the child can use these beliefs as excuses for any further inappropriate behavior.

During this stage, the counselor must be nonblaming but very active and directive in questioning and challenging parents' belief systems. When parents say, "The reason the boy can't sit still in class is that he is hyperactive and can't control himself," the counselor might ask them, "How do you account for this? Minimal brain damage? Blood sugar level? Biochemistry?" Based on their response, then ask, "Does he ever sit still? Under what circumstances? Does he sit still when the teacher is right beside him? The mother? The father? The principal? Does he act the same way in all of his classes at school? In your home? Weekends versus weekdays? At the dining room table? Watching TV? At the neighbors? At the grandparents? In church? In court? If his behavior changes under these different circumstances, how do you explain that in terms of biochemistry? Does he have two different biochemical systems—one to turn the sugar on, and one to turn it off only when Dad is around? Please explain that. How does that work?"

No matter what the parental belief system is, it is important to ask what evidence parents have to support the belief. The counselor must get parents to actively examine their belief system to see if there is a valid reason or excuse to let the child continue to misbehave. Usually, when parents systematically look for evidence, they find little or nothing to substantiate their position and, quite to the contrary, they find that the child has much more behavioral control than was initially believed. The counselor helps the parents through the maze of excuses for inappropriate behavior by using questioning techniques, looking for evidence, and pointing out inconsistencies of actual observable evidence that the parents have previously given about the child's demonstrated capability to control himself. Examples of this might be:

Counselor: You say John is hyperactive and can't control himself because of the sugar. Yet, you say he has the most trouble in school with Mr. Smith, the third period teacher, but has no trouble with Mr. Jones, the fourth period teacher. How do you explain that within 5 minutes from period three to period four he is able to control himself? Does he have two biochemical systems? One system that turns on the sugar and one that turns it off?

Counselor: Even in third period class you say he acts differently when you or the principal walks in. How do you explain that?

Counselor: You say he controls himself at church, at home when you and dad mean it, in the principal's office, first, third, fifth, and sixth period classes, and previously in fifth grade when he "had a good teacher." How do you explain that if he has minimal brain dysfunction and can't control himself?

As is common in counseling sessions, the parents initially might not bring up some of the "real" beliefs or reasons why the child is doing what he is doing. Again, the counselor must be very directive and use clinical experience and hunches to help draw out implicit beliefs, make them explicit, and dispel the beliefs as excuses for allowing the child to continue inappropriate behavior. Examples of this might be:

Example I:

Parent: I don't know why he is acting the way he is.

Counselor: Do you think it might be because he is emotionally disturbed or crazy? (Implicit message—parents bringing child to see a psychologist. Something must be "wrong" with child.)

Parent: No way.

Counselor: Well? That's good to know because some students think that if their parents take them to see a psychologist or shrink that something must be wrong with them and it is reassuring to know that that is not the case.

Example II:

Parent: I don't know why he is acting this way.

Counselor: Could it be that one of you is a terrible parent?

Father: Well! I keep telling her if she disciplined him better we wouldn't have this problem.

Counselor: Do you know any other mothers who do not discipline their children as well as your wife does and the children still go to school and get passing grades? Did your mother and father agree in everything when they disciplined you? Did you get failing grades and drop out of school? Do you know any married couples that agree on everything? Do their children go to school and get passing grades?

After exploring all the reasons why the parents think or feel that the child is doing what she is doing, after inquiring about any other hidden issues or hunches the counselor has regarding the reasons the child is acting out, and after exploring the evidence the parents have to substantiate these contentions, the counselor and family are ready to move to Step Three.

Step Three: Examples of What Parents Have Tried to Solve the Problem

Step Three of the model involves exploring actions parents have already taken to get their child to perform the goal behavior. Here, the counselor listens very carefully and takes notes to record what is actually being said and done to correct the problem. In analyzing parental communication patterns it is helpful to have parents give actual examples in the session. To do this, the counselor says, "Tell me, give me an example of what you actually say to him in the heat of battle." "Does that work?" "When that did not work, what did you say and do then?" "Did that work?"

If the child does something inappropriate in the session, the counselor observes what parents do to correct the problem right then and there. If the child talks back to parents or is "hyperactive," the counselor should note what parents do or say about the behavior in the session. These inquiries and observations usually give the counselor a fairly clear picture of the typical parent-child communication patterns in the home. The counselor needs to know how to analyze adult-child communication patterns similar to those previously described so that vague, abstract, indirect communications about child behavior can be identified.

Some researchers would argue that the interactions shown in the session are not typical of the ones shown at home. From my perspective, the typical messages given are close enough and it is not just the messages but the structure of the messages and the principles behind them that are important. Second, the messages given in the office are usually milder, toned down versions of the ones at home. And finally, it really does not matter if it is an accurate reflection of the interaction patterns or it is "real." We are interested in "solutions to problems" and creating change for the future. If the parents believe this is what they say and do; and we can put therapeutic blocks around their "typical interactions" so the parents cannot use them as often, and we get them to communicate differently; and they solve the problem; it really does not matter if it was ultimately "true or real"—it worked!

At this point in the parent conference, the counselor is making note of what language and behavioral patterns parents perceive they have actually used to correct the problem. By recording what parents have said and done, several things structurally become obvious to the counselor: The parents have not felt it appropriate to be in charge; they have left the decision to behave or not behave up to the child; they have used vague, indirect, and/or abstract communication patterns, which say to the child, "Continue the inappropriate behavior because I really don't expect you to do otherwise"; and they have inconsistently followed through with backup techniques. In Step Three, the counselor is only gathering information that helps set the stage for Step Five of the method (Summarizing, Comparing, and Contrasting Parental Interventions). After exploring what the parents have already tried and making notes using the parents' own language, the counselor is ready to move to Step Four.

Step Four: Analysis of Parental Successes

In Step Four, the counselor asks parents about situations in which they have successfully gotten their child to do what they wanted even though the child did not want to do it. Again, the counselor asks for actual examples of parental communications and behavior. During this step, some parents do not feel they are successful in anything and the counselor may need to help them see that they are successful in many areas. Some standard examples of inquiries that have proven helpful when parents are having difficulty with this step are: Does your child have chores she has to do around the house that she doesn't like to do? How do you get your child to do them? Did your child want to come to this counseling session? How did you get him to come? When you say your child does not do anything until the 10th time, what do

you say and do on the 10th time to be so successful? When you say you punish your child (e.g., restriction, spankings, sending him to his room, etc.), how do you do that? In all of these and in similar inquiries, the counselor is trying to draw out the fact that parents can make the behavior happen when they mean it, and when they communicate it clearly and specifically. When it is important enough to parents to make it happen, they take an active stand on the issue, they give clear and direct messages to the child, and they back up their language with behavior that says the child must do the desired behavior. In so doing, they are usually very successful at getting the child to do what they want.

At this point, the counselor is trying to help the parents recognize that they are successful parents in many areas. Further, the counselor helps them understand that their successes were contingent on their belief that the child was capable, and on their belief that it was reasonable to expect the child to behave. Based on those beliefs, the parents told the child to behave in clear, specific language, backed up their demands, and were consistent.

After the counselor has helped the parents to recognize the many areas in which they are successful at getting their children to do what they want and to understand how they have done so, the counselor is ready to move to the next step.

Step Five: Summary: Comparing and Contrasting Principles of Parental Intervention

In Step Five, all the information comes together in a way that challenges the parents to solve the goal behavior (Step One) if they so desire. Counselors are caring, empathetic, and nonblaming, yet clear and direct about what they see and understand to be happening. Begin by reviewing Step Four of the model. Stress how capable, competent, and successful the parents are. Give some examples of what parents said and did when they were successful. Use the parents' own words, if possible, because this technique helps to ensure ownership and responsibility for the action taken. Point out areas where parents have been successful, took an active leadership role, gave clear, specific, concrete directions, and consistently and systematically backed them up so that the student had to do the desired behavior.

Point out, however, that in the particular area of difficulty (Step One) they have been operating under completely different principles and communication patterns. By reviewing notes on Step Three, the counselor reiterates what the parents have tried in order to solve the concern. Make sure parents see that they have used completely different underlying principles and techniques in this area compared to Step Four where they were successful. Again, the counselor needs to make sure that the *exact* language of parents is used. This is done so parents cannot deny what they have said. Point out that these attempts, even though they were not successful, were *reasonable* because they were based on erroneous beliefs (Step Two) that the child was incapable of doing what was wanted or that a parental demand for the behavior was believed to be inappropriate.

At this point, review the many erroneous parental beliefs given, and give actual examples of contradictory evidence provided by the parents. Commend the parents for trying; after all, they have tried all kinds of things. However, point out that they have been using two completely different communication patterns and principles. When they have been unsuccessful, they have given vague, abstract, indirect, unclear messages, giving the child the choice of whether or not to comply, and have not backed up their expectations with behaviors that conveyed to the child that he had no choice in the matter. However, when they have been successful, they have communicated in clear, specific, direct terms; they were willing to lead and decide what the child was going to do; and they consistently backed up their demands with nonpunishing behaviors that said "There

is no way out; you are going to do what is expected, and you will be successful." So the parent does not feel blamed or put down, stress that the ineffective communication and backup techniques were reasonable, given their beliefs. Underscore that those beliefs have now been dispelled or eroded through their own observable evidence of the child's competence. Thus, the parents are now free, if they so desire, to use the same communication patterns and principles that have proven successful for the child to complete the desired goal behavior (Step One).

In most situations, the simple truth is that the parents have not told the student what to do, or they have not backed up their demand in a consistent fashion. In many cases, at this point of summarizing the process, the parents indicate that they understand what has happened and know what to do. Usually, the healthier the family is, and the more the child's problem really is just a school problem, the more effective the parents are in taking over and accomplishing quick results.

Many "normal" parents have been "psychologized" to the point of immobility, however. They want to do what is best for the child, but they do not know, or do not believe that they know, what to do. They are sure that they do not know enough and will cause great psychological harm to the child if they do the wrong thing. They are constantly bombarded with differing opinions on the latest causes and cures for inappropriate behavior. Many parents are looking for permission to be parents. They want to be told that it is okay to take an active stand and, if necessary, to make a reluctant student go to school and get at least straight Cs. When parents who love their children and want the best for them feel that they have permission to exert legitimate parental control, and know what to do, they are usually amazed at the remarkable changes in their child's behavior. Their child will make a complete turnaround and feel good about it. After the parents take over and finally set reasonable limits, the student ultimately gains more freedom and flexibility, and earns the family's trust. When the student is successful, the parents have little to fight over, like him better, grow to trust him more, and see him as being more mature and responsible. Because of the student's new "maturity" and "responsibility" the parents give him more independence: They "get off his back" and let him make most of his own decisions.

The family counseling session typically ends at this point (Step Five). Should additional reinforcement or clarification be deemed necessary, counselors should add Steps Six and Seven.

Step Six: Review of What the Parents Have Learned

Counselors use this optional step for parents who have not fully understood the principles of the method or are rather authoritarian, hostile, or abusive. Under these circumstances, the counselor asks parents to tell in their own words what they learned from the counseling session and what they plan to do. Listen carefully for any misinformation and clarify any misunderstood principles or messages.

For example, if a father says, "Yeah, I get the message—tell the kids what I want them to do, when I want them to do it, and if they don't do it the first time, let them have it, so they know I mean business." You might say, "No. That's not exactly what was said. What was said was . . . Can you see how this is different?" Or you might bluntly ask the father if he really wants to beat his children and hurt them, or wouldn't he, if given a choice, rather develop a way to get them to do what he wanted them to do without having to beat them?

As another option, tell the father that when he punishes or beats his children, it is a variation of the "if 'x' then 'y' contract," which says to the child that it is okay for him to behave inappropriately as long as he is willing to be punished. Ask the father which message he would rather give:

- Do "x" (be successful) or "y" (be a failure). Either choice is okay with

me; it is your choice. However, if you do choose "y," I am going to punish you; or

- Do "x." Be successful. There is no choice. I care about you and love you. I know that you can do it, and I'm willing to be a parent and help you in any way I can to ensure your success.

Highlighting and discussing these differences and options forces parents to clarify what they really want to do. Counselors should use this maneuver to try to build some therapeutic safeguards so that parents will not hurt or abuse the child after they leave the session. In any case you have made the choice clear: If you give a clear message for success and do everything in your power to make that happen without punishing or hurting your child, the message is that you love and care about your child, and wish your child to be successful. But if you do not follow through or beat your child after you have gone through this method, it is a clear message to the child and to others involved that you do not like and want to hurt your child, and want your child to be unsuccessful. If this latter message comes through loudly and clearly, active steps need to be taken to help safeguard the child's well-being.

Step Seven: Enactment, Plan Ahead, or Role-Play

Occasionally, families say that they want to change but are not sure they can without some structure. At this point, it is helpful to have them plan what they would do and say if the child does not do the goal behavior. Suggest that they develop an "individualized lesson plan" which is similar to a teacher's individual student discipline lesson plan (see Table 3), so that they can plan step by step what they will do. Counselors can guide parents' planning by asking: (a) What will be their first step? (b) What do they anticipate the child's response will be? (c) How will they handle the response? Have parents practice or role-play what they are going to say and do. If role-play or

TABLE 3
Parental Outline for Dealing with Discipline Problems

I. Set the Goal and the Standards

What must the child do or stop doing so that you will think that the problem is solved? State the rules and the solution to the problem in very clear, concrete, specific, objective, observable, behavioral terms, such as: Go to school; get to school on time; stay in school all day; do all your school work at school neatly and correctly; get nothing less than straight Cs in all subjects for the rest of your school career; turn in all assignments on time; and don't hit anyone.

Planned Parental Response—What is the problem? Describe the inappropriate behavior and the solution to the problem in clear behavioral terms:

Parental Goal: (See Table 4 for more information and helpful hints for parents to set the goal.)

REMEMBER: Stay focused on solving this problem and having the child achieve this goal. Do not get manipulated by the child (e.g., "your value system is over the hill," "you don't love me as much as you love my sister") or get sidetracked by other issues (e.g., "Are you a 'good' parent?").

II. Let the Child Know the Rules, Goals, and Standards

   A. Let the child know of any previous excuses or beliefs that you had about his assumed "incapabilities."
   B. Let the child know that you no longer believe these excuses because there is specific evidence to the contrary.
   C. Tell the child the new rules, goals, and standards.
   D. Let the child know that you love him and will do whatever it takes to make sure that he achieves these goals, even if he initially chooses not to do them on his own.

Planned Parent Response

   A. Write out any previous beliefs and excuses:

   Parental response: _____

   B. Write out evidence to the contrary:

   Parental response: _____

   C. State new rules, goals, and standards:

   Parental response: _____

   D. Let the child know that you love him but that from now on you expect him to be successful in this area and you will do whatever it takes to make this happen:

   Parental response: _____

REMEMBER: It is helpful if you practice saying statements A–D aloud a few times before you relate them to the child. Doing this will help you to make sure that your message is clear and specific.

III. General Plan When Child Does Not Comply

   A. First intervention strategy: What will you say when he doesn't do the stated behavior?

   Parental response: _____

   Anticipated response of the child (e.g., anger, pouting, swearing, fighting back) to your clear message: _____

   B. Second intervention strategy: What will you say and do if the child does not respond to the first intervention?

   Parental response: _____

   Anticipated response of the child: _____

   C. Third intervention strategy: What will you do and say now?

   Parental response: _____

REMEMBER: Stay focused on the solution to the problem. Do not get sidetracked by other issues or develop some new elaborate form of punishment. Work on expressing yourself clearly and with firm caring and concern.

(continued)

TABLE 3 *(continued)*

IV. Development of Backup Support

General Plan: If initial interventions do not work, what do you need to do to back up your statements to make your child successful? Who do you need to help you? Develop a plan with these individuals. Write out your plan:

Whose help do you need? Check off on the list:

_____ Support from spouse: The two of you have talked it over, agreed on a plan, and are willing to support each other for the child's well-being even if you strongly disagree with each other in other areas of your relationship.

_____ Support from other family members, such as sisters and brothers, grandparents, in-laws, and cousins.

_____ Support from hired aides, such as tutors, bodyguards, and escorts.

_____ Support from school personnel, such as principal, teachers, librarian, bus driver, custodian, and lunch aides.

_____ Support from neighbors if needed and if appropriate.

_____ Support from church or community support groups and agencies if needed and if appropriate.

_____ Support from police department, probation department, social workers, and court systems if needed and if appropriate.

REMEMBER: Devise backup techniques that say, "I love you and care about you so much that I will not let you fail, hurt yourself, or make a poor decision in this one area of your life. I will not hurt you, punish you, or belittle you. However, I will do whatever is necessary to make sure that you are successful." The choice of a good backup technique is a choice between success and success, not between success and failure. The bottom-line message conveyed to the child is this: "You must do the desired behavior. There is no way out of doing it." You—the parents—must be willing to put in the time and energy to make the goal behavior happen. You must be consistent, monitor the behavior, and follow through. You must convey to the child that you have a 100% commitment to this goal—and the goal will be achieved. There is no choice—it will happen.

enactments are not used, have them talk through what they plan to say and do.

At Steps Six and Seven it also helps to give parents examples of what other parents have tried. Relay techniques and backup strategies other parents have used as suggestions. If parents use such information successfully, then there is no problem, and counselors have saved a lot of time and energy. If they do not try any of the suggestions, or if they say that they tried them and they did not work, this parental response in and of itself can be used by the counselor as a diagnostic probe. This response would suggest that the counselor either needs to work longer with the family and intensify their interventions, begin exploring other belief systems that were not explored in the first session, or look for more complex and hidden dynamics or agendas that may be happening within the family. Remember, start with simple, straightforward interventions and thinking, and if

they do not work, then move to more complex interventions that take into account more subtle family dynamics.

Some parents find it helpful to plan what they would do if the student intensifies the situation and tries to manipulate them by anger, crying, sulking, or fighting back. The counselor needs to help parents mobilize what backup support systems they might need to succeed, both at home and at school. Teachers and/or the principal, in-laws, neighbors, or other family members may need to be enlisted to help to coordinate proper backup, follow-through, and consistency to ensure student success. In extreme situations, counselors may need to work with police and court systems. Some families have even used police handcuffs, probation officers, or bodyguards to make sure that truant, drug-taking, acting-out adolescents went to school, stayed there, and did what the parents expected until the student realized that the parents meant what they said and that the child had no choice but to obey and to be successful.

Counselors may wish to facilitate the parents' thinking about and planning for possible unforeseen consequences before they actually start their intervention plans. Ask parents questions such as: Can they do this together without getting angry at or blaming each other? Do they have the energy and persistence to make this happen, to follow through, and to be consistent 100% of the time—even if they are tired? Is it better to take a stand and possibly not have it work out, or not take a stand and know it will not work out?

Ask parents to think over and talk about their plan before they actually start their intervention. If the counselor feels that the parents really want to help their child achieve the goal behavior but may not follow through as consistently as hoped, she might force the situation by telling parents in the presence of their child, "Make sure you are 100% committed before you start the intervention because if you start it and then do not follow through, that tells your child that he can get away with it; that you don't love him, that you want him to be a failure; and, that you don't care about his education or his future well-being. So please don't start this unless you really are committed, because if you don't make it happen, that is a clear message to your child that you don't care." This last maneuver, if used, puts the parents in a definite position of making up their minds as to what they value and what they are willing to do to make sure that their child is successful in school.

As you finish the session, give parents materials that will help them to remember some of the general ideas expressed in the session. A handout of helpful hints for parents is found in Table 4.

Follow-Up Session

A follow-up session is arranged after completing the steps of this model. Usually, if the family functions well, counselors can set an appointment for a week or two later. However, indicate to parents that they can call any time they like or come in sooner if they are trying something and it does not seem to be working. Let them know that calling or coming in immediately is preferred to waiting a week or two and having the student continue to act inappropriately. In situations where families are high functioning, issues often can be settled in one session; in those situations, the success can be monitored by phone with parents or through feedback reports from teachers. In other situations, two or three sessions may be needed to help consult with parents to see where things are breaking down. This may entail examining or reexamining belief systems that were initially left out or were inadequately eroded, checking actual communication patterns, and, finally, checking on follow-through and consistency. Often in these latter cases, especially if the student has had a history of difficulties and manipulation of the parents, the main issue is supporting parents and encouraging them to follow through until the student is convinced that they mean business and will not back down. Once the student gets the message, things start to change rather quickly.

In extreme cases, it may be necessary for you to help to coordinate some community and school resources to help parents be successful. Keep parents in a position of power and control, but orchestrate other agencies to lend a short-term helping hand. For example, additional help is definitely needed for a single mother with a 16-year-old son who is threatening her with physical abuse if she tries to make him go to school. See if her ex-husband, other family members, neighbors, or church members can help. If none of them are available, have the mother hire a junior college football player or a bodyguard to help out initially. If necessary, get the police department, probation officers, or court system involved, especially if they are already involved, you have worked with them ahead of time, and they know and support the program. As a last resort, if the school system is supportive and the district has

TABLE 4
Helpful Suggestions for Getting Your Child to Do What You Want Him to Do

A. Decide on the Specific Behaviors of the Child that Are to Be Changed:
1. It is better if both parents agree and are willing to support each other on this.
2. Make the goal clear and specific: Go to school each day, stay in school, do all your work, and get nothing less than straight Cs instead of "He has an attitude problem" or "I want him to work up to his potential."
3. Break the goal into manageable units: "Do these 10 math problems neatly and correctly within the next 15 minutes; then I will check them with you".
4. Monitor behavior. If the student is not being successful, that is a clear message that he needs more help and guidance from you to ensure that he is successful.

B. Obstacles to Clear Demands:
1. Am I sure that he is capable of this behavior?
   a. What possible "excuses" for him have I been entertaining? Possibilities include: hyperactive; normal behavior ("boys will be boys"); stages of development ("terrible twos"); his friends make him do it, he can't help himself, he's bored, he is just like his Dad, it's because of the divorce, etc.
   b. What objective, observable evidence do I have to support these "excuses" to determine if, in fact, they are true?
   c. Have I ever seen my child do this goal behavior before? If so, then he is capable of doing it again.
2. Am I sure that this is a reasonable and essential goal?
   a. Am I willing to let my child make the decision on this (negotiable vs. non-negotiable)?
   b. Am I willing to let my child make the decision and if so can I do it without resentment, hostility, anger, or blaming? If not then I need to be the parent.
   c. Am I willing to put in the time and energy to follow through on this goal?
3. How is my child going to try to manipulate me? Possibilities include: arguing, crying, pouting, asks "why," questions parenting skills or rights, tantrums, threatens to run away or kill himself.
   Questions to keep in mind:
   a. Did I do this as a child? How did I react to my parents' attempts to deal with my manipulations?
   b. What will I say, and how might I deal with these manipulations? (What is my plan?)

C. Remember What the Bottom Line Is:
What is a very clear, specific, concrete, direct message and follow-up technique that tells my child that I love him so much that I will not allow him to be unsuccessful, that he must do this behavior, and that there is no way out of doing what is requested?

D. Types of Vague Communications to Stay Away From:
1. Ignoring inappropriate behavior, hoping it will go away.
2. Demanding honesty, concern, or sorrow versus stopping the inappropriate behavior.
3. Requesting that the child try to change, think about the behavior, or not get caught doing the behavior.
4. Using abstract terms such as "use common sense," "respect," "grow up," "maturity," "potential," "love," and so on.
5. Statements of fact: "I see that you didn't take out the trash."
6. Labeling or classifying: "You're a thief . . . a bad boy . . . a baby," and so on.
7. Questions such as these: "How many times do I have to tell you?" "Why are you hitting your sister?"
8. Wishes, wants, and shoulds.
9. If/then contracts: "If you don't do your homework, then you can't go to the dance."
10. Reasoning, inspiring, explaining, lecturing.

REMEMBER: Tell them once, then back it up—which means, do whatever it takes to get your child to do what you want him to do without punishing him or giving him a chance to fail. Care and love him enough to do what is necessary to make him successful.

---

worked out a plan to support teachers and parents in solving some of these problems, a support team backed by the district truant officer can be sent to the home on a short-term basis to protect mom and to help her get the student to school on time. If your counseling message to parents is, "If it is important, then make it happen," then your message to the school, community, and legal system should be, "If education is important, then develop support systems to help parents and teachers make it happen." This help is provided initially on a short-term basis with the parent in charge until the student is back on track and being successful. The more the student is successful and demonstrates independence and good decision making, the more freedom the student is given.

Remember, it is the parents' responsibility to solve the problem and they need to be in charge. The school's and community's role, if any, is only supportive and as a backup function on a short-term basis.

Finally, for parents who are not going to work to solve the problem or whose value system actively supports the child's inappropriate behavior, clarify this fact in a nonblaming, nonjudgmental way. Make it very explicit so that there is no misunderstanding on the parents' or the child's part that the inappropriate behavior is what they want to happen and they are very successful at it. As an example of this, a psychiatrist told me about a case of professional thieves who had a son on drugs. The family was referred to him from probation because the boy was arrested for stealing while he was under the influence of drugs. After going through family counseling, the family was very successful at getting the child off drugs (the parents' goal). When asked about stopping the boy from stealing (probation's goal), they were not interested. They had had three to four generations of professional thieves in their family, and they could see no reason to stop the tradition. However, it was pointed out to them how successful they really were in this particular area as parents, even though it was in direct contrast to society's and the school's point of view.

SUMMARY

In this chapter a brief overview of dealing with difficult discipline problems from a family-systems approach has been presented. This school-based discipline approach is based on the Brief Family Intervention Model, which states that what adults say to children in the heat of battle is a reflection of the adults' underlying beliefs about themselves or the child's capabilities. When using this model psychologists and counselors must develop skills to listen carefully and to analyze actual parent-child communication patterns, draw out implicit beliefs and make them explicit, and erode erroneous beliefs or put therapeutic blocks

around them to eliminate their use as excuses by parents or adults for allowing further inappropriate child behavior.

Examples of some typical popularly held beliefs about children's inappropriate behavior were explored and some standard questioning techniques showing that the belief had nothing to do with the inappropriate behavior were addressed. Examples of vague, abstract, indirect communication patterns were presented. A highly structured seven-step parent counseling approach, designed to help parents see they are capable of stopping the student's inappropriate behavior, was described.

One of the major underlying assumptions of this approach is that parents are very capable of getting their children to do what they want them to do. It was clearly pointed out that in the behavioral areas where parents are successful at getting their children to do what they want, they believe it is okay for them to be in charge as parents; they believe the child is capable; they communicate clearly; and they back up their demands. However, in the areas where they are having difficulty with the child, they operate under completely different techniques and principles because of their underlying belief systems. Under the latter situation the parents do not think they should be in charge or they do not see or believe the child is capable; they communicate in vague, abstract, indirect ways and they do not back up their requests as consistently as when they believe it and mean it. During counseling parents see and understand why they have not been taking a clear stand and communicating directly. Because of this new insight and understanding they are now free to apply the direct communication techniques and behavioral interventions that have proven to be successful in other areas.

The focus of this chapter is on the underlying philosophy and family counseling portion of a comprehensive school discipline approach. The assumptions, principles, and techniques of this approach can be used by teachers and administrators in the classroom or school

(Level One and Two), counselors/school psychologists working with families (Level Three), and community agencies working with the schools to solve difficult discipline problems (Level Four). Although the program has been used by schools and many districts have received staff development training in this approach, the efficacy of the approach has not been assessed at each of the individual levels or as a total program in a systematic research fashion. However, extensive case by case, school by school, and family by family success stories have been reported. A few examples of these successes are:

In Pennsylvania, where this model is getting extensive exposure at a teacher, school, district, and state level, it has been reported that:

- Behavior and academic performance of inner city minority students at one school has improved dramatically.

- A young lady, who had been sexually abused, provided foster care, kicked out of numerous schools, and thought to be emotionally disturbed, was helped to the point that she stayed in regular education classes; stopped all "weird and strange" behaviors, noises, and language; and got passing grades in all subjects.

- Twenty "at risk" students, who had significant behavior and academic problems, stopped most of their inappropriate school behavior and passed the seventh grade with Cs or better.

A Connecticut school psychologist, working predominantly with the family (Level Three) of a boy who was labeled "school phobic," failing school, kicked out of at least four schools, and in the process of being referred for out of district placement because of extreme emotional outbursts, successfully stopped all inappropriate behavior. The psychologist received a long letter of thanks at the end of the year from the parents along with a copy of the boy's report card with straight Cs or better, coupled with satisfactory or better marks on behavior and citizenship grades. The family and the school psy-

chologist stopped the inappropriate behavior, kept him in regular classes, had him pass in all his subjects, and never had to do a psychological evaluation for out of district placement or "label" the student.

A school psychologist in California worked with another student who was identified by a private practice psychologist as "school phobic." The boy rarely came to school, and when he did, he vomited and was sent home by the school nurse. After working with the family for one session, the boy was back in school and never missed another day of school that year.

These are only a few examples. Numerous others could be given. This approach is deceptively simple in its ideas and interventions but extremely powerful in its results and outcomes. I am looking forward to having researchers systematically evaluate the effectiveness of this model. Even more importantly, I am looking forward to school psychologists, counselors, and social workers learning this model so they can better meet the needs of students, work more effectively with parents, and solve discipline problems that face schools today.

REFERENCES

Haley, J. (1980). *Leaving home: The therapy of disturbed young people.* New York: McGraw-Hill.

Levant, R. (1984). *Family therapy: A comprehensive overview.* Englewood Cliffs, NJ: Prentice-Hall.

Minuchin, S., & Fishman, C. (1981). *Family therapy techniques.* Cambridge: Harvard University Press.

Okun, B. F., & Rappaport, L. J. (1980). *Working with families: An introduction to family therapy.* North Scituate, MA: Duxbury Press.

Petrie, P., & Piersel, W. C. (1982). Family therapy. In C. R. Reynolds & T. B. Gutkin (Eds.), *The handbook of school psychology* (pp. 580–590). New York: Wiley & Sons.

Valentine, M. (1987). *How to deal with discipline problems in the schools: A practical guide for educators.* Dubuque, IA: Kendall/Hunt.

Valentine, M. (1988). *Difficult discipline problems: A family systems approach.* Dubuque, IA: Kendall/Hunt.

17

INVOLVING PARENTS IN THE SPECIAL EDUCATION PROCESS

Joan Silverstein, Judith Springer, and Nancy Russo

INTRODUCTION

As indicated throughout this volume, parent-school collaboration has been widely advocated as a desirable educational goal. However, unlike other types of parent-school collaboration described elsewhere in this book, parent-school partnership in the domain of special education has been specifically mandated by federal law and regulation. For example, the Education of the Handicapped Act (EHA), also known as PL94–142, requires that parents give informed consent before a preplacement evaluation is conducted and before a handicapped child is initially placed in a program which provides special education and related services (34 CFR Part 300.504). Parent participation in the conference to develop the child's Individualized Education Program (IEP) is also mandated (34 CFR Part 300.345). Additionally, the EHA gives parents an oversight role in the special education of their children (Turnbull & Turnbull, 1986).

"Consent," as defined by the EHA regulations (34 CFR Part 300.500), requires that:

(a) The parent is fully informed of all information relevant to the activity for which consent is sought, in his or her native language, or other mode of communication; (b) The parent understands and agrees in writing to the carrying out of the activity for which his or her consent is sought, and the consent describes that activity and lists the records (if any) which will be released and to whom; and (c) The parent understands that the granting of consent is voluntary on the part of the parent and may be revoked at any time.

The EHA also requires that school districts take active steps to ensure the participation of parents in the meeting where the IEP is developed. Policy interpretations by the Office of Special Education in the U.S. Department of Education have clarified the expectation that:

The IEP meeting serves as a communication vehicle between parents and school personnel, and enables them as equal participants to decide jointly what the child's needs are, what services will be provided to meet those needs, and what the anticipated outcomes will be. (U.S. Office of Education; clarification of the IEP requirements in the Federal Register, 1981, p. 5462, cited in Turnbull & Turnbull, 1982)

The Supreme Court has reinforced the role of active parent participation by stating:

The IEP is to be developed jointly by a school official qualified in special education, the child's teacher, the parents or guardian, and, where appropriate, the child. In several places, the Act emphasized the participation of the parents in developing the child's educational program and assessing its effectiveness. (Burlington School Committee v. MA. Department of Education, 1985)

During the 12 years since the implementation of the EHA, there have been conflicting findings about parents' participation in, and satisfaction with, the IEP process. The picture of parents' interactions with multidisciplinary teams (MDTs) that emerges from the research literature generally is one of passive parent participation in short, pro forma meetings (e.g., Abramson, Willson, Yoshida, & Hagerty, 1983; Gilliam & Coleman, 1981; Goldstein, Strickland, Turnbull, & Curry, 1980; Lynch & Stein, 1982; Ysseldyke, Algozzine, & Allen, 1981). Parents who were surveyed immediately after the parent-team conference generally expressed high levels of satisfaction with the IEP meeting; however, some observers noted that parents often did not appear to fully understand what had actually occurred at the meeting (e.g., Goldstein et al., 1980; Hoff, Fenton, Yoshida, & Kaufman, 1978; Vaughn, Bos, Harrell, & Lasky, 1988; Ysseldyke et al., 1981; Ysseldyke & Thurlow, 1980). It is possible that overt signs of participation (e.g., how much parents say or don't say at meetings) and overt expressions of satisfaction at the time of the meeting (e.g., in response to exit surveys after the IEP meeting) may not be synonymous with substantive parent-team collaboration in the special education process.

Collaboration

As defined in this chapter, collaboration is a cooperative and nonhierarchical venture based on shared power and authority, in which power is based on knowledge and expertise rather than role and function (Kraus, 1980). The collaborative relationship is egalitarian and trusting, with an emphasis on "reciprocity of influence" (Tyler, 1983, p. 388) and persuasion rather than unidirectional influence and coercion. Consequently, all

partners change and gain as a result of the collaboration (Parsons & Meyers, 1984; Rosenfield, 1987; Tyler, 1983). Professional and parent each bring a unique perspective and different type of knowledge and expertise which is not readily available to the other. The school professional provides specialized knowledge and expertise in such areas as assessment and intervention for children's school-related problems; parents bring specific knowledge about their child's behavior in the home and other environmental contexts (Conoley, 1987). They also have information about the child's history and have experience in developing interventions in their child's life outside the school setting. Some parents, who are professionals or who have became educated in educational and mental health interventions, also bring specialized knowledge similar to the school professional. Both parent and professional thus provide different aspects of the total information necessary for diagnosis and for planning, implementing, and evaluating interventions.

THE SPECIAL EDUCATION PROCESS

Even though the IEP meeting has been the focal point of study and legislation regarding parent involvement, parents have indicated that the IEP meeting is embedded in a larger context, referred to in this chapter as "the special education process." As described below, this process begins when a problem is first identified. The process ends, for some parents, when the child leaves special education; for others, it may never end. In this chapter, parents' perceptions of the special education process will be discussed, based on the authors' qualitative research project studying the effects of the special education process on parents. First, the stages of the special education process, as identified by parents, will be reviewed. Within each stage, major themes identified from the data as affecting parent-school collaborative relationships will be discussed. Then, themes present across stages will be described and factors that impede or facilitate collaborative parent-professional relationships will be presented.

This discussion will focus primarily on parents' relationships with the "clinical members" of the multidisciplinary team (MDT): the learning consultant (a teacher with specialized training in learning and educational evaluation), the school psychologist, and the social worker. Working together with other school personnel, these clinicians generally played primary roles in assessment, development of IEPs, periodic reviews of children's progress in special education, and case management. When not otherwise specified, references to "the team" will be to these clinicians. Although some MDT members' roles are designated in the regulations accompanying the EHA, much room is left for variation. Therefore, the titles and composition of the teams vary somewhat among states (Kaiser & Woodman, 1985).

Although some common concerns and themes were raised by a number of parents, there was no single consistent perception shared by all parents. At times, different parents had strikingly varied perceptions of the same MDT members and of other school personnel. Parents' own perceptions also sometimes changed over time. One common theme, however, was that parents rarely told team members and other school professionals how they felt about the special education process or their treatment by team members, and rarely expressed to team members their feelings about themselves or their child. This chapter, therefore, raises issues which may be helpful to team members when they work with parents during the special education process.

METHODOLOGY

Grounded theory methodology. The findings discussed in this chapter are based on qualitative research using grounded theory methodology (Glaser & Strauss, 1967; Schatzman & Strauss, 1973; Strauss & Corbin, 1990; Strauss, 1987) to guide the collection and analysis of data. As described by Taylor and

Bogdan (1984), "The grounded theory approach is a method for discovering theories, concepts, hypotheses, and propositions directly from data, rather than from a priori assumptions, other research, or existing theoretical frameworks" (p. 126). Grounded theory methodology provides a means to "capture the complexity of reality (phenomena) we study, and . . . to make . . . sense of it. . . . The researcher's will not be the only possible interpretation of the data . . . but it will be plausible, useful, and allow its own further elaboration and verification" (A. L. Strauss, 1987, pp. 10–11). Data collection, coding, and other methods of analysis occur simultaneously. Analysis of existing data guides the theoretical sampling of incidents, events, activities, populations, and other data sources in order to make comparisons between and among those samples. Analytic methods used include induction, deduction, and verification.

The primary goal of the study discussed in this chapter was to understand the effects of the special education process from the parents' perspective. Parent "informants" with differing perspectives and experiences were sampled. "Secondary informants," such as MDT members and advocates, were also sought to provide additional viewpoints. Documents such as assessment reports, IEPs, parent handbooks developed by school districts, and other literature parents obtained from a variety of sources were also analyzed.

Parent "informants." Sixty-six parents and grandparents in 48 families (46 mothers, 17 fathers, one pair of custodial grandparents, and one noncustodial grandmother) were interviewed. Ten parents were interviewed only once; all others were interviewed a minimum of two times. Interviews were taped and transcribed. Parent-team meetings were also observed for six of the families. Parents in seven of the families were re-interviewed at 1 to 3 year intervals to provide a longitudinal perspective.

Parents were recruited directly through five school districts, one clinic, and two parent groups. Other parent

informants were recruited through referral by current parent participants and
professionals. They were sampled in order
to answer questions raised during the
data analysis. In total, 20 school districts
were represented. (Four of the families
had children in Catholic school at the
time of the initial interview). Eighteen of
the districts were suburban; two were
urban. Four of the parents were minority:
Asian-American (2), African-American
(1), and Hispanic (1). Working class,
middle class, and upper middle class
parents were interviewed.

STAGES OF THE SPECIAL EDUCATION PROCESS

The special education process may be
characterized as a problem-solving process (Skrtic, 1987; Springer, 1989) where
a problem is identified and analyzed;
solutions are generated and prioritized;
and interventions are selected, planned,
implemented, and evaluated (Gutkin &
Curtis, 1982). The special education process includes a number of stages. During
the *identification and referral stage,*
parents and teachers may feel the effects
of the problem but may not realize that
intervention by the MDT is warranted.
Interventions may be attempted by parents and other school personnel as well as
by other professionals in the medical and
mental health fields. Depending on the
nature of the problems, this stage may
begin at birth, before the child enters
school, or after the child is in an
academic environment. When the child is
referred, the problem is further clarified
and the child is referred to the MDT. In
the traditional model, prevalent for most
of the families in this study, referral
generally was followed by an assessment
by the MDT (*the assessment stage*).
Following the assessment, teams analyzed
the data and deliberated in private, after
which parents were given feedback about
the evaluation findings and recommendations for interventions (*feedback stage*). If
the child was classified and placed in
special education, an IEP was then developed during the parent-team *decision-
making stage*. This team—based on the

EHA and accompanying regulations—
included one or both parents, the child's
teacher, and other representatives of the
school district as well as at least one
evaluation team member. After the child
was placed in special education, parent
contacts with team members and with
other school personnel continued until
the child was declassified or completed
school (*postplacement stage*). In some
cases, parents then became involved with
professionals in post high school special
education programs or at the child's place
of employment. Parent-professional contacts during the special education process
included conferences; informal meetings;
phone conversations; and written documents such as handbooks, letters, reports, and IEPs.

The use of the term "problem" in this
chapter is not meant to imply that the
locus of the problem is necessarily found
within the child, as is assumed in the
medical model (Ysseldyke & Christenson,
1988). Instead, the term is being used
here to indicate that the child is not
benefiting optimally from the kinds of
experiences or instruction that are currently being provided. Although some of
the reasons for the problem may reside in
the child, it is likely that the problem may
be the result of the interaction between
the child and one or more of the child's
environmental contexts (Bronfenbrenner, 1979b; Conoley, 1987).

Identification and Referral

By the time parents enter the IEP
meeting they have had a number of
experiences which may influence their
perceptions of their child and themselves,
the school, professionals, and the special
education process. These influences include prior contacts of parents and others
(e.g., friends, relatives) with schools and
professionals, family circumstances and
stressors, and parents' prior experiences
with their children.

Themes Related to Parental and Family History

Some parents have had extensive
experience with education and mental

health professionals because of their own problems or friends' and relatives' problems, or because their child's difficulties were identified at birth or during preschool years. These prior contacts sometimes affected parents' expectations of the MDT and the special education process. For example, a parent whose own alcoholism was misdiagnosed by psychologists had little trust in the school psychologist and conveyed this to her child. As a result, the child resisted being assessed by the psychologist, thereby reducing the validity of the assessment. Another parent's reluctance to complain about her treatment by school personnel was due to her experiences as a youngster when she observed her teachers judging and disparaging parents who "made waves." Parents often cited conversations with other parents who had had either positive or negative experiences with the team and special education as influencing their initial approach to the team. One mother had heard so many negatives about the team's treatment of her neighbor that she decided to go in to the conference with a strategy of trying to meet the team halfway. This led to a very positive experience. Other parents approached their teams defensively because they had heard rumors such as that the district was trying to classify more children in order to obtain more money from the state.

Parents sometimes formed impressions about professionals based on the media. During interviews, parents cited talk shows, media columnists, newspaper or magazine articles, television programs, and movies as providing them with information about handicapping conditions, new interventions and fads, and the special education process. Some of this information was helpful. For example, when a newspaper article described the characteristics of Tourette's Syndrome, a father was able to diagnose the condition in his son who had previously been misdiagnosed by a number of professionals. In other cases, the media presentations may have been misleading, resulting in misinformation which later affected parents' understanding or acceptance of the team's communication.

Parents who had early positive, egalitarian experiences with professionals learned that it was possible to work collaboratively with clinicians and to advocate for their child. These experiences provided them with a model which served as a standard for their later relationships with MDTs. Parents sometimes felt excluded or dismayed when their child's next MDT did not seem to want the same level of participation from them. When these parents began to make requests based on their expertise about their child, they were sometimes viewed by team professionals as unreasonable and demanding.

Themes Related to the History of Identification of the Problem

The first stage of any problem-solving process is to recognize and identify the problem. As is common when dealing with complex issues, parental identification of the problem sometimes evolved slowly. Recognition of one part of the problem did not always guarantee understanding of the ramifications and scope of the entire problem. For example, several parents who appeared to have accepted their children's neurological impairment, which had been identified during preschool years, were still unprepared when their children later displayed signs of learning disabilities. Awareness of the existence of a problem may not occur simultaneously for both parents. A number of parents noted that they disagreed with their spouses about the existence or extent of their child's learning difficulty, with ramifications for their relationship with each other and with their child. Experiences which took place before the problem was clearly identified often appeared to generate strong emotions such as anger, anxiety, and guilt, which sometimes resulted in reactions such as defensiveness and denial.

Similar to parents' experiences, classroom teachers also appeared to vary in their ability to clearly identify the source of the problem. Based on parent reports, some teachers appear to have attributed the child's learning problems to such causes as laziness, lack of motivation, or lack of proper parental guidance. At times, these attributions seem to have resulted in teacher frustration with the child and, by extension, with the parents. In extreme cases, the resulting treatment was sometimes devastating to both parent and child and affected parent-child relationships. For example, as a result of teachers' comments, some parents began to view their learning disabled children as retarded or extremely slow. Other parents reported that their children felt angry and betrayed because their parents did not realize that they were being mishandled by teachers and did not act to prevent the mistreatment. Frequently, when parents brought their resulting guilt, anxiety, and other strong emotions into the parent-team meetings, they were in a "one down" position which affected their ability to process information and participate effectively.

Homework scenes. Pressures and frustrations from incorrectly diagnosed problems often surfaced during homework time, one of the major points of contact between school and parent. A number of parents reported painful, lengthy homework scenes—sometimes lasting as long as 3 or 4 hours—repeated night after night with serious consequences for family relationships. One mother described her nightly homework sessions with her son, who was later classified learning disabled. "The two of us would sit here in tears and I said, 'But I'm trying to help you,' and he'd say, 'but you're yelling at me.' Angry every night. I thought I was helping, but it was the wrong approach." Her husband added, "He became more resistant, we became more demanding. He became more upset. We became more angry. He became more depressed." Even when the homework experiences were far less traumatic, parents often stressed that the extensive amount of time spent on homework, "doesn't leave a lot of time for living." When neither parent nor teacher understood the causes of the child's problem, the effects of the frustrations at home and

in school sometimes took a toll, affecting the parents' perceptions of both their child and themselves. For example, after particularly frustrating homework scenes, a parent explained that she sometimes wondered, "What's in that empty head?"

Homework tensions sometimes created vicious cycles. For example, when some parents felt judged, they pushed the child harder for results so they could satisfy the teacher's requirements. Others tried to resolve the problem by doing the homework for the child. These approaches often backfired, resulting in the parents feeling even more judged and/or masking the extent of the child's difficulties so the difficulties were not evident to school personnel. In either case, the potential for effective collaborative problem solving between parents and school personnel was reduced.

Problem identification. Two patterns related to problem identification will be discussed: (a) when parents were the first to identify the problem and (b) when professionals were the first to notice the problem and inform the parent. In either case, the ways in which parents were treated by professionals—during the identification period and the time leading up to the referral for assessment—had the potential to affect parents' perceptions of school professionals, their child, and themselves, and to affect their predisposition to work collaboratively with the team.

When the classroom teacher was the first to identify a problem, the results appeared to vary depending on the teacher's diagnosis of the difficulty and the manner in which the parent was approached. When teachers identified a problem and had to inform the parents, the methods they used sometimes engendered high anxiety levels. Parents preferred to be given potentially stressful news concerning their children in person, rather than by telephone. Unfortunately, perhaps due to busy schedules, this was not always the case. Several parents reported that their first notification was a telephone call from the teacher who informed them that their child was being recommended for retention or for referral for special education evaluation. Telephone communications from teachers to parents relaying potentially distressing information tended to generate high levels of parental stress and anxiety.

When the school was the first to identify the problem, parents had a number of different reactions, depending on such factors as other support systems available in their life and the school's prior handling of the problem. Some parents initially did not acknowledge the existence of a problem. Clinicians and other professionals often appear to attribute this reaction to denial. In some cases, this attribution may be accurate; however, based on the data there may be an alternative explanation for some parents' responses. At times, parents' initial disagreement with the team's perception appears to have been due to differences in the team's and parents' attributions for the child's behavior, or differences between the child's behavior at home and behavior at school. Sometimes, when parents learned more about the handicapping condition and the school's definition of the problem, they began to "reframe" (Watzlawick, Weakland, & Fisch, 1974) their perception of the problem and to agree with the school. At other times, the school's identification of a problem validated parents' concerns. In these cases, despite the anxiety generated by the school's referral, parents often felt relieved to know that someone else perceived that something was tangibly wrong. For example, the mother of a learning disabled boy explained, "When I found out that he had this problem I was really sad about it, but I almost felt a little relieved . . . that he wasn't doing it on purpose. . . . I felt like a better mother because it wasn't my fault."

When parents were the first to identify the problem, the first professional with whom they talked was often either the pediatrician or the classroom teacher. Pediatricians sometimes played a key role as consultant and advisor for parents throughout the special education process. Their advice often influenced the parents' perceptions of the special education process and the team. Because the classroom teacher was often the first school professional with whom parents talked about their child's learning difficulties, teacher-parent contacts also tended to set the tone for future parent-school encounters.

When parents approached pediatricians and teachers with their suspicions, receptivity to parental concerns varied. Parents reported that they perceived professionals as wanting to work in partnership when they were responsive to parental anxieties, acknowledged the validity of their concerns, and either suggested further action—such as a referral—or recommended that the problem be monitored. Parents also responded more favorably when they felt that the professional had an accurate, well-rounded, compassionate perception of their child and a genuine liking for the youngster.

In some cases, the professional negated the problem, saying the parents had "jumped the gun" due to such factors as "overprotectiveness," "lack of experience as parents," "hysteria," "overanxiousness," or the child's (or parents') "immaturity." Fear of these negative labels served as a powerful control, often inhibiting parents from taking immediate action. At times, these "diagnoses" created serious doubts in parents. A typical example was presented by a mother who suspected that her daughter—the youngest of three—was having difficulty learning. "I had been told by . . . the kindergarten teacher that I was basically being neurotic over my last child. That she was my baby and I was not willing to let go. . . . I didn't perceive myself as being like that, but I started to have doubts. I mean, when so many people tell you 'You're ugly,' after a while you say, 'Maybe I'm wrong and I am.'"

When professionals minimized problems, this sometimes fed into the parents' wishes, raised false hopes, and delayed parents from seeking help. One mother—whose son was later diagnosed as having a learning disability—described her experiences when she and her husband approached their child's kindergarten teacher and asked if they should have their son's developmental delays checked.

"And she said 'No, no, no, no, no. I wouldn't go for that yet.' She was not overly concerned, chalking it up to immaturity—ours and his. And we didn't know if they were doing us a favor, or if they were avoiding it. The parental reaction I had was 'Oh, good. I'm glad she didn't want him tested. Everything seems to be fine. This *is* normal.' "

Occasionally, a school district refused to acknowledge that the child had a problem, even after the parent had obtained an outside opinion. Some parents described lengthy battles to have their concerns or their second opinion evaluations taken seriously by the district. Although their refusal was permissible under state regulations, when school districts refused to accept opinions that were different from theirs, parents reported that they found this occurrence to be very confusing and disturbing. The district's reaction heightened their feelings of suspicion about the school's motives and generated frustration and anger toward the district. Parents sometimes began to question every action or suggestion made by the team and administration and became extremely vulnerable to rumors circulating in the community about the special education process.

Assessment

The EHA does not require the same level of parent participation during the assessment as during the development of an IEP. In a policy letter written in 1987, the director of the federal Office of Special Education Programs stated, "The regulations do not require that parents be afforded a full participatory role in the evaluation process" (Bellamy, 1987, p. 437). The regulations do require that parents give written informed consent for the preplacement evaluation (i.e., the assessment before the child's first placement in special education). As indicated in a policy letter by the Chief of the State Policy and Administrative Review Branch of the Bureau of Education for the Handicapped, parents must be given information about any particular tests that will be used, if known in advance, or

descriptions of the general kinds of tests that will be used (Irvin, 1980). The lack of more extensive team contact with parents during the assessment stage may reduce the likelihood that collaborative decision making will occur during the development of the IEP.

Themes Related to the Social History Intake

One of the parents' initial contacts with team members was often the social history intake. If parents had prior positive contacts with team members, and if the purpose of potentially sensitive intake questions was clearly explained to them, the intake conference generally was not traumatic and was either positive or neutral.

The format of the social history intake conference sometimes conveyed the expectation that, whenever required by professionals throughout the child's special education career, parents would graciously cooperate by exposing themselves to the scrutiny of clinicians, repeating histories which might be painful or embarrassing. Parents told us they complied because they felt it would help their child. However, some parents noted that their compliance placed them in a one-down, vulnerable position, which was not conducive to the development of collaborative parent-professional relationships. Some professionals who were interviewed during the project noted that they saved the more personal and embarrassing questions until they knew the parent better, and only asked questions that were educationally relevant. However, the social intake questions were sometimes perceived by parents as intrusive and judgmental at a time when many parents already felt exposed and judged.

Some parents were afraid of the possible ramifications of the team's intrusion into their lives. Parents who had prior experience with the legal or social service systems were often, understandably, suspicious when their first team contact was with a clinician who asked them highly personal questions. Even when teams told parents how the information would be used, some parents did not trust or understand the explanations. For example, some parents wondered how information about their income could help diagnose or remediate their child's reading problem. Parents sometimes also feared that the information might be disclosed to some agency and, ultimately, used against them.

The process of questioning, itself, can create a negative set, producing blocking, reducing input, cutting off conversation, and inhibiting response (Dillon, 1979). This effect was sometimes amplified during the social history intake interview because of the stressful conditions under which the questions were asked and the implied negative judgment that some parents perceived. One advocate, who worked with parents of special education youngsters, summarized a recurrent theme: "Parents are never comfortable from the first day when they are handed a list of forms and somebody asks you what do you do for a living. . . . Do you have an elevator in your building? Does your child have his own room? Parents think, 'If I don't have an elevator, maybe they don't think I'm good.' Or, 'I have only one bedroom and I have three kids.' These are important things that parents think about. It's already something that makes parents very defensive. You feel you have to have certain answers, some pat answer that's the accepted norm in society. They already feel very exposed because there's something wrong with their child and you're asking these questions about themselves and where they live and what they do. . . . So you start the process feeling like they're judging you. . . . Some of it may be important to get a picture of the child's situation. But it makes you feel that you're not worth much as a parent."

Themes Concerning Parental Involvement

Effects of lack of parental involvement during the assessment process. In the experience of parents in the current study, the social history intake conference was often the only substantive contact between parents and team mem-

bers until the assessment was completed. Perhaps to allow flexibility in scheduling specific evaluation sessions, parents generally were not informed in advance about specific times when their child would be tested and were sometimes unaware that testing had been completed until the team contacted them for a feedback meeting. Thus, at a time when the team and the child were involved in a great deal of activity concerning the assessment, parents may have felt excluded from the process. Some parents indicated that the assessment stage was a very isolating time, particularly because they were generally new to the special education process and were not well acquainted (or were not acquainted at all) with the team members. Many of these parents also reported that they were reluctant to discuss the evaluation with their child's classroom teacher who, they felt, was not always informed about the assessment process.

Parental isolation hindered the collaborative problem-solving process in several ways. When teams did not seek parent input during the assessment stage, they sometimes missed valuable information which might have affected the results of their assessments. For example, the parents of a Down Syndrome youngster tried to tell the team that their son would be more comfortable if he were tested in his classroom. When team members, instead, took the boy to an office for testing, he refused to respond. Once the team agreed to test in the classroom, he became more cooperative. His refusal may also have been related to the parents' lack of knowledge about the specific dates on which testing would occur. Because they did not have the opportunity to inform their son that day about what would take place, the boy heeded his parents' repeated warnings not to talk to "strangers" and refused to talk to the team members, whom he did not know. Excluding parents from the assessment process may inadvertently send them a message about the hierarchical nature of the parent-professional relationship and may imply that parent input is not important, further reducing the possibility that collaborative problem solving will occur. Parental isolation during the assessment process may be reflective of a more pervasive, systemic isolation: School personnel appear to be isolated from each other and from the families and communities they serve and do not appear to engage in collaborative decision making (Bronfenbrenner, 1979a; Sarason, 1982, 1985).

Reasons for variations in parental involvement during the assessment and decision-making process. Parents were less likely to feel isolated or to be shocked by the findings when teams kept them involved and informed during the assessment process. Teams accomplished this important task through such means as asking parents to contribute to the referral questions, by frequent communication and updates, and by allowing parents to observe parts of the assessment. When parents understood the assessment process, they felt more capable of participating as equal partners in the decision making that followed.

The amount of involvement parents desired during the assessment and decision-making process depended on such factors as concurrent events and stressors in the family's life. As Turnbull and Turnbull (1986) also found, sometimes it was difficult for parents to find time and energy to deal with the decisions required during the special education process. People vary in the amount of control they want over events in their lives (Folkman, 1984); for some parents, the added responsibility of full participation in decision making was a burden at a time when they were already overextended and stressed. A number of parents also initially chose to leave the decision making to the team because they trusted school professionals unconditionally and assumed that team members would make the correct decisions for them and their child. As Turnbull and Turnbull (1982) also found, many of these parents initially did not feel that they had anything of substance to add to the educational decision-making process. As will be discussed below, other parents desired greater involvement in the decision-

making process, but felt intimidated by professionals.

Parents reported that team members set a positive tone for the parent-team relationship when they invited parent involvement and modeled collaborative behavior during the referral, assessment, and decision-making stages. When team members acted collaboratively with parents, it was more likely that parents gained sufficient information and understanding to make informed decisions and less likely that parents were vulnerable to unsubstantiated rumors and other information sources which might have harmed the parent-team relationship.

Parent-Team Feedback and Decision-Making Meetings

After the evaluation is completed, the EHA requires that parents and school personnel meet to "determine the child's needs and . . . discuss what special education and related services are appropriate to meet those needs" (Guard, 1986). In the current study, feedback about the assessment and classification and development of the IEP often took place during one meeting. In some cases, the tasks were divided into two sessions: one for feedback and discussion of the classification, and the other for development of the IEP.

Studies have indicated that the time devoted to feedback/IEP meetings is brief considering the complexity of the tasks to be accomplished. For example, the average length of the parent-team meetings observed by Ysseldyke, Algozzine, and Mitchell (1982) was 31 minutes, and the average length of meetings observed by Goldstein et al. (1980) was 36 minutes. The average length of meetings observed in the current study was one hour. As will be discussed below, even when the length of the meeting was increased to one hour, this was often insufficient time for collaborative problem solving to occur. Because feedback, classification, and placement decision making are so closely linked, all these activities will be discussed in this section.

Themes Concerning Parental Acquisition of Information, Understanding, and Skills

In order for parents to serve as equal partners in the decision-making process, they needed to have sufficient information and a clear understanding of that information. Based on data from the current study, parents required information about topics such as the following in order to work collaboratively: special education regulations, due process rights, classification systems, school culture, assessment and intervention methodologies, placement options (including alternatives to special education), curriculum, remediation methods, and their child's specific academic needs. Parents also needed skills such as negotiation, advocacy, collaboration, problem solving, IEP development, and stress management.

Frequently, parents did not acquire the necessary skills and information until long after the initial placement decision was made and the first IEP was signed. Parents who were experiencing the special education process for the first time often did not recognize their gaps in skills and information until long after they had agreed to a placement. One father explained, "When I went into my first meeting, I didn't even know what 'MDT' meant, let alone that I had rights." Another parent described her initial feedback and IEP meeting, which had taken place 3 years earlier. Although she felt that the team had been open to questions, she observed, "I really didn't know what kinds of questions to ask. . . . If it was now, I would know what to ask and what to do, but then I didn't know."

Brightman and Sullivan (1980) and D'Amato (1988) have also found that early in the special education process—when parents have to make informed decisions about consenting to preplacement evaluations and initial special education placements—they are often novices faced with a complex task for which they are ill-prepared. Parent participants in the current project described several factors at the parent-team feedback and IEP meetings that had affected their ability to comprehend information and to make informed decisions concerning their child's placement. These factors included: the emotion-laden content of topics related to the special education process, the limited amount of time allotted for the meeting, the highly technical language often used by team members, the amount of information presented during the meeting, and parents' lack of a framework to help them process information and make decisions.

Emotions generated by the assessment and classification. The child's assessment and classification appear to have tapped parental feelings of guilt, shame, self-blame, anger, doubt, and fear for the present and the future. These feelings seem to be pervasive throughout the special education process. Reactions specifically related to the assessment and classification will be described here. Emotions generated during the entire process will be discussed as a separate theme below.

Strong emotions were sometimes evoked during the meetings, particularly when parents were not prepared in advance for their child's classification label. One mother described her reactions when she and her husband first learned that the team was classifying her son as emotionally disturbed. "It just hit me like a ton of bricks. . . . There was no briefing on it. . . . I felt panicky. . . . I felt trapped." Another mother reported her reaction when her team first told her that her son had a learning disability. They decided not to classify him, but placed him in a transition class which served children who were not ready for the next grade but should not be retained. "I didn't know what they were going to say. I figured, 'Well, you know, Sam has a little problem and he's not reading that well.' I had no idea they were going to put him in this extra class and they considered him having a learning disability. It just boggled my mind, all these words that they were throwing at me. I was so upset." Conversely, when parents anticipated the findings—either because the parents had referred the child and suspected the diagnosis, or because the team had given them the opportunity during the assessment process to understand the nature of the problem and to absorb the ramifications of the diagnosis—the classification sometimes came as a relief and a validation of their perceptions.

Some parents referred to the assessment as "our evaluation," and indicated they felt that their competency as parents was being judged by the team and other school personnel. "Everybody hits you with the negatives. It's always what your child can't do. I just felt that I really made a boo boo when I had this kid." Another mother, told by the psychologist that her son had a learning disability and "minimal brain damage," commented, "Immediately the guilt comes in. What did I do? I went over my pregnancy. Could I have prevented this? . . . Should I have stopped work sooner? Maybe it was something I ate. Rationally I knew there was nothing I could have done to prevent this, but I still felt guilty."

As Featherstone (1980) also found, parental fears were sometimes a reflection of feelings of powerlessness and helplessness. At other times they were the result of shattered dreams and expectations. When strong emotions were generated during the meeting, parents reported feeling very vulnerable. They often focused their energies on holding themselves together and were no longer able to attend to the discussion. One mother explained that, after she heard the diagnosis, "Maybe more than half of what [the psychologist] said did not penetrate." Parents reported needing time to work through their emotional reactions before they could participate effectively in the decision-making process.

Many parents felt it was important that the team not see them cry or realize their shock or distress, because they would appear weak at a time when they felt it was important to look strong to protect their child. When parents felt that team members responded with humanity and allowed them to maintain their dignity, parents were more willing to expose their pain. A father described his experience in a district where the team was composed of skilled, caring clinicians. His older son had previously been classified learning disabled in another district where the father mistrusted the team. When he met with the team in his current district about his second son who was being referred for learning disabilities, he said, "I was a basket case going in. I was wiped out, and they knew it and said, 'What do you think?' I said, 'To have to do this again is very painful. I worry about [my son] as a person.' And [the learning consultant] got tears in her eyes. She was very upset for us."

Effects of methods teams use to communicate information to parents. The problems caused by the team's use of jargon and highly technical, complex language during feedback and decision-making meetings and in reports and other printed materials was a consistent theme identified by parent participants in the current study. Professionals' use of language affected parents' understanding of feedback data and prevented them from participating effectively in collaborative decision making with team members. The highly technical, complex language used at meetings and in reports and printed materials developed by state education agencies has also been observed by a number of researchers (Mehan, Hertweck, & Meihls, 1986; Roit & Pfohl, 1984; Weddig, 1984; Ysseldyke et al., 1982; Ysseldyke & Thurlow, 1980).

Data in the current study and in prior studies (e.g., Brightman & Sullivan, 1980) indicate that unexplained jargon often led to misunderstandings and had the effect of intimidating parents. This occurred particularly during the initial stages of the special education process when parents did not have the knowledge, experience, and language to help them interpret the information presented by the team. Consequently, teams may feel they have communicated information to parents, but parents may not have understood the message in the way the team members intended. Indeed, a number of other researchers who have observed parent-team decision-making meetings have also noted that parents often did not appear to understand adequately the information they were given by professionals about such aspects as interpretation of test findings; recommendations for eligibility, classification and placement, and IEP goals; the range of possible alternative placements, and review dates (Goldstein et al., 1980; Hoff et al., 1978; Vaughn et al., 1988; Ysseldyke & Thurlow, 1980). As Ysseldyke et al. (1982) have reported, the language used by professionals in the meetings they observed was at a level that parents could comprehend in only 27% of the meetings. "Technical terms simply are not defined; jargon (e.g., 'He has a visual sequential memory problem,' 'Her primary strength is in the auditory modality') abounded" (p. 311).

One result of using jargon and technical terms may be to alienate and confuse parents. One mother recalled her experiences at her first parent-team feedback meeting. "I felt frightened. I felt inadequate compared to the professionals. . . . I was telling them my feelings and didn't know the . . . words like 'cognitive' and 'CA.' . . . It doesn't make sense. If you're going to talk to a parent about their kid, don't you want him to understand it? When professionals talk mumbo jumbo, parents will back off. Professionals make you feel like they have the authority and they know it. Then you feel afraid."

The problem was not limited to parents meeting with the team for the first time. For example, the mother of a 14-year-old, who had been attending parent-team feedback meetings since her son was 9 months old, described her most recent 3-year reevaluation meeting. "When I go there I just freeze and the psychologist and [learning consultant] . . . read all of this to me and you blank out because they are in . . . big terms, you don't know what they're saying. . . . They'd talk above us. They didn't mean to. . . . We didn't understand, especially the abbreviations."

In general, parents did not want to admit their confusion to team members because they were afraid they would appear ignorant at a time when they felt they needed to appear competent. The leader of a parent organization explained, "If you asked them [the team], they would break it down for you, but you have to ask them and a lot of parents won't. They're afraid and they don't want to show that they're stupid. You know, [parents] figure, 'If [the team member's] saying this then they must think I know it.'" Because parents were reluctant to expose their feelings to team members, the professionals might not have been aware of parents' confusion. As some parents explained, "You nod your head to show that you heard, but it doesn't mean you understand."

A number of parents stated that the language in the teams' written reports and IEP summary statements was also intimidating and confusing. For example, one parent read to a researcher from her child's psychological report: "'He has difficulties with visual perception of missing detail and with part-to-whole configurations.' I read that sentence three times and have no idea what it meant." This conforms with Weddig's (1984) finding that the mean reading level required to comprehend the psychological reports she reviewed was above a 14.5 grade level.

The sheer quantity of information teams tried to convey during the meeting appears to have generated high levels of stress and emotionality for a number of parents. One mother described her experience at a parent-team meeting: "The overall atmosphere made me nervous; just trying to take in everything they were throwing at me. Even they said it; it was too much to hear at once. That made me nervous. I was trying to take it all in and it was a strain. They're talking on and on and you're trying to remember what they said at the beginning. You lose what they're saying and you don't want to interrupt them, but you are still back at the beginning trying to understand."

Parents' attempts to process extensive amounts of novel, complex, technical information in a short period of time under stressful conditions sometimes resulted in confusion and misinterpretation. A parent advocate explained: "A lot of parents wind up with the evaluation completed and not understanding what happened. You ask a parent what's wrong with their child and they won't know if the child is learning disabled, emotionally disturbed, or mentally retarded."

Similarly, same parents reported that they left the meeting assuming that the classification "learning disabled" actually meant "mentally retarded" and that the classification "emotionally disturbed" meant that the child was "crazy" or "nuts." One parent explained her reaction when she heard her son called learning disabled. "When I think of learning disabled, I think of somebody that's really either retarded or has some real problems." It sometimes took parents several years to understand fully the nature and ramifications of their child's problems.

If parents do not understand the information the team is trying to convey, there may be ramifications for the team, the parents, and the child. Informed parents can help the team to interpret their data within the context of the home environment; it is therefore in the team's best interest that parents understand the findings. When parents misunderstand the information, the ramifications for parent-child relationships and for parents' feelings of self-efficacy are also sometimes very serious. For example, one of the authors was present at a meeting when a single mother was told by the school psychologist that her son was basically well adjusted but seemed to "view his environment as harsh" and "took punishment seriously and very personally." The school psychologist reiterated, "This does not mean that you are being mean to him or beating him. . . . He is basically a well adjusted child." Although the parent appeared calm and collected throughout the meeting, she later disclosed to the researcher, "I thought he [the school psychologist] had meant physical abuse. I didn't know what was in his mind. I kept sitting there trying to figure out what [my son] meant by that, and I felt very shocked. . . . I think about it all the time. . . . But I have no one to ask and nowhere to go."

Without a sufficient knowledge base, many parents had no framework with which to interpret information accurately, ask relevant questions, or make meaningful decisions. Instead, as is fre-

quently true of new learners in complex situations (Heppner & Krauskopf, 1987), parents often relied on prior learning, past experience, and stereotypes of handicapped people to help them process the information presented by the team. For example, the mother quoted in the previous paragraph based her conclusions about the school psychologist's findings on her only prior experience with "psychiatrists": clinical interviews as portrayed in the media. Despite a brief explanation by the school psychologist about the nature of the tests, this parent, understandably, did not comprehend the inferential nature of the projective techniques on which the school psychologist had based his conclusions. Instead, she assumed that her son had told the psychologist directly that he was abused.

Parents' understanding appeared to increase when the team provided them with opportunities to absorb the information over time, allowed them to observe parts of the assessment, reviewed the assessment data on which their decisions were based, encouraged questions, and talked in "straight talk." Some team members included many illustrations from the testing in their presentations and incorporated descriptions of how the child's test performance might relate to home and classroom problems. Team members sometimes anticipated parents' questions and asked for clarification when they felt that the explanation made by one of their colleagues was unclear. This may have established a norm at the meeting that question-asking was positive and welcomed by the team. Some parents reported that team members were careful to talk "in English" and to treat parents with respect. When team members displayed a sensitivity for their feelings and situation and stepped out of role to respond as human beings, parents tended to respond more openly.

Factors affecting the decision-making process. Time pressures, high degrees of emotionality, and other stressors present during feedback/IEP meetings can affect people's ability to focus, to process and retain information, and to make effective decisions (Folkman, 1984;

Heppner & Krauskopf, 1987; Kienan, 1987; Norman, 1976; Wright, 1974). As parents in the current study noted, when a great deal of new information was presented during one session, information overload often resulted, reducing the possibility that information conveyed by the team was understood accurately by the parents.

Based both on the current findings and previous research conducted by Witt, Miller, McIntyre, and Smith (1984), the amount of time team members spend with parents appears to be extremely important to parents. However, data from the current study indicate that parents are not necessarily asking for longer formal meetings. Instead, they appear to be asking for more time to gain sufficient knowledge, to process information, and to make decisions. Parents gained more information and felt more comfortable when they had the opportunity to meet with team members throughout the entire special education assessment process, preferably in settings other than the formal MDT meetings. These less formal communications often fostered the development of mutually respectful, trusting relationships and provided a vehicle for parents to contribute information, admit confusions, ask questions, and address concerns. Such opportunities increased the likelihood that parents gained sufficient information and understanding.

Parents gave examples of factors that affected the extent to which they collaborated with team members in decision making. Factors identified by parents included: (a) the manner in which the team's decision was presented to parents; (b) the highly technical language and the titles and degrees, all of which conveyed a message of the superior expertise and authority of the professionals; and (c) the pressure exerted by teams to get parents to agree to the team's decision and to make decisions on the spot.

One parent explained why she felt that the manner in which the team presented their recommendations made her feel "uncomfortable, like your opinion may not mean anything even though it's your child. . . . Everything was all

written up in advance and typed . . . so when I went there I had a copy in front of me and they all had their copies right in front of them and they just read through it all and then elaborated on any parts they felt they should elaborate on."

Some parents feared there would be serious consequences if they "made waves" and challenged the team's decision, questioned their treatment by the team, or asked to take time to think about the decision before they signed. They were concerned that the team would perceive any question or challenge as an attack, and viewed the team as having a great deal of power over their child's academic future. For example, one parent explained that she had not told the team that they had inadvertently offended her because she felt that complaining to the team would affect "how you get dealt with, how they deal with [my son], and what they tell [me] about him."

Some parents were reluctant to challenge the team's decision because the team presented the appearance of a unified front which could be intimidating. One mother described her experience. "It was one person after another reporting and they all kept very quiet when one or the other was speaking. And you just sensed that even though one is in disagreement with the other or has other feelings, they're not going to say it. That's an unwritten rule: Any professional person is not going to disagree with a colleague in front of a parent. . . . You just don't do it. [If they do] that's going to cause a lot of problems. Because then the parent can turn around and say, 'Well, if you don't agree, then how do you know you're right?'" However, she would have found it less intimidating if team members "[spoke] out with their own opinions."

Parents who questioned their team's decision sometimes found themselves "diagnosed" by the team as "overprotective," "neurotic," "resistant," or "a troublemaker." When they tried to reject the team's recommendation and suggest an alternate solution, parents were sometimes told, "This is the worst thing you can do to your child." Teams may have felt ethically bound to point out their concerns about the parents' decision. However, expressing their reservations to parents during the formal, public forum of the feedback/IEP meeting appears to hinder the possibility of developing collaborative relationships. Often the result was to foster parents' perceptions that they were being coerced by the team and to increase their defensiveness and anger. Sometimes, parents' resolve to follow through with their original decision became even firmer.

Data from the current study indicate that parental anger and defensiveness may be avoided, reduced, or dissipated if parents feel they have been listened to by school professionals and their concerns taken seriously. Some parents noted that their teams included them in the decision-making process and emphasized that the final decision was up to the parent. Team actions that facilitated collaborative decision making at the meetings included three important elements: (a) The team demonstrated, by their words and behaviors, that they were considering several alternative solutions and that different viewpoints were legitimate; (b) the team made it clear that the parents would make the ultimate decision; and (c) the team requested that the parents delay their final decision until after they had observed the recommended placement.

After the IEP Meeting
Themes Concerning Obtaining
Information and Advice

After the meeting, parents needed to educate themselves quickly about the meaning and implications of their child's classification and placement. Although educating parents seems to be a natural way for the team to assist in the development of a collaborative relationship, parents in the current study reported that team members rarely served as information resources beyond providing a description of due process rights (often copied directly from the regulations) and a handbook describing special education in the district. Some team members provided parents with bibliographies and

reading materials and met with them outside of the formal meetings to answer questions, listen to concerns, and help them to interpret reports and other documents such as IEP recommendations. These positive actions enhanced the collaborative partnership by increasing parental levels of information and understanding and conveying a message to parents that the team members wanted them to be informed partners in the process.

When school professionals did not provide needed information, parent participants sought information and advice from a variety of sources such as the media (including newspaper articles, advice columnists, and television shows); unguided, often indiscriminate reading at the library; and friends, neighbors, relatives, co-workers, or other acquaintances. Parents also searched the yellow pages of the phone book for possible resources and sources of advice. One unfortunate consequence was that some of the information parents obtained in this manner was based on fads, rumors, and stereotypes. Inaccurate information sometimes fostered parents' mistrust of the motives and competency of the school professionals, further decreasing the possibility of collaboration.

Reading sometimes proved extremely helpful. One mother recalled, "I think all that reading saved me because I had nobody to talk to and I didn't understand what [my son's learning disability] meant. Now I understand it better." Some parents also obtained accurate information by contacting organizations such as the Association for Children with Learning Disabilities. They often learned about these organizations through their reading, through other media, or through acquaintances. For example, several parents cited Dear Abby as a valuable source for learning about parent organizations.

"It Never Ends"

Parents tended to assume that their child's problems would be solved when the child was classified. To their surprise, however, many parents discovered that a new set of problems was just beginning after the child was classified and placed. Even when the results were positive, parents reported feeling wary. One mother explained, "[My daughter is] doing fine now but when you have a child with learning disabilities, you never know when she is going to level off and stop making progress. I can never stop watching."

At times, the problems continued long after the IEP was developed and the child was placed. The mother of a boy who was classified learning disabled described her experience. "After my son was classified, I went to see his math teacher and said, 'Are you following the IEP?' And she said, 'What IEP?' Two of his primary teachers didn't know that he was classified. . . . [As a result of the difficulties and lack of progress he was making] he was sinking and this made us heartsick. He was getting nervous tics, getting depressed, withdrawing. We saw him withdraw from sports teams. His confidence was eroding. His self-esteem was going down the tubes. We were like two maniacs. . . . It was exhausting to us. We were still fighting with him."

As is often the case when professionals make recommendations (Gutkin & Conoley, 1990), parents in the current study reported that, even when teachers knew about the IEP, they did not necessarily follow it. For example; some teachers did not believe that children with mild or subtle learning disabilities really required accommodations and "special attention." Brightman and Sullivan (1980) also noted that parents in their study often had to continue to monitor their child's progress and program long after the IEP meeting.

Themes That Are Present Across Several Stages

Themes Concerning Having a Child Who Has a Handicapping Condition

At all stages of the special education process, parents reported experiencing a number of strong emotional reactions such as guilt, shame, embarrassment, anger, fear, and anxiety in response to

their child's problems. Some of these reactions had begun before the child was diagnosed; others came at the time of classification. In either case, these strong emotions tended to affect the parents' feelings of self-worth and competence as parents and tended to influence the parent-child relationship. For example, a mother described her reactions to her adolescent daughter who had a learning disability. "It does have a very profound effect on you that you can't produce a normal child. I know many people going through that now with children with learning disabilities. 'Should I have another child? Can I have a normal child? Will it be worse?' . . . When you have a child with a learning disability, you lose confidence in your own ability as a parent. Your child loses confidence also. You can become very angry at the child, 'Why aren't you normal? Why does this happen to me?' . . . You can reject the child if you let it get out of hand. You don't hug them. You don't say, 'I love you.' [You say] 'Don't be so dumb.' Things like that."

One mother explained the source of parental shame as "the ongoing difficulty of coping with the reality of a kid who has some kind of school disgrace. . . . Fundamentally I am embarrassed to have a kid who doesn't do well in school because it is a reflection on me. That is the ugly truth. I don't even like to say it."

Another mother described her reaction when she learned that her son, who had a seizure disorder, also had a learning disability. "It's like your child has something wrong with him like diabetes. It's a blow, a terrible blow. . . . It's like a mourning process, like when your mother or sister die. You never fully get over it."

When parents heard the diagnosis, many reported that they began to fear for the future—the child's and theirs. Similar to Featherstone's (1980) findings, parental concerns were both immediate and long term. Many parents noted that they stayed awake at night crying and worrying about whether they should allow their child to be placed in special education. Sleepless nights frequently continued

even after parents had made their decision, regardless of whether it was for or
against placement. The focus of parents'
anxieties varied somewhat with the type
and severity of the problem, but often
dealt with the quality of their child's
future life including such aspects as
education, employment, income levels,
potential marriage partners, independence, and the possible future impact of
the label and placement on the child.
More immediate parental issues included
fears about their children's vulnerability
to drugs, cults, gangs, and victimization
by more streetwise youngsters.

Parents also felt very responsible to
their child if they made the wrong
decision about classification or placement
in special education. For example, the
mother of an adolescent girl who had
been placed for the past 6 years in a
self-contained special education class explained why it was so important that her
daughter obtain a quality education. She
and her husband had been upset with her
child's team and with special education
because they saw their daughter falling
farther and farther behind academically.
"I get very disgusted. I want her to learn. I
want her to know that I am not going to
live forever. . . . And without the
knowledge and without the understanding, how is this girl going to survive on
the outside. . . . She can't even get a paper
route. Because you have to handle money
and she can handle dimes and nickles,
but not when so much is coming at her at
once. . . . Plus, you never know what's
going to happen to you tomorrow or the
next day. That's what I worry about. . . . I
want her to have a knowledge of an
education so that she can't come back to
me three years or ten years down the road
and say, 'Because of you I didn't learn.'
That's why I'm fighting so hard for her to
get the advancement in different grades of
school level so she'll have an education
like a normal child."

Themes Concerning Parent-Team Hierarchical Relationships

How parents and teams perceive each
other can affect their ability to work in an
egalitarian partnership. Based on data
from the current study and the writing of
other authors (e.g., Lightfoot, 1978; Sarason, 1985; Yoshida, Fenton, Kaufman, &
Maxwell, 1978), the parent-professional
relationship frequently appears to be
hierarchical and, therefore, not conducive to the building of close, trusting,
egalitarian relationships. Parents in the
current study often initially perceived
professionals as "the experts" who would
make decisions that were in their child's
best interest. For example, parents made
such comments as, "There's a whole aura
around the professionals. If the professional says it, it sounds right and it must
be right." Parents often deferred to the
professional's expertise, placing little
faith in their own knowledge and ability
and trusting the team members. For
example, a father explained why he and
his wife didn't question the team's intelligence test findings even though their
experience with the child at home led
them to believe that the IQ score was low.
"We accept the fact that this is an
established standard, so we're not gonna
question this. Maybe we feel that because
you have the title you know more than we
do."

When parents felt that their judgment was inferior to that of the professionals, parents tended not to offer opinions or information that contradicted the
team's judgment. This reticence resulted
in a reduction of the team's access to
information potentially important to the
decision-making process. Because most
team members met so infrequently with
parents, they were sometimes perceived
by parents as "relative strangers" whom
they saw once every 3 years—during the
reevaluation conference—for 1 hour. This
also contributed to parents' reluctance to
talk frankly to team members.

Because of the "professional aura,"
parents often entered the team-parent
relationship with an initial trust in
professionals which, at times, appeared to
be unconditional. This trust presumed an
unequal status between parents and professionals as opposed to the perception of
egalitarianism between partners necessary for the development of a collabora-

tive relationship. However, trust could quickly change to anger and mistrust if, because of the professional's actions and/or rumors in the community, parents began to suspect that the professional was not acting in the child's best interests.

One possible reason for a generally passive parental role may be the medical model prevalent in schools and inherent in the EHA (Sarason, 1982). When classification occurs, the locus of the problem is placed within the child, who must then be "repaired" (Mehan et al., 1986; Sarason, 1985). The child and, by extension, the parents may be viewed as deviant. Parents may inherit the child's status as "patient" (Roos, 1985) and be viewed as having little to offer in the decision-making process except for imparting information (Seligman, 1979; Yoshida et al., 1978). As also described poignantly by Roos (1985), parent participants in the current study—who were also professionals in the mental health and education fields—reported that their input into the assessment and development of recommendations was not solicited by team members even though these parents had substantial expertise to offer and were willing to work with the team.

When teams operate using the medical model of helping (Brickman et al., 1982), responsibility for diagnosing problems and generating and implementing solutions is left in the hands of the professional experts. Under this model, there is no possibility for the development of a collaborative relationship between school professionals and parents. One school psychologist speculated, "We *cooperate* with parents, but I think we don't generally *collaborate* with parents. We assume that they don't know as much as we do, that we are the expert. We assume the team knows best. It's a benevolent paternalism." This "paternalism" manifested itself in the terminology teams sometimes used to refer to parents and parents used to refer to themselves: "good," "informed," and "cooperative," as opposed to "resistant," "uncooperative," and "unconcerned." At times, team members complimented parents by saying, "You are concerned parents," sometimes

adding or implying, "unlike other parents."

Some parents worked exceptionally hard to maintain their status as good, reasonable, informed, concerned parents. Given the other demands and stresses in their lives, this effort appears to have taken a great deal of energy and emotional control and was quite draining at times. For example, in order to appear competent at parent-team conferences, one parent rehearsed her speeches numerous times before the meetings. She feared that if she lost control, even once, the team might no longer view her as a good parent. In fact, when her child changed schools and was assigned to a new team, the new team viewed the parent as unreasonable and demanding when she asked for services that were missing from the child's new IEP. For just this reason, parents have stated that they fear transitions which lead to changes in school personnel. Having worked very hard to establish positive relationships with their child's old team and with other school personnel, they now have to begin to build credibility and forge relationships all over again with the new team.

Some parents reported that the physical setting for the meetings affected the likelihood that the parent-team contacts would take place in an atmosphere conducive to collaborative decision making. One father described his meeting with the team. "I walked into this room and we were in this basement with plumbing pipes in the ceiling and the windows up above six feet high. Seven adults were sitting in chairs with their knees up to their chins. It's so stupid." In an urban district, parents described waiting in line to see their team during annual review conferences. Several conferences were being held simultaneously in the same large room with no opportunity for privacy. It is likely that these arrangements resulted from limited space. However, parents felt strongly that these environmental messages highlighted the inferior status of special education and the special education child and parent.

The issues identified above do not appear to be unique to parent-team

relationships during the special education process. In her review of the literature on family-school collaboration, Fish
(1990), noted that the schools' efforts to
encourage parents to become partners in
education have been limited. "Parent
involvement is enthusiastically supported, but not implemented" (p. 371).

Themes Related to Responsibility for Decisions Concerning the Child

One area of potential parent-team
conflict concerns the issue of who is
ultimately responsible for decisions concerning the child. This decision is affected by the issue of who is the clinician's client and who is the clinician's
primary responsibility (Pantaleo, 1983;
Trachtman, 1981). For example, the
NASP Principles for Professional Ethics
states that "School Psychologists consider
the pupils/clients to be their primary
responsibility and act as advocates of
their rights and welfare" (National Association of School Psychologists [NASP],
1990, p. 936). Although the ethical
principle also considers parents' rights,
the implementation of this professional
perspective may conflict, at times, with
the parents' assumption that they have
primary responsibility for the child and
are serving as their youngster's advocate.

During the current study, when parents and team members disagreed about
what was best for the child, parents
reported that school personnel sometimes presented themselves as the child's
protectors and treated the parents as
adversaries, acting as if the parents'
opinions were at best misguided and at
worst deliberately harmful to the child.
When teams conveyed this message, the
approach often led to antagonism, polar-
ization, and adversarial relationships.

Based on data from the research
project, there were a number of occasions
when parents disagreed strongly with the
team and, very likely, appeared antagonis-
tic to team members, but did so because
they genuinely disagreed about what
course of action would serve their child's
best interests. In some cases, conflicts
were dissipated when parents were given

a collaborative role in decision making for
their child and their opinion was sought.
In other cases, parents noted that conflicts might have been avoided or might
have ended sooner had they felt that team
members and other school personnel had
listened to their concerns and taken them
seriously. When conflicts were not resolved, children were often negatively
affected by the stress generated in the
parents.

Conflicts were sometimes exacer-
bated by the possibility that either side
might invoke due process proceedings.
For example, although the theme was not
raised by most parents, some parents
described how they were told by school
personnel that the district would proceed
to a hearing if the parents did not agree to
the referral. Although many parents did
not appear to clearly understand their
rights based on the materials they were
given to read, some parents noted that
they realized that they could invoke their
due process rights if they disagreed with
the team's findings. Based on interviews
conducted with team members at the
conclusion of the data collection, school
professionals also appeared to be very
conscious of the possibility of due process. Due process rights, as defined in
Subpart E of the regulations accompanying the EHA, provide important protec-
tions to the child and the parents.
However, in today's litigious society, team
members may, at times, feel compelled to
pursue their recommendations for fear of
later legal ramifications.

Themes Related to Increasing Collaborative Communication With Parents

Parents cited examples of team members' efforts to be supportive and to build
mutually respectful, trusting relationships which empowered parents. These actions generally required that team members step outside of their formal roles and
interact with parents with compassion and
warmth as fellow human beings, thus increasing the egalitarian nature of the parent-professional relationship. Team members' actions included:

- A caring touch during a stressful time at a meeting.

- A question or comment which indicated that the team member remembered and cared about the family. One father explained, "She asked us about Aunt Emily's operation. I don't care if she just looked it up in the folder five minutes ago. She remembered that it mattered to us."

- Suggesting opportunities to talk privately before or after a formal meeting.

- Providing reading lists, articles, and recommendations for resources.

- Demonstrating caring and liking for the child.

- Taking the time to "give away their skills" to parents. For example, some team members helped parents to learn to negotiate systems, to serve as co-diagnosticians and co-therapists for their children, and to understand the basis of the team's decision-making process.

Participants also described how some professionals showed respect for parents through words and actions. For example, one father described the behavior of the social worker who led his parent group. "You sensed it. Even if you had what you thought was something ridiculous to say, he never made small of that. He would explain it to you, why it was ridiculous. Instead of [saying], 'Oh, that's ridiculous; forget it,' he would say, 'Well, it's not practical. . . .' And then he would continue to explain it."

Caring, compassionate, mutually respectful relationships were more likely to occur when parents had opportunities to get to know team members in settings other than the formal parent-team meetings. Development of the relationship generally was fostered when the clinician stepped outside the formal role so that parent and professional could relate to each other as human beings. For example, one team member described by many parents as compassionate and helpful, often stopped to chat with parents at the local supermarket. Parents also explained that they felt more comfortable with team members after meeting them at school func-

tions unrelated to special education, such as Parent-Teacher Organization meetings. However, team members have noted that parents were sometimes uncomfortable talking publicly with them because the parents wanted to maintain their anonymity. When professionals and parents had opportunities to get to know each other over an extended period of time during such activities as a parent group or a school committee, or when the team member served as the child's case manager, parents were likely to feel more comfortable with the professional. Parents also became more trusting when they perceived team members as "taking risks" by stepping out of role to give them advice about how to deal with political situations in the district.

When professionals went beyond their roles and legal obligations and treated parents with care and respect, parents were often willing to reciprocate. One father described the school psychologist (who also served as special education administrator) in the district to which his family had just moved. "She really and truly made you feel like she cared and she was there for *your* kid and she knew what she was doing. She was bright, competent, efficient, knowledgeable, and she didn't disappear after the first diagnosis. She was there for all the IEP meetings. She'd call us on the phone. She'd say things like, 'I wouldn't try this. I might try that.' Even if I didn't agree, I'd say I didn't but then say I'd try it because I trusted her judgment. She demonstrated good skills, so we said we were going to believe her and do what she said. She engendered confidence, and if you engender confidence, until you learn otherwise, you are willing to trust a professional. Even before we moved to this district, she said, 'Bring him up and I'll check him out for you. . . .' He wasn't going to the school system yet, but she was going to deliver a service as a professional psychologist, and not solely as an agent of the school."

CONCLUSIONS

Parents in this study indicated, and authors and researchers (e.g., Conoley,

1987; Fish, 1990; Sarason, 1982) have noted, team members have the opportunity to play a significant role in facilitating collaboration between parents and professionals. One notable, overarching theme which influenced the team's ability to facilitate parent-team collaboration concerned issues involving time.

Parents needed time to reach the point where they could serve as effective, equal partners in a parent-team collaborative effort concerning the special education process. Just as it took time and training for professionals to understand the complexities of such topics as assessment, diagnosis, intervention, and regulation, parents needed time to gain the information and understanding they required. Parents also needed time to work through the strong emotions which may have been generated by the process. For example, some parents indicated that they entered a mourning process when they first heard their child's classification. They required time to work through their shock and denial before they could begin to relate effectively with the team.

Based on the accounts of parents in the current study, efforts to help parents gain information and understanding must begin long before parents enter the IEP meeting. Parent-professional collaborative efforts need to begin during the identification stage before a formal referral is initiated and, if the child is referred, continue throughout the stages of the special education process. In order to do so, it will be necessary for teams to educate the school professionals who often have the initial contact with parents—the classroom teachers (Anderson, 1983; Gutkin & Conoley, 1990). Through consultation and inservice training with teachers and school administrators, team members can help classroom teachers and other school personnel to identify potential problems and to discuss these concerns effectively with parents. Similarly, teams may also want to consider reaching out to pediatricians, the medical professionals to whom parents often turned when they first suspected a problem.

By working collaboratively from the time a problem is first suspected, teams can provide parents with a framework and language for thinking about the identified problems and a feeling of ownership in the process, resulting in a feeling of empowerment. As noted above, parents' ability to participate actively in this process will vary depending on such factors as the amount of physical and emotional energy available to them at any given time (Fish, 1990; Turnbull & Turnbull, 1982). If parents are viewed as experts about their children (Conoley, 1987), they can be active participants in such assessment activities as framing the assessment questions and collecting data from settings such as home, scouts, church, and after-school centers. These functions can serve several purposes including providing teams with valuable information about the child's performance outside the school setting, and helping to educate parents while including them in the assessment process. If a problem such as a learning disability does exist, parents will also be more gradually exposed to the ramifications, so that they have some preparation for what they will be told at the feedback meeting. If parents and team members can begin to work together collaboratively early in the process, parents will be more likely to have the information and understanding they need when the time comes to participate in placement decisions. If they have had extensive contact with team members before the IEP meeting, they will be more likely to make their decisions voluntarily.

In order to facilitate parent-professional collaboration in the early stages before a problem is clearly identified, clinical team members will have to broaden the scope of their role beyond special education in order to work with the entire school population (Anderson, 1983; Zins, Curtis, Graden, & Ponti, 1988) and to provide indirect service to children by working directly with the adults who play key roles in children's lives: parents, teachers, and other school professionals (Gutkin & Conoley, 1990), as well as reaching beyond the school to work collaboratively with professionals in the community, such as pediatricians (Mearig,

1982), who provide support and advice to parents.

AUTHOR NOTES

Research team members who contributed to the data collection and/or analysis are: Patricia Duarte Bunche, Buena Chilstrom, Patricia Carroll, Ingrid Wills Flannery, and Douglas Haan.

The project has been sponsored by the Montclair State College Separately Budgeted Research Project, the Montclair State College Alumni Association, the National Association of School Psychologists research grants program, and the New Jersey Psychological Trust.

REFERENCES

Abramson, M., Willson, V., Yoshida, R. K., & Hagerty, G. (1983). Parents' perceptions of their learning disabled child's educational performance. *Learning Disability Quarterly, 6,* 184–194.

Anderson, C. (1983). An ecological developmental model for a family orientation in school psychology. *Journal of School Psychology, 21,* 179–189.

Bellamy. G. T. (1987). Policy Letter. *Education for the Handicapped Law Report,* 211: 436–437.

Brickman, P., Rabinowitz, V. C., Karuza, J., Coates, D., Cohn, E., & Kidder, L. (1982). Models of helping and coping. 368–384.

Brightman, A. J., & Sullivan, M. B. (1980). *The impact of Public Law 94–142 on parents of disabled children: A report of findings.* Belmont, MA: Cambridge Workshop. (ERIC Document Reproduction Service No. ED 218 817)

Bronfenbrenner, U. (1979a). Contexts of child rearing: Problems and prospects. *American Psychologist, 34,* 844–850.

Bronfenbrenner, U. (1979b). *The ecology of human development: Experiments by nature and design.* Cambridge, MA: Harvard University Press.

Burlington School Committee v. Massachusetts Department of Education, 471 U.S. 359. (1985).

Conoley, J. C. (1987). Schools and families: Theoretical and practical bridges. *Professional School Psychology, 2,* 191–203.

D'Amato, E. (1988). *Informational needs of parents across the life cycle of their mentally retarded child.* Unpublished doctoral dissertation, Fordham University, New York.

Dillon, J. T. (1979). Defects of questioning as an interview technique. *Psychology in the Schools, 16,* 575–580.

Featherstone, H. (1980). *A difference in the family:*

Living with a disabled child. Middlesex, England: Penguin Books.

Fish, M. C. (1990). Best practices in family-school relationships. In A. Thomas & J. Grimes (Eds.), *Best practices in school psychology* (2nd ed., pp. 371–382). Washington, DC: National Association of School Psychologists.

Folkman, S. (1984). Personal control, stress and coping processes: A theoretical analysis. *Journal of Personality and Social Psychology, 46,* 839–852.

Gilliam, J. E., & Coleman, M. C. (1981). Who influences IEP committee decisions? *Exceptional Children, 47,* 642–644.

Glaser, B. G., & Strauss, A. L. (1967). *The discovery of grounded theory: Strategies for qualitative research.* Chicago: Aldine Publishing.

Goldstein, S., Strickland, B., Turnbull, A. P., & Curry, L. (1980). An observational analysis of the IEP conference. *Exceptional Children, 46,* 278–286.

Guard, P. (1986). Policy letter. *Education for the Handicapped Law Report,* 211: 384.

Gutkin, T. B., & Conoley, J. C. (1990). Reconceptualizing school psychology from a service delivery perspective: Implications for practice, training, and research. *Journal of School Psychology, 28,* 203–223.

Gutkin, T. B., & Curtis, M. J. (1982). School-based consultation: Theory and techniques. In C. R. Reynolds & T. B. Gutkin (Eds.), *The handbook of school psychology* (pp. 796–828). New York: John Wiley & Sons.

Heppner, P. P., & Krauskopf, C. J. (1987). An information-processing approach to personal problem solving. *The Counseling Psychologist, 15,* 371–447.

Hoff, M. K., Fenton, K. S., Yoshida, R. K., & Kaufman, M. S. (1978). Notice and consent: The school's responsibility to inform parents. *Journal of School Psychology, 16*(3), 265–273.

Kaiser, S. M., & Woodman, R. W. (1985). Multidisciplinary teams and group decision-making techniques: Possible solutions to decision-making problems. *School Psychology Review, 14,* 457–470.

Kienan, G. (1987). Decision making under stress: Scanning of alternatives under controllable and uncontrollable threats. *Journal of Personality and Social Psychology, 52,* 639–644.

Kraus, W. A. (1980). *Collaboration in organizations: Alternatives to hierarchy.* New York: Human Sciences Press.

Lightfoot, S. L. (1978). *Worlds apart: Relationships between families and schools.* New York: Basic Books.

Lynch, E. W., & Stein, R. (1982). Perspectives on parent participation in special education. *Exceptional Education Quarterly, 3,* 56–63.

Mearig, J. S. (1982). Integration of school and community services for children with special needs. In C. R. Reynolds & T. B. Gutkin (Eds.), *The handbook of school psychology* (pp. 748–773). New York: John Wiley & Sons.

Mehan, H., Hertweck, A., & Meihls, J. L. (1986). *Handicapping the handicapped: Decision making in students' educational careers.* Stanford, CA: Stanford University Press.

National Association of School Psychologists. (1990). NASP principles for professional ethics. In A. Thomas & J. Grimes (Eds.), *Best practices in school psychology* (2nd ed., pp. 931–940). Washington, DC: National Association of School Psychologists.

Norman, D. A. (1976). *Memory and attention: An introduction to human information processing* (2nd ed.). New York: John Wiley & Sons.

Pantaleo, A. P. (1983). Parents as primary clients of the school psychologist or why is it we are here? *Journal of School Psychology, 21,* 107–113.

Parsons, R. D., & Meyers, J. (1984). *Developing consultation skills.* San Francisco: Jossey-Bass.

Policy letter. *Education for the Handicapped Law Report,* 211: 188.

Roit, M., & Pfohl, W. (1984). The readability of P.L. 94–142 parent materials: Are parents truly informed? *Exceptional Children, 50,* 496–505.

Roos, P. (1985). Parents of mentally retarded children—Misunderstood and mistreated. In H. R. Turnbull & A. P. Turnbull (Eds.), *Parents speak out: Then and now* (2nd ed., pp. 245–257). Columbus, OH: Charles E. Merrill.

Rosenfield, S. A. (1987). *Instructional consultation.* Hillsdale, NJ: Lawrence Erlbaum.

Sarason, S. B. (1982). *The culture of the school and the problem of change* (2nd ed.). Boston: Allyn & Bacon.

Sarason, S. B. (1985). *Caring and compassion in clinical practice.* San Francisco: Jossey Bass.

Schatzman, L., & Strauss, A. (1973). *Field research.* Englewood Cliffs, NJ: Prentice-Hall.

Seligman, M. (1979). *Strategies for helping parents of exceptional children.* New York: The Free Press.

Skrtic, T. (1987). *An organizational analysis of special education reform.* Presented at a meeting of The National Inquiry Into the Future of Education for Students with Special Needs, Washington, DC.

Springer, J. (1989). *Project entry: A case study of a collaborative mainstreaming support program for special needs students in a public high school.*

Unpublished doctoral dissertation, Rutgers University, New Brunswick, NJ.

Strauss, A. L., & Corbin, J. (1990). *Basics of qualitative research: Grounded theory procedures and techniques.* Newbury Park, CA: Sage.

Strauss, A. L. (1987). *Qualitative analysis for social scientists.* Cambridge, England: Cambridge University Press.

Taylor, S. J., & Bogdan, R. (1984). *Introduction to qualitative research methods: The search for meanings* (2nd ed.). New York: John Wiley & Sons.

Trachtman, G. M. (1981). On such a full sea. *School Psychology Review, 10,* 138–181.

Turnbull, A. P., & Turnbull, H. R. (1982). Parent involvement in the education of handicapped children: A critique. *Mental Retardation, 20,* 115–122.

Turnbull, A. P., & Turnbull, H. R. (1986). *Families, professionals and exceptionality: A special partnership.* Columbus, OH: Merrill Publishing.

Tyler, F. B. (1983). The resource collaborator role: A model for interactions involving psychologists. *American Psychologist, 38,* 388–413.

Vaughn, S., Bos, C. S., Harrell, J. E., & Lasky, B. (1988). Parent participation in the initial placement/IEP conference ten years after mandated involvement. *Journal of Learning Disabilities, 21*(2), 82–89.

Watzlawick, P., Weakland, J. H., & Fisch, R. (1974). *Change: Principles of problem formation and problem resolution.* New York: W. W. Norton.

Weddig, R. (1984). Parental interpretation of psychoeducational reports. *Psychology in the Schools, 21,* 477–481.

Witt, J. C., Miller, C. D., McIntyre, R. M., & Smith, D. (1984). Effects of variables on parental perceptions of staffings. *Exceptional Children, 51,* 27–32.

Wright, P. (1974). The harassed decision maker: Time pressure, distractions, and the use of evidence. *Journal of Applied Psychology, 59,* 555–561.

Yoshida, R. K., Fenton, K. S., Kaufman, M. J., & Maxwell, J. P. (1978). Parental involvement in the special education pupil planning process: The school's perspective. *Exceptional Children, 44,* 531–534.

Ysseldyke, J. E., Algozzine, B., & Allen, D. (1981). Participation of regular education teachers in special education team decision making: A naturalistic investigation. *The Elementary School Journal, 82,* 160–165.

Ysseldyke, J. E., Algozzine, B., & Mitchell, J. (1982). Special education team decision making: An analysis of current practice. *The Personnel and Guidance Journal, 60,* 308–313.

Ysseldyke, J. E., & Christenson, S. L. (1988). Linking assessment to intervention. In J. L. Graden, J. E. Zins, & M. J. Curtis (Eds.), *Alternative educational delivery systems: Enhancing instructional options for all students* (pp. 91–109). Washington, DC: National Association of School Psychologists.

Ysseldyke, J. E., & Thurlow, M. L. (Eds.). (1980). *The special education assessment and decision-making process: Seven case studies.* (Research Report No. 44). Minneapolis: Institute for Research on Learning Disabilities, University of Minnesota.

Zins, J. E., Curtis, M. J., Graden, J. L., & Ponti, C. R. (1988). *Helping students succeed in the regular classroom.* San Francisco: Jossey-Bass.

18

LEADERSHIP SKILLS FOR SCHOOL PSYCHOLOGISTS: IMPROVING PARENTAL INVOLVEMENT IN MULTIDISCIPLINARY TEAM INTERACTIONS

E. Scott Huebner

Public Law 94-142 mandated that multidisciplinary teams (MDTs), composed of school professionals and parents, should provide the vehicle for the determination of eligibility and program development for children with handicapping conditions. A fundamental assumption underlying the passage of this aspect of the law was that parents of handicapped children should be actively involved in making decisions and implementing intervention efforts related to their children's educational needs (Turnbull, Turnbull, & Wheat, 1982). Such a premise is consistent with the well-documented positive effects of parental involvement in children's schooling (e.g., see Hawley & Rosenholtz, 1983; Epstein, 1987). Pfeiffer and Tittler (1983) have argued persuasively that such MDTs can serve as a major vehicle for developing ongoing home-school linkages.

School psychologists perform many of their functions as members or leaders of intra-agency and inter-agency teams. In addition to serving on special education placement teams, school psychologists perform other functions in the context of teams, including the widely-advocated prereferral intervention teams (Graden, Casey, & Christenson, 1985). Although the focus of this chapter will be on special education placement MDTs, the recommendations may also be appli-cable to other school-based MDTs and other meetings with parents.

The purpose of this chapter is thus to discuss leadership skills for improving parental involvement in special education placement MDTs. Many school psychologists report they serve as the leaders or coordinators of their MDTs (Huebner & Gould, 1991). Even if school psychologists do not serve as formal MDT leaders, they (as well as all team members) must be able to demonstrate effective team leadership and maintenance skills. Some authors (e.g., Anderlini, 1983) suggest that leadership should be distributed throughout the team to maximize the chances that the diverse resources of the members will be used most effectively. Whatever the case, MDTs require effective coordination to facilitate the active involvement of all members, including parents, in the development, implementation, and evaluation of services to school children.

CHALLENGES FACING MDT LEADERS

Before discussing different leadership tasks, it is important to examine the status of MDT functioning in the public schools. Research studies published shortly after the passage of PL 94-142 identified a number of serious problems affecting the functioning of MDT special education placement staffings. Such problems included, but were not limited to, lack of effective decision-making processes, inadequate time devoted to developing intervention strategies, role conflict, lack of clarity regarding goals, and inadequate interdisciplinary collaboration (Pfeiffer, 1981; Goldstein, Strickland, Turnbull, & Curry, 1980; Pugach, 1982; Yoshida, Fenton, Maxwell, & Kaufman, 1978; Ysseldyke, Algozzine, & Allen, 1982; Ysseldyke, Algozzine, Rostollan, & Shin, 1981). Of most importance to this chapter, such studies also suggested that parents (and regular class teachers) contributed little to MDT decision-making activities. Assessment specialists (e.g., school psychologists, special education teachers) reportedly dominated MDT activities (Gilliam, 1978). Hence, despite the numerous advantages of parental participation in MDT meetings, and contrary to the intent of P.L. 94-142, these studies indicated that parents played very passive roles on MDTs.

Recent research (e.g., Huebner & Gould, 1991; Silverstein, 1989; Vaughn, Bos, Harrell, & Lasky, 1988) suggests that many of these problems continue to plague school-based MDTs. For example, based on extensive parent interviews, Silverstein (1989) reported that MDTs often engender negative emotional reactions in parents. Furthermore, despite their distress, many parents indicated that they would be reluctant to express their feelings to MDT school personnel. Thus, many MDTs have not fulfilled the promise of effective home-school collaboration.

Numerous reasons for this relative lack of parental involvement in MDTs have been proposed including lack of knowledge (Goldstein et al., 1980), confusion over parents' roles on MDTs (Hoff, Fenton, Yoshida, & Kaufman, 1978), emotional reactions of parents following the diagnosis of a handicap (Hall & Richmond, 1984; Ormerod & Huebner, 1988), attribution of blame for children's problems as residing exclusively within the child and by extension, within the parents (Silverstein, 1989), and poor communication patterns on MDTs (Vaughn et al., 1988). Despite these factors, there has

been a consistently high level of parental satisfaction reported for MDT staffings (Goldstein et al., 1980; Goldstein & Turnbull, 1982; Witt, Miller, McIntyre, & Smith, 1984; Vaughn et al., 1988), suggesting that many parents *prefer* passive roles, at least given the conditions under which the typical MDT currently operates.

The development of effective MDT-based home-school partnerships is thus fraught with difficulties. MDTs apparently do not automatically provide an effective vehicle for promoting linkages with parents and significant others. Team leaders and members must display particular skills in order to develop a climate in which positive home-school linkages can be forged (Maher & Yoshida, 1985). Thus, MDTs would likely benefit from a systematic program of ongoing team building and evaluation activities, which includes the fostering of positive home-school partnerships as a major objective.

LEADERSHIP

The coordination of MDTs requires effective leadership and team building skills. Research in social and organizational psychology has described three general leadership styles (Seaman, 1981). The first style, authoritarian leadership, is characterized by leaders who primarily dictate decisions to group members, who are in turn expected to implement them. Under this leadership system, communication flows only in one direction. The second style, laissez-faire leadership, is characterized by leaders who actively avoid structuring or participating in the decision-making process, requiring the other team members to handle problems themselves. The final style, democratic leadership, allows communication to flow equally in all directions so that team members all provide input into decision making. Democratic leadership styles are generally recommended for MDT activities because team members have a higher probability of implementing decisions that they have helped to make, rather than decisions that others have made for them (Cooper & Wood, 1974; Reinking, Livesay, & Kohl, 1978). Nonetheless, given the aforementioned passive role of parents on many MDTs, it appears that nondemocratic leadership methods predominate on MDTs.

Consistent with this democratic philosophy, some authors (e.g., Christenson, Abery, & Weinberg, 1987; Mearig, 1982; Plas, 1981) have recommended that the overarching role of school psychologists (including their roles on MDTs) should be that of liaison or networker. This perspective and its associated role functions is concerned with the identification of a client's needs and the creation or enhancement of linkages among clients and formal (e.g., social service agency, school resource) and informal (e.g., neighbors) resources to meet those needs. From this perspective, the central task of the MDT leader concerns fostering a climate in which school personnel and parents can work together as equal partners in designing interventions that mobilize resources to meet the child's needs.

MDT leaders must facilitate the accomplishment of several specific team tasks to coordinate a problem-solving team in such a manner. These tasks, which are adapted from Dyer (1987), include (a) setting goals, (b) clarifying roles, (c) facilitating effective communication (d) developing a positive emotional climate, (e) facilitating collaborative problem solving and decision making, (f) developing collaboration of effort, (g) ensuring follow-through, and (h) evaluation. In the following section, I will discuss strategies to accomplish each of these tasks.

LEADERSHIP SKILLS
Setting Goals

The establishment of MDT meeting goals is a simple but important prerequisite for effective MDT meetings. Goals are needed to focus and organize team activities as well as to provide a basis for the evaluation of meetings. The major task of the leader is to ensure that the goals for the meeting are clear and agreed upon by the participants. For example, teams may choose to discuss eligibility decisions and develop formal IEPs in separate meetings.

Such a decision may be especially appropriate when a child's parents display strong feelings in response to a possible special education placement (see discussion of crisis reactions below). Whatever the case, goals for meetings need to be discussed and negotiated openly prior to the initiation of problem-solving activities.

The MDT leader may use formal agenda-setting procedures (e.g., Schmuck & Runkel, 1985) to set a reasonable number of goals and timelines for team meetings. Setting timelines, and adhering to them appropriately, may be critical for teams who characteristically spend too much time discussing assessment data and too little time discussing intervention plans, especially for those teams whose members simply manage time ineffectively.

Giving careful consideration to the development of a unique agenda for each MDT meeting may also contribute substantially to the improvement of MDT functioning. In this author's experience, many MDTs set aside the same amount of time for *all* meetings, which offers the opportunity for little flexibility in responding to the particular circumstances and needs of parents and school personnel alike. MDT leaders might be well advised to develop individualized meeting plans, including the *flexible* selection of agenda items and timelines according to the needs of each situation.

Clarifying Roles

The clarification of specific member roles is also a crucial prerequisite to subsequent team activities (e.g., decision making). In order to form a cooperative partnership with parents, MDT members need to clarify and agree upon their respective roles in team meetings and intervention activities. If the team itself does not function in an effective, collaborative manner, the home-school partnership is destined to fail from the outset. In order to circumvent such problems, some teams develop written policy statements that specify mutually agreed upon role descriptions for each team member, including the leader (Kabler & Carlton, 1982).

Effective MDT leaders need to address this issue explicitly during team meetings. The responsibilities of all participants, including parents, can be outlined briefly (and negotiated if necessary) by the leader prior to the start of problem-solving and decision-making activities. For example, in addition to describing the roles of each of the school professionals, team leaders may describe the team's expectations for parents' behavior in the meeting (e.g., encouraging parents to participate actively in the decision-making process). Of course, parental roles in intervention activities will need to be determined and clarified throughout the meeting(s).

Facilitating Effective Communication

A major task of leaders, which occurs throughout team activities, is to facilitate effective communication among *all* team members. Prior to effective problem solving and decision making, team members (including parents) must communicate openly, including expressing both positive and negative reactions to team proposals. For example, if parents are expected to collaborate effectively in implementing an intervention for their children, they must feel free to voice their dissatisfaction with recommendations with which they disagree.

To facilitate communication, MDT leaders must first be effective communicators themselves. Arends and Arends (1977) discuss the following communication skills, which are considered essential to the completion of the problem-solving tasks of MDTs. These skills include initiating discussion, information seeking, information giving, clarifying, summarizing, and consensus testing. See Arends and Arends for detailed descriptions of each of the skills.

In all cases, MDT leaders and members must ensure that they communicate in nontechnical language with parents and one another. The use of jargon not only impedes understanding but also can create an emotional distance between parents and school professionals and precludes successful, subsequent collaboration (Silverstein, 1989). Even when jargon is not used, team leaders should engage in frequent perception checking and summarizing to assess parental understanding of MDT discussions.

In addition to demonstrating effective communication skills, MDT leaders need to solicit communication from parents from the beginning of the staffing. Leaders can set the climate for active parental discussion by engaging in informal "chit chat" prior to the beginning of the meetings, both to develop rapport and to help the parents become comfortable conversing with the leader and/or members. The effective leader will tailor the conversation to topics of interest to the particular parents involved in order to communicate personal interest and concern.

From the beginning of the meeting, team leaders should also encourage parents to discuss their reactions in a forthright manner. For example, at a minimum, parents should be asked to (a) share any concerns they have about their child and her/his educational program, (b) provide information about the child's behavior at home, and (c) provide honest feedback regarding school professionals' assessments of their child's strengths and weaknesses and associated educational needs. Parents should be reinforced subsequently for their contributions (Turnbull & Leonard, 1981).

Once parents have begun to contribute to MDT discussions, MDT leaders must ensure that all members *listen* sensitively to parent responses. Effective listening communicates to parents that their input is truly valued by the team. Unfortunately, it has been this author's experience that many MDTs provide less than optimal listening environments due to leaders' and/or members' efforts to communicate their professional wisdom to the parents or simply to complete the meeting in the allotted time.

Facilitating a Positive Emotional Climate

Related to the above goal, the development of positive home-school partnerships through MDTs requires that MDT leaders be sensitive to the emotional needs of parents. Ormerod and Huebner (1988) discuss the many possible emotional reactions of parents to the diagnosis of a handicapping condition. These reactions can range from a sense of relief that professionals have confirmed what the parents have already suspected to crisis reactions in which parents experience a "temporary state of upset and disorganization" (Slakieu, 1984, p. 13) resulting in reduced coping skills. When confronted with parents who display a severe crisis reaction, Ormerod and Huebner (1988) suggest that team leaders adopt a crisis intervention perspective to help parents cope more effectively with the situation.

Facilitating a positive emotional environment first requires leaders to develop effective communication between parents and other members. In addition to the skills discussed in the previous section, Arends and Arends (1977) discuss several general communication skills that are essential to maintaining positive group interactions. These skills include encouraging (e.g., being warm and responsive to others; listening attentively to others' contributions), expressing group feelings (sensing and expressing feelings and interactions in group), harmonizing (attempting to reconcile differences), compromising (being willing to modify one's position to work cooperatively), gatekeeping (ensuring that everyone gets a chance to speak), and setting standards (expressing standards that will help the team to achieve its goals). Team leaders must thus display a variety of task and maintenance communication skills.

As noted by Ormerod and Huebner (1988), when confronted with parents displaying crisis reactions, however, more specialized counseling skills are needed to help parents resolve the crisis. Of perhaps most importance to this discussion, it should be noted that dealing effectively with such parents requires considerable time, support, and understanding from school personnel. Parents who demonstrate severe reactions involving protracted denial, anger, or guilt may

not be able to assume a key role in their children's educational programs immediately. For example, some parents may need to work through denial and anger reactions, which may temporarily impair their willingness and/or ability to work collaboratively with MDTs. MDT leaders may thus need to use multiple parent and MDT meetings to planfully design "therapeutic moments" (Simon, 1984, p. 14) to help parents assume gradually increasing responsibilities in their child's education. The length of team meetings (and presumably the number of meetings) has been identified as a major contributor to effective home-school interactions (Witt et al., 1984).

Perhaps the foremost task of the MDT leader is to guide the team in communicating to parents that she or he and the other team members truly care about them and their children. This task requires school professionals to demonstrate skills related to empathy, genuineness, and respect. Silverstein (1989) provides moving descriptions of simple ways in which MDT members can communicate such concern to parents.

Facilitating Effective Problem Solving

The major focus of most MDT meetings is solving problems. That is, MDTs must often develop intervention strategies to improve children's school functioning. The effective team leader thus needs to provide the structure to facilitate systematic, democratic problem solving and decision making among school personnel and parents. Such efforts should draw upon the resources of all participants, rather than allow one or more influential members to dominate the process. The structure for MDT problem solving can be provided by a problem-solving model composed of four components: (a) defining the problem, (b) generating intervention alternatives, (c) selecting an intervention plan, and (d) evaluating the plan. The first three components will be discussed next and the latter component will be discussed in a later section.

1. *Defining the problem.* First, MDT

leaders must guide team efforts to define the problem (i.e., identify the child's specific educational needs). MDT members must all agree upon the child's specific strengths and weaknesses and the need for an intervention prior to formulating intervention strategies. Jensen and Potter (1990) recommended that parents and school personnel are more likely to reach agreement when descriptions of a child's strengths and weaknesses are discussed in behavioral versus highly inferential language. For example, parents may resist describing their son as "unmotivated" but readily acknowledge that he seldom completes his homework. It should be noted that assessment techniques can be selected with this recommendation in mind. In this author's experience, providing parents with a child's classmates' handwritten copies of sociometric choices (e.g., number of children who select and reject a child as a potential playmate) can be more useful than telling the parents that their child has interpersonal problems on the basis of professional judgment of the child's responses to highly inferential assessment techniques (e.g., projectives), which are rarely shared with the parents.

The strengths of the child and relevant systems should also be highlighted as part of the problem definition stage (Plas, 1981). A focus on strengths should help maintain rapport between parents and school personnel. Also, the assessment of *system* strengths should provide an important foundation for the following stages of problem solving, which involve the identification and mobilization of system resources to meet the child's needs. By encouraging the use of a behavioral and systemic framework throughout assessment, MDT leaders can discourage parents and school professionals from attributing blame for the child's problem to a particular individual or individuals (e.g., parents, teachers).

The assessment of family and school characteristics is obviously an essential prerequisite to developing effective home-school interventions. However, MDT meetings have traditionally been dominated by discussions of individual (i.e.,

child) assessment data. To facilitate the development of meaningful home-school linkages, however, the effective team leader will need to help refocus assessment strategies toward an ecological or systems perspective. Conoley (1987) provides a useful overview of the application of systems theory to home-school partnerships, which includes a discussion of specific questions to guide the assessment of family and school system characteristics.

As noted in the introduction of this chapter, many MDT placement teams spend a disproportionate amount of time discussing assessment results during this component. MDT leaders must thus be skillful in the use and application of time management procedures (e.g., see Maher, 1981). For example, MDT leaders should help team members organize and streamline their presentations of assessment findings to allow more time for discussing interventions. Given the amount of information parents reportedly retain following MDT meetings (Silverstein, 1989), it is important for leaders to require assessment personnel to limit their verbal discussions to only the *most* important issues. Additional, less important findings and data can be provided in written reports, which the parents can read and digest at their leisure.

After agreement on the specific problem(s) has been obtained, objectives should be agreed upon. The objectives should also be defined in behavioral terms (e.g., Lauren will complete all of her math assignments with 80% accuracy during the allotted school time) so as to provide direction for subsequent problem-solving activities and to provide a clear basis for the evaluation of intervention efficacy.

There are special problems that should be noted when a child's needs are so extensive that some MDT members believe that special education services should be considered as an alternative. MDT leaders and/or other members must alert the parents to the fact that the diagnosis of a handicapping condition is required to provide special education services to a child. Given the state of the art of diagnostic procedures, classification systems, and interclinician reliability (McDermott, 1981), it is this author's suggestion that special education diagnoses (e.g., learning disability) should therefore be stated as tentative hypotheses and that parents be *clearly* informed of the potential advantages and disadvantages of labelling. In this manner, parents can be more informed decision makers.

2. *Generating alternative solutions.* The MDT leader must structure the discussion of intervention possibilities in this component. The development of effective home-school intervention plans often necessitates that MDT members generate novel and creative solutions to identified problems. Brainstorming is frequently recommended as a method to generate a large number of possible solutions to a problem (e.g., Zins, Curtis, Graden, & Ponti, 1988). Brainstorming requires that all members be encouraged to contribute suggestions. The individual suggestions are not discussed or evaluated in any way until after *all* the ideas have been recorded. Brainstorming may thus be a particularly effective method with those parents who feel unsure of their ability to contribute knowledgeably to MDT problem solving.

To facilitate thoughtful discussion of possible home-school interventions, the MDT leader may wish to provide a list of home-school activities that have been reported on in the literature. (See Ehly, Conoley, and Rosenthal, 1985, for an overview of frequently used strategies.) Also, parent advocates, who attend MDTs to provide support for parents, may be used to provide input and model appropriate problem-solving behaviors when the parents are particularly reticent (Goldstein & Turnbull, 1982).

3. *Selecting intervention plans.* During this stage of problem solving, the MDT leader must coordinate the process of selecting one or more of the proposed strategies to help the child. Democratic decision-making processes (e.g., consensus) are generally recommended to facilitate plan implementation. The interested reader should see Hare (1983) for specific leader behaviors to coordinate consensual

decision making. Arends and Arends (1977) provide a particularly useful description of consensual decision making as "solution shaping" as opposed to "people shaping." In the former case, team members who are opposed to a proposal are encouraged to indicate how the *solution* (rather than the person who proposed the solution) should be changed to make it more acceptable. MDTs may consequently spend more time trying to develop creative solutions to problems rather than trying to persuade others to change their views. This strategy may be particularly effective in preventing MDT meetings from resulting in adversarial relationships between parents and school personnel.

The selection of intervention plans and components should be guided not only by knowledge of the intervention effectiveness research, but also by the intervention acceptability research. The importance of creating intervention plans that are acceptable to all persons involved with the intervention is underscored by this literature. As Witt and Elliott (1985) note, if effective intervention plans are unacceptable to parents or school personnel, they are unlikely to be implemented with integrity or at all. Thus, it is crucial for MDT leaders to ensure that all intervention agents truly support the plan. Although this process may be very time consuming in the short run, careful attention in details at this stage may save considerable time in the long run. Several researchers (e.g., Elliott, 1988; Reimers, Wacker, & Koeppl, 1987) have recently reviewed the various factors related to acceptability. In addition to the effectiveness of the treatment, the factors include complexity, time, type, cost, and understanding of the intervention. All other things equal, interventions are preferred that are simple, brief, positive (vs. reductive or punishment-based), relatively inexpensive, and easily understood by the interventionist. Thus, the more the intervention is complicated, time consuming, and so forth, the more it is likely to be judged as unacceptable by the intervention implementers. Also, although little research has been conducted to examine the relationship between intervention acceptability and integrity (Reimers, Wacker, & Koeppl, 1987; Gresham, 1989), it seems prudent to assume that parents and other interventionists are unlikely to implement unacceptable interventions. It should be noted that most of the acceptability research has been conducted with teachers; however, it seems likely that these findings apply to parents as well.

During this component of problem solving, conflict is most likely to occur. Effective MDT leaders must be able to manage conflict in a way that promotes effective collaboration. Although conflict (e.g., between parents and teachers) can be stressful, MDT leaders must not seek to avoid the expression of conflict among members, but rather they must use the conflict as a positive influence in creating high quality solutions to problems. To do so, MDT leaders must first recognize the value of differences of opinion among team members. Studies have shown that groups experiencing conflict can produce more creative solutions to problems than groups in which conflict does not occur (Wall & Nolan, 1987). Effective conflict management strategies are described further in numerous sources (e.g., Dyer, 1987; Kindler, 1988; Wynn & Guditus, 1984).

Developing Collaboration of Effort

The goal of home-school partnerships is to encourage truly collaborative efforts between school personnel and parents to improve children's school functioning. MDT members must thus view the intervention process as a shared responsibility in which both parents and school personnel are expected to contribute. Such a goal requires that MDT leaders model an appreciation for the differing perspectives and values held by different team members (and associated disciplines) and parents on MDTs. Again, this behavior often necessitates a willingness to suspend judgments based upon disciplinary loyalties and/or theoretical preferences in order to recognize and consider the contributions of all team members. With regard to parents, leaders and members

must at times be willing to understand and accept parents' view of their roles even when they differ from their own. If school professionals are unable to do so, they are likely to promote intervention plans that are not congruent with parental expectations. If there is a mismatch between the "help" (i.e., change goals and strategy) offered by the school and the help sought by the parents, then parents are unlikely to accept the help and carry out their part in the plans (Dunst & Trivette, 1987).

At this point, it is important to consider what constitutes a desirable level of parental involvement in MDT collaborative change efforts. Although many school professionals advocate that *all* parents should be equal partners in determining and implementing their child's educational program, Simpson and Fiedler (1989) argue cogently that *more* parental involvement is not necessarily always *better* involvement. These authors suggest that the degree of parental involvement should be individualized (as IEPs are individualized for handicapped children) on the basis of family needs, resources, skills, and interests. Expecting greater or lesser involvement from parents than appropriate, given their particular family resources, is likely to have detrimental effects. For example, the expectations for a single parent of three children who has just moved to a new city should be different than expectations for an intact family composed of two parents and one child who have numerous supportive relatives nearby. Simpson and Fiedler further discuss general guidelines, based upon an analysis of family structure, functions, interactions, and life cycle stage, which can assist in determining appropriate levels of involvement for different families.

Thus, MDT leaders and members must be sensitive to individual differences in family resources and interests when developing home-school linkages. Turnbull (1983) discusses a variety of family involvement options, ranging from simple attendance at meetings to joint and independent interventions. Michaelis (1980) also provides a model of parental involvement that includes five stages in a progression toward parental understanding and readiness to work collaboratively with school personnel. These stages include (a) parent is apprehensive about school, (b) parent becomes more comfortable about school, (c) parent expresses concern about school, (d) parent is ready to listen to professional, and (e) parent becomes a partner in education. Taken together, these models of parental involvement illustrate that MDT leaders and members, who wish to develop joint home-school interventions, must be prepared to work with some parents over a period of time (not just one or two half-hour MDT meetings) to help them reach this level of interaction. The MDT leader must thus assist parents and other MDT members in the assessment and negotiation of an appropriate level of parental involvement from among the numerous available options.

Collaboration of effort can be facilitated through the use of written, behavioral contracts (Simon, 1984). Such contracts facilitate the development of effective linkages because they can be employed to prescribe systemic change, that is, behavioral change on the part of multiple key persons in the child's life (e.g., parents, teachers, child). As a simple example, a behavioral contract could be developed in which a child earns verbal praise and attention from his father (who typically criticizes him) and the opportunity to be "teacher's helper" for his teacher (who typically ignores him) for completing his math assignments during school hours (when the child typically finishes assignments at home, if at all). Each individual's behavior is thus altered to institute a significant change in the rules that determine their typical interactions. In this manner, MDTs can formalize home-school linkages in which the expectations and responsibilities of all parties are clearly outlined and which support a systems perspective and change efforts.

Ensuring Follow Through

MDTs must ensure that their intervention plans are carried out with integ-

rity if they hope to be successful. Many failures in MDT interventions may result from failures to actually implement interventions as intended (Gresham, 1989). Gresham (1989) discussed research findings related to the integrity of treatments in school settings, which are similar to the findings of the intervention acceptability research. In brief, the research suggests that interventions are most likely to be *implemented* effectively when they are relatively uncomplicated, require little time and few additional resources and intervention personnel, and are perceived as effective and implemented by highly motivated intervention agents. As suggested previously, careful attention to such factors during the phase when intervention strategies are selected should help ensure an acceptable degree of intervention integrity during the implementation phase.

Once developed, intervention plans should be recorded in *written* form (Yoshida, Fenton, Maxwell, & Kaufman, 1978). The written document should include the assignment of each person's responsibilities, timelines, review dates, and the signatures of all MDT members. The development of a written document should help ensure that each member understands her/his responsibilities with regard to the intervention and should also help increase her/his commitment to the plan's integrity and implementation.

MDT leaders should pay particular attention to encouraging shared responsibility among team members and other possible resource persons (e.g., CMHC therapist, child's grandmother, minister) for intervention assistance. MDTs have often relied exclusively on classroom teachers for program development and implementation (Pfeiffer, 1981). Dividing up responsibilities among more than one resource person may facilitate the completion of necessary tasks. However, MDTs must be careful to limit the number of intervention agents because there is likely to be an inverse relationship between the number of intervention agents and intervention integrity (Gresham, 1989).

Finally, one or more MDT members

should be delegated the responsibility of monitoring the implementation of intervention plans. This case manager role does not necessarily have to be carried out by the team leader, but could be determined individually for each case. Another possibility involves rotating this responsibility among team members, thereby further encouraging shared responsibility among team members (Ohio Department of Education, 1985). This task primarily involves monitoring of the intervention through phone contacts, visits (e.g., to the home and classroom), and scheduling follow-up meetings as necessary to see that MDT recommended activities are completed.

Evaluation

Formative and summative evaluation of the intervention program should be conducted routinely to determine the success of the intervention program and to determine the need for program modifications. Appropriate evaluation procedures are discussed in numerous sources including Maher and Bennett (1984). It is the role of the team leader to oversee the implementation of these activities.

MDTs and MDT leaders also need to conduct evaluations of *their* functioning. Given Silverstein's (1989) findings that many parents fail to express their true feelings in MDT meetings, it is essential that evaluations be conducted to elicit honest feedback from parents regarding their satisfaction with team activities. Evaluations should also be conducted to obtain feedback from other MDT members regarding their satisfaction as well.

It is this author's speculation that few MDTs actually conduct systematic evaluations of their effectiveness. Administrative support for team evaluation (and any subsequent team building efforts) is probably necessary to provide the motivation as well as time and resources to undertake such evaluations. Thus, school personnel who serve as MDT leaders, but who are not school administrators, should seek to obtain the support of relevant administrators prior to implementing evaluation activities.

The assessment of team and leader activities can subsequently be conducted in several ways. Questionnaires can be developed to allow participants (including parents) to provide anonymous feedback regarding the effectiveness of the leader and/or the team. For example, a rating scale might be developed in which respondents rate the team leader's effectiveness in facilitating each of the aforementioned team tasks, that is, setting goals, facilitating communication, developing a positive emotional climate, and so forth. Dyer (1987) provides numerous examples of checklists and questionnaires that could be modified for use with school-based MDTs. With regard to obtaining feedback from parents, formative evaluation can be accomplished by directly asking parents to share their perceptions of the usefulness of MDT meetings at appropriate times during and at the end of meetings. When there is concern that parents may not have revealed their true feelings during meetings, MDT leaders or members who have a particularly good rapport with the parents may also arrange for follow-up, face-to-face or phone interviews with parents to discuss MDT processes and outcomes.

When evaluation data indicate that the team and/or leader are not functioning as desired, then the MDT leader must organize intervention efforts. If the data suggest that team problems are primarily related to leader behavior, the leader must assume responsibility for improving her/his behavior through appropriate remedial actions (e.g., leadership training) or appointing a different leader. If the data suggest that difficulties should be conceptualized as a *team* problem, then a systematic program of team building efforts should be considered. Although a discussion of specific team building strategies is beyond the scope of this chapter, the interested reader can consult Dyer (1987) for an excellent overview of team building. It should be noted that team building efforts should be facilitated by an external consultant (rather than the MDT leader) when (a) the MDT leader is perceived as a major contributor to team problems, (b) major conflicts or relationship problems exist among team members, or (c) ineffective team behaviors have been maintained for a long time (Shonk, 1982).

SUMMARY

MDTs provide a major vehicle for the promotion of home-school partnerships for handicapped and nonhandicapped students. Unfortunately, school-based MDTs continue to be plagued by a variety of problems that impair the ability of MDTs to foster such partnerships. However, the ability of MDTs to promote effective home-school interventions could be increased significantly through improved coordination by MDT leaders.

In a recent national survey, numerous school psychologists reported that they served as MDT leaders in their schools (Huebner & Gould, 1991). However, more than one-quarter of the subjects indicated that they had received *no* formal preservice or inservice training in team leadership skills. University trainers and conference planners may thus wish to focus more attention on this important topic. Increased attention to the training of school psychologists in team building and leadership skills may improve overall MDT effectiveness and promote more effective home-school linkages.

REFERENCES

Anderlini, L. S. (1983). An inservice program for improving team participation in educational decisionmaking. *School Psychology Review, 12,* 160–167.

Arends, R. E., & Arends, J. H. (1977). *Systems change strategies in educational settings.* New York: Human Sciences Press.

Christenson, S., Abery, B., & Weinberg, R. (1987). An alternative model for the delivery of psychological services in the school community. In S. N. Elliott & J. C. Witt (Eds.), *The delivery of psychological services in schools: Concepts, processes and issues* (pp. 349–391). Hillsdale, NJ: Lawrence Erlbaum.

Conoley, J. C. (1987). Schools and families: Theoretical and practical bridges. *Professional School Psychology, 2,* 191–204.

Cooper, M. R., & Wood, M. T. (1974). Effects of member participation and commitment in group decision-making on influence, satisfaction, and decision riskiness. *Journal of Applied Psychology, 59,* 127–134.

Dunst, C. J., & Trivette, C. M. (1987). Enabling and empowering families: Conceptual and intervention issues. *School Psychology Review, 16,* 443–456.

Dyer, W. G. (1987). *Team building: Issues and alternatives* (2nd ed.). Reading, MA: Addison-Wesley Publishing Company.

Ehly, S., Conoley, J. C., & Rosenthal, D. (1985). *Working with parents of exceptional children.* St. Louis: Times Mirror/Mosby College Publishing.

Elliott, S. N. (1988). Acceptability of behavioral treatments in educational settings. In J. C. Witt, S. N. Elliott, & F. M. Gresham (Eds.), *Handbook of behavior therapy* (pp. 121–148). New York: Plenum Press.

Epstein, J. L. (1987). Parent involvement: What research says to administrators. *Education and Urban Society, 19,* 119–136.

Gilliam, J. E. (1978). Contributions and status rankings of educational planning participants. *Exceptional Children, 45,* 466–468.

Goldstein, S., Strickland, B., Turnbull, A. P., & Curry, L. (1980). An observational analysis of the IEP conference. *Exceptional Children, 46,* 278–286.

Goldstein, S., & Turnbull, A. P. (1982). Strategies to increase parent participation in IEP conferences. *Exceptional Children, 48,* 360–361.

Graden, J., Casey, A., & Christenson, S. (1985). Implementing a prereferral intervention system: Part I. The model. *Exceptional Children, 51,* 377–384.

Gresham, F. M. (1989). Assessment of treatment integrity in school consultation and prereferral intervention. *School Psychology Review, 18,* 37–50.

Hall, C. W., & Richmond, B. O. (1984). Consultation with parents of handicapped children. *Exceptional Child, 31,* 185–191.

Hare, A. (1983). *Creativity in small groups.* Beverly Hills, CA: Sage Publications.

Hawley, W., & Rosenholtz, S. (1983). *Education strategies that increase student achievement.* Washington, DC: U.S. Department of Education Office of Planning, Budget and Evaluation.

Hoff, M. K., Fenton, K. S., Yoshida, R., & Kaufman, M. J. (1978). Notice and consent: The school's responsibility to inform parents. *Journal of School Psychology, 16,* 265–273.

Huebner, E. S., & Gould, K. (1991). Multidisciplinary teams revisited: Current perceptions of school psychologists regarding team functioning. *School Psychology Review, 20,* 428–434.

Jensen, B. F., & Potter, M. C. (1990). Best practices in communicating with parents. In A. Thomas & J. Grimes (Eds.), *Best practices in school psychology* (vol. II, pp. 183–193). Kent, OH: National Association of School Psychologists.

Kabler, M., & Carlton, G. (1982). Education's exceptional students: A comprehensive team approach. *Theory into Practice, 21,* 88–96.

Kindler, H. S. (1988). *Managing disagreement constructively: Conflict management in organizations.* Los Altos, CA: Crisp Publications, Inc.

Maher, C. A. (1981). Time management training for school psychologists. *Professional Psychology, 12,* 613–620.

Maher, C. A., & Bennett, R. E. (1984). *Planning and evaluating special education services.* Englewood Cliffs, NJ: Prentice-Hall.

Maher, C. A., & Yoshida, R. K. (1985). Multidisciplinary teams in the schools: Current status and future possibilities. In T. R. Kratochwill (Ed.), *Advances in school psychology* (vol. IV, pp. 13–44). Hillsdale, NJ: Lawrence Erlbaum.

McDermott, P. A. (1981). Sources of error in the psychoeducational diagnosis of children. *Journal of School Psychology, 19,* 31–44.

Mearig, J. (1982). Integration of school and community services for children with special needs. In C. R. Reynolds & T. B. Gutkin (Eds.), *The handbook of school psychology* (pp. 748–773). New York: John Wiley and Sons.

Michaelis, C. T. (1980). *Home and school partnerships in exceptional education.* Rockville, MD: Aspen Publications.

Ohio Department of Education. (1985). *Intervention assistance teams.* Columbus, OH: Author.

Ormerod, J. J., & Huebner, E. S. (1988). Crisis intervention: Facilitating parental acceptance of a child's handicap. *Psychology in the Schools, 25,* 422–428.

Pfeiffer, S. I. (1981). The problems facing multidisciplinary teams: As perceived by team members. *Psychology in the schools, 18,* 330–333.

Pfeiffer, S. I., & Tittler, B. I. (1983). Utilizing the multidisciplinary team to facilitate a school-family systems orientation. *School Psychology Review, 12,* 168–173.

Plas, J. (1981). The psychologist in the school community: A liaison role. *School Psychology Review, 10,* 72–81.

Pugach, M. L. (1982). Regular classroom teacher involvement in the development and implementation of IEPs. *Exceptional Children, 48,* 371–374.

Reimers, T. M., Wacker, D., & Koeppl, G. (1987).

Acceptability of behavioral interventions: A review of the literature. *School Psychology Review, 16,* 212–227.

Reinking, R. H., Livesay, G., & Kohl, M. (1978). The effects of consultation style on consultee productivity. *American Journal of Community Psychology, 6,* 283–290.

Schmuck, R. A., & Runkel, P. J. (1985). *The handbook of organizational development in schools* (3rd ed.). Prospect Heights, IL: Waveland Press.

Seaman, D. F. (1981). *Working effectively with task-oriented groups.* New York: McGraw-Hill.

Shonk, J. H. (1982). *Working in teams: A practical manual for improving work groups.* New York: Amacon Co.

Silverstein, J. (1989). Fostering parent-professional partnerships: A role for school psychology educators. *Trainers Forum, 9,* 2, 4–7.

Simon, D. J. (1984). Parent conferences as therapeutic moments. *The Personnel and Guidance Journal, 62,* 612–616.

Simpson, R. L., & Fiedler, C. R. (1989). In M. Fine (Ed.), *The second handbook on parent education: Contemporary perspectives* (pp. 145–171). San Diego, CA: Academic Press.

Slakieu, K. A. (1984). *Crisis intervention: A handbook for practice and research.* Newton, MA: Allyn & Bacon.

Turnbull, A. (1983). Parental participation in the IEP process. In J. A. Mulick & S. M. Pueschel (Eds.), *Parent-professional partnerships in developmental disability services* (pp. 107–122). Cambridge, MA: Wave Press.

Turnbull, A. P., & Leonard, J. (1981). Parent involvement in special education: Emerging advocacy roles. *School Psychology Review, 10,* 37–44.

Turnbull, H. R., Turnbull, A. P., & Wheat, M. (1982). Assumptions about parental participation: A legislative history. *Exceptional Education Quarterly, 3,* 1–8.

Vaughn, S., Bos, C. S., Harrell, J. E., & Lasky, B. A. (1988). Parent participation in the initial placement/IEP conference ten years after mandated involvement. *Journal of Learning Disabilities, 21,* 82–89.

Wall, V. D., & Nolan, L. L. (1987). Small group conflict: A look at equity, satisfaction and styles of conflict management. *Small Group Behavior, 18,* 188–211.

Witt, J., & Elliott, S. N. (1985). Acceptability of classroom management strategies. In T. R. Kratochwill (Ed.), *Advances in school psychology* (vol. 4, pp. 251–288). Hillsdale, NJ: Lawrence Erlbaum.

Witt, J. C., Miller, C. D., McIntyre, R. M., & Smith, P.

(1984). Effects of variables on parental participation in staffings. *Exceptional Children, 51,* 27–32.

Wynn, R., & Guditus, C. W. (1984). *Team management: Leadership by consensus.* London: Charles E. Merrill Publishing Co.

Yoshida, R. K., Fenton, K. S., Maxwell, J. P., & Kaufman, M. J. (1978). Group decision-making in the planning team process: Myth or reality? *Journal of School Psychology, 16,* 178–183.

Ysseldyke, J. E., Algozzine, B., & Allen, P. (1982).

Participation of regular education teachers in special education decision-making. *Exceptional Children, 48,* 365–368.

Ysseldyke, J. E., Algozzine, B., Rostollan, D., & Shin, M. A. (1981). A content analysis of the data presented at special education placement team meetings. *Journal of Clinical Psychology, 37,* 655–622.

Zins, J. E., Curtis, M. J., Graden, J. L., & Ponti, C. R. (1988). *Helping students succeed in the regular classroom.* San Francisco, CA: Jossey-Bass.

19

A PUBLIC SCHOOL FOR STUDENTS WITH AUTISM AND SEVERE HANDICAPS

Andrew S. Bondy and
Kris O. Battaglini

The aim of this chapter is to introduce an approach to working with students with severe handicaps, including autism, and their families, within a public school context. The approach emphasizes team collaboration, with the school psychologist playing a central role in coordinating services within the school and between the school and the home. In order to describe the various elements of the approach, a portrayal will be made of the Delaware Autistic Program (DAP), where the components have been developed and implemented during the past decade.

The Delaware Autistic Program is part of the Department of Public Instruction and serves students with autism and pervasive developmental disorder throughout the state. The program is funded by state, federal, and local funds and is administered by one school district (the Christina District). Students may receive services in any type of education setting, from full-time placement in center-based programs to complete integration in regular classes with only consultative speech services. The program operates year round including almost 4 weeks of respite programming provided on a half-staff basis.

The State's financial commitment to DAP is considerable. This support was created partially in reaction to vocal parents who, several years ago, made the unique needs of their children clear. The funding formulas for teachers and certain specialists is fixed by state law under the State's Guidelines for Exceptional Children. A unit (four students) is supported by a teacher and a classroom assistant. Class size has typically consisted of five students. For every three units, one speech and language pathologist is funded and for every six units, one psychologist is funded. Other related services may include adaptive physical education, occupational therapy, physical therapy, and music classes. The program also has a community training specialist, a transition team leader, and a vocational specialist. Other special services may be required by individualized education plans. The program is also unique in that it directly provides residential services within two community-based group home settings. Each residence has its own staff on a 24-hour basis and provides services every day of the year.

FUNCTIONAL ORIENTATION OF EDUCATIONAL OBJECTIVES

All educational programs, regardless of the type of student served, must address two fundamental questions: (a) what to teach and (b) how to teach. The staff of DAP begin the selection of educational objectives by requiring that each objective has a clear functional purpose for the student. The general guidelines that help teachers and specialists determine what is currently functional for each student are derived in large part by the work done by Lou Brown and associates (Brown, Nietupski, & Hamre-Nietupski, 1976). Functional objectives are organized around key life domains, such as school-based objectives, domestic goals, and community and vocational objectives. There is no formal curriculum for all students because it is necessary to create an educational package that is uniquely sensitive to the student's skills and deficits, and living and work situation. A fundamental aspect of such planning is team work, which precludes any one staff member from being responsible for planning all aspects of the student's educational plan.

Another reason for the strong emphasis upon team planning is the interrelationship between various crucial elements of the educational effort. There are four areas that must be continuously integrated (Bondy, 1987).

1. At ALL times, each student must have a scheduled, functional activity. The purpose of this step is to ensure that the student and the staff are aware of what the student is to be doing. For each activity clear criteria are established for students and staff regarding what constitutes successful performance.

2. A reinforcement system that involves the use of powerful reinforcers must be in place at ALL times. Essentially, everything that the student does in school should be considered work and thus should be specifically reinforced. Powerful reinforcers (e.g., objects, edibles, activities, etc.) should be utilized to ensure sufficient motivation for each activity. Although the long-term goal is to develop reinforcers that naturally relate to functional activities, occasions exist in which additional reinforcement may be required to augment motivation. Whenever such reinforcers are necessary, a specific plan to fade the frequency or use of such rewards should be made. For example, a student may acquire certain

vocational skills while working on a reinforcement schedule which calls for fairly frequent sips of soda. The schedule and amount of soda would be gradually shifted (over months or even years) so that the student would be able to sustain working for 2 hours ending with a break and an entire can of soda. The last arrangement is the same as that self-selected by many non-handicapped people in a variety of work places. Fundamental to every lesson or activity is that the staff be aware of the potential reinforcer for a task prior to beginning the task. If staff do not know what would be reinforcing in the immediate context, then they should not begin the activity until they have made such a determination. (We use the phrase "let's make a deal" to remind staff and students of what is expected prior to each lesson.)

3. A communication system consisting of a minimum set of functional objectives must be created for each student. Such a system may require augmentative or alternative communication systems such as picture-based communication boards or similar arrangements. The communication system must be designed to be portable and readily available to the student. The system should permit the student to gain access to various reinforcers (e.g., social attention, specific objects or activities, etc.), to permit the student to avoid various events (e.g., the equivalents to "I need a break," "I need to get away from you," "I have a headache," "I need to go to the bathroom," etc.), and to generally call attention to needing help. The communication routine should also be designed to make more effective various staff instructions regarding what tasks are being assigned, what is the schedule of activities, and what is the reward associated with each activity.

4. Behavior management procedures that are effective and appropriate for each environment should be in effect. For example, procedures may differ depending upon whether the student was within the school, within a residential setting, or within a community setting. Behavior management plans (see below) must

include a specific plan for functionally equivalent alternative responses by the student as well as clear and uniform staff reactions to each behavior management target. Planned staff reactions would include ignoring the target as well as redirecting the student or other minimally reactive strategies. All reactions should be planned so that all staff will react to the student's behavior in a consistent manner.

The final component that links each of the above elements is a decision making process that is data based. Data must be routinely collected regarding progress on each IEP objective and each behavior management concern. Teams are expected to systematically review data and to designate when the next data review session will occur. Parents are given feedback on the specific level of performance for each objective rather than global descriptions, such as "good progress" or grades. The review teams must also decide prior to the next review what levels they are expecting. In this manner, criteria are set prior to each review rather than at the time of the review.

THE EDUCATIONAL CONTEXT

One of the unifying assumptions of DAP is that although an infinite number of skills to teach may exist, only a limited number of ways to teach actually exist. The program has a core set of prompting procedures (i.e., prompt hierarchy, modeling, shaping, fading, delayed prompt, etc.) from which teachers and specialists must choose to describe their lesson plans. A finite set of teaching arrangements can be selected by staff, such as whole-task presentation, partial-task presentation, forward and backward chaining, and incidental arrangements. Task analyses (TAs) may be developed for a variety of skills, and the program keeps a compendium of task analyses designed by staff. Staff are reminded that such TAs are to be used as general guidelines for their students as a TA pertains to an individual student and is not universally applicable. For example, several TAs have been

written that relate to public bus use because students with verbal abilities will be expected to follow a different sequence than students who use augmentative or alternative communication systems. Over 350 TAs are available for staff review, and are organized by domain.

In addition to identifying particular prompts and their structural organization, DAP has also developed a series of error correction strategies (Bondy, 1990). Several such strategies are described because there are a variety of errors that students may make that are directly related to the type of teaching methodology selected. The correction strategies include backstepping, model/prompt/switch/repeat, anticipatory prompt, peer reinforcement, etc. Each strategy has its own advantages and disadvantages (Bondy, Peterson, Tarleton, & Frangia, 1990). It is very helpful to have staff recognize that by carefully analyzing the lesson and how it is to be taught, they can anticipate the types of errors that students may produce, and can be prepared to respond to each type of error with effective corrective procedures.

The educational issues related to prompt selection and organization, combined with those issues pertaining to reinforcement use, generalization, and data collection are described on a single form called the Prescriptive Teaching Plan (PTP) cover sheet (see Figure 1). A PTP is prepared for each IEP objective by teachers and specialists. Because they are written in an essentially common language, all staff can pick up, read, and implement any PTP. Although certain aspects of PTPs may be similar across students, other aspects tend to remain unique to a student. For example, two students may be learning the same task for the same type of reward, but one student may respond better to corrective strategies that point out the appropriate behavior of a peer as opposed to more direct feedback after an error.

The dominant constituent of educational development is a motivational system that focuses upon positive reinforcement-based procedures. As noted earlier, students with autism often re-

FIGURE 1
PTP Cover Sheet

I.   Student: Teacher:
     Behavior Objective: Domain: Date Implemented:

II. Task Presentation Strategy:
     Prompt Strategy: Prompt pause:
     Parameter Details:

     Materials:

III. Behavior Specification:
     Task Analysis: Current Performance Level   Target Level:

IV. Consequence Procedure:
         Within Task> R+s:
     R+ Schedule> Initial: Final: Step size:
         Completed Task> R+s
     R+ Schedule> Initial: Final: Step size:

V.   Corrective Procedure:

     Number of repetitions: Corrective Prompt:

VI. Generalization/Maintenance Procedure:
     Stimulus Factors: Response Factors: Mastery Monitoring

VII. Data Collection System/Form:
     Continuous: Periodic (#/timeperiod):
     Minimum Data Collection Frequency: Initial Frequency:
     Final Frequency:

VIII. Special Comments:

quire the use of very powerful reinforcers before more socially mediated reinforcers gain effectiveness. The PTP also guides the teacher to review the differences between consequences that may be related to the completion of a task (i.e., the whole-task reinforcer) as opposed to the type of reinforcement that may be motivationally useful while the task is being performed (i.e., the within-task reinforcer). For example, a child may receive within-task rewards such as praise and pats on the back (or even a small snack) while tying his or her shoe and then receive the whole-task reward of going outside to play after his or her shoe is put on. The long-term goal would be to reduce all within-task rewards and have the natural consequence at the completion of the activity operate as sufficiently motivating. The point of all artificially added reinforcers is to have them reduced in number or replaced in kind with more

natural rewards over time. However, the removal of such reinforcers should be a planned activity of the teacher, and each point of reduction should be related to student progress.

The issue of generalizaiton is addressed next by the PTP format. Children with severe handicaps, and in particular, autistic children, frequently display difficulty in transferring what has been learned in one situation or with one person to other circumstances. Although such generalization is not impossible, teachers must anticipate the difficulty and incorporate long-term planning into their initial teaching efforts. This type of effective planning is critical if difficulties such as "prompt dependency" are to be avoided.

The PTP section on generalization asks staff to consider two broad categories of concern: stimulus generalization and response generalization. When environmental features, such as staff, classroom, materials, prompts, etc., change, stimulus generalization is being addressed. If response factors, such as duration, magnitude, frequency, etc., are at issue, response generalization is being addressed. Teachers must anticipate changes in each dimension to plan adequately for how a child's performance reasonably can be expected to change over time.

The last section of the PTP deals with issues concerning data collection. Taking data on every aspect of a student's performance is often not practical, feasible, or even useful. The salient point is to be certain that all data collected are used to assist in decision making with regard to the lesson plan. The fundamental question is always, "Should I keep teaching in the current manner or should I change procedures?" Only adequate data can provide support for maintaining an educational strategy in a manner that does not waste the child's or the teacher's time. Minimum guidelines should be selected for data collection, such as collecting data no less than once a week.

Behavior Management Procedures

The program's approach to behavior management parallels the orientation developed for educational objectives. Teachers are encouraged to determine the antecedents and consequences associated with each behavior management target and to thus complete a functional analysis of the target. Next, teachers are to consider teaching the student alternative actions that will serve the same function (i.e., the functionally equivalent alternative response). Furthermore, teachers must consider what specifically will happen following each occurrence of the target. The selection of particular procedures should generally follow the principles of choosing the least restrictive or intrusive procedure. This principle must be balanced by the principle that assures each student to the selection of effective procedures viewed as having a reasonable likelihood of success (Favell et al., 1982).

Within DAP, a unique orientation has been developed regarding behavior

management and its review by professionals and representatives from the community at large. State guidelines designate a Peer Review and Human Rights Committees to act as advisory groups concerning the implementation of behavior management procedures (BMPs; Delaware Administrative Manual, 1991). First, the guidelines define behavior management targets as behaviors that staff aim to decrease in rate, such as self-stimulation, aggression, self-injury, property destruction, and behaviors that may evoke strong community sanctions, such as public disrobing. Next, any procedure that is designed to decrease one of these behaviors is, by definition, a behavior management procedure, and thus must be reviewed by the two oversight committees. Staff do not determine if an intrusive or aversive component exists within the BMP. Rather, the two committees have the responsibility of making such evaluative recommendations.

Behavior Management Procedure Cover Sheet

Staff in DAP use a behavior management procedure (BMP) cover sheet in a manner similar to the PTP cover sheet (see Figure 2). It is organized to have teachers answer fundamental questions that guide the development of a complete plan to deal with behavior management targets. The first section of the BMP cover sheet addresses the description of the target in terms of topography and function. Other factors reviewed include prior attempts to reduce the target, significant people, places, and/or events associated with the presence and absence of the target, and long-term expectations for acceptable levels of the target.

The second section of this cover sheet deals with factors necessary to develop a replacement repertoire for the target response. The goal is to develop a new behavior or to enhance an existing behavior that, from the student's perspective, is functionally equivalent to the target and yet is socially acceptable. Thus, a student who runs around the classroom a great deal needs to be provided with an

FIGURE 2
Behavior Management Procedure Cover Sheet

I. Assessment and Background:
        Student: Teacher: Psychologist Init:
        Behavior Management Target   SLP Initials:
      Pre-Intervention or current level: Current date:
        Target level: Review Date(s):
      Prior Less Restrictive/Intrusive Procedure(s):

        a) Effectiveness and Limitations:
      FUNCTIONAL ANALYSIS:
        Antecedents and setting events:
        Behavior (patterns?):
        Functionally relevant consequences:
      Note: When and where does the BMT rarely occur?:
        Potential negative impact of BMT:

II. Positive/Educational Component
      A. 1. Proposed alternative (appropriate) response (AR) to BMT:
         1a. Function of AR:
         2.   Method of training AR:
         3.   Data collection system for AR:
            Pre-intervention/current level of AR: Target level:
      B. Accompanying reinforcement based procedure (DR__)
         1. Specify DR__ procedure:
           & other/incompatible/low rate behavior to be noted:
         2. DR__ interval   Initial:_____   Target:_____   Step size:_____
            Comments:
         3. Signaling device:
         4. Whole interval:_____ or Restart:_____
            Reinforcer Freeze: Statement after BMT or unsuccessful interval:
         5. Times of day and/or situations:
         6. Reinforcer(s):
         7. Frequency of Data collection and Review:

III. Behavior Management Procedure:
      H/PRC Review Status: A   AB   B   BC   C   (circle one)
      Potential Negative Side Effects:
      Parameter detail:
        Backup Procedure:
      Reinforcement System Changes:
      Special compliance prompting requirements:
        Special staffing requirements:
      Data Collection system: Minimum data requirement: Review:

IV. Progress Review   Date:_____ Initials: ___ ___ ___ ___ NEXT Review:
      BMT Goal Level:_____   AR Goal Level:_____
        Met:_____   Not Met:_____   Met:_____   Not Met:_____
        1. Monitor Only:_____
        2. Maintain Procedure:_____
        3. Within Acceptable Range:_____
        4. Select New Success Level:_____
          a. Same procedure:_____
          b. Modify procedure:_____
          c. New procedure:_____
        5. Drop Procedure:_____

alternative way to obtain whatever rein-forces running around, and should not be simply rewarded for staying in a seat. Obviously, a teacher would want the student to remain where he or she can best learn educational objectives but functionality is here determined from the student's, rather than the teacher's, per-spective. The input from a speech/ language pathologist, trained in behavior analysis, is often extremely important to ascertain the functional communicative impact of the student's behavior manage-ment target. This section of the BMP cover sheet also addresses the specifica-tion of alternative reinforcement proce-dures, indicating the type of differential reinforcement (DR__) procedure in place [e.g., DRO (Other), DRL (Low), DRA (Alternative), etc.]. These systems serve as a way to secure a minimum rate of reward for each student (Foxx, 1982b).

In the third section, emphasis is placed upon factors associated with the particular reaction by staff following a student's behavior management target. This section must be completed even if the overall plan is to use a DRO-based procedure and ignore specific occur-rences of the target. This section of the cover sheet also notes the level of review determined by the Peer Review and Human Rights Committees. Another as-pect of this portion of the cover sheet concerns back-up plans in the event that the student strenuously resists the imple-mentation of the primary procedure. Back-up plans may simply be another procedure or may involve requesting additional staff for assistance. Back-up plans may also be required when environ-mental factors preclude the use or accept-ability of a procedure. Each particular behavior management procedure has its own description, and the pertinent para-metric details must be provided in this section. For example, the length of a time-out procedure or the number of repetitions of a contingent exercise proce-dure are to be indicated in this section. Finally, this section requires staff to indicate how frequently they will collect data and how often progress will be reviewed.

The fourth section of the BMP cover sheet is used when progress is reviewed. Areas are available to indicate the current rate of the target and to indicate whether the procedure will be continued, modi-fied, changed, or dropped. This section also requires staff to review the data base regarding the alternative response (AR) and to review whether adequate progress in the development of the AR has been achieved.

EXTENDING THE CORE PROGRAM BEYOND THE SCHOOL SETTING

The aspects of DAP that have been described thus far are limited to develop-ment and implementation within the school setting. However, as indicated in the section regarding domains, a primary emphasis of education with students displaying severe disabilities is to bring the students into the real world, the world beyond the confines of the class-room and the school. All students, even the preschool children, within DAP have a community-based domain as part of their IEPs (Squittiere, 1990; Squittiere & Bondy, 1988). As students get older, both the number of community sites that they are expected to reasonably negotiate and the level of skill taught within a site increase. For example, very young chil-dren would be expected to learn to accompany adults while shopping in a supermarket; but as they get older, they would be taught to select foods and make direct purchases. In another situation, students in the middle-school years would be taught to accompany adults using public transportation but older students would be taught to use such systems independently as is safe and/or appropriate.

A major long-term goal of education is to adequately prepare students to join the work force. For too long a time, severely handicapped adults have been limited to large, often segregated and isolated, workshops as their only voca-tional option. During the past decade, a shift has emerged to introduce handi-capped students and adults into direct community-based employment with strong job support (Smith & Juhrs, 1985; Wehman, Kregel, & Barcus, 1985). Supported employment practices are started within DAP long before the students leave the program. Community-based objectives, begun while students are young teenagers, are designed to expose students to the types of situations they are likely to encounter in the future when they are working in the community. By introducing these objectives when the students are still young, and must go to a work site to begin specific training in vocational skills, they will not have to learn a different set of auxiliary or ancillary skills. Furthermore, by introducing students into the community before they learn work skills, reasonable procedures to deal with any behavior management targets will have had time to be developed, reviewed, and made more effective. Staff must be aware that certain classroom-based behavior management procedures may not be practical in community settings, either because of physical limitations or societal acceptability.

Guidelines for supported employment call for direct training of vocational skills at real job locations. Staff working with students functioning as job coaches need to know both how to teach the student and the requirements of the employer. Within DAP, teachers, specialists (including speech/language pathologists), and paraprofessionals all may serve as job coaches for a student during the early phases of skill acquisition. As the student approaches graduation, specific paraprofessionals whose primary function is job coaching, as opposed to classroom teaching, work with students in community settings.

All community training, whether vocational or otherwise, require staff to view the community as an extended classroom (Squittiere, 1990). All of the primary components noted earlier, including detailed lesson plans, powerful reinforcement procedures, and specified behavior managment plans, must be implemented in all community settings. Field trips that are oriented toward one-time exposure of students to a particular happening are not encouraged. If a community outing is

worthy of consideration, then a plan to teach specific skills is worthy of development for each student along with a corresponding plan to evaluate the student's progress on these skills.

Another unique aspect of the DAP regards its direct operation of a residential program (Bondy & McNelis, 1990). The program manages two community-based group homes with residential staff. Students may become part of the residential program if their IEP team determines a clear educational need for 24-hour-a-day programming. Such needs may be in terms of significant domestic skills deficits that preclude progress via a school program or home-based training, or significant behavior management targets wherein the absence of 24-hour-a-day programming prevents reasonable progress and interferes with educational progress. All of the guidelines described for classroom and community training are incorporated into the residential program. The long-term goal of the residential program is to increase students' time with their families, with the hoped for result being complete reintegration of the students into their own homes.

The remainder of this chapter describes how the fundamental aspects of DAP's educational orientation are conveyed to parents, introduced into a student's home, and implemented with family members.

SPECIFIC STRATEGIES FOR WORKING WITH PARENTS
General Orientation

Salient issues supporting a broad-based effort to serve the autistic population include child skill acquisition and family functioning (Bristol, 1980, 1985; Harris, 1982; Morgan, 1988; Strain, 1987). Teaching these children begins with the IEP process. An IEP is designed to help a student acquire effective skills that will impact upon increased independent functioning in the home and community (Sailor & Guess, 1983; Wehman, Kregel, & Barcus, 1985). Although most children learn about the real world in a classroom, autistic children are notoriously poor in generalizing skills from one environment to another. Learning via the traditional imitation process has been demonstrated to have relatively limited effectiveness with severely impaired populations (Brown, Nietupski, & Hamre-Nietupski, 1976). These children require direct teaching methodologies applied within relevant environments. The expansion of school services into the community and home necessitates interweaving several domains, including domestic, recreation/ leisure, and vocational concerns. To limit or isolate intervention to any single domain would seriously compromise the probability of maximizing long-term functioning. For example, skills acquired at home and school may influence fast-food (community) skills which may in turn relate to vocational adjustment (Mc-Carthy, Fender, & Fender, 1988; Smith & Juhrs, 1985). The focus in training across domains or environments is placed not only on specific skill development, but on communication and behavior management concerns as well. This multifaceted emphasis requires consistency of those with whom the child has direct contact in school and at home.

A second issue relative to a concerted school-family effort concerns family participation. Family participation in community-based activities is enhanced by the development of concurrent reduction/ elimination of problematic behaviors. This participation also has long-term impact as community-based experiences and exposure have been demonstrated to correlate highly with success in vocational activities. Families of autistic students are often under conditions of chronic stress and typically become more focused on short-term (survival) activities than long-term outcomes. In highly stressed families, parenting activities are initially focused on basic care needs and child safety issues. As the child grows older, parental activities shift to a focus on self-help issues and the disruptions related to behavior issues (e.g., affecting mealtime, family outings, recreation, va-cations, etc.). As the child grows into puberty, the community (and often the extended family) becomes less tolerant of behavior disruption and self-stimulating activities such as masturbation (Bristol, 1984; Bristol & Schopler, 1983; DeMeyer & Goldberg, 1983).

All of these factors can result in a family becoming "hostage" to an emerging pattern of avoidance of family trips into the community. Other stress-generating issues identified by various investigations (Agosta, Bass, & Spence, 1986; Cohen, Agosta, Cohen, & Warren, 1989; Morris, 1987) include limited family resources, concern for financial responsibilities, the lack of adequate professional services (educational, medical, and support services), and neglect of personal needs (affective and medical) on the part of the parents. The active participation of the family, preferably early in the autistic child's life, is a critical component in training, not only for the functioning of the child, but for the family system as well. The earlier the intervention, the more likely a number of the stress-related variables can be moderated or reduced in impact (Bristol, 1984; Bristol & Schopler, 1983; DeMeyer, 1978; Marcus, 1984).

There are a variety of issues pertaining to siblings that also influence the range of family participation in community activities. These can include (a) competition for parental attention, (b) dual discipline standards, (c) ambivalent feelings toward the handicapped sibling, (d) confusion and misinformation about the handicapping condition itself, and (e) at older ages, embarrassment in public settings (National Information Center for Children and Youth with Handicaps, 1988). Although there are no formal strategies for dealing with siblings, staff have worked with siblings within the family context or, at times, within separate groups identified just for siblings.

Relationship of Behavior Management, Communication, and Skill Development

In order to effect change within the family, a process is necessary to review the relationship of behavior management, communication, and skill development within the context of the family (see

Helm & Kozloff, 1986). The staff team begins the process of joining with the family on the first day of program contact with the child and family. The parents are encouraged to describe various aspects of the child's functioning in the home and community settings. A list of priorities is gradually established and the availability of staff to address home-based issues is made known. More often than not, the initially stated concerns of parents during the intake process focus on various aspects of problem behavior. Frequently, these are the concerns that lead to a referral, and have been the source of extended frustration in the home and other environments. Cases in which the child is somewhat older usually include some parental concern relative to communication patterns or deficits.

The parents (or in many instances one parent) have typically invested significant energy in attempting to evoke changes in the child's behavior, but may have, in fact, experienced repeated negative outcomes. Reports of "having been through six baby-sitters in the past three months" are not uncommon, nor are concerns relative to conflict with the extended family as a result of behavioral incidents or management. As the pattern of behavioral dysfunction increases, the family gradually becomes more limited in its activities in general, particularly as a family unit and/or marital dyad. Parental comments indicative of such problems include, "We haven't had a vacation since he was born," "One of us does the shopping while the other watches him," "Recreation? I don't have the time or energy, and besides who would babysit?" "We haven't been out together on a date for five years," etc. (see Wolf, Noh, Fisman, & Speechly, 1989).

Concurrent with such comments are descriptions of efforts to manage the child by way of any number of trial and error methods, most focusing exclusively on eliminating a behavior problem. Some parental observations are quite astute: "If he's quiet, we don't bother him, because he will just start shrieking." Rarely, if ever, is the link between the function of the behavior and the possibility of devel-

oping an alternative response considered by the untrained parent. This orientation typically can provide the opportunity for a relatively rapid development of credibility and entry into the family system on the part of staff when an effective intervention (also described as relief, hope, or both) is developed.

Consider, for example, a 3-year-old who on referral frequently exhibits extended tantrum behavior and uses no recognizable communicative speech (see Bebco, Konstantareas, & Springer, 1987). After the function of the behavior is systematically identified, an alternative communicative response (frequently in such cases a picture exchange communication system) is identified and trained concurrently with the implementation of a behavior management procedure (e.g.. sit-out time-out) as a consequence of the behavior target. The parent then observes the child interact with staff, typically first in the school setting, noting the reduction in tantrum as well as the often surprising exchange of a picture-card for an edible or other reinforcer. To the parent's surprise this exchange is even initiated by the child. The parent observes that specific skills are developed by linking a behavior or behavioral sequence to a rewarding outcome for the child. The key to this intervention package is the simultaneous integration of functional communication and skill development with effective and practical behavior management efforts. Borrowing from fishing lingo, the hook has been set, as the parent is typically most interested in how this change has happened. First by demonstration, then by information, training, and finally implementation rewarded by success, the parents and staff evolve into a team.

Domain Issues

The domain-based approach provides a framework in which the various efforts of home and school can be coordinated in a direct, problem-solving manner. It allows for the possibility of variability in priorities of focus and behavior functions in addressing a given individual's needs.

Although communication and behavior management issues are addressed across all domains, the specific application of these issues may be different from situation to situation. For example, a given disruptive behavior in the school setting, under a demand condition, may serve an escape function, while at home, especially in the late hours of the night, the same behavior may serve an entirely different function, such as attention seeking. An important skill in one setting may be of much lesser significance in another setting, such as for recognizing men's versus ladies' rooms in the community or vocational settings as opposed to toileting in the home. (A bathroom is not always a bathroom!) Certainly, although these distinctions may initially seem trivial, they become highly significant in the development of specific interventions as well as long-term objectives and sequencing.

Another frequently mentioned family difficulty is accomplishing community-based goals such as banking or shopping. Consider the parent who identifies a problem with his child while attempting to negotiate the local grocery market. The parent describes a series of attempts to complete shopping for necessities, but has given up on the idea of having the child accompany him, with the exception of "no-choice" situations. These trips are often viewed as traumatic because of some specific, probably repeated behavior sequence. As a result of repeated episodes, it has been deemed to be "easier" to arrange shopping trips without the child's company; thus the problem behavior is avoided, although not resolved, and may arise again in the next "no-choice" situation. A domain-and-setting-specific approach affords the opportunity for the staff to facilitate the parent's as well as the child's ability to negotiate the shopping environments comfortably. The school staff teach the child how to go shopping and then parents can maintain this skill. Parents begin by taking their child shopping when they do not really need to do shopping and can instead focus upon maintaining the child's new skills. One might think of this approach as something akin to a fire drill.

A significant aspect of the "chronic stress" issue can be diminished by this domain-based approach. Idiosyncratic routines that occur in the home, and are manifested as a component of a domestic activity, require direct intervention. The parental report of sleeping hours interrupted by a disruptive episode or an attempt or actual sojourn out of the house by the child provide other, more dramatic examples. Such problems may only be resolved when staff work with the family at the time of the difficulty. In this case, staff have shown up to work with the child in the middle of the night until parents can maintain the changes introduced.

DIRECT TRAINING OF PARENTS AND FAMILIES

Just as it is important to facilitate staff awareness of the interrelationships of communication and skill deficits, behavior functions and alternatives, and adequate reinforcement schedules, so too is it necessary to develop this perspective with parents. After all, children spend considerably more time with their family than they spend with staff.

In addition to the incidental and situation-specific exchanges that occur between staff and parents, a systematic and multifaceted parent program focusing on the development of a coordinated home and school team is offered. Three general components—education, training, and support—are included with respect to this effort. Each part is developed by way of group and individualized formats, both formally and informally. Various aspects of the program are associated with each of these components, and in reality, all three are addressed to some degree, simultaneously. Obviously, the educational and training components are better defined by way of their respective content. In addition to those efforts specifically targeted as supportive or stress reducing, the training process itself contributes to the support function.

Group Format

Groups of parents meet with staff at the school. Typically meetings are conducted on week nights, twice a month. Scheduling of sessions is developed by the parents at the beginning of the school year during a meeting specifically devoted to explanation and organization of the program. Sessions are led by the school psychologist, but include other staff (teacher and assistants, speech/language pathologist, OT, etc.). Guest speakers may be invited at times, contingent on the topic of the meeting.

Educational Component

The educational component is intended to provide the parents with an accurate information base on which their own "self-help" skills can be built. Although the on-going interaction with staff results in a natural, informal exposure, parents are invited to participate in group sessions that include discussion on basic behavior principles as well as behavior management techniques. A review of issues related to communication and functional analysis is emphasized prior to any discussion of consequence procedures, the latter in the context of a least-intrusive model (Foxx, 1982a). Examples drawn from the parents' experiences with their children are used to illuminate specific issues.

In addition to discussing behavioral principles, information related to autism is reviewed. A review of the general syndrome, its variations and similarities to other developmental disabilities, and its behavioral and physiological manifestations is presented. Discussion of such questions as what is and is not known about etiology and prognosis, what services are available to adult autistics, and legal issues is included. Guest speakers (e.g., Special Olympics coordinator, pediatrician, etc.) are also invited to present to the group on related topics. Throughout these discussions, staff and guests are encouraged to minimize technical terminology to avoid increasing the "distance" between staff and parents.

Training Component

The training component is intended to provide parents with hands-on demonstrations of various methods employed by the program relative to their child. It affords the opportunity for development of a consistent approach across settings while at the same time providing parents with an effective means of addressing troublesome behaviors, and communication and skill development issues.

Video tapes starring the child of one family are shown to demonstrate use of a particular procedure. These vignettes include the use of time-out procedures in response to tantrum behavior, and shaping procedures developing the approach to a swimming pool, or the tolerance of the presence of a large dog.

Informal group tours of classrooms during nonschool hours include review and discussion of classroom posted BMPs and task analyses. This review serves to strengthen several issues. First, staff stress that interventions can be systematically planned, described, and implemented. Second, the interrelationship of behavior targets, functional alternatives, reinforcement schedules, and general communication systems is re-emphasized. Third, a no-lose outcome occurs in that if the frequency of a problem behavior for a student is lower in the school an attribution of procedural effort occurs. If the rate is similar or lower at home, the importance of establishing behavioral priorities is demonstrated. Fourth, if the procedure is currently being applied at home by the parents, their use of the procedure is praised. Finally, the point that the child's behavior is directly affected by that of those in his/her surroundings is illuminated.

Group review of the various forms of communication systems is offered in concert with the respective case-specific discussions. The rationale and sequence of the development of a primary or augmentative communication system is presented. Discussion of picture exchange systems from basic to more sophisticated applications is included. Applications across domains are highlighted, and the importance of home-based implementation is stressed in the context of behavioral as well as skill-related impact.

The development and utilization of task analyses is included for several reasons. First of all, understanding of this technique involves acceptance of changing small behavioral steps along the path to progress. The use of the task analysis by parents promotes a consistent approach to teaching basic skills. Finally, the use of task analyses by parents facilitates the generalization of skill development (and IEP efforts) across settings and domains.

The ability of students to follow a schedule ultimately becomes critical with respect to their long-term independent functioning. Upon mastery of a given task analysis, the entire behavioral sequence can be reduced to a single descriptor such as "brush teeth." A schedule of activities is actually a collection of reduced task analyses and becomes increasingly useful as the number of activities across domains and settings are expanded.

Support Component

The support component is intended to reduce the impact of various stressors. A support group evolves as a function of the education and training activities. Although each session is structured with respect to topic, time is allocated to open discussion of experiences in the context of the respective topics. The group includes parents with a wide range of years of experience with an autistic child as well as representing significant variability with respect to functioning levels of their children. This mixture usually results in exchanges and comparisons of experiences. Open discussion of tough issues is common, as are suggestions regarding potential successful resolutions. The parent who has had the grocery store experience is exceptionally eager to hear of other parents who have "been there." The parent who has just entered the program is encouraged to recognize the long-term payoff for short-term efforts, even when the desired outcome seems out of reach. Community-based teaming,

in which families of two or more students meet for a specific outing (both with and without staff) has also materialized.

Individual (Family-Focused) Format

In addition to a standing invitation to visit the classroom, a variety of contacts is offered to each family. These contacts serve to bolster each of the respective issues of education, training, and support. Each contact is direct and leads to a focus on one or more aspects of the IEP.

Parents learn about their child's daily school performance via an informal notebook. Parents are encouraged to write in the same notebook on a daily basis. Staff typically attempt to provide a brief report of some positive aspect of the child's day. These notes serve to reinforce parent expectations that their child can, for example, use a picture communication system to express wants and/or needs in a specific situation (i.e., during mealtime). The notebook allows for a regular exchange regarding behavior management issues, and gives staff an opportunity to reinforce reported parental efforts on the home front. This format results in encouragement of staff efforts by indicating parental attempts to implement a technique (e.g., picture exchange). The home-school notebook also allows for direct and regular exchange of questions or concerns relative to various issues (e.g., questions about the presence or absence of a behavior; medical issues), or sharing reminders about the availability of resources (e.g., suggesting a community trip with staff, respite services, etc.).

Home visits are attempted as a matter of standard procedure, though the frequency may vary significantly, contingent on the openness of the family in question. A staff-team home visit typically involves the teacher, the speech/language pathologist, and the school psychologist, in various combinations, depending on the specific issues to be addressed. The purpose of these visits can be as broad as the scope of the IEP, and may follow a request by either the staff or parents. Implementation of communication systems, behavior management procedures, demonstration of the application of the steps of a task analysis, the development of a home-based activities schedule for evening or weekends, or response to a crisis situation are among the most frequent issues included. As the family and staff work directly in such problem-solving efforts, the team concept is strengthened, and the likelihood of additional contacts is increased. This contact often will facilitate the extension of the team efforts into community settings. The parents are now ready to return to the grocery store!

Respite Services

Respite services are offered to all parents by way of a co-payment, sliding scale funding arrangement and are available on a 24-hour, year-round basis. (The state provides 75% to 95% of the financial support.) Respite services are provided by the program staff, and in addition to providing the parents with a valuable resource, also afford the staff the opportunity to assess (and possibly intervene with) the child in new environments. Respite is provided in various settings including the home of the child, the home of the staff, and at times, by the residential group homes. The type of respite is determined on a case-by-case basis. Group-home respite is generally reserved for emergency situations.

Respite services are frequently a valuable backup to informal family-systems interventions. Respite provides the parent with the assurance that their child is being monitored by trained and competent staff, familiar with the specific needs of the child. This assurance may be crucial for parents, including those who, as quoted, no longer "date." Families often are amenable to in-home respite services, suggesting they do not experience the staff as intrusive. Respite may permit staff and parents to interact at the home thus strengthening important ties between the child's various contexts. Respite also may provide relief to certain stressors within family subsystems. This reduction may take the focus off the

child, thus decentralizing the child to some extent.

Community Resources

A variety of community-based agencies and providers including DAP form an integrated network of services to the autistic population. Assessment efforts, varying in degrees of procedural formality have been expanded via several avenues statewide, all of whom funnel referrals to the respective DAP centers. In addition to assessment, this network lends itself to coordinated intervention efforts as it includes a comprehensive medical and developmental medical center with satellite clinics in each county. The network also includes a statewide program for early identification and intervention for handicapped infants and toddlers, the early childhood screening programs of local school districts, various private medical and psychological practitioners, and DAP itself. Once a child has entered the system by any one of these referral points, access to other elements of the services network is enhanced. The services provided by particular elements of this network remain available and are usually well coordinated while the student remains within DAP.

A parent information center, located in the northern, more densely populated area of the state, operates throughout the state. The center's primary function is to disseminate crucial information to the parents. Activities engaged to achieve this function include providing parents with regular updates relative to the rights of the handicapped, access to services, various support groups, transition services, handicap-specific literature, and advocacy.

The transition process is viewed as a long-term endeavor requiring a coordinated effort across domains and among service providers. Planning in this area includes access to community-based residential programming and social/medical services as well as vocational issues. The school team coordinates a long-term effort to develop and maintain open lines of communication with the respective state agencies addressing adult-oriented issues (e.g., Division of Mental Retardation, Division of Vocational Rehabilitation, Post-21 Program, etc.). With respect to adult services, it is not unusual to initiate referral, planning, or at least a contact, 2 to 3 years in advance of graduating from the school system.

Unfortunately, some children reside in homes in which there are other problems that significantly impact upon family functioning. In such cases, referral and consultation with state child protective services may be necessary. Efforts relative to the coordination of behavior management plans, utilization of available resources, and crisis procedures (including temporary placement) become of the utmost importance in these situations.

CASE EXAMPLES

The following case examples illustrate various aspects of the home-school effort as described above. Each will describe an application of a particular component.

Peter: At the time of home-based intervention this student was 14 years old and had been with the program for several years. He presented as frail and fragile, and displayed relatively mild behavior management targets and very few adaptive skills across domains. His language functioning was significantly limited. He had come to DAP after being identified and after several years in another school as a student of trainable mentally handicapped status. Numerous attempts to engage the parents in various training activities finally paid off. They attended a parent training session, and after hearing other parents of 16–18-years-olds discuss the positive long-term impact of the program in the context of their concerns, they agreed to a home visit. Subsequently (and many training sessions and home visits later) a gradual shift in responsibilities for personal hygiene and domestic tasks occurred as a function of direct training (of the parents and the student, respectively). An increase in community exposure followed. Three years later, the student is now

placed at the district high school, enrolled in a computer skills class. His work resume includes work in a local restaurant, computer operation, operating the check sorting unit of a bank, and data-based entry for several employers including the school district.

Paul: He came to the program at the age of 31 months. At the time of placement he presented significant tantrum behavior, exhibited no verbal communication skills, and basically held the family hostage according to the parents' description. Paul's tantrum behaviors had resulted in reducing the social supports available to the family and had negatively impacted their marriage. These parents were the source of the previously mentioned comment regarding leaving the child alone if he was quiet. After six months in the program, during which time a picture communication capability was trained and faded as speech emerged, and after several home visits focused on behavior management, Paul is now using verbal communication as his primary means of communication. Tantrum behaviors are at a minimum. The parents report being more focused on raising both of the children rather than just the handicapped child, and attention to their marriage relationship is improved. Respite services are utilized regularly to afford social and other outings.

Marie: At the time of placement at age 3, Marie presented with significant language delay and an array of mild to moderate behavior management concerns. Although not classically autistic, consensus was to serve her via the program. The picture communication system and behavior management procedures were used in conjunction with skill development across domains, and a continued slow but steady progress was documented. Now age 6, she is served via a program specifically addressing language-impaired individuals and has been mainstreamed (previous and current school years) on a part-time basis. She is no longer classified as autistic, a "false-positive" in retrospect, but given the "needs" versus "labels" approach of the program, a success story nonetheless.

Josef: Identified for placement at the age of 2.5, Josef was not placed for services until 6 months later as a result of transience issues. He presented as a classically socially avoidant youngster who by all observations used zero verbal communication but by mother's report would in fact clearly articulate words in isolated incidents at home (selectively mute). Placement and programming with the picture communication techniques as well as a consistent behavior management program led to a relatively rapid development of expressive language. Triennial reevaluation last year (age 5) as language functioning emerged, revealed highly superior cognitive ability on tasks tapping simultaneous processing ability. Previous attempts at formal evaluations by several examiners had resulted in significant behavioral resistance and invalidated testing procedures. Now, at the age of 6, he is mainstreamed for reading and language groups as well as social and nonacademic activities, and will probably be declassified within the next year or two.

Henry: Identified for placement at the age of 3.5, Henry came to the program presenting with a variety of significant behavior management concerns (self-injurious behaviors, aggression, etc.) as well as minimal receptive and no expressive language in his repertoire. He demonstrated a strong capability for utilizing visually perceived information and responded quite favorably to the picture-based communication system developed for him. As he expanded his picture vocabulary (beyond the 250-picture range), printed words were added to the respective picture cards. The pictures were then faded and to date (now age 8.5) he has an expanded reading capability (2500+, and with a decoding ability) which has led to printed (vs. pictured) schedules of activities for the day, a reinforcement menu that is composed of sentences (vs. pictures), and an expressive capability that includes emotive statements and questions, all of which are used as augmentative to speech rather than in place of speech. The gradual and continued reduction in behavior management targets afforded part-time main-

streaming, commencing last school year. He also continues to expand his community activities as well as independent movement through the school complex. Schedules and a reinforcement menu are also part of his routine in the home setting on a daily basis. His parents depart for their respective employment setting approximately 1.5 hours before the arrival of his bus, leaving him in the charge of his 16-year-old sister. Henry typically completes a 12-task sequence, including personal hygiene, several domestic tasks, food preparation and clean-up, and leisure activity each morning. The printed schedule, with checkoffs entered by Henry and validated by his sister, is reviewed at school by his teacher, and reinforced on the basis of success.

Susan: Susan had been a student in the program for several months when her parents agreed to a home visit and interview. They described significant behavior management problems including aggressive and destructive behaviors, and went on to describe their most-effective control as including a belt. Additional probing revealed that there were apparently limited if any positive contingency arrangements in place. The staff then invested several additional visits to teach the parents the strategy of "let's make a deal." Involving on-site practice and training as well as the initial demonstrations. Parents were taught to find out what she wanted before telling her to do simple chores around the house. The belt has been put away.

Pat: At the time of the parent complaint, Pat was a 14-year-old who had been a student of the program for several years. Her mother reported that after about 2 weeks, she could no longer tolerate the nightly tantrums and disruption of the household sleep time. She went on to describe the tantrums as part of a sequence in which Pat would come into her mother's bedroom, stand by the bed, and demand that mother prepare her some oatmeal. Mother's attempts to lock her out and to ignore her resulted in extended tantrum behavior, and it became easier to just give her the oatmeal. Several staff (teacher, assistant, psychologist) visited the home for an on-site observation, anticipating the then nightly episode. The resulting management plan identified Pat coming out of her bedroom as the BMT, to be consequated via full prompt back into the room followed by a contingent work sequence. An assistant from the residential program staff was recruited to work with the family through the night for a period of less than 2 weeks, during which time mother assumed control of keeping Pat in her room. Pat was rewarded for staying in her room through the night by access to oatmeal first thing in the morning.

Andy: Andy at age 7 years presented as an obese lad with a variety of significant behavior management targets. He used a picture exchange system as his primary means of "formal" communication and had been a student with the program for about 4 years. Parent follow-up with behavior management procedures as well as the use of the picture exchange system at home had been suspect. His mother reported that she was having major difficulty negotiating community business in general, and particularly the grocery store. Andy would dart away from her unless held, as had been the practice for years, but size and evolving aggressive acts (hitting, biting) were interfering with her ability to control him. Staff had experienced very different (positive) trips to the community and offered to meet the parent and child in the community to address this problem. After observing the behaviors as accurately described by the parent, the staff developed a simple DRO schedule (initially F1:1) which was implemented by the staff and then taught and transferred to the mother's control. Andy now shops with mom not holding his hand, and has been doing so for about a year. The DRO is also doing fine as at last check it was up to V1:5.

CLOSING COMMENTS

We have described how staff from one program for children with severe developmental disabilities work with students and their families to design and implement an effective education. The key points established within the school context are associated with the (a) selection of functional activities, (b) development of individually sensitive, powerful reinforcement systems, (c) development of rapidly acquired functional communication systems, and (d) the design of behavior management procedures that aim to develop functionally equivalent alternative reactions. None of these factors can be properly developed in isolation from other factors and, in fact, behavior management interventions can be effectively implemented only if the other components are competently developed. Effective work with families relies upon the structure that the school program has established for individual students. The same set of factors designed for the school must be designed and refined for the home setting. Families must be able to promote reasonable activities, provide effective rewards, use effective communication systems, and consistently respond to behavior management concerns. In addition to these factors, a systems analysis regarding the impact that the identified child has upon individual family members, and the marital dyad, must also be considered by school staff. Adequate support may come from information, shared contact with other families, in-home support by staff, respite relief, either in-home or out-of-home, or community resources initiated by school contact.

The combination of providing effective in-school programming and effective family support by school personnel is a necessary coalition in order for children with severe developmental disabilities, including autism, to benefit fully from their educational experience.

REFERENCES

Agosta, J. M., Bass, A., & Spence, R. (1986). *The needs of families: Results of statewide survey in Massachusetts.* Cambridge, MA: Human Services Institute.

Bebco, J. M., Konstantareas, M. M., & Springer, J. (1987). Parent and professional evaluations of family stress associated with characteristics of autism. *Journal of Autism and Developmental Disorders, 17*(4), 565–576.

Bondy, A. (1987). Community-based education of autistic students. Paper presented at the Delaware Council for Exceptional Children convention, Dover, DE.

Bondy, A. (1990, May). Error correction: Three novel approaches. Paper presented at the Association for Behavior Analysis convention, Nashville, TN.

Bondy, A., & McNelis, M. (1990, May). Public-school operated group homes for autistic students. Paper presented at the Association for Behavior Analysis convention, Nashville, TN.

Bondy, A., Peterson, S., Tarleton, R., & Frangia, S. (1990, May). Error correction: Summary. Paper presented at the Association for Behavior Analysis convention, Nashville, TN.

Bristol, M. M. (1980). Maternal coping with autistic children: The effects of child characteristics and interpersonal support (Doctoral dissertation, UNC at Chapel Hill, 1979). *Dissertation Abstracts International, 40,* 3943A-3944A.

Bristol, M. M. (1985). Designing programs for young developmentally disabled children: A family systems approach to autism. *Remedial and Special education, 4*(6), 46–53.

Bristol, M. M., & Schopler, E. (1983). Coping and stress in families of autistic adolescents. In E. Schopler & G. B. Mesibov (Eds.), *Autism in adolescents and adults* (pp. 251–279). New York: Plenum Press.

Brown, L., Nietupski, J., & Hamre-Nietupski, S. (1976). The criterion of ultimate functioning and public school services for severely handicapped students. In M. A. Thomas (Ed.), *Hey, don't forget about me: Education's investment in the severely, profoundly, and multiply handicapped* (pp. 2–15). Reston, VA: Council for Exceptional Children.

Cohen, S., Agosta, J., Cohen, J., & Warren, R. (1989). Supporting families of children with severe disabilities. *Journal of the Association of Persons with Severe Handicaps, 14*(2), 155–162.

Delaware Administrative Manual: Programs for Exceptional Children (1991). Dover, DE: State Department of Education.

Delaware Autistic Program Staff Manual. (1991). Newark, DE: Author.

DeMeyer, M. K. (1978). *Parents and children in autism.* New York: Wiley.

DeMeyer, M. K., & Goldberg, P. (1983). Family needs of the autistic adolescent. In E. Schopler & G. B. Mesibov (Eds.), *Autism in adolescents and adults* (pp. 225–250). New York: Plenum Press.

Favell, J., Azrin, N., Baumeister, A., Carr, E., Dorsey, M., Forehand, R., Foxx, R., Lovass, O., Rincover, A., Risley, T., Romanczyk, R., Russo, D., Schroeder, S., & Solnick, J. (1982). The treatment of self-injurious behavior. *Behavior Therapy, 13,* 529–554.

Foxx, R. M. (1982a). *Decreasing behaviors of severely retarded and autistic persons.* Champagne, IL: Research Press.

Foxx, R. M. (1982b). *Increasing behaviors of severely retarded and autistic persons.* Champagne, IL: Research Press.

Harris, S. (1982). A family system approach to behavioral training with parents of autistic children. *Child and Family Behavior Therapy, 4*(1), 21–35.

Helm, D. T., & Kozloff, M. A. (1986). Research on PT: Shortcomings and remedies. *Journal of Autism and Developmental Disorders, 16*(1), 1–22.

Marcus, L. M. (1984). Coping with burnout. In E. Schopler & G. B. Mesibov (Eds.), *The effects of autism on the family* (pp. 312–326). New York: Plenum Press.

McCarthy, P., Fender, K. W., & Fender, D. (1988). Supported employment for persons with autism. In P. Wehman & M. S. Moon (Eds.), *Vocational rehabilitation and supported employment* (pp. 269–290). Baltimore: Brooks Co.

Morgan, S. B. (1988). The autistic child and family functioning: A developmental family systems approach. *Journal of Autism and Developmental Disorders, 18*(2), 263–280.

Morris, N. W. (1987). Health care: Who pays the bills? *Exceptional Parent, 17,* 39, 41–42.

National Information Center for Children and Youth with Handicaps. (1988). Children with disabilities: Understanding sibling issues. *News Digest, 11,* 11.

Sailor, W., & Guess, D. (1983). *Severely handicapped students: An instructional design.* Boston: Houghton Mifflin Co.

Scheifer, M. J. (1988). When are we ever going to be able to do something for ourselves? *Exceptional Parent, 18*(6), 102–108.

Smith, M. D., & Juhrs, P. (1985). *Achieving and maintaining community integrated training for persons severely disabled with autism.* Rockville, MD: Community Services for Autistic Adults and Children.

Squittiere, D. (1990, May). *The community is not just a big classroom: The new role for teachers.* Presented at the Association for Behavior Analysis convention, Nashville, TN.

Squittiere, D., & Bondy, A. (1988, May). Autistic students as consumers and providers of community services: Implementing community-based training within a public school system. Paper presented at the Association for Behavior Analysis convention, Philadelphia, PA.

Strain, P. S. (1987, February). Parent training with young autistic children: A report on the LEAP model. *Zero to Three,* 7–12.

Wehman, P., Kregel, J., & Barcus, J. M. (1985). From school to work: A vocational transition model for handicapped students. *Exceptional Children, 52*(1), 25–37.

Wolf, C. L., Noh, S., Fisman, S. N., & Speechly, M. (1989). Psychological effects of parenting stress on parents of autistic children. *Journal of Autism and Developmental Disorders, 19*(1), 157–166.

20

HOME-SCHOOL COLLABORATION FOR CHILDREN FROM SUBSTANCE-ABUSING FAMILIES

Margaret B. Walker

The purpose of this chapter is to discuss approaches to collaborating with families when at least one of the parents has a substance abuse problem. Characteristics of substance-abusing families and the characteristics and roles of the children from such families are also described. The final section of the chapter focuses on recommendations for school personnel who are targeting the involvement of substance-abusing parents in children's school programs.

School personnel discover that parents may be abusing a wide array of substances. Most of the experience reflected in this chapter, however, is based on work with families who are alcoholic. Often the terms "substance abuser" and "alcoholic" will be used interchangeably.

Literature and concern have grown regarding children from substance-abusing homes (e.g., Logan, 1991). Psychological and educational journals reflect an increasing awareness of the situation faced by millions of school-aged children. Because the school is the agency that touches the lives of the majority of young people, school personnel can play a key role in identification, education, and treatment of students from families in which a parent is addicted to alcohol or other drugs. Successful interactions with these families require a mastery of at least two important domains of informa-tion: (a) the effects of drug abuse on children, and (b) the roles that children and other family members play in such a family.

Although literature is cited when appropriate, readers should know the basis for this chapter has been my experiences as a teacher, consultant, and special education administrator in my school district. Issues identified from the work done by me and my colleagues in Nebraska may not be universally relevant to the work of other professionals, but our reading of national programs suggests that our experiences are not unique (Kirk, Chapman, & Sadler, 1990).

BACKGROUND STATISTICS

It is estimated that 7 million school-aged children in the United States are living in families in which substance abuse is a problem (National Clearing-house for Alcohol and Drug Information, 1989). In any elementary school class-room, 4 to 6 students out of every 25 could be children of alcoholics (O'Rourke, 1989). The most recent estimates from the National Council on Alcoholism are that there are between 10 and 20 million alcoholic adults in the U.S. today. Most often the alcoholic parent in the home is the father. In about 20% of the alcoholic homes in the U.S., both parents are alcoholic.

As staggering as these numbers are, the generational impact of having alcoholic parents is even more dismaying. Children of alcoholic parents may be at high risk for substance abuse themselves and for serious psychological problems (Edwards & Zander, 1985). Forty to 60% of these children will become alcoholics and 30% will marry alcoholics.

Family abuse of alcohol is also implicated as a correlate or cause for family violence, incest, and other forms of child abuse (e.g., Gabel & Shindledecker, 1990). Although all statistics bearing on these matters are merely estimates due to the secrecy and denial that permeate substance-abusing families, these estimates suggest that: (a) 55% of all reported family violence occurs in alcoholic homes; (b) incest is twice as likely to occur among daughters of alcoholics than among a similar sample with fathers who do not abuse alcohol; and (c) alcohol is found to be a significant factor in up to 90% of the child abuse cases.

SCHOOL-BASED INTERVENTIONS

Although there are many reports concerning the direct treatment of children from alcoholic homes (e.g., Palmer & Paisley, 1991; Schinke, Botvin, & Orlandi, 1991), there is little literature regarding ways and methods of involving parents in such treatment programs (DeMarsh & Kumpfer, 1985; Grady, Gersick, & Boratynski, 1985). Children have been offered programs that emphasize early identification, education about the effects of alcohol on a wide variety of variables (e.g., health, sexual behavior, school achievement, sports prowess), education about the roles occupied in alcoholic families (e.g., mascot, enabler), and group therapy for children with common family issues to confront. Educational programs have become available in many school districts, although little experimental information is available regarding the effectiveness of these child-centered approaches.

Hecht (1988) asserts:

It remains to devise methods for involving the parents who, as is typical of alcoholics, deny their own problems and its effect on their children. We believe, however, this integrated approach to early identification and intervention with children of alcoholics in a familiar setting such as the school will be helpful in arresting further pathological development. (p. 171)

The program described by Hecht (1988) is aimed at both elementary and middle school students from alcoholic families. It involves a group therapy approach for students that takes place during the school day. Parental approval for the therapy is mandatory, but Hecht obtains the permission "without labeling the problem as being related to alcoholism. Instead, the counselor used the children's school performance as the basis for their inclusion in the group" (p. 170).

The parents' approval is the extent of parental involvement in the program. This approach may be most typical of programs being initiated in schools. The failure to find many examples of successful collaboration is not surprising. Alcoholic parents are seen to be difficult to engage. Because children are at least present in the school building, interventions aimed at helping them clarify their feelings, experiences, and behavioral responses to family stresses are seen as the only available options.

Positive changes in children on an array of variables have been found with youngsters as young as age 5 (O'Rourke, 1989). Although such changes may be possible, the singular focus on children engenders, perhaps, an adversarial relationship between the school and parents and flies in the face of what is known about increasing the power (e.g., generalization) of child interventions.

CHARACTERISTICS OF SUBSTANCE-ABUSING FAMILIES

Family members of an alcoholic spend much of their energies reacting to situations caused by the alcoholic. Ackerman (1983) describes four stages of family response to alcoholism: reactive, active, alternative, and family unity stages.

Stages

Reactive stage. Reactive coping with alcoholism may characterize families for long periods of times or even be the only stage that is apparent in the life of the family. Reactive coping refers to family attempts to minimize the impact of the alcoholic member on the family. The unhealthy or difficult situations caused by the alcoholic member are denied or explained away. Because the behaviors and emotions of the alcoholic are inconsistent (e.g., promises are made when drunk that are later forgotten, extreme attitudes of concern are inexplicably replaced by abuse), the nonalcoholic family members may be observed to emit or experience very labile behaviors and emotions.

This inconsistency or unpredictability is especially difficult for children to interpret because it characterizes not just the drinking member's behavior but also that of the nonalcoholic parent. The nonalcoholic parent may remain in tense states of readiness unable to predict his or her mate's reactions. This tension may render the nonalcoholic parent unable to fulfill his/her parental roles adequately and consistently (Lerner, 1986). Little energy may be left to respond to children's needs. Children may be moved into positions of inappropriate responsibility to take care of younger siblings or household tasks. Some children become the confidantes of the nonalcoholic spouse, and consequently are asked to assume concerns far beyond their emotional or cognitive repertoires.

Denial is the primary coping strategy of family members in the reactive stage. Denial refers to the entire family's refusal to acknowledge the existence of the problem, not only to the outside world but even among themselves. Parents sometimes have good intentions when adopting this charade. They hope to protect their children from negative information. Ackerman (1983) states it is naive to assume that children in alcoholic homes do not experience the effects of alcoholism. They may not understand alcoholism, but they know their family life is painful.

Denial leads to the social disengagement of family members. They withdraw from interaction with others to protect themselves from embarrassment or from situations in which someone might find out about the alcoholic member. This can take the form of physical and/or emotional disengagement. Healthy relationships are denied or postponed indefinitely.

It is during the reactive stage that children learn that what is said in the family and what is done by family members do not match. Messages are distorted. The alcoholic may promise to quit drinking but does not do so. A parent may promise to show up for a school activity and because of drinking forget the activity. Children may learn that adults are not trustworthy. This perception is anxiety producing. It may be this anxiety that motivates the assumption of the roles (discussed in subsequent sections of this chapter) that a number of professionals have ascribed to children of alcoholics.

Active Stage. During the second or active phase (which, unfortunately, many families never reach), the family begins to decenter or disconnect itself from alcoholism (Ackerman, 1983). The denial weakens as family members begin to realize the ineffectiveness of this coping strategy. During this phase, the nonalcoholic family members attempt to pursue normal family activities as much as possible, both inside and outside of the home, in an effort to overcome the negative impacts of alcoholism. This is likely the stage during which children are encouraged to attend self-help groups and family members engage in conversations regarding the impact of the alcoholism on each member. These activities may not have an impact on the drinking behavior of the alcoholic per se, but they tend to create a better climate and healthier context for the nonalcoholic family members.

Alternative and family unity stages. The alternative phase is the one in which the family faces the question of whether or not separation is the only viable alternative to survive alcoholism. The final or the family unit phase comes about with the sobriety of the alcoholic and the acceptance of the sober alcoholic back into the mainstream of the family.

When the alcoholic member is in recovery, the family may develop normalized coping strategies. It is also possible that the alleviation of the drinking does not cause a change in the roles and behaviors adopted during earlier stages. The need for intervention with the family does not disappear with the sobriety of its members.

Varying Effects

Not all alcoholic families nor all members of the same family are affected in the same way by alcoholism. Ackerman (1983) suggests three variables to consider when looking at how people are affected. These are the degree of alcoholism, the type of alcoholic in the home, and the individual perception of potential harm from living with an alcoholic.

The degree of alcoholism refers to the severity of the problem, how often it occurs, and whether or not the alcoholic functions socially or on the job. The type of alcoholic in the family may be one who is belligerent, verbally abusive, and argumentative or one who is jovial while drinking or merely unavailable. Although the jovial alcoholic may not be physically or verbally harmful, the situation is emotionally stressful due to the inappropriateness of the behavior. These are just a few examples of the many types of alcoholics, but it is easy to see that a child growing up with a physically-abusive alcoholic parent may have a very different perspective on alcoholism compared to a child living with a passive or jovial alcoholic. The third variable is perception of the harmfulness of the situation by the nonalcoholic family members. Behavior and emotional reactions toward the alcoholic differ dramatically depending on each family member's assessment of the danger created by the drinking.

Another variable that has been suggested is that of the intactness of family rituals. Rituals refer to predictable patterns in families around eating, celebrating holidays, religious observances, and so on. Researchers reporting a longitudinal study at the George Washington University Center for Family Research have suggested that alcoholic families in which family rituals remain relatively undisturbed produce children who are less likely to become alcoholics themselves. In addition, other aspects of the child's development, for example, cognitive abilities, emotional-psychological functioning, and self-concept, may also be less disturbed by alcoholism in families in which families retain predictable behaviors to mark family events.

CHARACTERISTICS AND ROLES OF CHILDREN IN SUBSTANCE-ABUSING FAMILIES

There is general agreement that parental alcoholism or drug abuse can adversely affect the emotional, cognitive, and social functions of children who are exposed to substance abuse over a long period of time. A number of parental functions seen as essential to a child's healthy growth and development are damaged when one or both parents are substance abusers. These parental functions are role stability, environmental consistency, dependability, and emotional availability (Morehouse & Richards, 1983).

When these parental functions are not met in the home by either parent, children develop behaviors to cope with and compensate for family chaos, inconsistency, and neglect. Although the coping strategies adopted by family members may, in fact, be detrimental to them, they are meant to allow the child (or other family member) to remain in the home, that is, to maintain a homeostasis of sorts. A variety of authors have identified clusters of roles. Three role patterns labeled by Black (1981) are: (a) the responsible one; (b) the adjustor; and (c) the placater. According to Black, these roles may be adopted separately or in combination.

The Responsible One

This is the role most often adopted by an only or eldest child in the family. This child is the one who takes on the responsibility for the structure in the home or for meeting a variety of unmet parental functions. For example, the responsible one makes sure that meals are on the table, that children are in bed on time, or that dad gets to work. It is of some interest that Black (1981) suggests these roles generalize to other aspects of the child's life and continue to affect the children far into adulthood.

At school the responsible child may be an excellent student and a school leader as a result of having learned to plan, organize, and get others to do what is necessary. This person, although goal-oriented on a short-term basis, may be reluctant or unable to make long-term plans or goals. Cruse (1989) suggests the goals and the achievements of the responsible child are not to satisfy his or her own needs but are an attempt to bring normalcy and worth to the family, that is, a way to demonstrate the family is okay.

The responsible child rarely comes to the attention of school personnel as a problem. If problems do appear, they may be in the form of somatic complaints— headaches, allergies, and frequent upset stomachs.

The coping mechanisms of responsible children include both healthy and self-destructive patterns. The healthy patterns take the form of doing well in school, taking responsibility for things that need to be done, and putting others' needs before their own. However, self-destructive patterns that include being unable to recognize or assert their own needs or feelings, particularly feelings of anger and resentment, and an inability to be childlike (in other words, lighthearted or occasionally irresponsible or naughty) may have long-term effects on children's adjustment (Brenner, 1984).

The Adjustor

The adjustors appear to "go with the flow." They simply follow directions and do whatever is called for on a particular day, adapting behaviors and feelings as necessary in the home. Flexibility and detachment characterize their behaviors. At school such children are average, not calling attention to themselves through school work or activities. While associating with other children, adjustors do not assume leadership roles or form close attachments.

Like the responsible child and the placater, the adjustor develops a form of altruism that includes flexibility and subjugation of his or her needs to those of the parents. Although flexibility is a healthy pattern, like the placater and the responsible one, adjustors develop an inability to recognize and assert their own needs and feelings and may have little sense of self-worth or self-confidence.

The Placater

The placater is the child who takes on the role of helping others to adjust and to feel comfortable. This child smooths over conflicts in the home, working to lessen the fears or anger of other family members through listening and empathic responses. In school, placaters are often well liked because of their sensitivity to the needs of others.

Placaters continually monitor their parent's mood in order to be responsive. Although their sensitivity to others' moods and the ability to help others adjust and feel comfortable are healthy patterns, placaters also have difficulty recognizing and asserting their own needs and feelings.

Other Roles

Brenner (1984) refers to a fourth role or category that might include the acting-out child. She calls this child the "alkie kid." This is the child, according to Brenner, who identifies with the alcoholic parent and learns to manipulate others while being unresponsive to the needs of others. Teachers see this child as an impulsive troublemaker and a potential delinquent. Alkie kids may begin drinking in adolescence in vain but familiar attempts to cope and are at high risk for becoming adult alcoholics. Unlike the other three categories, the "alkie kid" learns to express his or her anger and resentment but often in a way that is dependent or demanding and invokes anger from other people. Alkie kids may also have a low frustration tolerance. They look for quick and easy solutions to problems, may do poorly in school, and have little sense of self-worth or self-control.

Ackerman (1983) suggests, however, there is another way to categorize children of alcoholics, that is, some are haves and some are havenots. His work suggests that alcoholism in the family creates a deficit in children's abilities to form positive relationships outside of the family. Constructive coping includes the ability to make lasting attachments to adults or others who are not family members. Havenots are unable to forge these bonds. On the other hand, the haves accept nurturance from adults. If there are adults willing to be consistently available to the children, there is the possibility that some of the trauma of living with an alcoholic is neutralized. The existence and use of an available adult gives the child a safe place to go, someone from whom comfort and permission to be a child can be received.

RECOMMENDATIONS
Important School Personnel Skills

Although a long list of skills could be generated for professional competencies in working with substance-abusing families, our experience has highlighted several skills that are critical to the success of any program. These include accepting attitudes, tolerance for ambiguity, and special communication skills.

Acceptance. The development of successful relationships with any parents requires the professional involved be *accepting* of the situation that alcoholic families experience (Apter & Conoley,

1984). Acceptance connotes an ability to suspend dogmatic judgments about what is right or wrong about other people. The ability to accept differences in values or lifestyles and to understand that blame and criticism are useless interventions are critical to developing a relationship with parents that is free of defensiveness from either party.

Parents interviewed about their lack of cooperation or collaboration with professionals or school personnel often state they feel as if they are being blamed for their child's problems and that school personnel believe them to be bad and uncaring parents. This perception can make a parent unwilling to meet or talk with school personnel. As one parent said, "Everybody blames me and tells me what to do, but nobody tells me how I'm going to manage to do it."

A strategy to counter these negative parent perceptions may be the belief on the part of school personnel *that parents are doing the best they can at that time.* When school professionals have been able to take that perspective, solutions, trust, and high expectations have tended to characterize interactions rather than suspicion and defensiveness.

Professionals must also realize the threat of family change. Apter and Conoley (1984), caution:

> Even the people who appear to be most villainous are also victims of their circumstances. The activities or interventions of the educational—mental health helpers are both facilitating and dangerous. Interventions that are aimed at changing dysfunctional patterns threaten familiar patterns. The patterns may seem terrible, but they are known and therefore are less frightening than the unknowns of change. Even at our best moments of helping others change, we must see that we are threats to stability. Even in a child's or parent's strongest moments of resistance, we must see struggles to maintain the only wholeness in system integrity that they know." (p. 250)

Tolerance for ambiguity. Tolerance for ambiguity is that characteristic that enables one to recognize there are no surefire cookbook solutions to difficult problems. Because people and systems are complex, a tolerance for ambiguity enables us to work with them without the need to have perfect control over what happens. It enables us to work toward solutions for problems without having to be sure that our solutions will necessarily solve the problem. Such a stance is important because it permits the school professional to feel comfortable in complex situations. If we attempt to simplify the experience of the child of the alcoholic into a few trite roles or truisms, we miss important intervention opportunities.

Communication skills. Another critical communication pattern in working with substance-abusing families is the ability to move family members from the "emotional state" to the "thinking state" (Faye & Cline, 1984). Family members must be in a thinking state before a successful conference can occur. Intense emotional states such as fear or anger stimulate the sympathetic nervous system to the extent that normal cognitive processes are impaired. The "fight or flight" response centers mental attention on the perceived danger making it difficult to remember or concentrate on other stimuli (Arnold, 1960). The statement "so scared/angry I couldn't think straight" is an accurate assessment of the physiological and psychological responses to perceived danger.

Parents may suffer a form of "stage fright" when asked to come to school to participate in a conference about their child. Substance-abusing parents have even more to fear (than sober parents do) when speaking with school professionals, that is, their secret may be discovered. Faye and Cline (1984) suggest that parental anxiety might be lessened by a willingness to meet with parents on their turf. We have found that visits to alcoholic families in their own homes or in coffee shops have seemed to arouse far less anxiety than those held in the school district offices.

We have discovered that many substance-abusing parents are intensely guilty about their drinking and its possible effects on their children. Even when this guilt is not openly shared, we have learned to build bridges with such parents by emphasizing their children's positive qualities (i.e., reduce anxiety) and by mapping out very specific and joint family and school intervention plans. The development of joint plans avoids the suggestion that only the parents are to blame for a child's behavioral or academic difficulties.

Promoting Interaction with Parents

Although it is critical that school personnel be well informed about the effects of substance abuse on a family, it is of equal importance that they be aware of their own feelings about substance abuse. If personal experiences or beliefs cloud professionals' abilities to respond objectively to substance-abusing families, an intervention role must be relinquished. Each school professional should examine religious and lifestyle beliefs to insure they are not equating substance-abusing families with bad families (Cruse, 1989).

There are several levels of possible interaction between school personnel and parents (Conoley, 1987). The levels are: Level 1—Information Provision and Sharing; Level 2—Parent Support for School Interventions; Level 3—Collaborative Home-School Programs; and Level 4—Parental Involvement in the Classroom. We have used this (and other) frameworks in conceptualizing some of our work with substance-abusing families.

Information provision and sharing. One activity at this level is a parent education program. Our parent education program on alcoholism is available to all parents. We make a special effort to recruit parents whose children have been identified as potentially substance abusing (School-Community Intervention Program). Our hope, however, is that a nonalcoholic spouse, in the reactive stage of alcoholism, already concerned but not willing to admit to alcoholism in the family, will attend. Such a parent may feel comfortable attending a general parent alcohol education program, particularly when invitations are worded in such a way that parents recognize that it may prevent alcohol or drug abuse in their own children. Offering a low-threat first step has proven successful in several instances in involving parents more closely in their children's academic programs. Once parents accept that alcoholism in one family member may be hurting another's academics or peer relationships, some change may be possible.

Even parents who do not attend sessions receive information about alcoholism. Written information is sent to homes of all children about preventing alcohol and drug problems and the effects of alcohol and drugs on the family system.

Another Level 1 activity involves sharing of information about other community agencies available for help with various child or family problems. Special attention is given to substance-abuse programs. Many parents have reported "not knowing where to turn" when they were finally ready to seek help. Keeping current on community resources is critical.

A child-centered approach that focuses on joint responsibility for problem solving is most effective with almost all families, but is particularly important with alcoholic families. Although family members are hard to contact, making and keeping the contact is the primary avenue for effecting change. In other words, approach the parents with a "What can we do together to work on Johnny's problem?" This "we" attitude, taking a nonjudgmental, nonblaming approach to the problem may move parents to see school personnel as allies rather than as adversaries. Establishing this connection may encourage the nonaddicted spouse to begin a process of self-disclosure. Such disclosure is the first and necessary step toward recovery. This can lead to opportunities for referral to other treatment sources, and more open discussions about collaborative programs for the student.

The information provision and sharing is a reciprocal process. Getting information from substance-abusing families is a particular challenge, however. Because denial of addiction is a common characteristic (Cruse, 1989), the information shared with you about the child or the home may be inaccurate. Do not view this as "lying" but as a part of the survival mechanism of the family. Parents may also appear defensive or unwilling to respond to your requests for information. It is critical that school personnel not respond with these same feelings but instead continue in attempting to establish rapport with the parent. Because family members are used to being disappointed and seem to expect inconsistency, we have found that persistence is a very powerful tool.

Whenever possible, seek information about the child from the nonaddictive parent or another nonaddictive adult in the family. An obvious advantage of this strategy is that information is likely to be more valid from this source. In addition, attention to nonaddictive parents may enhance their self-worth, and provide them with important out-of-family contacts. These are necessary precursors to change in the family system. In fact, school professionals should consider that much of their work with alcoholic families should be aimed at increasing the sense of self-efficacy felt by family members. Although having such a goal may seem rather ambiguous, it may be a significant accomplishment

The successful home-school programs we have implemented have shared several common assumptions about home-school or school-community relationships. These assumptions are based on mutual respect and collaboration and result in programs and practices that differ in accordance with family and community needs. First, we begin with the expectation that parents will be involved and plan on how to support this responsibility. Second, we provide families with information addressing the specific needs of their children. Third, we have tried to respond to family diversity and diverse parental needs, that is, avoiding a rigid protocol of action. Fourth, we have worked to encourage all members of the extended family to take an active role.

Schools must think of approaches that assist families to help one another. Parent-to-parent support may be as or more important than professional-to-parent support. Accessing available parent support groups in the community may be a very important service to offer parents.

Parent support for school interventions. At the most basic level, a Level 2 intervention may be one in which parents are simply asked for their input and for their support of school interventions. It may not require the parent to do anything other than verbally support the intervention or not consciously undermine the intervention.

It is critical to ask for parental support in such a way that we let parents know how important they are, that we value and will use their input. Apter (1982) states that when you involve parents in roles that allow them "to become important determiners of their children's behavior and learning," you also help to bring about changes in the parent's behavior.

In our work we have discovered that our willingness to work on child problems the parent identifies (not just expecting the parent to work on school-identified problems) has created some increased cooperation for future collaborative efforts. Sometimes the best thing you can say is, "I understand why you feel that way. What would you like to do and how can I help?" This enables us to start with the parent from where the parent is at that point in time.

Collaborative home-school programs. Collaborative programs between school and home may be very difficult to achieve with substance-abusing families. Even the simplest of the programs (e.g., monitoring homework or rewarding successful school experiences) may be beyond the resources of some parents. Extreme caution must be used to insure that you do not add further responsibilities to an already overburdened parent. Although school personnel may validly see this as part of the responsibility of the family, pushing too soon for home-school programs may result in the parents'

avoidance of school personnel due to guilt from not being able to carry out their role in the plan.

Parental involvement in the classroom. Asking the nonalcoholic spouse to take an active role in classroom or with other school activities (perhaps teaching a skill that they have or helping with a field trip) may help to promote changes in the parent as well as appropriate home-school relationships. Again, it is important to be careful, however, not to burden parents who already have more than they can do with one more thing. It has been our experience that even the most difficult or the most disturbed parent when made to feel valued and welcome, will become eager to cooperate.

One colleague has involved parents by inviting them to become part of a classroom social skills group as a model for appropriate behavior. A parent from a substance-abusing family joined the cooperative group and organized a carnival for younger children. Although she worked with a group other than the one her child was in (both mother and child were more comfortable with this) the interaction between them became increasingly positive over the 6-week period. The most noticeable change, however, was in the appearance and affect of the mother. Her posture, vocal quality, and eye contact reflected her increased feelings of self-worth and she began to take steps to seek professional help for herself and her children. This change occurred with no direct intervention regarding her alcoholic husband. She changed and was ready to be more active about the substance abuse perhaps because school staff saw her as competent and contributing.

Help from Other Agencies

When a parent acknowledges substance abuse in the home, school personnel should be prepared to recommend agencies or professionals who specialize in the treatment of drug or alcohol addiction. Encourage the parent to seek treatment for the nonabusing family members even if the abuser is not yet willing to take this step. If the child's school problems are significant it is wise to arrange with the parent for ongoing contact between the treatment agency and the school. In most states, written permission from the parent is necessary for this kind of information exchange.

Legal Issues

It is critical that school personnel be aware of state laws regarding the legal actions that may be taken on behalf of children who live with substance-abusing families. School personnel are required by law in all states to report suspected abuse or neglect of a child. In only a few states (i.e., New York, Nebraska, Iowa, and Rhode Island) can legal action be taken if a child lives with an alcoholic parent and is in danger of abuse. In these cases, there is also a criterion that the parent be habitually drunk (Brenner, 1984). In most states parental substance abuse is not grounds for legal action unless the child is also being abused or neglected.

Legal issues regarding confidentiality of information about children and families require that school personnel have parental permission to discuss their child with anyone outside of the school system. Therefore, unless neglect or abuse is suspected, school personnel cannot involve professionals from other agencies in the treatment of the child without parental permission. When school personnel know about the addictive behaviors of parents, it is often difficult not to seek help for the child. Occasionally children can be involved in groups that are not therapy groups (e.g., social skills, problem solving) that are regular parts of the curriculum without parental permission. School staff may investigate these options when other attempts to get help for a child fails.

Issues regarding confidentiality of information between students and their parents are less troublesome in certain situations. Minor children have very limited rights to confidentiality. The most recent amendment, however, of the American Psychological Association (1990) regarding *Ethical Principles of*

Psychologists includes the following principle:

Principal 5: Confidentiality

Psychologists have a primary obligation to respect the confidentiality of information obtained from persons in the course of their work as psychologists. They reveal such information to others only with the consent of the person or the person's legal representative, except in those unusual circumstances in which not to do so would result in clear danger to the person or others. Where appropriate, psychologists inform their clients of the legal limits or confidentiality. (APA, 1990)

Psychologists, counselors, or other school personnel who wish to maintain the trust of students in the interest of an ongoing relationship may be able to functionally hold much of the child's information in a confidential matter. Obviously, situations in substance-abusing families often push a psychologist toward reporting suspected abuse or neglect to the appropriate authorities. Children who have been betrayed before by the inconsistency of their parents may be especially sensitive to this difficult process. In addition, the norm to deny problems may make the public discussion of family dynamics even more traumatic than usual. All of these dynamics (and many others) make work with such children complex. It is of prime importance, however, that when it is necessary to report information from the student to parents or other professionals, the student should be informed. If allegations of abuse are to be made against the parent, the authorities should be informed about the suspected alcoholism or other drug use. Substance abuse is highly correlated with violent acts.

CONCLUSIONS

It was my hope to provide a long list of proven interventions for school personnel to attempt when working with substance-abusing families. Careful consideration of literature and our experience suggests that cookbook solutions are not available (Wills, 1990).

What seems vital is that school personnel be informed about substance abuse and its effects on children and all family members and that extraordinary efforts are made to involve substance-abusing families. These efforts involve attempts at many levels and will necessarily be characterized by remarkable persistence on the part of school personnel. The ethic of denial is so strong that isolated attempts at influence are likely doomed. Many forces act to keep such parents away from schools. Business as usual will never be effective in bringing them into productive partnerships.

REFERENCES

Ackerman, R. J. (1983). *Children of alcoholics: A guidebook for educators, therapists, and parents.* Holmer Beach, FL: Learning Publications.

American Psychological Association. (1990). Ethical principles of psychologists. *American Psychologist, 45*(3), 390–395.

Apter, S. J. (1982). *Troubled children, troubled systems.* New York: Pergamon.

Apter, S. J., & Conoley, J. C. (1984). *Childhood behavior disorders and emotional disturbance.* Englewood Cliffs, NJ: Prentice-Hall.

Arnold, M. B. (1960). *Emotions to personality: Neurological and physiological aspects.* New York: Columbia University Press.

Black, C. (1981). *It will never happen to me.* Denver: ACT Publishers.

Brenner, A. (1984). *Helping children cope with stress.* Lexington, MA: D. C. Health & Co.

Conoley, J. C. (1987). School and families: Theoretical and practical bridges. *Professional School Psychology, 2*(3), 191–203.

Cruse, S. W. (1989). *Another chance: Hope & health for the alcoholic family.* Palo Alto, CA: Science and Behavior Books, Inc.

DeMarsh, J., & Kumpfer, K. L. (1985). Family-oriented interventions for the prevention of chemical dependency in children and adolescents. *Journal of Children in Contemporary Society, 18,* 117–151.

Edwards, D. M., & Zander, T. A. (1985). Children of alcoholics: Background and strategies for the

counselor. *Elementary School Guidance and Counseling, 20*(2), 121–127.

Faye, J., & Cline, F. W. (1984). *Discipline with love and logic.* Evergreen, CO: Cline/Faye Institute.

Gabel, S., & Shindledecker, R. (1990). Parental substance abuse and suspected child abuse/maltreatment predict outcome in children's inpatient treatment. *Journal of the American Academy of Child & Adolescent Psychiatry, 29,* 919–924.

Grady, K., Gersick, K. E., & Boratynski, M. (1985). Preparing parents for teenagers: A step in the prevention of adolescent substance abuse. *Family Relations: Journal of Applied Family & Child Studies, 34,* 541–549.

Hecht, M. (1988). A cooperative approach toward children from alcoholic families. In W. M. Walsh & N. J. Giblin (Eds.), *Family counseling in school settings* (pp. 166–172). Springfield, IL: Charles C. Thomas.

Kirk, D. L., Chapman, T., & Sadler, O. W. (1990). Documenting the effectiveness of adolescent substance abuse treatment using public school archival records. *High School Journal, 74,* 16–21.

Lerner, R. (1986). Co-dependency: The swirl of energy surrounded by confusion. In R. J. Ackerman (Ed.), *Growing in the shadow: Children of alcoholics* (pp. 125–142). Pampano Beach, FL: Health Communications.

Logan, B. N. (1991). Adolescent substance abuse prevention: An overview of the literature. *Family & Community Health, 13*(4), 25–36.

Morehouse, E., & Richards, T. (1983). An examination of dysfunctional latency age children of alcoholic parents and problems in intervention. *Children in Contemporary Society, 15*(1), 21–33.

National Clearinghouse for Alcohol and Drug Information. (1989). *It's elementary: Meeting the needs of high-risk youth in the school setting* (No. PH 265). Rockville, MD: Office for Substance Abuse Prevention, U.S. Department of Health and Human Services.

O'Rourke, K. (1989). *Young children of alcoholics: Little people with big needs.* (Report No. PS-017–890). (ERIC Document Reproduction Service No. ED 307 173)

Palmer, J. H., & Paisley, P. O. (1991). Student assistance programs: A response to substance abuse. *School Counselor, 38,* 287–293.

Schinke, S. P., Botvin, G. J., & Orlandi, M. A. (1991). *Substance abuse in children and adolescents: Evaluation and intervention.* Newbury Park, CA: Sage Publications.

Wills, T. A. (1990). Multiple networks and substance use. *Journal of Social & Clinical Psychology, 9,* 78–90.

21

NURTURING CHILDREN OF DIVORCE: A SHARED RESPONSIBILITY

Jane Close Conoley and
Theresa Bahns

Children who experience a divorce that involves conflict, economic deprivation, instability, and bitter legal contests are put at risk for behavioral and emotional disorders (Amato & Keith, 1991b). These disorders may be acting out behaviors, depression, academic difficulties, somatic complaints, or general feelings of low self-esteem. The duration of such disorders may be brief or quite long lasting depending on the ways in which the adults involved in the divorce manage the separation process and which important life decisions are influenced by the divorce (Amato, 1988; Amato & Keith, 1991a).

Because parents are often absorbed by their own emotional needs during a conflictual marriage and divorce, the psychological attention available for children may be minimal (Wallerstein, 1983). Somewhat more than one million children a year experience divorce (i.e., 38% of White children and 75% of Black children born to married parents experience divorce before the age of 16). In any classroom in the United States a significant number of the children may be from divorced, single-parent, or blended (e.g., step) families (U.S. Bureau of the Census, 1989, p. 87). The general education teacher may therefore be facing a significant number of children with very special psychological needs that are, at least temporarily, unheeded by their parents.

Research in the area of divorce adjustment for children has supported the effectiveness of school-based treatment. Counselors and school psychologists have been successful in offering group counseling to children at various stages in the divorce process and have found consistent reductions in school-identified problem behaviors.

Researchers have found improvement on such psychological variables as self-esteem, locus of control, and adjustment to divorce as a result of group treatment. Others have found the effects of treatment in school have generalized to the home insofar as parents notice a reduction in problematic behaviors (Alpert-Gillis, Pedro-Carroll, & Cowen, 1989; Bornstein, Bornstein, & Walters, 1988; Cowen, Hightower, & Pedro-Carroll, 1989; Crosbie-Burnett & Newcomer, 1989; Garvin, Leber, & Kalter, 1991; Gwynn & Brantley, 1987; Kalter, Pickar, & Lesowitz, 1984; Lesowitz, Kalter, Pickar, Chethik, & Schaefer, 1987; Omizo & Omizo, 1987; Pedro-Carroll & Cowen, 1985; Stolberg & Mahler, 1989). Overall, the research base is supportive of school personnel forming collaborative arrangements with parents to assist children in coping with a difficult developmental challenge—the separation of the family.

The organization and activities included in all the divorce adjustment programs (noted above) are quite familiar to school-based mental health personnel. Professionals who have been successful in other group efforts with children (e.g., social skills training) should have no difficulty in mastering a divorce adjustment curriculum.

It would be an error, however, to limit attempts to collaborate with families stressed by divorce and its related difficulties to direct treatment of children. Other systemic or organizational adjustments may be necessary to keep the school responsive to the realities of America's changing families.

Some adjustments include information-gathering and information-sharing procedures, expectations toward parents regarding attendance at school functions, care of sick children, before- and after-school daycare, educational experiences for parents, education of teachers about both the possible effects of divorce on children and the bias in language and curriculum that can make children of divorce feel stigmatized, and the role of the school in providing children with significant adult models.

The objectives of this chapter are therefore to:

1. Explore ways to intervene directly with children who are experiencing divorce or divorce-related trauma;

2. Analyze ways that schools have changed in response to a major sociological event in American culture; and

3. Suggest ways in which mental health professionals in schools (e.g., school psychologists, counselors, social workers) may change their daily roles to accommodate the new challenges faced by children.

THE EFFECTS OF DIVORCE ON CHILDREN

A significant amount of research has accumulated concerning the impact of divorce on children (Amato & Keith, 1991b) and the longer term impact of parental divorce on adult well-being (Amato & Keith, 1991a). As is so often the case, the more information that becomes available, the less simple the relationships among variables become.

Using the Amato and Keith (1991a & b) meta-analyses as a basic source, what seems to be true about the effects of divorce might be summarized as follows:

1. Family conflict prior to, during, and after a divorce is the critical factor creating risk for children (Amato, 1986; Emery, 1982; Hetherington, Cox, & Cox, 1982; Johnston, Kline, & Tschann, 1989; Kline, Johnston, & Tschann, 1991; Maccoby & Martin, 1983; Wallerstein & Kelly, 1980).

2. Children can experience a wide array of potential problems following a divorce (or while living in a conflictual home) that include disrupted academic achievement, conduct disorders, poor psychological adjustment, impaired self-concept, social adjustment concerns, and damaged mother-child and father-child relations. Although most of the research suggests that children of divorce are at a disadvantage in these areas, the effect sizes tend to be rather small.

3. Sex differences are not too pronounced in terms of differential effects of divorce (Wallerstein, 1984). Although boys seem to experience more social adjustment problems, an analysis across many studies shows no other sex differences. This particular finding from the Amato and Keith (1991b) meta-analysis flies in the face of conventional wisdom and some widely cited research (e.g., Guidubaldi, Cleminshaw, Perry, & McLoughlin, 1983; Hetherington et al., 1982; Wallerstein & Kelly, 1980).

4. School-aged children (elementary to secondary) appear to show the greatest vulnerability to negative effects in terms of psychological adjustment, social adjustment, and mother-child and father-child relations (Amato, 1987; Amato & Ochiltree, 1987; Brady, Bray, & Zeeb, 1986; Tuckman & Regan, 1966).

5. Although the research on the

long-term effects of divorce is tenuous for a number of reasons, available studies suggest that adults who experienced parental divorce exhibit lower levels of well-being than adults whose parents were continuously married. Living in a single-parent family seems to be related to lower educational attainment for females and a greater likelihood that males will be in a single-parent status as adults. Problems of confounds between the occupational status and parental educational achievement of the families of origin make these latter findings quite tentative (McLanahan & Bumpass, 1988).

7. Race may mediate some of the effects of divorce. White children seem to show greater negative effects than do Black children. This finding may relate to the socioeconomic status and prevailing family structure norms in the different ethnic/racial groups. That is, children of color may be stressed by many sociocultural factors and have their quality of life only marginally disrupted by divorce (Hetherington, Camara, & Featherman, 1983).

All of the above may suggest that although divorce is not the worst event a child can experience, it does have implications for a child's sense of well-being and behavioral and academic experiences. In addition, it is possible that even longer term effects may accrue based on reduced educational attainment or the socialization into one-parent family norms.

DIVORCE ADJUSTMENT GROUPS

Several therapy group formats are available to psychologists who choose to target children who may be experiencing divorce-related difficulties. No research is available, as yet, that compares the effectiveness of one approach over another. Their similarities are so great that it is likely comparative research will involve student characteristics, length of the intervention, or parent involvement practices rather than highlighting dramatic differences in the treatment packages.

Group Goals

Wallerstein (1983) has outlined what she believes to be the child's divorce-related challenges: (a) acknowledging the marital disruption; (b) regaining a sense of direction and freedom to pursue customary activities; (c) dealing with loss and feelings of rejection; (d) forgiving the parents; (e) accepting the permanence of the divorce and relinquishing longings for the restoration of the predivorce family; and (f) resolving issues of relationship, that is, achieving realistic hopes regarding future relationships and the enduring ability to love and be loved.

This framework has served as the basis of Pedro-Carroll's (1985) Children of Divorce Intervention Program (CODIP) that is highlighted below. The Pedro-Carroll program is closely related to the work done by Stolberg and his associates (Stolberg & Cullen, 1983; Stolberg, Cullen, & Garrison, 1982; Stolberg & Garrison, 1985; Stolberg & Mahler, 1989) who developed the Divorce Adjustment Project.

We have implemented the CODIP at the University of Nebraska Clinic for Psychological and Educational Services for the past 4 years (Pedro-Carroll, 1985; Pedro-Carroll, Alpert-Gillis, & Sterling, 1987). The elements of CODIP, like most other programs described in the research literature or available commercially, include the following: (a) identification of feeling words and feelings associated with divorce; (b) social problem solving around predictable events and dilemmas faced by children (e.g., parental fighting, transitions between homes, parents' emotional unavailability, pressures to inform on one parent to another); (c) identification of issues and concerns that cannot be solved by children (e.g., the finality of the divorce, appearance of new partners for the parents, parents' depression); (d) exploration of the wide array of family structures; (e) self-esteem-building exercises; (f) practice of coping strategies for the many changes that occur in a child's life because of divorce (e.g., communication skills, anger management, impulse control, relaxation); and (g) promotion of a group process that connects children with helpful peers and concerned adults.

Implementation

Most often implemented during the school day, divorce adjustment groups have been offered in 6- to 16-week intensities for about 30 to 50 minutes per week. The Pedro-Carroll program is organized in a 12-week format with meetings lasting about 50 minutes. Existing programs are appropriate for elementary-aged children and young adolescents. The groups reported in studies cited earlier have been led by school psychologists, school counselors, and school social workers. Paraprofessionals have been used as co-leaders.

Our experience using the Pedro-Carroll program at our University clinic has illustrated a number of hands-on guidelines.

1. Pacing is very important. Children must be listened to very carefully, but the activities (e.g., games, role-plays, problem solving) must move rather quickly to keep children's enjoyment and attention.

2. Children (even in our oldest groups of about 9- to 12-year-olds) do not enjoy long discussion periods. They prefer a mixture of activities that are not heavily verbally mediated.

3. The video and slide shows suggested in the Pedro-Carroll manuals are very popular with the children. The elementary-aged groups love to read or be read a variety of children's divorce books.

4. Parents benefit from regular involvement with the program. If two leaders are assigned to the children, one can be available frequently to parents to keep them up-to-date on group objectives and to gather input. In our Clinic, parents are involved in the groups themselves for one or two activities over an 11-week format. Parents cannot attend the majority of the sessions, however, because they often are still rather focused on their own needs and divert attention away from meeting the children's agendas.

5. School involvement has been facilitated by asking for teacher input on each child using the Teacher Report Form (Achenbach & Edelbrock, 1986). Often the parent permits the final report concerning group goals, strategies, and outcomes to be shared with the teachers. The mere request for information has prompted several teachers to offer assistance to parents.

6. Children may not want to talk about divorce all the time, but benefit from an atmosphere that allows for identification of their many victories and difficulties.

7. Our best results have emerged when group size has been limited to about six older (ages 9–12) children and four younger (ages 6–8) children.

8. Activities from CODIP have been adapted for use with 4-year-olds. This adaptation included parent observation and extensive parent involvement in the group meetings. These groups have been kept to a limit of three children. Helpful adaptations to the CODIP are available from Rossiter (1988).

CHANGING AMERICAN SCHOOLS

Apart from offering services to children who are experiencing the process of divorce, what other modifications might schools make that would be responsive to the changing structures of American families? A school interested in supporting the adjustment of families who are experiencing separation and divorce might consider changes in information transfer, intensity of shared involvement, interaction and shared responsibility, and decision making.

Information Transfer

Information provision and sharing is a basic level of joining with distressed parents. Traditionally, this has meant providing parents with report cards, notes, or phone calls in addition to infrequent parent-teacher meetings. It has also involved getting fairly superficial information from parents about their children. To make this a meaningful exchange several things could happen at a school (Alexander, Kroth, Simpson, & Poppelreiter, 1982; Conoley, 1987; Ehly, Conoley, & Rosenthal, 1985; Hughes & Baker, 1990; Lombard, 1979; Losen & Diament, 1978; Loven, 1978):

Forms. Forms that collect information about families should include queries about the address, phone number, and involvement of noncustodial parents. Some noncustodial parents are prevented by court order from interacting with their children, but most would benefit from being on school mailing lists to receive notices of activities. School personnel must insure that noncustodial parents are permitted to pick up sick children and attempt to use the noncustodial parent as a helpful backup for the custodial parent.

Communication skills. Teachers and administrators can be trained in appropriate communication skills that emphasize a need to include many different forms of families. For example, children should not always be told to go home and tell their mothers and fathers about something. Overt acknowledgment of the number of single parents may be experienced as supportive to the children.

Content information about divorce. Teachers can receive specialized training about holding parent/teacher meetings and other forms of parent communication with a special focus on the stresses and strains of single parenting or the particular aspects of the divorce process that put children at-risk. Understanding the context of single parenting or the emotional demands of a divorce may assist teachers to frame communication in supportive and helpful ways.

Parental expertise. Parents must be seen and responded to as experts on their own children and as such be asked to provide the school with continuous feedback on the status of their children. For example, parents might be encouraged to keep the school informed about legal activities (e.g., custody disputes, visitation modifications) that involve the children, moves to new living quarters, visitation schedules, and so on. This information may be very useful for school personnel in interpreting child behavior and may assist parents and children by focusing attention on children's experiences.

Communication alternatives. Every school should have a regular method of communicating with parents, for example, newsletters, phone committees, community bulletin boards, regular features in newspapers, and monthly meetings. School bulletins could highlight especially appropriate TV, movie, or book resources for parents to access with their children. Unless otherwise instructed, schools might play a role in keeping parents involved with children by routinely sending both parents all announcements. A variety of communication approaches may be especially helpful in one-parent homes. Often the work schedules of single parents make regular attendance at school functions very difficult.

Case manager. A coordinator of information and services should be available to every parent, so the parent has one person to contact to help through the school bureaucracy. Noncustodial parents may be especially helped by the existence of a "case-manager" role because their information about their children may be incomplete.

Reading materials. Specialized bibliographies should be made available to parents depending on their particular needs. There are many good books for children and for parents about divorce and stepfamilies. These would be useful in the school library, but equally helpful if disseminated to parents (Pardeck, 1989).

Parental visits. Parents should routinely be invited to speak to children in their areas of expertise. This should happen very frequently. A special effort to invite single moms, noncustodial dads, stepdads, and stepmoms would seem to normalize the experience of both the parents and the children.

Intense Collaboration

Another aspect of partnership with divorced families involves collaborative home/school programs. The programs might include instructions for actually tutoring a child, teaching prosocial skills, or implementation of solutions or rewards.

Although most families can benefit from this kind of collaboration with teachers and other school-based professionals, single-parent families in particular are in great need of adult support. A most common concern of single parents is the lack of another adult with whom to problem solve about children's issues (Jenson, Bloedau, & Davis, 1990).

Hallmarks of successful collaborative efforts are as follows:

1. All parties understand exactly the changes expected of each. Everyone, teacher, parent, child, etc., must agree to a change. Already overwhelmed single parents cannot be asked to make dramatic changes in their typical coping styles. Some sensitive approaches that rely on small adjustments coupled with support are necessary.

2. A feasible communication system between parents and teachers must be established. Divorced or divorcing parents can be difficult to contact. Often it is useful to have alternative contacts such as child-care workers or grandparents.

3. Consistent follow-through on the parts of teachers and parents in terms of their behaviors and any rewards that have been agreed upon must be facilitated. A psychologist facilitating a collaborative program that targets a child of divorce may need to allot more time than usual to support the parents in making changes. The parents' own agendas can make it difficult to follow through on behavioral contracts.

Often, cooperation is aimed at fairly discrete child behaviors, but can be the vehicle for classroom and family change if all parties live up to their contracts. For example, parents who follow through with positive attention to a child who performs well at school are likely to improve not only the child's school work, but also the parent/child relationship. Analogously, a teacher who communi-cates frequently with parents is likely to both be more successful with individual children and feel more supported by parents in doing difficult work (Luster-man, 1985).

Interaction and Shared Responsibility

The active involvement of parents at the school represents an important way to enhance home/school collaboration. Unfortunately, most American families no longer include a parent who is routinely available for school duties. Divorced families are even less likely to have such a person. Lightfoot (1978) emphasizes the importance of such interaction, however:

> Not only does the working collaboration of parents and teachers transform the educational environment and cultural medium of the school, it also changes the adult perceptions of their roles and relationships.(p. 173)

Volunteer programs. Lightfoot goes on to say that school volunteer mothers reported that many behavioral and learning problems in school disappeared when their children experienced an alliance between mothers and teachers. In addition, they were able to share important information with teachers about neighborhood children, they reduced the workload of teachers, they gained an appreciation of how complex and burdensome teaching is, and finally, they began to perceive the school as belonging to them. These outcomes have been replicated in several inner-city schools (Comer, 1984, 1987; Comer & Haynes, 1991; Lightfoot, 1976).

To make a volunteer program work with families stressed by divorce, everyone will have to agree that it is important to do. Mothers and fathers must be trained in diverse roles (Cowen, Trost, Lorion, Dorr, Izzo, & Isaacson, 1975); childcare must be engineered for non-school-aged children; some kind of real reward or motivational system must be in place for volunteers; teachers must be convinced and then trained to utilize help effectively; and, someone must be in charge of coordinating.

In addition, volunteers must be organized with parents' limited time taken into account. For example, over the course of an academic year parents might be asked to help with one field trip, bake cookies for one party, read stories in the library for only one 30-minute period, or supervise the crosswalk on only one morning. Although this kind of program involves complex organization, the payoffs could be significant.

Childcare. Many American families have difficulty arranging for high quality daycare for their children. Predictably, single-headed homes are particularly stressed with childcare needs before and after school and when children are ill. Many schools now offer early morning programs and care until about 5 p.m. These programs, although not evaluated to our knowledge, seem to offer parents peace of mind and children a significantly safer environment than that of an empty house.

Childcare should also be made available during parent/teacher conferences and school plays or concerts. Often such care is free but even a nominal charge might be acceptable to parents. That is, if every parent paid only a dollar for an hour of care, junior or senior high students could still receive attractive pay for entertaining a group of children. If parents know they can attend functions without finding care for their other children and can look forward to an enjoyable time, their participation might increase in the lives of school-aged children.

Finally, Swap (in Chapter 3 of this volume) reports on a school facilitating a partnership among the school, parents, and local businesses to arrange for care for mildly ill children. The model she presents illustrates a home-based approach for children who were between ages 9–12. Other possible models include shared sponsorship of centers that care for children with colds, ear infections, and other fairly routine illnesses.

Such programs are established with joint funding from parents and from local private industry. The businesses have often been approached and influenced by school personnel who advocate for the contributions based both on family needs and the benefits to industry from decreased worker absenteeism.

Decision Making

Ultimately, children and families are assisted through difficult divorce situations by receiving support to get on with their lives. This means coming to grips with inevitable losses and changes and establishing personally fulfilling agendas. The exact path for any particular family toward these goals will be impossible for school personnel to recognize without input from parents. In like manner, parents have difficulty making optimal decisions because of the emotionality that can surround the divorce. Together, however, in real partnership with each other, professionals and parents might assist children in important ways. Some suggestions include:

1. Schools can sponsor parent-training workshops that are based on needs actually identified by parents. These workshops may be about learning games, nutritional snacks, or life after divorce. Bringing people together in problem-solving groups increases their abilities to deal with stress (Pilisuk, 1982). A study by Lindblad-Goldberg and Dukes (1985) suggested that more adaptive mothers had more nonfamily supports than less adaptive mothers. Family members, mentioned often by both groups, provided support, but also made intense demands upon the mothers. Schools, never mentioned as supportive by either group (this despite the fact that both groups were receiving services from a clinic because of school-related problems of their children), could be a wellspring of such nonfamily support if someone thought it was worthwhile.

2. The school building can be used as a community center where exercise, decorating, food preparation, shopping, sewing, and crafts classes are taught. Creating a community center for families who have lost important emotional an-

chors may be a very important contribution.

3. School buses could be made available to carry mothers or fathers and their school children to libraries, museums, or special exhibits. The economic stress experienced by many families following divorce can limit their activities and their energy to organize events with their children.

4. Brief family consultation/counseling could become an integral part of the educational programming for children. Some change in procedures is necessary if important information is to be gotten and given to parents. Solution-focused brief therapy models might be useful and are garnering increasing research support (Conoley, 1989; deShazer, 1985; Griest, Forehand, Rogers, Breiner, Furey, & Williams, 1982; Madanes, 1981).

Solution-focused therapy is a somewhat novel approach squarely based on the functional analysis of behavior. Some of its appealing elements are: (a) its focus on a family's past successes, that is, both family strengths and exceptions to the rules governing the complaint; (b) the acceptance of several problem formulations while challenging people's tendency to see situations as "either/or" (i.e., both of you are right but the results are wrong); (c) the simple but profoundly important mandate to insert doubt about any element of the complaint, so the family members have a way to change their behaviors; and (d) the insistence that therapists must have no doubt that change will occur.

Perhaps one, some, or none of the above might be useful with a particular group of parents or in a particular community. The critical issue is that parents and school professionals come together to identify concerns and solutions. Shared decision making increases investment (Lundquist, 1982).

SCHOOL PSYCHOLOGISTS AND DIVORCE ADJUSTMENT

Woven through the previous paragraphs are hints as to changes in role and function well-trained psychologists in schools might make to better support families distressed by divorce. There is a growing body of important work on families by school psychologists (Abidin, 1980; Anderson, 1983; Bergan, Neumann, & Karp, 1983; Carlson, 1987; Christenson & Cleary, 1990; Conoley, 1987, 1989; Fine, 1990; Guidubaldi, 1980; Guidubaldi et al., 1983; Knoff, 1987; Pfeiffer & Tittler, 1983; Shellenberger, 1981), but the volume of studies in individual assessment techniques is overwhelming in comparison to serious theoretical or research consideration of families (Reynolds & Clark, 1984). And the percentage of time devoted to family versus individual child assessment is minuscule.

Psychologists can find practice and research literature available to support them in implementing groups for children and in doing brief, solution-focused work with families. They can access information about the short- and long-term consequences of divorce on children to educate teachers and administrators. In order to accomplish the work needed to support families, however, a new kind of psychology in the schools is called for.

Cowen et al. (1975) have called for a "quarterback"—a psychologist who manages people and programs that anticipate and meet the needs of children. This psychologist is an expert about children: who they are, where they live, what they need, and what can go wrong. He or she is a family and school systems expert because to not know families and schools is to not know children.

The quarterback psychologist can assist all facets of the system to work in concert. Comer (1984, 1987, 1989; Comer & Haynes, 1991) used teams of teachers, administrators, parents, and social services and mental health workers to effect school reform. Only when all groups were engaged in promoting positive school experiences did the system begin to change. Comer and his associates' work is an inspirational example of what can be done when consultation, social support, and collaboration are verbs rather than abstract constructs (Conoley & Conoley, 1992). It is work, however, that depends on someone taking a leadership role in making a system work for children and their families.

Psychologists who would practice a family-oriented brand of school psychology would require flexibility in terms of actual roles and functions and in terms of operational levels. The schools must have clinicians who can work from micro to macro systems levels piecing together comprehensive, coordinated service packages for children and families. Psychologists must be important members of many teams and plan interventions for children based on children's particular needs and their special potentials.

Children identified as vulnerable or at-risk in the school environment absorb a good portion of psychologists' time, but the future of psychology in the schools depends on the development of an ecological framework in which to conceptualize and intervene with such children. Only when such a frame is in place does the family structure that nurtures a child get appropriate attention from the psychologist. Only when such a frame is used does family intervention become a necessity, not a luxury. And only with such a frame does serious school change become an obvious step to take.

A family-oriented school psychology would likely be quite a novelty in terms of the activities and priorities of the school psychologist. Traditional norm-referenced testing would become optional and infrequently used. Children would be known by their strengths and weaknesses and their match to their family and classroom contexts, not by shorthand descriptions of their problems. Psychologist recommendations would be tied to the daily behavior of teachers and parents and be based on well-tested cognitive-behavioral principles.

Psychologists also would become far more active in teacher and parent consultation. Overall, Stallings (1975) reports that about 40% of children's achievement can be accounted for by classroom instructional procedures (and 30% by their entry abilities). If 40% of children's achievement is explained by teacher instructional behavior then teachers and psychologists belong together working on producing optimal instructional environments for children (Ysseldyke & Christenson, 1986). And, if another 30% is explained by entry skills, then parents are prime targets for intervention as well (Conoley, 1987; Hansen, 1986). Children from divorced families should be embedded in school environments that are optimal. Only with serious adult cooperation, flexibility, and collaboration can such environments be engineered.

CONCLUSIONS

The key points in this paper argue for a shift in practice—an increase in direct therapeutic work with children of divorce; a focus on family service; and an initiation of school change to be responsive to the situations faced by millions of divorced or blended families. School psychologists say they are for children. In most situations, what is good for children is to help their families function more adaptively. This help may be in the form of brief family counseling, information sharing, collaboration on a behavioral plan, education, invitations to be meaningfully involved in the schooling process, training of school personnel to deal more effectively with distressed parents, and activity at administrative and governmental levels to monitor policy that affects children.

Divorce is not necessarily a psychopathological event for children. It is, however, a stress that may create some short- and long-term negative consequences (Borduin & Henggeler, 1987; Glenn & Kramer, 1987). Successful interventions are available. However schools and parents devise their team work, an important motivation might be that their ability to cooperate, learn from each other, and accomplish significant work for child welfare can serve as a model for all the adults who are responsible for troubled children and for the children themselves. Being a part of a cooperative and caring network of adults may be a new and healing experience for children of divorce.

REFERENCES

Abidin, R. R. (1980). *Parent education and intervention handbook.* Springfield, IL: Charles C. Thomas.

Achenbach, T. M., & Edelbrock, C. (1986). *Manual for the Teacher Report Form and the teacher version of the Child Behavior Profile.* Burlington, VT: University Associates in Psychiatry.

Alexander, R. N., Kroth, R. L., Simpson, R. L., & Poppelreiter, T. (1982). The parent role in special education. In R. L. McDowell, G. W. Adamson, & F. W. Wood (Eds.), *Teaching emotionally disturbed children* (pp. 300–316). New York: Little Brown.

Alpert-Gillis, L. J., Pedro-Carroll, J. L., & Cowen, E. L. (1989). The children of divorce intervention program: Development, implementation, and evaluation of a program for young, urban, children. *Journal of Consulting and Clinical Psychology, 57,* 583–589.

Amato, P. R. (1986). Marital conflict, the parent-child relationship, and child self-esteem. *Family Relations, 35,* 103–110.

Amato, P. R. (1987). Family process in one-parent, stepparent, and intact families: The child's point of view. *Journal of Marriage and the Family, 49,* 327–337.

Amato, P. R. (1988). Long-term implications of parental divorce for adult self-concept. *Journal of Family Issues, 9,* 201–213.

Amato, P. R., & Keith, B. (1991a). Parental divorce and adult well-being: A meta-analysis. *Journal of Marriage and the Family, 53,* 43–58.

Amato, P. R., & Keith, B. (1991b) Parental divorce and the well-being of children: A meta-analysis. *Psychological Bulletin, 110,* 26–46.

Amato, P. R., & Ochiltree, G. (1987). Child and adolescent competence in intact, one-parent, and stepfamilies: An Australian study. *Journal of Divorce, 10,* 75–96.

Anderson, C. (1983). An ecological developmental model for a family orientation in school psychology. *Journal of School Psychology, 21,* 179–189.

Bergan, J. R., Neumann, A. J., II, & Karp, C. L. (1983). Effects of parent training on parent instruction and child learning of intellectual skill. *Journal of School Psychology, 21,* 31–39.

Borduin, C. M., & Henggeler, S. W. (1987). Post divorce mother-son relations of delinquent and well-adjusted adolescents. *Journal of Applied Developmental Psychology, 8,* 273–288.

Bornstein, M. T., Bornstein, P. H., & Walters, H. A. (1988). Children of divorce: Empirical evaluation of a group-treatment program. *Journal of Clinical Child Psychology, 17,* 248–254.

Brady, C. P., Bray, J. H., & Zeeb, L. (1986). Behavior problems of clinic children: Relation to parental marital status, age and sex of child. *American Journal of Orthopsychiatry, 56,* 399–411.

Carlson, C. I. (1987). Family assessment and intervention in the school setting. In T. R. Kratochwill (Ed.), *Advances in school psychology* (Vol. 6, pp. 81–129). Hillsdale, NJ: Lawrence Erlbaum.

Christenson, S. L., & Cleary, M. (1990). Consultation and the parent-educator partnership: A perspective. *Journal of Educational and Psychological Consultation, 1,* 219–241.

Comer, J. P. (1984). Home-school relationships as they affect the academic success of children. *Education and Urban Society, 16,* 323–337.

Comer, J. P. (1987). New Haven's school-community connection. *Educational Leadership, 44,* 13–16.

Comer, J. P. (1989). Child development and education. *Journal of Negro Education, 58,* 125–139.

Comer, J. P., & Haynes, N. M. (1991). Parent involvement in schools: An ecological approach [Special issue]. Educational partnerships. *Elementary School Journal, 91,* 271–277.

Conoley, J. C. (1987). Families and schools: Theoretical and practical bridges. *Professional School Psychology, 2,* 191–203.

Conoley, J. C. (1989). The school psychologist as a community/family service provider. In R. Dean & R. D'Amato (Eds.), *The school psychologist in nontraditional settings* (pp. 33–65). Hillsdale, NJ: Erlbaum.

Conoley, J. C., & Conoley, C. W. (1992). *School consultation: Practice and training.* Boston: Allyn and Bacon.

Cowen, E. L., Hightower, A. D., & Pedro-Carroll, J. (1989). School based models for primary prevention programming with children. *Prevention in Human Services, 7,* 133–150.

Cowen, E. L, Trost, M. A., Lorion, R. P., Dorr, D., Izzo, L. D., & Isaacson, R. V. (1975). *New ways in school mental health: Early detection and prevention of school maladaption.* New York: Human Science Press.

Crosbie-Burnett, M., & Newcomer, L. L. (1989). A multimodal intervention for group counseling with children of divorce. *Elementary School Guidance & Counseling, 23,* 155–166.

deShazer, S. (1985). *Keys to solution in brief therapy.* New York: W. W. Norton.

Ehly, S., Conoley, J. C., & Rosenthal, D. (1985). *Working with parents of exceptional children.* St. Louis, MO: Mosby.

Emery, R. E. (1982). Interparental conflict and the

children of discord and divorce. *Psychological Bulletin, 92,* 310–330.

Fine, M. J. (1990). Facilitating home-school relationships: A family-oriented approach to collaborative consultation. *Journal of Educational and Psychological Consultation, 1,* 169–187.

Garvin, V., Leber, D., & Kalter, N. (1991). Children of divorce: Predictors of change following preventive interventions. *American Journal of Orthopsychiatry, 61,* 438–447.

Glenn, N. D., & Kramer, K. B. (1987). The marriages and divorces of the children of divorce. *Journal of Marriage and the Family, 49,* 811–825.

Griest, D. L., Forehand, R., Rogers, T., Breiner, J., Furey, W., & Williams, C. A. (1982). The effects of parent enhancement therapy on the treatment outcome and generalization of a parent training program. *Behavior Research and Therapy, 20,* 429–436.

Guidubaldi, J. (Ed.). (1980). Families: Current status and emerging trends [Special issue]. *School Psychology Review, 9.*

Guidubaldi, J., Cleminshaw, H. K., Perry, J. D., & McLoughlin, C. S. (1983). The impact of parental divorce on children: Report of the nationwide NASP study. *School Psychology Review, 12,* 300–323.

Gwynn, C. A., & Brantley, H. T. (1987). Effect of a divorce group intervention for elementary school children. *Psychology in the Schools, 21,* 161–164.

Hansen, D. A. (1986). Family-school articulations: The effects of interaction rule mismatch. *American Educational Research Journal, 23,* 643–659.

Haynes, N. M., Comer, J. P., & Hamilton-Lee, M. (1989). School climate enhancement through parental involvement. *Journal of School Psychology, 27,* 87–90.

Hetherington, E. M., Camara, K. A., & Featherman, D. L. (1983). Achievement and intellectual functioning in children in one-parent households. In J. T. Spence (Ed.), *Achievement and achievement motives* (pp. 205–284). San Francisco: W. H. Freeman.

Hetherington, E. M., Cox, M., & Cox, R. (1982). Effects of divorce on parents and children. In M. Lamb (Ed.), *Nontraditional families* (pp. 233–288). Hillsdale, NJ: Erlbaum.

Hughes, J. N., & Baker, D. B. (1990). *The clinical child interview.* New York: Guilford Press.

Jenson, P., Bloedau, L., & Davis, H. (1990). Children at risk: II. Risk factors and clinic utilization. *Journal of the American Academy of Child and Adolescent Psychiatry, 29,* 804–812.

Johnston, J. R., Kline, M., & Tschann, J. M. (1989). Ongoing postdivorce conflict: Effects on children

of joint custody and frequent access. *American Journal of Orthopsychiatry, 59,* 576–592.

Kalter, N., Pickar, J., & Lesowitz, M. (1984). School-based developmental facilitation groups for children of divorce: A preventive intervention. *American Journal of Orthopsychiatry, 54,* 613–623.

Kline, M., Johnston, J. R., & Tschann, J. M. (1991). The long shadow of marital conflict: A model of children's postdivorce adjustment. *Journal of Marriage and the Family, 53,* 297–309.

Knoff, H. (1987). Children and divorce. In A. Thomas & J. Grimes (Eds.), *Children's needs: Psychological perspectives* (pp. 173–181). Washington, DC: National Association of School Psychologists.

Lesowitz, M., Kalter, N., Pickar, J., Chethik, M., & Schaefer, M. (1987). School based developmental facilitation groups for children of divorce: Issues of group process. *Psychotherapy, 24,* 90–95.

Lightfoot, S. L. (1976). *A school in transition: Stories of struggles and hope.* Unpublished manuscript.

Lightfoot, S. L. (1978). *Worlds apart: Relationships between families and schools.* New York: Basic Books.

Lindblad-Goldberg, M., & Dukes, J. (1985). Social support in black, low-income single-parent families: Normative and dysfunctional patterns. *American Journal of Orthopsychiatry, 55,* 42–58.

Lombard, T. (1979). Family-oriented emphasis for school psychologists: A needed orientation for training and professional practice. *Professional Psychology, 10,* 687–696.

Losen, S. N., & Diament, B. (1978). *Parent conferences in the schools. Procedures for developing effective partnership.* Boston: Allyn & Bacon.

Loven, M. (1978). Four alternative approaches to the family/school liaison role. *Psychology in the Schools, 15,* 553–559.

Lundquist, G. W. (1982). Needs assessment in organizational development. In C. R. Reynolds & T. B. Gutkin (Eds.), *The handbook of school psychology* (pp. 936–968). New York: Wiley.

Lusterman, D.D. (1985). An ecosystemic approach to family school problems. *The American Journal of Family Therapy, 13,* 22–30.

Maccoby, E., & Martin, J. A. (1983). Socialization in the context of the family: Parent-child interaction. In E.M. Hetherington (Ed.), *Handbook of child psychology, Vol. IV: Socialization, personality, and social development* (pp. 1–101). New York: Wiley.

Madanes, C. (1981). *Strategic family therapy.* San Francisco: Jossey-Bass.

McLanahan, S., & Bumpass, L. (1988). Intergenerational consequences of family disruption. *American Journal of Sociology, 94,* 130–152.

Omizo, M. M., & Omizo, S. A. (1987). Group counseling with children of divorce: New findings. *Elementary School Guidance and Counseling, 22,* 46–52.

Pardeck, J. T. (1989). Bibliotherapy and the blended family. *Child Psychiatry Quarterly, 22*(1), 1–15.

Pedro-Carroll, J. L. (1985). *Children of divorce intervention program procedures manual.* Rochester, NY: Center for Community Study.

Pedro-Carroll, J. L., Alpert-Gillis, L., & Sterling, S. (1987). *Children of divorce intervention program procedures manual for conducting support group with second and third grade children.* Rochester, NY: Center for Community Study.

Pedro-Carroll, J. L., & Cowen, E. L. (1985). The children of divorce intervention program: An investigation of the efficacy of a school-based prevention program. *Journal of Consulting and Clinical Psychology, 53,* 603–611.

Pfeiffer, S., & Tittler, B. (1983). Utilizing the multidisciplinary team to facilitate a school family systems orientation. *School Psychology Review, 12,* 168–173.

Pilisuk, M. (1982). Delivery of social support: The social inoculation. *American Journal of Orthopsychiatry, 52,* 20–31.

Reynolds, C. R., & Clark, J. (1984). Trends in school psychology research: 1974–1980. *Journal of School Psychology, 22,* 43–52.

Rossiter, A. B. (1988). A model for group intervention with preschool children experiencing separation and divorce. *American Journal of Orthopsychiatry, 58,* 387–396.

Shellenberger, S. (Ed.). (1981). Services to families and parental involvement with interventions [Special issue]. *School Psychology Review, 10.*

Stallings, J. (1975). Implementation and child effects of teaching practices in follow-through classroom. *Monograph of the Society for Research in Child Development, 40*(7–8, Serial No. 163).

Stolberg, A. L., & Cullen, P. M. (1983). Preventing psychopathology in children of divorce: The divorce adjustment project. In L. Kurdek (Ed.), *New directions for child development: Children and divorce* (pp. 71–81). San Francisco: Jossey-Bass.

Stolberg, A. L., Cullen, P. M., & Garrison, K. M. (1982). The divorce adjustment project: Preventive programming for children of divorce. *Journal of Preventive Psychiatry, 1,* 365–368.

Stolberg, A. L., & Garrison, K. M. (1985). Evaluating a primary prevention program for children of divorce: The Divorce Adjustment Project. *American Journal of Community Psychology, 13,* 111–124.

Stolberg, A. L., & Mahler, J. L. (1989). Protecting children from the consequences of divorce: An empirically derived approach. *Prevention in Human Services, 7,* 151–175.

Tuckman, J., & Regan, R. (1966). Intactness of the home and behavioral problems in children. *Journal of Child Psychology and Psychiatry, 7,* 225–233.

United States Bureau of the Census. (1989). *Statistical abstract of the United States: 1989* (109th ed.). Washington, DC: Author.

Wallerstein, J. S. (1983). Children of divorce: Stress and developmental tasks. In N. Garmezy & M. Rutter (Eds.), *Stress, coping and development in children* (pp. 265–302). New York: McGraw-Hill.

Wallerstein, J. S. (1984). Children of divorce: Preliminary report of a ten-year follow-up of young children. *American Journal of Orthopsychiatry, 54,* 444–459.

Wallerstein, J. S., & Kelly, J. B. (1980). *Surviving the breakup: How children and parents cope with divorce.* London: Grant McIntyre.

Ysseldyke, J., & Christenson, S. (1986). *The Instructional Environment Scale.* Austin, TX: PRO-ED.

22

FAMILY-SCHOOL PARTNERSHIPS: THE RESPONSE TO CHILD SEXUAL ABUSE AS A CHALLENGING EXAMPLE

Deborah Tharinger and
Connie Burrows Horton

This book calls for efforts to be made by school psychologists and other school-based mental health and education professionals to bridge home and school influences to promote learning and development for children. Although this may seem like a small shift in thinking and practice, in actuality it demands adopting a fundamentally distinct perspective from that guiding traditional school psychology practice. Existing practice has focused on assessing the child and offering interventions to the child and/or to others within the school system who impact the child (e.g., consultation with teachers). Involvement with the child's family typically has been limited to inviting parents to attend meetings, including parents in developmental and family history interviews for child-focused psychological assessment purposes, providing brief parental consultations, and making referrals for family-related services outside of the school. A family-school perspective of practice demands a view of families as *partners* with the school for problem solving and effecting change regarding children.

In the past two decades, theoretical frameworks to guide a shift to a family-school perspective have been laid down by general systems theory applied to psychology (Bertalanffy, 1975), buttressed by work in family systems theory and therapy (Haley, 1978; Hoffman, 1981; Minuchin, 1974), and applied to the child's development through the ecological theory of Bronfenbrenner (1979). These basics have been reviewed in an earlier part of this book and are integrated in an upcoming section of this chapter. Service delivery models for school psychology, based on the above theoretical influences, have further laid the foundation for systems-oriented school psychology practice, with the family seen as a major system with which the school can coordinate to effect change (Anderson, 1983a; Christenson, Abery, & Weinberg, 1986). Although the emphasis of this book and this chapter is on the family-school bridge, it is important to recognize that the system approach and ecological theory speak to the influence of multiple systems on children's development, recognizing, to use Bronfenbrenner's terminology, a series of micro, meso, exo, and macro systems that jointly and transactionally impact the development of the child (Bronfenbrenner, 1979). Addressing the bridge between family and schools is but one piece of the overall picture. For example, attention also has been paid to utilizing a system's model and family-school-community public policy collaboration to more effectively meet the needs of seriously emotionally disturbed children and adolescents (Knitzer, Steinberg, & Fleisch, 1990).

With a theoretical base in place and the continuing entry of systems models and resulting practices within school psychology training programs (Carlson, 1987; Green & Fine, 1988; Willan & Hugman, 1988), many family-school collaborative practices are ready to be put in place to affect the child's educational and psychological development. Although shifting to a family-school mode of functioning as a school psychologist or school mental health professional raises training, practice, pragmatic, and political challenges, efforts are likely to be more easily achieved in problem areas that are primarily in the domain of the educational system, for example, school achievement, school behavior, and special education assessment, entry, and programming. The partnership to be established involves the school and the family, with little direct involvement needed from other systems.

However, the shift applied to responding to child sexual abuse will be exceptionally challenging. In fact, there may not be a more complex issue that impacts the psychological development of children and families and challenges professionals than the sexual abuse of children, especially when the abuse has been committed by a family member. Child sexual abuse is simultaneously (a) *a child welfare or social services issue*, in terms of securing child protection; (b) *a legal issue*, in that it is a crime to commit child abuse and a crime to fail to report it; (c) *a child mental health issue*, in that the psychological consequences to the child victim often are extensive and long term; (d) *a family mental health issue*, in that the psychological consequences to the family can be devastating and also often long term; (e) *a child educational issue*, in that the effects of child sexual abuse on the victim can be disruptive to her or his learning and development; (f) *a larger educational issue*, in that educational efforts directed at offenders, professionals, caretakers, and children will help prevent the occurrence and reoccurrence of sexual abuse; (g) *a sociological/societal issue,* in terms of conditions that may be maintaining the occurrence of sexual abuse; and (h) *a policy issue*, in terms of assignment of resources to identify, treat, and research child sexual abuse. In addition, it can be an extremely *emotional issue*, rendering many people, including mental health and educational professionals, uncomfortable, hesitant, and unprepared to respond.

Thus, child sexual abuse is a child protection issue and a crime that demands a response from multiple systems, including social service, legal (police and courts), mental health, and educational agencies. Responding systems usually have distinct goals that may even be contradictory (Pogge & Stone, 1990). Following disclosure or discovery of sexual abuse, the family often is factionalized, particularly in the case of intrafamilial abuse. Attempts to form bridges to the family system, or more often to pieces of the family system, may be made by each of the involved agencies, but unfortunately, due to differences in goals, philosophies, and lack of resources, coordination among the systems is rare. Furthermore, with the exception of identifying and reporting child abuse and being the major setting for educational or prevention efforts targeted at children, the school, in its educational and/or mental health capacities, typically has not been perceived as a central or even a recognized ongoing respondent to children who have been sexually abused, let alone a respondent to their families. Thus, the challenging task for school psychologists involves more than establishing partnerships with families whose children have been sexually abused. The task also requires fostering new perceptions as well as actively collaborating with the other involved systems.

School psychologists have begun to address their role in meeting the needs of sexually abused children. In the past decade they have been designated as being important figures in schools' responses to child sexual abuse (Brassard, Tyler, & Kehle, 1983; Caterino, 1987; Tharinger, Russian, & Robinson, 1988b; Vevier & Tharinger, 1986). In addition, examples have appeared in the school psychology literature delineating how school psychologists can offer services to maltreated children *and* their parents (Germain, 1988) and to abusive *families* (Brassard & Apellaniz, in press). The latter chapter urged psychologists working in schools to view child abuse systematically and to intervene with a child-school-family-community perspective. However, as mentioned earlier, child *sexual* abuse and *sexually* abusive families appear to raise additional emotional obstacles and challenges for school-based mental health professionals. Practicing school-based school psychologists do not report having as yet gained extensive experience and confidence in responding to child sexual abuse from a child-focused perspective (Tharinger et al., 1988b, reviewed below). With this in mind, proposing that school psychologists need to move toward bridging school, family, and community resources to promote identification and recovery of children who have been sexually abused may seem premature and unreachable. However, if children are to be identified and assisted in their recovery process, coordination of aims and services is required and new models of effective service delivery systems involving the school are demanded. Given: (a) the number of children who have been sexually abused; (b) the finding that most children who are victims of child sexual abuse and their families receive few or inadequate intervention services; (c) the evidence that the effects of sexual abuse can be long lasting for some victims and their families, including possibly having an impact on the next generation; (d) the limits of existing resources in most communities to provide ongoing services for these children and families; and (e) the knowledge of the key function that family members appear to play in the recovery of the child, it is extremely important that the schools examine the role they can play in working with these children and their families. Schools, under the leadership of school psychologists and other school-based mental health professionals, need to determine how they can assist children and families in the identification and recovery

processes and how they can coordinate with other systems, typically the mental health and social service systems, who also are attempting to address the psychological and social needs of this population.

Thus, there is a multiple challenge for school psychologists who attempt to expand their roles to include forming partnerships between families and schools to promote identification and recovery of children who have been sexually abused. First, they must shift to a systems perspective and reconceptualize the recipients of their services, their methods of service delivery, and the coordination of their services with other systems. Second, they must examine their readiness to respond as well as identify and overcome emotional and professional obstacles that may prevent them from being effective. Third, they must obtain extensive education, training, and supervision in the area of sexual abuse, including a theoretical and empirical understanding of factors that promote recovery from sexual abuse. And finally, they must respond with creative initiatives that establish working partnerships between families and schools, utilizing and coordinating with community resources, with the aim of identifying children who have been sexually abused and fostering their recovery process. This chapter sets out to provide a blueprint for reaching this multiple challenge.

A SYSTEMS PERSPECTIVE: IMPACT ON SERVICE CONCEPTUALIZATION AND DELIVERY

A systems perspective has at its core the concept that individuals (e.g., children, parents, and teachers) within a system (e.g., home, school, or community) are interrelated and interdependent. Further, a change in one individual necessarily affects the system and change in the system affects the individual (Carlson & Hickman, 1990). Those working from a systems perspective, especially when it is incorporated into an ecological model, appreciate further that each individual is a part of multiple intertwining systems. Thus, "a holistic view of an individual is dependent upon appreciating and understanding the interrelationships of these systems, their mutual influences, and reciprocal effects" (Christenson et al., 1986, p. 367).

From a systems perspective, new techniques per se are not the focus (although practical applications exist and are discussed below). Instead, there is a fundamental paradigm shift. A systems perspective "provides a framework for organizing the reciprocal influences of the various ecosystems of the developing child" (Christenson et al., 1986, p. 374). Although a school psychologist conceptualizing from a systems framework will continue to work with a variety of individuals, at times providing traditional services, the perspective is what changes. Using a systems perspective a school psychologist does not lose sight of the fact that the individual being interviewed or provided with consultation is not isolated but is part of a child's ecosystem. As part of this perspective school psychologists may view themselves as a link between the child's ecosystems (Christenson et al., 1986). This commonly may be between family and school ecosystems, but also may include links between family and community mental health service providers, family and child protective services, and school and community agencies, among others. Truly viewing oneself as a systems' link involves more than reporting child abuse, providing parents with a referral for outside counseling, and inviting parents to a school conference. Instead, the goal is to create a connected network of systems mobilized on the child's behalf. The multidisciplinary orientation of Armer and Thomas (1978) includes constructs applicable to intersystems networking: *sharing* of suggestions and ideas, *joint* planning, *mutual* decision making, and *reciprocal* teaching and learning. However, creating such a service network can be a complicated task.

Part of what makes the task difficult is the age-old question of who is the client. Over the years, school psychologists have debated the issue and have argued whether the client is the child, the parents, the teacher, or the school (see Christenson et al., 1986). A systems perspective adds an additional complexity. If there is truly to be a paradigm shift, the child, or any other individual can no longer be viewed as the sole client. Instead, the family and other systems must be viewed as clients as well. The strength of the incorporation of Bronfenbrenner's model is that the ultimate focus remains on the developing child. Thus, with this shift, the ultimate concern is still the child's best interest. However, the child's interest may be best served through providing services for other clients whose functioning directly or indirectly impacts the child's functioning. As a result, the targets of a school psychologist's interventions may change as a result of utilizing a systems perspective, just as a systems therapist's alliances shift and change through joining and counterbalancing (Minuchin & Fishman, 1981). Resulting interventions may be targeted in micro, meso, exo, or macro systems levels (Anderson, 1983a).

The basic tenets of a systems perspective, the concepts of *circularity, communication, rules, equifinality, morphostasis, nonsummativity,* and *multifinality* have been explicated previously, and examples of family-school applications provided (Christenson et al., 1986). Although all of the systems principles may effectively be applied to child sexual abuse, examples of two of these systems principles, *nonsummativity* and *multifinality,* applied to child sexual abuse will be used to illustrate the use of the paradigm shift for these sensitive situations. Nonsummativity, the view that the whole system is greater than the sum of its parts, is a key principle in systems theory and highlights the importance of relationship to the parts. Applied to sexual abuse, imagine a not so atypical case in which, among many others, three individuals are greatly impacted: the sexually abused child, the mother who is an adult survivor of sexual abuse and married to her child's offender, and a teacher who is uncomfortable with children's sexuality and its expression, healthy or distorted. The child has been directly traumatized and exhibits a variety of symptoms, including nightmares, frequent crying, fear of adult males, and sexually aggressive behavior with peers. The mother is overwhelmed as she is flooded with memories of her own victimization that she had previously repressed and experiences intense conflicts of loyalty between her allegiance to her husband and to her daughter. The teacher becomes very distressed when she observes the child masturbating and sexually aggressing toward peers. Thus, each individual in the scenario is separately and significantly impacted.

However, the whole is more than the sum of its parts. The relationships tell more of the story. The child, depressed and anxious, becomes more needy of the mother's attention. The mother, however, is overwhelmed with all that she is dealing with herself and is psychologically unavailable to her daughter. The daughter, in turn, acts out more at school, which becomes very distressing to the teacher. The teacher becomes nervous and upset and overreacts punitively to the child's sexual behaviors and sends notes home to the mother stating that the child's behavior must change or she will be removed from the classroom. The child's already vulnerable self-esteem is further compromised by the teacher's reactions and she again becomes more demanding at home. The mother continues to be unable to cope with the increased demands she perceives from her daughter and the school, becomes further depressed, and is virtually immobilized and unable to provide a supportive environment within which her daughter can begin to recover from the abuse and its aftermath. A school psychologist, hoping to intervene on behalf of this child, clearly must recognize the multiple systems involved and the importance of the relationships between them.

On a more hopeful note, another key principle of systems theory is the notion of multifinality, which suggests that similar initial conditions may lead to dissimilar ends. Thus, two children may have experienced similar sexual abuse trau-

mas, but depending on how the multiple systems that impact the child respond, the outcomes may be very different. In the scenario above, without a systems intervention the outcome is not promising. However, if the school psychologist is able to mobilize multiple systems (school- and community-based service providers) in support of the child and in partnership with the family, recovery for the child is more likely. The systems principle of multifinality offers motivation for the school psychologist who realizes that negative outcomes are not inevitable even in cases of child sexual abuse.

The shift to a systems perspective will not be without obstacles within the schools. School administrators will need to give school psychologists freedom to try creative new networking interventions that may require different working hours, clients, and techniques. School psychologists, while attempting to create such networks, may be accused of "not doing their job" as they may provide less direct intervention to children. Parents may be afraid that their family business will become public knowledge if so many systems are involved. Children too may sense the lack of privacy and control. These concerns are real and must be addressed sensitively and professionally. It is worth overcoming the obstacles, however, because the potential impact, according to systems theory, is greater because a positive intervention at one level of a system affects the entire system. If multiple ecosystems can be positively integrated and mobilized through family-school partnerships to assist children's recovery from sexual abuse, many people and systems will have been positively impacted.

READINESS OF SCHOOL PSYCHOLOGISTS

As mentioned earlier, school psychologists have been called upon to be leaders in the schools' response to child sexual abuse. A framework for responding to child sexual abuse has been proposed by Vevier and Tharinger (1986) and provides that school psychologists: (a) be informed resources, by being knowledgeable about child sexual abuse, establishing themselves as resources within their districts, and educating their staffs; (b) respond appropriately to the disclosure of sexual abuse, including providing crisis intervention for the child; (c) evaluate the presence and validity of emotional and behavioral indicators of sexual abuse; (d) report suspected abuse to the proper authorities; (e) provide ongoing indirect intervention, such as teacher and parent consultation, inservice training, and follow-up and monitoring activities; (f) provide direct intervention, such as individual or group supportive counseling with child victims of sexual abuse; and (g) be informed about sexual abuse prevention activities, such as educational programs for children and parents.

Although this framework outlines necessary roles and functions, it falls short of taking a systems driven family-school perspective and a coordinated community view, and lacks a recovery focus that includes families. With the exception of providing parental consultation and education, it fails to call for constructing an active bridge between schools, families, and the community. Without explicitly designating such roles and activities, it sets the standard to practice in a fairly traditional, child-focused manner. The practice standard needs to go beyond this limited view. However, the majority of school psychologists have not had sufficient experience and confidence in performing the roles outlined above and are asking for education and training opportunities. A national sample of practicing school psychologists was surveyed to ascertain their readiness and experience with the roles outlined in the above framework (Tharinger et al., 1988). Questionnaires were obtained from over 400 regular members of the National Association of School Psychologists. The findings revealed that the respondents were only in the first phase of establishing themselves as informed resources and educating others, that is, they were in the process of securing knowledge and professional preparation themselves. They were not yet in the position of feeling established as resources, nor did they feel comfortable educating teachers or other school personnel. Results supported that many school psychologists were responding appropriately and moderately comfortably to disclosures by children and almost half of the surveyed school psychologists reported having supported a child through the crisis following disclosure.

In terms of evaluating indicators of possible child sexual abuse, respondents reported confidence in their basic awareness about identification, but less confidence in their ability to evaluate indicators of sexual abuse. Results also indicated that respondents felt well prepared for reporting and that their school districts support such activity. The role of providing indirect intervention services, primarily to teachers and parents, had been adopted by many of the respondents, but typically was limited to consultation focused on identification of a child as having been sexually abused. The great majority of respondents reported that they had not provided direct services to children who have been sexually abused. They viewed direct service provision to the child as less important than their other roles, felt little school district support for it, and reported little confidence in their ability to provide such service. At the same time they reported a desire to obtain education and training in providing crisis intervention and counseling to sexually abused children, suggesting an interest in moving in the direction of school-based provision of some of the direct services needed to promote recovery. Respondents viewed the role of supporting or participating in sexual abuse prevention education programs for children and parents as important and most indicated that their districts were providing some educational programs. Approximately one third reported having supported or participated in prevention education programs for children but fewer than 1 in 10 stated that they have supported or participated in prevention education programs for parents. Most stated that their confidence in their knowledge base in this area is low and that they want additional education and training.

The results of this one study indicate that many of the school psychologists sampled are identifying and providing initial support to sexually abused children. Although the school psychologists are not as yet prepared to respond to the ongoing recovery needs of children who have been abused, they are open to education and training experiences that will prepare them. This openness creates an opportunity for educators, trainers, and supervisors to function from a systemic model of child development and of professional practice, with a focus on school-family-community intervention and collaboration in response to child sexual abuse. Awareness of emotional and professional obstacles to responding to child sexual abuse may facilitate the preparation process.

Identifying and Overcoming

There are many obstacles that school psychologists and other mental health and educational professionals must identify and address before attempting to respond to the needs of sexually abused children and developing family-school partnerships. These apply to educators, trainers, supervisors, practitioners, and students.

Emotional Obstacles

There are multiple emotional reactions that can constitute obstacles to involvement in the response to child sexual abuse. They are not unique to school psychologists and may apply to all persons confronting the problem. One of the first emotional conflicts encountered involves accepting the fact that children *are* sexually abused, usually by adults charged with their care and protection. The idea that children are sexually abused may produce a number of extremely uncomfortable feelings, including horror (Herman, 1981), repulsion and dread (Justice & Justice, 1979), fear and anger (Lee, 1980), and possibly resulting disbelief (Conte & Berliner, 1981). These emotional reactions can constitute a basis for denying the existence of child sexual abuse. Resultant denial may take the form of minimizing the seriousness of the problem, being reluctant to accept the prevalence of the problem, or expressing disbelief in the credibility of the child's report (Conte & Berliner, 1981; Frenken & Van Stolk, 1990). These responses can seriously undermine the individual's capacities to respond effectively to the psychological needs of sexually abused children and their families.

A second emotional conflict involves the difficult task of sorting through personal values and feelings about sexuality and sexual behavior. This includes recognizing one's own sexual feelings, fantasies, and impulses; reviewing familial, religious, and societal teachings about sexuality; examining one's ability to communicate with others about sexual matters (Gottlieb & Dean, 1981); being alert and ready to respond to the possible sexualized behavior presented by many sexually abused children (Tharinger, 1990); and examining personal views on sexuality education and sexual abuse education for children and adolescents in the schools (see Friedrich, 1990; Tharinger et al., 1989; Tharinger, 1987).

A third emotional conflict involves countertransference reactions that may surface when learning about child sexual abuse or working with children who have been abused or with families where abuse has occurred. Memories or discoveries of an individual's own abuse or abuse of a family member may arise, possibly causing much pain and confusion and rendering the individual unable to respond appropriately to the needs of a sexually abused child and those of the family. Countertransference reactions may necessitate seeking out psychotherapy, supervision, and/or consultation from other mental health professionals (Frenken & Van Stolk, 1990; Pollak & Levy, 1990).

Another common emotional conflict involves fear or ambivalence about reporting suspected or confirmed abuse. There is fear of the pain that will be created for children and families by calling attention to the possible existence of child sexual abuse, along with the fear of the damage that will continue if nothing is done (the fact that reporting by professionals is legally mandated in all states does not preclude this struggle). Accompanying this fear is the concern that the systems that investigate reports of child sexual abuse, child protective services agencies and/or police departments, will fail to substantiate the abuse, leaving the child in danger of further abuse. Countertransference feelings of guilt and shame, anger, and sympathy also have been linked to practitioners failing to report child abuse (Pollak & Levy, 1990).

An additional emotional obstacle involves the perception of the degree of psychopathology present in sexually abusing families, including within the offender, the nonoffending caretaker, and the child victim. There have been numerous theories put forth to attempt to explain the etiology of child sexual abuse, including the sociological perspective, the intra-individual perspective, the family systems view, the feminist view, and Finkelhor's model of what constitutes necessary and sufficient motivation to sexually abuse a child (see Finkelhor, 1984; Vevier & Tharinger, 1986; Walker, 1988). Historically there have been interpretations ranging from seeing all offenders as psychotic or psychopathic to viewing sexual abuse as simply a manifestation of a dysfunctional family system. Although none of the etiological models fully account for the multiple paths that can lead to sexual abuse, it is helpful to have a grasp of etiological perspectives in order to appreciate the broad range of psychopathology, from slight to extreme, that can exist within the individuals in these families.

A final emotional obstacle involves the fear of being stressed, overwhelmed, and rapidly burnt out from working with sexually abused children and their families. It certainly is true that the nature of the offense, multiple system involvement, possible legal involvement, complexity of needs of the children and families, and countertransference issues tend to make working in the area of child abuse a highly stressful experience. Efforts to prevent burnout need to be put in place, such as involvement in professional consultation, supervision, and support activities. Thus, emotional reactions by professionals to the act of child sexual abuse and to the process that follows are pervasive. These emotional reactions or obstacles demand attention if denial is to be overcome, personal issues on sexuality addressed, countertransference reactions confronted, and burnout prevented.

Professional Obstacles

There also are multiple professional issues that can constitute obstacles to involvement in the response to child sexual abuse. These include the lack, until recently, of an adequate information base, the absence of formal education and training in professional psychology training programs, and the lack of professional guidelines for training and practice. These three obstacles contribute to limiting competence on the part of practitioners and students in training.

Until recently there has been an inadequate information base regarding sexually abused children and their families, including a lack of theoretical models and empirical research findings concerning etiology, effects, and recovery, as well as an underrepresentation of psychologists contributing to the field (Alpert & Paulson, 1990). However, in the past 10 years and especially the last 5 years, the number of publications on child sexual abuse has exploded, the quality has improved, and the empirical base of understanding has been made more evident. Recent books by psychologists include Briere (1989), Cicchetti and Carlson (1989), Friedrich (1990), Haugaard and Reppucci (1988), MacFarlane and Waterman (1986), Walker (1988), Walker, Bonner, and Kaufman (1988), and Wyatt and Powell (1988). In addition, journals in psychology, social work, education, psychiatry, nursing, pediatrics, and especially those of an interdisciplinary nature (e.g., *Child Abuse & Neglect: The International Journal; Journal of Interpersonal Violence*), feature recent empirical findings in the field. A recent 1990 issue of the journal *Professional Psychology: Research and Practice*, published by the American Psychological Association and edited by Judie Alpert, a school psychologist, is an excellent example of the serious attention now being paid to the topic by psychologists. Thus, although the knowledge base in child sexual abuse is relatively new and rapidly expanding, at this time there is an adequate theoretical and empirical base to guide practice, including identification, intervention, and prevention activities.

Despite the existing and growing knowledge base, most professional programs in psychology, including school psychology training programs, have not formally incorporated education and training in child sexual abuse and there is no literature addressing training issues at the graduate level (Alpert & Paulson, 1990). This raises the questions of where and how students and current practitioners can receive training and by whom. It can be assumed that most psychologists working and teaching in this area at this time are self-taught and in addition have sought out the expertise and supervision of other mental health professionals, often from other disciplines. Given the number of children who are abused and in need of identification and intervention, it is essential for professional psychology training programs to make a commitment to foster research, education, and training in this area. An excellent example of such an effort in one school psychology training program is provided by Alpert and Paulson (1990). It also is important for professional associations, such as APA and NASP, to develop standards for education, training, and practice (for recommendations made to the APA, see Walker et al., 1989). In addition, practicing school psychologists need to seek out inservice training opportunities at the local and national level. As these professional obstacles are overcome, the confidence and competence of practitioners will enable them to provide more effectively for the needs of sexually abused children and their families. The following section provides a summary of

knowledge needed to enhance basic competence and guide the choice of intervention efforts.

CHILD SEXUAL ABUSE

Provided in this section is a brief overview of the nature and incidence of sexual abuse of children, the initial and long-term effects, a theoretical model addressing how sexual abuse impacts development and the recovery process, and empirical evidence on variables that appear to mediate the impact of and recovery from child sexual abuse. An understanding of the recovery process and factors that mediate recovery will help guide the establishment of family-school partnerships.

General Description

Behaviorally, sexual abuse is seldom restricted to attempted or actual intercourse (Finkelhor, 1979). Rather, sexual abuse may consist of any one or a progression of the following acts: nudity, disrobing, genital exposure, observation of the child, kissing, fondling, masturbation, oral-genital contact, digital penetration, and vaginal or anal intercourse (Sgroi, Blick, & Porter, 1982). In addition, contrary to the stereotype of the "friendly stranger," children usually know the people who sexually abuse them (Mrazek, 1983). Males are reported to be the abusers in 80% to 95% of cases (American Humane Association [AHA], 1982; Conte & Berliner, 1981; NCCAN, 1982). Girls are reported victims of sexual abuse at significantly higher rates than boys, four to one (AHA, 1982; Conte & Berliner, 1981; Kempe & Kempe, 1984; NCCAN, 1982). However, data are emerging suggesting that boys may be victims of sexual abuse more often than reports indicate (Crewdson, 1988; Vander Mey, 1988), and possibly as often as girls. The majority of sexual abusers of girls are members of the child's nuclear or extended family (De Francis, 1969; Garbarino & Gilliam, 1980), whereas male children are more likely to be abused by nonfamily rather than family members (Vander Mey,

1988). Lastly, effects of sexual abuse on female and male victims appear to be serious and long lasting, and although there are differences between the effects on boys and girls, there appear to be more similarities than differences (Finkelhor, 1990).

Incidence and Prevalence

Although general consensus exists that sexual abuse is a much more frequent childhood experience than previously thought, accurate and reliable data on the incidence and prevalence of child sexual abuse in the United States are nonexistent. Further, there is agreement that child sexual abuse remains largely undisclosed and is grossly underreported even if disclosed (Mayhall & Norgard, 1983). A number of large retrospective surveys indicate that between 20% and 38% of all women have had a childhood sexual encounter with an adult male (Crewdson, 1988; Finkelhor, 1979; Fromuth, 1986; Russell, 1983).

The concern has been voiced that handicapped persons, especially mentally retarded individuals, are particularly vulnerable to being victims of child sexual abuse and that the incidence of assault in handicapped populations is higher than it is in the nonhandicapped population (Ammerman, Van Hasselt, & Hersen, 1988; Anderson, 1983; Tharinger, Horton, & Millea, 1990). However, accurate information describing the prevalence of sexual abuse and exploitation in handicapped populations and with the mentally retarded also do not exist. It has been proposed that mentally retarded children, and possibly other handicapped individuals, may be extra vulnerable to sexual abuse because they are often dependent on caregivers their whole life, are relatively powerless in society, are easily coerced, are emotionally and socially insecure and needy, and often are not educated about sexuality and sexual abuse (Tharinger et al., 1990). In the schools, special care needs to be made to identify and promote recovery in sexually abused handicapped children.

Effects of Child Sexual Abuse

Professionals who come in contact with sexually abused children agree that sexual abuse has "widespread consequences for the child's subsequent psychological and social life" (Conte & Berliner, 1981, p. 603). Sexually abused children have been described in the clinical literature since the late 1930s, but only recently have empirical investigations (e.g., Conte & Schuerman, 1987; Gomes-Schwartz, Horowitz, & Cardarelli, 1990; Runyan, Everson, Edelsohn, Hunter, & Coulter, 1988; Tufts, 1984) been conducted to examine the impact and developmental sequelae of this experience on children.

Initial effects. Empirical research has consistently supported the existence of a variety of initial symptoms in many girls who have been sexually abused, the most common being fear, anxiety, depression, anger, aggression, and sexually inappropriate behavior (Finkelhor, 1990). Recent research comparing boys and girls indicates many similarities, although boys tend to evidence more externalizing symptoms and girls more internalizing ones (Friedrich, Urquiza, & Beilke, 1986; Friedrich, Beilke, & Urquiza, 1987, 1988; Gomes-Schwartz, Horowitz, & Cardarelli, 1990; Tufts, 1984). A recent review on the impact of sexual abuse on the sexual behavior of children (Tharinger, 1990) concluded that: 16% to 41% of sexually abused children manifest overt sexual behavior problems and that the problems vary according to age; and more sexually abused children display sexual problems than comparison groups of normal children, nonabused clinic children, nonabused hospitalized children, diagnosed externalizing children, physically abused clinic children, and physically abused hospitalized children.

It is apparent that a significant number of children abused as children show serious psychological problems. Tufts researchers (1984) found that 40% of the 7- to 13-year-old children in their study met their criteria as seriously disturbed. Friedrich et al. (1986) found that 46% of sexually abused girls in their sample had significantly elevated scores on an Internalizing scale (including fearful, inhibited, depressed, and overcontrolled behaviors) and 46% on an Externalizing scale (aggressive, antisocial, and undercontrolled behaviors). Browne and Finkelhor (1986) concluded that in the immediate aftermath of sexual abuse, from one-fifth to two-fifths of abused children seen by clinicians manifest pathological disturbance.

Long-term effects. The most frequently noted patterns associated with a history of child sexual abuse for women include depression, self-destructive behavior, anxiety, feelings of isolation and stigma, poor self-esteem, difficulty in trusting others, a tendency toward revictimization, substance abuse, and sexual maladjustment (Brown & Finkelhor, 1986). Four overall dynamics that result from sexual victimization are proposed by Finkelhor and Browne (1985) and include: traumatic sexualization, betrayal, stigmatization, and powerlessness. When studied as adults, female victims of sexual abuse as a group demonstrate impairment when compared with their nonvictimized counterparts, and approximately one-fifth evidence serious psychopathology. An understanding of the long-term impact on males is beginning to appear, with most studies reporting similar long-term findings for male victims as with females (Finkelhor, 1990).

Recovery from Child Sexual Abuse

Although most research studies to date have focused on understanding the initial and long-term effects of child sexual abuse, attention is shifting to both theoretical and empirical efforts to understand the process of recovery from child sexual abuse. This is in part because of the more methodologically sophisticated longitudinal research that is now appearing, as well as the existence of viable theoretical frameworks.

A developmental, organizational theoretical perspective. In considering the impact of child sexual abuse on development over time and possible mediating influences, a theoretical perspective is needed that can integrate the existing body of knowledge, guide future research, and help inform intervention decisions. A theoretical framework also must be sufficiently complex to reflect the multifaceted ways in which constitutional and environmental factors, as well as their resulting transactions, affect the social, emotional, cognitive, behavioral, and sexual development of children who have been sexually abused. A developmental, organizational theoretical perspective may be useful in this regard. Developmental, organizational models are not new to the area of child maltreatment (Brassard, Germain, & Hart, 1987). They have been proposed to account for the etiology and developmental consequences of physical abuse (Belsky, 1980; Cicchetti & Rizley, 1981) and psychological abuse (Egeland, Sroufe, & Erickson, 1983; Erickson & Egeland, 1987). These models have their roots in ecological theory of human development (Bronfenbrenner, 1979) and the organismic (structural) approach to development (Piaget, 1971; Sroufe, 1979; Werner, 1948; White, 1976).

Theoreticians and researchers in the past decade have conceptualized a child's developmental outcomes as having multiple historical and causal determinants rather than single-factor etiologies. For maltreated children, including children who have been sexually abused, development is related to many factors, but particularly the type and severity of the maltreatment and the subsequent quality of care the child receives. The transactional model views the multiple transactions among environmental forces, caregiver characteristics, and child characteristics as dynamic, reciprocal contributions to the events and outcomes of child development. This model discounts the efficacy of simple, linear "cause-effect" models of causality and suggests that it is impossible to understand a child's development by focusing on single pathogenic events (such as having been sexually abused). It is argued that how the environment responds to a particular child's characteristics at a particular time must be analyzed in a dynamic fashion (Sameroff & Chandler, 1975).

Thus, the organizational model is transactional and conceptualizes the environment and the child as mutually influencing each other. This perspective views maltreatment phenomena as an expression of underlying dysfunction in the parent-child-environment system, rather than solely the result of aberrant parental personality traits, environmental stress, or deviant child characteristics. It also conceptualizes the recovery process as a reflection of what occurs in the parent-child-environment system following the occurrence and disclosure of abuse, recognizing that it is influenced by features of the child, parents, and the environment that existed during and prior to the abuse, as well as the nature of the abuse itself. Because the child and the environment are seen as reciprocally influencing each other, it follows that behavior at a later point reflects not only the quality of earlier adaptation but also the intervening environmental inputs and supports. As the child develops, both the match between child and caretaker as well as salient child and caretaker characteristics may change. If a child demonstrates deviant development across time, it is assumed that the child has been involved in a *continuous* maladaptive process. The continued manifestation of maladaptation depends primarily on environmental support, though the child's characteristics, reciprocally, partially determine the nature of the environment. Thus, maladapted children contribute to their own environment and their own development.

From the developmental, organismic point of view, normal or healthy development is defined as structural changes among the child's behavioral systems that reflect the dynamic interactions of changing familial, social, and environmental variables and that allow the child to attain competence (Cicchetti & Schneider-Rosen, 1987). Competence is defined as the ability to utilize environmental and personal resources to attain a satisfactory, age-appropriate adaptation. Competence at one period of development prepares the way for the formation of competence at the next (Sroufe & Rutter, 1984). Moreover, normal development is marked by the integration of earlier competencies into later modes of functioning. In addition, early competence also exerts a subtle influence toward adaptation throughout the life span because each developmental issue, although perhaps most salient at one developmental period, is of continuing importance throughout the life cycle.

Pathological development, in contrast, is conceived of as a lack of effective integration and organization of the social, emotional, and cognitive competencies that are important to achieving adaptation at a particular developmental level (Cicchetti & Schneider-Rosen, 1987). Pathological development leads to personal distress and cognitive, affective, or social incompetence. Because early structures often are incorporated into later structures, an early deviation or disturbance in functioning ultimately may cause a much larger disturbance to emerge later on. However, just as early competence may lead to later adaptation and incompetence to later maladaptation, this isomorphism in functioning is not the only expectable outcome, as pointed out earlier by the systems theory principle of multifinality. There are many factors that may mediate between early and later adaptation or maladaptation that may permit alternative outcomes to occur; that is, early problems or deviations in the successful resolution of a developmental task may be countered by major changes in the child's experience that could result in the successful negotiation of subsequent developmental tasks. For example, a major family change, such as the child receiving consistent and appropriate support from the caretaking parent, could enable the child to successfully master upcoming developmental tasks.

Longitudinal findings on effects of sexual abuse. Although clinical and empirical evidence has accumulated on common initial and long-term effects of being a victim of child sexual abuse (reviewed earlier), the empirical information has resulted from cross-sectional research methodologies. Results from longitudinal research studies that have followed children who have been sexually abused are beginning to appear and have recently been reviewed by Finkelhor (1990). It appears that over an initial period of time from 5 months to a year and in some cases several years, approximately one-quarter to one-half of the children appear to improve, measured by decreased symptomatology. Findings also indicate that some children get worse, ranging from 14% to 28%. These results raise the question of what is known about factors that facilitate or mediate the recovery process in children who have been sexually abused.

Factors that mediate impact and recovery. Research findings on variables that mediate the impact of child sexual abuse have been reviewed by Browne and Finkelhor (1986). They concluded that sexual abuse experiences that involve fathers or stepfathers, genital contact, and force appear to result in more trauma to the victims, whereas the relation between traumatic impact and age when the abuse began and the duration of the abuse is seen as complex and unclear. These mediating variables, the first three of which appear to affect impact and possibly long-term recovery, cannot in and of themselves be changed. It is important to examine what is known about mediating factors, typically post-abuse factors, that can be altered through intervention efforts and that appear to promote ongoing recovery. Several research studies (reviewed below) have investigated the relationship between impact and recovery and the following factors: response to the abuse by the nonoffending caretaker; quality of the caretaker-child relationship; response to the abuse by the offender; quality of the offender-child relationship; psychological functioning of the caretaker; quality of the child's other relationships; child's perception of responsibility for the abuse; quality of family functioning; and number of stressful life events experienced by the child in addition to the abuse itself. Although initial responses to the abuse by the

caretaking parent and the offender cannot be altered through subsequent interventions, the remaining influences are open to change, positively or negatively. All of these factors constitute the quality of care the child receives, as discussed in the previous theoretical discussion, and will impact the child developing toward competence or pathology.

The response to the abuse by the nonoffending caretaker has been found to be significantly related to initial and ongoing recovery in several studies. It was found that when mothers reacted to disclosure with anger and punishment, children manifested more behavioral disturbances (Tufts, 1984). In addition, in another study children who had encountered negative reactions from their parents were found to have 2½ times the number of symptoms compared with children whose parent(s) responded positively (Anderson, Bach, & Griffith, 1981). The aid of family support in recovery also has been reported by Finkelhor (1990) and supported by Browne and Finkelhor (1986). Furthermore, the child's view of the quality of her relationship with her mother significantly affected outcome in a study of girls sexually abused by an adult male in their families (Tharinger et al., 1989). Those who viewed their relationship with their mother as trusting, safe, and supportive were experiencing fewer emotional and behavioral problems a year after the abuse was disclosed.

The response to abuse by the offender also appears to be related to the child's recovery. It has been found that the offender's denial that the abuse took place negatively mediated the impact of the abuse on the child's adjustment (Conte & Schuerman, 1987). Not surprisingly, it also has been found by the same researchers that the victim's perception of bearing some responsibility for the abuse negatively mediated adjustment. They also reported that the closer the degree of relationship between the child and the abuser the more negative the impact on adjustment.

The psychological functioning of the nonoffending caretaker also serves as a key variable in the recovery of the child, as documented by several studies. The tendency for the caretaker to have a negative outlook on life was related to severity or seriousness of impact of the abuse in Conte and Schuerman's 1987 study. In addition, degree of maternal depression was found to negatively impact behavioral and emotional functioning following sexual abuse (Tharinger et al., 1989). It also has been reported that victims are adversely affected by negative relationships with their siblings (Conte, 1984) and that having a supportive relationship with an adult (other than a caretaker) or a sibling mediates the impact of the abuse (Conte & Schuerman, 1987).

General aspects of the family's functioning also have been related to impact of the abuse on the child's recovery. Research has supported a relationship between problems in living, including unemployment, substance abuse, and lack of social support, and the impact of sexual abuse (Conte, 1984). In addition, the number of characteristics of the victim's family characteristic of a poorly functioning and unhealthy family has been found to negatively mediate the impact of the abuse (Conte & Schuerman, 1987), as has the number of stressful life events the child has experienced following the abuse (Tharinger et al., 1989).

Summary: Child Sexual Abuse, the Recovery Process, and Targets for Intervention

Many children, both girls and boys, are sexually abused, resulting in significant symptomatology in the internalizing, externalizing, and sexual domains. Research from cross-sectional studies indicates that approximately 40% of children show significant initial disturbance, with 20% of adults abused as children showing such severity. This shift fits with the findings from recent longitudinal studies that up to one-half of sexually abused children are showing improvement with time (although it fails to account for the percentage of children who appear to get worse with time). The developmental, organizational model de-

scribed earlier is a helpful framework from which to understand the central mediating variables that may account for the multiple developmental paths that are followed by sexually abused children. The quality of care the child receives from her or his caregivers following the abuse, as well as the environment's ongoing response, viewed in dynamic transaction with the child's characteristics, are seen as key to the child's developing competence and recovery. Empirical findings from the few longitudinal studies available support the theoretical model and demonstrate the importance of the quality of the child's relationships, the mental health of the caretaker, the child's perceptions, and the quality of the family and environmental functioning. The invasiveness and forceful nature of the abuse itself cannot be altered, nor can the identified relationship of the offender to the child. However, through intervention efforts, individual, relationship, family, and environmental functioning and their transactions can be changed to promote the child's competence and recovery. Family-school partnerships, coordinated with community resources, are part of the effort that can foster this positive path.

ESTABLISHING FAMILY-SCHOOL PARTNERSHIPS TO PROMOTE IDENTIFICATION AND RECOVERY

The goal of establishing family-school partnerships is to identify children who have been sexually abused and to foster their competence and recovery. The partnerships targeted at identification efforts are seen as being school wide and group oriented, whereas the partnerships targeted at recovery are conceived of as being set up uniquely and individually with each abused child and her or his family. As will be evident, the partnerships benefit from collaboration and coordination with local community agencies. Prior to explicating these two levels of family-school partnerships, numerous preparatory steps need to be identified and discussed.

Preparatory Steps

First, involved school psychologists and other school mental health professionals need to address the emotional and professional obstacles presented and discussed earlier. Next, they need to assist other involved school staff (e.g., teachers and administrators) in examining and confronting their own emotional and competence issues that may render them knowingly or unknowingly resistant to a school-based response to child sexual abuse. It is important that teachers and administrators explore their views of the role of the school as regards identification efforts and promotion of recovery through school-based and community coordinated interventions. Resulting administrative and school staff support needs to be assessed and school policies set forth. In addition, personnel and financial resources need to be secured for planned family-school partnership efforts. It may be helpful to create a school-and/or district-wide child sexual abuse task force composed of psychologists, administrators, teachers, and other school personnel charged with addressing the needs of children who have been sexually abused and of their families, as well as the preparation of the school and community to respond to these identified needs. The inclusion of parents and possibly adolescents on the task force (i.e., families), could be an excellent first step in establishing family-school partnerships. Following, or concurrently with such school-based efforts, groundwork needs to be laid for collaborating and coordinating with other involved agencies, such as child protective services and mental health centers. These efforts could include plans for coordinated case management and possibly the establishment of an interagency/school task force to address needs, as well as service delivery and collaboration issues.

In addition, each involved school needs to work toward creating an atmosphere where children and families feel they can be safe and can trust school professionals to treat them with respect, compassion, and partnership status.

Reaching this goal will require school staff to function with a high level of professionalism (e.g., demonstrating appropriate handling of issues of confidentiality). Extending a respectful, compassionate, and professional hand to children who have been abused and to their families also will require that all involved school professionals closely examine the ways they may tend to define and respond to "dysfunctional" families and the split that is created between "them" and "us." If working partnerships are to be formed between families and schools, especially with those where abuse has occurred, the capacity to respect and appropriately empower these families must be present.

Family-School Partnerships to Promote Identification and Initial Positive Response to Disclosure/Discovery

Identification of sexually abused children will be assisted through educating adults who are in contact with children to recognize common behavioral, emotional, familial, and disclosure signs that are suggestive of a child having been sexually abused. Most educational efforts to date have been targeted directly at children in schools, through child abuse prevention programs. The programs claim to assist children in preventing abuse, whereas in actuality, children cannot prevent their own abuse (see Reppucci & Haugaard, 1989 and Tharinger et al., 1988a for a discussion of central issues). At most children can limit the extent of the abuse after they have been approached or disclose that they have been abused. Schools, knowingly or unknowingly, have entered into *partnerships with children* to identify (and prevent) sexual abuse, but they have failed, with some exceptions, to enter into such partnerships with parents and families. Parents and children together, that is families, need to be educated about how to identify and respond to child sexual abuse.

It is not easy to involve parents and families in any school-based activities, let alone in family-focused educational activities about child sexual abuse. The first step may be to partner with a core group of interested parents and families, perhaps those who have had professional or personal experience with sexual abuse (and are in their own recovery process). As a group of committed parents, families, school-based psychological staff, and possibly community-based experts, plans can then be made regarding the most effective ways to expand the partnership to other parents and families. The goal, through educational activities offered by family-school partners, is to provide many families with: (a) ways to overcome emotional obstacles that can lead to denial, minimization, or exaggeration of child sexual abuse, as well as overidentification with child victims; (b) knowledge of how to identify signs of sexual abuse; (c) knowledge of how to report abuse; (d) the means to respond appropriately and positively to children and families when disclosures and discoveries of sexual abuse are made; and (e) competencies to cope with the aftermath of the report, including investigations by police department and child protective services, legal action against the perpetrator, and pressures on the child to recant. In addition, it is hoped that participating families that are at risk of sexually abusing their children will be encouraged to take needed action to prevent such an occurrence.

Family-School Partnerships to Promote Ongoing Positive Response and Recovery

In contrast with the school-wide family-school partnership efforts that have as their goal identification of sexually abused children and promotion of initial appropriate and positive response to children and families, individual family-school partnerships are unique, case based, and have as their goal promoting the recovery process of each abused child. This goal may be approached by providing and/or coordinating services to the child, individual family members, the family as a whole, and other concerned and significant persons, such as the child's teacher. The partnership aspect requires that the family have an active role in co-assessing their needs, co-determining a contract, co-managing their services, and co-evaluating their progress.

Drawing on the developmental, organization model applied to the recovery process and the supportive research findings discussed earlier, it is important to set into place a cooperative plan to: (a) promote positive relationships between the child and the caretaking parent(s), the child and siblings, and the child and other adults; (b) support positive mental health of the caretaking parent(s); (c) address the child's perceptions; (d) stabilize the family's functioning; and (e) reduce stressful life events in the child's and family's life. These goals can be addressed through numerous intervention plans. Possible school-based services may include crisis intervention for the child and family, individual or group counseling for the child, special educational services for the child, parent consultation, family education and consultation, family counseling/therapy, support groups, and teacher education and consultation. Excellent resources for mental health efforts targeted at abused children and their families include Friedrich (1990), Garbarino, Stott, and Faculty of the Erikson Institute (1989), and James (1989). In addition, coordinated planning among the family, school, and involved community agencies is necessary, with the family being an active participant in their own case management.

Although the aim of this chapter has been to provide a theoretical and empirical rationale for establishing family-school partnerships to identify and promote the recovery of sexually abused children, it is important to acknowledge that a percentage of families where abuse has occurred will not be open to entering into a family-school partnership or to receiving school-based services although the child may be open to and asking for assistance. In this case, partnerships between the child and the school may be all that can be estabished. As stated in the Survey on Child Abuse and Neglect: A Report by the Committee on Professional Practice and Standards (COPPS) of the American Psychological Association:

> For some children, parental involvement, especially in the initial stages of disclosure or treatment, may involve considerable risk of a variety of sorts. There is need for legal, logistical, and psychological accessibility of services for children without parental involvement. If services are available or connected to a school system, for example, in order for those services to be effectively utilized the following would need to be in place: some contact could exist without parental consent; students would have logistical access to the psychologist; and the psychological atmosphere within the school would be such that it would feel acceptable for students to have contact with psychologists. (COPPS, 1989, p. 7)

This point is an important one. School psychologists need to be involved in responding to situations where child-school partnerships are the only available option to securing needed interventions, that is, when family-school partnerships are not possible.

SUMMARY AND CONCLUSIONS

Efforts need to be made by school psychologists and other school-based mental health and education professionals to bridge home and school influences to promote learning and development for children. This shift in practice focus demands adopting a fundamentally distinct theoretical perspective from that guiding traditional school psychology practice. The theoretical and pragmatic shift in school psychology from child-focused practice to child-family-community-focused practice is a challenging one, especially when directed toward responding to complex societal issues such as child sexual abuse. Child sexual abuse demands a coordinated response from multiple systems, including social service, legal, mental health, and educational agencies. An effective coordinated response presently is rare for a variety of

reasons, one of which is the lack of education and training for school psychologists in working with sexually abused children and their families and coordinating their work with other involved agencies. However, if children are to be identified and assisted in their recovery process, coordination of services is required and new models of effective service delivery systems involving the family-school partnerships are needed.

It has been maintained in this chapter that to meet this goal school psychologists must shift to a systems perspective and reconceptualize the recipients of their services, their methods of service delivery, and the coordination of their services with other systems. They also must examine their readiness to respond as well as to identify and overcome emotional and professional obstacles that may prevent them from being competent, confident, and effective. In addition, they must obtain extensive education, training, and supervision in the area of sexual abuse, including theoretical and empirical understanding of factors that promote recovery from sexual abuse. With these objectives met, school psychologists will be able to respond with creative initiatives that, coordinated with community resources and taking into account emotional resistances of children and families, establish (a) school-wide family-school partnerships that aim to identify sexually abused children and facilitate positive initial family response, and (b) individual family-school partnerships that aim to foster the recovery process of children by targeting the children's key relationships, the children's perceptions, the mental health of the caretaking parent(s), the stability of the family, and the reduction of stressful life events for the child. These efforts by school psychologists will serve to reduce the initial and long-term trauma experienced by children who have been sexually abused and allow these children to take advantage more fully of the opportunities for learning and development provided by schooling.

REFERENCES

Alpert, J., & Paulson, A. (1990). Graduate-level education and training in child sexual abuse. *Professional Psychology: Research and Practice, 21,* 366–371.

American Humane Association. (1982). *Estimated number of sexual maltreatment victims in the United States reported to child protective services.* Denver: American Humane Association.

Ammerman, R. T., Van Hasselt, V. B., & Hersen, B. (1988). Maltreatment of handicapped children: A critical review. *Journal of Family Violence, 3,* 53–72.

Anderson, C. (1983a). An ecological developmental mode for a family orientation in school psychology. *Journal of School Psychology, 21,* 179–189.

Anderson, C. (1983b). *Teaching people with mental retardation about sexual abuse prevention.* Santa Cruz, CA: Network Publications.

Anderson, S. C., Bach, S. M., & Griffith, S. (1981). *Psychosocial sequelae in intrafamilial victims of sexual assault and abuse.* Paper presented at the Third International Conference on Child Abuse and Neglect, Amsterdam, The Netherlands.

Armer, B., & Thomas, B. K. (1978). Attitudes toward interdisciplinary collaboration in pupil personnel service teams. *Journal of School Psychology, 16,* 167–176.

Belsky, J. (1980). Child maltreatment: An ecological integration. *American Psychologist, 35,* 320–335.

Bertalanffy, L. (1975). General systems theory and psychiatry. In S. Arieti (Ed.), *American handbook of psychiatry* (Vol. 1, 2nd ed., pp. 1095–1117). New York: Basic Books.

Brassard, M. R., & Apellaniz, I. (in press). The abusive family: Theory and intervention. In M. J. Fine & C. I. Carlson (Eds.), *Handbook of family school problems and interventions: A systems perspective.* New York: Allyn & Bacon.

Brassard, M. R., Germain, R., & Hart, S. N. (Eds.). (1987). *Psychological maltreatment of children and youth.* New York: Pergamon Press.

Brassard, M. R., Tyler, A. H., & Kehle, T. J. (1983). Sexually abused children: Identification and suggestions for intervention. *School Psychology Review, 12,* 93–97.

Briere, J. (1989). *Therapy for adults molested as children: Beyond Survival.* New York: Springer.

Bronfenbrenner, U. (1979). *The ecology of human development.* Cambridge, MA: Harvard University Press.

Browne, A., & Finkelhor, D. (1986). The impact of child sexual abuse: A review of the research *Psychological Bulletin, 99,* 66–77.

Carlson, C. I., & Hickman, J. (1990). Family consultation in schools in special services. In C. A. Maher & R. E. Greenberg (Eds.), *Effective teams and groups: Vital contribution to special needs students* [Special issue]. *Special Services in the Schools, 6.*

Caterino, L. C. (1987). Children and sexual abuse. In A. Thomas & J. Grimes (Eds.), *Children's needs: Psychological perspectives* (pp. 522–532). Kent, OH: National Association of School Psychologists.

Christenson, A., Abery, B., & Weinberg, R. A. (1986). An alternative model for the delivery of psychological services in the school community. In S. N. Elliott & J. C. Witt (Eds.), *The delivery of psychological services in schools* (pp. 349–388). Hillsdale, NJ: Lawrence Erlbaum.

Cicchetti, D., & Carlson, V. (1989). *Child maltreatment: Theory and research on the causes and consequences of child abuse and neglect.* Cambridge, England: Cambridge University Press.

Cicchetti, D., & Rizley, R. (1981). Developmental perspectives on the etiology, intergenerational transmission, and sequelae of child maltreatment. In W. Damon (Ed.), *New directions for child development* (pp. 31–55). San Francisco: Jossey-Bass.

Cicchetti, D., & Schneider-Rosen, K. (1987). An organizational approach to childhood depression. In M. Rutter, C. Izard, & P. Reed (Eds.), *Depression in young people: Developmental and clinical perspectives* (pp. 71–134). New York: Guilford Press.

Committee on Professional Practice and Standards. (1989). *Survey on child abuse and neglect.* Washington, DC: American Psychological Association.

Conte, J. (1984). The effects of sexual abuse on children: A critique and suggestions for future research. *Victimology, 10,* 110–130.

Conte, J., & Schuerman, J. R. (1987). The effects of sexual abuse on children: A multidimensional view. *Journal of Interpersonal Violence, 2,* 380–390.

Conte, J. R., & Berliner, L. (1981). Sexual abuse of children: Implications for practice. *Social Casework, 62,* 601–606.

Crewdson, J. (1988). *By silence betrayed: Sexual abuse of children in America.* Boston: Little, Brown & Company.

De Francis, V. (1969). *Protecting the child victim of sex crimes committed by adults.* Denver: American Humane Society.

Egeland, B., Sroufe, L. A., & Erickson, M. F. (1983). Developmental consequences of different patterns of maltreatment. *International Journal of Child Abuse, 7,* 459–469.

Erickson, M. F., & Egeland, B. (1987). A developmental view of the psychological consequences of maltreatment. *School Psychology Review, 16,* 156–168.

Finkelhor, D. (1979). *Sexually victimized children.* New York: Free Press.

Finkelhor, D. (1984). *Child sexual abuse: New theory and research.* New York: Free Press.

Finkelhor, D. (1990). Early and long-term effects of child sexual abuse: An update. *Professional Psychology: Research and Practice, 21,* 325–330.

Finkelhor, D., & Browne, A. (1985). The traumatic impact of child sexual abuse: A reconceptualization. *Journal of Orthopsychiatry, 55,* 530–541.

Frenken, J., & Van Stolk, B. (1990). Incest victims: Inadequate help by professionals. *Child Abuse and Neglect, 14,* 253–263.

Friedrich, W., Beilke, R., & Urquiza, A. (1987). Children from sexually abusive families: A behavioral comparison. *Journal of Interpersonal Violence, 2,* 391–402.

Friedrich, W., Beilke, R., & Urquiza, A. (1988). Behavior problems in young sexually abused boys: A comparison study. *Journal of Interpersonal Violence, 3,* 21–28.

Friedrich, W. N. (1990). *Psychotherapy of sexually abused children and their families.* New York: W. W. Norton.

Friedrich, W. N., Urquiza, A. J., & Beilke, R. (1986). Behavioral problems in sexually abused young children. *Journal of Pediatric Psychology, 11,* 47–57.

Fromuth, M. E. (1986). The relationship of childhood sexual abuse with later psychological and sexual adjustment in a sample of college women. *Child Abuse & Neglect, 10,* 5–15.

Garbarino, J., & Gilliam, G. (1980). *Understanding abusive families.* Lexington, MA: D. C. Heath & Company.

Garbarino, J., Stott, F. M., & Faculty of the Erikson Institute. (1989). *What children can tell us.* San Francisco: Jossey-Bass.

Germain, R. B. (1988). Maltreatment of children. In J. Sandoval (Ed.), *Crisis counseling, intervention, and prevention in the schools* (pp. 73–92). Hillsdale, NJ: Lawrence Erlbaum.

Gomes-Schwartz, B., Horowitz, J., & Cardarelli, A. (1990). *Child sexual abuse: The initial effects.* Newbury Park, CA: Sage.

Gottlieb, B., & Dean, J. (1981). The co-therapy relationship in group treatment of sexually mistreated girls. In P. B. Mrazek & C. H. Kempe (Eds.), *Sexually abused children and their families* (pp. 211–218). New York: Pergamon.

Green, K., & Fine, M. J. (1988). Family therapy: A case for training for school psychologists. In W. M. Walsh & N. J. Giblin (Eds.), *Family counseling in*

school settings (pp. 15–25). Springfield, IL: Charles C. Thomas.

Haley, J. (1987). *Problem solving therapy.* San Francisco: Jossey-Bass.

Haugaard, J. J., & Reppucci, N. D. (1988). *The sexual abuse of children: A comprehensive guide to current knowledge and intervention strategies.* San Francisco: Jossey-Bass.

Herman, J. L. (1981). *Father-daughter incest.* Cambridge, MA: Harvard University Press.

Hoffman, L. (1981). *Foundations of family therapy.* New York: Basic Books.

James, B. (1989). *Treating traumatized children: New insights and creative interventions.* Lexington, MA: Lexington Books.

Justice, B., & Justice, R. (1979). *The broken taboo: Sex in the family.* New York: Human Sciences Press.

Kempe, R. S., & Kempe, C. H. (1984). *The common secret: Sexual abuse of children and adolescents.* New York: Freeman.

Knitzer, J. Steinberg, Z., & Fleisch, B. (1990). *At the schoolhouse door: An examination of programs and policies for children with behavioral and emotional problems.* New York: Bank Street College of Education.

Lee, B. (1980). The use of interdisciplinary problem-solving groups in educational settings. In R. Volpe, M. Breton, & J. Mitton (Eds.), *The maltreatment of the school-aged child* (pp. 121–128). Lexington, MA: D. C. Heath.

MacFarlane, F., & Waterman, J. (1986). *Sexual abuse of the young child.* New York: Guilford Press.

Mayhall, P. D., & Norgard, K. E. (1983). *Child abuse and neglect: Sharing responsibility.* New York: Wiley.

Minuchin, S. (1974). *Families and family therapy.* Cambridge, MA: Harvard University Press.

Minuchin, S., & Fishman, H. C. (1981). *Family therapy techniques.* Cambridge, MA: Harvard University Press.

Mrazek, P. B. (1983). Sexual abuse of children. In B. B. Lahey & A. E. Kazdin (Eds.), *Advances in clinical child psychology* (Vol. 6, pp. 199–215). New York: Plenum.

National Center on Child Abuse and Neglect (NCCAN). (1982). *Profile of child sexual abuse.* Rockville, MA: Clearinghouse on Child Abuse and Neglect Information.

Piaget, J. (1971). *Biology and knowledge.* Chicago: University of Chicago Press.

Pogge, D. L., & Stone, K. (1990). Conflicts and issues in the treatment of child sexual abuse. *Profes-*

sional Psychology: Research and Practice, 21, 354–361.

Pollak, J., & Levy, S. (1990). Counter transference and failure to report child abuse and neglect. *Child Abuse and Neglect, 13,* 515–522.

Reppucci, N. D., & Haugaard, J. J. (1989). Prevention of child sexual abuse: Myth or reality. *American Psychologist, 44,* 1266–1275.

Runyan, D. K., Everson, M. D., Edelsohn, G. A., Hunter, W. M., & Coulter, M. L. (1988). Impact of legal intervention on sexually abused children. *Journal of Pediatrics, 113,* 647–653.

Russell, D. E. H. (1983). The incidence and prevalence of intrafamilial and extrafamilial sexual abuse of female children. *Child Abuse and Neglect, 7,* 133–146.

Sameroff, A. J, & Chandler, M. J. (1975). Reproductive risk and the continuum of caretaking casualty. In F. Horowitz (Ed.), *Review of child development research* (Vol. 4, pp. 187–244). Chicago: University of Chicago Press.

Sgroi, S. M., Blick, L. C., & Porter, F. S. (1982). A conceptual framework for child sexual abuse. In S. M. Sgroi (Ed.), *Handbook of clinical intervention in child sexual abuse* (pp. 9–37). Lexington, MA: Ballinger.

Sroufe, L. A. (1979). Socioemotional development. In J. Osofsky (Ed.), *Handbook of infant development* (pp. 462–513). New York: Wiley.

Sroufe, L. A., & Rutter, M. (1984). The domain of developmental psychology. *Child Development, 55,* 17–29.

Tharinger, D. (1987). Children and sexual interest. In A. Thomas & J. Grimes (Eds.), *Children's needs: Psychological perspectives* (pp. 532–542). Kent, OH: National Association of School Psychologists.

Tharinger, D. (1990). Impact of child sexual abuse on developing sexuality. *Professional Psychology: Research and Practice, 21,* 331–337.

Tharinger, D., Horton, C. B., & Millea, S. (1990). Sexual abuse and exploitation of children and adults with mental retardation and other handicaps. *Child Abuse & Neglect, 14,* 301–312.

Tharinger, D., Krivacska, J. J., Laye-McDonough, M.,

Jamison, L., Vincent, G. G., & Hedlund, A. D. (1988a). Prevention of child sexual abuse: An analysis of issues, educational programs, and research findings. *School Psychology Review, 17,* 614–634.

Tharinger, D., Russian, T., & Robinson, P. (1988b). School psychologists' involvement in the response to child sexual abuse. *School Psychology Review, 18,* 386–399.

Tharinger, D., Vincent, G., Aussiker, A., Horton, C. B., Madrey, K., Robinson, P., Reeder, V., & Russian, T. (1989, August). *Children's recovery from sexual abuse: Stage one results.* Paper presented at the Annual Meeting of the American Psychological Association, New Orleans, LA.

Tufts' New England Medical Center, Division of Child Psychiatry. (1984). *Sexually exploited children: Service and research project* (Final report for the Office of Juvenile Justice and Delinquency Prevention). Washington, DC: U.S. Department of Justice.

Vander Mey, B. J. (1988). The sexual victimization of male children: A review of previous research. *Child Abuse & Neglect, 12,* 61–72.

Vevier, E., & Tharinger, D. (1986). Child sexual abuse: A review and intervention framework for the school psychologist. *Journal of School Psychology, 24,* 293–311.

Walker, C. E., Bonner, B. L., & Kaufman, K. L. (1988). *The physically and sexually abused child: Evaluation and treatment.* New York: Pergamon.

Walker, L. E. A. (1988). *Handbook on sexual abuse of children.* New York: Springer.

Werner, H. (1948). *Comparative psychology of mental development.* Chicago: Follett Press.

White, S. H. (1976). The active organism in theoretical behaviorism. *Human Development, 19,* 99–107.

Willan, S., & Hugman, Y. (1988). Family therapy within a school's psychological service. In W. M. Walsh & N. J. Giblin (Eds.), *Family counseling in school settings* (pp. 7–14). Springfield, IL: Charles C. Thomas.

Wyatt, G. E., & Powell, G. J. (Eds.). (1988). *Lasting effects of child sexual abuse.* Beverly Hills, CA: Sage.

Part IV:

Implications for Facilitating Change Toward Home-School Collaboration

23

UTILIZATION OF COMMUNITY RESOURCES: AN IMPORTANT VARIABLE FOR THE HOME-SCHOOL INTERFACE

Dianne Apter

Children do not exist in a vacuum. A child is part of a family that functions to meet the needs of the child as well as those of the other family members. In most cases families make use of both informal (family, friends, and neighbors) and formal (doctors, day care centers, schools) supports to assist them in their child-rearing tasks. When a child has special needs which cause his caretaking to be difficult or extended, the use of formal supports may need to increase. The family's needs, as well as those of their child, may be more complex or specialized. Many innovative programs have been developed to attempt to broaden the school's domain beyond academics (Apter, 1982; Fiske, 1989; Marriott, 1990; Knitzer, Steinberg, & Brahm, 1990). Knitzer et al. (1990), in their examination of programs and policies for children with behavioral and emotional problems, give an excellent presentation of some exemplary efforts across the country. In their discussion of model programs they make mention of many that involve multiple agencies involved in collaborative initiatives within the school building (see especially Chapters 4 and 5). Other chapters in this volume describe other such models.

Beyond the schoolhouse door there exists an array of systems, services, and private practitioners within our commu-

nities. However, the task of finding and accessing these resources seems almost impossible, not only for families but also for the persons who are trying to assist them. The piecemeal delivery and narrow boundaries of each service often make it difficult to decipher just what it is an agency does. Understanding the eligibility criteria and the application process creates what sometimes seems to be insurmountable barriers. The school is a natural place for families to turn for guidance through the maze of the "helping" services. One parent put it poignantly: "While the school district was trying to figure out what to do and how to do it [serve the child], we as a family were struggling emotionally and financially . . . and no one really seemed to give a hoot. . . . No one was really looking at us as a whole, no one really saw the problems" (Brown, 1988). The school *is* in the position of seeing the "whole." The school and the school psychologist in particular can take the lead in building the linkages between school and home, school and the community, and home and the community.

Figure 1 helps dramatize the merry-go-round many families of disabled children must ride. Each agency may have something to offer, but each also has its own sets of rules as to who can access it and for what purpose. The staff frequently

Figure 1

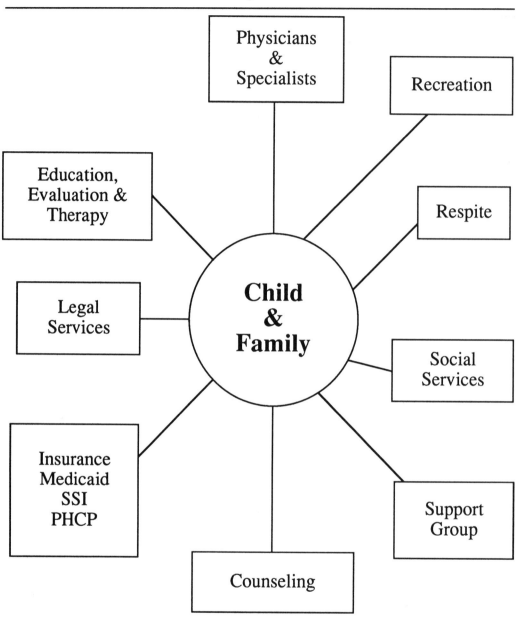

has little or no idea what the other agencies do or can do for their clients. It is little wonder the helpers often cause more problems and more stress than the problems and stress they are attempting to ameliorate. Many service systems have policies that require or recommend that families receive some sort of "case management" service (Gilkerson, Hilliard, Schrag, & Shonkoff, 1987; Knitzer et al., 1990; NASDSE, 1979; Shelton, Jeppson, & Johnson, 1987). A study of the merry-go-round demonstrates that the "case" that needs managing is the system of services and not the family per se. It is also clear that the linkage process is far more involved than merely suggesting or passing out a list of services.

Bailey (1989) extensively discusses the role of case management in his literature review. He found a multitude of descriptions of case management and mentions several titles ascribed to the person doing the managing: "broker, advocate, systems agent, expediter, community agent, service coordinator, patient representative, helper, partner, synthesizer, and human development liaison specialist" (p. 121). Young (1990) presents a model of case management for emotionally disturbed youngsters, which he describes as "therapeutic case advocacy," which includes direct clinical work with children and families as well as advocacy and care management. A similar model, the BRIDGE program, was developed in 1973 under a National Institute of Mental Health Grant (Apter et al., 1978). Many agencies would describe themselves as providing case management. Yet rarely is the concept discussed in terms of the school personnel assuming such roles. Some exceptions are the models for school based case management mentioned in Snitzer et al., (1990). The Washington State Educational Service District, for example, has established multi-agency teams of school personnel, social service agencies, and private providers coordinated by a school-based case manager. If one thinks of case management in terms of linkage, who better to provide such help than school personnel?

Rationale for School-based Community Linkage

The problem with coordination exists largely because of the organization of our systems at the federal, state, and local level. Healy, Keesee, and Smith (1985) make the point that despite the need for coordinated efforts in assisting disabled children and their families, funding policies tend to create rigid boundaries between agencies. Other administrative policies provide little incentive or financial reward for linkage between one system and another or one professional and another. Hazel gives an excellent summary of the barriers to interagency

linkages. He states that agencies, institutions or organizations:

- may not have a means for communication with one another and with other professionals who are in private practice about the children and families they serve.

- may be protective of their professional or agency "turf" or be hesitant about trusting one another.

- may not have formal mechanisms for referring children and families to one another and for following up on those they refer.

- may consider themselves primarily responsible to their employing agency, rather than to the children and families they serve. (adapted from Hazel et al., 1988, p. 19)

Our educational systems could (and in some cases already do) take the lead in overcoming these barriers to more coordinated, accessible services. Other agencies already may look to school personnel to provide information about a specific child. The school may already be making referrals to outside agencies, for example to social services when there is suspected child abuse or to a mental health clinic for psychotherapy or counseling. It is a logical extension for schools to take on the linkage role in a more formal sense. Schools, along with families, are expected to take on the responsibilities of contributing to every child's social/emotional and academic development. If a child is handicapped, the "responsibility" of helping that child reach his potential is shared not only by school and family but by a collection of other public and private agencies, professionals, and institutions. Schools are the only agent of society that exists for everyone. As such, schools are in the best position to coordinate the systems that will ultimately impact on a child and his family.

Existing legislation implies a role for the school in this linkage process (NASDSE, 1979; Zeller, 1980). P.L. 94-142 requires that "each handicapped child must be provided all services necessary to meet his or her special education and related need" (P.L. 94-142, Section 121a.4). In addition to speech, physical, and occupational therapies, "related services" are defined in regulations as including: "recreation, counseling service, medical services for diagnostic or evaluative purposes, school health services, social work services and parent counseling and training" (Section 121a.13). Further, the regulations provide the impetus for linkage services by authorizing the "mobilizing (of) school and community resources to enable the child to receive maximum benefits from his or her educational program" (P.L. 94-142 Regulations, 121a.4; NASDSE, 1979). There is no requirement that schools should recommend and plan only for services they will provide and pay for, nothing in the law prohibits the school from utilizing other nonschool community services and funding where they are available. The passage of P.L. 99–457, which is an extension of P.L. 94-142 downward to birth, implies rather dramatically that families are *entitled* to services. Part H (dealing with ages birth to 3) requires the development of an Individualized Family Service Plan. The IFSP not only assumes that families are entitled to services but that they have the *primary* role in determining what those services should be (Gilkerson et al., 1987; Krauss, 1990). This legislation focusing on the youngest disabled children is already having impact on the school-aged population. In the 1990 state legislative session, New York introduced a bill that would require informing the child's parent or person in a parental relationship as to the availability of any additional services which can assist the child's family (State of New York Assembly Bill 9228).

School systems have much to gain and much to offer by assuming the leadership in linkage and coordination. However, there are many considerations and issues involved in doing so. One linkage model is discussed in depth in the section that follows. The intricacies of referring and linking, as well as other ideas for the school as a clearinghouse, conclude the chapter.

The Early Childhood Direction Model

Some parents know exactly what they need, and a few even know where to get it. Others never hear of—or ever imagine—services that might improve their lives immeasurably. It is remarkably difficult for parents to locate the services that do exist. No one seems to know exactly what is available for whom under what circumstances. (Featherstone, 1980)

In 1978, the New York State Education Department funded the first of what would become a statewide network of information, support, and referral centers to address this all-too-common concern. The model was based on the direction service programs, funded by the Federal Bureau for the Education of the Handicapped, which were set up in 25 sites between 1976 and 1979 (Davidson et al., 1984; Zeller, 1980; NASDSE, 1979). (The National Direction Service Assistance Project continues to exist and offers technical assistance to those seeking to develop their own models.) The Early Childhood Direction Centers, as they were named, were designed to serve families of children from birth to age 5. The concept of "direction service" has to do with a family-centered, single coordinating entity designed to assist families in negotiating the maze of services and developing a coordinated plan to meet their needs and those of their disabled child.

The ECDC network was, and still is, the only state funded, statewide direction service in the country. The original request for proposals for the Early Childhood Direction Centers (ECDCs) were sent to a variety of community agencies, including school districts, and several were located at Boards of Cooperative Educational Services (B.O.C.E.S.). Others were housed at universities, private agencies, and hospitals. The model has proved so successful that plans are being considered to increase the age span through the school-age years and beyond (State of New York Legislative Bills A11651 & S8050).

Although each ECDC functions in a slightly different manner, all must meet the same objectives as set out by the State Education Department. In brief, each center is responsible for: (a) conducting an active child-find by continual public service announcements, presentations, outreach to primary referral sources, etc.; (b) maintaining current, accurate resource information which includes comprehensive (generic and specialized) service descriptions, updated legislative and regulatory information, and other relevant literature for parents and professionals; (c) assisting school districts and parents with transition between various educational programs (i.e., toddler to preschool, preschool to school age); and (d) providing "direction" (i.e., information, referral, support, and follow-up) to parents and professionals.

The heart of each ECDC is assisting families with identification of their specific issues and problems, and then locating, selecting, and accessing the services they need. Referrals are comprehensive and are made to a variety of agencies and service systems including medical, educational, social services, financial assistance, family support, respite, mental health, day care, etc. The ECDCs are not tied to a direct service provider, even though they may be physically located in a private or public agency that does provide direct service. This independence enables the staff of an ECDC to be objective problem solvers and also helps in the building of trust. The trust emanates not only from families, but also from the agencies and professionals with whom the ECDC must coordinate. Each ECDC in the network of 15 has formal and informal agreements with intensive care nurseries, health departments, early education programs, diagnostic clinics, and other service agencies. Referrals come to the ECDC not only from families themselves, but from a wide group of professionals. Included in the group are all the "generic" community resources, such as clergy, nursery and day care teachers, and even real estate agents. Basically, the Center serves anyone with a concern about a young child with diagnosed or suspected handicapping conditions or at risk for handicapping conditions.

The level of support given to a family is dependent upon the family request, the nature of the needs, and to some extent the nature of the family. The ECDC rarely requests medical or agency records. The *parents' perception of the problem* is generally more understandable, more to the point, and more accurate than reams of agency paperwork. Spending time building rapport and trust and assisting parents in reaching decisions about what they want to happen for their child is far more productive than spending time poring over someone else's notes. When a call comes in, there is no foolproof method to anticipate how complicated or involving the case will be. However, there are certain factors that help the caseworker determine how much will be required of her to resolve the presented problems. These factors are:

- the amount of service required;

- the level of parent sophistication (i.e., a parent who is less articulate or assertive might need ECDC to "walk through" the steps toward receiving service or lay groundwork with an agency);

- the caller's state of mind (i.e., a parent who is distraught, emotionally upset, or confused about the service system may require more involvement);

- the type of problem (i.e., certain problems stand out as being more complicated, less clear-cut, and thus making the determination as to what is "best" requires lots of talking time and perhaps more research time on the part of ECDC staff).

Professional intuition necessarily plays a part in determining the type, level, or intensity of involvement with a family.

A key aspect to this process of locating and accessing services is that the parents are given options whenever they exist and they are given information about those options so that they are able to make educated decisions on behalf of their child. Direction services is shared problem solving where parent and "helper" jointly determine what the problem is, what the possible solutions might be, and then how to go about obtaining services to effect those solutions. Zeller (1980) provides an excellent concept analysis of direction (Figure 2).

A final important component of the model is extensive follow-along and follow-up. ECDC staff stay involved with a family until a "match" occurs and thereafter every 6 months to a year. This ensures the recommendations were appropriate and lets that family know they can reconnect as needs change or other issues emerge.

Direction Service in Schools

The Early Childhood Direction Center and other models of "direction services" clearly require some additional staff, resources, and financial support. Earlier in this chapter, rationale were presented for why schools should be involved in the linkage "business." Direction service is an effective model for helping school districts to implement the components of IEPs for its students. Although it is crucial that direction service personnel have independence from their host agency, existing and past

models have demonstrated that conflict of interest issues can be overcome (Zeller, 1980). It must be clear to all concerned that "allegiance" is to the family. However, because the direction service worker is knowledgeable about how things are *supposed* to work as well as how things *actually* work, he/she is in a position to provide a reality base for families. The role of a good advocate is to listen to all sides of an issue and provide the most accurate information possible, not to tell the parent what to do.

As noted in the NASDSE (1979) report, "the strength of the Direction Service [model] has been in the functions performed to provide information and assistance to target families and school personnel identifying, assessing and utilizing community resources" (p. 14). The ability to assume these functions, using school staff, could involve merely reassigning existing staff or changing their current job descriptions. For example, the school psychologist could assume a supervisory role to a staff of paraprofessionals, including parents, who provide the direction. Several ECDCs make use of parents and graduate student interns as part of their staff. Districts could pursue cooperative funding at the state and/or local levels. Several districts could join together and share costs of supporting a linkage center. The ECDC model in New York State has been estimated to cost

FIGURE 2
Concept Analysis of Direction

Direction is . . .	Direction is not . . .
Obtaining relevant information from family and (with permission) professionals involved with child/family	Preparing extensive family histories using a set format
Identifying as many potentially appropriate needs-to-service matches as possible	Making decisions about which is the best service for a particular child or family
Systematic, comprehensive matching of needs-to-service over time	An information and referral service
Resource linking and referral facilitation	Assignment to services
Child/family centered (needed services to family regardless of which system or agency provides them)	Program centered (concerned with efficient management of programs for groups

Adapted from Zeller (1980).

approximately $300 per child. It is difficult to assign a dollar figure to the value of direction services to families, children, school personnel, and the community at large. The advantages of better coordinated services, improved family coping, less duplications, and shared responsibility for a child's development cannot easily be matched with a dollar amount. There is ample evidence that ECDCs serve a useful function for both parents and professional. A 1982 independent evaluation of the Early Childhood Direction Centers concluded: "Parents and agencies feel that the Direction Centers play a vital role in the service delivery system. Contact with ECDCs helps handicapped children attain needed services. Most (70%) of the parents and agencies surveyed were successful in attaining the services they requested; furthermore, most of those users who were not able to get services indicated their lack of success was largely due to gaps in the service system rather then the work of the Direction Centers" (Musumeci & Koen, 1982).

The Referral Process

Not all ECDC work with families is intensive, nor does every child with disabilities need the services of a multisystem nature. Figure 3 is a flow chart demonstrating the assistance process at the ECDC based at Syracuse University's Center on Human Policy. This particular ECDC services a large geographic area in Central New York which consists of urban and rural demographic locales. To accommodate families from such a diverse and widespread region the Center maintains a toll free number. Most referrals are accepted and handled by telephone, or the staff work closely with someone involved and trusted by the family to deliver information and resources. Staff members attend interagency meetings and visit services in all nine counties it serves. The ECDC is also assisted by an advisory board consisting of members from each county, which helps with keeping resources and information about services up to date. (The files are updated every 6 months to a year.) Referrals are accepted from families, physicians, teachers, public health nurses, protective case workers, etc. The Syracuse ECDC also has agreements with medical facilities as well as the 96 school districts in the region. The Syracuse Early Childhood Direction Center consists of a staff of five (2.5 FTE), two of whom are parents of children with disabilities and one who is a graduate student in special education. The center functions much as described previously in the chapter. Two case examples will serve as illustration.

Case Examples

Janet Berwel was referred to the ECDC by the Pediatric Clinic for help with her son Ben, age 3. Ben had been a premature baby and needed help in several areas. He was developmentally delayed in motor skills, in speech and language, and in self-help skills. He was difficult for his mom to handle because he was often cranky and cried frequently. Ms. Berwel was a single parent and agreed with the pediatrician that she needed help. Yet the intervention program she was involved with reported that Ben rarely made it to school, that Ms. Berwel was unresponsive to their notes home, and that from their point of view she was uncooperative and Ben was suffering because of it. They had even considered reporting Ms. Berwel to the Child Abuse Hotline. ECDC staffperson met with Ms. Berwel several times to get her perspective of what Ben's needs were, what her needs were, and what types of services would be helpful. She had a very good perception of her own child and some legitimate concerns with the program he was involved with. She did lack the skill to express her concerns directly, and thus had been "uncooperative." Based on their discussions, information was presented to Ms. Berwel so she could make some choices for a more suitable service for Ben. The new program was a better match to Ms. Berwel's values and needs and was actually more appropriate for Ben, too. The ECDC staff person called Ms. Berwel several weeks after Ben began the program to make sure things were going

Figure 3

ECDC Assistance Flow Chart

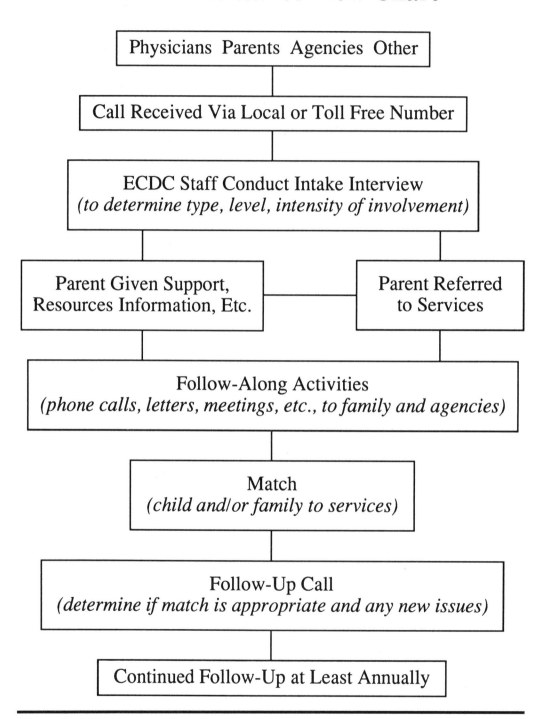

okay. Ms. Berwel was satisfied and reported that she liked and trusted the staff there. She was now ready to focus on some of her own issues and the staff person gave her information about a parent support group that met at the neighborhood center near her home. She was also linked to a respite program so she could have some leisure time away from Ben.

The parents of Marci Stockter, a 4-year-old child with Down's Syndrome, were referred to the ECDC by Marci's teacher. The youngest of three children, Marci had a history of health problems. Although the family's health insurance picked up the major expenses, Marci's frequent visits to the pediatrician and much of her medication was adding quite a financial burden to the family resources. Marci was still not toilet trained and the expense of diapers was significant. Since Marci's birth, the family had never had a real vacation and Mr. and Mrs. Stockter very rarely got out together as a couple. The parents were beginning to have concerns that their other children were becoming resentful of Marci. The ECDC staff person knew of several resources and services she thought might be helpful to the Stockters. She was sure they would qualify for a financial assistance program in their state because of their unusual medical expenses. She was able to point out to Mr. Stockter that this assistance wasn't "welfare" or "charity" and that his tax dollars had been contributing to the program for years. She also mentioned a respite program which was designed for children with disabilities. The Stockters chose to make the calls to both programs themselves and took advantage of the service and assistance each offered. During the time period of regular contact the staff person was also able to help the Stockters learn to be more assertive at the next IEP meeting and insist that toilet training be a top priority in Marci's plan. Six months later, ECDC called back and the Stockters assured her that things were much less tense at home and that they were pleased with the support they were getting.

These two cases represent several key elements in the ECDC model:

- single coordinating agency matching specific PARENT IDENTIFIED needs to specific combinations of services
- independence from direct service providers and provision
- options and information given to parents so that they have the ultimate say in the course of action they wish to pursue
- extensive follow-along until a match occurs
- extensive follow-up after a match occurs

The two case situations also demonstrate several important features, not only of the ECDC model, but of any successful referral process. The coordinator took time to listen. That enabled her to clarify the problem and have a better chance of making suggestions that were "in sync" with the family's expressed need, as well as their cultural and value systems. She drew from a variety of service systems, both specialized and generic, to find appropriate help. She shared the information she knew, but the family chose the services they felt would be of use and they decided how much assistance they required from the caseworker. It is important to know what the parent has already attempted to help solve the problem. There may be obvious sources of help that have been overlooked or that the family was not aware of. They may have approached the appropriate agency but not articulated their needs in the "right" way. Much direction service involves "scripting" families so they can make their needs known to potential helpers. Once the family is assisted with their identified problem, it is helpful to mention other resources and services that might be of use. The quotation from Helen Featherstone highlights the fact that some families do not even know what the possibilities of assistance might be. Broad, open-ended questions such as "what do you need?" are usually not helpful. How can one ask for respite to provide some break time for personal and family benefit, if one has never heard the word "respite" and has no idea what such a service can do? Finally, the caseworker in the two examples followed up to make sure all went well and to ascertain any new issues.

There is another side to the referral process that cannot be overlooked. An effective coordinator must not only have an intimate knowledge of the family perspective but must also have an in-depth awareness of agencies and how each operates. Beyond the name, address, phone, contact person and purpose that distinguishes one resource from another, each has its own method of doing things. The more the coordinator knows about the subtle and not so subtle workings of an agency the better position she is in to assist a parent and insure that a referral will "take." The coordinator should know the answers to the following questions:

- Is an appointment necessary or can a "client" walk in or call in?

- Does the parent have to make direct contact or can someone call on his/her behalf?

- Is there a waiting list? What is the turnover time from first call until service is received?

- Does the agency require that application forms be filled out and returned before appointments are scheduled? What provisions are made or must be made for a parent that doesn't read or write?

- Does the parent have to go to an office or does the service come to the family's home?

- What written documentation or information should the parent have available in order to receive the services being sought?

- Is the agency accessible to public transportation?

- What is the cost? What third party payments are accepted (e.g., insur-ance, Medicaid)? Is there a sliding fee schedule? (adapted from Lubker, p. 124, 1983)

Other Strategies

Obviously this author's position is that schools should adapt the direction services model. However, there are other activities that a school can undertake to assume their responsibilities to link families to resources. One such activity is to establish a family resource library (Steele & Willard, 1983). Such a library can house printed and/or audiovisual information on a variety of topics determined by families and school staff. These can include such issues as child rearing, coping, handicaps, educational rights, etc. The library can also serve as a central data bank for services in the local region. Thus the staff in the school and parents would know where such information was available for their use.

Another method of providing linkage to community supports is to compile and organize community resource inventories, which can be made available at parent/school conferences and planning meetings. There are several ways to locate the resources and services to be included in the guide. It is useful to inquire from various government and charitable organizations if any guides currently exist. These can be collected and housed in the school resource library. In addition, community resources can be located through telephone directories and suggestions from school support staff.

To be useful, the resource guides must be comprehensive and include a broad scope of services. Some categories to consider are: medical services (including practitioners willing and able to work with disabled children), diagnostic and evaluation centers, specialty clinics, child care services, counseling and psychotherapy services, parent support groups, recreation and summer camping opportunities, legal and advocacy services, financial assistance programs, and social service programs. This list, though lengthy, is certainly not exhaustive. Surveys can be mailed to identified resources to obtain more complete information that would address, as well as possible, the questions posed in the previous section. Once collected, the service guides can be organized into computerized data banks or booklets with the services arranged alphabetically or by category. It must be cautioned that even the simplest resource guide needs constant updating as the information contained within changes frequently and new resources need to be added. The data collection forms themselves should be clear and as brief as possible in order to gain the information needed but not be burdensome for service providers to complete.

Some practical resources to assist in compiling a thorough and useful service guide are listed at the end of this chapter.

CONCLUSION

The community in which children and their families live, where their school and homes are located, offers a wealth of support and assistance. It is not enough for school specialists to be competent in assessing educational strengths and deficits and planning an individualized program. The ability to know and use the resources a community has to offer is a crucial skill for those who work with children. The ability to teach families how to access those supports is equally important. This chapter offered some suggestions for school psychologists to consider. The activities and strategies to provide collaboration and linkage between home, school, and community will provide benefit both to the families and the school.

SUGGESTED RESOURCES

A Community Approach to an Integration Service System for Children with Special Needs by Robin Hazel et al., 1988. Brookes Publishing Co., Baltimore, MD. See especially Appendix G, pp. 203–216 and Section IV for sample forms and methodologies.

Developing Community Networks: A Guide to Resources and Strategies by Barbara Steele, 1989. Association for the Care of Children's Health, 3615 Wisconsin Avenue, N.W., Washing-

ton, DC 20006. See especially Appendix A through E for sample forms for gathering data information.

A Community Workbook for Collaborative Services to Preschool Handicapped Children by Phyllis Magrab, Elynor Kazuk, & Lorna Green, 1981. HEW Task Force Grant # P-71476/3–02.

The Direction Voice. The National Direction Service Assistance Project Newsletter, published by the National Parent Chain, Inc., 867-C High Street, Worthington, OH 43085, (614) 431–1911.

REFERENCES

Apter, S. (1982). *Troubled children/troubled systems.* New York: Pergamon Press.

Apter, S., Apter D., Trief, P., Cohen, N., Woodlock, D., & Harrootunian, B. (1978). *The bridge program.* Washington, DC: NIMH.

Bailey, D. (1989). Case management in early intervention. *Journal of Early Intervention, 13*(2), 120–134.

Brown, L. (1988). Let's do it right: A parent's eye view of P.L. 99–457. *The Networker, 1*(3), pp. 1, 11.

Davidson, P., Reif, M., Shapiro, D., Griffith, B., Shapiro, P., & Crocker, A. (1984). Direction services: A model facilitating secondary prevention of developmental handicapping conditions. *Mental Retardation, 22*(1), 21–27.

The Direction Voice. The National Direction Service Assistance Project Newsletter. (Published by the National Parent CHAIN, Inc., 867-C High Street, Worthington, OH 43085, 614–431–1911).

Featherstone, H. (1980). *A difference in the family.* Middlesex, England: Penguin Books.

Fiske, E. (1989, March 1). Lessons. *The New York Times,* Section A.

Gilkerson, L., Hilliard, A., Schrag, E., & Shonkoff, J. (1987). *Report accompanying the education of the handicapped act, amendments of 1986 and comments on P.L. 99–457.* Washington, DC: National Center for Clinical Infant Programs.

Hazel, R., Barber, P. A., Roberts, S., Behr, S., Helmstetter, E., & Guess, D. (1988). *A community approach to an integrated service system.* Baltimore: Paul H. Brookes Publishers.

Healy, A., Keesee, M. S., & Smith, B. (1985). *Early services for children with special needs: Transactions for family support.* Iowa City, IA: University of Iowa.

Knitzer, J., Steinberg, Z., & Brahm, F. (1990). *At the schoolhouse door.* New York: Bank Street College of Education.

Krauss, M. W. (1990). New precedent in family

policy: Individualized family service plan. *Exceptional Children, 56*(5), 388–385.

Lubker, B. (1983). The community: Its services and service providers. In J. Paul (Ed.), *The exceptional child* (pp. 107–132). Syracuse, NY: Syracuse University Press.

Magrab, P., Kazuk, E., & Green, L. (1981). *A community workbook for collaborative services to preschool handicapped children.* HEW Task Force Grant No. P-71476/3–02.

Marriott, M. (1990, June 13). A new road to learning: teaching the whole child. *The New York Times,* p. A1.

Musumeci, M., & Koen, S. (1982). *New York State Early Childhood Direction Centers: 1981–82 evaluation report.* Yorktown Heights, NY: Center for Resource Management, Inc. (Available from the NYS Education Department)

National Association of State Directors of Special Education. (1979). *Direction service: From concept to reality.* Washington, DC: NASDSE.

Shelton, T., Jeppson, E., & Johnson, B. (1987). *Family-centered care for children with special health care needs.* Washington, DC: Association for the Care of Children's Health.

State of New York Assembly Bill 9228, February 6, 1990, introduced by Hevesi, Griffith, & Cooke.

State of New York Assembly Bill A11651 and Senate Bill S8050.

Steele, B. (1989). *Developing community networks: A guide to resources and strategies.* Washington, DC: Association for the Care of Children's Health.

Steele, B., & Willard, C. (1983). *Guidelines for establishing a family resource library.* Washington, DC: Association for the Care of Children's Health.

Young, T. (1990). Therapeutic case advocacy: A model for interagency collaboration in serving emotionally disturbed children and their families. *American Journal of Orthopsychiatry, 60*(1), 118–124.

Zeller, R. (1980). Direction service: Collaboration one case at a time. In J. O. Elder & P. R. Magrab (Eds.), *Coordinating services to handicapped children: A handbook for interagency collaboration* (pp. 69–82). Baltimore: Paul H. Brookes.

24

SCHOOL AND FAMILY PARTNERSHIPS: LEADERSHIP ROLES FOR SCHOOL PSYCHOLOGISTS

Joyce L. Epstein

INTRODUCTION

This is a time for school reform. Like others in education, school psychologists are beginning to think about new models—new directions—for their work. Many of the topics about children that concern school psychologists also are about families—the diversity of families, the problems and needs of families, and the influence of families on children.

These two components—a recognition that schools must improve to become more responsive to students and a history of interest in families—make school psychologists potential leaders in the growing field of school and family connections.

There is high agreement that school and family connections are important for schools, children, and families (see literature reviews in Epstein, 1992; Henderson, 1987). Despite high rhetoric, however, practices have lagged. Although there has been real progress in some states, districts, and schools (Paths to Partnership, 1991), in most places family involvement still is incidental, infrequent, and uncoordinated with children's needs or school programs. Where progress has been made, it is because someone has had a deep understanding of what is possible, a clear vision of the work needed, and time, finances, and social support to build strong programs for family involvement. The leaders in the field have, in different places, been state supervisors, school superintendents, principals, district leaders with various responsibilities for families or for students, community educators, and teachers in schools. Surprisingly, few leaders have been school psychologists. This is curious because there are natural connections between the skills and interests of school psychologists and the needs of schools for better school and family connections.

Dedicated professionals are key to the success of effective school and family partnerships. The strongest leadership should come from those who have:

- knowledge of child development and an understanding of how children benefit from coordinated efforts of the many influences in their lives;

- an appreciation of and experience with "systems" approaches to preventing and solving problems; and

- an awareness of the distinctions between prevention and treatment activities to encourage healthy child and adolescent development.

School psychologists are among those whose education, training, and responsibilities provide this knowledge. They are, therefore, candidates for leadership in school and family connections.

Family-School Connections and the Work of School Psychologists

Research on the organization and effects of school and family connections yields five broad conclusions (Davies, 1991; Epstein, 1988; Epstein & Scott-Jones, in press; Swap, 1990). See how strong is the fit of these basic perspectives with the work of school psychologists.

School and family connections are about children. The main purpose of partnerships organized by schools or initiated by families is to help more children to succeed in school and to measure up to their potential. The partnerships help by sending students common messages from parents, teachers, and others about the importance of school. If partnerships are positive, more students, regardless of their initial ability, will be motivated to learn, work hard, and enjoy learning with support from home and from school. Students' stress and confusion should be reduced when children see that their parents and teachers communicate regularly, when schools recognize the importance of all families, and when families understand school and schoolwork. When partnerships are strong, problems that students have with schoolwork, behavior, or attitudes toward school and learning can be solved in the early stages. Should serious problems arise, they can be more easily solved on a base of long-standing, positive connections.

School psychologists focus on children. They study and serve the "whole child" and understand the important linkages between the support systems of children and their progress in schoolwork. They recognize that achievement test scores are important, but so are other skills, talents, and other developmental outcomes.

Too often students have been the forgotten members of school and family partnerships, resulting in what may seem to be teacher-parent conspiracies. The unique focus of school psychologists on children's well-being assures that students would be viewed as important and active "connectors" between school and home.

School and family connections are important at all grade levels. Across the school years, through high school, families need information to understand their children's developmental changes and the changes that occur in their children's schools. Toddlers become school age children, and children mature into early and late adolescence. They move from preschool to elementary, middle, and high schools, all of which are organized differently and make new demands on children and families.

Families maintain their influence on children, even as parent-child relationships change and even as parents' interactions with teachers and schools change. If families stay informed and involved at all grade levels, their children have better chances for success, and the schools have greater support for high quality programs.

School psychologists are trained in child and adolescent development, and have a deep understanding of the changing relationships across the grades of children and parents, children and peers, teachers and students, and schools and families. They can assist educators at all school levels—elementary, middle, and high—to develop strong and appropriate programs of family involvement.

School and family connections include all families not just those who are easy to talk with or easy to reach. Families of students who are at risk of failing may be the most difficult to reach, require more responsive communications, clearer information, and more specific guidelines in understandable language about how to work with the school and teachers to help their children pass a course or grade.

It is not only families of children at risk of failing who request better information from the schools. Just about all families say they need and want information from the schools on how to help their own children do better each year (Bauch, 1988; Dornbusch & Ritter, 1988; Epstein, 1986). There is a feeling of loss in families when they do not know how to talk with, assist, guide, and monitor their own children's schoolwork. This sense of inadequacy grows each year as families receive less information as children proceed from grade to grade (Dauber & Epstein, in press; Stevenson & Baker, 1987; Useem, 1991). This pattern is correctable if school and family partnerships establish cumulative, continuous practices of communication and interaction to benefit students.

School psychologists understand families and work with those whom others may find "hard to reach" and whose children have serious problems in school. School psychologists are likely to be aware of and accepting of family differences, and can identify and use the strengths in all families to help children solve their problems.

School and family connections reflect a process, not an event. A comprehensive program of family involvement is not developed overnight, nor in one year. Much like partners in business, partners in education must work hard at understanding their mutual interests, developing trust, organizing their shared responsibilities, and appreciating each others' investments and contributions. A strong program develops step by step, over time, from different starting points for schools and families. There must be time to assess strengths and needs, set goals, plan projects, implement practices, evaluate results, and revise activities so that they work well for most or all families (Comer, 1980; Epstein & Dauber, 1991). There are no shortcuts to the process.

Experience shows that investments of leadership and support for 3 to 5 years is a minimum time for building a strong partnership of schools and families. Even more time is needed to assure a lasting structure. At the end of that time, a comprehensive program of family involvement should include so many educators (teachers, administrators, guidance counselors, school psychologists, and others) and so many families that the process becomes a regular part of school practice.

School psychologists are experienced in working with families and with other educators using a systems approach—

recognizing that children's development and success in learning are products of cumulative processes, not isolated events.

School and family connections do not take the place of other school reform or school improvement initiatives. Establishing families as partners with the school will not, by itself, *solve* children's learning problems or increase school achievement. The process of developing excellent schools and excellent students is far more complex. To raise reading and math test scores, for example, will, in most schools, require better curricula, texts, and other learning materials, better instructional strategies in reading and math classes, *and* family involvement in helping students practice and maintain high interest in reading and math. Similar requirements will produce improvements in other subjects (Epstein & Salinas, 1992). Educators have the major responsibility for increasing students' opportunities to learn and to succeed in school subjects at each grade level with new and better curricula, challenging thinking skills, more responsive school and classroom organization with more support, encouragement, and recognition for all students. They also have the responsibility to implement practices that inform, guide, and enable all families to support and enrich those efforts.

School psychologists know the importance of the interdependence of academic programs and support services. They know that their work with children supports the efforts of classroom teachers. They are aware that students are successful when they are motivated to learn, to "buy into" school goals as their own, and when they are encouraged to work hard by all of the important people in their lives.

Ironically, although the perspectives and skills of school psychologists are clearly tied to the basic conclusions about school and family connections, most of the actual work of school psychologists focuses on other tasks. Consider these facts:

● Just about all educators and all

families recognize the importance of school and family connections.

- These connections are, typically, undeveloped because of the lack of leadership and time of school professionals.

- School psychologists may have the strongest educational base and closest ties in practice for providing leadership to help school staffs develop comprehensive programs of school and family connections.

- There is one major obstacle to activating this leadership. Tradition.

Traditionally, school psychologists assist individual children with special needs, meet with groups of children to discuss problems, develop and conduct testing programs for schools, oversee special education programs and processes, and assist students in other ways. Most do not work with total populations of students and families nor provide staff development and assistance to other teachers regularly.

From School Psychologist to Psychologist of the School

There has been considerable discussion in recent years about the importance of "paradigm shifts" in education to describe radically different approaches for improving education (Finn, 1990; Kuhn, 1970; Laosa, 1979). Perhaps more than most examples, revisions in the work and leadership of school psychologists would produce a true paradigm shift—a redirection of investments from treatment to prevention activities, from attention to some children and families to all children and families, from isolation from other teachers to interaction with and assistance to the teaching staff, from being the school psychologist to being the psychologist of the school.

Related Theoretical and Practical Frameworks

A brief review of our theoretical model and practical framework for school

and family connections shows how school psychologists' work could fill a serious gap in leadership and program development.

The model of "overlapping spheres of influence" extends other ecological models by providing external and internal (or interpersonal) structures for understanding and examining school and family connections (Epstein, 1987a). The model recognizes that although some practices of families and schools are conducted independently, other practices reflect the shared responsibilities of parents and educators for children's learning and development. The spheres of influence can be pushed closer together to enable schools and families to increase their interactions and share more responsibilities. Or the spheres may be pulled apart to separate responsibilities and reduce interactions. The changes in overlap are evident in the philosophies and practices of schools and families.

Across the grades as children, families, and schools change, the nature and extent of "overlap" in practices and the interpersonal relationships among partners also change. Practices required for partnerships to benefit young children will differ from those required to benefit older students. The task for research is to identify practices that are appropriate at each grade level or level of schooling and to study the effects of school and family connections on students, parents, teaching practice, and school climate. The task for practice is to consider, select, adapt, and implement practices of partnership that will help schools reach specific goals they set.

School psychologists may be particularly interested in the internal structure of the model of overlapping spheres of influence. The internal structure assumes that there are interpersonal interactions between and among the members of school and family organizations that influence students' learning and development. These include interactions with all families, such as communications about school policies or events, and specific interactions between parents and teachers that concern an individual child, such as a parent-teacher conference on a child's academic, social, or other needs or problems.

When teachers are partners with parents, they increase their attention to children's home life, to the development of student self-esteem, aspirations, social skills, and talents—some of the traditional responsibilities of families. When parents are partners with teachers, they increase their attention to their children's education, school life, mastery of skills, and learning progress—some of the traditional responsibilities of schools. Increasing the overlap of home and school spheres of influence leads to more "school-like families" and more "family-like schools" (Epstein, 1987a)—settings that are mutually responsible for and more responsive to the needs of children as students.

The model recognizes the interlocking histories of the institutions that educate and socialize children, and the changing and accumulating skills of the individuals in these institutions—children, parents, teachers, administrators. The overlapping spheres of influence recognizes that multiple contexts and the interpersonal relations of all participants in those contexts may positively or negatively influence children's learning and development.

Within the area of overlap of home and school, we have identified five major types of involvement that create partnerships with families: Basic Obligations of Families, Communications from the School, Volunteers, Learning Activities at Home, and Decision Making, Committees, Advocacy, and other Leadership Roles. The types are described in detail in other sources (Brandt, 1989; Epstein, 1987b). When guided by schools, practices of all types help all families participate as knowledgeable partners in their children's education (Dauber & Epstein, in press). A sixth type of school and family partnership, Collaboration and Exchange with Community Organizations, is being explored in new research and practice (Center on Families, Communities, Schools and Children's Learning, 1990; California State Board of Education,

1988). Examples of leadership roles for applying this framework for school and family partnerships include:

TYPE 1—*Basic Obligations of Families* refers to the responsibilities of families for their children's health and safety, parenting and child rearing skills at each age level, and positive home conditions for learning at each grade level.

- Organize a cumulative, educationally and psychologically sound series of workshops on child and adolescent development, with pertinent information for families at each grade level. These could include parenting skills and information for helping children develop positive personal qualities, values, behaviors that help children succeed in life (e.g., self-confidence, perseverance, independence, respect for others, to name a few [Epstein, 1989; Rich, 1988]). The workshops also may focus on what schools want families to know about home conditions needed to support students each year in school.

- Also, arrange ways to disseminate this information to all families who cannot attend workshops. This may involve creating a library of videotapes, tape recordings, summary sheets, or booklets for parents to use at convenient times. If workshops were tape/video recorded at each grade level, the information still would be available to parents and students without having to conduct the same workshops every year.

- Help all families obtain the information they need in words they can understand to support their children as students each year.

- Help teachers and administrators establish practices that increase their understanding and appreciation for families, for their goals, customs, and cultures, and for tapping family strengths to support children as students.

- Develop the leadership of counselors, teachers, community volunteers, parents, and others so that they can continue organizing and conducting effective workshops and other Type 1 practices to assist families in helpful ways to support their children as students.

TYPE 2—*Communications from the School* refers to the responsibilities of schools for communications from school-to-home about school programs and children's progress in forms and words all families can understand, and for options for home-to-school communications.

- Establish a structure and routine for discussing with parents test scores, report card grades, student behavior, and other indicators of progress.

- Establish print and nonprint methods of communicating about meetings, school programs, facilities, and other events and opportunities.

- Establish procedure to evaluate the "readability" of all memos, notices, and other communications, and the clarity of all print or nonprint information that goes home, with sensitivity for parents who do not speak English well, do not read well, need large type, etc.

- Design a useful structure and schedule for conferences. Work with teachers to improve the content of conferences so that some time is spent discussing how each teacher involves parents as partners each year, and so that some time is spent discussing parents' observations and expectations for their own children.

- Improve communications with non-English-speaking families, families with less formal education, and other groups that are often ignored by the schools.

- Establish parent-to-parent options for sharing information, raising questions, and other communications.

- Establish procedures for two-way communications so that families can contact school, teachers, counselors, administrators for information, and so that families can provide information or observations about their children that may help the school increase responsiveness to individual needs.

- Develop the leadership of adminis-

trators, teachers, and parents so that they can continue effective two-way communications and other Type 2 practices.

TYPE 3—*Volunteers* refers to those who assist teachers, administrators, and children in classrooms, parent rooms, or other areas of the school; to those who assist at home; and to those who come to school to support student performances and events.

- Establish an effective volunteer program including the recruitment of families and others, training, matching volunteers to teacher and school needs.

- Develop the leadership of teachers, other educators, and parents so that they can continue to organize and conduct effective volunteer programs and practices, and other Type 3 activities.

TYPE 4—*Learning Activities at Home, and Connections to Curriculum* refers to parent-initiated, child-initiated, or teacher-initiated ideas to monitor, discuss, or assist children at home on learning activities that are coordinated with children's classwork.

- Help teachers understand how to implement effective and frequent communications about homework. This includes homework policies, how to monitor homework, and ways to discuss schoolwork in each subject. Surveys show that most parents want to know how to help their own children at home. They want to know how to influence their children to work hard, do their best in school, and stay in school.

- Help teachers to organize other curriculum-related connections to families. This includes assisting teachers to understand, design, and implement interactive homework such as TIPS (Epstein, Jackson, Salinas, & Associates, 1991), or assisting administrators, teachers, parents, or others to understand and organize family math, science, reading, or other curriculum related events with families.

- Also, help teachers across the grades to provide parents with information about course requirements, grading processes, course choices (Useem, 1991), program decisions, and other curriculum-related decisions that have important consequences for children and for their families. In the earlier grades, information on grouping procedures and their consequences should be shared with families.

- Develop the leadership of teachers so that they can continue effective practices to involve families in their children's learning activities and other curriculum-related Type 4 activities.

TYPE 5—*Decision Making, Committees, Advocacy, and other Leadership Roles* refers to parent participation in decisions in PTA/PTO, advisory councils, other committees or groups at the school, or independent advocacy groups.

- Establish a structure and processes for successful school-site management teams, committees, and other decision making to include families.

- Develop the leadership of counselors, administrators, teachers, and parents so that they can continue effective practices of involving parents in decisions that affect their children, and other Type 5 activities.

TYPE 6—*Collaboration and Exchange with Community Organizations* refers to school actions and programs that provide or coordinate student and family access to community and support services. Also collaborations with businesses, cultural organizations, and other groups to improve school programs for children, services for families to support their child rearing and guidance of children as students, and to improve the effectiveness of the other types of involvement.

- Establish a structure and processes for business-school or community-school partnerships. Draw on community resources to enrich school programs, students' experiences, and family interactions with their children in the community.

- Assist families with information about community resources that can help them strengthen home condi-

tions to assist children's learning and development.

- Develop the leadership of counselors, administrators, teachers, and parents so that they can continue effective practices of integrating the services of the community with the needs of children, families, and schools, and other Type 6 activities.

To accomplish the work outlined above, school psychologists would have to draw upon several roles and skills including:

- *synthesizer* of information about parent involvement in forms useful to educators at each grade level and useful to parents of each age child.

- *disseminator* of good ideas, new information, new programs and practices, to assist schools and families to improve practice.

- *coordinator* of plans for action, including multi-year goals and plans.

- *facilitator/trainer* to help teachers and other school staffs understand and implement new programs, and to assume leadership for continuing practices.

- *demonstrator* of helpful or successful practices and approaches.

- *communicator* with parents, organizer of workshops, parent rooms or "clubs" for parent-to-parent interactions, volunteer work, and other family-initiated, and family-based exchanges.

- *evaluator* of programs including needs assessments, evaluations of implementations, and evaluations of effects.

These are all common talents of school psychologists. Success in these roles and skills depends on knowledge and sensitivity about the work of teachers, the developmental characteristics and needs of students, and the hopes and strengths of families. Few other educators are prepared by their education to assume these roles that are needed for the development of strong, cumulative, and successful school and family connections. A few examples show how school psychologists would exercise these roles in implementing practices of the major types of involvement:

EXAMPLES: *synthesizer and disseminator.*

- Collect information from research and practical examples of school and family connections. Present an in-service program for teachers and administrators.

- Plan and facilitate a workshop series for parents in cooperation with teachers at each grade level, and distribute the information from the workshop in useful and understandable forms. One useful series of workshops might focus on topics of "transition," such as preparing children and families for changes to new grade levels, new schools, or children's stages of development.

- Arrange annual or semiannual sessions for teachers and parents to share the practices and results of their partnerships so that others could adapt or adopt the practices.

EXAMPLES: *coordinator and facilitator.*

- Brainstorm with teachers, parents, and administrators to outline their common goals for parent involvement.

- Establish committees to design plans to reach selected goal(s) each year, and arrange for needed supplies, materials, or extra services or support to help implement the practices to attain the goals.

- Assist teachers to implement communications with families about school programs in general, and classwork and homework in particular.

EXAMPLES: *demonstrator and communicator.*

- Organize and implement a "parent room" and work with and train a parent room coordinator to take over the leadership of this practice.

- Organize and implement a parent volunteer program and processes to invite, recruit, train, and match volunteers to assist teachers and others at school, and to develop volunteer work to be conducted at home. Work with and train a coordinator of volunteers to take over the leadership of this practice.

- Allocate time one day each week to meet with teachers about new practices that may help them communicate better with families.

EXAMPLES: *evaluator.*

- Use skills in tests and measurement to design responsive evaluation forms to assess family, teacher, and student reactions to school practices to involve parents, and to monitor, document, and evaluate the results of particular practices and overall school climate. Continue to work with committees of teachers, administrators, parents, and students in this role as the program for involving families continues over the years.

Three conditions for this work are necessary so that the tasks are not oppressive and so that the school psychologist is not solely responsible for all of the work:

- *Leadership in school and family connections does not mean that the school psychologist works alone.* Because the goal is to build the school staff's understanding and capabilities to continue to conduct strong partnerships with families, it is important for the school psychologist to work with teams of educators and parents from the outset. Developing strong programs and practices is not a personal mission, but a *team effort* to produce a positive school climate that fully supports student progress and success.

- *The school psychologist's leadership in school and family connections may be scheduled for 3 years, at which time other educators take over the leadership, continuations, and extensions of the activities.* Because most educators presently enter their schools without preservice or advanced education in school and family connections, someone must take the lead in making these practices of partnership understandable and accessible. Part of that leadership is training and guidance or assistance in the design, implementation, and assessments of practices so that other professional colleagues can assume leadership for the program. As teachers, guidance counselors, parent liaisons, other parent volunteers, administrators, community educators, speech and language therapists, school social workers, and others on a school staff begin to understand and share the "big picture" and specific practices, they should be able to coordinate and continue the programs and practices to involve families. The school psychologist would then provide oversight and periodic assessments to assist those in charge, and to assure the continuation and development of parent involvement activities.

- *After family and school connections have been established and others in the school have taken over the leadership of these activities, the school psychologist would direct attention to other topics to promote the mental health of the school.* Leadership on school and family connections is just one example of an investment in the psychology of the school. For instance, the school psychologist could, over 3 to 5 years, accomplish the development of a structure for school and family connections. As others assume continuing leadership on these topics, the school psychologist would continue to contribute and conduct helpful assessments of

school and family partnerships, but turn attention to other topics to strengthen the mental health of the school. Some examples include:

- new procedures and practices for marking, grading, and rewarding or recognizing students;
- new directions for developing all children's individual talents;
- new partnerships with communities to support school programs, children's learning, and family capacities;
- promotion and retention policies and practices for increasing student success (to complement the school psychologist's traditional work in promotion and retention decisions);
- and many others.

How To Initiate These New Emphases

The school psychologist's work might be organized in this way:

- For about half of the time, the school psychologist would conduct "business as usual," on responsibilities and tasks that are presently done including crisis intervention and management, problem solving with children and with families, testing, organizing and overseeing special education, or other psychological services or counseling for individual students or small groups.
- For about half of the time, the school psychologist would promote and maintain a psychologically healthy school, as it affects all students, all teachers, and all families—a basic building block for student success and for a positive and productive school climate. This would start with a 3-to-5-year plan for school and family partnerships. The work would continue with attention to other topics to benefit the psychology of the school.

Competing Realities

It is true that most school psychologists do not have enough time or resources to conduct adequately their present assignments. The problems children face today are serious and some seem intractable. Drugs, violence, sexual and physical abuse, other traumas or injuries, and many other special needs remain important and time-consuming concerns. Also, conducting tests and other assessments of groups and individuals, and arranging special education placements and providing these services take time and require the special talents of school psychologists. Thus, some may question the wisdom of limiting traditional activities to half time.

There is, however, a competing argument that justifies a new direction toward the psychology of the school and leadership on school and family connections. Schools, students, and families today face difficult-to-desperate challenges to assure that all students succeed in school so that they can contribute to society as citizens, workers, and family members. Children are at risk of failing in school. Families are at risk of losing touch with their children and their children's schools. Schools are at risk of failing in their programs for students. Major investments are needed in better communications between schools and families to enhance children's mental health and to prevent learning and motivation problems before they occur.

If more families understood their children's schooling each year, many of the minor problems that arise with children's motivation, homework completion, test failure, and attitudes toward learning could be prevented. If more families understood their ongoing partnership with schools, more children would understand that their families believe education is important, thereby reducing the inconsistencies that some children experience in the messages they receive from school and home. Thus, school and family connections create a support structure that should help to prevent problems that presently require

treatment from school psychologists or other educators.

School psychologists aim to develop psychologically healthy and competent children. The question is: How can they best reach that goal—by serving a few children with special needs, or by serving all children and their families? The answer, we suggest, is by allocating equal time to the two groups. Half time for diagnoses and treatment and half time for prevention activities would provide the equivalent of about 10 days per month for each responsibility. This would add up to between 90–120 days per school year, depending on the length of the school psychologist's contract year. Although still a small investment, 3 years is enough time to make a real difference in the development of partnerships of schools with all families.

Changes in the Work of School Psychologists

The expectation is that more systematic and inclusive parent involvement will produce greater success for more students. Also, the school psychologist's influence will be greater overall. To invest half time in prevention and half time in treatment activities, school psychologists will need to revise the time they spend on certain tasks. For example, to equalize time on treatment and prevention activities and to focus on school and family connections, the reallocations of less time and more time shown in Table 1 may be considered.

These examples of equal time allocations clarify the dual emphases of school psychologists: to assist children with special needs using case management or crisis intervention approaches, and to prevent problems for children by assisting the rest of the school staff to conduct more effective and consistent school and family connections at every grade level.

Another way to examine the changing work of school psychologists needed for developing school and family partners as a general program for all children and all families is to see how specific topics are divided for the dual emphases of

TABLE 1
Reallocating Time to Develop School and Family Partnerships

less time: (down to half time)	more time: (up to half time)
treating individual children's problems	developing a positive school climate for all children
conducting crisis interventions to treat students' acute and chronic problems with school and family	helping all students to cope with normal developmental changes, and to understand the school's appreciation of their families
focusing on problems and weaknesses of families	focusing on and using strengths of families; strengthening all families' skills as partners in their children's education
empowering individual families	empowering teachers to inform and involve all families on a regular basis; enabling all teachers to understand families and to work confidently and productively with them
systems approaches for special education students and families	taking systems approaches for all students and the involvement of their families; including teachers in systems approaches
working alone	working with other educators as a leader and as a colleague in order to multiply efforts to produce a healthy school climate and positive schools and family partnerships
meeting one-on-one	meeting with small and large groups of teachers, parents, students, others
developing one-year plans or short-term goals	developing multi-year (3–5 year) plans and long-term goals; this includes processes for developing leadership skills so that other educators can eventually take over leadership on school and family connections, as the school psychologist gives attention to other topics

prevention and treatment. A few examples are provided in Table 2. There are many other practices that operationalize the six types of involvement; all can be similarly examined as those in Table 2 to identify their prevention and treatment components.

How are these activities different from what most school psychologists presently do? They include not only communications and meetings about problems or concerns, but also standards for two-way communications with all families to establish and maintain a healthy, positive dialogue between home and school. They include not only information and meetings at times of crises, but also the slow and steady exchange and accumulation of information and skills to help all families understand the school, their children's work, and their children's progress. There is not only an attempt to help children succeed, but also orchestrated efforts to help all families help their children to succeed at each grade level. There is not only the development of the professional status of the school psychologist, but also planned and thoughtful efforts to share knowledge with families.

Changes in the Education of School Psychologists

It would be a bold step for school psychologists to change their work and assume new leadership in family and school connections. Only some will understand the rationale, agree, and take action. If the dual emphases make sense, it will be necessary to add these perspectives and capacities to the university programs that prepare school psychologists and other educators.

Even though school psychologists come with skills and knowledge that make them more ready than many others to assume immediate leadership in school and family connections and other activities, they would be a stronger, surer force if their education and training directly and systematically addressed the role and practice of leaders for promoting the healthy psychology of the school, and for developing programs of family and school partnerships, in particular.

TABLE 2
Examples of Prevention Practices to Increase School and Family Partnerships

Topic for family involvement	Practices that emphasize prevention focus on:	Practices that emphasize treatment focus on:
Topics of concern to families and schools including drug abuse, alcohol use, early sexual behavior, discipline problems, peer pressure, and others	Establishing prevention programs including information and discussion sessions on challenges to children and adolescents	Conducting crisis interventions to assist children with special needs
Report card grades and school success	Helping families understand report cards, grading systems, steps needed for improvement (how to interpret report cards, grading systems, and steps for students to improve their grades)	Working with children who fail courses and with their families in partnership to prevent future failure on report cards
Parent-teacher conferences	Helping teachers organize responsive schedules and useful content for conferences	Establishing procedures to contact families who do not attend scheduled conferences; assist in designing follow-up contacts after conferences
Developmental needs and characteristics of children at each grade level	Conducting workshops to provide information in print and nonprint forms to families on child development to assist families and students to cope with normal growth and development	Provide services to students with special problems
Cultural diversity in schools	Helping teachers make the best uses for student learning of the customs, cultures, skills, and talents of students and families	Dealing with difficulties, conflict, or discrimination in connection with racial and ethnic differences
Diversity of families	Helping teachers understand and draw on the strengths of families, however they are structured	Discussion groups with students experiencing family crises; individual meetings with students or families with special needs
Peer relations	Arranging opportunities for developing strong and positive peer influence	Negotiating or arbitrating peer conflicts, group counseling for resolving peer disputes
Study skills	Helping students and families build skills that help students study successfully as they move to increasingly complex information each year	Conduct individual follow-up or tutorial sessions to assist students who need extra help in mastering study skills
Understanding each academic subject	Providing students and families with understandable information about the content and requirements for each subject each year	Review and information in clearer or different forms for those who need it

In addition to the traditional courses and topics, new studies of family, school, and community connections would include theory and research on school and family environments and their connections; family backgrounds and cultures, family structures and conditions of family life; family strengths and needs; changing relationships between children and parents; developmental patterns in the connections of families to schools and other community institutions; practices for involving families in children's education; effects on family life of school practices; effects on school life of family backgrounds, needs, and practices; the meaning of transitions for student development, student success, and family involvement; and other topics (Epstein, 1990). The expanded education would be useful to school psychologists who are placed in schools, districts, or state departments of education.

Even with education and training in school and family partnerships, school psychologists cannot do the job without the support of others in a team effort in program development. Principals, for example, will have to support the school psychologists' new role. Teachers, counse-

TABLE 2 (continued)

Topic for family involvement	Practices that emphasize prevention focus on:	Practices that emphasize treatment focus on:
Achievement test scores	Helping students and families understand test scores and options for increasing skills	Providing tutoring opportunities or referrals for tutoring
Homework	Helping students and families understand homework policies, schedules, purposes and content; helping teachers design new and creative forms for homework, including interactive homework that requires children to interact with family about work	Identifying students who are not completing their homework; providing help to students and communicating with families to improve the rate and quality of completion
Grouping practices	Helping students and families understand grouping practices and options for changing or working into groups	Serving as advocate for students or families with requests for grouping practices
Course requirements, and consequences of course choices	Providing information to students and families about their options for courses and their importance for helping students reach their goals and aspirations	Serving as advocate for students whose courses do not yet match their goals, or assisting students to examine and revise goals or choices that are not successful
Planning for careers	Establishing programs for career exploration and providing information to students and families about career choice requirements for education	Assisting students who have difficulties identifying career options
Parent input	Establishing working arrangements for committees (e.g., curriculum, safety, buildings, hospitality, volunteers, library, program enrichment, school improvement, and others)	Serving as advocate for family committees to assure their input is taken seriously by administrators and teachers as their decisions are made
Community resources, agencies, and other groups	Producing directories of community resources, potential volunteers, and contributors	Providing references to families who need special community services; some families are themselves at risk and may benefit from information on social services in the community

lors, and other educators will benefit only if they see the value of increasing information to and the involvement of families at each grade level. In the long run, we also will have to revise the education of teachers, principals, guidance counselors, and other educators so that they are ready for partnerships.

Discussion: Paradigm Shift or Renewal?

In the 1980s the work of school psychologists was extended by increasing attention to children in context and the ecological model and by adding a "family orientation" to better serve children with problems (Bronfenbrenner, 1979; Phillips, 1985). A focus on "systems approaches" to solve problems encouraged psychologists to work with families rather than trying to solve learning or adjustment problems by working with children alone (Dowling & Osborne, 1985; Petrie & Piersel, 1982). These added perspectives increased the influence of school psychologists as they integrated social services, applied family therapy strategies, and orchestrated services for handicapped children or others with special needs. But these extensions did not change the school psychologists' influence on schools as a whole, on parents as a group, or on students' success overall.

In this chapter, we are suggesting that school psychologists can exercise leadership in promoting the healthy psychology of the school. Put this way, the suggestions—to equalize investments in prevention and treatment activities, and to begin with school and family partnerships to build interinstitutional support for students—seem more an evolution than a revolution in the work of school psychologists.

The suggested revisions build on the changes in the 1980s and renew some early expectations for the field. Early on, school psychologists were asked to use their knowledge and skills in assessment, learning, and interpersonal relations "to *assist school personnel* to enrich the experiences and growth of *all children, and* to recognize and deal with *exceptional children*" (emphases added) (Ysseldyke & Schakel, 1983, citing a 1955 conference decision).

Historically, some school psychologists worked to provide scientific information to other educators (Bergan, 1985), served as liaisons between the administration and staff (Harrington, 1985), provided in-service training to teachers and school personnel on a variety of topics such as tests and measurements (Bardon, 1982), including working with single parents, noncustodial parents, and stepparents (Carlson, 1985), and offered leadership to school staffs on other topics.

There have been long-standing debates about ways for school psychologists to broaden their influence by working with all staff, students, and families to develop emotionally supporting school climates (Bardon, 1982; Schmuck, 1982; Wilson, 1985). Harrington (1985), for example, calls attention to the school's mental health and prevention activities when the school itself is the "client" of the school psychologist.

There is a long-standing record of school psychologists' attention to families, particularly their involvement in special education plans, decisions, and placements (Bergan, 1985). An evolutionary step would operationalize and extend to all children and families the best arrangements of special education that link schools, students, and families for improving children's learning. This might involve helping teachers design the equivalent of IEPs for all children (as

some of Utah's teachers in selected schools are demonstrating with SEPs— Student Education Plans). It should also be possible to provide information on student assessments to all families (Henderson & Valencia, 1985; Teglasi, 1985), and to share information and organize the involvement of families in all student placement or grouping decisions.

It would be an important step forward to extend good special education practices of communications and involvement with all families. Just as important, however, is involving families with children in special education in the major types of involvement that have been discussed in this chapter. Also, it is crucial to integrate families with children in special education and other special and categorical programs with all other families in a comprehensive program of school and family connections.

Many connections with families, particularly in special education, are codified in the National Association of School Psychologists' Standards for the Provision of School Psychological Services (1984). This is an important base on which to build more general leadership in school and family partnerships.

There are many examples that support the dual investments by school psychologists in prevention *and* treatment activities, in work as an individual professional *and* in providing expertise and in-service education to other educators; in work with all children *and* children with special needs, in promoting the mental health of the greatest number of children *and* in correcting problem behavior, in recognizing the importance of parent support for children *and* in informing and assisting families in language that is understandable and involving them in decisions and activities that affect their children.

For over three decades, and longer by some counts, the field of school psychology has continued to debate its roles and goals. How much prevention and how much treatment should school psychologists emphasize in their orientation and activities (Bergan, 1985; Martin, 1983)? In

1985, this was still a "nebulously defined field" (Bergan, 1985). One reason for the continued debates has been the either/or decisions that have been set before the field. Either prevention or treatment. Either all children or some children. Either families or staff. We have taken a different course to suggest that school psychologists assume a leadership role in the school, assign half time for prevention and half for treatment activities, start with family and school connections as a topic basic to the psychology of the school, engage in team-building activities so that others assume leadership roles on this topic, and move on to other topics that contribute to a positive and productive school climate for all students, teachers, and families.

Setting Goals for Action

The field of school psychology prides itself on its receptivity to change to meet professional challenges, become more responsive to clients, and more relevant to society (Bergan, 1985; Ysseldyke & Schakel, 1983). With awareness of the need for change, it should be possible to move in more influential directions.

Thus, the goal: to assure that school and family connections and productive partnerships take root and begin to grow in schools in which school psychologists work. And, the challenge to school psychologists: to take an active role in assisting educators and families in their schools to join forces to develop and to continue a comprehensive program of school and family connections for all children and their families across the grades.

This "modest proposal" to revise the work of school psychologists will not be agreeable to all. There will be some, perhaps many, who are not ready to leave tradition, reapply skills to prevention, reach out to all families and students, assist all teachers in their partnerships with families, or focus on the psychology of the school. In the schools with school psychologists who continue only their traditional work, the goals and practices

discussed here must be assigned to and accomplished by other educators.

But, there may be some, perhaps many, school psychologists who see that education in the United States is at a critical juncture. The combination of great needs of children, changing family structures and family lifestyles, and low federal, state, and district budgets for school improvement, calls for unusual measures and new designs for work in education.

It is very clear that the success of school reform and the progress on family and school partnerships depends on leadership. If we are to change the sporadic, idiosyncratic, and charismatic nature of program development for school and family connections, leadership must become more routine and more equitable for all families at all grade levels. The pattern of incidental leadership will continue until we systematize responsibilities, duties, and schedules.

This leadership must come from talented staff already in the schools, because few schools, districts, or states have new or extra money to create new positions such as school and family coordinator.

Because of the school psychologists' special knowledge, training, and a responsibility to provide leadership to promote a school's positive climate, they are natural leaders of successful school and family connections. Those who take these new directions can importantly influence healthy and more successful schools, students, and families.

REFERENCES

Bardon, J. I. (1982). The psychology of school psychology. In C. R. Reynolds & T. B. Gutkin (Eds.), *The handbook of school psychology* (pp. 3–14). New York: John Wiley.

Bauch, P. A. (1988). Is parent involvement different in private schools? *Educational Horizons, 66,* 78–82.

Bergan, J. R. (Ed.) (1985). *School psychology in contemporary society: An introduction.* Columbus, OH: Charles E. Merrill.

Brandt, R. (1989). On parents and schools: A

conversation with Joyce Epstein. *Educational Leadership, 47,* 24–27.

Bronfenbrenner, U. (1979). *The ecology of human development.* Cambridge, MA: Harvard University Press.

California State Board of Education. (1988). *Parent involvement initiative: A policy and plan for action.* Sacramento: California State Department of Education.

Carlson, C. I. (1985). Working with single parent and step families. In A. Thomas & J. Grimes (Eds.), *Best practices in school psychology* (pp. 43–60). Kent, OH: National Association of School Psychologists.

Center on Families, Communities, Schools and Children's Learning. (1990). Proposal to the Office of Educational Research and Improvement. Washington, DC: Department of Education.

Comer, J. P. (1980). *School power: Implications of an intervention project.* New York: Free Press.

Dauber, S. L., & Epstein, J. L. (in press). Parents' attitudes and practices of involvement in inner-city elementary and middle schools. In N. Chavkin (Ed.), *Minority parent involvement in education.* Albany, NY: SUNY Press.

Davies, D. (1991). Schools reaching out: Family, school, and community partnerships for student success. *Phi Delta Kappan, 72,* 376–383.

Dornbusch, S. M., & Ritter, P. L. (1988). Parents of high school students: A neglected resource. *Educational Horizons, 66,* 75–77.

Dowling, E., & Osborne, E. (1985). *The family and the school: A joint systems approach to problems with children.* London: Routledge & Kegan Paul.

Epstein, J. L. (1986). Parents' reactions to teacher practices of parent involvement. *The Elementary School Journal, 86,* 277–294.

Epstein, J. L. (1987a). Toward a theory of family-school connections: Teacher practices and parent involvement. In K. Hurrelmann, F. Kaufmann, & F. Losel (Eds.), *Social intervention: Potential and constraints* (pp. 121–136). New York: DeGruyter.

Epstein, J. L. (1987b). What principals should know about parent involvement. *Principal, 66,* 6–9.

Epstein, J. L. (1988). How do we improve programs in parent involvement? *Educational Horizon, 66*(2), 58–59.

Epstein, J. L. (1989). Family structures and student motivation: A developmental perspective. In C. Ames & R. Ames (Eds.), *Research on motivation in education: Goals and cognitions* (pp. 259–295). San Diego: Academic Press.

Epstein, J. L. (1990). School and family connections: Theory, research, and implications for integrating sociologies of education and family. In D. Unger &

M. Sussman (Eds.), *Families in community settings: Interdisciplinary perspectives* (pp. 96–126). New York: Haworth Press.

Epstein, J. L. (1992). School and family partnerships. In M. Alkin (Ed.), *Encyclopedia of educational research* (pp. 1139–1151). New York: MacMillan.

Epstein, J. L., & Dauber, S. L. (1991). School programs and teacher practices of parent involvement in inner-city elementary and middle schools. *The Elementary School Journal, 91*(3), 289–303.

Epstein, J. L., Jackson, V. E., Salinas, K. C., & Associates. (1991). *Manual for teachers: Teachers Involve Parents in Schoolwork (TIPS)—Interactive homework in the middle grades, language arts and science/health.* Baltimore, MD: Center on Families, Communities, Schools and Children's Learning, The Johns Hopkins University.

Epstein, J. L., & Salinas, K. C. (1992). *Promising programs in the middle grades.* Reston, VA: National Association of Secondary School Principals.

Epstein, J. L., & Scott-Jones, D. (in press). School, family, and community connections for accelerating student progress in elementary and middle grades. In H. M. Levin (Ed.), *Accelerating the education of at-risk students.* Philadelphia: Falmer Press.

Finn, C. E. (1990). The biggest reform of all. *Phi Delta Kappan, 71,* 584–592.

Harrington, R. G. (1985). Best practices in facilitating organizational change in the schools. In A. Thomas & J. Grimes (Eds.), *Best practices in school psychology* (pp. 193–206). Kent, OH: National Association of School Psychologists.

Henderson, A. (1987). *The evidence continues to grow: Parent involvement improves student achievement.* Columbia, MD: National Committee for Citizens in Education.

Henderson, R. W., & Valencia, R. R. (1985). Nondiscriminatory school psychological services: Beyond nonbiased assessment. In J. R. Bergan (Ed.), *School psychology in contemporary society: An introduction* (pp. 340–377). Columbus, OH: Charles E. Merrill.

Kuhn, T. S. (1970). *The structure of scientific revolutions* (2nd ed.). Chicago: University of Chicago Press.

Laosa, L. M. (1979). Social competence in childhood: Toward a developmental, socioculturally relativistic paradigm. In M. W. Kent & J. E. Rolf (Eds.), *Primary prevention of psychopathology, Vol 3. Social competence in children* (pp. 253–279). Hanover, NH: University Press of New England.

Martin, R. P. (1983). Consultation in the schools. In G. W. Hynd (Ed.), *The school psychologist: An introduction* (pp. 269–292). Syracuse, NY: Syracuse University Press.

NASP standards for training field placement and credentialling. (1984). Washington, DC: National Association of School Psychologists.

Paths to partnership: What we can learn from federal, state, district, and school initiatives. (1991). *Phi Delta Kappan, 72* [Special issue].

Petrie, P., & Piersel, W. (1982). Family therapy. In C. R. Reynolds & T. B. Gutkin (Eds.), *The handbook of school psychology* (pp. 580–590). New York: John Wiley.

Phillips, B. (1985). Family intervention. In J. R. Bergan (Ed.), *School psychology in contemporary society: An introduction* (pp. 92–115). Columbus, OH: Charles E. Merrill.

Rich, D. (1988). *MegaSkills.* Boston: Houghton Mifflin.

Schmuck, R. A. (1982). Organizational development in the schools. In C. R. Reynolds & T. B. Gutkin (Eds.), *The handbook of school psychology* (pp. 829–857). New York: John Wiley.

Stevenson, D., & Baker, D. (1987). The family-school relation and the child's school performance. *Child Development, 58,* 1348–1357.

Swap, S. M. (1990). Comparing the philosophies of home-school collaboration. *Equity and Choice, 6*(3), 9–19.

Teglasi, H. (1985). Best practices in interpreting psychological assessment data to parents. In A. Thomas & J. Grimes (Eds.), *Best practices in school psychology* (pp. 415–429). Kent, OH: National Association of School Psychologists.

Useem, E. L. (1991). Student selection into course sequences in mathematics: The impact of parent involvement and school policies. *Journal of Research on Adolescence, 1*(3), 231–250.

Wilson, M. (1985). Best practices in improving school climate. In A.Thomas & J. Grimes (Eds.), *Best practices in school psychology* (pp. 485–492). Kent, OH: National Association of School Psychologists.

Ysseldyke, J. E., & Schakel, J. A. (1983). Directions in school psychology. In G. W. Hynd (Ed.), *The school psychologist: An introduction* (pp. 3–26). Syracuse, NY: Syracuse University Press.

Epilogue

Are school psychologists willing to assume leadership in the growing field of school and family connections? We hope so. Epstein (this volume) not only has challenged school psychologists to assume leadership, but also has provided a theoretical and practical framework that is consistent with the concept of alternative service delivery. Her chapter was not altered by us as co-editors. Also, Dr. Epstein is a Professor of Sociology and Co-Director of the Center on Families, Communities, Schools, and Children's Learning. While her challenge is validation from an outside discipline for a role change, her message is consistent with current roles and functions of many school psychologists (e.g., consultation, program development) and the work of many school psychologists (e.g., Christenson and Clearly, 1990; Conoley, 1987; Fine and Carlson, 1991; Fish, 1990).

Is it time to operationalize Bronfenbrenner's (1979) model to enhance human development? We believe so. To do so requires a new kind of psychologist: a quarterback (Cowen et al., 1975, cited by Conoley, 1989). According to Conoley (1989), "This psychologist is an expert about children: who they are, where they live, what they need, and what can go wrong. He or she is a family and school systems expert because to fail to know families and schools is to fail to know children (p. 556)." This quarterback is synonymous with Epstein's concept, Psychologist of the School.

To do so requires a reconceptualization of providing services to children, youth, and their families. To do so requires preservice and staff development training. Systematic research of the effects of family-school interventions on children's academic and social development is needed. We hope this book has served to stimulate school psychologists' discussion about and action in working with school and family connections.

S.L.C.
J.C.C.

REFERENCES

Bronfenbrenner, U. (1979). *The ecology of human development.* Cambridge, MA: Harvard University Press.

Christenson, S. L., & Clearly, M. (1990). Consultation and the parent-educator partnership. *Journal of Educational and Psychological Consultation, 1*(3), 219–241.

Conoley, J. C. (1989). Cognitive-behavioral approaches and prevention in the schools. In J. N. Hughes & Robert J. Hall (Eds.), *Cognitive and behavioral psychology in the schools: A comprehensive handbook.* New York: Guilford Press.

Conoley, J. C. (1987). Schools and families: Theoretical and practical bridges. *Professional School Psychology, 2*, 191–203.

Fine, M. J., & Carlson, C. (Eds.). (1992). *The handbook of family-school intervention: A systems perspective.* Boston, MA: Allyn and Bacon.

Fish, M. C. (1990). Family-school relationships: In A. Thomas & J. Grimes (Eds.), *Best practices in school psychology* (pp. 371–378). Washington, DC: National Association of School Psychologists.

Appendix A
Home-School Collaboration Resources

Selected resources for professionals to use in developing school-family connections are provided in four areas: (a) Resource organizations and associations, (b) Federal agencies, (c) Publications, and (d) Parenting books. The list of resources in the categories of the resource organizations and associations and federal agencies was developed by Educational Resources Information Center (ERIC) (Swanson, 1991, pp. 8–9).

ORGANIZATIONS AND ASSOCIATIONS

Alliance for Parental Involvement in Education (AllPIE)
This parent-to-parent organization provides information about family education options (pubic school, private school, and home education), and parent and student rights within those options. Services include a newsletter, a book and resources catalog, a referral services, pamphlets, workshops, and conferences. P.O. Box 59, East Chatham, New York, NY 12060-0059. (518) 392-6900 Program Contacts: Seth Rockmuller and Katharine Houk.

ASPIRA Association, Inc.
A National Hispanic education leadership development organization, ASPIRA administers a national parent involvement demonstration project in Hispanic communities in nine cities and produces booklets to help Hispanic parents with their children's education. 1112-16th Street N.W., Suite 340, Washington, DC 20036 (202) 835-3600. Program Contact: Lisa Colón.

Council for Educational Development and Research
The members of this association are long-term educational research and development institutions that create programs and materials, including information on parent involvement useful for educators and parents. 1201-16th Street N.W., Washington, DC 20036. (202) 223-1593. Program Contact: Diane Schwartz.

Hispanic Policy Development Project (HPDP)
This nonprofit organization encourages the analysis of public and private policies and policy proposals affecting Hispanics in the United States. After conducting a nationwide grant program, it produced a publication highlighting successful strategies for working with Latino parents. 250 Park Avenue South, Suite 5000A, New York, NY 10003. (212) 523-9323. Program Contact: Carmen Lydia Ramos.

The Home and School Institute (HSI)
For more than two decades, HSI has developed practical self-help programs to unite the educational resources of the home, the school, and the community. HSI is currently presenting MegaSkills seminars nationally to train parent workshop leaders. Special Projects Office, 1201-16th Street N.W., Washington, DC 20036. (202) 466-3633. Program Contact: Dorothy Rich.

Institute for Responsive Education (IRE)
This national research and advocacy organizaiton studies schools and helps them become more responsive to citizen and parent involvement and concerns. IRE publishes the journal Equity and Choice and various reports and is principal contact for the new National Center on Families. 605 Commonwealth Avenue, Boston, MA 02215. (617) 353-3309. Program Contact: Owen Heleen.

International Reading Association
This organization works with parents, educators, and researchers to improve reading instruction and increase literacy. IRA also offers information to parents on how to develop lifelong reading habits with their children. 800 Barksdale Road, Newark, DE 19704-8139. (302) 731-1600. Program Contact: Peter Mitchell, Executive Director.

Mexican American Legal Defense and Educational Fund (MALDEF)
This civil rights organization conducts a Parent Leadership Program for promoting the participation of Latino parents as leaders at their children's schools. The program involves a 12-week course, including parent-teacher conferences and meetings with school district officials. 634 South Spring Street, 11th Floor, Los Angeles, CA 90014. (213) 629-2512. Program Contact: Luisa Perez-Ortega.

National Association for the Education of Young Children (NAEYC)
NAEYC offers many resources for educators on all aspects of child development and early childhood education, including parent involvement. A free catalog is available. 1834 Connecticut Avenue N.W., Washington, DC 20009. (202) 232-8777. Program Contact: Pat Spahr.

National Association of Partners in Education
This organization helps individuals and groups start and manage school volunteer programs and business-education partnerships. 209 Madison Street, Suite 401, Alexandria, VA 22314. (703) 836-4880. Program Contact: Daniel W. Merenda, Executive Director.

National Black Child Development Institute
This organization provides direct services and conducts advocacy campaigns to improve the quality of life for black children and youth. Family and early childhood education are emphasized, and speakers and publications are available. 1463 Rhode Island Avenue N.W., Washington, DC 20005. (202) 387-1281. Program Contact: Sherry Deane.

National Coalition for Parent Involvement in Education (NCPIE)
This organization, composed of more than 25 national education and community life associations, is dedicated to developing effective family and school partnerships. To receive a free brochure, "Developing Family/School Partnerships: Guidelines for Schools and School Districts," other information about NCPIE, and additional parent involvement resources, send a stamped (45 cents), self-addressed, business-sized envelope to NCPIE, Box 39, 1201-16th Street N.W., Washington, DC 20036.

National Coalition of Title 1/Chapter 1 Parents (National Parent Center)
This organization provides a voice for Chapter 1 parents at the federal, regional, state, and local levels. The Coalition publishes a newsletter, provides training, and sponsors conferences. Edmonds School Building, 9th & D Streets N.E., Washington, DC 20002. (202) 547-9286. Program Contact: Robert Witherspoon.

National Committee for Citizens in Education
This organization has many publications for parents and also provides free information and help for parents with school problems. Request a free bookmark with information on parent involvement in the middle school. 10840 Little Patuxent Parkway, Suite 301, Columbia, MD 21044. 1-800-NETWORK.

National Council of La Raza (NCLR)
This research and advocacy organization works on behalf of the U.S. Hispanic population and provides technical assistance to community-based organizations. NCLR's Project EXCEL is a national education demonstration project which includes tutoring services and parental education. 810-1st Street N.E., Suite 300, Washington, DC 20002-4205. (202) 289-1380. Program Contact: Denise De La Rosa.

National Information Center for Children and Youth with Handicaps (NICHCY)

This organization provides free information to assist parents, educators, caregivers, advocates, and others in helping children and youth with disabilities. NICHCY provides information on local, state, and national disability groups for parents and professionals and maintains databases with current information on disability topics. Publications include *News Digest* and *Parent Guides*. P.O. Box 1492, Washington, DC 20013. 1-800-999-5599.

Parent-Teacher Associations

National, state, and local PTAs have many resources and materials that can be used at home and at school to support children's learning. For a free list of publications, send a stamped, self-addressed, business-sized envelope to Publications List, National PTA, Department D, 700 North Rush Street, Chicago, IL 60611-2571. Local PTAs may also have the list.

Parents as Teachers National Center (PAT)

PAT encourages parents of chidlren from birth to age 3 to think of themselves as their children's first and most influential teachers. It provides information and training to parents, supports public policy initiatives, and offers parent educator certification. University of Missouri-St. Louis Marillac Hall, 8001 Natural Bridge Road, St. Louis, MO 63121-4499. (314) 553-5738. Program Contact: Claire Eldredge.

Parent Training and Information Centers, and Technical Assistance to Parent Projects

The Office of Special Education Programs supports a network of 60 parent Training and Information Centers in all 50 states and Puerto Rico to enable parents to participate more effectively with professionals in meeting the educational needs of children with disabilities. Technical Assistance to Parents Projects (TAPP) provides technical assistance and coordination to the 60 PTIs and to developing minority programs in urban and rural locations. 95 Berkeley Street, Suite 104, Boston, MA 02116. (617) 482-2915. Program Contact: Martha Ziegler.

FEDERAL AGENCIES

Department of Health and Human Services

Office of Human Development Services
200 Independence Avenue S.W.
Washington, DC 20201
- Administration for Children, Youth, and Families (202) 245-0347

Department of Agriculture

Extension Service
3443 South Building
Washington, DC 20025
- Human Development and Family Relations (202) 447-2018

Department of Education

400 Maryland Avenue S.W.
Washington, DC 20202-7240
- Office of Educational Research and Improvement (202) 219-2050
- Center on Families, Communities, Schools, and Children's Learning (617) 353-3309
- National Research Center on Education in the Inner Cities (215) 787-3001
- Southwest Educational Development Laboratory (512) 476-6861
- Compensatory Education Programs, Office of Elementary and Secondary Education (202) 401-1682
- Office of Bilingual Education and Minority Languages Affairs (202) 732-5063
- White House Initiative on Hispanic Education (202) 401-3008

PUBLICATIONS

Chrispeels, J., Boruta, M., Daugherty, M. (1988). *Communicating with parents*. San Diego, CA: San Diego County Office of Education.

Collins, C., Moles, O., & Cross, M. (1982). *The home-school connection: Selected partnership programs in large cities.* Boston, MA: Institute for Responsive Education.

Council of Chief State School Officers (1989). *Family support, education, and involvement: A guide for state action.* Washington, DC: Author.

ERIC Clearinghouse on Handicapped and Gifted Children (1991). *Communicating with culturally diverse parents of exceptional children.* Reston, VA: Council for Exceptional Children.

Henderson, A. T., Marburger, C. L., & Ooms, T. (1988). *Beyond the bake sale: An educator's guide to working with parents.* Columbia, MD: National Committee for Citizens in Education.

Rich, D. (1987a). *Teachers and parents: An adult-to-adult approach.* Washington, DC: National Education Association.

Rich, D. (1987b). *Schools and families: Issues and actions.* Washington, DC: National Education Association.

Swap, S. M. (1987). *Enhancing parent involvement in schools.* New York: Teachers College Press.

U.S. Department of Education (1991). *Working with families: Promising programs to help parents support young children's learning.* Washington, DC: Author.

Wikelund, K. R. (1990). *Schools and communities together: A guide to parent involvement.* Portland, OR: Northwest Regional Educational Laboratory.

PARENTING BOOKS

Albert, L. (1984). *Coping with kids and school.* NY: Ballantine Books.

Canter, L., & Hauser, L. (1985). *Homework without tears: A parents guide for motivating children to do homework and to succeed in schools.* NY: Harper & Row.

Cutright, M. J. (1989). *The national PTA talks to parents: How to get the best education for your child.* NY: Doubleday.

Eyre, L., & Eyre, R. (1984). *Teaching children responsibility.* NY: Ballantine Books.

Ferguson, S., & Mazin, L. (1989). *Parent power.* NY: Clarkson N. Potter, Inc.

Greene, L. J. (1987). *Smarter kids.* NY: Fawcett Crest.

Johnson, E. W. (1984). *Raising children to achieve: A guide for motivating success in school and in life.* NY: Walker Publishing.

Kuepper, J. (1987). *Homework helper: A guide for parents offering assistance.* Education Media Corp.

Levine, F. M., & Anesko, K. M. (1987). *Winning the homework war.* NY: Prentice-Hall.

Maeroff, G. I. (1989). *The school smart parent.* NY: Times Books.

Rich, D. (1988). *MegaSkills: How families can help children succeed in school and beyond.* Boston: Houghton-Mifflin.

Solomon, A. M., & Grenoble, P. B. (1988). *Helping your child get top grades.* Chicago: Contemporary Books.

Stainback, W., & Stainback, S. (1988). *How to help your child succeed in school.* NY: Meadowbrook.

Thiel, A., Thiel, R., & Grenoble, P. B. (1988). *When your child isn't doing well in school.* Chicago: Contemporary Books.

REFERENCES

Swanson, B. (1991). *The ERIC Review.* 1(3). U.S. Department of Education. Office of Educational Research and Improvement. Educational Resources Information Center.

Subject Index